CCNA Security
Official Exam Certification Guide

Michael Watkins
Kevin Wallace, CCIE No. 7945

Cisco Press

800 East 96th Street
Indianapolis, IN 46240 USA

CCNA Security Official Exam Certification Guide

Michael Watkins
Kevin Wallace, CCIE No. 7945

Copyright© 2008 Cisco Systems, Inc.

Published by:
Cisco Press
800 East 96th Street
Indianapolis, IN 46240 USA

Printed in the United States of America

First Printing June 2008

Library of Congress Cataloging-in-Publication data is on file.

ISBN-13: 978-1-58720-220-9

ISBN-10: 1-58720-220-4

Warning and Disclaimer

This book is designed to provide the information necessary to be successful on the Cisco IINS (640-553) exam. Every effort has been made to make this book as complete and accurate as possible, but no warranty or fitness is implied.

The information is provided on an "as is" basis. The authors, Cisco Press, and Cisco Systems, Inc. shall have neither liability nor responsibility to any person or entity with respect to any loss or damages arising from the information contained in this book or from the use of the discs or programs that may accompany it.

The opinions expressed in this book belong to the authors and are not necessarily those of Cisco Systems, Inc.

Trademark Acknowledgments

All terms mentioned in this book that are known to be trademarks or service marks have been appropriately capitalized. Cisco Press or Cisco Systems, Inc., cannot attest to the accuracy of this information. Use of a term in this book should not be regarded as affecting the validity of any trademark or service mark.

Corporate and Government Sales

Cisco Press offers excellent discounts on this book when ordered in quantity for bulk purchases or special sales. For more information, please contact:

U.S. Corporate and Government Sales

1-800-382-3419   corpsales@pearsontechgroup.com

For sales outside of the U.S. please contact:

International Sales

international@pearsontechgroup.com

Feedback Information

At Cisco Press, our goal is to create in-depth technical books of the highest quality and value. Each book is crafted with care and precision, undergoing rigorous development that involves the unique expertise of members of the professional technical community.

Reader feedback is a natural continuation of this process. If you have any comments about how we could improve the quality of this book, or otherwise alter it to better suit your needs, you can contact us through e-mail at feedback@ciscopress.com. Please be sure to include the book title and ISBN in your message.

We greatly appreciate your assistance.

Publisher: Paul Boger	**Cisco Press Program Manager:** Jeff Brady
Associate Publisher: Dave Dusthimer	**Copy Editor:** Gayle Johnson
Executive Editor: Brett Bartow	**Technical Editors:** Ryan Lindfield and Anthony Sequeira
Managing Editor: Patrick Kanouse	
Development Editor: Andrew Cupp	
Senior Project Editor: Tonya Simpson	
Editorial Assistant: Vanessa Evans	
Book and Cover Designer: Louisa Adair	
Composition: Mark Shirar	
Indexers: Tim Wright and Heather McNeil	
Proofreader: Debbie Williams	

Americas Headquarters	Asia Pacific Headquarters	Europe Headquarters
Cisco Systems, Inc.	Cisco Systems, Inc.	Cisco Systems International BV
170 West Tasman Drive	168 Robinson Road	Haarlerbergpark
San Jose, CA 95134-1706	#28-01 Capital Tower	Haarlerbergweg 13-19
USA	Singapore 068912	1101 CH Amsterdam
www.cisco.com	www.cisco.com	The Netherlands
Tel: 408 526-4000	Tel: +65 6317 7777	www-europe.cisco.com
800 553-NETS (6387)	Fax: +65 6317 7799	Tel: +31 0 800 020 0791
Fax: 408 527-0883		Fax: +31 0 20 357 1100

Cisco has more than 200 offices worldwide. Addresses, phone numbers, and fax numbers are listed on the Cisco Website at **www.cisco.com/go/offices**.

About the Authors

Michael Watkins, CCNA/CCNP/CCVP/CCSP, is a full-time senior technical instructor with SkillSoft Corporation. With 13 years of network management, training, and consulting experience, he has worked with organizations such as Kraft Foods, Johnson and Johnson, Raytheon, and the U.S. Air Force to help them implement and learn about the latest network technologies. In addition to holding more than 20 industry certifications in the areas of networking and programming technologies, he holds a bachelor of arts degree from Wabash College.

Kevin Wallace, CCIE No. 7945, is a certified Cisco instructor working full time for SkillSoft, where he teaches courses in the Cisco CCSP, CCVP, and CCNP tracks. With 19 years of Cisco networking experience, he has been a network design specialist for the Walt Disney World Resort and a network manager for Eastern Kentucky University. He holds a bachelor of science degree in electrical engineering from the University of Kentucky. He is also a CCVP, CCSP, CCNP, and CCDP, with multiple Cisco security and IP communications specializations.

About the Technical Reviewers

Ryan Lindfield is an instructor and network administrator with Boson. He has more than ten years of network administration experience. He has taught many courses designed for CCNA, CCNP, and CCSP preparation, among others. He has written many practice exams and study guides for various networking technologies. He also works as a consultant, where among his tasks are installing and configuring Cisco routers, switches, VPNs, IDSs, and firewalls.

Anthony Sequeira, CCIE No. 15626, completed the CCIE in Routing and Switching in January 2006. He is currently pursuing the CCIE in Security. For the past 15 years, he has written and lectured to massive audiences about the latest in networking technologies. He is currently a senior technical instructor and certified Cisco Systems instructor for SkillSoft. He lives with his wife and daughter in Florida. When he is not reading about the latest Cisco innovations, he is exploring the Florida skies in a Cessna.

Dedications

For their support and encouragement throughout this process, I dedicate my contribution to this book to my family.
—Michael

I dedicate my contribution to this book to my best friend (and wife of 14 years), Vivian.
—Kevin

Acknowledgments

From Michael Watkins:

I want to thank the team at Cisco Press for their direction and support throughout the writing process. For their support and encouragement throughout this process, I wish to thank and acknowledge Tom Warrick and the instructor team at SkillSoft. I also wish to thank Kevin Wallace, who brought his talent and experience to this project and was an enormous help each step of the way.

Finally, I want to thank my family for their continued support through this project, especially my children, Abigail, Matthew, and Addison, who are always an inspiration in all that I do.

From Kevin Wallace:

I wish to express my sincere thanks to the team at Cisco Press. You guys are a class act, and I'm honored to be associated with you. Also, I give a huge thank-you to Michael Watkins for inviting me to participate in writing this book.

On a personal note, I know all the good things in my life come from above, and I thank God for those blessings. Also, my wife, Vivian, and my daughters, Sabrina and Stacie, have become accustomed to seeing me attached to my laptop over the past few months. Thank you for your love and support throughout this process.

This Book Is Safari Enabled

The Safari® Enabled icon on the cover of your favorite technology book means the book is available through Safari Bookshelf. When you buy this book, you get free access to the online edition for 45 days.

Safari Bookshelf is an electronic reference library that lets you easily search thousands of technical books, find code samples, download chapters, and access technical information whenever and wherever you need it.

To gain 45-day Safari Enabled access to this book:

- Go to http://www.informit.com/onlineedition.

- Complete the brief registration form.

- Enter the coupon code 35C1-WTME-WMIT-F7ED-JNPY

If you have difficulty registering on Safari Bookshelf or accessing the online edition, please e-mail customer-service@safaribooksonline.com.

Contents at a Glance

Contents

Icons Used in This Book

 Router

 Switch

 PC

 Server

 IDS/IPS Sensor

 IEEE 802.1x-Enabled Switch

 Modem

 PSTN Network

 Dial-Up Link

 Data Network

 Adaptive Security Appliance (ASA)/PIX

 IOS Router with Firewall Feature Set

 IPsec-Protected Tunnel

 Network Management Station (NMS)

 VPN Termination Device

 Headquarters

 Remote Office

 Analog Phone

 Voice Gateway

 PBX

 IP Phone

 Cisco Unified Communications Manager

 Shared Media Hub

 WAN Link

 Cisco NAC Appliance

 Access Gateway

 Server Protected by Cisco Security Agent

 Management Center for Cisco Security Agent with Internal or External Database

 Fibre Channel Switch

 Physical SAN Island

 Firewall

 ASA Device

 Generic Firewall

 SSL Tunnel

 Encryption Key

 VPN Concentrator

 Cisco MDS 9000

Command Syntax Conventions

The conventions used to present command syntax in this book are the same conventions used in the IOS Command Reference. The Command Reference describes these conventions as follows:

- **Bold** indicates commands and keywords that are entered literally as shown. In actual configuration examples and output (not general command syntax), bold indicates commands that the user enters (such as a **show** command).

- *Italic* indicates arguments for which you supply actual values.

- Vertical bars (|) separate alternative, mutually exclusive elements.

- Square brackets ([ ]) indicate an optional element.

- Braces ({ }) indicate a required choice.

- Braces within brackets ([{ }]) indicate a required choice within an optional element.

Foreword

CCNA Security Official Exam Certification Guide is an excellent self-study resource for the Cisco IINS (640-553) exam. Passing the IINS exam validates the knowledge and skills required to successfully secure Cisco network devices.

Gaining certification in Cisco technology is key to the continuing educational development of today's networking professional. Through certification programs, Cisco validates the skills and expertise required to effectively manage the modern enterprise network.

Cisco Press exam certification guides and preparation materials offer exceptional—and flexible—access to the knowledge and information required to stay current in your field of expertise or to gain new skills. Whether used as a supplement to more traditional training or as a primary source of learning, these materials offer users the information and knowledge validation required to gain new understanding and proficiencies.

Developed in conjunction with the Cisco certifications and training team, Cisco Press books are the only self-study books authorized by Cisco, and they offer students a series of exam practice tools and resource materials to help ensure that learners fully grasp the concepts and information presented.

Additional authorized Cisco instructor-led courses, e-learning, labs, and simulations are available exclusively from Cisco Learning Solutions Partners worldwide. To learn more, visit http://www.cisco.com/go/training.

I hope that you find these materials to be an enriching and useful part of your exam preparation.

Erik Ullanderson
Manager, Global Certifications
Learning@Cisco
May 2008

Introduction

Congratulations on your decision to pursue a Cisco Certification! If you're reading far enough to look at the introduction to this book, you likely already have a sense of what you ultimately would like to achieve—the Cisco CCNA Security certification. Achieving Cisco CCNA Security certification requires that you pass the Cisco IINS (640-553) exam. Cisco certifications are recognized throughout the networking industry as a rigorous test of a candidate's knowledge of and ability to work with Cisco technology. Through its quality technologies, Cisco has garnered a significant market share in the router and switch marketplace, with more than 80 percent market share in some markets. For many industries and markets around the world, networking equals Cisco. Cisco certification will set you apart from the crowd and allow you to display your knowledge as a networking security professional.

Historically speaking, the first entry-level Cisco certification is the Cisco Certified Network Associate (CCNA) certification, first offered in 1998.

With the introduction of the CCNA Security certification, Cisco has for the first time provided an area of focus at the associate level. The CCNA Security certification is for networking professionals who work with Cisco security technologies and who want to demonstrate their mastery of core network security principles and technologies.

Format of the IINS Exam

The 640-553 IINS exam follows the same general format of other Cisco exams. When you get to the testing center and check in, the proctor gives you some general instructions and then takes you into a quiet room with a PC. When you're at the PC, you have a few things to do before the timer starts on your exam. For instance, you can take a sample quiz, just to get accustomed to the PC and the testing engine. If you have user-level PC skills, you should have no problems with the testing environment. Additionally, Chapter 16 points to a Cisco website where you can see a demo of the actual Cisco test engine.

When you start the exam, you are asked a series of questions. You answer the question and then move on to the next question. *The exam engine does not let you go back and change your answer.* When you move on to the next question, that's it for the earlier question.

The exam questions can be in one of the following formats:

- Multiple-choice (MC)

- Testlet

- Drag-and-drop (DND)

- Simulated lab (Sim)

- Simlet

The first three types of questions are relatively common in many testing environments. The multiple-choice format simply requires that you point and click a circle beside the correct answer(s). Cisco traditionally tells you how many answers you need to choose, and the testing software prevents you from choosing too many answers. Testlets are questions with one general scenario, with multiple MC questions about the overall scenario. Drag-and-drop questions require you to click and hold, move a button or icon to another area, and release the mouse button to place the object somewhere else—typically in a list. For example, to get the question correct, you might need to put a list of five things in the proper order.

The last two types both use a network simulator to ask questions. Interestingly, these two types allow Cisco to assess two very different skills. Sim questions generally describe a problem, and your task is to configure one or more routers and switches to fix the problem. The exam then grades the question based on the configuration you changed or added. Interestingly, Sim questions are the only questions that Cisco (to date) has openly confirmed that partial credit is given for.

The Simlet questions may well be the most difficult style of question on the exams. Simlet questions also use a network simulator, but instead of answering the question by changing the configuration, the question includes one or more MC questions. The questions require that you use the simulator to examine the current behavior of a network, interpreting the output of any **show** commands that you can remember to answer the question. Whereas Sim questions require you to troubleshoot problems related to a configuration, Simlets require you to analyze both working networks and networks with problems, correlating **show** command output with your knowledge of networking theory and configuration commands.

What's on the IINS Exam?

Cisco wants the public to know both the variety of topics and the kinds of knowledge and skills that are required for each topic, for every Cisco certification exam. To that end, Cisco publishes a set of exam topics for each exam. The topics list the specific subjects, such as ACLs, PKI, and AAA, that you will see on the exam. The wording of the topics also implies the kinds of skills required for that topic. For example, one topic might start with "Describe...", and another might begin with "Describe, configure, and troubleshoot...". The second objective clearly states that you need a thorough and deep understanding of that topic. By listing the topics and skill level, Cisco helps you prepare for the exam.

Although the exam topics are helpful, keep in mind that Cisco adds a disclaimer that the posted exam topics for all its certification exams are *guidelines*. Cisco makes an effort to keep the exam questions within the confines of the stated exam topics. I know from talking to those involved that every question is analyzed to ensure that it fits within the stated exam topics.

IINS Exam Topics

Table I-1 lists the exam topics for the 640-553 IINS exam. Although the posted exam topics are not numbered at Cisco.com, Cisco Press does number the exam topics for easier reference. Notice that the topics are divided among nine major topic areas. The table also notes the part of this book in which each exam topic is covered. Because it is possible that the exam topics may change over time, it may be worthwhile to double-check the exam topics as listed on Cisco.com (http://www.cisco.com/go/certification). If Cisco later adds exam topics, you may go to http://www.ciscopress.com and download additional information about the newly added topics.

Table I-1 *640-553 IINS Exam Topics*

Reference Number	Exam Topic	Book Part(s) Where Topic Is Covered
1.0	**Describe the security threats facing modern network infrastructures**	
1.1	Describe and mitigate the common threats to the physical installation	I
1.2	Describe and list mitigation methods for common network attacks	I
1.3	Describe and list mitigation methods for Worm, Virus, and Trojan Horse attacks	II
1.4	Describe the main activities in each phase of a secure network lifecycle	I
1.5	Explain how to meet the security needs of a typical enterprise with a comprehensive security policy	I
1.6	Describe the Cisco Self Defending Network architecture	I
1.7	Describe the Cisco security family of products and their interactions	I, II, III
2.0	**Secure Cisco routers**	
2.1	Secure Cisco routers using the SDM Security Audit feature	I
2.2	Use the One-Step Lockdown feature in SDM to secure a Cisco router	I
2.3	Secure administrative access to Cisco routers by setting strong encrypted passwords, exec timeout, login failure rate and using IOS login enhancements	I
2.4	Secure administrative access to Cisco routers by configuring multiple privilege levels	I
2.5	Secure administrative access to Cisco routers by configuring role based CLI	I

Table I-1 *640-553 IINS Exam Topics (Continued)*

Reference Number	Exam Topic	Book Part(s) Where Topic Is Covered
2.6	Secure the Cisco IOS image and configuration file	I
3.0	**Implement AAA on Cisco routers using local router database and external ACS**	
3.1	Explain the functions and importance of AAA	I
3.2	Describe the features of TACACS+ and RADIUS AAA protocols	I
3.3	Configure AAA authentication	I
3.4	Configure AAA authorization	I
3.5	Configure AAA accounting	I
4.0	**Mitigate threats to Cisco routers and networks using ACLs**	
4.1	Explain the functionality of standard, extended, and named IP ACLs used by routers to filter packets	II
4.2	Configure and verify IP ACLs to mitigate given threats (filter IP traffic destined for Telnet, SNMP, and DDoS attacks) in a network using CLI	II
4.3	Configure IP ACLs to prevent IP address spoofing using CLI	II
4.4	Discuss the caveats to be considered when building ACLs	II
5.0	**Implement secure network management and reporting**	
5.1	Describe the factors to be considered when planning for secure management and reporting of network devices	I
5.2	Use CLI and SDM to configure SSH on Cisco routers to enable secured management access	I
5.3	Use CLI and SDM to configure Cisco routers to send Syslog messages to a Syslog server	I
5.4	Describe SNMPv3 and NTPv3	I
6.0	**Mitigate common Layer 2 attacks**	
6.1	Describe how to prevent layer 2 attacks by configuring basic Catalyst switch security features	II
7.0	**Implement the Cisco IOS firewall feature set using SDM**	
7.1	Describe the operational strengths and weaknesses of the different firewall technologies	II
7.2	Explain stateful firewall operations and the function of the state table	II
7.3	Implement Zone Based Firewall using SDM	II
8.0	**Implement the Cisco IOS IPS feature set using SDM**	
8.1	Define network based vs. host based intrusion detection and prevention	II

Table I-1 *640-553 IINS Exam Topics (Continued)*

Reference Number	Exam Topic	Book Part(s) Where Topic Is Covered
8.2	Explain IPS technologies, attack responses, and monitoring options	II
8.3	Enable and verify Cisco IOS IPS operations using SDM	II
9.0	**Implement site-to-site VPNs on Cisco Routers using SDM**	
9.1	Explain the different methods used in cryptography	III
9.2	Explain IKE protocol functionality and phases	III
9.3	Describe the building blocks of IPSec and the security functions it provides	III
9.4	Configure and verify an IPSec site-to-site VPN with pre-shared key authentication using SDM	III

IINS Course Outlines

Another way to get some direction about the topics on the exams is to look at the course outlines for the related courses. Cisco offers one authorized CCNA Security-related course: Implementing Cisco IOS Network Security (IINSv1.0). Cisco authorizes Certified Learning Solutions Providers (CLSP) and Certified Learning Partners (CLP) to deliver these classes. These authorized companies can also create unique custom course books using this material, in some cases to teach classes geared toward passing the 640-553 IINS exam.

About the CCNA Security Official Exam Certification Guide

As mentioned earlier, Cisco has outlined the topics tested on the 640-553 IINS exam. This book maps to these topic areas and provides some background material to give context and to help you understand these topics.

This section lists this book's variety of features. A number of basic features included in this book are common to all Cisco Press *Official Exam Certification Guides*. These features are designed to help you prepare to pass the official certification exam, as well as help you learn relevant real-world concepts and procedures.

Objectives and Methods

The most important and somewhat obvious objective of this book is to help you pass the 640-553 IINS exam. In fact, if the primary objective of this book were different, the book's title would be misleading! However, the methods used in this book to help you pass the exams are also designed to make you much more knowledgeable about how to do your job.

This book uses several key methodologies to help you discover the exam topics on which you need more review, to help you fully understand and remember those details, and to help you prove to yourself that you have retained your knowledge of those topics. So, this book does not try to help you pass the exams only by memorization, but by truly learning and understanding the topics. The CCNA Security certification is the foundation of the professional level Cisco certification in security, the CCSP, so it is important that this book also help you truly learn the material. This book is designed to help you pass the CCNA Security exam by using the following methods:

- Helping you discover which exam topics you have not mastered

- Providing explanations and information to fill in your knowledge gaps

- Supplying exercises that enhance your ability to recall and deduce the answers to test questions

- Providing practice exercises on the topics and the testing process via test questions on the CD

Book Features

To help you customize your study time using this book, the core chapters have several features that help you make the best use of your time:

- **"Do I Know This Already?" quiz**: Each chapter begins with a quiz that helps you determine how much time you need to spend studying that chapter.

- **Foundation Topics**: These are the core sections of each chapter. They explain the protocols, concepts, and configuration for the topics in that chapter.

- **Exam Preparation Tasks**: At the end of the "Foundation Topics" section of each chapter, the "Exam Preparation Tasks" section lists a series of study activities that you should do at the end of the chapter. Each chapter includes the activities that make the most sense for studying the topics in that chapter.

    — **Review All the Key Topics**: The Key Topic icon appears next to the most important items in the "Foundation Topics" section of the chapter. The Review All the Key Topics activity lists the Key Topics from the chapter, along with their page numbers. Although the contents of the entire chapter could be on the exam, you should definitely know the information listed in each Key Topic, so you should review these.

    — **Complete the Tables and Lists from Memory**: To help you memorize some lists of facts, many of the more important lists and tables from the chapter are included in a document on the CD. This document lists only partial information, allowing you to complete the table or list.

— **Definition of Key Terms**: Although the exam may be unlikely to ask a question such as "Define this term," the CCNA exams do require that you learn and know a lot of networking terminology. This section lists the most important terms from the chapter, asking you to write a short definition and compare your answer to the glossary at the end of the book.

— **Command Reference Tables:** Some chapters cover a large number of configuration and EXEC commands. These tables list and describe the commands introduced in the chapter. For exam preparation, use these tables for reference, but also read them when performing the Exam Preparation Tasks to make sure you remember what all the commands do.

■ **CD-based practice exam**: The companion CD contains an exam engine (From Boson software, http://www.boson.com), that includes two question databases. One database has a copy of all the "Do I Know This Already?" quiz questions from the book, and the other has unique exam-realistic questions. To further help you prepare for the exam, you can take a simulated IINS exam using the CD.

How This Book Is Organized

This book contains 15 core chapters—Chapters 1 through 15. Chapter 16 includes some preparation tips and suggestions for how to approach the exam. Each core chapter covers a subset of the topics on the IINS exam. The core chapters are organized into parts. They cover the following topics:

■ **Part I: Network Security Concepts**

— **Chapter 1, "Understanding Network Security Principles"**: This chapter explains the need for network security and discusses the elements of a secure network. Additionally, legal and ethical considerations are discussed. You are also introduced to various threats targeting the security of your network.

— **Chapter 2, "Developing a Secure Network"**: This chapter explains the day-to-day procedures for deploying, maintaining, and retiring information security components. You are also provided with considerations and principles for authoring a security policy, in addition to creating user awareness of the security policy. Finally, this chapter describes the Cisco Self-Defending Network, which is Cisco's vision for security systems.

— **Chapter 3, "Defending the Perimeter"**: This chapter describes methods of securely accessing a router prompt for purposes of administration. Additionally, you are given an overview of the Cisco Integrated Services Router (ISR) line of routers. In this chapter you also examine the Cisco Security Device Manager (SDM) interface. The graphical interface provided by SDM allows administrators to configure a variety of router features using a collection of wizards, which use best-practice recommendations from the Cisco Technical Assistance Center (TAC).

— **Chapter 4, "Configuring AAA"**: This chapter explores the uses of AAA, including the components that make it up, as well as the steps necessary to successfully configure AAA using the local database. The role of Cisco ACS is also examined as it relates to configuring AAA, including a discussion of working with both RADIUS and TACACS+.

— **Chapter 5, "Securing the Router"**: This chapter discusses various router services that attackers might target. To help you harden the security of a router, this chapter also describes the AutoSecure feature and Cisco SDM's One-Step Lockdown feature. Next the chapter focuses on securing and monitoring router access using syslog, SSH, and SNMPv3 technologies. Finally, this chapter distinguishes between in-band and out-of-band network management and how to use Cisco SDM to configure a variety of management and monitoring features.

■ **Part II: Constructing a Secure Infrastructure**

— **Chapter 6, "Securing Layer 2 Devices"**: This chapter explains how Cisco Catalyst switches can be configured to mitigate several common Layer 2 attacks. Then you are introduced to how Cisco Identity-Based Networking Services (IBNS) uses IEEE 802.1x, RADIUS, and Extensible Authentication Protocol (EAP) technologies to selectively allow access to network resources based on user credentials.

— **Chapter 7, "Implementing Endpoint Security"**: This chapter examines a variety of threats faced by endpoints in a network environment and introduces a series of techniques that can be used to help safeguard systems from common operating system vulnerabilities. This chapter also explores various Cisco-specific technologies that may be used to defend endpoints from a variety of attacks. Specifically, technologies such as IronPort, the Cisco NAC Appliance, and the Cisco Security Agent are discussed.

— **Chapter 8, "Providing SAN Security"**: This chapter outlines the basics of SAN operation and looks at the benefits that a SAN brings to the enterprise as a whole. A variety of security mechanisms, such as LUN masking, SAN zoning, and port authentication, are also explored as steps that may be taken to safeguard data in a SAN environment.

— **Chapter 9, "Exploring Secure Voice Solutions"**: This chapter introduces you to voice over IP (VoIP) networks. You learn what business benefits VoIP offers, in addition to the components and protocols that support the transmission of packetized voice across a data network. You are made aware of specific threats targeting a VoIP network. Some threats (such as toll fraud) are found in traditional telephony networks, but others are specific to VoIP.

Finally, this chapter identifies specific actions you can take to increase the security of VoIP networks. For example, you will consider how to use firewalls and VPNs to protect voice networks and how to harden the security of Cisco IP Phones and voice servers.

— **Chapter 10, "Using Cisco IOS Firewalls to Defend the Network"**: This chapter begins by exploring the evolution of firewall technology and the role of firewalls in constructing an overall network defense. This chapter also examines how to use access control lists (ACL) to construct a static packet-filtering mechanism for the enterprise environment. Finally, zone-based firewalls are discussed because they represent a significant advance in firewall technology. Their role in defending the network is examined.

— **Chapter 11, "Using Cisco IOS IPS to Secure the Network"**: This chapter distinguishes between intrusion detection and intrusion prevention. Various Intrusion Prevention System (IPS) appliances are introduced, and the concept of signatures is discussed. Also, this chapter examines how to configure a Cisco IOS router to act as an IPS sensor, as opposed to using, for example, a dedicated IPS appliance. Specifically, the configuration discussed uses a wizard available in the Cisco SDM interface.

■ **Part III: Extending Security and Availability with Cryptography and VPNs**

— **Chapter 12, "Designing a Cryptographic Solution"**: This chapter initially explores the basics of cryptographic services and looks at their evolution. This chapter also examines the use of symmetric encryption, including a variety of symmetric algorithms such as DES, 3DES, AES, SEAL, and various Rivest ciphers. This chapter concludes with a discussion of the encryption process and what makes for a strong, trustworthy encryption algorithm.

— **Chapter 13, "Implementing Digital Signatures"**: This chapter begins with a look at hash algorithms and explores their construction and usage. This includes a discussion of their relative strengths and weaknesses in practical application. The components that make up a digital signature are also explored in depth, along with a discussion of their application as a means of proving a message's authenticity.

— **Chapter 14, "Exploring PKI and Asymmetric Encryption"**: This chapter looks at the use of asymmetric algorithms in a PKI and examines the features and capabilities of RSA specifically. The Diffie-Hellman (DH) algorithm is also discussed, as to how it is used for key exchange. This chapter also explores the makeup of the PKI infrastructure and discusses the various components and topologies that may be employed.

— **Chapter 15, "Building a Site-to-Site IPsec VPN Solution"**: This chapter introduces you to an IPsec virtual private network (VPN) and its components. Additionally, you explore specific devices in the Cisco VPN product family. Then you are presented with Cisco best-practice recommendations for VPNs. This chapter then walks you through the process of configuring an IPsec site-to-site VPN on an IOS router, using both the command-line interface and the Cisco Security Device Manager (SDM) interface.

■ **Part IV: Final Preparation**

— **Chapter 16, "Final Preparation"**: This chapter identifies tools for final exam preparation and helps you develop an effective study plan.

■ **Part V: Appendixes**

— **Appendix A, "Answers to the 'Do I Know This Already?' Questions"**: Includes the answers to all the questions from Chapters 1 through 15.

— **Appendix B, "Glossary"**: The glossary contains definitions of all the terms listed in the "Definition of Key Terms" section at the conclusion of Chapters 1 through 15.

— **Appendix C, "CCNA Security Exam Updates: Version 1.0"**: This appendix provides instructions for finding updates to the exam and this book when and if they occur.

— **Appendix D, "Memory Tables"**: This CD-only appendix contains the key tables and lists from each chapter, with some of the contents removed. You can print this appendix and, as a memory exercise, complete the tables and lists. The goal is to help you memorize facts that can be useful on the exams. *This appendix is available in PDF format on the CD; it is not in the printed book.*

— **Appendix E, "Memory Tables Answer Key"**: This CD-only appendix contains the answer key for the memory tables in Appendix D. *This appendix is available in PDF format on the CD; it is not in the printed book.*

How to Use This Book to Prepare for the IINS Exam

Using this book to prepare for the IINS exam is pretty straightforward—read each chapter in succession, and follow the study suggestions in Chapter 16, "Final Preparation."

For the core chapters of this book (Chapters 1 through 15), you do have some choices about how much of the chapter you read. In some cases, you may already know most or all of the information covered in a given chapter. To help you decide how much time to spend on each chapter, the chapters begin with a "Do I Know This Already?" quiz. If you get all the quiz questions correct, or you miss just one question, you may want to skip to the end of the chapter and the "Exam Preparation Tasks" section, and do those activities. Figure I-1 shows the overall plan.

Figure I-1   *How to Approach Each Chapter of This Book*

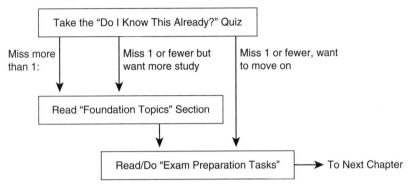

When you have completed Chapters 1 through 15, you can use Chapter 16 for exam preparation guidance. That chapter includes the following suggestions:

■   Check http://www.ciscopress.com for the latest copy of Appendix C, which may include additional topics for study.

■   Repeat the tasks in all the chapters' "Exam Preparation Tasks" chapter-ending section.

■   Review all DIKTA questions using the exam engine.

■   Practice for the exam using the exam engine.

This book is broken into parts and chapters that address the key areas of the IINS exam. Each chapter begins with a series of "Do I Know This Already?" questions. You should work through these to get a sense of your current knowledge of the subject matter being discussed. Each chapter contains memory tables that you should work through. At the end of each chapter is a list of all the key topics, as well as terms central to the topic. It is a good idea to focus on these key topic areas and to be familiar with all the terms listed in each chapter. After you have completed this book, you may further prepare for the exam and test your knowledge by working through the practice exam on the CD. Tracking your score on the practice exam and noting areas of weakness will allow you to review these areas in the text to further solidify your knowledge before the actual IINS exam.

For More Information

If you have any comments about this book, you can submit them at http://www.ciscopress.com. Just go to the website, click Contact Us, and enter your message.

Cisco might occasionally make changes that affect the CCNA Security certification. You should always check http://www.cisco.com/go/certification for the latest details.

IINS exam topics covered in this part:

- Describe and mitigate the common threats to the physical installation
- Describe and list mitigation methods for common network attacks
- Describe the main activities in each phase of a secure network lifecycle
- Explain how to meet the security needs of a typical enterprise with a comprehensive security policy
- Describe the Cisco Self Defending Network architecture
- Describe the Cisco security family of products and their interactions
- Secure Cisco routers using the SDM Security Audit feature
- Use the One-Step Lockdown feature in SDM to secure a Cisco router
- Secure administrative access to Cisco routers by setting strong encrypted passwords, exec timeout, login failure rate and using IOS login enhancements
- Secure administrative access to Cisco routers by configuring multiple privilege levels
- Secure administrative access to Cisco routers by configuring role-based CLI
- Secure the Cisco IOS image and configuration file
- Explain the functions and importance of AAA
- Describe the features of TACACS+ and RADIUS AAA protocols
- Configure AAA authentication
- Configure AAA authorization
- Configure AAA accounting
- Describe the factors to be considered when planning for secure management and reporting of network devices
- Use CLI and SDM to configure SSH on Cisco routers to enable secured management access
- Use CLI and SDM to configure Cisco routers to send Syslog messages to a Syslog server
- Describe SNMPv3 and NTPv3

Part I: Network Security Concepts

This chapter covers the following topics:

Exploring security fundamentals: This section explains the need for network security and discusses the elements of a secure network. Additionally, legal and ethical considerations are discussed.

Understanding the methods of network attacks: This section makes you aware of various threats targeting the security of your network and describes specific attacks that could be launched against a network.

CHAPTER 1

Understanding Network Security Principles

As networks grow and interconnect with other networks, including the Internet, those networks are exposed to a greater number of security risks. Not only does the number of potential attackers grow along with the size of the network, but the tools available to those potential attackers are always increasing in terms of sophistication.

This chapter begins by broadly describing the necessity of network security and what should be in place in a secure network. Legal ramifications are addressed. Also, this chapter walks you through several specific types of attacks that could threaten your network. Finally, you are provided with a list of best-practice recommendations for mitigating such attacks.

"Do I Know This Already?" Quiz

The "Do I Know This Already?" quiz helps you determine your level of knowledge of this chapter's topics before you begin. Table 1-1 details the major topics discussed in this chapter and their corresponding quiz questions.

Table 1-1   *"Do I Know This Already?" Section-to-Question Mapping*

Foundation Topics Section	Questions
Exploring Security Fundamentals	1 to 6
Understanding the Methods of Network Attacks	7 to 15

1. Where do most attacks on an organization's computer resources originate?

   a. From the Internet

   b. From the inside network

   c. From universities

   d. From intruders who gain physical access to the computer resources

2. What are the three primary goals of network security? (Choose three.)

   a. Confidentiality

   b. Redundancy

   c. Integrity

   d. Availability

3. The U.S. government places classified data into which classes? (Choose three.)

   a. SBU

   b. Confidential

   c. Secret

   d. Top-secret

4. Cisco defines three categories of security controls: administrative, physical, and technical. Individual controls within these categories can be further classified as what three specific types of controls? (Choose three.)

   a. Preventive

   b. Deterrent

   c. Detective

   d. Reactive

5. Litigators typically require which three of the following elements to present an effective argument when prosecuting information security violations? (Choose three.)

   a. Audit trail

   b. Motive

   c. Means

   d. Opportunity

6. Which type of law typically involves the enforcement of regulations by government agencies?

   a. Criminal law

   b. Tort law

   c. Administrative law

   d. Civil law

7. Which of the following is a weakness in an information system that an attacker might leverage to gain unauthorized access to the system or data on the system?

    a. Risk

    b. Exploit

    c. Mitigation

    d. Vulnerability

8. What type of hacker attempts to hack telephony systems?

    a. Script kiddy

    b. Hacktivist

    c. Phreaker

    d. White hat hacker

9. Which of the following is a method of gaining access to a system that bypasses normal security measures?

    a. Creating a back door

    b. Launching a DoS attack

    c. Starting a Smurf attack

    d. Conducting social engineering

10. What security design philosophy uses a layered approach to eliminate single points of failure and provide overlapping protection?

    a. AVVID

    b. Defense in Depth

    c. SONA

    d. IINS

11. What are two types of IP spoofing attacks? (Choose two.)

    a. Nonblind spoofing

    b. Promiscuous spoofing

    c. Autonomous spoofing

    d. Blind spoofing

12. What term refers to the electromagnetic interference (EMI) that can radiate from network cables?

   a.   Doppler waves

   b.   Emanations

   c.   Gaussian distributions

   d.   Multimode distortion

13. What kind of integrity attack is a collection of small attacks that result in a larger attack when combined?

   a.   Data diddling

   b.   Botnet attack

   c.   Hijacking a session

   d.   Salami attack

14. Which of the following best describes a Smurf attack?

   a.   It sends ping requests to a subnet, requesting that devices on that subnet send ping replies to a target system.

   b.   It sends ping requests in segments of an invalid size.

   c.   It intercepts the third step in a TCP three-way handshake to hijack a session.

   d.   It uses Trojan horse applications to create a distributed collection of "zombie" computers, which can be used to launch a coordinated DDoS attack.

15. Which of the following are Cisco best-practice recommendations for securing a network? (Choose three.)

   a.   Deploy HIPS software on all end-user workstations.

   b.   Routinely apply patches to operating systems and applications.

   c.   Disable unneeded services and ports on hosts.

   d.   Require strong passwords, and enable password expiration.

Foundation Topics

Exploring Security Fundamentals

A "secure network" is a moving target. As new vulnerabilities and new methods of attack are discovered, a relatively unsophisticated user can potentially launch a devastating attack against an unprotected network. This section begins by describing the challenges posed by the current security landscape. You will learn about the three primary goals of security: confidentiality, integrity, and availability.

This section also explains traffic classification and security controls. You will learn how to respond to a security violation and consider the legal and ethical ramifications of network security.

Why Network Security Is a Necessity

Network attacks are evolving in their sophistication and in their ability to evade detection. Also, attacks are becoming more targeted and have greater financial consequences for their victims.

Types of Threats

Connecting a network to an outside network (for example, the Internet) introduces the possibility that outside attackers will exploit the network, perhaps by stealing network data or by impacting the network's performance (for example, by introducing viruses). However, even if a network were disconnected from any external network, security threats (in fact, most of the probable security threats) would still exist.

Specifically, according to the Computer Security Institute (CSI) in San Francisco, California, approximately 60 to 80 percent of network misuse incidents originate from the inside network. Therefore, although network isolation is rarely feasible in today's e-business environment, even physical isolation from other networks does not ensure network security.

Based on these factors, network administrators must consider both internal and external threats.

Internal Threats

Network security threats originating inside a network tend to be more serious than external threats. Here are some reasons for the severity of internal threats:

- Inside users already have knowledge of the network and its available resources.

- Inside users typically have some level of access granted to them because of the nature of their job.

- Traditional network security mechanisms such as Intrusion Prevention Systems (IPS) and firewalls are ineffective against much of the network misuse originating internally.

External Threats

Because external attackers probably do not have intimate knowledge of a network, and because they do not already possess access credentials, their attacks tend to be more technical in nature. For example, an attacker could perform a *ping sweep* on a network to identify IP addresses that respond to the series of pings. Then, those IP addresses could be subjected to a *port scan*, in which open services on those hosts are discovered. The attacker could then try to exploit a known vulnerability to compromise one of the discovered services on a host. If the attacker gains control of the host, he could use that as a jumping-off point to attack other systems in the network.

Fortunately, network administrators can mitigate many of the threats posed by external attackers. In fact, the majority of this book is dedicated to explaining security mechanisms that can defeat most external threats.

Scope of the Challenge

The "2007 CSI/FBI Computer Crime and Security Survey" is a fascinating document that provides insight into trends in network attacks from 2004 to 2007. A copy of this document can be downloaded from http://i.cmpnet.com/v2.gocsi.com/pdf/CSISurvey2007.pdf.

As an example of the information contained in this document, Figure 1-1 shows the average number of security incidents reported by 208 respondents for the years 2004 to 2007. Notice that the percentage of respondents reporting more than 10 incidents in a year dramatically increased in 2007.

Figure 1-1 *Incidents in the Past 12 Months (Source: "2007 CSI/FBI Computer Crime and Security Survey")*

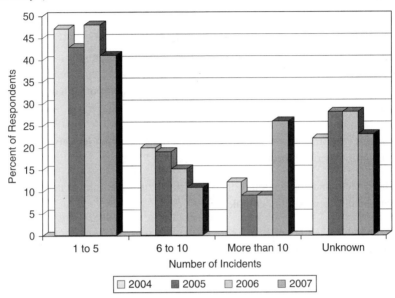

The following is a further sampling of information contained in the survey:

■ The average financial loss from computer crime/security incidents increased from $168,000 in 2006 to $350,424 in 2007.

■ Of the survey respondents who reported one or more attacks, 18 percent of those attacks were "targeted" attacks (that is, an attack not targeting the general population).

■ Before the 2007 report, viruses were the leading contributor to financial losses for seven years in a row. However, in the 2007 report, viruses fell to the second leading cause of financial losses, with financial fraud rising to the number one factor.

Nonsecured Custom Applications

The vast majority (approximately 75 percent) of network attacks target specific applications, as opposed to lower-layer attacks. One reason attacks have become more targeted is the trend of attackers to be more motivated by profit, rather than by the fame or notoriety generated by creating a virus, for example. Unfortunately, because many organizations use custom applications (often not written with security in mind), these applications can be prime attack targets.

Attacks on custom applications are not as preventable as attacks on "well-known" applications, which periodically release security patches and updates. Another concern for some organizations is complying with regulatory mandates about protecting company data (for example, customer credit card information).

The Three Primary Goals of Network Security

For most of today's corporate networks, the demands of e-commerce and customer contact require connectivity between internal corporate networks and the outside world. From a security standpoint, two basic assumptions about modern corporate networks are as follows:

- Today's corporate networks are large, interconnect with other networks, and run both standards-based and proprietary protocols.

- The devices and applications connecting to and using corporate networks are continually increasing in complexity

Because almost all (if not all) corporate networks require network security, consider the three primary goals of network security:

- Confidentiality

- Integrity

- Availability

Confidentiality

Data confidentiality implies keeping data private. This privacy could entail physically or logically restricting access to sensitive data or encrypting traffic traversing a network. A network that provides confidentiality would do the following, as a few examples:

- Use network security mechanisms (for example, firewalls and access control lists [ACL]) to prevent unauthorized access to network resources.

- Require appropriate credentials (for example, usernames and passwords) to access specific network resources.

- Encrypt traffic such that an attacker could not decipher any traffic he captured from the network.

Integrity

Data integrity ensures that data has not been modified in transit. Also, a data integrity solution might perform origin authentication to verify that traffic is originating from the source that should be sending it.

Examples of integrity violations include

- Modifying the appearance of a corporate website

- Intercepting and altering an e-commerce transaction

- Modifying financial records that are stored electronically

Availability

The availability of data is a measure of the data's accessibility. For example, if a server were down only five minutes per year, it would have an availability of 99.999 percent (that is, "five nines" of availability).

Here are a couple of examples of how an attacker could attempt to compromise the availability of a network:

- He could send improperly formatted data to a networked device, resulting in an unhandled exception error.

- He could flood a network system with an excessive amount of traffic or requests. This would consume the system's processing resources and prevent the system from responding to many legitimate requests. This type of attack is called a denial-of-service (DoS) attack.

Categorizing Data

Different data requires varying levels of security (for example, based on the data's sensitivity). Therefore, organizations often adapt a data classification system to categorize data. Each category can then be treated with a specific level of security. However, sometimes this data classification is not just a convenience. Sometimes organizations are legally required to protect certain classifications of data.

Classification Models

Although no single standard exists for data classification, organizations often benefit from examining classification models commonly used by government and many businesses.

Government and Military Classification Model

Table 1-2 provides an example of a data classification model, which is used by multiple governments and militaries.

**Key
Topic**

Table 1-2   *Government and Military Data Classification Example*

Data Category	Description
Unclassified	Data that has few or no privacy requirements
Sensitive but unclassified (SBU)	Data that could cause embarrassment but not constitute a security threat if revealed
Confidential	Data that has a reasonable probability of causing damage if disclosed to an unauthorized party
Secret	Data that has a reasonable probability of causing serious damage if disclosed to an unauthorized party
Top-secret	Data that has a reasonable probability of causing exceptionally grave damage if disclosed to an unauthorized party

NOTE   In the U.S., Executive Order 12958 (available at http://www.whitehouse.gov/news/releases/2003/03/20030325-11.html) states that the U.S. government shall classify classified information into one of three levels: (1) Confidential, (2) Secret, and (3) Top-Secret.

Organizational Classification Model

Table 1-3 provides an example of an organizational data classification model.

Table 1-3   *Organizational Data Classification Example*

Data Category	Description
Public	Information made available to the public (for example, through marketing materials)
Sensitive	Data that could cause embarrassment but not constitute a security threat if revealed
Private	Organizational information that should be kept secret and whose accuracy should be maintained
Confidential	Sensitive organizational information (for example, employee records) that should be protected with great care

Data Classification Characteristics

Table 1-4 offers a few characteristics by which data can be classified.

Table 1-4 *Data Classification Characteristics*

Key
Topic

Characteristic	Description
Value	How valuable the data is to the organization
Age	How old the data is
Useful life	How long the data will be considered relevant
Personal association	How personal the data is

When determining a classification approach, define how many classification levels you need. Having too many classification levels can prove difficult to administer, whereas having too few classification levels lacks the granularity needed to classify a wide spectrum of data. As part of documenting your classification approach, you should also indicate who is responsible for securing data classified using your defined security levels.

NOTE Some occasions necessitate the release of classified data. Such occasions include the need to comply with a court order, when working with certain government agencies, and when the release of the information is ordered by senior management.

Classification Roles

Different members of an organization must assume different roles to ensure the proper protection of classified data. Examples of these roles include the following:

■ Owner

Key
Topic

— Initially determines the classification level

— Routinely reviews documented procedures for classifying data

— Gives the custodian the responsibility of protecting the data

■ Custodian

— Keeps up-to-date backups of classified data

— Verifies the integrity of the backups

— Restores data from backups on an as-needed basis

— Follows policy guidelines to maintain specific data

■ User

— Accesses and uses data in accordance with an established security policy

— Takes reasonable measures to protect the data he or she has access to

— Uses data for only organizational purposes

Controls in a Security Solution

As just mentioned, the work of actually securing data is the responsibility of the *custodian*. However, if security is applied only through technical means, the results will not be highly effective. Specifically, because most attacks originating inside a network are not technical attacks, nontechnical mitigation strategies are required to thwart them. Cisco defines three security controls contained in a more all-encompassing security solution:

- **Administrative controls** are primarily policy-centric. Examples include the following:

  — Routine security awareness training programs

  — Clearly defined security policies

  — A change management system, which notifies appropriate parties of system changes

  — Logging configuration changes

  — Properly screening potential employees (for example, performing criminal background checks)

- **Physical controls** help protect the data's environment and prevent potential attackers from readily having physical access to the data. Examples of physical controls are

  — Security systems to monitor for intruders

  — Physical security barriers (for example, locked doors)

  — Climate protection systems, to maintain proper temperature and humidity, in addition to alerting personnel in the event of fire

  — Security personnel to guard the data

- **Technical controls** use a variety of hardware and software technologies to protect data. Examples of technical controls include the following:

  — Security appliances (for example, firewalls, IPSs, and VPN termination devices)

  — Authorization applications (for example, RADIUS or TACACS+ servers, one-time passwords (OTP), and biometric security scanners)

> **NOTE**   Because this book focuses on Cisco-based security solutions, most of the mitigation strategies presented use technology controls.

Individual administrative, physical, and technical controls can be further classified as one of the following control types:

■ **Preventive**: A preventive control attempts to prevent access to data or a system.

■ **Deterrent**: A deterrent control attempts to prevent a security incident by influencing the potential attacker not to launch an attack.

■ **Detective**: A detective control can detect when access to data or a system occurs.

Interestingly, each category of control (administrative, physical, and technical) contains components for these types of controls (preventive, deterrent, and detective). For example, a specific detective control could be one of the following:

■ An administrative control, such as a log book entry that is required by a security policy

■ A physical control, such as an alarm that sounds when a particular door is opened

■ A technical control, such as an IPS appliance generating an alert

Responding to a Security Incident

Many *deterrent* controls might display warnings such as "Violators will be prosecuted to the fullest extent of the law." However, to successfully prosecute an attacker, litigators typically require the following elements to present an effective argument:

■ **Motive**: A motive describes *why* the attacker committed the act. For example, was he a disgruntled employee? Also, potential motives can be valuable to define during an investigation. Specifically, an investigation might begin with those who had a motive to carry out the attack.

■ **Means**: With all the security controls in place to protect data or computer systems, you need to determine if the accused had the *means* (for example, the technical skills) to carry out the attack.

■ **Opportunity**: The question of whether the accused had the *opportunity* to commit the attack asks if the accused was *available* to commit the attack. For example, if the accused claims to have been at a ball game at the time of the attack, and if witnesses can verify this statement, it is less likely that the accused did indeed commit the attack.

Another challenge with prosecuting computer-based crime stems from the fragility of data. For example, a time stamp can easily be changed on a file without detection. To prevent such evidence tampering, strict policies and procedures for data handling must be followed. For example, before any investigative work is done on a computer system, a policy might require that multiple copies of the hard drive be made. One or more *master copies* could be locked up, and copies could also be given to the defense and prosecution for their investigation.

Also, to verify the integrity of data since a security incident occurred, you should be able to show a *chain of custody*. A chain of custody documents who has been in possession of the data (that is, the evidence) since a security breach occurred.

Legal and Ethical Ramifications

Some businesses must abide by strict government regulations for security procedures. Therefore, information security professionals should be familiar with a few fundamental legal concepts. For example, most countries classify laws into one of the following three types:

■ **Criminal law** applies to crimes that have been committed and that might result in fines and/or imprisonment for someone found guilty.

■ **Civil law** addresses wrongs that have been committed. However, those wrongs are not considered crimes. An example of civil litigation might involve patent infringement. Consequences to someone found to be in violation of a civil law might include an order to cease and desist the illegal activity and/or to pay damages.

■ **Administrative law** typically involves the enforcement of regulations by government agencies. For example, a company that misappropriated retirement funds might be found in violation of an administrative law. If a party is found to be in violation of an administrative law, the consequences typically are monetary, with the money being divided between the government agency and the victim.

In addition to legal restrictions, information security professionals should be bound by ethical guidelines. Ethical guidelines deal more with someone's intent and conduct, as opposed to whether an act was technically legal.

Although the issue of ethics might seem more difficult to define, information security professionals have several formalized codes of conduct:

■ International Information Systems Security Certification Consortium, Inc. Code of Ethics

■ Computer Ethics Institute

■ Internet Activities Board (IAB)

■ Generally Accepted System Security Principles (GASSP)

Legal Issues to Consider

As a provider of network connectivity to customers, a service provider needs to be aware of potential liability issues. For example, if an e-commerce company lost a certain amount of business because of a service provider outage, the service provider might be found liable and have to pay damages.

Also, some countries are passing laws dictating how companies handle privacy issues. For example, the Notification of Risk to Personal Data Act in the U.S. requires companies and government agencies that conduct commerce between states to alert anyone whose personal data was revealed to someone not authorized to see it.

U.S. Laws and Regulations

With increased levels of terrorist activity on the Internet and an ever-increasing percentage of Internet connectivity for the world's citizens, governments are forced to develop regulations and legislation covering information security. As a few examples, the U.S. government created the following regulations, which pertain to information security:

- **Gramm-Leach-Bliley Act (GLBA) of 1999**: Did away with antitrust laws that disallowed banks, insurance companies, and securities firms from combining and sharing their information.

- **Health Insurance Portability and Accountability Act (HIPAA) of 2000**: Provides assurance that the electronic transfer of confidential patient information will not be less secure than the transfer of paper-based patient records.

- **Sarbanes-Oxley (SOX) Act of 2002**: Responded to corporate accounting scandals in an attempt to increase public trust in accounting and reporting practices.

- **Security and Freedom through Encryption (SAFE) Act**: Permits any form of encryption to be used by people in the U.S.

- **Computer Fraud and Abuse Act**: Developed to reduce malicious computing hacking, with an amendment to accommodate the Uniting and Strengthening America by Providing Appropriate Tools Required to Intercept and Obstruct Terrorism (USA PATRIOT) Act.

- **Privacy Act of 1974**: Protects the privacy of individuals and requires that they provide written permission for their information to be released.

- **Federal Information Security Management Act (FISMA) of 2002**: Requires annual audits of network security within the U.S. government and affiliated parties.

- **Economic Espionage Act of 1996**: States that the misuse of trade secrets is a federal crime.

International Jurisdiction Issues

A unique legal challenge for prosecuting information security offenses deals with jurisdictional issues. For example, an attacker in one country could launch an attack from a computer in another country that targets a computer in yet another country. The international boundaries that were virtually crossed could pose significant challenges to litigators.

Fortunately, governments are beginning to collaborate on such investigations and prosecutions. For example, organizations that share law enforcement information between countries include G8, Interpol, and the European Union.

Understanding the Methods of Network Attacks

You might have noticed that this book has thus far referred to computer criminals as "attackers" rather than "hackers." This wording is intentional, because not all hackers have malicious intent, even though the term "hacker" often has a negative connotation. In this section, you will gain additional insight into the mind-set and characteristics of various hackers.

Additionally, you will be introduced to a variety of methods that attackers can use to infiltrate a computing system. To help mitigate such attacks, Cisco recommends the Defense in Depth design philosophy, which also is covered in this section, in addition to a collection of best practices for defending your network.

Vulnerabilities

A *vulnerability* in an information system is a weakness that an attacker might leverage to gain unauthorized access to the system or its data. In some cases, after a vulnerability is discovered, attackers write a program intended to take advantage of the vulnerability. This type of malicious program is called an *exploit*.

However, even if a system has a vulnerability, the likelihood that someone will use that vulnerability to cause damage varies. This likelihood is called *risk*. For example, a data center might be vulnerable to a fire breaking out in the building. However, if the data center has advanced fire suppression systems and hot standby backups at another physical location, the risk to the data is minimal.

When you make plans to address vulnerabilities, consider the varied types of vulnerabilities. For example, consider the following broad categories of vulnerabilities:

■   Physical vulnerabilities, such as fire, earthquake, or tornado

■   Weaknesses in a system's design

■   Weaknesses in the protocol(s) used by a system

■ Weaknesses in the code executed by a system

■ Suboptimal configuration of system parameters

■ Malicious software (for example, a virus)

■ Human vulnerabilities (whether intentional or unintentional)

For example, consider human vulnerabilities. Because most attacks against information systems are launched from people on the "inside," controls should be set up to prevent the intentional or unintentional misuse of information systems.

Social engineering is an example of unintentional misuse. To illustrate this concept, consider a situation in which an outside attacker calls a receptionist. The attacker pretends to be a member of the company's IT department, and he convinces the receptionist to tell him her username and password. The attacker then can use those credentials to log into the network.

To prevent a single inside user from accidentally or purposefully launching an attack, some organizations require that two users enter their credentials before a specific act can be carried out, much like two keys being required to launch a missile.

Also, many employees are concerned with accomplishing a particular task. If stringent security procedures seem to stand in their way, the employees might circumnavigate any safeguards to, in their minds, be more productive. Therefore, user education is a critical component of any organizational security policy.

Potential Attackers

Another element of defending your data is identifying potential attackers who might want to steal or manipulate that data. For example, a company might need to protect its data from corporate competitors, terrorists, employees, and hackers, to name just a few.

The term "hacker" is often used very generically to describe attackers. However, not all hackers have malicious intent.

Table 1-5 lists various types of "hackers."

Key Topic

Table 1-5 *Types of Hackers*

Type of "Hacker"	Description
White hat hacker	A white hat hacker has the skills to break into computer systems and do damage. However, he uses his skills to help organizations. For example, a white hat hacker might work for a company to test the security of its network.
Black hat hacker	A black hat hacker, also known as a "cracker," uses his skills for unethical reasons (for example, to steal funds).
Gray hat hacker	A gray hat hacker can be thought of as a white hat hacker who occasionally strays and acts unethically. For example, a gray hat hacker might be employed as a legitimate network security tester. However, in the course of his ethical duties, he finds an opportunity for personal gain and acts unethically to obtain that personal gain.
Phreaker	A phreaker is a hacker of a telecommunications system. For example, a phreaker known as "Captain Crunch" used a toy whistle he found in a box of Captain Crunch cereal (which generated a 2600-Hz tone) to trick phone systems into letting him place free long distance calls. Convincing a telecommunications carrier to permit free long distance calls in this manner is an example of "phreaking."
Script kiddy	A script kiddy is a user who lacks the skills of a typical hacker. Rather, he downloads hacking utilities and uses those utilities to launch attacks, rather than writing his own programs.
Hacktivist	A hacktivist is a hacker with political motivations, such as someone who defaces the website of a political candidate.
Computer security hacker	A computer security hacker is knowledgeable about the technical aspects of computer and network security systems. For example, this person might attempt to attack a system protected by an IPS by fragmenting malicious traffic in a way that would go undetected by the IPS.
Academic hacker	An academic hacker typically is an employee or student at an institution of higher education. The academic hacker uses the institution's computing resources to write "clever" programs. Typically, these hackers use their real names (unlike the pseudonyms often used by computer security hackers), and they tend to focus on open-standards-based software and operating systems (for example, Linux).
Hobby hacker	A hobby hacker tends to focus on home computing. He might modify existing hardware or software to, for example, use software without a legitimate license. For example, code that "unlocks" an Apple iPhone might be the work of a hobby hacker.

As shown in Table 1-5, "hackers" come in many flavors, which leads to the question, "What motivates a hacker?" Some hackers might work for governments to try to gather intelligence from other governments. Some attackers seek financial gain through their attacks. Other hackers simply enjoy the challenge of compromising a protected information system.

This book details several specific attacks that an attacker can launch. However, at this point, you should be familiar with five broad categories of attacks:

■ **Passive**: A passive attack is difficult to detect, because the attacker isn't actively sending traffic (malicious or otherwise). An example of a passive attack is an attacker capturing packets from the network and attempting to decrypt them (if the traffic was encrypted originally).

■ **Active**: An active attack is easier to detect, because the attacker is actively sending traffic that can be detected. An attacker might launch an active attack in an attempt to access classified information or to modify data on a system.

■ **Close-in**: A close-in attack, as the name implies, occurs when the attacker is in close physical proximity with the target system. For example, an attacker can bypass password protection on some routers, switches, and servers if he gains physical access to those devices.

■ **Insider**: An insider attack occurs when legitimate network users leverage their credentials and knowledge of the network in a malicious fashion.

■ **Distribution**: Distribution attacks intentionally introduce "back doors" to hardware or software systems at the point of manufacture. After these systems have been distributed to a variety of customers, the attacker can use his knowledge of the implanted back door to, for example, access protected data, manipulate data, or make the target system unusable by legitimate users.

The Mind-set of a Hacker

Hackers can use a variety of tools and techniques to "hack" into a system (that is, gain unauthorized access to a system). Although these methods vary, the following steps illustrate one example of a hacker's methodical process for hacking into a system:

Step 1   Learn more about the system by performing reconnaissance. In this step, also known as "footprinting," the hacker learns all he can about the system. For example, he might learn the target company's domain names and the range of IP addresses it uses. He might perform a port scan to see what ports are open on a target system.

Step 2   Identify applications on the system, as well as the system's operating system. Hackers can use various tools to attempt to connect to a system, and the prompt they receive (for example, an FTP login prompt or a default web page) could provide insight into the system's operating system. Also, the previously mentioned port scan can help identify applications running on a system.

Step 3   Gain access to the system. Social engineering is one of the more popular ways to obtain login credentials. For example, public DNS records provide contact information for a company's domain name. A hacker might be able to use this information to convince the domain administrator to reveal information about the system. For example, the hacker could pretend to be a representative of the service provider or a government agency. This approach is called *pretexting*.

Step 4   Log in with obtained user credentials, and escalate the hacker's privileges. For example, a hacker could introduce a Trojan horse (a piece of software that appears to be a legitimate application but that also performs some unseen malicious function) to escalate his privileges.

Step 5   Gather additional usernames and passwords. With appropriate privileges, hackers can run utilities to create reports of usernames and/or passwords.

Step 6   Configure a "back door." Accessing a system via a regular username/ password might not be how a hacker wants to repeatedly gain access to a system. Passwords can expire, and logins can be logged. Therefore, hackers might install a back door, which is a method of gaining access to a system that bypasses normal security measures.

Step 7   Use the system. After a hacker gains control of a system, he might gather protected information from that system. Alternatively, he might manipulate the system's data or use the system to launch attacks against other systems with which the system might have an established trust relationship.

Defense in Depth

Because a security solution is only as strong as its weakest link, network administrators are challenged to implement a security solution that protects a complex network. As a result, rather than deploying a single security solution, Cisco recommends multiple, overlapping solutions. These overlapping solutions target different aspects of security, such as securing against insider attacks and securing against technical attacks. These solutions should also be subjected to routine testing and evaluation. Security solutions should also overlap in a way that eliminates any single point of failure.

Defense in Depth is a design philosophy that achieves this layered security approach. The layers of security present in a Defense in Depth deployment should provide redundancy for one another while offering a variety of defense strategies for protecting multiple aspects of a network. Any single points of failure in a security solution should be eliminated, and weak links in the security solution should be strengthened.

The Defense in Depth design philosophy includes recommendations such as the following:

- Defend multiple attack targets in the network.

    — Protect the network infrastructure.

    — Protect strategic computing resources, such as via a Host-based Intrusion Prevention System (HIPS).

- Create overlapping defenses. For example, include both Intrusion Detection System (IDS) and IPS protections.

- Let the value of a protected resource dictate the strength of the security mechanism. For example, deploy more resources to protect a network boundary as opposed to the resources deployed to protect an end-user workstation.

- Use strong encryption technologies, such as AES (as opposed to DES) or Public Key Infrastructure (PKI) solutions.

Consider the sample Defense in Depth topology shown in Figure 1-2. Notice the two e-mail servers—external and internal. The external e-mail server acts as an e-mail relay to the internal e-mail server. Therefore, an attacker attempting to exploit an e-mail vulnerability would have to compromise both e-mail servers to affect the internal corporate e-mail.

Also notice the use of a Network-based Intrusion Detection System (NIDS), a Network Intrusion Prevention System (NIPS), and a Host-based Intrusion Prevention System (HIPS). All three of these mitigation strategies look for malicious traffic and can alert or drop such traffic. However, these strategies are deployed at different locations in the network to protect different areas of the network. This overlapping yet diversified protection is an example of the Defense in Depth design philosophy.

However, if all security solutions in a network were configured and managed by a single management station, this management station could be a single point of failure. Therefore, if an attacker compromised the management station, he could defeat other security measures.

Figure 1-2 *Defense in Depth*

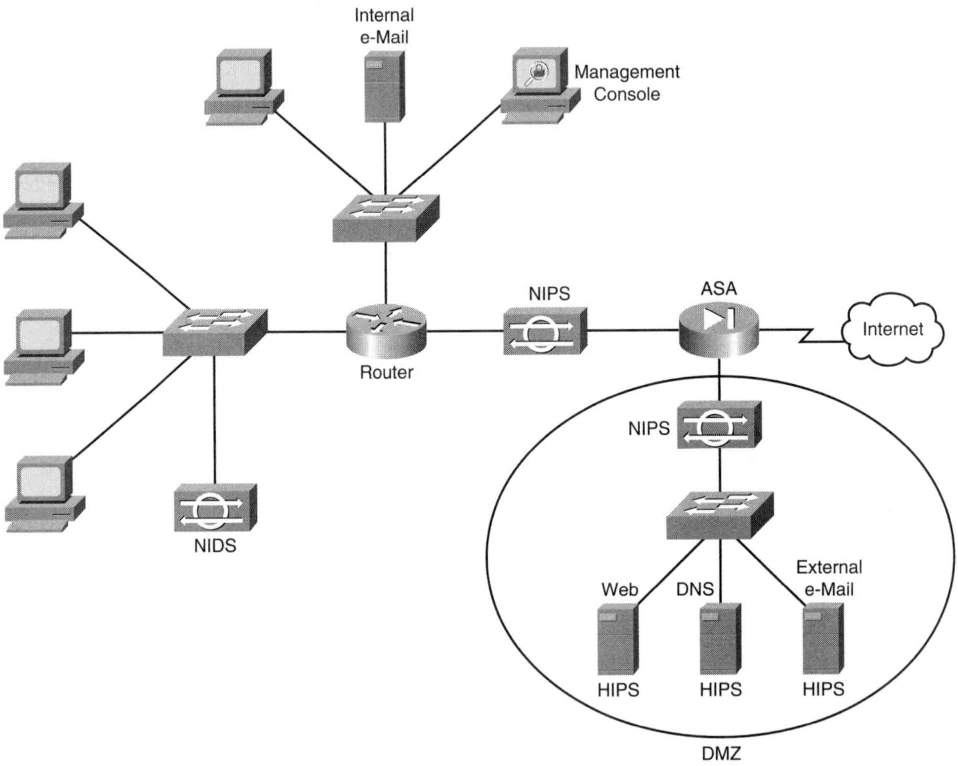

In the "Potential Attackers" section you read about five classes of attacks; Table 1-6 provides examples of overlapping defenses for each of these classes.

Table 1-6 *Defending Against Different Classes of Attacks*

Attack Class	Primary Layer of Defense	Secondary Layer of Defense
Passive	Encryption	Applications with integrated security
Active	Firewall at the network edge	HIPS
Insider	Protecting against unauthorized physical access	Authentication
Close-in	Protecting against unauthorized physical access	Video monitoring systems
Distribution	Secured software distribution system	Real-time software integrity checking

Understanding IP Spoofing

Attackers can launch a variety of attacks by initiating an IP spoofing attack. An IP spoofing attack causes an attacker's IP address to appear to be a trusted IP address. For example, if an attacker convinces a host that he is a trusted client, he might gain privileged access to a host. The attacker could also capture traffic, which might include credentials such as usernames and passwords. As another example, you might be familiar with denial-of-service (DoS) and distributed denial-of-service (DDoS) attacks. The perpetrators of such attacks might use IP spoofing to help conceal their identities.

To understand how an IP spoofing attack is possible, consider the operation of IP and TCP. At Layer 3, the attacker can easily modify his packets to make the source IP address appear to be a "trusted" IP address. However, TCP, operating at Layer 4, can be more of a challenge.

From your early studies of TCP, you might recall that a TCP session is established using a three-way handshake:

1. The originator sends a SYN segment to the destination, along with a sequence number.

2. The destination sends an acknowledgment (an ACK) of the originator's sequence number along with the destination's own sequence number (a SYN).

3. The originator sends an ACK segment to acknowledge the destination's sequence number, after which the TCP communication channel is open between the originator and destination.

Figure 1-3 illustrates the TCP three-way handshake process.

Figure 1-3   *TCP Three-Way Handshake*

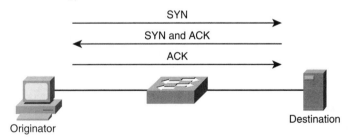

For an attacker to "hijack" a session being set up between a legitimate originator and a destination, the attacker needs to know the TCP sequence numbers used in the TCP segments. If the attacker successfully guesses or predicts the correct TCP sequence numbers, he can send a properly constructed ACK segment to the destination. If the attacker's ACK segment reaches the destination before the originator's ACK segment does, the attacker becomes trusted by the destination, as illustrated in Figure 1-4.

Figure 1-4   *IP Spoofing*

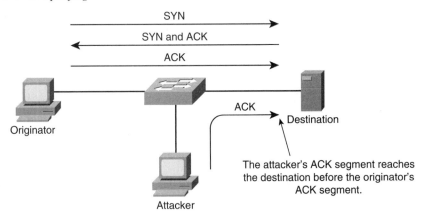

How an attacker guesses or predicts correct TCP sequence numbers depends on the type of IP spoofing attack being launched. Table 1-7 describes two categories of IP spoofing attacks.

Table 1-7   *Types of IP Spoofing Attacks*

Type of Attack	Description
Nonblind spoofing	Nonblind spoofing occurs when the attacker and the destination are on the same subnet. By being on the same subnet, the attacker might be able to use a packet-capture utility to glean sequence numbers.
Blind spoofing	Blind spoofing occurs when the attacker is not on the same subnet as the destination. Therefore, obtaining correct TCP sequence numbers is more difficult. However, using techniques such as *IP source routing* (described next), an attacker can accurately determine those sequence numbers.

Launching a Remote IP Spoofing Attack with IP Source Routing

If an attacker uses a feature known as IP source routing, he can specify a complete routing path to be taken by two endpoints. Consider Figure 1-5. The attacker is on a different subnet than the destination host. However, the attacker sends an IP packet with a source route specified in the IP header, which causes the destination host to send traffic back to the spoofed IP address via the route specified. This approach can overcome the previously described challenge that an attacker might have when launching a remote IP spoofing (blind spoofing) attack.

Figure 1-5 *IP Source Routing*

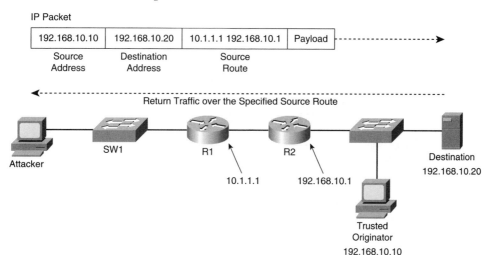

Source routing has two variations:

- **Loose**: The attacker specifies a list of IP addresses through which a packet must travel. However, the packet could also travel through additional routers that interconnect IP addresses specified in the list.

- **Strict**: The IP addresses in the list specified by the attacker are the only IP addresses through which a packet is allowed to travel.

Launching a Local IP Spoofing Attack Using a Man-in-the-Middle Attack

If an attacker is on the same subnet as the target system, he might launch a man-in-the-middle attack. In one variant of a man-in-the-middle attack, the attacker convinces systems to send frames via the attacker's PC. For example, the attacker could send a series of gratuitous ARP (GARP) frames to systems. These GARP frames might claim that the attacker's Layer 2 MAC address was the MAC address of the next-hop router. The attacker could then capture traffic and forward it to the legitimate next-hop router. As a result, the end user might not notice anything suspicious.

Another variant of a man-in-the-middle attack is when the attacker connects a hub to a network segment that carries the traffic the attacker wants to capture, as shown in Figure 1-6. Alternatively, an attacker could connect to a Switch Port Analyzer (SPAN) port on a Catalyst switch, which makes copies of specified traffic and forwards them to the configured SPAN port. The attack could then use a packet-capture utility to capture traffic traveling between end systems. If the captured traffic is in plain text, the attacker might be able to obtain confidential information, such as usernames and passwords.

Figure 1-6   *Man-in-the-Middle Attack*

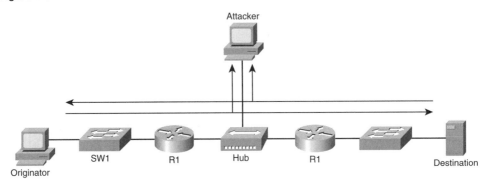

Protecting Against an IP Spoofing Attack

The following approaches can be used to mitigate IP spoofing attacks:

■ Use access control lists (ACL) on router interfaces. As traffic comes into a router from an outside network, an ACL could be used to deny any outside traffic claiming to be addressed with IP addressing used internally on the local network. Conversely, ACLs should be used to prevent traffic leaving the local network from participating in a DDoS attack. Therefore, an ACL could deny any traffic leaving the local network that claimed to have a source address that was different from the internal network's IP address space.

■ Encrypt traffic between devices (for example, between two routers, or between an end system and a router) via an IPsec tunnel. In Figure 1-7, notice that the topology is now protected with an IPsec tunnel. Even though the attacker can still capture packets via his rogue hub, the captured packets are unreadable, because the traffic is encrypted inside the IPsec tunnel.

Figure 1-7   *Protecting Traffic in a Tunnel*

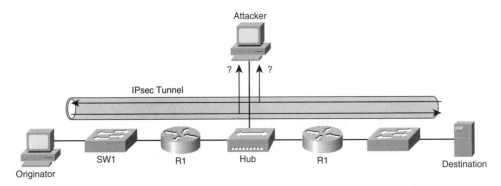

■   Use cryptographic authentication. If the parties involved in a conversation are authenticated, potential man-in-the-middle attackers can be thwarted. Potential attackers will not be successfully authenticated by the other party in the conversation.

Understanding Confidentiality Attacks

A confidentiality attack (see Figure 1-8) attempts to make "confidential" data (such as personnel records, usernames, passwords, credit card numbers, and e-mails) viewable by an attacker. Because an attacker often makes a copy of the data, rather than trying to manipulate the data or crash a system, confidentiality attacks often go undetected. Even if auditing software to track file access were in place, if no one suspected an issue, the audit trail might never be examined.

Figure 1-8   *Confidentiality Attack*

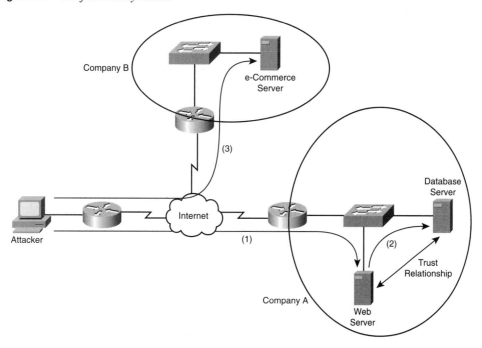

In Figure 1-8, a web server and a database server have a mutual trust relationship. The database server houses confidential customer information, such as credit card information. As a result, Company A decides to protect the database server (for example, patching known software vulnerabilities) better than the web server. However, the attacker leverages the trust relationship between the two servers to obtain customer credit card information and then make a purchase from Company B using the stolen information. The procedure is as follows:

Step 1   The attacker exploits a vulnerability in Company A's web server and gains control of that server.

Step 2   The attacker uses the trust relationship between the web server and the database server to obtain customer credit card information from the database server.

Step 3   The attacker uses the stolen credit card information to make a purchase from Company B.

Table 1-8 identifies several methods that attackers might use in a confidentiality attack.

Table 1-8   *Confidentiality Attack Strategies*

Tactic	Description
Packet capture	A packet-capture utility (such as Wireshark, available at http://www.wireshark.org) can capture packets visible by a PC's network interface card (NIC) by placing the NIC in promiscuous mode. Some protocols (for example, Telnet and HTTP) are sent in plain text. Therefore, an attacker can read these types of captured packets, perhaps allowing him to see confidential information.
Ping sweep and port scan	A confidentiality attack might begin with a scan of network resources, to identify attack targets on a network. A ping sweep could be used to ping a series of IP addresses. Ping replies might indicate to an attacker that network resources can be reached at those IP addresses. As soon as a collection of IP addresses is identified, the attacker might scan a range of UDP and/or TCP ports to see what services are available on the host at the specified IP addresses. Also, port scans often help attackers identify the operating system running on the target system.
Dumpster diving	Because many companies throw away confidential information, without proper shredding, some attackers rummage through company dumpsters in hopes of discovering information that could be used to compromise network resources.
Electromagnetic interference (EMI) interception	Because data is often transmitted over wire (for example, unshielded twisted-pair), attackers can sometimes copy information traveling over the wire by intercepting the EMI being emitted by the transmission medium. These EMI emissions are sometimes called "emanations."

Table 1-8 *Confidentiality Attack Strategies (Continued)*

Tactic	Description
Wiretapping	If an attacker gains physical access to a wiring closet, he might physically tap into telephone cabling to eavesdrop on telephone conversations. Or he might insert a shared media hub inline with a network cable. This would let him connect to the hub and receive copies of packets flowing through the network cable.
Social engineering	Attackers sometimes use social techniques (which often leverage people's desire to be helpful) to obtain confidential information. For example, an attacker might pose as a member of the IT department and ask a company employee for her login credentials "for the IT staff to test the connection."
Sending information over overt channels	An attacker might send or receive confidential information over a network using an overt channel. An example of using an overt channel is tunneling one protocol inside another (for example, sending instant messaging traffic via HTTP). *Steganography* is another example of sending information over an overt channel. An example of steganography is sending a digital image made up of millions of pixels, with "secret" information encoded in specific pixels. Only the sender and receiver know which pixels represent the encoded information.
Sending information over covert channels	An attacker might send or receive confidential information over a network using a covert channel, which can communicate information as a series of codes and/or events. For example, binary data could be represented by sending a series of pings to a destination. A single ping within a certain period of time could represent a binary 0, and two pings within that same time period could represent a binary 1.

Understanding Integrity Attacks

Integrity attacks attempt to alter data (that is, compromise its integrity). Figure 1-9 shows an example of an integrity attack.

Figure 1-9 *Integrity Attack*

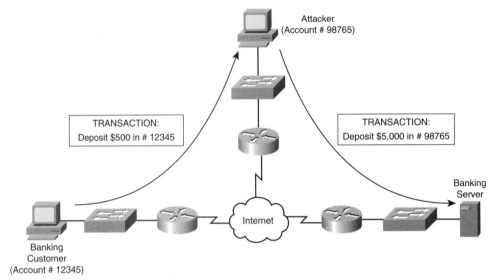

Traffic diverted to attacker due to a man-in-the-middle attack.

In the figure, an attacker has launched a man-in-the-middle attack (as previously described). This attack causes data flowing between the banking customer and the banking server to be sent via the attacker's computer. The attacker then can not only intercept but also manipulate the data. In the figure, notice that the banking customer attempts to deposit $500 into her account. However, the attacker intercepts and changes the details of the transaction, such that the instruction to the banking server is to deposit $5,000 in the attacker's account.

The following list describes methods that attackers might leverage to conduct an integrity attack:

- **Salami attack**: This is a collection of small attacks that result in a larger attack when combined. For example, if an attacker had a collection of stolen credit card numbers, he could withdraw small amounts of money from each credit card (possibly unnoticed by the credit card holders). Although each withdrawal is small, they add up to a significant sum for the attacker.

- **Data diddling**: The process of data diddling changes data before it is stored in a computing system. Malicious code in an input application or virus could perform data diddling. For example, a virus, Trojan horse, or worm could be written to intercept keyboard input. It would display the appropriate characters on-screen so that the user would not see a problem. However, manipulated characters would be entered into a database application or sent over a network.

■ **Trust relationship exploitation**: Different devices in a network might have a trust relationship between themselves. For example, a certain host might be trusted to communicate through a firewall using specific ports, while other hosts are denied passage through the firewall using those same ports. If an attacker could compromise the host that had a trust relationship with the firewall, the attacker could use the compromised host to pass normally denied data through a firewall. Another example of a trust relationship is a web server and a database server mutually trusting one another. In that case, if the attacker gained control of the web server, he might be able to leverage that trust relationship to compromise the database server.

■ **Password attack**: A password attack, as the name suggests, attempts to determine a user's password. As soon as the attacker gains the username and password credentials, he can attempt to log into a system as that user, and therefore inherit that user's set of permissions. Various approaches are available for determining passwords:

— **Trojan horse**: A program that appears to be a useful application captures a user's password and then makes it available to the attacker.

— **Packet capture**: A packet-capture utility can capture packets seen on a PC's NIC. Therefore, if the PC can see a copy of a plain-text password being sent over a link, the packet-capture utility can be used to glean the password.

— **Keylogger**: A keylogger is a program that runs in the background of a computer, logging the user's keystrokes. After a user enters a password, it is stored in the log created by the keylogger. An attacker then can retrieve the log of keystrokes to determine the user's password.

— **Brute force**: A brute-force password attack tries all possible password combinations until a match is made. For example, the brute-force attack might start with the letter a and go through to the letter z. Then the letters aa through zz are attempted, until a password is determined. Therefore, using a mixture of uppercase and lowercase letters in passwords, in addition to special characters and numbers, can help mitigate a brute-force attack.

— **Dictionary attack**: A dictionary attack is similar to a brute-force attack, in that multiple password guesses are attempted. However, the dictionary attack is based on a dictionary of commonly used words, rather than the brute-force method of trying all possible combinations. Picking a password that is not a common word can help mitigate a dictionary attack.

- **Botnet**: A software "robot" typically is thought of as an application on a machine that can be controlled remotely (for example, a Trojan horse or a back door in a system). If a collection of computers is infected with such software robots, called "bots," this collection of computers (each of which is called a "zombie") is known as a "botnet." Because of the potentially large size of a botnet, it might compromise the integrity of a large amount of data.

- **Hijacking a session**: Earlier in this chapter, you read about how an attacker could hijack a TCP session (for example, by completing the third step in the three-way TCP handshake process between an authorized client and a protected server). If an attacker successfully hijacked a session of an authorized device, he might be able to maliciously manipulate data on the protected server.

Understanding Availability Attacks

Availability attacks attempt to limit a system's accessibility and usability. For example, if an attacker could consume the processor or memory resources on a target system, that system would be unavailable to legitimate users.

Availability attacks vary widely, from consuming the resources of a target system to doing physical damage to that system. Attackers might employ the following availability attacks:

- **Denial of service (DoS)**: An attacker can launch a DoS attack on a system by sending the target system a flood of data or requests that consume the target system's resources. Alternatively, some operating systems and applications might crash when they receive specific strings of improperly formatted data, and the attacker could leverage such operating system and/or application vulnerabilities to render a system or application inoperable. The attacker often uses IP spoofing to conceal his identity when launching a DoS attack, as shown in Figure 1-10.

Figure 1-10 *Denial-of-Service Attack*

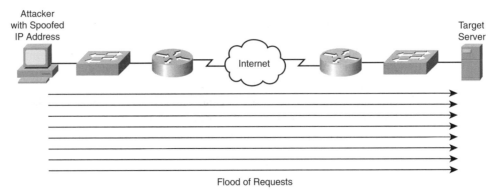

■ **Distributed denial of service (DDoS)**: DDoS attacks can increase the amount of traffic flooded to a target system. Specifically, the attacker compromises multiple systems. The attacker can instruct those compromised systems, called "zombies," to simultaneously launch a DDoS attack against a target system.

■ **TCP SYN flood**: Earlier in this chapter you reviewed the three-way TCP handshake process. One variant of a DoS attack is for an attacker to initiate multiple TCP sessions by sending SYN segments but never completing the three-way handshake. As illustrated in Figure 1-11, the attack can send multiple SYN segments to a target system, with false source IP addresses in the header of the SYN segment. Because many servers limit the number of TCP sessions they can have open simultaneously, a SYN flood can render a target system incapable of opening a TCP session with a legitimate user.

Figure 1-11   *TCP SYN Flood Attack*

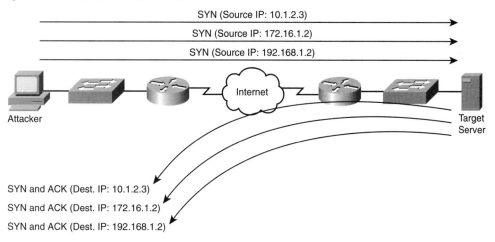

■ **ICMP attacks**: Many networks permit the use of ICMP traffic (for example, ping traffic), because pings can be useful for network troubleshooting. However, attackers can use ICMP for DoS attacks. One ICMP DoS attack variant called "the ping of death" uses ICMP packets that are too big. Another variant sends ICMP traffic as a series of fragments in an attempt to overflow the fragment reassembly buffers on the target device. Also, a "Smurf attack" can use ICMP traffic directed to a subnet to flood a target system with ping replies, as shown in Figure 1-12. Notice in the figure that the attacker sends a ping to the subnet broadcast address of 172.16.0.0/16. This collection of pings instructs devices on that subnet to send their ping replies to the target system at IP address 10.2.2.2, thus flooding the target system's bandwidth and processing resources.

> **NOTE**   For illustrative purposes, Figure 1-12 shows only three systems in the subnet being used for the Smurf attack. However, realize that thousands of systems could potentially be involved and send ping replies to the target system.

Figure 1-12   *Smurf Attack*

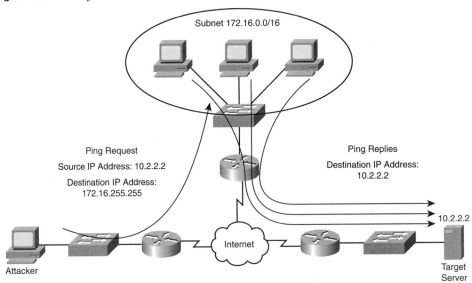

- **Electrical disturbances**: At a physical level, an attacker could launch an availability attack by interrupting or interfering with the electrical service available to a system. For example, if an attacker gained physical access to a data center's electrical system, he might be able to cause a variety of electrical disturbances:

    — **Power spike**: Excess power for a brief period of time

    — **Electrical surge**: Excess power for an extended period of time

    — **Power fault**: A brief electrical outage

    — **Blackout**: An extended electrical outage

    — **Power sag**: A brief reduction in power

    — **Brownout**: An extended reduction in power

To combat such electrical threats, Cisco recommends that you install uninterruptible power supplies (UPS) and generator backups for strategic devices in your network. Also, you should routinely test the UPS and generator backups.

■ **Attacks on a system's physical environment**: Attackers could also intentionally damage computing equipment by influencing the equipment's physical environment. For example, attackers could attempt to manipulate such environmental factors as the following:

— **Temperature**: Because computing equipment generates heat (for example, in data centers or server farms), if an attacker interferes with the operation of the air conditioning system, the computing equipment could overheat.

— **Humidity**: Because computing equipment is intolerant of moisture, an attacker could, over time, cause physical damage to computing equipment by creating a high level of humidity in the computing environment.

— **Gas**: Because gas can often be flammable, if an attacker injects gas into a computing environment, small sparks in that environment could cause a fire.

Consider the following recommendations to mitigate such environmental threats:

— Computing facilities should be locked (and inaccessible via a dropped ceiling, a raised floor, or any other way other than a monitored point of access).

— Access should require access credentials (for example, via a card swipe or a fingerprint scan).

— Access points should be visually monitored (for example, via local security personnel or remotely via a camera system).

— Climate control systems should maintain temperature and humidity and send alerts if specified temperature and humidity thresholds are exceeded.

— The fire detection and suppression systems should be designed not to damage electronic equipment.

Best-Practice Recommendations

You now have a fundamental understanding of threats targeting network and computing environments. Cisco recommends the following best practices to help harden the security of your network:

- Routinely apply patches to operating systems and applications.

- Disable unneeded services and ports on hosts.

- Require strong passwords, and enable password expiration.

- Protect the physical access to computing and networking equipment.

- Enforce secure programming practices, such as limiting valid characters that can be entered into an application's dialog box.

- Regularly back up data, and routinely verify the integrity of the backups.

- Train users on good security practices, and educate them about social engineering tactics.

- Use strong encryption for sensitive data.

- Defend against technical attacks by deploying hardware- and software-based security systems (for example, firewalls, IPS sensors, and antivirus software).

- Create a documented security policy for company-wide use.

Exam Preparation Tasks

Review All the Key Topics

Review the most important topics from this chapter, denoted with the Key Topic icon. Table 1-9 lists these key topics and the page where each is found.

Key Topic

Table 1-9 *Key Topics for Chapter 1*

Key Topic Element	Description	Page Number
List	Reasons for the severity of internal threats	10
List	The three primary goals of network security	12
Table 1-2	Government and military data classification example	14
Table 1-4	Data classification characteristics	15
List	Classification roles	15
List	Security controls	16
List	Control types	17
List	Legal elements needed to make a case	17
List	Three types of law	18
Table 1-5	Types of hackers	22
List	Categories of attacks	23
List	Defense in Depth recommendations	25
Table 1-6	Defending against different classes of attacks	26
List	Three-way TCP handshake	27
Table 1-7	Types of IP spoofing attacks	28
List	Types of source routing	29
Table 1-8	Confidentiality attack strategies	32-33
List	Integrity attack methods	34
List	Availability attack methods	36
List	Best-practice recommendations	40

Complete the Tables and Lists from Memory

Print a copy of Appendix D, "Memory Tables," (found on the CD) or at least the section for this chapter, and complete the tables and lists from memory. Appendix E, "Memory Tables Answer Key," also on the CD, includes completed tables and lists so that you can check your work.

Definition of Key Terms

Define the following key terms from this chapter, and check your answers in the glossary:

confidentiality, integrity, availability, preventive control, deterrent control, detective control, vulnerability, exploit, phreaker, Defense in Depth, IP spoofing, data diddling, salami attack, denial of service (DoS)

This chapter covers the following topics:

Increasing operations security: This section explains the day-to-day procedures for deploying, maintaining, and retiring information security components.

Constructing a comprehensive network security policy: This section discusses considerations and principles for writing a security policy, in addition to making users aware of the policy.

Creating a Cisco Self-Defending Network: This section describes the Cisco Self-Defending Network, which is the Cisco vision for security systems.

CHAPTER 2

Developing a Secure Network

Day-to-day network operations include adding new components to the network, monitoring and maintaining existing components, and retiring other components. While you perform these operations, security should be a consideration, so this chapter discusses how security practices can be integrated into such day-to-day operations. Also, network security practices and procedures should be governed by a documented security policy, so this chapter discusses the elements and use of an effective security policy.

Finally, because a security threat (such as a worm) can spread rapidly through a network, a security solution needs to be able to react quickly. The Cisco approach to protecting a network from such threats is called the *Cisco Self-Defending Network*, which is examined in this chapter.

"Do I Know This Already?" Quiz

The "Do I Know This Already?" quiz helps you determine your level of knowledge of this chapter's topics before you begin. Table 2-1 details the major topics discussed in this chapter and their corresponding quiz questions.

Table 2-1 *"Do I Know This Already?" Section-to-Question Mapping*

Foundation Topics Section	Questions
Increasing operations security	1 to 4
Constructing a comprehensive network security policy	5 to 10
Creating a Cisco Self-Defending Network	11 to 13

1. What are the five phases of the System Development Life Cycle (SDLC)? (Choose five.)

   a. Termination

   b. Operations and maintenance

   c. Acquisition and development

   d. Initiation

   e. Implementation

   f. Execution

   g. Disposition

2. Which of the following attempts to ensure that no one employee becomes a pervasive security threat, that data can be recovered from backups, and that information system changes do not compromise a system's security?

   a. Strategic security planning

   b. Implementation security

   c. Disaster recovery

   d. Operations security

3. Which three of the following are network evaluation techniques? (Choose three.)

   a. Using Cisco SDM to perform a network posture validation

   b. Scanning a network for active IP addresses and open ports on those IP addresses

   c. Performing end-user training on the use of antispyware software

   d. Using password-cracking utilities

   e. Performing virus scans

4. What are three phases of disaster recovery? (Choose three.)

   a. Emergency response phase

   b. Return to normal operations phase

   c. Threat isolation phase

   d. Recovery phase

5. Which of the following is a continually changing document that dictates a set of guidelines for network use?

   a. Security policy

   b. Best-practice recommendations

   c. Identity-based networking policy

   d. Acceptable-use executive summary

6. Which security policy component contains mandatory practices (as opposed to recommendations or step-by-step instructions)?

   a. Guidelines

   b. Standards

   c. Procedures

   d. Tenets

7. Which three individuals are the most likely to be intimately involved with the creation of a security policy? (Choose three.)

   a. Chief Security Officer (CSO)

   b. Chief Executive Officer (CEO)

   c. Chief Information Officer (CIO)

   d. Chief Information Security Officer (CISO)

8. The following formula can be used to calculate annualized loss expectancy:

   ALE = AV * EF * ARO

   Which component of the formula represents the percentage of loss of an asset that is experienced if an anticipated threat occurs?

   a. ALE

   b. AV

   c. EF

   d. ARO

9. All of the following are common elements of a network design. Which one is the most important?

   a. Business needs

   b. Risk analysis

   c. Security policy

   d. Best practices

   e. Security operations

   f. They are all equally important.

10. Which of the following makes the end-user community conscious of security issues without necessarily giving any in-depth procedural instruction?

   a. Education

   b. Training

   c. Awareness

   d. Remediation

11. What type of threat combines worm, virus, and Trojan horse characteristics?

   a. Heuristic threat

   b. Blended threat

   c. Morphing threat

   d. Integrated threat

12. What are the three core characteristics of a Cisco Self-Defending Network? (Choose three.)

   a. Integrated

   b. Collaborative

   c. Autonomous

   d. Adaptive

13. Which of the following offers a variety of security solutions, including firewall, IPS, VPN, antispyware, antivirus, and antiphishing features?

   a. Cisco IOS router

   b. Cisco ASA 5500 series security appliance

   c. Cisco PIX 500 series security appliance

   d. Cisco 4200 series IPS appliance

Foundation Topics

Increasing Operations Security

After a network is installed, network operations personnel monitor and maintain it. From a security perspective, *operations security* attempts to secure hardware, software, and various media while investigating anomalous network behavior.

System Development Life Cycle

A computer network is a dynamic entity, continuously changing to meet the needs of its users. New network components are added and eventually retired.

The life of these components can be defined by the System Development Life Cycle (SDLC), which consists of five phases:

- Initiation

- Acquisition and development

- Implementation

- Operations and maintenance

- Disposition

Initiation

SDLC's initiation phase consists of two security procedures:

- **Security categorization**: Security categorization, as the name suggests, categorizes the severity of a security breach on a particular network component. For example, a newly added network device might be categorized as having either a high, medium, or low security level.

- **Preliminary risk assessment**: Although a more formalized risk assessment follows in the SDLC, the preliminary risk assessment offers a high-level overview of a system's security requirements.

Acquisition and Development

SDLC's acquisition and development phase consists of multiple security procedures:

- **Risk assessment**: The risk assessment performed in the SDLC's initiation phase serves as the foundation for this more formalized risk assessment, which specifies protection requirements.

■ **Security functional requirement analysis**: This analysis identifies what is required to properly secure a system such that it can function in its intended capacity. For example, a requirement might state that a corporate security policy has to be written.

■ **Security assurance requirements analysis**: Based on legal and functional security requirements, this analysis provides evidence that the network resource in question will be protected at the desired level.

■ **Cost considerations and reporting**: A report is created that details the costs of securing a system. Included costs might include expenses for hardware, applications, personnel, and training.

■ **Security planning**: A report is created that details what security controls are to be used.

■ **Security control development**: A report is created detailing how the previously determined security controls are to be designed, developed, and implemented.

■ **Developmental security test and evaluation**: Testing is performed to validate the operation of the implemented security controls.

Implementation

SDLC's implementation phase consists of the following security procedures:

■ **Inspection and acceptance**: The installation of a system and its functional requirements are verified.

■ **System integration**: The system is integrated with all required components at its operational site, and its operation is verified.

■ **Security certification**: The operation of the previously specified security controls is verified.

■ **Security accreditation**: After the operation of required security controls is verified, a system is given appropriate administrative privileges to process, store, and/or transmit specific data.

Operations and Maintenance

SDLC's operations and maintenance phase consists of the following security procedures:

■ **Configuration management and control**: Before a configuration change is made to one part of a network, the potential impact on other parts of the network is considered. For example, change management software might be used to notify a variety of information security employees before a change is made to one of the integrated systems. Those employees could then evaluate the potential impact that such a change would have on the portion of the information system they are responsible for.

■ **Continuous monitoring**: Even after a security solution is in place, it should be routinely monitored and tested to validate its operation.

Disposition

SDLC's disposition phase consists of the following security procedures:

■ **Information preservation**: Some information needs to be preserved because of legal restrictions. Also, archived information should periodically be transferred to more modern storage technologies, to ensure that, over time, the medium used to store the archived information is not an obsolete technology.

■ **Media sanitation**: When storage media that contain sensitive information are disposed of, they should be "sanitized" so that no one can retrieve the information. For example, simply deleting a file from a hard drive does not necessarily prevent someone from retrieving it. A better practice might be to overwrite the old data to prevent its retrieval.

■ **Hardware and software disposal**: When hardware and software components are retired, a formalized disposal procedure should be used. Such a procedure could help prevent someone with malicious intent from retrieving information from those components.

Operations Security Overview

Operations security recommendations attempt to ensure that no one employee will become a pervasive security threat, that data can be recovered from backups, and that information system changes do not compromise a system's security. Table 2-2 provides an overview of these recommendations.

Table 2-2 *Operations Security Recommendations*

Recommendation	Description
Separation of duties	Information security personnel should be assigned responsibilities such that no single employee can compromise a system's security. This could be accomplished through a *dual operator* system (in which specific tasks require two people) or a *two-man control* system (in which two employees have to approve one another's work).

continues

Key Topic

Table 2-2 *Operations Security Recommendations (Continued)*

Recommendation	Description
Rotation of duties	The potential for a single employee to cause an ongoing security breach is lessened by having multiple employees periodically rotate duties. This rotation results in a "peer review" process in which employees check one another's work. However, smaller organizations with limited staff might have difficulty implementing this recommendation.
Trusted recovery	Trusted recovery implies making preparations for a system failure (for example, backing up sensitive data and securing those backups) and having a plan to recover data in the event of a failure. The recovery procedures should ensure that data is secured during the backup process (for example, running an operating system in a single-user mode or safe mode while restoring the data). Also, data should be restored such that its original permissions are in effect.
Configuration and change control	When making changes to an information system, multiple personnel should review the changes beforehand to anticipate any issues that could result. For example, a change in one system might open a security hole on another system. The primary goals of configuration and change management are minimizing system disruptions, being able to quickly back out of a change, and using network resources more efficiently and effectively.

Evaluating Network Security

To verify that a network's security solutions are acting as expected, you should test them occasionally. This network security evaluation typically occurs during the implementation phase and the operations and maintenance phase of SDLC.

During the implementation phase you should evaluate network security on individual system components, in addition to the overall system. By performing a network security evaluation during the implementation stage, you are better able to discover any flaws in your security design, implementation strategy, or operational strategy. You can also get a sense of whether your security solution will meet the guidelines of your security policy.

After a system enters its operation and maintenance phase, you should continue to perform periodic security evaluations to verify the performance of your security solution. In addition to regularly scheduled evaluations, Cisco recommends that evaluations be performed after you add a component (for example, a web server) to the information system.

The results of your security evaluations can be used for a variety of purposes:

- Creating a baseline for the information system's level of protection

- Identifying strategies to counter identified security weaknesses

- Complementing other SDLC phases, such as performing risk assessments

- Conducting a cost/benefit analysis when evaluating additional security measures

A variety of network evaluation techniques are available. Some of them can be automated, and others are manual procedures. Consider the following approaches to evaluating network security:

- Scanning a network for active IP addresses and open ports on those IP addresses

- Scanning identified hosts for known vulnerabilities

- Using password-cracking utilities

- Reviewing system and security logs

- Performing virus scans

- Performing penetration testing (perhaps by hiring an outside consultant to see if he or she can compromise specific systems)

- Scanning for wireless SSIDs to identify unsecured wireless networks

Several tools and utilities are available for performing a security evaluation. Some are available as freeware, and other packages require the purchase of a license. The following is a sample of these tools and utilities:

- Nmap

- GFI LANguard

- Tripwire

- Nessus

- Metasploit

- SuperScan by Foundstone, a division of McAfee

Nmap

To gain a sense of the features available in such evaluation tools, consider the Nmap utility. Nmap is a publicly available scanner that can be downloaded from http://www.insecure.org/nmap. Nmap offers features such as the following:

■ It has scanning and sweeping features that identify services running on systems in a specified range of IP addresses.

■ It uses a stealth approach to scanning and sweeping, making the scanning and sweeping less detectible by hosts and IPS technology.

■ It uses operating system (OS) fingerprinting technology to identify an operating system running on a target system (including a percentage of confidence that the OS was correctly detected).

Figure 2-1 shows a GUI version of Nmap called Zenmap, which can be downloaded from the link just provided.

Figure 2-1 *Nmap*

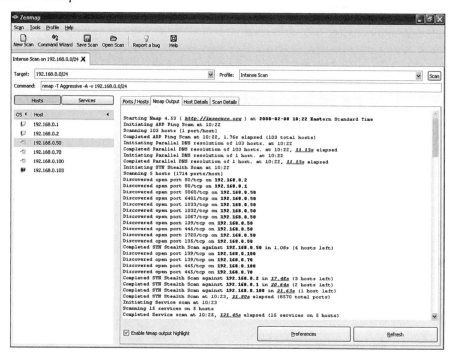

Disaster Recovery Considerations

With the potential for natural disasters (such as hurricanes, floods, and earthquakes) and man-made disasters (such as terrorist attacks) looming over today's networks, network administrators need to have contingency plans in place. Although these plans are sometimes called *business continuity plans* or *disaster recovery plans*, disaster recovery planning tends to address actions taken during and immediately after a disaster.

Specifically, disaster recovery (which is just a subset of business continuity planning) is concerned with allowing personnel to again access the data, hardware, and software they need to do their jobs. Also keep in mind that although a disaster recovery plan often conjures up thoughts of redundant hardware and backup facilities, a comprehensive disaster recovery plan also considers the potential loss of key personnel.

The two primary goals of business continuity planning are

■   Moving critical business operations to another facility while the original facility is under repair

■   Using alternative forms of internal and external communication

The overall goal of these plans is to allow an organization to perform critical business operations after a disaster. Three phases of recovery include

■   Emergency response phase

■   Recovery phase

■   Return to normal operations phase

Because these plans cannot possibly address all conceivable scenarios, disaster recovery and business continuity plans typically target the events that are most likely to occur. To illustrate the severity of a critical data loss, consider that some companies reportedly spend approximately 25 percent of their IT budget on business continuity and disaster recovery plans. Cisco also offers the following statistics about companies that lose most of their computerized records:

■   43 percent never reopen.

■   51 percent close within two years.

■   6 percent survive long-term.

Types of Disruptions

Business continuity and disaster recovery plans should address varying levels of disruptions by specifying different responses based on the severity of the disruption. To assist you in quantifying a disruption, consider the categories presented in Table 2-3.

Table 2-3 *Disruption Categories*

Disruption	Description
Nondisaster	Normal business operations are briefly interrupted.
Disaster	Normal business operations are interrupted for one or more days. However, not all critical resources at a site are destroyed.
Catastrophe	All resources at a site are destroyed, and normal business operations must be moved to an alternative site.

Types of Backup Sites

Redundancy is key to recovering from a disaster. For example, if a server is destroyed, you need a replacement server to assume its role. However, on a larger scale, you should also consider redundant sites, from where critical business operations can be resumed. Consider the three types of redundant sites described in Table 2-4.

Table 2-4 *Backup Sites*

Site	Description
Hot site	A hot site is a completely redundant site, with very similar equipment to the original site. Data is routinely copied from the primary site to the hot site. As a result, a hot site can be up and functioning within a few minutes (or even seconds) after a catastrophe at the primary site.
Warm site	A warm site, like a hot site, is a facility that has very similar equipment to the original site. However, a warm site is unlikely to have current data because of a lack of frequent replication with the original site. Therefore, disaster recovery personnel typically need to physically go to the warm site and manually bring all systems online. As a result, critical business operations might not be restored for days.
Cold site	Although a cold site does offer an alternative site where business operations can be conducted, unlike a hot or warm site, a cold site typically does not contain redundant computing equipment (such as servers and routers). As a result, the data network would need to be rebuilt from scratch, which might require weeks. Therefore, although a cold site is less expensive initially, as compared to hot or warm sites, a cold site could create more long-term consequences. In fact, the financial consequences could be far greater than the initial cost savings.

Constructing a Comprehensive Network Security Policy

One of the main reasons security breaches occur within an organization is the lack of a security policy or, if a security policy is in place, the lack of effectively communicating that security policy to all concerned. This section discusses the purpose of a security policy, what should be addressed in that policy, how to maximize its effectiveness, and how to create awareness and understanding of the policy.

Security Policy Fundamentals

A security policy is a continually changing document that dictates a set of guidelines for network use. These guidelines complement organizational objectives by specifying rules for how a network is used.

The main purpose of a security policy is to protect an organization's assets. An organization's assets include more than just tangible items. Assets also entail such things as intellectual property, processes and procedures, sensitive customer data, and specific server functions (for example, e-mail or web functions).

Aside from protecting organizational assets, a security policy serves other purposes, such as the following:

- Making employees aware of their obligations as far as security practices

- Identifying specific security solutions required to meet the goals of the security policy

- Acting as a baseline for ongoing security monitoring

One of the more well-known components of a security policy is an *acceptable use policy* (AUP), also known as an *appropriate use policy*. An AUP identifies what users of a network are and are not allowed to do on the network. For example, retrieving sports scores during working hours via an organization's Internet connection might be deemed inappropriate by an AUP.

Because an organization's security policy applies to various categories of employees (such as management, technical staff, and end users), a single document might be insufficient. For example, managerial personnel might not be concerned with the technical intricacies of a security policy. Technical personnel might be less concerned with why a policy is in place. End users might be more likely to comply with the policy if they understand the reasoning behind the rules. Therefore, a security policy might be a collection of congruent, yet separate, documents.

Security Policy Components

As previously mentioned, an organization's security policy typically is composed of multiple documents, each targeting a specific audience. Figure 2-2 offers a high-level overview of these complementary documents.

Figure 2-2   *Components of a Security Policy*

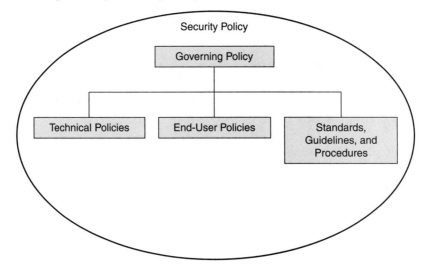

Governing Policy

At a very high level, a governing policy addresses security concepts deemed important to an organization. The governing policy is primarily targeted at managerial and technical employees. Following are typical elements of a governing policy:

- Identifying the issue addressed by the policy

- Discussing the organization's view of the issue

- Examining the relevance of the policy to the work environment

- Explaining how employees are to comply with the policy

- Enumerating appropriate activities, actions, and processes

- Explaining the consequences of noncompliance

Technical Policies

Technical policies provide a more detailed treatment of an organization's security policy, as opposed to the governing policy. Security and IT personnel are the intended targets of these technical policies, and these personnel use these policies in performing their day-to-day tasks. Typical components of technical policies include specific duties of the security and IT staff in areas such as the following:

- E-mail

- Wireless networks

- Remote access

End-User Policies

End-user policies address security issues and procedures relevant to end users. For example, an end user might be asked to sign an acceptable use policy (AUP) for Internet access. That AUP might state that Internet access is only for business purposes. Then, if an end user is found using the Internet for personal reasons, he or she could face the consequences outlined in the governing policy.

More-Detailed Documents

Because the governing policy, technical policies, and end-user policies each target a relatively large population of personnel, they tend to be general in nature. However, a comprehensive security policy requires a highly granular treatment of an organization's procedures. Therefore, more-detailed documents, such as the following, are often contained in a security policy:

- **Standards**: Standards support consistency within a network. For example, a standard might specify a limited number of operating systems to be supported in the organization, because it would be impractical for the IT staff to support any operating system that a user happened to select. Also, standards could apply to configuring devices, such as routers (for example, having a standard routing protocol).

- **Guidelines**: Whereas standards tend to be mandatory practices, guidelines tend to be suggestions. For example, a series of *best practices* might constitute a security policy's guidelines.

- **Procedures**: To support consistency in the network, and as dictated by the previously mentioned standards, a security policy might include a collection of procedures. These procedures are very detailed documents providing step-by-step instructions for completing specific tasks (such as steps for configuring port security on a Cisco Catalyst switch).

Security Policy Responsibilities

The ultimate responsibility for an organization's security policy rests on the shoulders of senior management (for example, the Chief Executive Officer [CEO]). However, senior management typically oversees the development of a security policy, as opposed to being intimately involved with the policy's creation.

Senior security or IT personnel usually are directly involved with the creation of the security policy. These individuals might create the policy themselves or delegate its creation. Examples of senior security or IT personnel include

- Chief Security Officer (CSO)

- Chief Information Officer (CIO)

- Chief Information Security Officer (CISO)

As soon as a security policy is created, the security and IT staff are responsible for implementing it within the organization's network. End users are responsible for complying with the security policy.

Risk Analysis, Management, and Avoidance

Network security concerns mitigating risks to the network. Therefore, network security designers need to identify threats facing the network. This process is known as *threat identification*.

However, beyond basic identification of threats, a key design decision revolves around analyzing the probability that a threat will occur and the severity of the consequences if that threat does occur. This analysis is called *risk analysis*.

When performing risk analysis, one of two broad approaches can be used: *quantitative* or *qualitative*.

Quantitative Analysis

A quantitative analysis mathematically models the probability and severity of a risk. As an example of one quantitative analysis formula, consider the following:

ALE = AV * EF * ARO

This formula calculates the annualized loss expectancy (ALE). The ALE produces a monetary value that can be used to help justify the expense of security solutions. The factors contributing to the ALE value are defined in Table 2-5.

Table 2-5 *Annualized Loss Expectancy Factors*

Key
Topic

Factor	Description
Asset value (AV)	The asset value is the total cost of an asset, including a purchase price, recurring maintenance expenses, and all other costs associated with acquiring an asset.
Exposure factor (EF)	The exposure factor is a percentage that represents the percentage of loss that an asset experiences if an anticipated threat occurs.
Annualized rate of occurrence (ARO)	The annualized rate of occurrence represents how many times per year a specific threat occurs.

From two of these factors, another metric can be calculated. The single loss expectancy (SLE) value represents the expected monetary loss from a single occurrence of an anticipated risk. The SLE can be calculated from the following formula:

SLE = AV * EF

Qualitative Analysis

A qualitative analysis is often more appropriate than a quantitative analysis because of the large scale of the network being analyzed. For example, in a nationwide network deployment, it might be considered impractical to list all the assets installed in all facilities across the country. Therefore, a qualitative analysis uses a scenario model, in which scenarios of risk occurrence are identified.

Risk Analysis Benefits

The exercise of performing a risk analysis yields a variety of benefits:

- It identifies a cost/value ratio for the cost of security measures versus the anticipated value of the security measures.

- It justifies requested capital expenditures for security solutions.

- It identifies areas in the network that would benefit most from a security solution.

- It provides statistics for future security planning.

Risk Analysis Example: Threat Identification

As an example of the threat identification process, consider an e-commerce company that sells products online and collects customer credit card information as part of its transactions. Potential risks to such an e-commerce company might include the following:

- An attacker could compromise one of the e-commerce servers and potentially gain access to customer credit card information.

- An attacker could falsify transactions. This could, for example, cause the e-commerce server to inaccurately charge customers for products that customers did not purchase.

- An attacker could launch a denial-of-service attack on one of the e-commerce servers, rendering it unusable for legitimate transactions.

Managing and Avoiding Risk

Risk mitigation involves *risk management* and/or *risk avoidance*:

- **Risk management**: Risk management assumes that not all potential threats can be eliminated. It attempts to reduce the anticipated damage from risks to an acceptable level. For example, in the previous lists of potential threats, IPS, IDS, HIPS, and firewall solutions might be introduced to reduce the likelihood and impact of the identified threats.

- **Risk avoidance**: Risk avoidance can eliminate the identified risks by not exposing a system to end users. This would be impractical for the e-commerce application just mentioned. However, if network designers can identify a way to deploy a service while simultaneously eliminating potential risks, that approach could prove highly lucrative.

Factors Contributing to a Secure Network Design

A common temptation when designing a security solution for a network is to make the network so secure that it cannot easily be used for its intended purpose. Therefore, when designing a network security solution, designers should recognize that business needs supersede all other needs. However, other factors do enter into the design equation. Consider the following elements of a secure network design:

- **Business needs**: Business needs dictate what an organization wants to accomplish with its network. Note that this need is the most important of all the needs.

- **Risk analysis**: As previously discussed, a comprehensive risk analysis can be used to assign an appropriate level of resources (for example, an appropriate amount of money) to a potential security risk.

- **Security policy**: Earlier in this chapter you read about the elements of a security policy. A security policy typically contains multiple documents, targeting specific audiences within an organization. These individual documents provide day-to-day guidance, relating to network security, for all organizational employees.

- **Best practices**: Rather than the mandatory rules imposed by a security policy, a set of best practices (developed internally and/or externally) can offer proven methods for achieving a desired result.

- **Security operations**: Day-to-day security operations entail responding to an incident, monitoring and maintaining a system, and auditing a system (to ensure compliance with an organization's security policy).

Design Assumptions

A system's security often becomes compromised because of incorrect assumptions made by the network designer or the person responsible for the initial network configuration. For example, the group of users assumed to be the routine users of a system might be incorrect. Also, the types of attacks to which a network might be subjected could be incorrectly assumed. To avoid making incorrect assumptions about network design and implementation, consider the following recommendations from Cisco:

- Analyze how the failure of one system component impacts other system components.

- Determine which elements in a network *fail open*. Specifically, suppose a security component of a network (such as an IPS appliance) fails. If that component defaults to a mode in which it forwards traffic, rather than performing its previous security function on that traffic, the component is said to be operating in fail-open mode. However, if a security component denies traffic that it cannot inspect, the component is said to be operating in *fail-closed* (also known as *fail-safe*) mode, which would be the more secure of the two modes.

- Identify all possible attacks to which a network might be exposed.

- Evaluate the likelihood that a particular attack will be launched against a network.

- If an attack seems unlikely because of required processor resources, extrapolate to consider the fact that processor resources will be more readily available in the future.

- Consider the inevitability of user error in compromising a system's security.

- Subject your assumptions to review by other knowledgeable parties within your organization.

Minimizing Privileges

One approach to securing a network is to assign users the minimum privileges they require to complete their assigned duties. This approach, called the *least-privilege concept*, helps reduce potential system vulnerabilities resulting from a user being assigned too many privileges. Also, the least-privilege concept can expedite the identification of security weaknesses in a system.

In actual practice, however, the least-privilege concept is often challenging to implement consistently. For example, users might occasionally require a level of permission beyond that which they are currently assigned to accomplish a legitimate task. These "exceptions to the rule" might result in an unacceptable level of day-to-day configuration on the part of administrators and might also result in an overall loss of productivity.

To understand the least-privilege concept, consider Figure 2-3. The firewall only allows the user to communicate with the e-mail server via SMTP and/or POP3. This example of the least-privilege concept could result in an issue if web-based e-mail access were added. In such an instance, the user might attempt to connect to the e-mail server using HTTP to connect to the newly configured web-based e-mail feature. However, the user would be denied, because the firewall permits only SMTP and POP3 access to the e-mail server. Additional firewall configuration would then be required by the administrator to enable the web-based e-mail access.

Figure 2-3   *Least-Privilege Concept*

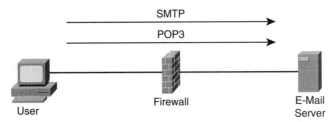

Simplicity Versus Complexity

A final principle of security network design considers the complexity of a security solution. A complex security solution, by its nature, can make it difficult for network administrators to effectively troubleshoot security-related issues. Additionally, if users are faced with a complex security procedure they must perform to accomplish their tasks, they might seek a simpler work-around to improve their productivity.

Therefore, Cisco recommends the simplest solution possible that still accomplishes the desired results. A comparatively simple security solution can do the following:

■ Help administrators more effectively troubleshoot security issues

■ Encourage users to follow security practices

■ Make security vulnerabilities more visible

User Awareness and Training

A properly written security policy and proper installment of security mechanisms can be rendered largely ineffective if the users of a system do not use security best practices.

Therefore, a critical component of an effective security deployment is a security awareness program.

For example, administrative assistants, accountants, and human resources employees might need periodic reminders to follow recommended security practices, because security is not the focus of their daily tasks. A security awareness program, which can provide continual reinforcement of security concepts for all end users, should do the following:

- **Identify the scope of the program**: A comprehensive program should provide training to all users of a system and/or network.

- **Select trainers**: The trainers should be competent at communicating current security issues.

- **Identify groups of users to receive training**: Because different categories of users require different training (for example, different users require varying levels of technical training), the end-user community should be categorized into different audiences.

- **Encourage full participation**: Obtaining management buy-in to a security awareness program can help motivate other users to participate.

- **Continually administer, maintain, and evaluate the program**: As a system's security needs evolve, a security awareness program must be subjected to periodic review and be updated accordingly.

Table 2-6 lists the core components of a security awareness program.

Table 2-6 *Components of a Security Awareness Program*

Key Topic

Component	Description
Awareness	Awareness makes the end-user community conscious of security issues, without necessarily any in-depth procedural training. For example, distributing an e-mail or pamphlet describing the issue of viruses and the importance of virus protection creates awareness of the issue.
Training	Training creates competence on the part of the end user to perform a specific task or serve in a specific role. Conducting a class to educate network administrators about features on a Cisco Adaptive Security Appliance (ASA) is an example of training.
Education	Education is more comprehensive than training, in that it covers a larger body of knowledge. Obtaining a college degree focusing on IT security would be an example of a comprehensive security education.

With proper awareness training in place, all categories of end users (such as executives, managers, staff, and temporary employees) can contribute to the network's overall security. Note that awareness training, a security policy, and properly installed network defenses are insufficient when used in isolation. However, these security elements complement one another when used together.

Creating a Cisco Self-Defending Network

Many modern security threats rapidly propagate across the Internet and internal networks. As a result, security components need to be able to respond rapidly to emerging threats. To combat these threats, Cisco offers the *Cisco Self-Defending Network*, which is its vision for using the network to recognize threats and then prevent and adapt to them. This section describes the implementation of the Cisco Self-Defending Network approach, which leverages Cisco products and solutions.

Evolving Security Threats

As computing resources have evolved over the past couple of decades, security threats have kept pace. For example, in the 1980s, boot viruses presented a threat to computer systems. However, such viruses took weeks to propagate throughout an individual network. During the 1990s, more-advanced viruses, denial-of-service (DoS) attacks, and other hacking attacks evolved. These attacks could impact multiple networks and propagate in a matter of days.

Modern networks face threats such as *blended threats*, which combine worm, virus, and Trojan horse characteristics. Such advanced threats can spread throughout regional networks in a matter of minutes. Future threats are anticipated to spread globally within just a few seconds.

One of the challenges of protecting against these evolving threats is the ambiguity of network boundaries. For example, consider the following:

- Port 80 traditionally is thought of as the port used for web traffic. Because it is often an open conduit entering "secured" networks, attackers can attempt to send malicious traffic in the form of port 80 payloads.

- Because traffic is often sent in an encrypted format (for example, using Secure Socket Layer [SSL] or Transport Layer Security [TLS]), malicious traffic can often escape recognition (for example, by Intrusion Prevention System [IPS] or Intrusion Detection System [IDS] appliances).

■ Clients often have multiple network connections (for example, a wireless laptop connected to a corporate wireless access point and also acting as a peer in a wireless ad-hoc network). Therefore, those clients might act as conduits for malicious users to access a "secured" network.

Constructing a Cisco Self-Defending Network

When a Cisco Self-Defending Network is constructed, consideration is given to how the individual security products work together. As a result, a Cisco Self-Defending Network integrates a collection of security solutions to identify threats, prevent those threats, and adapt to emerging threats.

Figure 2-4 highlights the three core characteristics of a Cisco Self-Defending Network, which are described in Table 2-7.

Figure 2-4 *Cisco Self-Defending Network Core Characteristics*

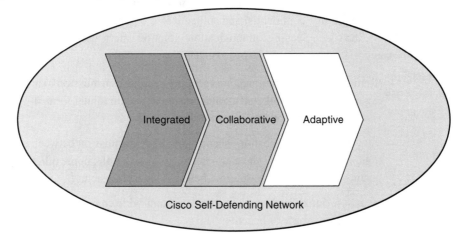

Table 2-7 *Cisco Self-Defending Network Core Characteristics*

Characteristic	Description
Integrated	Security is built in to the network, as opposed to being added to an existing network.
Collaborative	IT personnel focusing on security collaborate with IT personnel focusing on network operations.
Adaptive	Security solutions can adapt to evolving threats.

Cisco Self-Defending Networks can be more cost-effective, as compared to merely implementing a series of standalone solutions (also known as *point solutions*). This is because a complementary infrastructure simplifies management and administrative tasks. Similarly, equipment upgrade cycles can be better coordinated. Construction of a Cisco Self-Defending Network begins with a network platform that has integrated security. Then, strategic security features such as the following are layered on top of the already secure foundation:

■ **Threat control**: Strategies to contain and control threats include the following:

— Endpoint threat control defends endpoints against threats, typically sourced from the Internet, such as viruses and spyware.

— Infrastructure threat control protects servers and shared applications from internal and external threats.

— E-mail threat control blocks security threats sourced from e-mail, such as malicious attachments.

■ **Confidential and authenticated communication**: Technologies such as IPsec and SSL VPNs can provide confidential and authenticated communications channels. Specifically, the Cisco Secure Communications solution offers a set of products that can be categorized into one of two broad categories:

— Remote-access communications security secures transmission to an organization's network and applications via a secure tunnel formed across the Internet on an as-needed basis.

— Site-to-site communications security secures transmission between an organization's primary site and other sites (for example, home offices or business partners) via an Internet-based WAN infrastructure.

■ **Management solutions**: Products that provide system-wide control of policies and configuration offer a variety of benefits:

— Efficiency of rolling out a new policy to multiple devices while maintaining consistency of the configuration

— Comprehensive view of a network's end-to-end security status

— Quick response to attacks

— Improved congruity with an organizational security policy

Figure 2-5 shows the hierarchical structure of a Cisco Self-Defending Network.

Figure 2-5 *Cisco Self-Defending Network Hierarchical Structure*

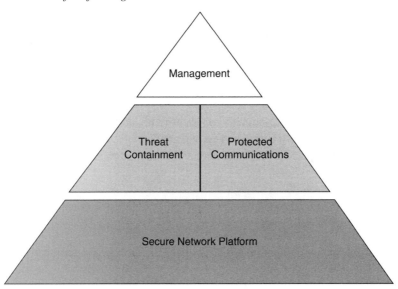

Cisco Security Management Suite

As an organization's network begins to grow, end-to-end security management becomes a more daunting task. Fortunately, Cisco offers a suite of security management tools, the main components of which are Cisco Security Manager and Cisco Security Monitoring, Analysis, and Response System (MARS).

Cisco Security Manager

The Cisco Security Manager application can be used to configure security features on a wide variety of Cisco security products. From a scalability perspective, Cisco Security Manager can be useful on smaller networks (for example, networks with fewer than ten devices), and it can also help more efficiently manage networks containing thousands of devices. As a few examples, the Cisco Security Manager application offers these features:

- Provisioning security on a variety of Cisco platforms, including Cisco IOS-based routers, Cisco ASA 5500 series security appliances, Cisco PIX 500 series security appliances, Cisco IPS 4200 sensors, and the Advanced Inspection and Prevention Security Services Module (AIP-SSM), available for the Cisco Catalyst 6500 series switch platform

- Performing configuration tasks via a graphical interface

- Applying a centralized policy, which maintains consistency throughout a network and that can be inherited by newly installed devices

■ Interoperates with Cisco Secure Access Control Server (ACS) to provide different sets of permissions to different users

NOTE   The following URL offers a flash-based introduction to Cisco Security Manager: http://www.cisco.com/cdc_content_elements/flash/sec_manager/index.html

Cisco Security MARS

The Cisco Security MARS product offers security monitoring for security devices and applications. In addition to Cisco devices and applications, Cisco Security MARS can monitor many third-party devices and applications. As a few examples, Cisco Security MARS performs these functions:

■ It uses event correlation to collect events from multiple devices in the network, thereby reducing the number of false positives.

■ It identifies appropriate mitigation strategies for specific security challenges.

■ It uses Cisco NetFlow technology to more readily identify network anomalies.

NOTE   The following URL offers a flash-based introduction to Cisco Security MARS: http://www.cisco.com/cdc_content_elements/flash/security_mars/demo.htm

Cisco Integrated Security Products

A Cisco Self-Defending Network relies on a collection of complementary security solutions. Table 2-8 identifies some of the products available in the Cisco product line that could contribute to a Cisco Self-Defending Network.

Table 2-8   *Examples of Cisco Security Products*

Product	Description
Cisco IOS router	Many Cisco IOS routers can be configured with Intrusion Prevention System (IPS), virtual private network (VPN), and firewall features.
Cisco ASA 5500 series security appliance	The Cisco 5500 series of Adaptive Security Appliances (ASA) offers a wide variety of security solutions, such as firewall, IPS, VPN, antispyware, antivirus, and antiphishing. Figure 2-6 shows a collection of Cisco ASA 5500 series security appliances.
Cisco PIX 500 series security appliance	The Cisco PIX 500 series of security appliances offer firewall and VPN-termination features. As an example, Figure 2-7 shows a Cisco PIX 535 security appliance.

Table 2-8 *Examples of Cisco Security Products (Continued)*

Product	Description
Cisco 4200 series IPS appliances	The Cisco 4200 series of IPS appliances can analyze traffic inline. If this inline analysis identifies traffic believed to be malicious, the IPS appliance can perform such operations as dropping the traffic, sending an alert, and instructing another network device (such as a Cisco PIX security appliance) to block connections from the offending host. Figure 2-8 shows a selection of Cisco 4200 series IPS appliances.
Cisco Security Agent (CSA)	Cisco Security Agent (CSA) is an application that provides IPS services on a host. Therefore, CSA is called a *Host-based Intrusion Prevention System* (HIPS) application.
Cisco Secure Access Control Server	The Cisco Secure Access Control Server (ACS) application can provide an authentication, authorization, and accounting (AAA) function, thus allowing different sets of permissions to be applied to different users.
Cisco Catalyst 6500 series switch and Cisco 7600 series router modules	Cisco Catalyst 6500 series switches and Cisco 7600 series routers use a modular chassis with multiple interchangeable modules. Some of these modules provide security features to the chassis. For example, you could insert a Firewall Services Module (FWSM) into a chassis to provide firewall services between various VLANs defined on a Cisco Catalyst 6500 series switch.
Cisco Router and Security Device Manager (SDM)	Cisco SDM provides a graphical interface for configuring a variety of security features (for example, IPS, IPsec site-to-site VPN, and firewall features), in addition to multiple router configuration features. Figure 2-9 shows the home screen of the SDM application.

Figure 2-6   *Cisco ASA 5500 Series Security Appliances*

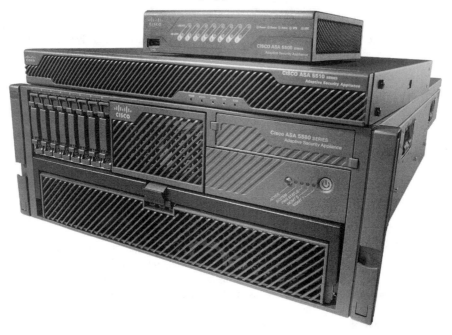

Figure 2-7   *Cisco PIX 535 Security Appliance*

Figure 2-8   *Cisco 4200 Series IPS Appliances*

Figure 2-9 *SDM Interface*

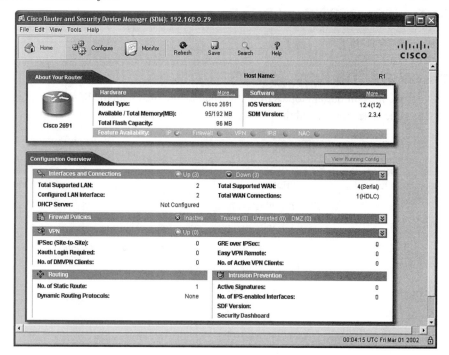

Exam Preparation Tasks

Review All the Key Topics

Key Topic

Review the most important topics from this chapter, denoted with the Key Topic icon. Table 2-9 lists these key topics and the page where each is found.

Table 2-9 *Key Topics for Chapter 2*

Key Topic Element	Description	Page Number
List	The five phases of SDLC	49
List	SDLC's initiation phase procedures	49
List	SDLC's acquisition and development phase procedures	49
List	SDLC's implementation phase procedures	50
List	SDLC's operations and maintenance phase procedures	50
List	SDLC's disposition phase procedures	51
Table 2-2	Operations security recommendations	51-52
List	Three phases of recovery	55
Table 2-3	Disruption categories	56
Table 2-4	Backup sites	56
List	Detailed documents included in a security policy	59
Table 2-5	Annualized loss expectancy factors	61
List	Components of risk mitigation	62
Table 2-6	Components of a security awareness program	65
Table 2-7	Cisco Self-Defending Network core characteristics	67
Table 2-8	Examples of Cisco security products	70-71

Complete the Tables and Lists from Memory

Print a copy of Appendix D, "Memory Tables," (found on the CD) or at least the section for this chapter, and complete the tables and lists from memory. Appendix E, "Memory Tables Answer Key," also on the CD, includes completed tables and lists so that you can check your work.

Definition of Key Terms

Define the following key terms from this chapter, and check your answers in the glossary:

System Development Life Cycle (SDLC), disaster recovery plan, nondisaster, disaster, catastrophe, hot site, warm site, cold site, security policy, threat identification, risk analysis, awareness, training, education, Cisco Self-Defending Network, Cisco Security Manager, Cisco Security MARS

This chapter covers the following topics:

ISR overview and providing secure administrative access: This section describes methods of securely accessing a router prompt for purposes of administration. Additionally, this section provides an overview of the Cisco Integrated Services Router (ISR) line of routers.

Cisco Security Device Manager overview: This section examines the Cisco Security Device Manager (SDM) interface. The graphical interface provided by SDM allows administrators to configure a variety of router features using a collection of wizards and other configuration aids, which use best-practice recommendations from the Cisco Technical Assistance Center (TAC).

CHAPTER 3

Defending the Perimeter

In addition to Cisco firewall, virtual private network (VPN), and intrusion prevention system (IPS) appliances that can sit at the perimeter of a network, Cisco IOS routers offer perimeter-based security. For example, the Cisco Integrated Services Routers (ISR) can be equipped to provide high-performance security features, including firewall, VPN termination, and IPS features, in addition to other services such as voice and quality-of-service (QoS) services. This chapter introduces various ISR models.

Because perimeter routers can be attractive targets for attack, they should be configured to secure administrative access. Therefore, this chapter also discusses specific approaches to "harden" administrative access to ISRs.

Configuring advanced ISR router features can be a complex process. Fortunately, many modern Cisco routers can be configured using the graphical Cisco Security Device Manager (SDM) interface. SDM contains multiple wizard-like configuration utilities, which are introduced in this chapter.

"Do I Know This Already?" Quiz

The "Do I Know This Already?" quiz helps you determine your level of knowledge of this chapter's topics before you begin. Table 3-1 details the major topics discussed in this chapter and their corresponding quiz questions.

Table 3-1 *"Do I Know This Already?" Section-to-Question Mapping*

Foundation Topics Section	Questions
ISR Overview and Providing Secure Administrative Access	1 to 10
Cisco Security Device Manager Overview	11 to 13

1.   Which of the following are considered IOS security features? (Choose four.)

   a.   Stateful firewall

   b.   MARS

   c.   IPS

   d.   VRF-aware firewall

   e.   VPN

   f.   ACS

2.   Some ISRs include a USB port, into which a flash drive can connect. What are three common uses for the flash drive? (Choose three.)

   a.   Storing configuration files

   b.   Storing a digital certificate

   c.   Storing a copy of the IOS image

   d.   Storing a username/password database

3.   The enable secret password appears as an MD5 hash in a router's configuration file, whereas the enable password is not hashed (or encrypted, if the password-encryption service is not enabled). Why does Cisco still support the use of both enable secret and enable passwords in a router's configuration?

   a.   Because the enable secret password is a hash, it cannot be decrypted. Therefore, the enable password is used to match the password that was entered, and the enable secret is used to verify that the enable password has not been modified since the hash was generated.

   b.   The enable password is used for IKE Phase I, whereas the enable secret password is used for IKE Phase II.

   c.   The enable password is considered to be a router's public key, whereas the enable secret password is considered to be a router's private key.

   d.   The enable password is present for backward compatibility.

4.   What is an IOS router's default response to multiple failed login attempts after the **security authentication failure** command has been issued?

   a.   The login process is suspended for 10 seconds after 15 unsuccessful login attempts.

   b.   The login process is suspended for 15 seconds after 10 unsuccessful login attempts.

   c.   The login process is suspended for 30 seconds after 10 unsuccessful login attempts.

   d.   The login process is suspended for 10 seconds after 30 unsuccessful login attempts.

5. What line configuration mode command would you enter to prevent a line (such as a console, aux, or vty line) connection from timing out because of inactivity?

   a. no service timeout

   b. timeout-line none

   c. exec-timeout 0 0

   d. service timeout default

6. An IOS router's privileged mode, which you can access by entering the **enable** command followed by the appropriate password, has which privilege level?

   a. 0

   b. 1

   c. 15

   d. 16

7. How is a CLI view different from a privilege level?

   a. A CLI view supports only commands configured for that specific view, whereas a privilege level supports commands available to that level and all the lower levels.

   b. A CLI view can function without a AAA configuration, whereas a privilege level requires AAA to be configured.

   c. A CLI view supports only monitoring commands, whereas a privilege level allows a user to make changes to an IOS configuration.

   d. A CLI view and a privilege level perform the same function. However, a CLI view is used on a Catalyst switch, whereas a privilege level is used on an IOS router.

8. To protect a router's image and configuration against an attacker's attempt to erase those files, the Cisco IOS Resilient Configuration feature keeps a secure copy of these files. What are these files called?

   a. The bootset

   b. The configset

   c. The backupset

   d. The backup-config

9. When you configure Cisco IOS login enhancements for virtual connections, what is the "quiet period"?

    a. The period of time between successive login attempts

    b. A period of time when no one is attempting to log in

    c. The period of time in which virtual login attempts are blocked, following repeated failed login attempts

    d. The period of time in which virtual logins are blocked as security services fully initialize

10. In the **banner motd #** command, what does # represent?

    a. A single text character that will appear as the message of the day

    b. A delimiter indicating the beginning and end of a message of the day

    c. A reference to a system variable that contains a message of the day

    d. The enable mode prompt from where the message of the day will be entered into the IOS configuration

11. What Cisco IOS feature provides a graphical user interface (GUI) for configuring a wide variety of features on an IOS router and also provides multiple "smart wizards" and configuration tutorials?

    a. QPM

    b. SAA

    c. SMS

    d. SDM

12. What are two options for running Cisco SDM? (Choose two.)

    a. Running SDM from a router's flash

    b. Running SDM from the Cisco web portal

    c. Running SDM from within CiscoWorks

    d. Running SDM from a PC

13. Which of the following are valid SDM configuration wizards? (Choose three.)

    a. Security Audit

    b. VPN

    c. ACS

    d. NAT

    e. STP

Foundation Topics

ISR Overview and Providing Secure Administrative Access

This section begins by introducing the security features offered in the Cisco line of ISR routers. Additional hardware options for these routers are also discussed. Then, with a foundational understanding of the underlying hardware, you will learn a series of best practices for security administrative access to a router. For example, a router can be configured to give different privilege levels to different administrative logins.

IOS Security Features

Although they are not a replacement for dedicated security appliances in large enterprise networks, modern Cisco routers, such as the ISR series, offer multiple integrated security features. Table 3-2 provides examples of these features, which vary by IOS feature set.

Table 3-2 *IOS Security Features*

Feature	Description
Stateful firewall	The Cisco IOS firewall feature allows an IOS router to perform stateful inspection of traffic (using Context-Based Access Control [CBAC]), in addition to basic traffic filtering using access control lists (ACL).
Intrusion Prevention System	The IOS Intrusion Prevention System (IPS) feature can detect malicious network traffic inline and stop it before it reaches its destination.
VPN Routing and Forwarding-aware (VRF-aware) firewall	A VRF-aware firewall maintains a separate routing and forwarding table for each VPN, which helps eliminate issues that arise from more than one VPN using the same address space.
Virtual private networks	Cisco IOS routers can participate in virtual private networks (VPN). For example, a router at a headquarters location and at a branch office location could interconnect via an IPsec-protected VPN. This approach would allow traffic to pass securely between those sites, even if the VPN crossed an "untrusted" network, such as the Internet.

Cisco Integrated Services Routers

Cisco offers a series of routers called *Integrated Services Routers* (ISR). As their name suggests, these routers integrate various services (such as voice and security services) into the router architecture. Although Cisco offers a wide range of router platforms, ISR models are easy to identify, because the last three digits of their model begin with the number 8. As shown in Figure 3-1, the ISR family of routers includes the 800 series, 1800 series, 2800 series, and 3800 series.

Figure 3-1 *800 Series, 1800 Series, 2800 Series, and 3800 Series ISRs*

Cisco 2800 Series Router   Cisco 3800 Series Router

Cisco 800 Series Router   Cisco 1800 Series Routers

Cisco 800 Series

The Cisco 800 series of ISRs is designed for teleworkers and small-office environments. These routers can connect to the Internet via a cable modem or DSL modem connection and offer secure connections over the Internet. Table 3-3 contrasts some of the features available in the Cisco 850 and 870 series of ISRs.

Table 3-3 *Cisco 800 Series of ISRs*

Feature	Cisco 850 Series	Cisco 870 Series
WAN technology support	ADSL Annex A (Cisco 857)	ADSL Annex B (Cisco 876), ADSL Annex A (Cisco 877), G.SHDSL (Cisco 878)
Built-in routed/WAN Ethernet	One 10/100 WAN (Cisco 851)	One 10/100 WAN (Cisco 871)
Integrated cryptographic hardware	Yes	Yes
Maximum flash memory	20 MB	52 MB
Maximum SRAM	64 MB	256 MB
Support for Cisco Security Device Manager (SDM)	Yes	Yes

Table 3-3 *Cisco 800 Series of ISRs (Continued)*

Feature	Cisco 850 Series	Cisco 870 Series
Maximum number of VPN tunnels	10	20
Stateful firewall support	Yes	Yes
Intrusion Prevention System (IPS) support	No	Yes

Cisco 1800 Series

The Cisco 1800 series of ISRs is designed for small businesses and smaller enterprise branch offices. These routers are designed for connectivity via cable modem/DSL, Metro Ethernet, and wireless technologies. Table 3-4 contrasts some of the features available in the Cisco 1800 and 1841 series of ISRs.

Table 3-4 *Cisco 1800 Series of ISRs*

Feature	Cisco 1800 Series (Fixed Interface)	Cisco 1841 Series (Modular)
WAN technology support	ADSL Annex A (Cisco 1801), ADSL Annex B (Cisco 1802), G.SHDSL (Cisco 1803)	ADSL and optional G.SHDSL WICs
Built-in routed/WAN Ethernet	One 10/100 (Cisco 1801-1803) Two 10/100 (Cisco 1811, 1812)	Two 10/100
Integrated cryptographic hardware	Yes	Yes
Maximum flash memory	128 MB	128 MB
Maximum SRAM	384 MB	384 MB
Support for Cisco Security Device Manager (SDM)	Yes	Yes
Maximum number of VPN tunnels	50	800
Stateful firewall support	Yes	Yes
Intrusion Prevention System (IPS) support	Yes	Yes

Cisco 2800 Series

The Cisco 2800 series of ISRs is designed for small-to-medium businesses and enterprise branch offices. These routers can securely provide voice, data, and video services. Table 3-5 contrasts some of the features available in the Cisco 2801, 2811, 2821, and 2851 series of ISRs.

Table 3-5   *Cisco 2800 Series of ISRs*

Feature	Cisco 2801 Series	Cisco 2811 Series	Cisco 2821 Series	Cisco 2851 Series
WAN technology support	ADSL and optional G.SHDSL WICs	ADSL and optional G.SHDSL WICs	ADSL and optional G.SHDSL WICs	ADSL and optional G.SHDSL WICs
Built-in routed/ WAN Ethernet	Two 10/100	Two 10/100	Two 10/100/1000	Two 10/100/1000
Integrated cryptographic hardware	Yes	Yes	Yes	Yes
Maximum flash memory	128 MB	256 MB	256 MB	256 MB
Maximum SRAM	384 MB	769 MB	1024 MB	1024 MB
Support for Cisco Security Device Manager (SDM)	Yes	Yes	Yes	Yes
Maximum number of VPN tunnels	1500	1500	1500	1500
Stateful firewall support	Yes	Yes	Yes	Yes
Intrusion Prevention System (IPS) support	Yes	Yes	Yes	Yes

Cisco 3800 Series

The Cisco 3800 series of ISRs is designed for medium to large businesses and enterprise branch offices. These routers offer multiple security, IP telephony, video, network analysis, and web application features. Table 3-6 contrasts some of the features available in the Cisco 3825 and 3845 series of ISRs.

Table 3-6 *Cisco 3800 Series of ISRs*

Feature	Cisco 3825 Series	Cisco 3845 Series
WAN technology support	ADSL and optional G.SHDSL WICs	ADSL and optional G.SHDSL WICs
Built-in routed/WAN Ethernet	Two 10/100/1000	Two 10/100/1000
Integrated cryptographic hardware	Yes	Yes
Maximum flash memory	256 MB	256 MB
Maximum SRAM	1024 MB	1024 MB
Support for Cisco Security Device Manager (SDM)	Yes	Yes
Maximum number of VPN tunnels	2000	2500
Stateful firewall support	Yes	Yes
Intrusion Prevention System (IPS) support	Yes	Yes

ISR Enhanced Features

Although traditional Cisco routers (that is, non-ISRs) offer features similar to those highlighted in the preceding tables, ISRs are unique in that they contain integrated hardware components (that vary by platform) to enhance performance. For example, most ISR models include the following enhancements:

■ **Integrated VPN acceleration**: By using dedicated hardware for VPN encryption, ISRs reduce the overhead placed on a router's processor, thereby increasing VPN performance and scalability. Specifically, the built-in VPN acceleration hardware supports 3DES and Advanced Encryption Standard (AES).

■ **Dedicated voice hardware**: IP telephony applications often use digital signal processors (DSP) to mix multiple voice streams in a conference. They also encrypt voice packets and convert between high-bandwidth and low-bandwidth codecs (that is, a coder/decoder, such as G.711 and G.729, which specify how voice samples are digitally represented in a voice packet). Voice traffic uses Real-time Transport Protocol (RTP), a Layer 4 protocol, to transport voice in a network. For increased security, Secure RTP (SRTP) can be used, which provides AES encryption for voice. However, because of the processor overhead required for SRTP's encryption, dedicated DSP hardware is required. Fortunately, ISRs can use packet voice DSP modules (PVDM) to take over the processing of such tasks.

The Cisco 2800 series of ISRs can use PVDM2 modules with onboard voice interface cards (VIC). Additionally, PVDM2 modules can be inserted into Cisco High-Density Analog (HDA) network modules and the Cisco Digital Extension Module for Voice and Fax, which can be inserted into the Cisco 2821, 2851, 3825, and 3845 ISR models.

- **Advanced Integration Modules**: Cisco offers a variety of Advanced Integration Modules (AIM), which can offload processor-intensive tasks from a router's processor. For example, AIMs can be used for VPN processing, including a variety of standards for encryption, authentication, and data integrity. The following are some AIM models:

  — **AIM-VPN/BPII-PLUS**: Used in Cisco 1800 series ISRs, which can support a single AIM

  — **AIM-VPN/EPII-PLUS**: Used in Cisco 2800 series ISRs and the Cisco 3825 ISR, all of which can accommodate two AIMs

  — **AIM-VPN/HPII-PLUS**: Used in the Cisco 3845 ISR, which supports two AIMs

- **USB port**: All Cisco ISRs, with the exception of the Cisco 850 ISR, include one or two Universal Serial Bus (USB) ports. These ports can be used with a USB flash drive to store IOS images or configuration files. Also, from a security perspective, a USB eToken containing a signed digital certification can be inserted for VPN use.

WAN connectivity network modules such as the WIC-2T, WIC-1B, and VWIC-1MFT offer flexibility in how various ISRs connect to the WAN. Here are some examples of other network modules supported on various ISR models:

- **Cisco HWIC-AP**: An IEEE 802.11 wireless module supporting a variety of wireless standards.

- **Cisco IDS Network Module**: Includes a hard drive containing multiple signatures of well-known attacks. Can be used to detect and subsequently prevent malicious traffic.

- **Cisco Content Engine**: Includes either a 40-GB or 80-GB hard drive for caching web content. This makes it available for quick retrieval by local clients, as opposed to the client's having to retrieve all the information from the web.

- **Cisco Network Analysis Module (NAM)**: Provides a detailed analysis of traffic flow.

Password-Protecting a Router

Administrators can access a router for administrative purposes in a variety of ways. For example, as shown in Figure 3-2, a PC running terminal emulation software can telnet into a router. The Telnet connection is considered to be using a vty line (a "virtual tty" line). Alternatively, a PC using terminal emulation software can connect directly to a router's console ("con") line over a serial connection. For remote administrative access, many Cisco routers also have an auxiliary line ("aux") that might connect to a modem.

Figure 3-2 *Administrative Access to a Router*

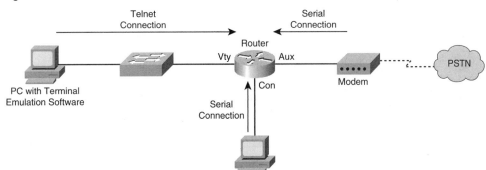

Telnet sends data in clear text. Therefore, if an attacker intercepted a series of Telnet packets, he could view their contents, such as usernames and passwords. For a more secure connection, administrators might choose to use Secure Shell (SSH) for access over a vty line. Modern Cisco routers also offer a graphical interface called Cisco Security Device Manager (SDM), which is accessible over the network using HTTP or HTTPS.

However, regardless of how an administrator chooses to access a router, the router typically challenges the administrator to provide either a password or a username/password combination before access is granted. As soon as an administrator is granted access to the router, she might be in *user mode,* where she has a limited number of commands she can issue. However, most router administration is performed from *privileged mode.* To access privileged mode from user mode, the administrator enters the **enable** command. Typically, the administrator then is prompted to enter another password, sometimes called the enable password. Interestingly, by default, a router has no password protection of any kind.

To protect a router from unauthorized access, a "strong" password should be selected. A strong password is one that is difficult for an attacker to guess or compromise by launching a *dictionary attack* or *brute-force attack.* A dictionary attack occurs when an attacker tries to use passwords from a file containing commonly used passwords. A brute-force attack occurs when an attacker tries all combinations of characters until a match is found. Recommended Cisco guidelines for selecting a strong router password include the following:

■   Select a password that is at least ten characters long. The **security password min-length 10** global configuration mode command can be used to enforce this password length recommendation.

- Use a mixture of alphabetic (both uppercase and lowercase), numeric, and special characters.

- The password should not be a common word found in a dictionary.

- Create a policy that dictates how and when passwords are to be changed.

NOTE   A space is a valid special character that can be used in a password. However, any leading space (that is, one or more spaces at the beginning of the password) is ignored.

When an administrator initially either sets up a router from the factory and chooses to run the setup script or issues the **setup** command, the System Configuration dialog appears. The administrator is prompted to enter basic router configuration parameters, including the passwords described in Table 3-7.

Table 3-7   *Passwords Configured During the SETUP Script*

Password Type	Description
Enable secret password	This password is used to permit access to a router's privileged mode. The password is stored in the router's configuration as an MD5 hash value, making it difficult for an attacker to guess and impossible to see with the naked eye.
Enable password	This password is not encrypted (or hashed) by default. Therefore, the enable password is considered weaker than the enable secret password. However, Cisco IOS still supports the enable password for backward compatibility. For example, if the IOS version on a router were rolled back to a version that supported the enable password but not the enable secret password, the enable password would offer some level of security.
vty password	When an administrator connects to a router over a network connection (such as a Telnet or SSH connection), she might be prompted to enter a vty password to have access to the virtual tty line to which she is connecting.

Even after the System Configuration dialog completes, and the router is functioning in a production environment, administrators can still change the router passwords. For example, the **enable secret** *password* global configuration mode command can be used to set the router's enable secret password. Consider Example 3-1, which shows an enable secret password being set to Cisc0Pr3$$. Notice how the enable secret password then appears in the running configuration. The string of characters shown is not an *encrypted* version of the password. Rather, the string is the result of an MD5 hash function, which always yields a 128-bit hash value that is also known as a "digest."

Example 3-1 *Setting the Enable Secret Password*

```
R1(config)# enable secret Cisc0Pr3$$
R1(config)# end
R1# show running-config

!
hostname R1
!
enable secret 5 $1$kmOB$rL419kUxmQphzVVTgO4sP1
!
```

To configure a password for a router's console, the administrator enters line configuration mode for **con 0** and specifies a password with the **password** command. Then, to force console connections to require a password, the **login** command is issued, as shown in Example 3-2.

Example 3-2 *Setting the Console Password*

```
R1(config)# line con 0
R1(config-line)# password 1mA$3cr3t
R1(config-line)# login
```

Similarly, you can set a password for the auxiliary port. Enter line configuration mode for **aux 0** and specify a password and require a login, like the console port configuration illustrated in Example 3-3.

Example 3-3 *Setting the Auxiliary Port Password*

```
R1(config)# line aux 0
R1(config-line)# password @uxP@$$w0rd
R1(config-line)# login
```

In addition to physically connecting to a router via the console or auxiliary port, administrators can connect to a router using a Telnet or SSH connection. Instead of connecting to physical ports, these types of connections use virtual ports. Specifically, by default a router has five virtual tty lines (that is, "vty"), vty 0 to vty 4, over which administrators can remotely connect. Similar to the console and auxiliary ports, passwords can be assigned to these vty lines, as shown in Example 3-4.

Example 3-4 *Setting the vty Line Password*

```
R1(config)# line vty 0 4
R1(config-line)# login
R1(config-line)# password MyP@$$w0rd
```

The enable secret password appears in the running configuration as an MD5 hash value. However, the console, auxiliary, and vty line passwords appear in the running configuration as plain text, as shown in Example 3-5.

Example 3-5 *Line Passwords Appearing in Plain Text*

```
R1# show running-config

!
line con 0
 password 1mA$3cr3t
 login
line aux 0
 password @uxP@$$w0rd
 login
line vty 0 4
 password MyP@$$w0rd
 login
```

To better secure these passwords, a *password encryption* service can be enabled on the router. This service uses a Cisco-proprietary algorithm that is based on a Vigenere cipher. This algorithm is far from secure. Its password can be easily compromised with downloadable utilities freely available on the Internet (such as the GetPass utility from Boson Software). However, enabling the password encryption service does help prevent someone from obtaining a password from the casual inspection of a router's configuration.

The password encryption service is enabled in global configuration mode using the **service password-encryption** command. After enabling this service, the console, auxiliary, and vty line passwords appear in an encrypted format. The 7 that appears after the **password** command indicates that the password has been encrypted using this Cisco-proprietary encryption algorithm, as shown in Example 3-6.

Example 3-6 *Cisco-Proprietary Password Encryption Results*

```
R1(config)# service password-encryption
R1# show run

!
line con 0
 password 7 091D43285D5614005818
 login
line aux 0
 password 7 06261A397C6E4D5D1247000F
 login
line vty 0 4
 password 7 09615739394153055B1E00
 login
```

Aside from having a single password for all administrators, individual user accounts can be used to give different login credentials (that is, username/password combinations) to different administrators. Although an external user database (such as a Cisco Secure Access Control Server [ACS]) could be used, a simple way to configure a user database is to add the username/password combinations to a router's configuration. Example 3-7 shows the addition of a username and password using the **username kevinw secret $up3r$3cr3t** command. The password will appear in the router's configuration as an MD5 hash value.

Example 3-7 *Configuring a Local User Database*

```
R1(config)# username kevinw secret $up3r$3cr3t
R1(config)# end
R1# show run

!
username kevinw secret 5 $1$geU5$vc/uDRS5dWiOrpQJTimBw/
!
```

> **NOTE** If you already know the MD5 hash value of the password you are setting for a user, you can enter the hash value, instead of the password, using the **username** *username* **secret 5** *hash_value* command. The 5 indicates that the string you are entering for the password is the result of an MD5 hash of the password, as opposed to the plain-text password. You could optionally indicate the plain-text password with a 0 in place of the 5.

If an attacker gains physical access to a router, he could connect to the router's console port and reboot the router. During the bootup process, the attacker could generate a break sequence, causing the router to enter ROM monitor (ROMMON) mode. From ROMMOM mode, the attacker could reset the router's password and thereby gain access to the router's configuration.

Although the ability to perform this type of *password recovery* often proves useful to administrators, if the router's physical security cannot be guaranteed, this feature opens a vulnerability for attackers. To mitigate this threat, an administrator can disable the password recovery feature by issuing the **no service password-recovery** command in global configuration mode. After entering this command, the administrator is cautioned not to execute this command without another plan for password recovery, because ROMMON will no longer be accessible.

Limiting the Number of Failed Login Attempts

If an attacker uses a brute-force attack or a dictionary attack when attempting to log in to a device, such as a router, multiple login attempts typically fail before the correct credentials are found. To mitigate these types of attacks, a Cisco IOS router can suspend the login process for 15 seconds, following a specified number of failed login attempts. By default, a 15-second delay is introduced after ten failed login attempts. However, the **security authentication failure** *rate number_of_failed_attempts* **log** configuration command (issued in global configuration mode) can be used to specify the maximum number of failed attempts (in the range of 2 to 1024) before introducing the 15-second delay.

Example 3-8 illustrates setting the maximum number of attempts to five. Also, notice the **log** command, which causes a TOOMANY_AUTHFAILS syslog message to be written to a syslog server.

Example 3-8   *Setting the Number of Failed Login Attempts*

```
R1# conf term
R1(config)# security authentication failure rate 5 log
R1(config)# end
```

Setting a Login Inactivity Timer

After an administrator provides appropriate credentials and successfully logs into a router, the router could become vulnerable to attack if the administrator walks away. To help prevent an unattended router from becoming a security weakness, a 10-minute inactivity timer is enabled by default. However, Cisco recommends that inactivity timers be set to no more than 3 minutes. Fortunately, administrators can adjust the inactivity windows with the **exec-timeout** *minutes* [*seconds*] command, issued in line configuration mode. Consider Example 3-9, which shows setting the inactivity timer for the console, auxiliary, and vty lines to 2 minutes and 30 seconds.

Example 3-9   *Setting an Inactivity Timer*

```
R1# conf term
R1(config)# line con 0
R1(config-line)# exec-timeout 2 30
R1(config-line)# exit
R1(config)# line aux 0
R1(config-line)# exec-timeout 2 30
R1(config-line)# exit
R1(config)# line vty 0 4
R1(config-line)# exec-timeout 2 30
```

> **NOTE**   Although it isn't recommended, you can disable the inactivity timer by entering a 0 for both the *minutes* and *seconds* arguments in the **exec-timeout** command (that is, **exec-timeout 0 0**).

Configuring Privilege Levels

Larger enterprise environments might need to support multiple administrative privilege levels for router configuration. For example, help desk staff might need access to a subset of the IOS commands available to the primary router configuration team.

Cisco IOS routers normally use two of the 16 supported privilege levels. Specifically, Cisco IOS routers support privilege levels in the range 0 to 15. By default, when you attach to a router, you are in *user* mode, which has a privilege level of 0. After entering the **enable** command and providing appropriate credentials, you are moved to *privileged* mode, which has a privilege level of 15.

However, for a finer granularity of administrative privileges, you can configure privilege levels in the range 1 to 14 using the **privilege** *mode* {**level** *level command* | **reset** *command*} command in global configuration mode. **reset** is used to reset the privilege level of a command to its original privilege level. To illustrate, Example 3-10 shows how to configure the **debug** command to be a privilege level 5 command and how to set the enable secret password for level 5 administrative access.

Example 3-10   *Configuring a Privilege Level*

```
R1# config term
R1(config)# privilege exec level 5 debug
R1(config)# enable secret level 5 L3v3l5P@55
R1(config)# end
```

After additional privilege levels are configured, an administrator can specify the privilege level she wants to change to using the **enable** *level* command. For example, for an administrator to switch to the previously configured privilege level of 5, she would enter the **enable 5** command. After switching to a privilege level of 5, the administrator would have access to all commands associated not only with privilege level 5, but also all lower privilege levels.

Creating Command-Line Interface Views

Similar to making different commands available to different administrators using privilege levels, role-based *command-line interface (CLI) views* can be used to provide different sets of configuration information to different administrators. However, unlike making commands available via privilege levels, using role-based CLI views you can control exactly what commands an administrator has access to. Following are the steps required to configure these views:

Step 1   **Enable AAA**: Authentication, authorization, and accounting (AAA) is discussed in detail in Chapter 4, "Configuring AAA." For now, just realize that AAA must be enabled to support views. Example 3-11 shows how to enable AAA on an IOS router.

Example 3-11   *Enabling AAA*

```
R1# conf term
R1(config)# aaa new-model
R1(config)# end
```

Step 2   **Enable the root view**: The root view is represented by the set of commands available to an administrator logged in with a pri'vilege level of 15. You might be required to provide the enable secret password to enable the root view, as shown in Example 3-12.

Example 3-12   *Enabling the Root View*

```
R1# enable view

Password:
R1#
```

Step 3   **Create a view**: Use the **parser view** *name* command to create a new view, as shown in Example 3-13.

Example 3-13   *Creating a View*

```
R1# config term
R1(config)# parser view HELPDESK

R1(config-view)#
```

Step 4   **Set a password for the view**: Use the **secret 0** *password* command to set the password required to invoke the view. The 0 in the command indicates that the password provided is in plain text, as opposed to an MD5 hash value. Example 3-14 shows how to configure a view's password.

Example 3-14   *Setting a Password for a View*

```
R1(config-view)# secret 0 H31pD3skP@55

R1(config-view)#
```

Step 5   **Add available commands to the view**: The **commands** *parser_mode*
{**include** | **include-exclusive** | **exclude**} [**all**] [**interface**
interface_identifier | *command*] command, issued in view configuration
mode, allows an administrator to specify a command (or interface)
available to a particular view. Example 3-15 shows how to specify that
the **copy** command (followed by any keywords), the **traceroute**
command, and the **ping** command will be available to a specific view
(HELPDESK in this example).

Example 3-15   *Specifying Commands Available to a View*

```
R1(config-view)# commands exec include all copy
R1(config-view)# commands exec include traceroute
R1(config-view)# commands exec include ping
```

Step 6   **Verify the role-based CLI view configuration**: After creating a view,
you can switch to that view with the **enable view** *name* command. After
switching to the new view, you enter a **?**, for context-sensitive help, to see
what commands are available in your new view, as demonstrated in
Example 3-16.

Example 3-16   *Confirming Role-Based CLI Configuration*

```
R1# enable view HELPDESK

Password:

R1#?
Exec commands:
  <1-99>      Session number to resume
  copy        Copy from one file to another
  enable      Turn on privileged commands
  exit        Exit from the EXEC
  ping        Send echo messages
  show        Show running system information
  traceroute  Trace route to destination
```

Protecting Router Files

To protect a router's image and configuration from an attacker's attempt to erase those files,
the *Cisco IOS Resilient Configuration* feature keeps a secure copy of these files. These files
are called the *bootset*. Table 3-8 details the steps required to configure Cisco IOS Resilient
Configuration.

Table 3-8 *Cisco IOS Resilient Configuration Steps*

Step	Description
Step 1: Enable image resilience	The **secure boot-image** command, issued in global configuration mode, secures the Cisco IOS image. The secured image is hidden so that it does not appear in a directory listing of files.
Step 2: Secure the boot configuration	The **secure boot-config** command, issued in global configuration mode, archives the running configuration of a router to persistent storage.
Step 3: Verify the security of the bootset	The **show secure bootset** command can be used to verify that Cisco IOS Resilient Configuration is enabled and that the files in the bootset have been secured.

Enabling Cisco IOS Login Enhancements for Virtual Connections

Administrators, and therefore attackers, can create virtual connections to an IOS router using Telnet, SSH, and HTTP. Because an attacker does not need physical access to a router to attempt one of these "virtual" connections, you should further secure these connection types using the Cisco IOS Login Enhancements feature. This feature adds the following requirements to the login process:

■ Create a delay between repeated login attempts.

■ Suspend the login process if a denial-of-service (DoS) attack is suspected.

■ Create syslog messages upon the success and/or failure of a login attempt.

These login enhancements are not enabled by default. To enable the login enhancements with their default settings, you can issue the **login block-for** command in global configuration mode. The default login settings specify the following:

■ A delay of 1 second occurs between successive login attempts.

■ No virtual connection (that is, a connection using Telnet, SSH, or HTTP) can be made during the "quiet period," which is a period of time in which virtual login attempts are blocked, following repeated failed login attempts.

You, as an administrator, might want to alter the supported virtual login parameters to better detect and protect against DoS and/or dictionary attacks. Table 3-9 provides a command reference for these parameters.

Table 3-9 *Commands for Enhancing Virtual Login Support*

Command	Description
Router(config)# **login block-for** *seconds* **attempts** *attempts* **within** *seconds*	Specifies the number of failed login attempts (within a specified time period) that trigger a *quiet period*, during which login attempts would be blocked.
Router(config)# **login quiet-mode access-class** {*acl-name* | *acl-number*}	Specifies an ACL that identifies exemptions from the previously described quiet period.
Router(config)# **login delay** *seconds*	Specifies a minimum period of time that must pass between login attempts. The default time period is 1 second.
Router(config)# **login on-failure log** [**every** *login_attempts*]	Creates log messages for failed login attempts.
Router(config)# **login on-success log** [**every** *login_attempts*]	Creates log messages for successful login attempts.
Router# **show login**	Can be used to verify that enhanced support for virtual logins is configured and to view the login parameters.

Consider the enhanced support for virtual logins configuration shown in Example 3-17. After entering global configuration mode, the **login block-for 30 attempts 5 within 10** command is used to block login attempts for 30 seconds after five failed login attempts occur within a 10-second time period. If logins are then blocked based on the first command, the period of time that logins are blocked is called the quiet period. However, in this example, the **login quiet-mode access-class 101** command specifies that during the quiet period, traffic permitted by ACL 101 still is allowed to log in via Telnet, SSH, or HTTP. The delay between successive login attempts is configured to 3 seconds with the **login delay 3** command. This configuration specifies that log messages should be generated upon every failed or successful login attempt using the **login on failure log** and **login on-success log** commands. Finally, the **show login** command is issued to confirm the configuration of these virtual login parameters.

Example 3-17 *Configuring Enhanced Support for Virtual Logins*

```
R1# conf term
R1(config)# login block-for 30 attempts 5 within 10
R1(config)# login quiet-mode access-class 101
R1(config)# login delay 3
R1(config)# login on failure log
R1(config)# login on-success log
R1(config)# end
R1# show login

    A login delay of 3 seconds is applied.
    Quiet-Mode access list 101 is applied.
    All successful login is logged.
    All failed login is logged.

    Router enabled to watch for login Attacks.
    If more than 5 login failures occur in 10 seconds or less,
    logins will be disabled for 30 seconds.

    Router presently in Normal-Mode.
    Current Watch Window
        Time remaining: 9 seconds.
        Login failures for current window: 0.
    Total login failures: 0.
R1#
```

Creating a Banner Message

When someone connects to one of your routers, he sees some sort of message or prompt. For legal reasons, Cisco suggests that a banner message be displayed to warn potential attackers not to attempt a login. For example, you wouldn't want to use a banner message that says, "Welcome! You are connected to Router 1." An attacker could use such a message as part of his legal defense, stating that he was told that he was welcomed to your router.

Please consult competent legal counsel when phrasing the banner message. However, as soon as you have the appropriate verbiage for your banner message, you can apply the message to your router with the **banner motd** *delimiter message_body delimiter* command. The **motd** parameter stands for "message of the day," and the *delimiter* is a character you choose to indicate the beginning and end of the banner message. Therefore, you should choose a delimiter that will not appear in the message body. Example 3-18 shows how to create a banner message. Notice that the $ character is used as the delimiter. Example 3-19 shows the new banner message presented to a user who just connected to the router via Telnet.

Example 3-18 *Creating a Message-of-the-Day Banner*

```
R1# conf term

Enter configuration commands, one per line.  End with CNTL/Z.
R1(config)# banner motd $

Enter TEXT message.  End with the character '$'.
WARNING: This router is the private property of Cisco Press.
    Disconnect now if you are not an authorized user.
    Violators will be prosecuted.
$
R1(config)#end
```

Example 3-19 *Login Prompt with a Banner Message*

```
WARNING: This router is the private property of Cisco Press.
    Disconnect now if you are not an authorized user.
    Violators will be prosecuted.

User Access Verification

Password:
```

Cisco Security Device Manager Overview

Cisco IOS routers support many features (including security features) that require complex configurations. To aid in a number of these configuration tasks, Cisco introduced the Cisco Security Device Manager (SDM) interface. This section introduces SDM, discusses how to configure and launch SDM, and how to navigate the SDM wizards.

Introducing SDM

Cisco SDM provides a graphical user interface (GUI) for configuring a wide variety of features on an IOS router, as shown in Figure 3-3. Not only does SDM offer multiple "smart wizards," but configuration tutorials also are provided. Even though SDM stands for Security Device Manager, several nonsecurity features also can be configured via SDM, such as routing and quality-of-service (QoS) features.

Figure 3-3 *SDM Home Screen*

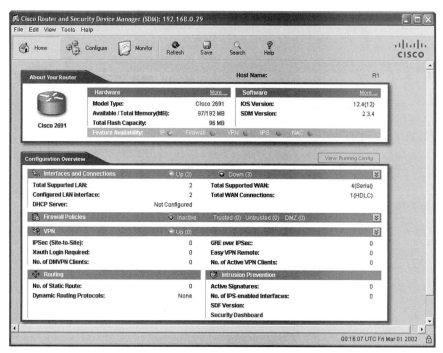

Some newer Cisco routers come with SDM preinstalled, but SDM needs to be installed on other supported platforms. Go to http://www.cisco.com/pcgi-bin/tablebuild.pl/sdm to download the current version of SDM and its release notes. Cisco SDM offers the following benefits:

■   SDM's smart wizards use Cisco TAC best-practice recommendations for a variety of configuration scenarios.

■   SDM intelligently determines an appropriate security configuration based on what it learns about a router's configuration (for example, a router's interfaces, NAT configuration, and existing security configuration).

■   SDM supports multiple security features such as wizard-based VPN configuration, router security auditing, and One-Step Lockdown configuration.

■   SDM, which is supported in Cisco IOS 12.2(11)T6 and later, does not impact a router's DRAM or CPU.

Preparing to Launch Cisco SDM

If you plan to run SDM on a router that does not already have SDM installed, you need to install SDM either from a CD accompanying the router or from a download from the Cisco IOS Software Center. The installation is wizard-based. You are prompted to install SDM either on an administrator's PC, in the router's flash, or both.

SDM can connect to the managed router using secure HTTP (that is, HTTPS). The commands shown in Table 3-10 can be used to configure the router for HTTP support. Example 3-20 illustrates the use of these commands.

Table 3-10 *HTTPS Configuration Commands*

Command	Function
Router(config)# **ip http server**	Enables an HTTP server on a router
Router(config)# **ip http secure-server**	Enables a secure HTTP (HTTPS) server on a router
Router(config)# **ip http authentication local**	Configures a local authentication method for accessing the HTTPS server
Router(config)# **username** *name* **privilege 15 secret 0** *password*	Configures a username and password to be used for authentication local to the router

Example 3-20 *HTTPS Server Configuration for R1*

```
R1(config)# ip http server
R1(config)# ip http secure-server
R1(config)# ip http authentication local
R1(config)# username kevin privilege 15 secret 0 cisco
```

To verify that the required SDM files are installed on a router, you can issue the **show flash** command. The output of this command should show, at a minimum, the following SDM files:

- sdmconfig-*router_platform*.cfg

- sdm.tar

- es.tar

- common.tar

- home.shtml

- home.tar

If you run SDM from a router's flash, as opposed to running SDM from a PC, the first time you connect to the router via a browser, you are taken to the Cisco SDM Express interface. Specifically, on a new router that has SDM installed, you point your browser to http://10.10.10.1. Alternatively, on an existing router, you point your browser to an active IP address on the router. Cisco SDM Express guides you through the initial SDM configuration on a router. Subsequent connections to your router via a browser take you directly to SDM, as opposed to Cisco SDM Express. However, if you run SDM from a PC, you can launch Cisco SDM by choosing **Start > Programs > Cisco Systems > Cisco SDM**.

Exploring the Cisco SDM Interface

Notice the toolbar across the top of the SDM page, as highlighted in Figure 3-4. You can use this toolbar to navigate between the Home, Configure, and Monitor views.

Figure 3-4   *SDM Toolbar*

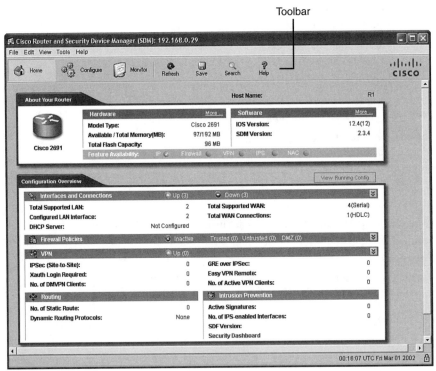

The Home view provides summary information about the router platform. For example, this summary information shows you the router model, memory capacity, flash capacity, IOS version, and an interface summary.

After clicking the **Configure** button, you see a screen similar to the one shown in
Figure 3-5. Notice the wizards available in the Tasks bar. Available configuration wizards
are described in Table 3-11.

Figure 3-5   *Configuration Tasks Bar*

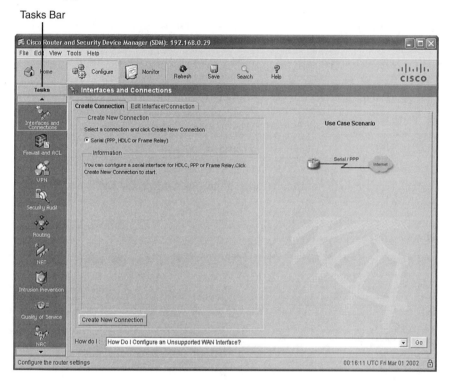

Table 3-11   *Cisco SDM Wizards*

Cisco SDM Wizard	Description
Interfaces and Connections	Helps you configure LAN and WAN interfaces
Firewall and ACL	Supports the configuration of basic and advanced IOS-based firewalls
VPN	Helps you configure a secure site-to-site VPN, Cisco Easy VPN Server, Cisco Easy VPN Remote, and DMVPN
Security Audit	Identifies potential security vulnerabilities in a router's current configuration and tweaks the router's configuration to eliminate those weaknesses

continues

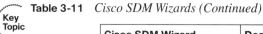

Table 3-11   *Cisco SDM Wizards (Continued)*

Cisco SDM Wizard	Description
Routing	Allows an administrator to modify and view routing configurations for the RIP, OSPF, or EIGRP routing protocols
NAT	Helps you configure Network Address Translation (NAT)
Intrusion Prevention	Walks an administrator through the process of configuring an IOS-based IPS
Quality of Service	Provides wizards for configuring Network Admission Control (NAC) features such as Extensible Authentication Protocols (EAP)
NAC	Helps you configure NAC

In addition to the configuration wizards, notice the **Additional Tasks** button, as shown in Figure 3-6.

Figure 3-6   *Additional Tasks Button*

Additional Tasks Button

Advanced administrators can use graphical interfaces to configure these additional tasks. Examples of these tasks are DHCP configuration, DNS configuration, and AAA configuration.

After clicking the **Monitor** button, you see a screen similar to the one shown in Figure 3-7. Clicking the various buttons in the Tasks bar allows you to monitor the status of various router features. Examples are firewall status, VPN status, and IPS status.

Figure 3-7 *Monitoring Tasks*

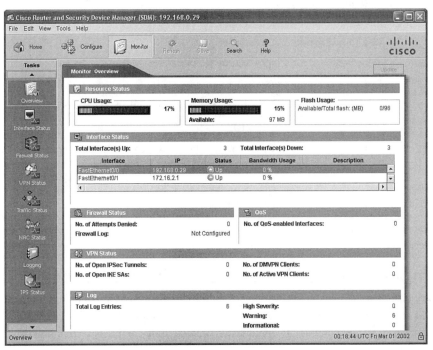

This chapter has introduced SDM. Subsequent chapters will detail how you can leverage SDM to configure a variety of security options. For exam purposes, you should be comfortable with navigating the various SDM screens and performing basic configuration tasks.

Exam Preparation Tasks

Review All the Key Topics

Review the most important topics from this chapter, denoted with the Key Topic icon. Table 3-12 lists these key topics and the page where each is found.

Table 3-12   *Key Topics for Chapter 3*

Key Topic Element	Description	Page Number
Table 3-2	IOS security features	81
List	ISR enhancements	85
Table 3-7	Passwords configured during the SETUP script	88
Table 3-8	Cisco IOS Resilient Configuration steps	96
List	Requirements added by Cisco IOS Login Enhancements for Virtual Connections	96
Example 3-18	Creating a message-of-the-day banner	99
List	Cisco SDM benefits	100
Table 3-11	Cisco SDM wizards	103-104

Complete the Tables and Lists from Memory

Print a copy of Appendix D, "Memory Tables," (found on the CD) or at least the section for this chapter, and complete the tables and lists from memory. Appendix E, "Memory Tables Answer Key," also on the CD, includes completed tables and lists so that you can check your work.

Definition of Key Terms

Define the following key terms from this chapter, and check your answers in the glossary:

Integrated Services Router (ISR), dictionary attack, brute-force attack, privilege level, role-based command-line interface (CLI) view, bootset, Cisco Security Device Manager (SDM)

Command Reference to Check Your Memory

This section includes the most important configuration and EXEC commands covered in this chapter. To see how well you have memorized the commands as a side effect of your other studies, cover the left side of the table with a piece of paper, read the descriptions on the right side, and see whether you remember the commands.

Table 3-13   *Chapter 3 Configuration Command Reference*

Command	Description
enable secret *password*	A global configuration mode command that configures a router's enable secret password
password *password*	A line configuration mode command that configures a password for a line (such as a con, aux, or vty line)
login	A line configuration mode command that configures a line to require a login
service password-encryption	A global configuration mode command that encrypts plain-text passwords in a router's configuration
exec-timeout *minutes* [*seconds*]	A line configuration mode command that specifies an inactivity period before logging out a user
security authentication failure *rate number_of_failed_attempts* **log**	A global configuration mode command used to specify the maximum number of failed attempts (in the range of 2 to 1024) before introducing a 15-second delay; also generates a log message if the specified threshold is exceeded
privilege *mode* {**level** *level command* | **reset** *command*}	A global configuration mode command used to associate a command (issued in a specific mode) with a specified privilege level, in the range 0 to 15 (although custom privilege levels are in the range 1 to 14), or to reset a command to its default level
aaa new-model	A global configuration mode command used to enable authentication, authorization, and accounting (AAA)
parser view *view_name*	A global configuration mode command used to create a new view
secret 0 *password*	A view configuration mode command used to set the password required to invoke the view
commands *parser_mode* {**include** | **include-exclusive** | **exclude**} [**all**] [**interface** *interface_identifier* | *command*]	A view configuration mode command that allows an administrator to specify a command (or interface) available to a particular view

continues

Table 3-13   *Chapter 3 Configuration Command Reference (Continued)*

Command	Description
secure boot-image	A global configuration mode command used to enable image resilience
secure boot-config	A global configuration mode command that archives the running configuration of a router to persistent storage
login block-for *seconds* **attempts** *attempts* **within** *seconds*	A global configuration mode command that specifies the number of failed login attempts (within a specified time period) that trigger a quiet period, during which login attempts will be blocked
login quiet-mode access-class {*acl-name*	*acl-number*}	A global configuration mode command that specifies an ACL that identifies exemptions from the previously described quiet period
login delay *seconds*	A global configuration mode command that specifies a minimum period of time that must pass between login attempts
login on-failure log [**every** *login_attempts*]	A global configuration mode command that creates log messages for failed login attempts
login on-success log [**every** *login_attempts*]	A global configuration mode command that creates log messages for successful login attempts
banner motd *delimiter message_body delimiter*	A global configuration mode command that configures a message to be displayed when a user administratively connects to a router
ip http server	A global configuration mode command that enables an HTTP server on a router
ip http secure-server	A global configuration mode command that enables a secure HTTP (HTTPS) server on a router
ip http authentication local	A global configuration mode command that configures a local authentication method for accessing the HTTPS server
username *name* **privilege 15 secret 0** *password*	A global configuration mode command that configures a username and password to be used for authentication local to the router

Table 3-14 *Chapter 3 EXEC Command Reference*

Command	Description
enable view	Enables the root view, which is represented by the set of commands available to an administrator logged in with a privilege level of 15
enable view *view_name*	Switches to the specific view (after the required credentials are provided)
show secure bootset	Used to verify that Cisco IOS Resilient Configuration is enabled and that the files in the bootset have been secured
show login	Can be used to verify that enhanced support for virtual logins is configured and to view the login parameters

This chapter covers the following topics:

Configuring AAA using the local user database: This section discusses the components of AAA, as well as the steps necessary to successfully configure AAA using the local user database.

Configuring AAA using Cisco Secure ACS: This section discusses the role of Cisco Secure ACS in configuring AAA, including a discussion of working with both RADIUS and TACACS+.

Configuring AAA

As a network administrator, you must provide network access, as well as guard your network against improper access. The authentication, authorization, and accounting (AAA) model helps you securely manage who and what accesses the network, as well as provides a means of determining when, where, and how this network access can occur. AAA is made up of a series of network security services that together provide a framework for setting up Network Access Control (NAC). This chapter examines the modular nature of AAA and discusses how it provides authentication, authorization, and accounting services. This chapter also examines how to troubleshoot AAA on Cisco routers using the CLI and discusses configuring local user database authentication using AAA from the Cisco Security Device Manager (SDM).

"Do I Know This Already?" Quiz

The "Do I Know This Already?" quiz helps you determine your level of knowledge of this chapter's topics before you begin. Table 4-1 details the major topics discussed in this chapter and their corresponding quiz questions.

Table 4-1 *"Do I Know This Already?" Section-to-Question Mapping*

Foundation Topics Section	Questions
Configuring AAA Using the Local User Database	1 to 6
Configuring AAA Using Cisco Secure ACS	7 to 12

1. Which of the following commands is used in global configuration mode to enable AAA?

   a. aaa EXEC

   b. aaa new-model

   c. configure aaa-model

   d. configure-model aaa

2. How do you define the authentication method that will be used with AAA?

   a. With a method list

   b. With a **method** statement

   c. With the **method** command

   d. With the **method aaa** command

3. Which of the following are authentication methods that may be used with AAA? (Choose three.)

   a. Local

   b. Remote

   c. TACACS+

   d. RADIUS

   e. IPsec

4. To configure accounting in AAA, from which mode should the **aaa accounting** command be issued?

   a. Privileged EXEC

   b. Command mode

   c. Global configuration

   d. Admin EXEC

5. What does the **aaa authentication login console-in** local command do?

   a. It specifies the login authorization method list named console-in using the local username-password database on the router.

   b. It specifies the login authentication list named console-in using the local user-name-password database on the router.

   c. It specifies the login authentication method list named console-in using the local user database on the router.

   d. It specifies the login authorization method list named console-in using the local RADIUS username-password database.

6. Which command should be used to enable AAA authentication to determine if a user can access the privilege command level?

   a. **aaa authentication enable level**

   b. **aaa authentication enable method default**

   c. **aaa authentication enable default local**

   d. **aaa authentication enable default**

7. Which of the following are features provided by Cisco Secure ACS 4.0 for Windows? (Choose three.)

   a. Cisco NAC support

   b. IPsec support

   c. Network access profiles

   d. NTVLM profiles

   e. Machine access restrictions

8. Which of the following browsers are supported for use with Cisco Secure ACS? (Choose three.)

   a. Opera 9.2

   b. Microsoft Internet Explorer 6 with SP1

   c. Netscape 7.1

   d. Firefox 2.0

   e. Netscape 7.2

9. Which of the following ports are used with RADIUS authentication and authorization? (Choose two.)

   a. UDP port 2000

   b. TCP port 2002

   c. UDP port 1645

   d. TCP port 49

   e. UDP port 1812

10. Which of the following are valid responses that the TACACS+ daemon might provide the NAS during the authentication process? (Choose three.)

    a. Accept

    b. Reject

    c. Approved

    d. Continue

    e. Failed

11. Which RADIUS message type contains AV pairs for username and password?

   a. Access-Request

   b. Access-Accept

   c. Access-Reject

   d. Access-Allow

12. To enable AAA through the SDM, you choose which of the following?

   a. **Configure > Tasks > AAA**

   b. **Configure > Authentication > AAA**

   c. **Configure > Additional Tasks > AAA**

   d. **Configure > Additional Authentication > AAA**

Foundation Topics

Configuring AAA Using the Local User Database

Unauthorized access to a network creates the potential for network intruders to gain access to sensitive network equipment and services. The Cisco AAA architecture provides a means to address this threat through systematic, scalable access security. Of course, network users and would-be intruders are not the only ones to try to access the network. Network administrators also need access to network equipment, and AAA offers a secure means to provide this.

Authentication, Authorization, and Accounting

Providing network and administrative access in a Cisco environment—regardless of whether it involves campus, dialup, or Internet access—is based on a modular architecture that is composed of three functional components—authentication, authorization, and accounting:

- **Authentication**: Authentication is the process by which users and administrators prove that they are who they claim to be. The network environment has a variety of mechanisms for providing authentication, including the use of a username and password, token cards, and challenge and response.

- **Authorization**: After the user or administrator has been authenticated, authorization services are used to decide which resources he is allowed to access, as well as which operations he may perform.

- **Accounting and auditing**: After being authenticated and authorized, the user or administrator begins to access the network. It is the role of accounting and auditing to record what the user or administrator actually did with this access, what he accessed, and how long he accessed it.

AAA for Cisco Routers

Cisco provides three ways to implement AAA services for Cisco routers:

- **Cisco Secure ACS Solution Engine**: In this implementation, AAA services on either the router or network access server (NAS), which acts as a gateway to guard access to protected resources, contact an external Cisco Secure ACS Solution Engine for both user and administrator authentication. The Cisco Secure ACS SE is an appliance that contains CSA. This can be an easier approach for some organizations, rather than purchasing hardware, an OS license, CSA license, and ACS license. In this more complex configuration, the administrator would also have to take steps to lock down the server, whereas the ACS SE is already secure.

■ **Cisco Secure Access Control Server (ACS) for Windows Server:** This software package may be used for user and administrator authentication. AAA services on the router or NAS contact an external Cisco Secure ACS for Microsoft Windows systems. You need a separate license for CSA if this is what you want.

■ **Self-contained AAA:** AAA services are self-contained in either a router or NAS. Implemented in this fashion, this form of authentication is also known as local authentication.

One common implementation of AAA is its use in authenticating users accessing the corporate LAN through a remote connection such as dialup or over the Internet via an IPsec VPN. Another is authenticating an administrator's access to a router console port, auxiliary port, or vty ports.

AAA access control is supported on Cisco networking products using either a local username-password database or through a remote security server database. To provide access to a small group of network users, a local security database can be configured in the router using the **username** *xyz* **password** *strongpassword* command. The **username secret** command may also be used to configure a **username** and an associated MD5-encrypted **secret**.

A remote security server may also be used. This implementation uses a remote security database on a separate server running an AAA security protocol. This can provide AAA services for multiple network devices and a large number of network users.

Router Access Authentication

Three general steps are required to configure a Cisco router to perform AAA using a local user database for authentication. It is critical that you secure the interfaces of all your routers—most importantly, network access servers and perimeter routers connecting to the Internet. AAA commands are used to configure the router to secure administrative access and remote LAN network access. Table 4-2 compares the router access modes, port types, and AAA command elements.

Table 4-2 *AAA Commands to Secure Administrative and Remote LAN Access*

Key Topic

Access Type Mode	Mode	Network Access Server Ports	AAA Command Element
Remote administrative access	Character (line or EXEC mode)	TTY, vty, auxiliary, and console	**login**, **exec**, and **enable** commands
Remote network access	Packet (interface mode)	async, group-async, BRI, and PRI	**ppp** and **network** commands

Six steps are required to configure a Cisco router for local authentication:

Step 1   Secure access to privileged EXEC mode.

Step 2   Use the **aaa new-model** command to enable AAA globally on the perimeter router.

Step 3   Configure AAA authentication lists.

Step 4   Configure AAA authorization for use after the user has passed authentication.

Step 5   Configure the AAA accounting options.

Step 6   Verify the configuration.

Using AAA to Configure Local User Database Authentication

To configure a router to use the AAA process, you must begin by issuing the **aaa new-model** command. This command is a critical first step in establishing a local AAA user authentication account. By establishing the local authentication method, you can reestablish your Telnet or console session and use the locally defined authentication list to access the router should a connection be lost while you're configuring AAA. Failing to do this causes the administrator to be locked out of the router. If this is the case, you need physical access to the router (console session), and you are required to perform a password recovery sequence. In the most extreme cases, the entire configuration saved in NVRAM may be lost.

At a minimum, these commands should be entered, in this order:

```
Router(config)# aaa new-model
Router(config)# username username password password
Router(config)# aaa authentication login default local
```

The following is a complete list of **aaa authentication** commands for Cisco IOS Release 12.2 and later:

```
aaa authentication arap
aaa authentication banner
aaa authentication enable default
aaa authentication fail-message
aaa authentication local-override
aaa authentication login
aaa authentication nasi
aaa authentication password-prompt
aaa authentication ppp
aaa authentication username-prompt
```

For a complete description of each **aaa authentication** command, refer to Table 4-3.

Key Topic

Table 4-3 *AAA Authentication Commands*

Command	Description
aaa authentication arap	AppleTalk Remote Access Protocol (ARAP) users using RADIUS or TACACS+ use the **aaa authentication arap** global configuration command to enable an AAA authentication method. The **no** form of this command is used to disable this authentication.
aaa authentication banner	Use this command to create a personalized login banner.
aaa authentication enable default	Use the **aaa authentication enable default** global configuration command to enable AAA authentication to determine if a user can access the privileged command level. The **no** form of this command may be used to disable this authorization method.
aaa authentication fail-message	This command creates a message that is displayed when a user login fails.
aaa authentication local-override	This command is used to configure the Cisco IOS software to check the local user database for authentication before attempting another form of authentication. The **no** form of this command may be used to disable the override.
aaa authentication login	Use the **aaa authentication login** global configuration command to set AAA authentication at login. The **no** form of this command is used to disable AAA authentication.
aaa authentication nasi	To specify AAA authentication for NetWare Access Server Interface (NASI) clients who connect using the access server, use the **aaa authentication nasi** global configuration command. The **no** form of this command is used to disable authentication for NASI clients.
aaa authentication password-prompt	Use the **aaa authentication password-prompt** global configuration command to change the text displayed when users are prompted for a password. The **no** form of this command is used to return to the default password prompt text.

Table 4-3 *AAA Authentication Commands (Continued)*

Key
Topic

Command	Description
aaa authentication ppp	Use the **aaa authentication ppp** global configuration command to specify one or more AAA authentication methods for use on serial interfaces running PPP. The **no** form of this command is used to disable authentication.
aaa authentication username-prompt	Use the **aaa authentication username-prompt** global configuration command to change the text displayed when users are prompted to enter a username. The **no** form of this command is used to return to the default username prompt text.

Although understanding all these commands can be quite useful, it is important that you learn the following three commands and how to implement them in an AAA environment:

■ The **aaa authentication login** command

Key
Topic

■ The **aaa authentication ppp** command

■ The **aaa authentication enable default** command

After you have enabled AAA globally on the access server, you need to define the authentication method lists and apply them to lines and interfaces. These are security profiles that indicate the service, PPP, dot1x, or login and authentication method. You may specify up to five authentication methods (local, group TACACS+, group RADIUS, line, or enable authentication) to apply to a line or interface. Although our focus in this section is on the local user database, if you are working with multiple authentication methods, it is a best practice to have either local or enable authentication as the final method to recover from a severed link to the chosen method server.

Defining a Method List

To define an authentication method list using the **aaa authentication** command, you need to follow three steps:

Step 1 In global configuration mode, use the **aaa authentication** command to configure an AAA authentication method list:

   • Indicate the service (PPP, dot1x, and so on) or login authentication.

   • Either use the default method list name or specify a method list name. Be aware that a defined method list overrides the default method list after it is applied to an interface. If this is not applied, the default method list applies.

- A list name may be any alphanumeric string you want to use. You may configure multiple strings on the router, but each must have a unique name.

- Method lists are sequential lists that describe the authentication methods that should be queried when authenticating a user. These allow an administrator to designate one or more security protocols to be used for authentication, allowing for a backup system for authentication should the initial method have an error or not be reachable.

Step 2   Specify the authentication method (local, group TACACS+, group RADIUS, line, or enable authentication), and how the router should handle requests when a method is not operating. For instance, is a AAA server down?

Up to four methods may be specified.

Step 3   Apply the authentication method lists to each of the following:

a. **Lines**: TTY, vty, console, auxiliary, and async lines, or the console port for login and asynchronous lines (in most cases) for ARAP

b. **Interfaces**: Interfaces sync, async, and virtual configured for PPP, Serial Line Interface Protocol (SLIP), NASI, or ARAP

Setting AAA Authentication for Login

The **aaa authentication login** command is issued in global configuration mode to set AAA authentication for login to a router's administration port. The following is a list of these commands:

- **aaa authentication login default enable** is used to specify a default login authentication method list using the enable password.

- **aaa authentication login console-in local** specifies the login authentication method list named console-in using the local username-password database on the router.

- **aaa authentication login tty-in** is used to specify a login authentication list named tty-in using the line password configured on the router.

The following is an example of the syntax to be used for the **aaa authentication** command:

```
aaa authentication login {default | list-name} method1 [method2...]
```
Table 4-4 lists the **aaa authentication login** command elements and details their usage.

Table 4-4 **aaa authentication login** *Command Elements*

Command Element	Description
Default	Specifies the default list of methods to be used when a user logs in based on the methods that follow this argument.
list-name	Used to name the list of authentication methods activated when a user logs in.
Method	One keyword must be specified. To use the local user database, use the **local** keyword.
	enable: The enable password is used for authentication.
	krb5: Kerberos 5 is used for authentication.
	krb5-telnet: Kerberos 5 Telnet authentication protocol is used when using Telnet to connect to the router.
	line: The line password is used for authentication.
	local: The local username database is used for authentication.
	local-case: Provides case-sensitive local username authentication.
	none: No authentication is used.
	group radius: The list of all RADIUS servers is used for authentication.
	group tacacs+: The list of all TACACS+ servers is used for authentication.
	group *group-name*: Uses either a subset of RADIUS or TACACS+ servers for authentication as defined by the **aaa group server radius** or **aaa group server tacacs+** command.

Configuring AAA Authentication on Serial Interfaces Running PPP

You may specify one or more AAA authentication methods for use on serial interfaces running PPP. To do this, you use the **aaa authentication ppp** command from global configuration mode. Here are the choices:

■ **aaa authentication ppp default local**: This command is used to specify a default PPP authentication method list using the local username-password database on the router.

■ **aaa authentication ppp dial-in local none**: This command is used to specify a PPP authentication method list named dial-in. It should be used on the initial login attempt, using the local username-password database on the router. If the local username is not defined, no authentication is used.

Using the aaa authentication enable default Command

To enable AAA authentication to determine if a user can access the privileged command level, you use the **aaa authentication enable default** command. This command should be issued from global configuration mode.

The following is an example of the syntax to be used for this command:

```
aaa authentication enable default method1 [method2...]
```

Authentication commands may be applied to both router lines and interfaces. As a best practice, you should always define a default list for AAA to provide a means of "last resort" authentication on all lines and interfaces protected by AAA. Example 4-1 shows the application of the authentication commands to router lines and interfaces.

Example 4-1 *Applying Authentication Commands to Router Lines and Interfaces*

```
router(config)# line console 0
router(config-line)# login authentication console-in
router(config)# int s3/0
router(config-if)# ppp authentication chap dial-in
```

Let's examine these commands:

■ **line console 0** is issued to enter line console configuration mode.

■ **login authentication console-in** specifies an authentication list named console-in for login authentication on console port 0.

■ **int s3/0** is issued to enter interface configuration mode on port 0 of serial interface slot number 3.

■ **ppp authentication chap dial-in** specifies an authentication method list named dial-in for use with PPP CHAP authentication on interface s3/0.

Implementing the aaa authorization Command

To set parameters that will restrict administrative EXEC access to the routers or user access to the network, you may use the **aaa authorization** command from global configuration mode. The following is the syntax:

```
aaa authorization {network | exec | commands level |
   reverse-access | configuration} {default | list-name}
   method1 [method2...]
```

Table 4-5 explains the syntax of the **aaa authorization** command.

Table 4-5   **aaa authorization** *Command Elements*

Command Element	Description
Network	Used to implement authorization for all network-related service requests, such as SLIP, PPP Network Control Protocol (NCP), and ARAP.
Exec	Used to implement authorization to determine if the user is allowed to run an EXEC shell.
Commands	Used to implement authorization for all commands for a specific privilege level.
Level	Used to specify the command level that should be authorized. Values may range from 0 to 15.
reverse-access	Used to implement authorization for reverse access connections, such as reverse Telnet.
configuration	Used to download the configuration from the AAA server.
Default	Used to list the authentication methods, *list-name* and *method*, as the default list of methods for authorization.
list-name	Provides a character string used to name the list of authorization methods.
method	Specifies the method to be used for authentication using one of the following keywords: **group** *group-name*: Specifies a subset of RADIUS or TACACS+ servers to be used for authentication. These are defined with the **aaa group server RADIUS** or **aaa group server tacacs+** commands. **if-authenticated**: The user is permitted to access the requested function if he or she has been validly authenticated. **krb5-instance**: Used in conjunction with the Kerberos **instance map** command to specify the instance to be used. **local**: Specifies the use of the local user database for authorization. **none**: Authorization is not performed.

Additionally, you can name authorization lists after specifying the service. You may list up to four failover methods.

Here are some examples of the **aaa authorization** command:

```
router(config)# aaa authorization commands 15 default local
router(config)# aaa authorization commands 1 mickey local
router(config)# aaa authorization commands 15 goofy local
router(config)# aaa authorization network pluto local none
router(config)# aaa authorization exec donald if-authenticated
```

These commands are as follows:

- **aaa authorization commands 15 default local**: The local user database is used to authorize the use of all level 15 commands for the default method list.

- **aaa authorization commands 1 mickey local**: The local username database is used to authorize all level 1 commands for the mickey method list.

- **aaa authorization commands 15 goofy local**: The local user database is used to authorize the use of all level 15 commands for the goofy method list.

- **aaa authorization network pluto local none**: The local user database is used to authorize the use of all network services, such as SLIP, PPP, and ARAP, for the method list named Pluto. If no local username is defined, this command does not perform authorization, and the user can use all network services.

- **aaa authorization exec donald if-authenticated**: If the user has already been authenticated, this command allows the user to run the EXEC process.

Working with the aaa accounting Command

In addition to authorization and authentication, AAA provides accounting capabilities for either billing or security purposes, or both. To enable AAA accounting of a requested service when you are working with RADIUS or TACACS+, you issue the **aaa accounting** command from global configuration mode:

```
aaa accounting {auth-proxy | system | network | exec |
  connection | commands level} {default | list-name} [vrf vrf-name]
  {start-stop | stop-only | none} [broadcast] group
  group-name
```

Table 4-6 explains the options that can be used with the **aaa accounting** command.

Table 4-6   aaa accounting *Command Elements*

Command Element	Description
auth-proxy	Provides information about all authenticated proxy user events.
system	Performs accounting for all system-level events that are not associated with users.
network	Runs accounting for all network-related service requests, including SLIP, PPP, PPP NCP, and ARAP.

Table 4-6 **aaa accounting** *Command Elements*

Command Element	Description
exec	Provides accounting for EXEC shell sessions.
connection	Provides information about all outbound connections made from the NAS.
commands *level*	Runs accounting for all commands at the specified privilege level. Privilege level entries are integers and may range from 0 to 15.
default	Sets the default list of methods for accounting services based on the listed accounting methods specified by *list-name*.
list-name	The list of at least one of the accounting methods.
vrf *vrf-name*	This optional command element, used only with system accounting, may be used to specify a VPN routing and forwarding (VRF) configuration.
start-stop	Sends a "start" accounting notice at the beginning of a process and a "stop" accounting notice at the end of a process. The start accounting record is sent in the background. Regardless of whether the start accounting notice was received by the accounting server, the requested user process begins.
stop-only	Sends a stop accounting notice at the end of the requested user process.
none	Disables accounting services on this line or interface.
broadcast	This optional command element allows the sending of accounting records to multiple AAA servers. Accounting records are simultaneously sent to the first server in each group. Should the first server be unavailable, failover occurs using the backup servers defined within that group.
group *group-name*	Defines the character string used to name the group of accounting methods.

The following are a couple of examples of how this command may be implemented:

```
router(config)# aaa accounting commands 15 default stop-only group tacacs+
router(config)# aaa accounting auth-proxy default start-stop group tacacs+
```

The first example defines a default command accounting method list. Accounting services in this case are provided by a TACACS+ security server, and it has been set for privilege level 15 commands. A stop-only restriction is also implemented in this example.

The second example defines a default authentication proxy accounting method list in which accounting services are provided by a TACACS+ security server for authentication proxy events with a start-stop restriction. If you are unfamiliar with authentication proxy or the **auth-proxy** command, it is used to authenticate inbound or outbound users, or both.

Using the CLI to Troubleshoot AAA for Cisco Routers

The primary command used when troubleshooting AAA on Cisco routers is the **debug** command. Three separate **debug** commands may be used to troubleshoot the various aspects of AAA:

- **debug aaa authentication**: Use this command to display debugging messages for the authentication functions of AAA.

- **debug aaa authorization**: Use this command to display debugging messages for the authorization functions of AAA.

- **debug aaa accounting**: Use this command to display debugging messages for the accounting functions of AAA.

Each of these commands should be executed from privileged EXEC mode to display the required information. To disable debugging for any of these functions, use the **no** form of the command, such as **no debug aaa authentication**.

Example 4-2 shows sample output from the **debug aaa authentication** command.

Example 4-2   *Using the* **debug aaa authentication** *Command*

```
router# debug aaa authentication

113123: Feb 4 10:11:19.305 CST: AAA/MEMORY: create_user (0x619C4940) user=''
ruser='' port='tty1' rem_addr='async/81560' authen_type=ASCII service=LOGIN
  priv=1
113124: Feb 4 10:11:19.305 CST: AAA/AUTHEN/START (2784097690): port='tty1'
  list=''
action=LOGIN service=LOGIN
113125: Feb 4 10:11:19.305 CST: AAA/AUTHEN/START (2784097690): using "default"
  list
113126: Feb 4 10:11:19.305 CST: AAA/AUTHEN/START (2784097690): Method=LOCAL
113127: Feb 4 10:11:19.305 CST: AAA/AUTHEN (2784097690): status = GETUSER
113128: Feb 4 10:11:26.305 CST: AAA/AUTHEN/CONT (2784097690): continue_login
(user='(undef)')
113129: Feb 4 10:11:26.305 CST: AAA/AUTHEN (2784097690): status = GETUSER
113130: Feb 4 10:11:26.305 CST: AAA/AUTHEN/CONT (2784097690): Method=LOCAL
113131: Feb 4 10:11:26.305 CST: AAA/AUTHEN (2784097690): status = GETPASS
113132: Feb 4 10:11:28.145 CST: AAA/AUTHEN/CONT (2784097690): continue_login
(user='diallocal')
113133: Feb 4 10:11:28.145 CST: AAA/AUTHEN (2784097690): status = GETPASS
113134: Feb 4 10:11:28.145 CST: AAA/AUTHEN/CONT (2784097690): Method=LOCAL
113135: Feb 4 10:11:28.145 CST: AAA/AUTHEN (2784097690): status = PASS
```

In Example 4-2, a user has attempted to log in to the router using the ttyl port. The user tries to access user mode (privilege level 1) using a plain-text authentication method (PAP in this case). The router identifies the default list to be used for authentication. The default list has been configured for authentication against the local user database. Status messages of GETUSER and GETPASS indicate that the router collects the username and password. A check of the local user database, denoted as LOCAL in the debugging output, verifies that the credentials are correct and the user is permitted to access the router. This is indicated in the PASS status in the debugging output.

Using Cisco SDM to Configure AAA

In addition to working with the CLI, you can configure and edit AAA using the Cisco Router and Security Device Manager (SDM). To configure or edit AAA using the Cisco SDM, first you issue the **aaa new-model** command from the CLI. Then you can configure or edit AAA using Cisco SDM by choosing **Additional Tasks > AAA**. Next, click the **Enable AAA** button in the upper-right corner to enable AAA on the router. The SDM takes precautionary steps to prevent locking the router or disconnecting the SDM session.

Figure 4-1 shows the process of enabling AAA with Cisco SDM.

Figure 4-1   *Enabling AAA with Cisco SDM*

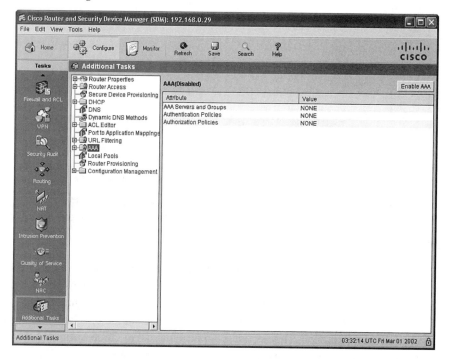

Figure 4-2 shows the AAA Authentication Login Screen with two login authentication method lists configured on the router. One is the default method list, and the other is the sdm_vpn_xauth_ml_l method list. Each of these method lists uses the local user database to provide login authentication. The screen shown is where you can configure new login authentication method lists, as well as edit or delete existing login authentication method lists on the router.

Figure 4-2   *AAA Authentication Login Screen*

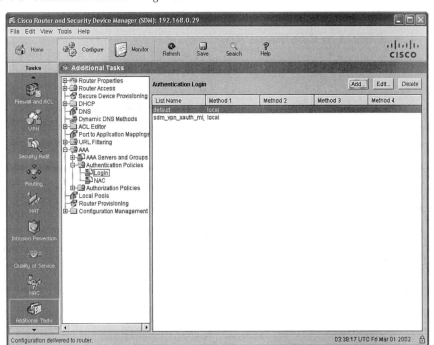

Configuring AAA Using Cisco Secure ACS

Cisco Secure ACS provides administrators with a centralized identity networking solution and simplified user management experience, whether they are working with Cisco devices or security management applications.

Through Cisco Secure ACS, administrators can ensure the enforcement of assigned policies by controlling who can log into the network, the privileges a user may have on the network, and securing access to the administrative web interface for each configuration administrator. Cisco Secure ACS also can provide documentation of security audits and account billing information. This section examines the role of Cisco Secure ACS in configuring AAA and explores working with RADIUS and TACACS+.

Overview of Cisco Secure ACS for Windows

Cisco Secure ACS for Windows allows you to manage and administer user access for Cisco IOS routers, virtual private networks (VPN), firewalls, dialup and DSL connections, cable access solutions, storage, content, VoIP, Cisco wireless solutions, and Cisco Catalyst switches using IEEE 802.1x access control. Cisco NAC is an industry initiative sponsored by Cisco Systems. It uses the network infrastructure to enforce security policy compliance on all devices seeking to access network computing resources. It relies on Cisco Secure ACS as an important component. In NAC deployments, Cisco Secure ACS 4.0 for Windows acts as a policy decision point by allowing the evaluation of credentials, determining the state of the host, and providing per-user authorization to the network access devices.

Cisco Secure ACS 4.0 for Windows provides a number of advanced features:

- Lightweight Directory Access Protocol (LDAP) and Open Database Connectivity (ODBC) user authentication support

Key Topic

- 802.1x authentication type support, including Extensible Authentication Protocol Transport Layer Security (EAP-TLS), Protected EAP (PEAP), Cisco Lightweight EAP (LEAP), EAP-Flexible Authentication via Secure Tunneling (EAP-FAST), and EAP Message Digest 5 (EAP-MD5)

- Access control lists (ACL) that may be downloaded for any Layer 3 device, including Cisco routers, Cisco PIX Firewalls, and Cisco VPNs

- Automatic service monitoring, database synchronization, and importing of tools for large-scale deployments

- Device command set authorization

- Dynamic quota generation

- User and device group profiles

- User and administrative access reporting

- Network access restrictions

- Restrictions such as time of day and day of week

Cisco Secure ACS 4.0 for Windows provides a scalable, high-performance RADIUS and TACACS+ security server. Cisco Secure ACS provides a comprehensive identity-based NAC solution for Cisco intelligent information networks by acting as the centralized control point for managing enterprise network users, network administrators, and network infrastructure resources. Cisco Secure ACS combines traditional authentication, authorization, and accounting (AAA) with policy control to effectively extend network access security. Through implementing Cisco Secure ACS, you can enforce a uniform network access security policy for network administrators and other network users.

Cisco Secure ACS supports a wide range of Cisco and other network access devices (NAD), sometimes called AAA clients:

- Wired and wireless LAN switches and access points

- Edge and core routers

- Dialup and broadband terminators

- Content and storage devices

- VoIP

- Firewalls

- VPNs

Additional Features of Cisco Secure ACS 4.0 for Windows

Cisco Secure ACS 4.0 for Windows provides a number of additional features that you might want to use:

- **Cisco NAC support**: In NAC deployments, Cisco Secure ACS 4.0 for Windows acts as a policy decision point. Cisco Secure ACS 4.0 provides configurable policies that it uses to evaluate and validate the credentials received from the Cisco Trust Agent (posture). With these it also determines the state of the host and sends a per-user authorization to the NAD: ACLs, a policy-based ACL, or a private VLAN assignment. This evaluation of the host credentials can enforce many specific policies, such as OS patch level and antivirus digital audio tape (DAT) file version. Cisco Secure ACS also records the results of this policy evaluation for use with monitoring systems. For hosts without the appropriate agent technology, Cisco Secure ACS 4.0 for Windows makes it possible for these hosts to be audited by third-party vendors before granting network access. External policy servers also make it possible to extend Cisco Secure ACS policies.

- **Improvements to scalability**: The 4.0 version of Cisco Secure ACS for Windows supports an industry-standard relational database management system (RDBMS), increasing the number of devices (AAA clients) ten times while increasing the number of users by three times the previous number. Improvements have also been made in performance, including significant performance increases in the number of transactions per second across the full protocol portfolio supported by Cisco Secure ACS.

■ **Network Access Profiles (NAP)**: One new feature provided by Cisco Secure ACS 4.0 for Windows is Network Access Profiles. Using these, administrators may classify access requests based on network location, membership in a network device group (NDG), protocol type, or other RADIUS attribute values sent by the NAD used by the user to connect. AAA policies may be mapped to specific profiles. Using this feature allows you as an administrator to apply a different access policy based on, for instance, wireless access.

■ **Extended replication components**: Through the improved replication provided by Cisco Secure ACS 4.0 for Windows, administrators may now replicate NAPs and all related configurations, including

— Posture validation settings

— AAA clients and hosts

— External database configuration

— Global authentication configuration

— NDGs

— Dictionaries

— Shared-profile components

— Additional logging attributes

■ **EAP-FAST enhanced support**: Cisco has developed EAP-FAST as a publicly accessible IEEE 802.1x EAP type to support customers who cannot enforce a strong password policy. EAP-FAST is also for those who want to deploy an 802.1x EAP type that has the following characteristics:

— No digital certificate is required

— Versatile supports for user and password database types

— Support for password expiration and change

— Flexible and easy to deploy and manage

■ **Machine access restrictions (MARs)**: MARs is offered as an enhancement of Microsoft Windows machine authentication. Administrators can use MARs to control authorization of EAP-TLS, EAP-FASTv1a, and Microsoft PEAP users who authenticate with a Microsoft Windows external user database when Microsoft Windows machine authentication is enabled. With this feature, users who access the network with a computer that has not passed machine authentication within a configurable length of time are given the authorizations of a user group that you specify. You can configure this to limit authorization as needed, or you may choose to deny network access.

- **NAFs**: Network access filters (NAF), a new type of shared profile component, give administrators a flexible way to apply network access restrictions and downloadable ACLs on network device names, NDGs, or their IP address. When NAFs are applied by IP addresses, you may use IP address ranges and wildcards. This new feature allows for granular application of network access restrictions (NAR) and downloadable ACLs. Previously, these supported only the use of the same access restrictions or ACLs to all devices.

- **Downloadable IP ACLs**: Per-user ACL support is extended to any Layer 3 network device that supports downloadable IP ACLS, such as Cisco ASA, Cisco PIX Firewalls, Cisco VPN solutions, and Cisco IOS routers. Sets of ACLs may be defined that can be applied per user or per group. This works hand in hand with NAC by enforcing the correct ACL policy. Further, these may be used along with NAFs to apply downloadable ACLs differently on a per-device basis, tailoring ACLs uniquely per user, per access device.

- **Certificate revocation list (CRL) comparison**: An X.509 CRL profile is used to support certificate revocation in this version of Cisco Secure ACS for Windows.

Cisco Secure ACS 4.0 for Windows Installation

You may install Cisco Secure ACS 4.0 on either Microsoft Windows 2000 Server or Microsoft Windows Server 2003. Before you undertake this installation on either operating system, however, you need to do a few things to prepare.

You need to be sure that the minimum hardware, OS, and third-party software requirements have been met before the installation. What follows is a general overview of these requirements; we will review each in greater detail later:

- Hardware configuration of the server

- Software currently on the server

- Compatible browser types used to administer Cisco Secure ACS

- Network requirements

- Ports used to communicate with Cisco Secure ACS

- Answers to installation questions, including the administrator and database passwords

The server on which Cisco Secure ACS will be installed must meet the following minimum hardware requirements:

- IBM PC-compatible with a minimum of a 1.8 GHz or faster Pentium 4 processor

- 1 GB of RAM

- Minimum of 1 GB of free disk space (if you are running the database on the same computer, more disk space is required)

- Minimum graphics resolution of 256 colors at 800×600 pixels

- CD-ROM drive

- 100BASE-T or faster connection

Cisco Secure ACS 4.0 supports the following operating systems. Note the service pack levels and other necessary services beyond the base OS. Also note that the OS and the service pack must be English-language versions.

- Microsoft Windows 2000 Server (Service Pack 4 [SP4])

- Microsoft Windows 2000 Advanced Server, with the following conditions:

    — SP4 must be installed.

    — Microsoft Windows 2000 Cluster Service must *not* be installed.

    — Other features specific to Microsoft Windows 2000 Advanced Server, such as Microsoft Windows 2000 Terminal Services, should *not* be installed.

- Microsoft Windows Server 2003 Enterprise Edition with Service Pack 1

- Microsoft Windows Server 2003 Standard Edition (SP1)

Specific to Windows 2000 Advanced Server, Cisco has not yet tested the multiprocessor feature of this OS; therefore, it cannot be considered to be supported. Further, Microsoft Windows 2000 Data Center Server is *not* a supported OS.

You may use the following browsers with Cisco Secure ACS:

- Microsoft Internet Explorer 6 SP1 and Microsoft Internet Explorer 5.5 for Microsoft Windows (English and Japanese version)

- Netscape 7.0, 7.1, and 7.2 for Microsoft Windows (English and Japanese version)

A number of known issues are related to using Netscape Communicator with Cisco Secure ACS. If this is your preferred browser, see the "Release Notes for Cisco Secure ACS for Windows" on Cisco.com.

You also need either the Sun Java Runtime Environment (JRE) 1.4.2_04 or Microsoft Java Virtual Machine (JVM) installed.

Before you deploy Cisco Secure ACS 4.0 for Windows, your network should meet the following requirements:

■ The Cisco Secure ACS computer should be able to ping all AAA clients.

■ All dial-in, VPN, or wireless clients must be able to connect to the applicable AAA clients.

■ Gateway devices between the Cisco Secure ACS and AAA clients must permit communication over the ports needed to support the necessary feature or protocol.

■ All network cards must be enabled in the computer that is running Cisco Secure ACS.

■ AAA clients must run Cisco IOS Release 11.1 or later to have full TACACS+ and RADIUS support on Cisco IOS devices.

■ Other vendors' AAA clients must be configured with TACACS+, RADIUS, or both.

■ For Cisco Secure ACS to use the Grant Dial-in Permission to User feature in Microsoft Windows when authorizing network users, this option must be selected in the Windows User Manager or Active Directory Users and Computers for the required user accounts.

■ One of the supported web browsers must be installed on the computer that is running Cisco Secure ACS.

Table 4-7 lists the ports used by Cisco Secure ACS for communicating with AAA clients, other Cisco Secure ACS machines and applications, and web browsers. Additionally, other ports are used to communicate with external user databases, but Cisco Secure ACS initiates those communications rather than listening to specific ports. For instance, if Cisco Secure ACS initiates communications with LDAP or RADIUS token server databases, these destination ports may be configured in Cisco Secure ACS.

Key Topic

Table 4-7 *Ports Used by Cisco Secure ACS for Client Communication*

Feature	Protocol	Port(s)
RADIUS authentication authorization	UDP	1645, 1812
RADIUS accounting	UDP	1646, 1813
TACACS+	TCP	49

Table 4-7 *Ports Used by Cisco Secure ACS for Client Communication (Continued)*

Key
Topic

Feature	Protocol	Port(s)
Cisco Secure ACS database replication	TCP	2000
RDBMS synchronization	TCP	2000
User-changeable password web application	TCP	2000
Logging	TCP	2001
Administrative HTTP port for new sessions	TCP	2002
Administrative HTTP port range	TCP	Configurable

As you begin the installation, you are asked a series of questions. For instance, you are asked to check the following:

■ Confirm that end-user clients can successfully connect to AAA clients.

■ Confirm that the Microsoft Windows server can ping the AAA clients.

■ Confirm that Cisco IOS Release 11.1 or later is running on the Cisco IOS clients.

■ Confirm that Microsoft Internet Explorer 6 SP1 or Netscape 7.02 is installed.

An administration password and database password also need to be created for the installation. The following is a detailed list of the steps necessary to install Cisco Secure ACS 4.0 for Windows for the first time:

Step 1 Log on to the computer using a local administrator account.

Step 2 Click **setup.exe** in the root directory of the CD-ROM.

Step 3 Read the software license agreement, and accept it by clicking **Accept**.

Step 4 After reading the Welcome screen, click **Next**. The Before You Begin dialog box appears.

Step 5 After you have completed all items in the Before You Begin dialog box and checked the corresponding check box for each item, click **Next**. The Choose Destination Location dialog box appears.

Step 6 If you do not want to change the destination folder, click **Next**. The Authentication Database Configuration dialog box appears.

Step 7   You have two options:

1. If you want to authenticate users with the Cisco Secure ACS internal database only, click **Check the Cisco Secure ACS Database Only**.

2. If you want to authenticate users with a Windows Security Access Manager (SAM) user database or Active Directory user database in addition to the Cisco Secure ACS internal database, you can do the following:

   • Click **Also Check the Windows User Database**. The **Grant Dial-in Permission to User** setting check box becomes available.

   • Click **Yes** for the **Grant Dial-in Permission to User** setting if you want to allow access by users who are authenticated by a Microsoft Windows domain user database only when they have dial-in permission in their Microsoft Windows account.

NOTE   The **Yes, Grant Dial-in Permission to User** setting check box applies to all forms of access that Cisco Secure ACS controls, not just dial-in access.

Step 8   Click **Next**. The setup program installs Cisco Secure ACS and updates its configuration.

Step 9   The Advanced Options dialog box has several features of Cisco Secure ACS displayed that are not enabled by default. Select each feature you want to enable by checking the corresponding check box for each feature, and click **Next**. The Active Service Monitoring dialog box appears.

Step 10 Click **Next**. The Database Encryption Password dialog box appears.

Step 11 Enter a password to be used for database encryption, and click **Next**. The setup program ends. The Cisco Secure ACS Service Initiation dialog box appears.

Step 12 Check the corresponding check box for each option you require, and then click **Next**. Select from the following options:

   • Yes, I Want to Start the Cisco Secure ACS Service Now

   • Yes, I Want Setup to Launch the Cisco Secure ACS Administrator from My Browser Following Installation

   • Yes, I Want to View the Readme File

Step 13 Click **Finish**. The setup program exits. You can access the Cisco Secure ACS HTML interface, on the computer running Cisco Secure ACS, by using the Cisco Secure ACS Admin desktop icon, or you can use one of the following URLs:

http://127.0.0.1:2002

or

http://localhost:2002

If you will be administering the Cisco Secure ACS from the network, you need to create and enable an administrator first, because an administrative account is not created by default.

To create an administrative account, follow these steps:

Step 1 Click **Administration Control**.

Step 2 Click **Add Administrator**.

Step 3 Complete the boxes in the Administrator Details table:

- Enter the login name (up to 32 characters) in the Administrator Name box.

- Enter the password (up to 32 characters) in the Password box.

- Enter the password a second time in the Confirm Password box.

Step 4 Click **Grant All** to choose all privileges, including user group editing privileges for all user groups.

If all privilege options are selected, all user groups move to the Editable groups list. To clear all privileges, including user group editing privileges for all user groups, click **Revoke All**.

Overview of TACACS+ and RADIUS

TACACS+ and RADIUS are the two most widely used AAA protocols. Although TACACS+ and RADIUS are quite popular, each has different features that make them suitable for different situations.

The Internet Engineering Task Force (IETF) created and maintains the RADIUS standard. TACACS+ is a proprietary Cisco Systems technology that encrypts data and replaces older versions such as TACACS and XTACACS. These protocols also differ in the protocols that they run on. TACACS+ runs in TCP, and RADIUS operates in User Datagram Protocol (UDP). Furthermore, TACACS+ can control the authorization level of users, but RADIUS cannot. Unlike RADIUS, TACACS+ also separates authentication and authorization. This feature allows administrators to use TACACS+ for authorization and accounting while giving them the flexibility to implement a different method for authentication, such as Kerberos, if they want to.

TACACS+ Authentication

The TACACS+ protocol is more flexible than RADIUS communication. TACACS+ allows an arbitrary conversation to be held between the daemon and the user. It continues until the daemon receives enough information to authenticate the user. Typically this is accomplished by prompting for a username and password combination, but this may include additional methods as well. For instance, the user might be prompted for something like her mother's maiden name. This is all done under the control of the TACACS+ daemon.

The following is a detailed list of the steps involved in the authentication process used with TACACS+, as shown in Figure 4-3:

1. The user requests access.

2. The NAC requests a username from the TACACS+ server.

3. The TACACS+ server provides a username prompt.

4. NAC prompts the user.

5. The user provides a username.

6. NAC forwards the username to the TACACS+ server.

7. NAC requests the password prompt from the TACACS+ server.

8. The TACACS+ server provides a password prompt.

9. NAC prompts the user for the password.

10. The user submits the password.

11. NAC forwards the password to the TACACS+ server.

12. The TACACS+ server accepts or rejects the user.

Figure 4-3 *TACACS+ Authentication Process*

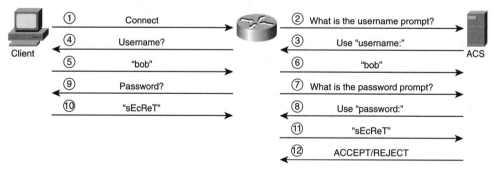

The TACACS+ daemon provides the NAS with one of the following responses:

- **ACCEPT**: The user is authenticated, and authorization begins at this point if the NAS has been configured to require it.

- **REJECT**: Authentication has failed for the user. The user either is prompted to retry the login sequence or is denied further access, depending on the TACACS+ daemon.

- **ERROR**: At some point during the authentication process, an error occurred. This may have occurred at either the daemon or in the network connection between the daemon and the NAS. If an ERROR response is received, the NAS usually attempts to use an alternative method to authenticate the user.

- **CONTINUE**: The user is prompted for further authentication information before acceptance or rejection.

As soon as authentication has occurred, the user must complete an authorization phase if authorization has been enabled on the NAS. Successful TACACS+ authentication is required of the user before he goes on to TACACS+ authorization.

The TACACS+ daemon is contacted again if TACACS+ authorization is required, and it returns an ACCEPT or REJECT authorization response. If it returns an ACCEPT response, it contains attributes that are used to direct the EXEC or NETWORK session for that user. This determines which services the user can access.

The services that may be available include

- PPP, Telnet, rlogin, SLIP, or EXEC services

- Connection parameters, such as the host or client IP address, ACL, and user timeouts

Figure 4-4 shows the authorization process with TACACS+ after the user has successfully authenticated.

Figure 4-4 *TACACS+ Authorization Process*

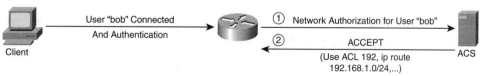

TACACS+ can be used to upload a per-user ACL and static route to the NAS, as well as for a variety of other parameters. The steps involved in this process are as follows:

1. NAC submits an authorization request for network access to the TACACS+ server.

2. The request is either accepted or denied by TACACS+. Authorization parameters are sent to the NAC if the access is permitted and are applied to the user connection.

Command Authorization with TACACS+

Access control over services available to a user is an important aspect of authorization. By controlling access to configuration commands, infrastructure security in large enterprise networks is simplified considerably. The ACS allows per-user permissions to be easily configured, and this simplifies the configuration on network devices.

Figure 4-5 shows the authorization process involved when a network administrator issues the **configure terminal** command on the router. In this example, the router queries the ACS for permission to execute the command on behalf of the user. During this process, TACACS+ establishes a new TCP session. By default, a new TCP session is established for each authorization request; this may lead to delays when users enter commands. To improve performance, Cisco Secure ACS supports persistent TCP sessions. To realize this benefit, both the Cisco Secure ACS and the router have to be configured for this functionality.

Figure 4-5   *TACACS+ Command Authorization Process*

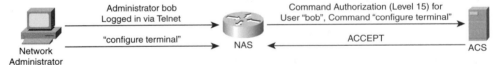

TACACS+ Attributes

TACACS+ frequently uses a number of attributes for authentication and authorization:

■ **ACL (EXEC authorization)**: Lists an access class number that will be applied to a line.

■ **ADDR (SLIP, PPP/IP authorization)**: When using a SLIP or PPP/IP connection, this is used to specify the IP address of the remote host that should be assigned.

■ **CMD (EXEC)**: The attribute-value (AV) pair is used to start an authorization request for an EXEC command.

■ **Priv-lvl (EXEC authorization)**: This may be an integer between 0 and 15. It is used to specify the current privilege level for command authorization.

- **Route (PPP/IP, SLIP authorization)**: Used to specify a route to be applied to an interface.

- **InACL (PPP/IP, SLIP authorization)**: Used with SLIP or PPP/IP connections to list an inbound IP ACL.

- **OutACL**: Used with SLIP or PPP/IP connections to list an outbound IP ACL.

- **Addr-pool**: Used to specify the name of a local address pool from which to obtain the address of the remote host.

- **Autocmd**: Used to specify a command to be automatically executed at EXEC startup.

In addition to these attributes, a number of other attributes exist for most network applications.

TACACS+ is a Cisco-proprietary protocol that uses TCP port 49 as the default transport layer. TACACS+ is supported on IOS routers, switches, and the Cisco PIX Firewall. It is the primary protocol used with Cisco AAA implementations.

When TACACS+ is used with AAA, typically each AAA transaction uses a dedicated TCP connection. By using a single session, there should be less server load and better detection of a break in communication. This single session persists as long as the server or network device is operational.

Authentication and Authorization with RADIUS

Like TACACS+, RADIUS may be used as a AAA protocol. Unlike TACACS+, it operates using UDP/IP rather than TCP/IP and provides only password encryption. However, unlike TACACS+, a Cisco-proprietary protocol, RADIUS was created by the Internet Engineering Task Force (IETF). The following list describes the steps involved in the authentication process with RADIUS (see Figure 4-6):

1. The NAS prompts the client for a username.

2. The client provides a username to the NAS.

3. The NAS prompts the client for a password.

4. The client provides the password.

5. An Access-Request datagram containing all the necessary AV pairs is used to send the information about the username and the password to the RADIUS server.

6. If the information provided by the user is correct, the server responds with an Access-Accept datagram. This Access-Accept message also contains authorization parameters in the form of AV pairs. For instance, this might be the IP address to be assigned, and so on. On the other hand, if the information that the user has provided is incorrect, an Access-Reject message is returned, and NAS terminates the connection.

Figure 4-6 *Authentication Process Using RADIUS*

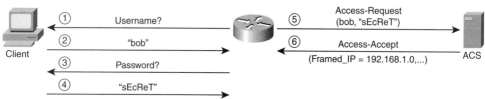

RADIUS Message Types

The four RADIUS message types are as follows:

■ **Access-Request**: Contains AV pairs for the username and password that are encrypted by RADIUS, as well as additional information such as the NAS port.

■ **Access-Challenge**: Used for authentication methods that employ a challenge-based approach such as Challenge Handshake Authentication Protocol (CHAP), Microsoft CHAP (MS-CHAP), and Extensible Authentication Protocol-Message Digest 5 (EAP-MD5).

■ **Access-Accept**: Indicates that the user-provided information is correct.

■ **Access-Reject**: Indicates that the user-provided information is incorrect.

RADIUS Attributes

All RADIUS messages can contain a number of AV pairs. Some of the pairs are used for authentication, and others are used for authorization purposes.

Here are some of the most commonly used RADIUS AV pairs:

■ User-Name

■ User-Password (encrypted)

■ CHAP-Password

■ NAS-IP-Address

■ NAS-Port

■ Service-Type

■ Framed-IP-Address

Roughly 50 AV pairs are defined in IETF standards. To these, Cisco has added several vendor-specific attributes on the server side. Cisco AV pairs are always used by default by Cisco IOS devices, but you may configure these devices to use only IETF attributes for standard compatibility if you like.

Features of RADIUS

You can augment the standard attributes we discussed with either proprietary attributes or extensions to RFC 2865. When we think in terms of RADIUS (Cisco), it is actually RADIUS (IETF) support plus IETF attribute 26, the vendor-specific attribute (VSA) for Cisco. It is via this VSA that any authorization request specified in the TACACS+ specification can be sent to an access device through RADIUS.

However, limitations exist, even with this extension of RADIUS. The most notable are the following:

- Limited security features

- The combination of authentication and authorization in one function

Table 4-8 describes the primary differences between RADIUS and TACACS+.

Table 4-8 *Comparison of RADIUS and TACACS+*

Key Topic

Topic	TACACS+	RADIUS
Packet delivery	TCP.	UDP.
Packet encryption	Encrypts the entire body of the packet but leaves a standard TCP header.	Encrypts only the password in the Access-Request packet from the client to the server.
AAA support	Uses the AAA architecture, separating authentication, authorization, and accounting.	Combines authentication and authorization.
Multiprotocol support	Supports other protocols, such as AppleTalk, NetBIOS, and IPX.	None.
Router management	Enables network administrators to control which commands can be executed on a router.	Can pass a privilege level down to the router, which can then be used locally for command authorization.
Responses	Uses multiple-challenge response for each of the AAA processes. Uses the AAA architecture and separates each process.	Uses single-challenge response. Combines authentication and authorization.

Configuring TACACS+

This section explores how to configure an IOS router to use TACACS+ as a AAA protocol using both the CLI and Cisco SDM. Let's begin by looking at the steps involved in this configuration using the CLI.

Here are the first steps of configuring the network access server:

Step 1   Enable AAA globally to allow the use of all AAA elements. This is a prerequisite for all other AAA commands.

Step 2   Specify which Cisco Secure ACS will provide AAA services for the network access server.

Step 3   Configure an encryption key to be used to encrypt the data transfer between the network access server (NAS) and the Cisco Secure ACS.

Example 4-3 shows these steps being used with TACACS+.

Example 4-3   *Configuring the Network Access Server with TACACS+*

```
router(config)# aaa new-model
router(config)# tacacs-server host 192.168.10.75 single connection
router(config)# tacacs-server key shared1
```

Table 4-9 lists commonly used AAA configuration commands and their functions.

Table 4-9   *Commonly Used AAA Configuration Commands*

Command	Description
aaa new-model	Used to enable AAA on the router. This is a prerequisite for all other AAA commands.
tacacs-server host *ip-address* **single-connection**	Used to indicate the address of the Cisco Secure ACS server and to specify the use of the TCP single-connection feature of Cisco Secure ACS. Performance is improved by maintaining a single TCP connection for the life of the session between the network access server and the Cisco Secure ACS server, rather than opening and closing TCP connections for each session, which is the default.
tacacs-server key *key*	Used to establish a shared secret encryption key between the network access server and the Cisco Secure ACS server.

Using the CLI to Configure AAA Login Authentication on Cisco Routers

To enable the AAA authentication process, the **aaa authentication login** command is issued in global configuration mode. Here is an example of the syntax that is used:

```
aaa authentication login {default | list-name} group
    {group-name | radius | tacacs+}
    [method2 [method3 [method4]]]
```

Table 4-10 lists the **aaa authentication login** parameters, along with the details of their usage.

Table 4-10   aaa authentication login *Parameters*

Key
Topic

Parameter	Description
Default	Used to create a default that is automatically applied to *all* lines and interfaces to specify the method or sequence of methods used for authentication.
list-name	Used to create a list (you may choose the name) that is applied explicitly to a line or interface using the method or methods specified. This list overrides the default when applied to a specific line or interface.
group *group-name* **group radius** **group tacacs+**	Used to specify the use of a AAA server. The **group radius** and **group tacacs+** methods refer to previously defined RADIUS or TACACS+ servers. The *group-name* string is used to specify a predefined group of RADIUS or TACACS+ servers for authentication (created with the **aaa group server radius** or **aaa group server tacacs+** command).
method2 *method3* *method4*	Used to execute authentication methods in the order listed. If an error is returned by the authentication method, such as a timeout error, the Cisco IOS software attempts to execute the next method. Access is denied if the authentication fails. Up to four methods may be configured for each operation. The method must be supported by the authentication operation specified. A general list of methods includes the following: **enable**: The enable password for authentication **group**: Uses server-group **krb5**: Kerberos version 5 is used for authentication **line**: The line password is used for authentication **local**: The local username and password database is used for authentication **local-case**: Specifies the use of case-sensitive local username authentication **none**: No authentication is used

Configuring Cisco Routers to Use TACACS+ Using the Cisco SDM

In addition to using the CLI to configure your routers to use TACACS+ as a AAA protocol, you may use the graphical user interface of the Cisco Security Device Manager (SDM). The first task when configuring AAA using the Cisco Security Device Manager is to enable AAA.

To enable AAA through the SDM, choose **Configure > Additional Tasks > AAA**. Figure 4-7 shows this process in the interface.

Figure 4-7   *Enabling AAA in the Cisco SDM*

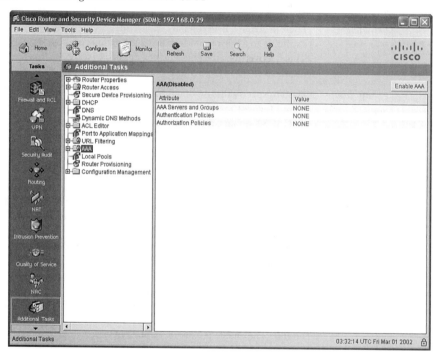

Click the **Enable AAA** button in the upper-right corner to enable AAA on the router. The SDM performs a series of precautionary tasks to prevent locking the router or disconnecting the SDM session. Figure 4-8 shows the Enable AAA dialog box.

Figure 4-8 *Enable AAA Dialog Box*

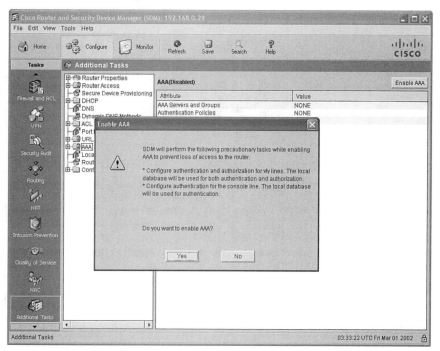

Defining the AAA Servers

After you have enabled AAA on the router, you can define the AAA servers to be used. To do this, choose **Configure > Additional Tasks > AAA > AAA Servers and Groups**. Click the **Add** button in the upper-right corner to create a new AAA server entry.

Figure 4-9 shows how to define a TACACS+ server. After you have clicked the **Add** button in the AAA Servers configuration section, the Add AAA Server window appears. You may select either RADIUS or TACACS+ from the **Server Type** drop-down box. When you choose TACACS+, you have the option of configuring the key to be used, as shown in the figure.

Figure 4-9 *Defining the TACACS+ Server in the SDM*

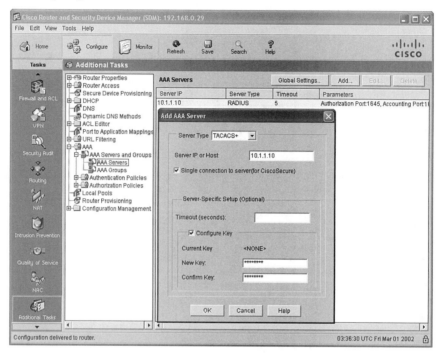

Exam Preparation Tasks

Review All the Key Topics

Review the most important topics from this chapter, denoted with the Key Topic icon. Table 4-11 lists these key topics and the page where each is found.

Key
Topic

Table 4-11   *Key Topics for Chapter 4*

Key Topic Element	Description	Page Number
List	Description of AAA components	115
List	Three ways to implement AAA services	115
Table 4-2	AAA commands to secure administrative and remote LAN access	117
Table 4-3	AAA authentication commands	118
List	Key AAA authentication commands	119
List	Commands to set AAA authentication for login	120
Table 4-4	**aaa authentication login** command elements	121
Table 4-5	**aaa authorization** command elements	123
Table 4-6	**aaa accounting** command elements	124-125
List	**debug** command for AAA	126
List	Cisco Secure ACS 4.0 for Windows advanced features	129
List	Cisco Secure ACS 4.0 for Windows additional features	130
List	Requirements to install Cisco ACS for Windows	133
Table 4-7	Ports used by Cisco Secure ACS for client communication	134-135
Figure 4-3	TACACS+ authentication process	138
List	TACACS+ daemon responses	139
Figure 4-4	TACACS+ authorization process	139
Figure 4-5	TACACS+ command authorization process	140
List	TACACS+ authentication and authorization attributes	140
Figure 4-6	Authentication process using RADIUS	142
List	RADIUS message types	142
List	RADIUS AV pairs	142

continues

Table 4-11 *Key Topics for Chapter 4 (Continued)*

Key Topic Element	Description	Page Number
Table 4-8	Comparison of RADIUS and TACACS+	**143**
List	Steps involved in configuring the network access server	**144**
Example 4-3	Configuring the network access server with TACACS+	**144**
Table 4-9	Commonly used AAA configuration commands	**144**
Table 4-10	AAA authentication login parameters	**145**
Figure 4-7	Enabling AAA in the Cisco SDM	**146**
Figure 4-9	Defining the TACACS+ server in the SDM	**148**

Complete the Tables and Lists from Memory

Print a copy of Appendix D, "Memory Tables," (found on the CD) or at least the section for this chapter, and complete the tables and lists from memory. Appendix E, "Memory Tables Answer Key," also on the CD, includes completed tables and lists so that you can check your work.

Definition of Key Terms

Define the following key terms from this chapter, and check your answers in the glossary:

authentication, authorization, and accounting (AAA); authentication; authorization; accounting; auditing; Challenge Handshake Authentication Protocol (CHAP); Extensible Authentication Protocol-Flexible Authentication via Secure Tunneling (EAP-FAST); Extensible Authentication Protocol-Message Digest 5 (EAP-MD5); Extensible Authentication Protocol-Transport Layer Security (EAP-TLS); Lightweight Extensible Authentication Protocol (LEAP); method list; Microsoft Challenge Handshake Authentication Protocol (MS-CHAP); network admission control (NAC); network access device (NAD); network access server (NAS); Point-to-Point Protocol (PPP); Remote Authentication Dial-In User Service (RADIUS); Terminal Access Controller Access-Control System Plus (TACACS+); Transmission Control Protocol (TCP); user datagram protocol (UDP); virtual private network (VPN)

Command Reference to Check Your Memory

This section includes the most important configuration and EXEC commands covered in this chapter. To see how well you have memorized the commands as a side effect of your other studies, cover the left side of the table with a piece of paper, read the descriptions on the right side, and see whether you remember the commands.

Table 4-12 *Chapter 4 Configuration Command Reference*

Command	Description
aaa new-model	Enables AAA on the router. This is a prerequisite for all other AAA commands.
aaa authentication arap	A global configuration command used by AppleTalk Remote Access Protocol (ARAP) users using RADIUS or TACACS+ to enable an AAA authentication method.
aaa authentication banner	Creates a personalized login banner.
aaa authentication enable default	A global configuration command that enables AAA authentication to determine if a user can access the privileged command level.
aaa authentication fail-message	Creates a message that is displayed when a user login fails.
aaa authentication localoverride	Configures the Cisco IOS software to check the local user database for authentication before attempting another form of authentication.
aaa authentication login {**default** | *list-name*} **group** {*group-name* | **radius** | **tacacs+**} [*method2* [*method3* [*method4*]]]	A global configuration command that sets AAA authentication at login.
aaa authentication nasi	A global configuration command that specifies AAA authentication for NetWare Access Server Interface (NASI) clients who connect using the access server.
aaa authentication passwordprompt	A global configuration command that changes the text displayed when users are prompted for a password.
aaa authentication ppp	A global configuration command that specifies one or more AAA authentication methods for use on serial interfaces running PPP.
aaa authentication usernameprompt	A global configuration command that changes the text displayed when users are prompted to enter a username.
aaa authentication ppp default local	A global configuration command that specifies a default PPP authentication method list using the local username-password database on the router.

continues

Table 4-12 *Chapter 4 Configuration Command Reference (Continued)*

Command	Description
aaa authentication ppp dial-in local none	A global configuration command that specifies that a PPP authentication method list named dial-in should be used on the initial login attempt, using the local username-password database on the router. If the local username is not defined, no authentication is used.
aaa authorization {**network** | **exec** | **commands** *level* | **reverse-access** | **configuration**} {**default** | *list-name*} *method1* [*method2*. . .]	A global configuration command that may be used to set parameters that restrict administrative EXEC access to the routers or user access to the network.

Table 4-13 *Chapter 4 EXEC Command Reference*

Command	Description
debug aaa authentication	Displays debugging messages for the authentication functions of AAA
debug aaa authorization	Displays debugging messages for the authorization functions of AAA
debug aaa accounting	Displays debugging messages for the accounting functions of AAA

This chapter covers the following topics:

Locking down the router: This section discusses various router services that attackers might target. To help you harden the security of a router, this section also describes the AutoSecure feature and Cisco SDM's One-Step Lockdown feature.

Using secure management and reporting: This section focuses on securing and monitoring router access using syslog, SSH, and SNMPv3 technologies. Also, this section distinguishes between in-band and out-of-band network management and shows you how to use Cisco SDM to configure a variety of management and monitoring features.

CHAPTER 5

Securing the Router

Newly installed Cisco IOS routers might have multiple services and interfaces enabled that do not need to be enabled. Therefore, they present potential security vulnerabilities. The process of turning off unnecessary services is called "hardening" a router, and this chapter discusses Cisco best-practice recommendations for router hardening. Cisco SDM's One-Step Lockdown feature is explored, in addition to the **auto secure** command.

Besides disabling unneeded services and interfaces, unsecured router management traffic can pose a security threat. For example, an attacker could compromise router security by intercepting login credentials. Therefore, this chapter also addresses management and reporting protocols and applications such as syslog, Secure Shell (SSH), and Simple Network Management Protocol v3 (SNMPv3). Interestingly, just as Cisco SDM can help harden a router, it can also be used to enable a variety of Cisco IOS management features.

"Do I Know This Already?" Quiz

The "Do I Know This Already?" quiz helps you determine your level of knowledge of this chapter's topics before you begin. Table 5-1 details the major topics discussed in this chapter and their corresponding quiz questions.

Table 5-1   *"Do I Know This Already?" Section-to-Question Mapping*

Foundation Topics Section	Questions
Locking Down the Router	1 and 2
Using Secure Management and Reporting	3 to 8

1. If you need to use Simple Network Management Protocol (SNMP) on your network, what version does Cisco recommend?

   a. Version 2

   b. Version 2c

   c. Version 3

   d. Version 3c

2. What are two automated approaches for hardening the security of a Cisco IOS router? (Choose two.)

   a. AutoQoS

   b. AutoSecure

   c. Cisco SDM's One-Step Lockdown

   d. Cisco IPS Device Manager (IDM)

3. Which of the following router services can best help administrators correlate events appearing in a log file?

   a. Finger

   b. TCP small services

   c. CDP

   d. NTP

4. What management topology keeps management traffic isolated from production traffic?

   a. OOB

   b. OTP

   c. SAFE

   d. MARS

5. What syslog logging level is associated with warnings?

   a. 3

   b. 4

   c. 5

   d. 6

6. Information about a managed device's resources and activity is defined by a series of objects. What defines the structure of these management objects?

   a. LDAP

   b. CEF

   c. FIB

   d. MIB

7. When SSH is configured, what is the Cisco minimum recommended modulus value?

    a. 256 bits

    b. 512 bits

    c. 1024 bits

    d. 2048 bits

8. If you click the **Configure** button along the top of Cisco SDM's graphical interface, which Tasks button allows you to configure such features as SSH, NTP, SNMP, and syslog?

    a. Additional Tasks

    b. Interfaces and Connections

    c. Security Audit

    d. Intrusion Prevention

Foundation Topics

Locking Down the Router

This section begins by identifying router services that are susceptible to attack and by explaining how security can be compromised by various router management services. You will learn two approaches for hardening a Cisco IOS router against attacks:

- Using Cisco SDM's One-Step Lockdown feature

- Using the **auto secure** CLI command

Identifying Potentially Vulnerable Router Interfaces and Services

One of the most obvious steps to secure a router is to administratively shut down any unused router interfaces using the **shutdown** command in interface configuration mode. Another approach to securing a router involves turning off unneeded services.

Fortunately, hardening a router against attack does not require a thorough understanding of how an attacker can compromise router security through specific services. However, you should be acquainted with the services that are potentially running on your router, which might or might not be needed. If a service is not needed, typically it should be disabled to prevent it from inadvertently becoming a security hole. Table 5-2 provides an overview of several services and features available on many Cisco IOS routers.

Key Topic

Table 5-2 *Cisco IOS Features*

IOS Feature	Description
Bootstrap protocol (BOOTP) server	Allows a router to serve as a BOOTP server for other routers
Cisco Discovery Protocol (CDP)	A Layer 2 protocol that permits adjacent Cisco devices to learn information about one another (for example, protocol and platform information)
Configuration autoloading	Supports a router loading its configuration information from a network server
FTP server	Causes a router to act as an FTP server for file transfer
TFTP server	Permits a router to act as a TFTP server, which does not require authentication
Network Time Protocol (NTP)	Allows a router to act as a time source for other network devices

Table 5-2 *Cisco IOS Features (Continued)*

IOS Feature	Description
Packet Assembler/ Disassembler (PAD)	Permits access to X.25 commands
TCP/UDP minor services	Allows various daemons to be used for diagnostics
Maintenance Operation Protocol (MOP)	Used as a maintenance protocol in a Digital Equipment Corporation (DEC) environment
Simple Network Management Protocol (SNMP)	Allows a router to communicate with an SNMP-speaking network management station
HTTP/HTTPS configuration and monitoring	Supports the monitoring and configuration of a router via a web interface (for example, the Cisco SDM interface)
Domain Name Service (DNS)	Allows a router to send DNS queries for name-to-IP address resolution
Internet Control Message Protocol (ICMP) redirects	Tells a router to send an ICMP redirect message in case the router resends a packet out the same interface the packet was received on
IP source routing	Permits the sender of a packet to dictate the route that the packet will take to its destination
Finger service	Displays users currently logged into a router
ICMP unreachable notifications	Notifies the sender of a packet if the packet was destined for an invalid destination
ICMP mask	Causes a router to send an ICMP mask reply message, which contains an interface's IP address mask, in response to an ICMP mask request
IP identification service	Identifies the initiator of a TCP connection to the other party in the connection
TCP keepalives	Helps a router close inactive TCP connections
Gratuitous ARP	Allows a router to accept replies to Address Resolution Protocol (ARP) requests that the router did not request
Proxy ARP	Supports a router functioning as a Layer 2 bridge by responding to ARP requests on behalf of another network device (for example, a network server)
IP-directed broadcast	Allows a router to propagate a broadcast message originating in one subnet and destined for another subnet

NOTE   SNMP version 1 and SNMP version 2c use *community strings* for authentication. These community strings, which are often set to a default of "public" (which provides read access) and "private" (which provides read-write access) are sent in clear text, and SNMPv1 and SNMPv2c can easily be spoofed. Therefore, Cisco recommends that SNMP be disabled. However, if SNMP is needed, Cisco recommends using SNMP version 3, which is more secure. Specifically, SNMP version 3 offers authentication, encryption, and access control features.

NOTE   Although Cisco SDM supports either HTTP or HTTPS, Cisco recommends using HTTPS, because HTTPS encrypts the data exchanged between a router and the Cisco SDM workstation. For additional security, access to a router's HTTPS service can be limited by an access control list (ACL), which can restrict the subnet(s) allowed to access a router via HTTPS.

NOTE   By default, when a Cisco IOS router sends a DNS name query, the router sends the query to a broadcast address of 255.255.255.255. Attackers could leverage this default behavior by pretending to be a DNS server and responding to the router's name queries with incorrect information.

Locking Down a Cisco IOS Router

Next, consider how you can follow the Cisco best-practice recommendations for disabling services and further securing a router. Instead of individually enabling or disabling selected services, you can use one of two automated approaches that Cisco offers, as summarized in Table 5-3.

Table 5-3   *Methods for Locking Down a Cisco Router*

Methods	Configuration
AutoSecure	The AutoSecure IOS feature is invoked by issuing the **auto secure** command from the CLI.
Cisco SDM One-Step Lockdown	The Cisco SDM One-Step Lockdown method for securing a router uses a wizard in the Cisco SDM graphical interface.

AutoSecure

The AutoSecure feature can be enabled from privileged EXEC mode by issuing the **auto secure** command, as shown in Example 5-1.

Example 5-1 *Enabling AutoSecure*

```
R1# auto secure

                --- AutoSecure Configuration ---

*** AutoSecure configuration enhances the security of
the router, but it will not make it absolutely resistant
to all security attacks ***

AutoSecure will modify the configuration of your device.
All configuration changes will be shown. For a detailed
explanation of how the configuration changes enhance security
and any possible side effects, please refer to Cisco.com for
Autosecure documentation.
At any prompt you may enter '?' for help.
Use ctrl-c to abort this session at any prompt.


Gathering information about the router for AutoSecure

Is this router connected to internet? [no]: yes
Enter the number of interfaces facing the internet [1]:

Interface            IP-Address     OK? Method Status                   Protocol
FastEthernet0/0      192.168.0.29   YES NVRAM  up                       up

FastEthernet0/1      172.16.2.1     YES NVRAM  up                       up

Serial1/0            172.16.1.1     YES NVRAM  up                       up

Serial1/1            unassigned     YES NVRAM  administratively down down

Serial1/2            unassigned     YES NVRAM  administratively down down

Serial1/3            unassigned     YES NVRAM  administratively down down

Enter the interface name that is facing the internet: FastEthernet0/1

Securing Management plane services...

Disabling service finger
Disabling service pad
Disabling udp & tcp small servers
Enabling service password encryption
Enabling service tcp-keepalives-in
```

continues

Example 5-1   *Enabling AutoSecure (Continued)*

```
Enabling service tcp-keepalives-out
Disabling the cdp protocol

Disabling the bootp server
Disabling the http server
Disabling the finger service
Disabling source routing
Disabling gratuitous arp

Here is a sample Security Banner to be shown
at every access to device. Modify it to suit your
enterprise requirements.

Authorized Access only
  This system is the property of So-&-So-Enterprise.
  UNAUTHORIZED ACCESS TO THIS DEVICE IS PROHIBITED.
  You must have explicit permission to access this
  device. All activities performed on this device
  are logged. Any violations of access policy will result
  in disciplinary action.

Enter the security banner {Put the banner between
k and k, where k is any character}:
%
WARNING: This router is the property of Cisco Press.
Any unauthorized access is monitored. Violators will be prosecuted.
%
Enter the new enable password:
Confirm the enable password:
Configuring AAA local authentication
Configuring Console, Aux and VTY lines for
local authentication, exec-timeout, and transport
Securing device against Login Attacks
Configure the following parameters

Blocking Period when Login Attack detected: 30

Maximum Login failures with the device: 3

Maximum time period for crossing the failed login attempts: 10

Configure SSH server? [yes]:
Enter the domain-name: ciscopress.com

Configuring interface specific AutoSecure services
Disabling the following ip services on all interfaces:
```

Example 5-1 *Enabling AutoSecure (Continued)*

```
 no ip redirects
 no ip proxy-arp
 no ip unreachables
 no ip directed-broadcast
 no ip mask-reply
Disabling mop on Ethernet interfaces

Securing Forwarding plane services...

Enabling CEF (This might impact the memory requirements for your platform)
Enabling unicast rpf on all interfaces connected
to internet

Configure CBAC Firewall feature? [yes/no]: yes

This is the configuration generated:

no service finger
no service pad
no service udp-small-servers
no service tcp-small-servers
service password-encryption
service tcp-keepalives-in
service tcp-keepalives-out
no cdp run
no ip bootp server
no ip http server
no ip finger
no ip source-route
no ip gratuitous-arps
no ip identd
banner motd ^C
WARNING: This router is the property of Cisco Press.
Any unauthorized access is monitored. Violators will be prosecuted.
^C
security passwords min-length 6
security authentication failure rate 10 log
enable password 7 095F4B0A0B0003022B1F17
aaa new-model
authentication login local_auth local
line con 0
 login authentication local_auth
 exec-timeout 5 0
 transport output telnet
line aux 0
 login authentication local_auth
 exec-timeout 10 0
```

continues

Example 5-1   *Enabling AutoSecure (Continued)*

```
 transport output telnet
line vty 0 4
 login authentication local_auth
 transport input telnet
login block-for 30 attempts 3 within 10
ip domain-name ciscopress.com
crypto key generate rsa general-keys modulus 1024
ip ssh time-out 60
ip ssh authentication-retries 2
line vty 0 4
 transport input ssh telnet
service timestamps debug datetime msec localtime show-timezone
service timestamps log datetime msec localtime show-timezone
logging facility local2
logging trap debugging
service sequence-numbers
logging console critical
logging buffered
interface FastEthernet0/0
 no ip redirects
 no ip proxy-arp
 no ip unreachables
 no ip directed-broadcast
 no ip mask-reply
 no mop enabled
interface FastEthernet0/1
 no ip redirects
 no ip proxy-arp
 no ip unreachables
 no ip directed-broadcast
 no ip mask-reply
 no mop enabled
interface Serial1/0
 no ip redirects
 no ip proxy-arp
 no ip unreachables
 no ip directed-broadcast
 no ip mask-reply
interface Serial1/1
 no ip redirects
 no ip proxy-arp
 no ip unreachables
 no ip directed-broadcast
 no ip mask-reply
interface Serial1/2
 no ip redirects
 no ip proxy-arp
```

Example 5-1 *Enabling AutoSecure (Continued)*

```
 no ip unreachables
 no ip directed-broadcast
 no ip mask-reply
interface Serial1/3
 no ip redirects
 no ip proxy-arp
 no ip unreachables
 no ip directed-broadcast
 no ip mask-reply
ip cef
access-list 100 permit udp any any eq bootpc
interface FastEthernet0/1
 ip verify unicast source reachable-via rx allow-default 100
ip inspect audit-trail
ip inspect dns-timeout 7
ip inspect tcp idle-time 14400
ip inspect udp idle-time 1800
ip inspect name autosec_inspect cuseeme timeout 3600
ip inspect name autosec_inspect ftp timeout 3600
ip inspect name autosec_inspect http timeout 3600
ip inspect name autosec_inspect rcmd timeout 3600
ip inspect name autosec_inspect realaudio timeout 3600
ip inspect name autosec_inspect smtp timeout 3600
ip inspect name autosec_inspect tftp timeout 30
ip inspect name autosec_inspect udp timeout 15
ip inspect name autosec_inspect tcp timeout 3600
ip access-list extended autosec_firewall_acl
 permit udp any any eq bootpc
 deny ip any any
interface FastEthernet0/1
 ip inspect autosec_inspect out
 ip access-group autosec_firewall_acl in
!
end

Apply this configuration to running-config? [yes]:

Applying the config generated to running-config
The name for the keys will be: R1.ciscopress.com

% The key modulus size is 1024 bits
% Generating 1024 bit RSA keys, keys will be non-exportable...[OK]

R1#
```

> **NOTE**   In Example 5-1, the administrator is prompted for a variety of input. However, adding the **no-interact** option to the end of the **auto secure** command eliminates this interactivity and simply applies default configurations without any further prompts.

Cisco SDM One-Step Lockdown

Most of the actions performed by the AutoSecure feature can be configured graphically using Cisco SDM's One-Step Lockdown feature. The following steps describe how to configure One-Step Lockdown:

Step 1   Click the **Configure** button in the Cisco SDM interface, as shown in Figure 5-1.

Figure 5-1   *Entering the Cisco SDM Configure Screen*

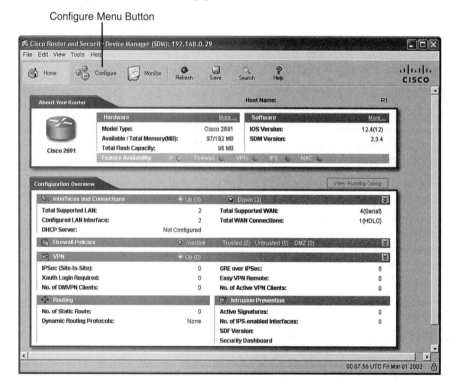

Step 2   Click the **Security Audit** button in the Tasks pane, as shown in Figure 5-2.

Figure 5-2 *Selecting the Security Audit Task*

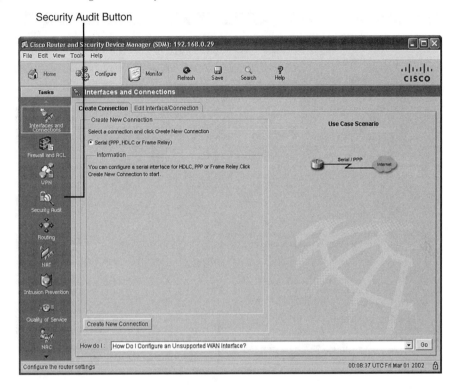

Step 3 Click the **One-step lockdown** button, as shown in Figure 5-3.

Figure 5-3   *Initiating a Security Audit*

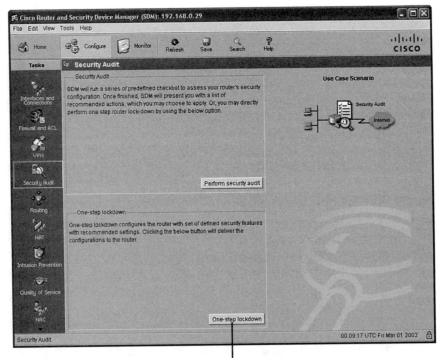

One-Step Lockdown Button

Step 4   Click the **Yes** button on the SDM Warning screen, as shown in Figure
5-4. It explains how to undo some of the settings about to be applied by
the One-Step Lockdown feature.

Figure 5-4   *SDM Warning Window*

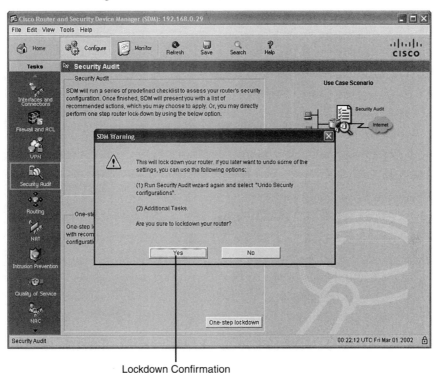

Lockdown Confirmation

Step 5   After the One-Step Lockdown feature generates a set of recommended
security settings, click the **Deliver** button, as shown in Figure 5-5, to
apply the recommended configuration to the router.

Figure 5-5 *Delivering a Recommended Configuration to the Router*

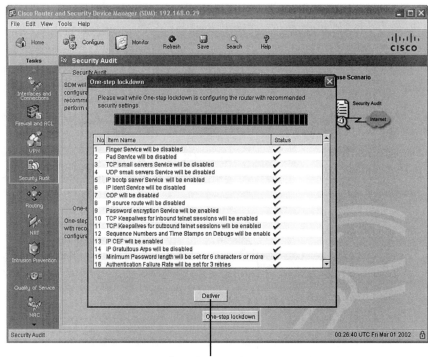

Prompt to Send Configuration to Router

Step 6   Click the **OK** button after the recommended commands are delivered to
the router, as shown in Figure 5-6.

Be aware that Cisco SDM's One-Step Lockdown feature does not perform all the same
actions as the Cisco AutoSecure feature. Following are a few distinctions to keep in mind:

■ One-Step Lockdown does not support the disabling of NTP.

■ One-Step Lockdown does not support the configuration of AAA.

■ One-Step Lockdown does not support the setting of Selective Packet Discard (SPD)
values.

■ One-Step Lockdown does not support the enabling of TCP intercepts.

■ One-Step Lockdown does not configure antispoofing ACLs.

Figure 5-6 *Completing the One-Step Lockdown Process*

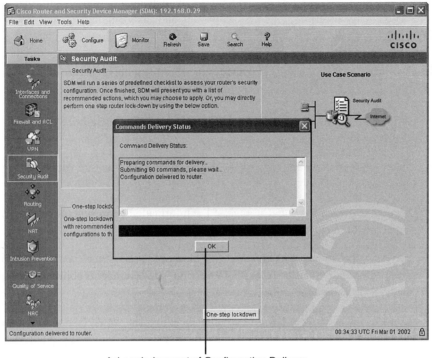

Acknowledgement of Configuration Delivery

- Although One-Step Lockdown does support the disabling of SNMP, it does not support the configuration of SNMP version 3.

- Although One-Step Lockdown supports the configuration of Secure Shell (SSH) access, it does not support the enabling of Service Control Point or the disabling of other access services and file transfer services (for example, FTP).

Using Secure Management and Reporting

Network management and reporting applications help network administrators proactively monitor and configure their network. However, left unsecured, management and reporting traffic can be used by potential attackers to compromise network security. For example, captured management and reporting traffic might contain administrative credentials for logging onto a system. Therefore, this section focuses on securing such traffic types.

Specifically, you will learn about securing syslog, SSH, and SNMPv3. In-band and out-of-band network management will be contrasted, and you will see how Cisco SDM can be used to monitor log messages and enable management features.

Planning for Secure Management and Reporting

Because smaller networks generate a relatively small amount of logging information, as compared to large enterprise networks, collecting and analyzing logging and reporting information poses an increasing challenge as a network grows larger. Similarly, the challenge of configuring network devices, and limiting administrative access to those devices, increases as a network's size increases. When planning for secure management and reporting, consider the following recommendations:

- With feedback from network and security team members, determine the most important information to log.

- Select appropriate syslog logging levels to collect an appropriate volume of log information.

- Secure the transmission and storage of log information to prevent the malicious tampering of the logs.

- Use Network Time Protocol (NTP) to synchronize logging time stamps, which aids in event correlation. Preferably, use NTP version 3, to leverage its ability to provide authentication for time updates.

- Consult your security policy to determine what log data would be required to provide appropriate evidence for a criminal investigation.

- Allocate sufficient storage capacity for anticipated logging demands.

- Identify an enterprise management system for managing multiple devices.

- Develop a change management plan for tracking configuration changes.

Secure Management and Reporting Architecture

Two primary schools of thought exist about how management traffic should be sent between a management station and a managed device. One approach is to allow management traffic to traverse a production data network. The other approach is to use a separate network to transport management traffic. This approach, where management traffic is isolated from production data traffic, is called *out-of-band (OOB) management*.

Obviously, allowing management traffic on a production network poses a security risk. Therefore, Cisco recommends that management traffic usually be relegated to a separate network, in an OOB management configuration. However, design constraints might necessitate situations in which management traffic must flow over a production network.

When such a requirement exists, you should take precautions to further secure the management traffic.

> **NOTE**   Even though OOB management is usually preferred over in-band management, some management applications benefit from in-band management. For example, consider a network management application that checks the reachability of various hosts and subnets. To check this reachability, an application might send a series of pings to a remote IP address, or check the availability of various Layer 4 services on a remote host. To perform these "availability" checks, the network management application needs to send traffic across a production data network. Also, in-band network management often offers a more economic solution for smaller networks.

Figure 5-7 illustrates a network using both in-band and OOB management approaches.

Figure 5-7   *Network Using In-Band and Out-of-Band Management*

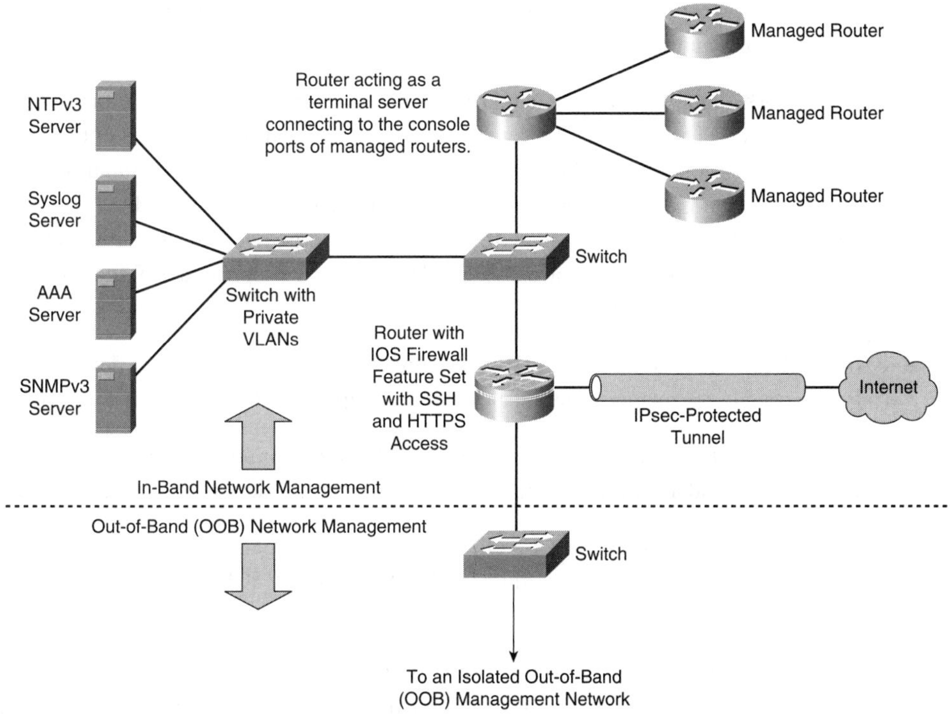

Notice the following characteristics of this mixed-management-style network:

- Even though the servers (that is, the NTP, syslog, AAA, and SNMPv3 servers) are attached to the same Cisco Catalyst switch, they are isolated from one another through the use of private VLANs (PVLAN). Using PVLANs, if an attacker compromised one of the servers, he would be unable to use that server to obtain access to another server.

- The IOS router running the Firewall Feature Set supports configuration via Secure Shell (SSH) and Secure HTTP (HTTPS), both of which provide encryption for management traffic.

- Any management traffic coming from an untrusted network (the Internet in the figure) is sent via an IPsec-protected tunnel. Additionally, you should use ACLs to limit what devices (or subnets) are allowed to initiate an IPsec tunnel with the IOS router. If an IPsec tunnel is unfeasible, consider another secure method of transport, such as Secure Sockets Layer (SSL).

- SNMP is being used in the network. Specifically, SNMPv3 is used because of its encryption and authentication features.

- The network contains three managed routers that are connected to a router acting as a terminal server. This terminal server provides asynchronous connectivity to the console ports of the managed routers. Because the router acting as a terminal server is part of the production network, access to that router should be protected via an access class, which determines which IP addresses, or subnets, are allowed to administratively connect to the router. Also, the access should be via SSH, as opposed to Telnet, because Telnet does not encrypt traffic.

- Although not illustrated in its entirety, the figure indicates that managed devices are also accessible for management purposes over a separate OOB management network.

- A AAA server is provided to give a centralized location for authentication, authorization, and accounting functions for administrative access to managed devices.

- A syslog server is used to store log information from the managed devices. Access to the syslog server should be limited (using VLAN ACLs [VACL] and ACLs) to specified managed devices.

- A Network Time Protocol (NTP) server is used to synchronize the time on the managed devices. Time synchronization is critical for event correlation purposes. For example, after an attack, an administrator might examine log messages stored on a syslog server. To map out the sequence of events that occurred during the attack, the devices involved need a common clock so that they can appropriately time stamp their syslog messages. Sometimes, attackers can send invalid NTP traffic as part of their attack. Incorrect NTP information can cause valid digital certificates to appear invalid or can cause the routers to incorrectly time stamp syslog messages. Fortunately, the network shown in Figure 5-7 uses NTPv3, which supports cryptographic authentication between NTP peers, helping mitigate NTP attacks.

Keep in mind that some networks might require unsecured protocols to be used from time to time. For example, TFTP occasionally might be required to update a router's IOS image. Consider allowing such unsecured applications on an as-needed basis, in which you configure permissions for the application when required and then remove the permissions after the application finishes.

Configuring Syslog Support

Administrators analyze router logs, in addition to logs from other network devices, for a variety of reasons. For example, log information can provide insight into the nature of an attack. Log information can be used for troubleshooting purposes. Viewing logs from multiple devices can provide event correlation information (that is, the relationship between events occurring on different systems).

Cisco IOS routers can send log output to a variety of destinations:

■ **Console**: A router's console port can send log messages to an attached terminal.

Key Topic

■ **Vty lines**: Virtual tty (vty) connections (such as Telnet connections) can also send log information to a remote terminal (such as a Telnet client). However, the **terminal monitor** command should be issued to cause log messages to be sent out of a vty line.

■ **Buffer**: When log messages are sent to a console or a vty line, those messages are not later available for detailed analysis. However, log messages can be stored in router memory. This "buffer" area can store messages until a router is rebooted.

■ **SNMP server**: When configured to run an SNMP agent, a router can send log messages, in the form of SNMP traps, to an SNMP server. Although this approach to logging can preserve log messages for an extended time, considerable setup and configuration are required.

■ **Syslog server**: A very popular choice for storing log information is a syslog server, which is easily configured and can store a large volume of logs.

A syslog logging solution consists of two primary components: syslog servers and syslog clients. A syslog server receives and stores log messages sent from syslog clients. As shown in Figure 5-8, various types of network devices can act as syslog clients and send logging information to a syslog server.

Figure 5-8 *Syslog System*

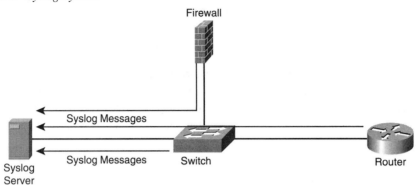

Not all syslog messages are created equal. Specifically, they have different levels of severity. Table 5-4 lists the eight levels of syslog messages. The higher the syslog level, the more detailed the logs. Keep in mind that more-detailed logs require additional storage space, and also consider that syslog messages are transmitted in clear text.

Table 5-4 *Syslog Severity Levels*

Level	Name	Description
0	Emergencies	The most severe error conditions, which render the system unusable
1	Alerts	Conditions requiring immediate attention
2	Critical	A less severe condition as compared to alerts, which should be addressed to prevent an interruption of service
3	Errors	Notifications about error conditions within the system that do not render the system unusable
4	Warnings	Notifications that specific operations failed to complete successfully
5	Notifications	Nonerror notifications that alert an administrator about state changes within a system
6	Informational	Detailed information about the normal operation of the system
7	Debugging	Highly detailed information (for example, information about individual packets) that is typically used for troubleshooting purposes

Consider the format of a syslog message, as illustrated in Figure 5-9. The syslog log entries contain time stamps, which are helpful in understanding how one log message relates to another. The log entries include severity level information in addition to the text of the syslog messages.

Figure 5-9 *Structure of a Syslog Message*

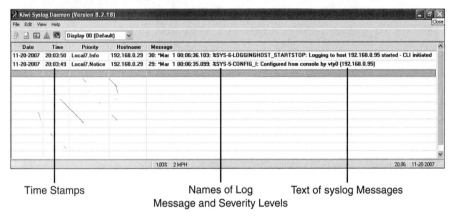

Time Stamps   Names of Log   Text of syslog Messages
                           Message and Severity Levels

> **NOTE**   A variety of systems can be used to act as a syslog server (for example, a CiscoWorks server). In Figure 5-9, the Kiwi Syslog Daemon is used. This freeware utility can be downloaded from http://www.kiwisyslog.com/kiwi-syslog-daemon-download.

Syslog messages can also be viewed from within Cisco SDM. As shown in Figure 5-10, you click the **Monitor** button along the top of the Cisco SDM window, and then click the **Logging** button in the Tasks pane, to view a variety of router logs, including syslog messages.

Figure 5-10 *Cisco SDM's Logging Window*

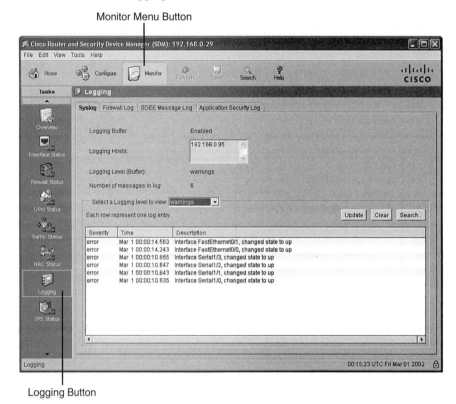

Monitor Menu Button

Logging Button

As shown in Figure 5-11, you can drop down the **Select a Logging level to view** menu and filter the logs displayed based on their severity level. After you select an appropriate severity level, click the **Update** button to display all syslog messages with a severity level greater than or equal to the severity level you selected. The log messages are displayed in a pane at the bottom of the Cisco SDM interface, in columnar format, showing the severity level, time-stamp information, and a description of each syslog message.

Figure 5-11 *Filtering Syslog Messages by Severity Level*

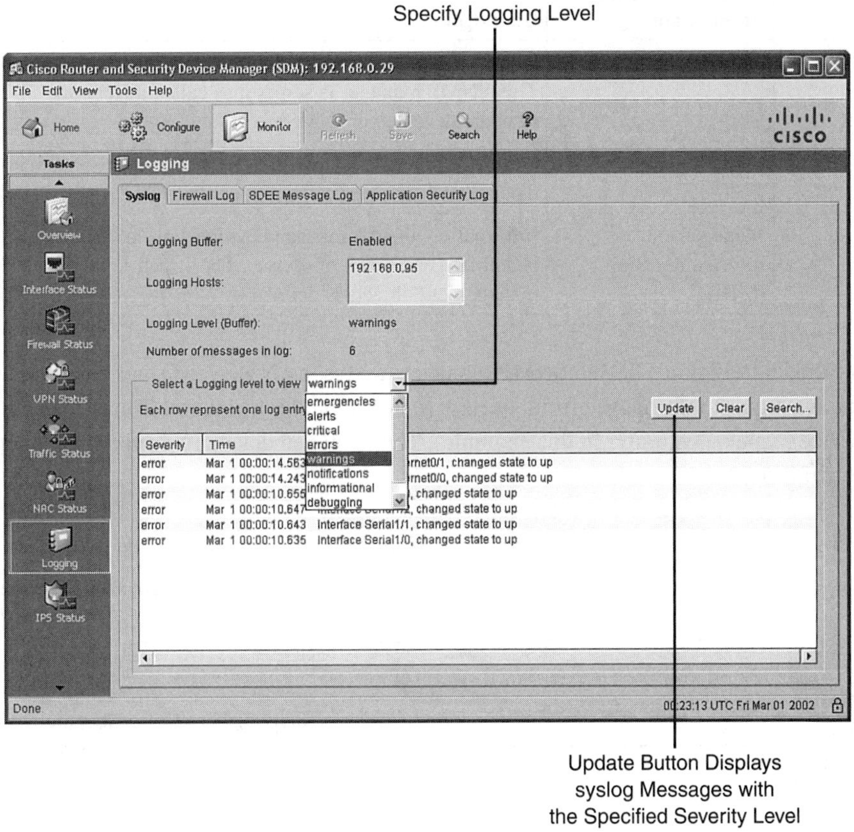

Securing Management Traffic with SNMPv3

The first Request for Comments (RFC) for SNMP came out in 1988. Since then, SNMP has become the de facto standard for network management protocols. The original intent of SNMP was for it to manage network nodes, such as network servers, routers, switches, and hubs. SNMP version 1 (SNMPv1) and SNMP version 2c (SNMPv2c) specify three major components of an SNMP solution, as detailed in Table 5-5.

Table 5-5   *Components of an SNMPv1 and SNMPv2c Network Management Solution*

Component	Description
SNMP manager	An SNMP manager runs a network management application. This SNMP manager is sometimes called a Network Management Server (NMS).
SNMP agent	An SNMP agent is a piece of software that runs on a managed device (such as a server, router, or switch).
Management Information Base (MIB)	Information about a managed device's resources and activity is defined by a series of *objects*. The structure of these management objects is defined by a managed device's MIB.

As shown in Figure 5-12, an SNMP manager (that is, an NMS) can send information to, receive request information from, or receive unsolicited information from a managed device (a managed router in this example). The managed device runs an SNMP agent and contains the MIB.

Figure 5-12   *SNMPv1 and SNMPv2c Network Management Components and Messages*

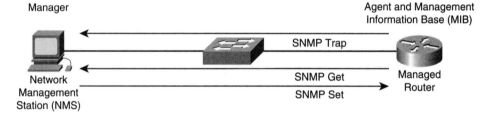

Even though multiple SNMP messages might be sent between an SNMP manager and a managed device, consider the three broad categories of SNMP message types:

■ **GET**: An SNMP GET message is used to retrieve information from a managed device.

■ **SET**: An SNMP SET message is used to set a variable in a managed device or to trigger an action on a managed device.

■ **Trap**: An SNMP trap message is an unsolicited message sent from a managed device to an SNMP manager. It can be used to notify the SNMP manager about a significant event that occurred on the managed device.

Unfortunately, the ability to get information from or send configuration information to a managed device poses a potential security vulnerability. Specifically, if an attacker introduced a rogue NMS into the network, the attacker's NMS might be able to gather information about network resources by polling the MIBs of managed devices.

Additionally, the attacker could launch an attack against the network by manipulating the configuration of managed devices by sending a series of SNMP SET messages.

Although SNMP does offer some security against such an attack, the security integrated with SNMPv1 and SNMPv2c is considered weak. Specifically, SNMPv1 and SNMPv2c use *community strings* to gain read-only access and/or read-write access to a managed device. You can think of a community string much like a password. Also, be aware that multiple SNMP-compliant devices on the market today have a default read-only community string of "public" and a default read-write community string of "private."

> **NOTE**   Notice that this section refers to SNMPv2c as opposed to SNMPv2. SNMPv2 did contain security enhancements, in addition to other performance enhancements. However, few network administrators adopted SNMPv2 because of the complexity of the newly proposed security system. Instead, Community-Based Simple Network Management Protocol version 2 (SNMPv2c) gained widespread acceptance because it included the performance enhancements of SNMPv2 without using SNMPv2's complex security solution. Instead, SNMPv2c kept the SNMPv1 concept of community strings.

Fortunately, the security weaknesses of SNMPv1 and SNMPv2c are addressed in SNMPv3. To better understand these security enhancements, consider the concept of a *security model* and a *security level*:

- **Security model**: A security model defines an approach for user and group authentications. Cisco IOS supports the SNMPv1, SNMPv2c, and SNMPv3 security models.

- **Security level**: A security level defines the type of security algorithm performed on SNMP packets. Three security levels are discussed here:

    - **noAuthNoPriv**: The noAuthNoPriv (no authorization, no privacy) security level uses community strings for authorization and does not use encryption to provide privacy.

    - **authNoPriv**: The authNoPriv (authorization, no privacy) security level provides authorization using Hashed Message Authentication Code (HMAC) with Message Digest 5 (MD5) or Secure Hash Algorithm (SHA). However, no encryption is used.

    - **authPriv**: The authPriv (authorization, privacy) security level offers HMAC MD5 or SHA authentication and also provides privacy through encryption. Specifically, the encryption uses the Cipher Block Chaining (CBC) Data Encryption Standard (DES) (DES-56) algorithm.

As summarized in Table 5-6, SNMPv3 supports all three of the previously described security levels. Notice that SNMPv1 and SNMPv2 support only the noAuthNoPriv security level.

Key Topic

Table 5-6   *Security Models and Security Levels Supported by Cisco IOS*

Security Model	Security Level	Authentication Strategy	Encryption Type
SNMPv1	noAuthNoPriv	Community String	None
SNMPv2c	noAuthNoPriv	Community String	None
SNMPv3	noAuthNoPriv	Username	None
	authNoPriv	MD5 or SHA	None
	authPriv	MD5 or SHA	CBC-DES (DES-56)

Through the use of the security algorithms, as shown in Table 5-6, SNMPv3 dramatically increases the security of network management traffic as compared to SNMPv1 and SNMPv2c. Specifically, SNMPv3 offers three primary security enhancements:

- **Integrity**: Using hashing algorithms, SNMPv3 can ensure that an SNMP message was not modified in transit.

- **Authentication**: Hashing allows SNMPv3 to validate the source of an SNMP message.

- **Encryption**: Using the CBC-DES (DES-56) encryption algorithm, SNMPv3 provides privacy for SNMP messages, making them unreadable by an attacker who might capture an SNMP packet.

In addition to its security enhancements, SNMPv3 differs architecturally from SNMPv1 and SNMPv2c. SNMPv3 defines *SNMP entities*, which are groupings of individual SNMP components. As shown in Figure 5-13, SNMP applications and an SNMP manager combine into an *NMS SNMP entity*, and an SNMP agent and a MIB combine into a *managed node SNMP entity*.

Figure 5-13 *SNMPv3 Entities*

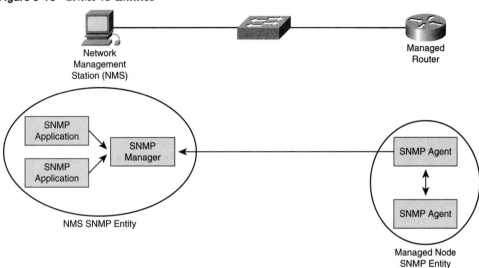

Enabling Secure Shell on a Router

When administrators remotely connect to a router to perform configuration, monitoring, and troubleshooting tasks, Cisco recommends that the administrators connect using Secure Shell (SSH), as opposed to using Telnet. Telnet is not considered secure, and the contents of the Telnet session are transmitted in clear text. SSH, however, uses encryption to protect transmissions between an administrator's workstation and a router.

> **NOTE**   Cisco IOS 12.1(1)T and later support SSH version 1, and SSH version 2 is supported in Cisco IOS 12.3(4)T and later.

When you configure SSH on a Cisco router, the router acts as an SSH server. You then can use SSH client software (such as PuTTY) to securely connect to the router. Following are the steps required to configure a Cisco IOS router to act as an SSH server:

Step 1   Configure a domain name on your router using the **ip domain-name** *name* command in global configuration mode.

Step 2   Use the **crypto key generate rsa general-keys modulus** *modulus-size*
command in global configuration mode to generate the security keys
used by SSH. Cisco recommends that the minimum value for the
modulus be 1024 bits.

> **NOTE**   After generating the keys, you can issue the **show crypto key mypubkey rsa**
> command from privileged EXEC mode to view the generated public key.

Step 3   Specify the SSH timeout (that is, the number of seconds the router waits
on the SSH client) with the **ip ssh timeout** *seconds* command from
global configuration mode.

Step 4   Issue the **ip ssh authentication-retries** *number* command from global
configuration mode to specify the number of SSH authentication retries
before an interface is reset.

Step 5   To prevent Telnet sessions, issue the **no transport input telnet** command
in line configuration mode for all your vty lines.

Step 6   Permit SSH connections using the **transport input ssh** command, still in
line configuration mode, for all your vty lines.

Example 5-2 illustrates the configuration of an SSH server. Notice the use of the **crypto key
zeroize rsa** command issued in global configuration mode. This command can be used to
delete any existing RSA keys on a router. Also note that Example 5-2 uses the **ip ssh timeout** command, as opposed to the **ip ssh timeout** command previously described. This
command varies by IOS version. IOS 12.4(12) is used in the example.

Example 5-2   *Enabling SSH*

```
R1# conf term

Enter configuration commands, one per line.  End with CNTL/Z.
R1(config)# ip domain-name ciscopress.com
R1(config)# crypto key zeroize rsa

% All RSA keys will be removed.
% All router certs issued using these keys will also be removed.
Do you really want to remove these keys? [yes/no]: yes
R1(config)#
*Mar  1 01:33:35.455: %SSH-5-DISABLED: SSH 1.99 has been disabled
R1(config)# crypto key generate rsa general-keys modulus 1024

The name for the keys will be: R1.ciscopress.com

% The key modulus size is 1024 bits
```

Example 5-2 *Enabling SSH (Continued)*

```
% Generating 1024 bit RSA keys, keys will be non-exportable...[OK]

R1(config)#
*Mar  1 01:34:20.235: %SSH-5-ENABLED: SSH 1.99 has been enabled
R1(config)# ip ssh time-out 120
R1(config)# ip ssh authentication-retries 4
R1(config)# line vty 0 4
R1(config-line)# transport input ssh
R1(config-line)# end
R1#
```

Example 5-3 provides the output of the **show crypto key mypubkey rsa** command, which displays the generated keys.

Example 5-3 *Viewing the Generated Keys*

```
R1# show crypto key mypubkey rsa

% Key pair was generated at: 01:34:20 UTC Mar 1 2007
Key name: R1.ciscopress.com
 Usage: General Purpose Key
 Key is not exportable.
 Key Data:
  30819F30 0D06092A 864886F7 0D010101 05000381 8D003081 89028181 009C3542
  26FDD40C C0CEA5DE 8D4AEC7E 2AB70ECB 1F5EAC60 1459AA16 0EE4059B FD95C548
  29126EC0 522501E3 6AEF0581 BDFF46FC 1C145B94 6590C7BB 931C1734 0BC90ACE
  57A726ED 5E233A92 02F2B5A6 DE10BA2A 99D7EC00 2646FC20 39BB4298 55B4DED1
  ED6F7D3F 289FFB3F 8F1F014B 2252BC49 45D27160 0C50AC02 E51B1C1A 9F020301 0001
% Key pair was generated at: 01:34:21 UTC Mar 1 2007
Key name: R1.ciscopress.com.server
 Usage: Encryption Key
 Key is not exportable.
 Key Data:
  307C300D 06092A86 4886F70D 01010105 00036B00 30680261 00D811FD 3CF9D04F
  33A7D951 93ED5C01 90E3515B B9C23EF6 268E638F 868D2AD2 3A7722BC 52DF0CAF
  DC33C7F8 54208F5B 147CAB1E 9B634B69 4D44F556 43482BB5 7B3A447B 397F6E7E
  5C423F7C 903A391A B8970A32 51F7D9EB 91FBE954 D7AEC02D 31020301 0001
R1#
```

Using Cisco SDM to Configure Management Features

Several management features available on Cisco IOS routers (for example, syslog logging, SNMP, NTP, and SSH) can be configured using Cisco SDM's graphical interface. These features, however, are not separate wizards available in the Tasks pane of Cisco SDM. Rather, you can configure these features by clicking the **Additional Tasks** button in the Tasks pane.

Configuring Syslog Logging with Cisco SDM

The following steps describe how to configure syslog logging using Cisco SDM:

Step 1   Click the **Configure** button, near the top of the Cisco SDM window, and then click the **Additional Tasks** button in the Tasks pane, as shown in Figure 5-14.

Figure 5-14   *Accessing the Additional Tasks Screen in Cisco SDM*

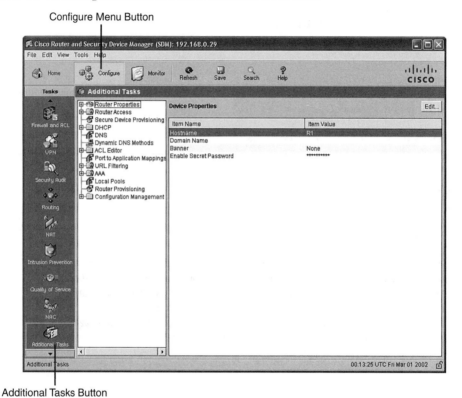

Step 2   Click the + next to **Router Properties** to expand the selection, and then click the **Logging** option, as shown in Figure 5-15.

Figure 5-15 *Accessing the Logging Configuration Screen*

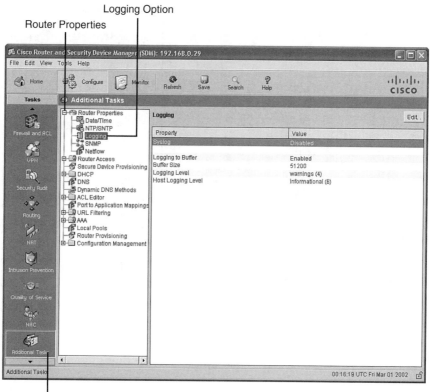

Step 3 In the Logging configuration screen, click the **Edit** button in the upper-
right corner of the Cisco SDM screen to open a separate Logging
window, shown in Figure 5-16.

Figure 5-16 *Opening the Logging Editing Window*

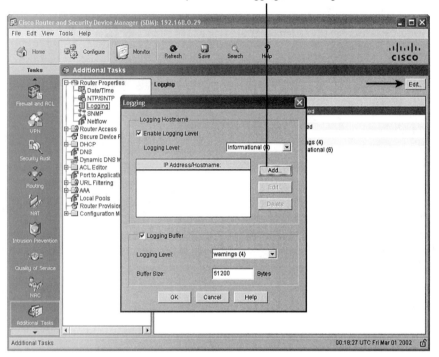

Open an Add Logging Host Dialog Box

Step 4 Click the **Add** button to open the Add logging host window. Use the dialog box in this window to enter the IP address or hostname of your syslog server, as shown in Figure 5-17. Then click **OK** to close this window.

Figure 5-17   *Adding a Syslog Server*

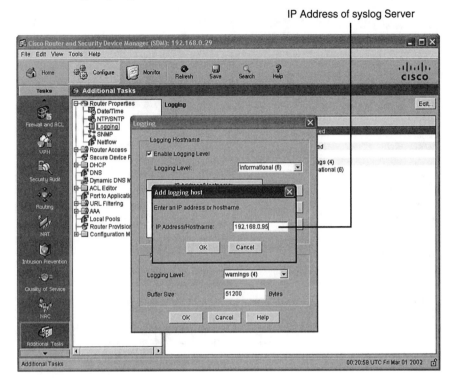

IP Address of syslog Server

Step 5   After you return to the Logging window, you can optionally select the level of severity for the messages you want to log, using the **Logging Level** drop-down menu shown in Figure 5-18. When your configuration is complete, click the **OK** button.

Figure 5-18   *Specifying a Logging Level*

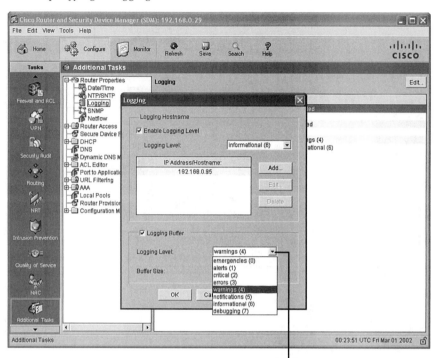

Select Message Severity Level

Configuring SNMP with Cisco SDM

The following steps explain how to enable a Cisco IOS router for SNMP using Cisco SDM:

Step 1   Expand the **Router Properties** option available in the Additional Tasks window as previously described. Then click the **SNMP** option, as shown in Figure 5-19. To enable and configure SNMP, click the **Edit** button in the upper-right corner of the Cisco SDM screen.

Figure 5-19 *Accessing the SNMP Configuration Screen*

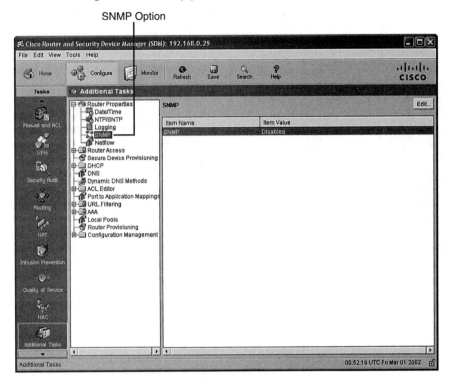

SNMP Option

Step 2 From the SNMP Properties window, click the **Enable SNMP** checkbox, as shown in Figure 5-20. Then click the **Add** button in the Password area of the window to open the Add a Community String window. Enter a community string to be used as your password, and click either the **Read-Only** or **Read-Write** radio button to specify the privilege level accessible with this community string. Click the **OK** button when you are finished. You might want to add both a read-only and read-write community string.

Figure 5-20 *Enabling SNMP*

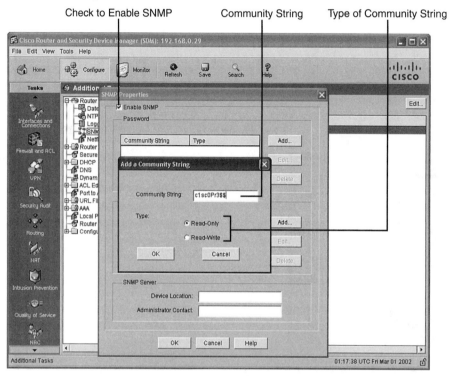

Step 3   After adding the community string(s), click the **Add** button in the Trap receiver area of the SNMP Properties window, as shown in Figure 5-21. Enter the IP address or hostname of the SNMP server and a corresponding password. When you are finished, click the **OK** button.

Figure 5-21 *Configuring a Trap Receiver*

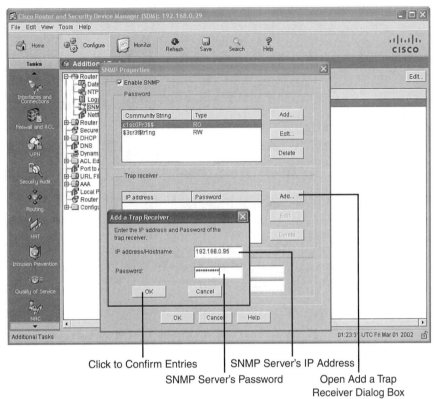

Click to Confirm Entries   SNMP Server's IP Address
           SNMP Server's Password   Open Add a Trap
                                              Receiver Dialog Box

Step 4   You can optionally enter location and contact information for the SNMP
server, as shown in Figure 5-22. Click the **OK** button when you are
finished entering this information.

Figure 5-22   *Entering Location and Contact Information*

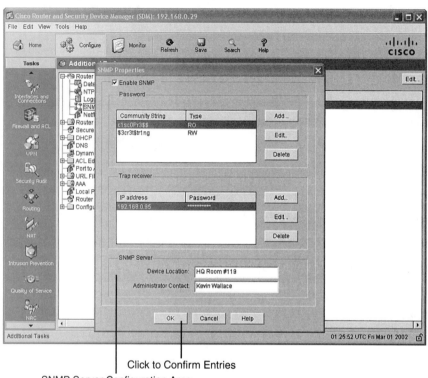

Click to Confirm Entries

SNMP Server Configuration Area

Configuring NTP with Cisco SDM

As a best practice, you should synchronize the time on your routers using NTP. For example, having your router clocks in sync allows you to better identify and correlate events by viewing syslog messages. The following steps explain how to enable a Cisco IOS router for NTP using Cisco SDM:

Step 1   Expand the **Router Properties** option available in the Additional Tasks window as previously described. Then click the **NTP/SNTP** option, as shown in Figure 5-23.

Figure 5-23 *Accessing the NTP Configuration Screen*

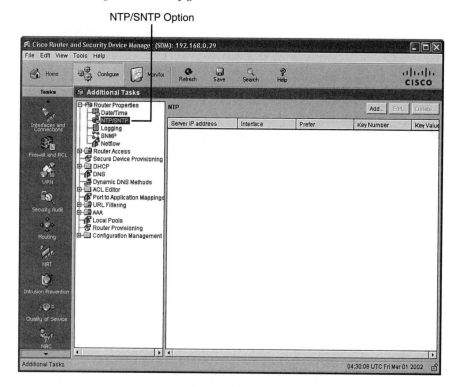

Step 2 Click the **Add** button to bring up the Add NTP Server Details window, as
shown in Figure 5-24. From this window you can specify the IP address
or hostname of the NTP server and select the router interface that is used
to connect to the NTP server. If you configure more than one NTP server,
you can use the **Prefer** checkbox to indicate which server is the preferred
server. Optionally, you can check the **Authentication Key** checkbox to
provide information used to secure your NTP communication. When you
are finished, click **OK**.

Figure 5-24   *Adding an NTP Server*

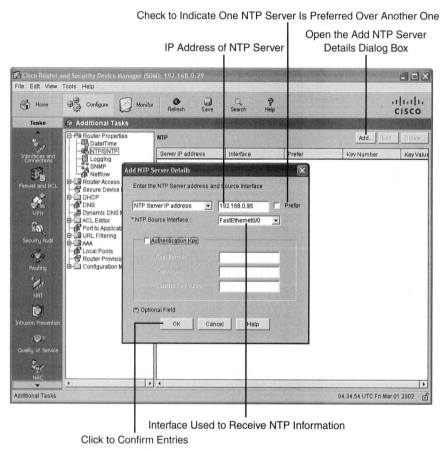

Check to Indicate One NTP Server Is Preferred Over Another One

Open the Add NTP Server
Details Dialog Box

IP Address of NTP Server

Interface Used to Receive NTP Information

Click to Confirm Entries

Configuring SSH with Cisco SDM

As discussed earlier, using SSH to access a router prompt is preferred to using Telnet, because Telnet uses clear text, whereas SSH provides encryption. Although you can enable SSH on a router using the CLI, as previously demonstrated in Example 5-2, Cisco SDM can alternatively be used to enable SSH. The following steps show you how to enable a Cisco IOS router for SSH using Cisco SDM:

Step 1   Navigate to the Additional Tasks window as previously described. Then double-click the **Router Access** option to expand it, as shown in Figure 5-25.

Figure 5-25 *Navigating to the Router Access Option*

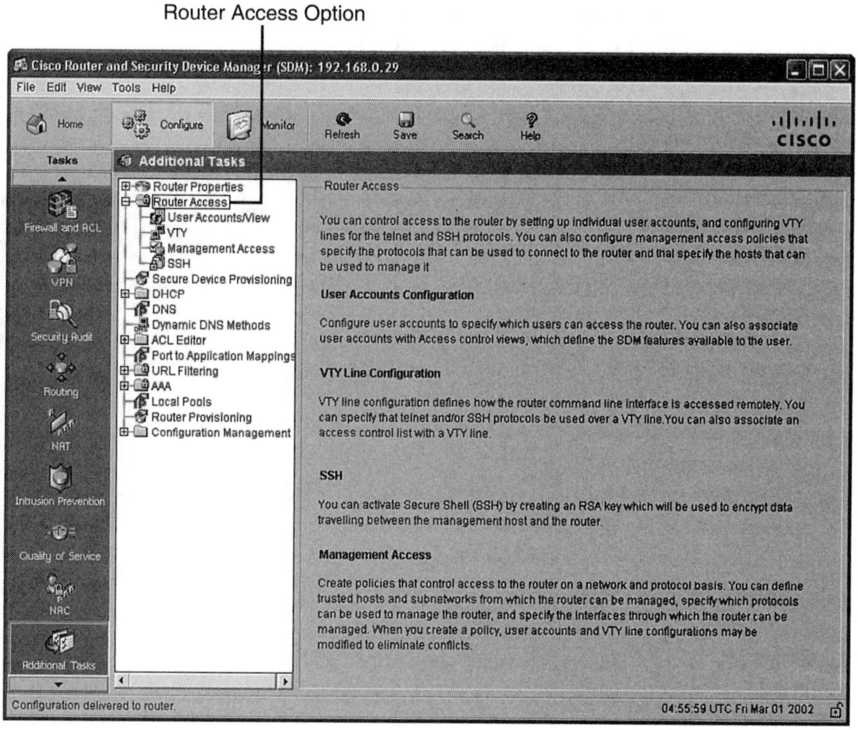

Step 2   Click the **SSH** option. If the router is not already configured for SSH, you
see a **Generate RSA Key** button, as shown in Figure 5-26.

Figure 5-26 *Accessing the SSH Configuration Screen*

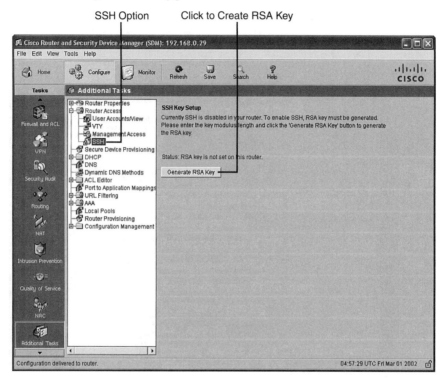

Step 3   Click the **Generate RSA Key** button to begin the key generation process. After clicking the button, you see the Key modulus size window, as shown in Figure 5-27. Cisco recommends that you specify a value of at least 1024 bits for this field. However, if you enter a value in the range 512 to 1024, the value must be a multiple of 64. If you want to use a value greater than 1024, you can select either 1536 or 2048. After entering your desired modulus size, click the **OK** button.

Figure 5-27 *Setting the Modulus Size*

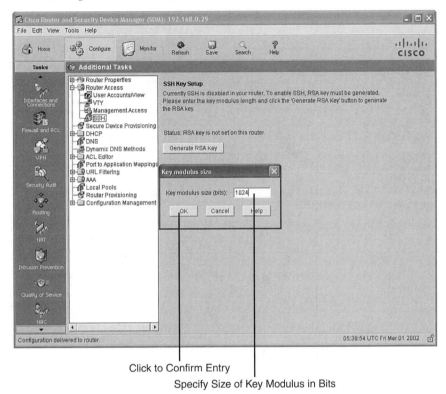

Click to Confirm Entry
Specify Size of Key Modulus in Bits

NOTE   To successfully generate an RSA key, a router first must have been configured with a domain name. You can configure a router's domain name by clicking the **Edit** button in the Router Properties configuration screen, which is available from the previously described Additional Tasks window.

Step 4   You are prompted to enter your SSH username and password credentials, as shown in Figure 5-28. After entering the appropriate credentials, click **OK**.

Figure 5-28   *Providing SSH Username and Password Credentials*

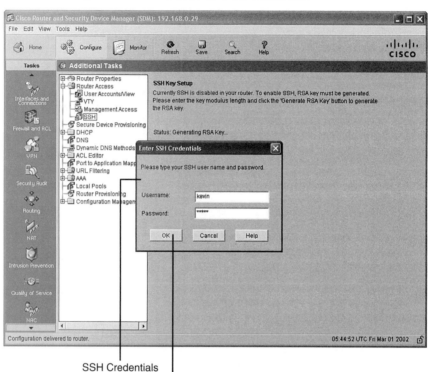

SSH Credentials

Click to Confirm Entries

Exam Preparation Tasks

Review All the Key Topics

Review the most important topics from this chapter, denoted with the Key Topic icon. Table 5-7 lists these key topics and the page where each is found.

Key Topic

Table 5-7 *Key Topics for Chapter 5*

Key Topic Element	Description	Page Number
Table 5-2	Cisco IOS features	**158-159**
Table 5-3	Methods for locking down a Cisco router	**160**
List	Limitations of Cisco SDM's One-Step Lockdown feature	**170**
List	Recommendations for secure management and reporting	**172**
List	Characteristics of a mixed-management-style network	**174**
List	Log output destinations	**175**
Table 5-4	Syslog severity levels	**176**
Table 5-5	Components of an SNMPv1 and SNMPv2c network management solution	**180**
List	SNMP message types	**180**
List	Security models and security levels	**181**
Table 5-6	Security models and security levels supported by Cisco IOS	**182**

Complete the Tables and Lists from Memory

Print a copy of Appendix D, "Memory Tables," (found on the CD) or at least the section for this chapter, and complete the tables and lists from memory. Appendix E, "Memory Tables Answer Key," also on the CD, includes completed tables and lists so that you can check your work.

Definition of Key Terms

Define the following key terms from this chapter, and check your answers in the glossary:

Cisco Discovery Protocol (CDP), Network Time Protocol (NTP), AutoSecure, out-of-band (OOB) management, in-band management, syslog, Simple Network Management Protocol (SNMP), SNMP GET, SNMP SET, SNMP Trap, SNMP Manager, SNMP Agent, Management Information Base (MIB), security model, security level, Secure Shell (SSH)

Command Reference to Check Your Memory

This section includes the most important configuration and EXEC commands covered in this chapter. To see how well you have memorized the commands as a side effect of your other studies, cover the left side of the table with a piece of paper, read the descriptions on the right side, and see whether you remember the commands.

Table 5-8 *Chapter 5 Configuration Command Reference*

Command	Description
shutdown	An interface configuration mode command used to administratively shut down an interface
ip domain-name *name*	A global configuration mode command used to set a router's domain name
crypto key generate rsa general-keys modulus *modulus-size*	A global configuration mode command used to generate the security keys used by SSH
ip ssh timeout *seconds*	A global configuration mode command used to specify the SSH timeout (that is, how many seconds the router waits on the SSH client)
ip ssh authentication-retries *number*	A global configuration mode command used to specify the number of SSH authentication retries before an interface is reset
no transport input telnet	A line configuration mode command used to prevent Telnet sessions on vty lines
transport input ssh	A line configuration mode command used to permit SSH connections on vty lines
crypto key zeroize rsa	A global configuration mode command used to delete any existing RSA keys on a router

Table 5-9 *Chapter 5 EXEC Command Reference*

Command	Description
auto secure [no-interact]	Used to invoke a configuration script that applies best-practice security recommendations to a router, where the **no-interact** option does not prompt the administrator for any additional input
show crypto key mypubkey rsa	Used to view generated RSA keys, which are used for SSH

IINS exam topics covered in this part:

- Describe and list mitigation methods for Worm, Virus, and Trojan horse attacks

- Describe the Cisco security family of products and their interactions

- Explain the functionality of standard, extended, and named IP ACLs used by routers to filter packets

- Configure and verify IP ACLs to mitigate given threats (filter IP traffic destined for Telnet, SNMP, and DDoS attacks) in a network using CLI

- Configure IP ACLs to prevent IP address spoofing using CLI

- Discuss the caveats to be considered when building ACLs

- Describe how to prevent Layer 2 attacks by configuring basic Catalyst switch security features

- Describe the operational strengths and weaknesses of the different firewall technologies

- Explain stateful firewall operations and the function of the state table

- Implement Zone Based Firewall using SDM

- Define network based vs. host based intrusion detection and prevention

- Explain IPS technologies, attack responses, and monitoring options

- Enable and verify Cisco IOS IPS operations using SDM

Part II: Constructing a Secure Infrastructure

This chapter covers the following topics:

Defending against Layer 2 attacks: This section explains how Cisco Catalyst switches can be configured to mitigate several common Layer 2 attacks.

Cisco Identity-Based Networking Services: This section examines how Cisco Identity-Based Networking Services (IBNS) uses IEEE 802.1x, RADIUS, and Extensible Authentication Protocol (EAP) technologies to selectively allow access to network resources, based on user credentials.

CHAPTER 6

Securing Layer 2 Devices

The characteristics of Layer 2 LAN devices frequently make these devices attractive targets for attackers. If an attacker can compromise Layer 2, he has access to the upper layers. This chapter explores these Layer 2 vulnerabilities and describes methods of mitigating such weaknesses using features available on Cisco Catalyst switches.

Cisco Catalyst switches also play an integral role in the Cisco Identity-Based Networking Services (IBNS) technology. IBNS offers per-user access control to network resources. This chapter examines the components of IBNS, including IEEE 802.1x and various Extensible Authentication Protocol (EAP) types.

"Do I Know This Already?" Quiz

The "Do I Know This Already?" quiz helps you determine your level of knowledge of this chapter's topics before you begin. Table 6-1 details the major topics discussed in this chapter and their corresponding quiz questions.

Table 6-1   *"Do I Know This Already?" Section-to-Question Mapping*

Foundation Topics Section	Questions
Defending against Layer 2 attacks	1 to 11
Cisco Identity-Based Networking Services	12 to 17

1. A Cisco Catalyst switch stores port MAC address assignments in what type of table?

   a. ARP cache

   b. FIB table

   c. Adjacency database

   d. CAM table

2. What Cisco Catalyst switch feature can isolate ports from one another, even though those ports belong to the same VLAN?

   a. Private VLAN

   b. Policing

    c. Per-VLAN Spanning Tree (PVST)

    d. Dynamic ARP Inspection (DAI)

3. What are the two main approaches for launching a VLAN hopping attack? (Choose two.)

    a. Gratuitous ARP (GARP)

    b. Switch spoofing

    c. Double tagging

    d. DHCP spoofing

4. What Spanning Tree Protocol (STP) protection mechanism disables a switch port if the port receives a Bridge Protocol Data Unit (BPDU)?

    a. Root Guard

    b. BPDU Guard

    c. PortFast

    d. UplinkFast

5. What Cisco Catalyst switch feature can help protect against DHCP server spoofing?

    a. DAI

    b. GARP

    c. DHCP snooping

    d. VACLs

6. What type of message might an attacker send to a host to convince the host that the attacker's MAC address is the host's next-hop MAC address?

    a. GARP

    b. DAI

    c. BPDU

    d. DHCPACK

7. If a switch is running in the fail-open mode, what happens when the switch's CAM table fills to capacity and a new frame arrives?

    a. The frame is dropped.

    b. A copy of the frame is forwarded out all switch ports other than the port the frame was received on.

    c. The frame is transmitted on the native VLAN.

    d. The switch sends a NACK segment to the frame's source MAC address.

8. What kind of MAC address is dynamically learned by a switch port and then added to the switch's running configuration?

    a. Static secure MAC address

    b. Dynamic secure MAC address

    c. Sticky secure MAC address

    d. Pervasive secure MAC address

9. What Cisco Catalyst switch feature can be used in an Intrusion Detection System (IDS) solution to cause the switch to send a copy of traffic for analysis by an IDS sensor?

    a. GARP

    b. DHCP snooping

    c. DAI

    d. SPAN

10. What are three potential responses of a switch port to a port security violation? (Choose three.)

    a. Protect

    b. Isolate

    c. Restrict

    d. Shut down

11. What two Cisco Catalyst switch features can be used to mitigate man-in-the-middle attacks? (Choose the two best answers.)

    a. DAI

    b. Private VLANs

    c. DHCP snooping

    d. VACLs

12. In an IEEE 802.1x deployment, EAPOL messages typically are sent between which two devices?

    a. Between the authenticator and the authentication server

    b. Between the supplicant and the authentication server

    c. Between the RADIUS server and the authenticator

    d. Between the supplicant and the authenticator

13. A RADIUS server acts as which component in an IEEE 802.1x deployment?

   a. Supplicant

   b. Authentication server

   c. Authenticator

   d. Method list

14. What EAP type usually leverages MS-CHAPv2 as its authentication protocol?

   a. PEAP

   b. EAP-TLS

   c. EAP-MD5

   d. LEAP

15. What happens to a client that successfully authenticates with a Cisco Catalyst switch port using 802.1x but also creates a port security violation?

   a. The client can transmit regardless of the port security settings, because of the successful 802.1x authentication.

   b. After the client authenticates, it is allowed to transmit on the network if the switch is configured for AAA authorization, which explicitly permits network access for the client.

   c. The client cannot transmit because of the port security violation, even though it successfully authenticated.

   d. This is an invalid configuration, because port security and 802.1x features on a port are mutually exclusive.

16. When is a Cisco Catalyst switch port placed in a restricted VLAN?

   a. When a connected client fails to authenticate after a certain number of attempts

   b. If a connected client does not support 802.1x

   c. After a connected client exceeds a specified idle time

   d. When 802.1x is not globally enabled on the Cisco Catalyst switch

17. Which command configures a Cisco Catalyst switch port to operate in multiple-host mode?

   a. Switch(config)# **dot1x host-mode multi-host**

   b. Switch(config-if)# **enable dot1x multi-host**

   c. Switch(config)# **no host-mode single-host**

   d. Switch(config-if)# **dot1x host-mode multi-host**

Foundation Topics

Defending Against Layer 2 Attacks

This section begins by exploring the nature of Layer 2 switch operation and why it is such an attractive target for attackers. Then, approaches for mitigating a variety of Layer 2 attacks are addressed. These strategies include best practices for securing a Layer 2 network, protecting against VLAN hopping attacks, preventing an attacker from manipulating Spanning Tree Protocol (STP) settings, stopping DHCP server and ARP spoofing, preventing Content Addressable Memory (CAM) table overflow attacks, and disallowing MAC address spoofing. Other switch-related security topics include port security, Switch Port Analyzer (SPAN), Remote SPAN (RSPAN), VLAN access control lists (VACL), private VLANs, rate limiting, and MAC address notification.

Review of Layer 2 Switch Operation

Shared media hubs have largely been eliminated from today's corporate networks, with Ethernet switches taking their place. An Ethernet switch learns the MAC addresses connected off each of its ports. Then, when a frame enters the switch, the switch forwards the frame based on the frame's destination MAC address. However, if the switch does not have the frame's destination MAC address stored in its CAM table (also known as a *MAC address table*), or if the frame's destination MAC address is a broadcast address of all Fs (that is, FFFF.FFFF.FFFF), the frame is forwarded out all ports other than the port it was received on.

Many Ethernet switches can also logically group ports to form a Virtual LAN (VLAN), where each VLAN is its own broadcast domain. Traffic must be routed to travel from one VLAN to another VLAN.

Cisco Catalyst switches operate at Layer 2 of the OSI model (the Data Link Layer), as illustrated in Figure 6-1. If an attacker were to gain control of an Ethernet switch operating at Layer 2, all the upper layers could be compromised. As a result, Layer 2 switches, such as a series of Cisco Catalyst switches, might appear to be an attractive target of attacks.

Figure 6-1   *Compromising Layer 2*

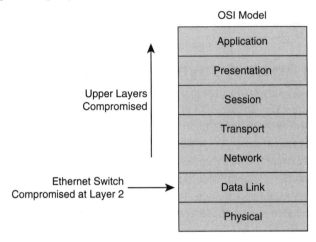

Basic Approaches to Protecting Layer 2 Switches

Although this chapter explores several advanced approaches to securing Ethernet switches, for now, consider the following basic approaches to Layer 2 protection, which should be applied to switches throughout the network:

■ **Telnet access**: Administrators can connect to a Cisco Catalyst switch using Telnet. Unfortunately, Telnet is not a secure protocol. If an attacker intercepted the Telnet packets, he might be able to glean the password credentials necessary to gain administrative access to the switch. Therefore, Secure Shell (SSH) is preferred as an alternative to Telnet, because it offers confidentiality and data integrity. Administrators alternatively can configure the switch via a switch's console port. Therefore, this console port should have physical security (for example, it should be locked away from physical access by a user).

■ **SNMP access**: Simple Network Management Protocol (SNMP) is often used by a network management station to collect information about network devices. Older versions of SNMP (for example, version 1 and version 2c) lack strong security mechanisms. If these older versions are used, consider allowing SNMP to only read information, rather than read and write information. Alternatively, you might consider using SNMP version 3, which does implement strong security mechanisms.

■ **Reducing exposure**: Just as server administrators can reduce their server's exposure to attacks by turning off unneeded services, switch administrators can reduce a switch's exposure to attacks by disabling any unneeded services and any unused Ethernet ports. Additionally, administrators can limit the number of MAC addresses that ports can learn.

- **Logging**: As with routers, logging attempts to access the switch. Regularly reviewing those logs can alert switch administrators to potential threats.

- **Change control**: In enterprise networks, multiple switch administrators might share the responsibility for switch configuration. Therefore, consider a formalized change control policy to better coordinate administrative activity.

- **VLAN configuration**: Consider the following recommendations when configuring switch VLANs:

  — Configure ports that do not need to form a trunk to a trunk setting of "off," as opposed to "auto."

  — Do not send user data over an IEEE 802.1Q trunk's native VLAN.

  — Use private VLANs to prevent an attacker from compromising one host in a VLAN and then using that host as a jumping-off point to attack other hosts within the VLAN.

Preventing VLAN Hopping

A VLAN hopping attack allows traffic from one VLAN to pass into another VLAN, without first being routed. An attacker could use a VLAN hopping attack to, for example, eavesdrop on traffic that the attacker's PC is supposed to be isolated from or to send traffic to a VLAN that the attacker's PC should not be able to reach. The two main approaches for launching a VLAN hopping attack are *switch spoofing* and *double tagging*.

Switch Spoofing

By default, Ethernet trunks on Cisco Catalyst switches carry traffic for all VLANs. Therefore, if an attacker can persuade a switch to go into trunking mode, the attacker could then see traffic for all VLANs. In some cases this type of attack could be used to discover username and password credentials that the attacker could use for a later attack.

Some Cisco Catalyst switch ports default to *auto* mode for trunking, which means that the ports automatically become trunk ports if they receive Dynamic Trunking Protocol (DTP) frames. An attacker could attempt to make his switch port enter trunking mode either by spoofing DTP frames or by connecting a rogue switch to his switch port. To combat switch spoofing, you can disable trunking on all ports that do not need to form trunks, and disable DTP on ports that do need to be trunks.

Example 6-1 illustrates how to disable trunking on a Cisco Catalyst 3550 switch port, and Example 6-2 demonstrates how to configure a port to act as a trunk port, without the use of DTP.

Example 6-1 *Disabling Trunking*

```
Cat3550(config)# interface gigabitethernet 0/3
Cat3550(config-if)# switchport mode access
Cat3550(config-if)# exit
```

Example 6-2 *Preventing the Use of DTP*

```
Cat3550(config)# interface gigabitethernet 0/4
Cat3550(config-if)# switchport trunk encapsulation dot1q
Cat3550(config-if)# switchport mode trunk
Cat3550(config-if)# switchport nonegotiate
```

Double Tagging

On an IEEE 802.1Q trunk, one VLAN is designated as the *native* VLAN. The native VLAN does not add any tagging to frames traveling from one switch to another switch.

If an attacker's PC belonged to the native VLAN, the attacker could leverage this native VLAN characteristic to send traffic that has two 802.1Q tags. Specifically, the traffic's outer tag is for the native VLAN, and the traffic's inner tag (which is not examined by the switch's ingress port) is for the target VLAN to which the attacker wants to send traffic.

As illustrated in Figure 6-2, the first switch (SW1) removes the outer tag from the frame before forwarding the frame to its neighboring switch (SW2), because the outer tag specifies the native VLAN (VLAN 1 in this example), which is not tagged by a switch. As a result, when the frame is transmitted from switch SW1 to SW2, the inner tag becomes visible to SW2. This inner tag specifies the target VLAN (VLAN 100 in this example). As a result, SW2 sends the traffic out to the target VLAN.

To help prevent a VLAN hopping attack using double tagging, do not use the native VLAN to send user traffic. You can accomplish this by creating a VLAN in your organization that does not have any ports. This unused VLAN is solely for the purpose of native VLAN assignment. Example 6-3 shows a configuration on a Cisco Catalyst 3550 in which the native VLAN has been set to an unused VLAN.

Figure 6-2 *VLAN Hopping Using Double Tagging*

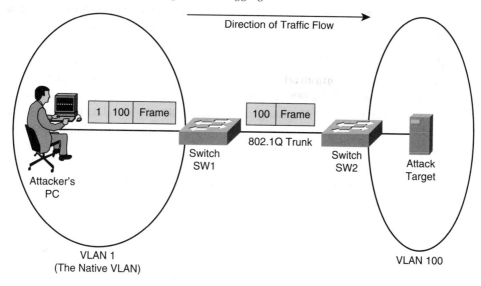

Example 6-3 *Setting the Native VLAN*

```
Cat3550(config)# interface gigabitethernet 0/4
Cat3550(config-if)# switchport trunk native vlan 400
```

Key
Topic

Protecting Against an STP Attack

Redundant links can be introduced into a Layer 2 switch topology to increase the network's availability. However, redundant links can potentially cause Layer 2 loops, which can result in broadcast storms. Fortunately, Spanning Tree Protocol (STP) can allow you to physically have redundant links while logically having a loop-free topology, thus preventing the potential for broadcast storms.

STP achieves this loop-free topology by electing one switch as the *root bridge*. The network administrator can influence which switch becomes the root bridge by manipulating a switch's bridge priority, in which the switch with the lowest bridge priority becomes the root bridge. Every other switch in the network designates a *root port*, which is the port on the switch that is "closest" to the root bridge, in terms of "cost." The bridge priorities of switches are learned through the exchange of Bridge Protocol Data Units (BPDU). After the election of a root bridge, all the switch ports in the topology are either in the *blocking* state (where user data is not forwarded) or in the *forwarding* state (where user data is forwarded).

If the root bridge fails, the STP topology reconverges by electing a new root bridge. Note that a port does not immediately transition from the blocking state to the forwarding state. Rather, a port transitions from blocking, to *listening*, to *learning*, to forwarding.

If an attacker has access to two switch ports (each from a different switch), he can introduce a rogue switch into the network. The rogue switch can then be configured with a lower bridge priority than the bridge priority of the root bridge. After the rogue switch announces its "superior BPDUs," the STP topology reconverges. All traffic traveling from one switch to another switch now passes through the rogue switch, thus allowing the attacker to capture that traffic.

For example, consider the topology shown in Figure 6-3. Data traveling from PC1 to Server1 passes through SW2 and SW3 (the root bridge).

Figure 6-3 *Converged STP Network*

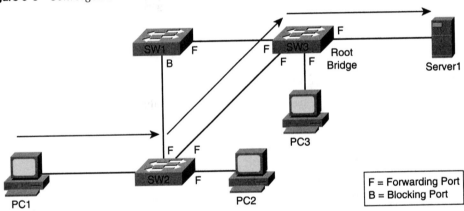

Notice PC2 and PC3. If an attacker gained access to the switch ports of these two PCs, he could introduce a rogue switch that advertised superior BPDUs, causing the rogue switch to be elected as the new root bridge. The new data path between PC1 and Server1, as shown in Figure 6-4, now passes through the attacker's rogue switch. The attacker can configure one of the switch ports as a Switch Port Analyzer (SPAN) port. A SPAN port can receive a copy of traffic crossing another port or VLAN. In this example, the attacker could use the SPAN port to receive a copy of traffic crossing the switch destined for the attacker's PC.

Figure 6-4 *Introducing a Rogue Switch*

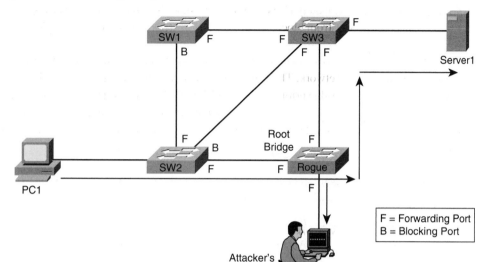

Consider two approaches for protecting a network from this type of STP attack:

- **Protecting with Root Guard**: The Root Guard feature can be enabled on all switch ports in the network off of which the root bridge should not appear (that is, every port that is not a *root port*, the port on each switch that is considered to be closest to the root bridge). If a port configured for Root Guard receives a superior BPDU, instead of believing the BPDU, the port goes into a *root-inconsistent* state. While a port is in the root-inconsistent state, no user data is sent across it. However, after the superior BPDUs stop, the port returns to the forwarding state. Example 6-4 illustrates the configuration of Root Guard on a port.

Example 6-4 *Configuring Root Guard*

```
Cat3550(config)# interface gigabitethernet 0/1
Cat3550(config-if)# spanning-tree guard root
```

- **Protecting with BPDU Guard**: The BPDU Guard feature is enabled on ports configured with the Cisco PortFast feature. The PortFast feature is enabled on ports that connect to end-user devices, such as PCs. It reduces the amount of time required for the port to go into forwarding state after being connected. The logic of PortFast is that a port that connects to an end-user device does not have the potential to create a topology loop. Therefore, the port can go active sooner by skipping STP's listening and learning states, which by default take 15 seconds each. Because these PortFast ports are connected to end-user devices, they should never receive a BPDU. Therefore, if a port enabled for BPDU Guard receives a BPDU, the port is disabled. Example 6-5 shows a sample BPDU Guard configuration.

Example 6-5 *Configuring BPDU Guard*

```
Cat3550(config)# interface gigabitethernet 0/2
Cat3550(config-if)# spanning-tree portfast bpduguard
```

Table 6-2 summarizes the actions of Root Guard and BPDU Guard.

Table 6-2 *Root Guard Versus BPDU Guard*

STP Attack Mitigation Method	Description
Root Guard	After receiving a superior BPDU, a port configured for Root Guard goes into a root-inconsistent state. While in this state, the port stops forwarding. After the superior BPDUs stop, the port returns to forwarding state.
BPDU Guard	BPDU Guard is designed to work on ports configured for the PortFast feature. If a port enabled for BPDU Guard receives a BPDU, the port is disabled.

Combating DHCP Server Spoofing

On today's networks, most clients obtain their IP address information dynamically, using Dynamic Host Configuration Protocol (DHCP), rather than having their IP address information statically configured. To dynamically obtain IP address information, a client (for example, a PC) sends out a DHCP request. A DHCP server sees the request, and a DHCP response (including such information as an IP address, subnet mask, and default gateway) is sent to the requesting client.

However, if an attacker connects a rogue DHCP server to the network, the rogue DHCP server can respond to a client's DHCP request. Even though both the rogue DHCP server and the actual DHCP server respond to the request, the client uses the rogue DHCP server's response if it reaches the client before the response from the actual DHCP server. This is shown in Figure 6-5.

Figure 6-5 *DHCP Server Spoofing*

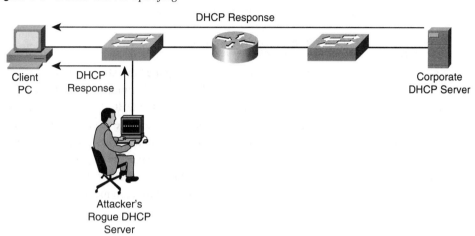

The DHCP response from an attacker's DHCP server might assign the attacker's IP address as the client's default gateway or DNS server. As a result, the client could be influenced to send traffic to the attacker's IP address. The attacker can then capture the traffic and forward the traffic to an appropriate default gateway. Because, from the client's perspective, everything is functioning correctly, this type of DHCP server spoofing attack can go undetected for a long period of time.

The *DHCP snooping* feature on Cisco Catalyst switches can be used to combat a DHCP server spoofing attack. With this solution, Cisco Catalyst switch ports are configured in either the *trusted* or *untrusted* state. If a port is trusted, it is allowed to receive DHCP responses (for example, DHCPOFFER, DHCPACK, or DHCPNAK). Conversely, if a port is untrusted, it is not allowed to receive DHCP responses, and if a DHCP response attempts to enter an untrusted port, the port is disabled.

Fortunately, not every switch port needs to be configured to support DHCP snooping. If a port is not explicitly configured as a trusted port, it is implicitly considered to be an untrusted port. To configure DHCP snooping, the feature must first be enabled. Use the following command to globally enable DHCP snooping:

```
Cat3550(config)# ip dhcp snooping
```

You can also enable DHCP snooping for specific VLANs. For example, to enable DHCP snooping for VLANS 1 and 100, in addition to VLANs in the range of 200 to 210, use the following global configuration mode command:

```
Cat3550(config)# ip dhcp snooping vlan 1,100,200-210
```

After you enable the DHCP snooping feature, specific switch interfaces can be configured as trusted ports, as the following syntax demonstrates:

```
Cat3550(config)# interface gigabitethernet 0/4
Cat3550(config-if)# ip dhcp snooping trust
```

Another type of DHCP attack is more of a DoS attack against the DHCP server. Specifically, the attacker can repeatedly request IP address assignments from the DHCP server, thus depleting the pool of addresses available from the DHCP server. The attacker can accomplish this by making the DHCP requests appear to come from different MAC addresses. To mitigate such a denial-of-service (DoS) attack, the previously mentioned DHCP snooping feature can be used to limit the number of DHCP messages per second that are allowed on an interface, thus preventing a flood of spoofed DHCP requests. For example, to limit the number of DHCP messages on a port to three messages per second, use the following syntax:

```
Cat3550(config)# interface gigabitethernet 0/5
Cat3550(config-if)# ip dhcp snooping limit rate 3
```

Using Dynamic ARP Inspection

The DHCP snooping feature dynamically builds a DHCP binding table, which contains the MAC addresses associated with specific IP addresses. Additionally, this feature supports static MAC address to IP address mappings, which might be appropriate for network devices, such as routers. This DHCP binding table can be used by the Dynamic ARP Inspection (DAI) feature to help prevent Address Resolution Protocol (ARP) spoofing attacks.

Recall the purpose of ARP requests. When a network device needs to determine the MAC address that corresponds to an IP address, the device can send an ARP request. The target device replies to the requesting device with an ARP reply. The ARP reply contains the requested MAC address.

Attackers can attempt to launch an attack by sending gratuitous ARP (GARP) replies. These GARP messages can tell network devices that the attacker's MAC address corresponds to specific IP addresses. For example, the attacker might be able to convince a PC that the attacker's MAC address is the MAC address of the PC's default gateway. As a result, the PC starts sending traffic to the attacker. The attacker captures the traffic and then forwards the traffic to the appropriate default gateway.

To illustrate, consider Figure 6-6. PC1 is configured with a default gateway of 192.168.0.1. However, the attacker sends GARP messages to PC1, telling PC1 that the MAC address corresponding to 192.167.0.1 is BBBB.BBBB.BBBB, which is the attacker's MAC address. Similarly, the attacker sends GARP messages to the default gateway, claiming that the MAC address corresponding to PC1's IP address of 192.168.0.2 is BBBB.BBBB.BBBB. This *ARP cache poisoning* causes PC1 and Router1 to exchange traffic via the attacker's PC. Therefore, this type of ARP spoofing attack is considered to be a *man-in-the-middle* attack.

Figure 6-6 *ARP Spoofing*

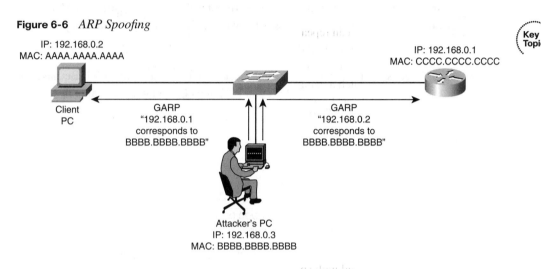

Client PC — IP: 192.168.0.2 MAC: AAAA.AAAA.AAAA

GARP "192.168.0.1 corresponds to BBBB.BBBB.BBBB"

GARP "192.168.0.2 corresponds to BBBB.BBBB.BBBB"

IP: 192.168.0.1 MAC: CCCC.CCCC.CCCC

Attacker's PC IP: 192.168.0.3 MAC: BBBB.BBBB.BBBB

Key Topic

Networks can be protected from ARP spoofing attacks using the DAI feature. DAI works similarly to DHCP snooping by using *trusted* and *untrusted* ports. ARP replies are allowed into the switch on trusted ports. However, if an ARP reply enters the switch on an untrusted port, the contents of the ARP reply are compared to the DHCP binding table to verify its accuracy. If the ARP reply is inconsistent with the DHCP binding table, the ARP reply is dropped, and the port is disabled.

The first step in configuring DAI is to enable DAI for one or more VLANs. For example, to enable DAI for VLAN 100, enter the following global configuration mode command:

```
Cat3550(config)# ip arp inspection vlan 100
```

By default, the DAI feature considers all switch ports to be untrusted ports. Therefore, trusted ports must be explicitly configured. These trusted ports are the ports on which ARP replies are expected. For example, to configure port Gigabit 0/6 to be a DAI trusted port, use the following syntax:

```
Cat3550(config)# interface gigabitethernet 0/6
Cat3550(config-if)# ip arp inspection trust
```

Mitigating CAM Table Overflow Attacks

A Cisco Catalyst switch uses a Content Addressable Memory (CAM) table to store the information used by the switch to make forwarding decisions. Specifically, the CAM table contains a listing of MAC addresses that have been learned from each switch port. Then, when a frame enters the switch, the switch interrogates the frame's destination MAC address. If the destination MAC address is known to exist off one of the switch ports, the frame is forwarded out only that port.

For example, consider Figure 6-7. PC1 sends packets to PC2 via switch SW1. Because the switch knows the MAC addresses of PC1 and PC2 in its CAM table, the traffic flows only between interface Gig 0/1 and Gig 0/2.

Figure 6-7   *Normal Switch Operation*

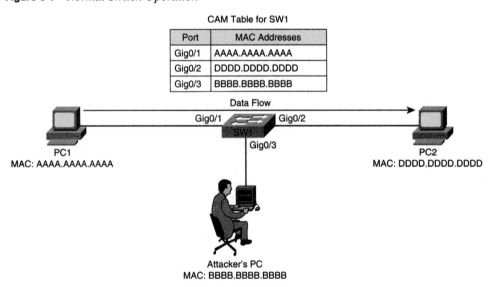

The switch's CAM table, however, does have a finite size. Therefore, if the CAM table ever fills to capacity, the switch is unable to learn new MAC addresses. As a result, when frames arrive destined for these unlearned MAC addresses, the switch floods a copy of these frames out all other switch interfaces, other than the interfaces they were received on.

The attacker's PC is connected to interface Gig 0/3, and the attacker wants to receive a copy of the traffic flowing between PC1 and PC2. If the attacker had caused the switch's CAM table to overflow before the switch learned the MAC addresses of PC1 and PC2, traffic between these two PCs would be flooded out all other switch ports, other than the ports the traffic was received on, allowing the attacker's PC to see and capture the traffic, as shown in Figure 6-8. This behavior of flooding frames with an unlearned destination MAC address is called *fail-open mode*.

Figure 6-8 *Flooding Behavior After a CAM Table Overflow Attack*

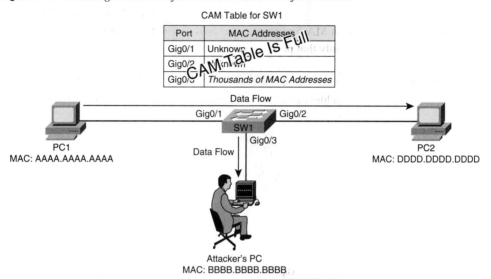

An attacker could launch a CAM table overflow attack using a utility such as macof, which is a component of a suite of utilities called dsniff. The macof utility can generate as many as 155,000 MAC addresses in a minute. After a short time, the switch learns so many MAC addresses from the attacker's PC that the switch's CAM table overflows, thus forcing the flooding of frames with unlearned MAC addresses. This type of attack noticeably impacts network performance, potentially causing applications to drop packets or even crash. As a result, a CAM table overflow attack is by no means a stealth attack, which an attacker might expect to launch without detection.

Keep in mind that the CAM table size can vary by switch model. Fortunately, Cisco Catalyst switches support a port security command, discussed later in this chapter. It allows the switch administrator to specify the maximum number of MAC addresses that can be learned on a port, thus preventing a CAM table overflow attack.

Spoofing MAC Addresses

Another type of attack targeted at the switch's CAM table is a MAC address spoofing attack. An attacker sends a frame with a false source MAC address—specifically, the MAC address of another device on the network. Under normal conditions, as shown in Figure 6-9, the switch's CAM table contains the correct MAC address of the stations attached to the switch's ports.

Figure 6-9 *CAM Table Under Normal Operation*

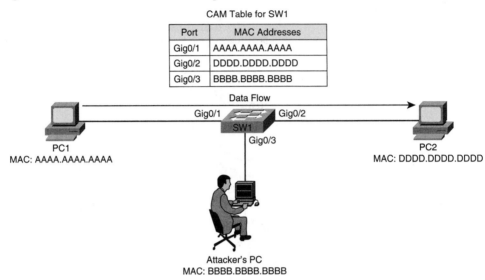

However, Figure 6-10 shows the attacker's PC sending a frame to the switch. It incorrectly shows a source MAC address of DDDD.DDDD.DDDD, which is actually the MAC address of PC2. This frame causes the switch to update its CAM table to show that DDDD.DDDD.DDDD is available off port Gig 0/3, which allows the attacker's PC to start capturing traffic destined for PC2.

Figure 6-10 *MAC Address Spoofing Attack*

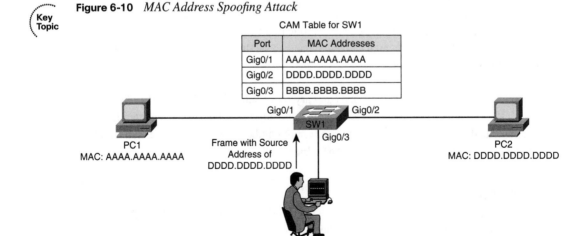

This condition of the attacker's PC receiving traffic for PC2, as shown in Figure 6-11, is a temporary condition. When PC2 sends another source frame into the switch, the switch relearns PC2's MAC address of DDDD.DDDD.DDDD on port Gig 0/2. However, even though the problem corrects itself, in the interim, the attack disrupts the normal traffic flow and allows the attacker to receive traffic intended for another device (that is, PC2 in this example).

Figure 6-11 *Diverted Traffic Flow*

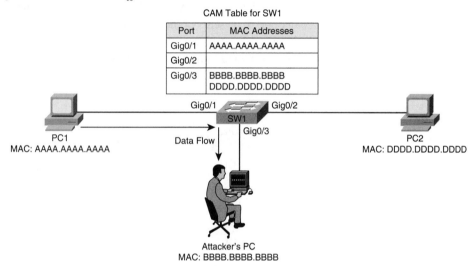

To mitigate MAC address spoofing attacks, a switch administrator can configure the Cisco Catalyst switch to use *sticky secure MAC addresses*. When configured for sticky secure MAC addresses, a Catalyst switch dynamically learns MAC addresses connected to various ports. These dynamically learned MAC addresses are added to the switch's running configuration, thus preventing an attacker from spoofing a previously learned address. Port security configuration is covered in great detail later in this chapter.

Additional Cisco Catalyst Switch Security Features

No single network device secures an entire network from all potential attacks. Rather, multiple hardware and/or software solutions work in tandem to help secure the overall network. For example, virtual private networks (VPN) and firewalls can help protect sensitive traffic from eavesdroppers and prevent unwanted traffic from entering a network. As described earlier in this chapter, a Layer 2 Cisco Catalyst switch can also aid in network security. The additional Cisco Catalyst switch security features described in the following sections can further secure a network infrastructure.

Using the SPAN Feature with IDS

Chapter 11, "Using Cisco IOS IPS to Secure the Network," discusses the Cisco Intrusion Detection System (IDS) technology. With IDS, a sensor receives a copy of traffic for analysis. If the sensor recognizes the traffic as being malicious or suspicious, the IDS sensor can take a preconfigured action, such as generating an alarm or dynamically configuring a firewall to block the sender.

One way to cause an IDS sensor to receive a copy of network traffic is to configure a port on a Cisco Catalyst switch for the Switched Port Analyzer (SPAN) feature. SPAN allows a copy of traffic destined for another port to be sent out the SPAN port, thus allowing an attached IDS sensor to receive a copy of the traffic, as illustrated in Figure 6-12. Example 6-6 demonstrates how to configure port Gig 0/2 as a SPAN source and port Gig 0/3 as a SPAN destination port.

Figure 6-12   *SPAN*

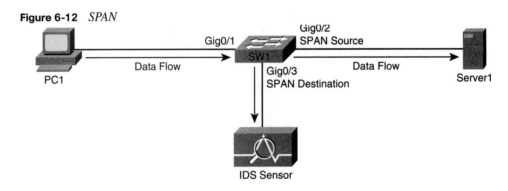

Example 6-6   *Configuring a SPAN Port*

```
Cat3550(config)# monitor session 1 source interface gigabitethernet0/2
Cat3550(config)# monitor session 1 destination interface gigabitethernet0/3
Cat3550(config)# end
```

Example 6-6 shows the SPAN port residing on the same switch as the destination port. However, Cisco Catalyst switches also support the Remote SPAN (RSPAN) feature, which allows a SPAN port to be configured on a different switch.

Enforcing Security Policies with VACLs

Routers can use IP access control lists (ACL) to permit or deny specific traffic from entering or exiting a network interface. Therefore, ACLs are used as traffic travels between network address spaces.

However, a Cisco Catalyst switch can have an ACL applied *within* a VLAN. This intra-VLAN ACL is called a *VLAN access control list* (VACL). Example 6-7 shows the configuration of a VACL that permits Telnet traffic to be sent to a host at IP address 10.1.1.2 while denying all other traffic. Notice that a *vlan access-map* named ALLOWTELNET is configured to match access list 100. For sequence number 10, the specified action is to forward traffic matching that access list. All other traffic is dropped because of a default implicit drop instruction, which drops all traffic not explicitly permitted. Finally, the VLAN filter (that is, the VACL) is applied to VLANs in the range 1 to 100.

Example 6-7 *Configuring a VACL*

```
Cat3550(config)# access-list 100 permit tcp any host 10.1.1.2 eq telnet
Cat3550(config)# vlan access-map ALLOWTELNET 10
Cat3550(config-access-map)# match ip address 100
Cat3550(config-access-map)# action forward
Cat3550(config-access-map)# exit
Cat3550(config)# vlan filter ALLOWTELNET vlan-list 1-100
```

Isolating Traffic Within a VLAN Using Private VLANs

Another way for a Cisco Catalyst switch to provide security is through the use of private VLANs (PVLAN). These PVLANs can provide privacy between groups of Layer 2 ports on a Cisco Catalyst switch. A PVLAN domain has a single primary VLAN. Additionally, the PVLAN domain contains secondary VLANs that provide isolation between ports in a PVLAN domain. Cisco Catalyst switches support two categories of secondary VLANs:

- **Isolated VLANs**: Ports belonging to an isolated VLAN lack Layer 2 connectivity between one another.

- **Community VLANs**: Ports belonging to a community VLAN can communicate with one another, but not with ports in other community VLANs.

PVLAN ports fall into one of three categories, as described in Table 6-3.

Table 6-3 *PVLAN Ports*

PVLAN Ports Category	Description
Promiscuous	Promiscuous ports typically are used to communicate with network devices (for example, routers or backup servers). These ports can communicate with all other PVLAN ports.
Isolated	Isolated ports can communicate with only promiscuous ports.
Community	Community ports can communicate with other ports in their community and also with promiscuous ports.

To learn more about private VLANs and their configuration, consult *Building Cisco Multilayer Switched Networks (BCMSN) Authorized Self-Study Guide*, Fourth Edition, available from Cisco Press.

Traffic Policing

To prevent an attacker from flooding a network with traffic in a DoS attack, Cisco Catalyst switches can rate-limit traffic using a traffic policing mechanism. Specifically, a traffic policing configuration allows an administrator to configure a committed information rate (CIR), which can be thought of as a "speed limit" on specific traffic. If traffic conforms to the speed limit, typically it is transmitted. However, traffic policing can alternatively transmit the conforming traffic and set a quality of service (QoS) marking (for example, a Differentiated Services Code Point [DSCP] marking) for the traffic. If traffic exceeds the speed limit, it can be dropped, or the switch can attempt to transmit the traffic while optionally setting the traffic's priority value to a lower priority value.

The configuration of traffic policing is performed using the three-step Modular QoS CLI (MQC) approach. For more information on the MQC approach, consult *Cisco Catalyst QoS: Quality of Service in Campus Networks*, available from Cisco Press.

Notifying Network Managers of CAM Table Updates

Cisco Catalyst switches can proactively notify network administrators when CAM table updates occur. For example, if a switch learns a new MAC address and adds it to the CAM table, the Cisco Catalyst switch could send a Simple Network Management Protocol (SNMP) trap (that is, a notification) to a network management station (NMS). Similarly, a trap could be sent when a MAC address is deleted from the CAM table. The **mac address-table notification** command is used to enable this notification feature.

Port Security Configuration

Earlier in this chapter you saw that Cisco Catalyst port security features can be used to combat CAM table overflow attacks and MAC address spoofing attacks. Cisco recommends that port security be configured on a switch before a switch is deployed in the network, to be proactive instead of reactive. When a switch port security violation occurs, you can configure the switch port to respond in one of three ways:

- **Protect**: When configured for protect, a switch port drops frames with an unknown source MAC address after the switch port reaches its configured maximum number of secure MAC addresses. However, frames with known (that is, learned) source MAC addresses are transmitted. Also, no notifications are sent if a port security violation occurs.

- **Restrict**: The restrict option operates similarly to the *protect* option. However, the restrict option sends an SNMP trap and a syslog message and increments a violation counter when a port security violation occurs.

- **Shutdown**: The shutdown option is the strictest approach. Not only does the shutdown option generate the same notifications as the restrict option, but it also shuts down the port. Therefore, after a port security violation occurs, no traffic is transmitted on that port.

A port security violation doesn't occur only after a port learns a maximum number of MAC addresses or after an unknown source MAC address attempts to enter the port. A violation also can occur when a MAC address on one secure port appears on a different secure port. Ports support one of three types of secure MAC addresses:

- **Static secure MAC address**: An administrator can statically configure which MAC addresses exist off specific ports using the **switchport port-security mac-address** *address* command issued in interface configuration mode. These statically configured MAC addresses are added to a switch's running configuration and CAM table.

- **Sticky secure MAC address**: Similar to static secure MAC addresses, ports configured for sticky secure MAC addresses also store MAC address-to-port associations in their switch's running configuration and CAM table. However, the MAC addresses do not need to be statically configured. Rather, a switch port dynamically learns the MAC addresses that exist off its ports.

- **Dynamic secure MAC address**: Similar to sticky secure MAC addresses, ports configured for dynamic secure MAC addresses dynamically learn which MAC addresses exist off specific ports. However, dynamic secure MAC addresses are stored only in a switch's CAM table, not in a switch's running configuration.

By default, port security is not enabled on a Cisco Catalyst switch port. After enabling port security with the **switchport port-security** interface configuration mode command, the maximum number of secure MAC addresses on a port defaults to one, and the violation mode defaults to shutdown.

Example 6-8 offers a comprehensive example of configuring port security on a Cisco Catalyst switch. Commands might vary somewhat based on the switch platform. This example is configured on a Cisco Catalyst 3550 switch.

Example 6-8 *Comprehensive Port Security Configuration*

```
Cat3550(config)# interface gigabitethernet 0/5
Cat3550(config-if)# switchport mode access
Cat3550(config-if)# switchport port-security
Cat3550(config-if)# switchport port-security maximum 5
Cat3550(config-if)# switchport port-security violation protect
Cat3550(config-if)# switchport port-security mac-address 1234.1234.1234
Cat3550(config-if)# switchport port-security mac-address sticky
Cat3550(config-if)# end
```

Notice that the administrator enters interface configuration mode for interface Gigabit Ethernet 0/5. In interface configuration mode, the administrator prevents the port from forming a trunk by issuing the **switchport mode access** command. Next, port security is enabled using the **switchport port-security** command. Recall that with port security enabled for a port, only one MAC address can be learned on that port. That number is increased to five in this example with the **switchport port-security maximum 5** command. The default action to take in the event of a security violation is to shut down the port. The **switchport port-security violation protect** command is used to override the default behavior of shutting down. It also allows the learned (or configured) MAC addresses to be transmitted while not allowing unknown (that is, not learned or configured) MAC addresses to be transmitted. Also, notice that the **switchport port-security mac-address 1234.1234.1234** command trains the switch about a MAC address available off interface Gigabit Ethernet 0/5. Finally, the **switchport port-security mac-address sticky** command causes learned MAC addresses to be dynamically entered into the switch's running configuration, thus mitigating a MAC address spoofing attack.

Multiple **show** commands can be used to verify and troubleshoot an interface's port security configuration. Example 6-9 shows the output from the **show port-security** command.

Example 6-9   *Output from the* **show port-security** *Command*

```
Cat3550# show port-security

Secure Port  MaxSecureAddr  CurrentAddr  SecurityViolation  Security Action
             (Count)        (Count)      (Count)
-----------------------------------------------------------------------------
     Gi0/5         5             1              0            Protect
-----------------------------------------------------------------------------
Total Addresses in System (excluding one mac per port)    : 0
Max Addresses limit in System (excluding one mac per port) : 6176
```

Example 6-10 shows output from the **show port-security address** command.

Example 6-10   *Output from the* **show port-security address** *Command*

```
Cat3550# show port-security address

        Secure Mac Address Table
----------------------------------------------------------------------
Vlan    Mac Address    Type                 Ports  Remaining Age
                                                   (mins)
----    -----------    ----                 -----  -------------
  1    1234.1234.1234  SecureConfigured     Gi0/5      -
----------------------------------------------------------------------
Total Addresses in System (excluding one mac per port)    : 0
Max Addresses limit in System (excluding one mac per port) : 6176
```

As an additional illustration, Example 6-11 shows how the **show port-security interface** *interface-id* command can be used to view detailed port security configuration information for an interface.

Example 6-11   *Output from the* **show port-security interface** *Command*

```
Cat3550# show port-security interface gigabitethernet 0/5

Port Security              : Enabled
Port Status                : Secure-down
Violation Mode             : Protect
Aging Time                 : 0 mins
Aging Type                 : Absolute
SecureStatic Address Aging : Disabled
Maximum MAC Addresses      : 5
Total MAC Addresses        : 1
Configured MAC Addresses   : 1
Sticky MAC Addresses       : 0
Last Source Address:Vlan   : 0000.0000.0000:0
Security Violation Count   : 0
```

Configuration Recommendations

Based on the Layer 2 attack mitigation strategies discussed earlier, the following list summarizes the recommended Cisco procedures for securing Layer 2 networks:

- Limit management access for a Layer 2 switch to trusted administrators.

- If management protocols are used on a switch, use secure management protocols (such as SNMPv3) as opposed to management protocols that transmit information in plain text (such as SNMPv1 and SNMPv2c).

- Disable any services running on the switch that are not necessary.

- Use a port security configuration to limit the number of allowable MAC addresses that a port can learn.

- Do not send user data over a native VLAN on an IEEE 802.1Q trunk.

- Administratively shut down any unused ports.

- Use STP protection mechanisms such as Root Guard and BPDU Guard.

- Enable DHCP snooping and DAI to combat man-in-the-middle attacks.

Cisco Identity-Based Networking Services

Cisco Catalyst switches can also participate in a Cisco Identity-Based Networking Services (IBNS) solution. Cisco IBNS is not provided by a single security feature. Rather, it is made available by combining multiple technologies to provide authentication, access control, and user-based policies. This section discusses how IBNS leverages IEEE 802.1x, RADIUS, and Extensible Authentication Protocol (EAP) technologies.

Introduction to Cisco IBNS

Cisco IBNS can be deployed on an end-to-end Cisco network, which includes components such as Cisco Catalyst switches, wireless LAN (WLAN) devices (such as wireless access points and controllers), and a RADIUS server (such as a Cisco Secure Access Control Server [ACS]).

However, for a client to directly benefit from IBNS, the client operating system needs to support IEEE 802.1x. Fortunately, many modern operating systems (such as Microsoft Windows Vista) support 802.1x. For greater scalability, an IBNS solution might operate in conjunction with a Public Key Infrastructure (PKI). Here X.509 certificates are issued to validate a host's identity and to provide the host's public key to any other device that wants to securely communicate with that host. Figure 6-13 shows a Cisco IBNS-enabled network. Notice that the authenticated user receives an IP address from one address pool, and the nonauthenticated user receives an IP address from a different address pool.

Figure 6-13   *Cisco IBNS Network Example*

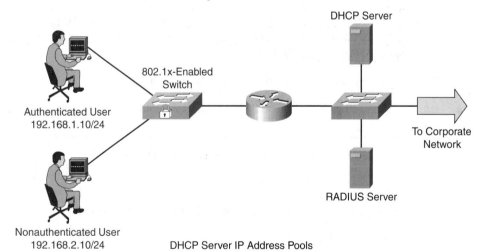

DHCP Server

802.1x-Enabled
Switch

Authenticated User
192.168.1.10/24

To Corporate
Network

RADIUS Server

Nonauthenticated User
192.168.2.10/24

DHCP Server IP Address Pools

Pool	Address Space
Authenticated	192.168.1.0/24
Nonauthenticated	192.168.2.0/24

Benefits of a Cisco IBNS-enabled network include the following:

- Cisco IBNS can authenticate individual users and/or devices.

- After authentication, a user's or device's permission on the network can be controlled by a configured policy.

- Using 802.1x, Cisco Catalyst switches can permit or deny access to the network at the switch port level.

- After users or devices are initially granted access to the network, additional policies can limit access to specified network resources.

- Cisco IP phones can operate in an IBNS network.

> **NOTE**   Cisco IP Phones can be recognized via Cisco Discovery Protocol (CDP).

- Cisco IBNS supports multiple authentication types, including EAP-MD5, PEAP, and EAP-TLS.

To illustrate the operation of IBNS, consider Figure 6-14, which shows a PC that boots up and wants to connect to a network. On many networks, a PC sends a DHCP request to obtain an IP address for use on the network. However, with IBNS, an 802.1x-enabled PC initially sends an Extensible Authentication Protocol over LAN (EAPOL) request. The Cisco Catalyst switch connected to the PC sees the EAPOL request and responds to the PC with a challenge. The challenge asks the PC to provide credentials for network access, such as a valid username and password combination. The switch forwards these credentials to a RADIUS server for verification. Upon verification of the supplied credentials, the switch grants the PC access to the network.

Figure 6-14   *IEEE 802.1x Port-Based Access Control*

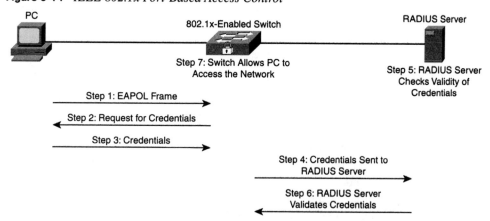

Overview of IEEE 802.1x

IEEE 802.1x (commonly just called "802.1x") is a standards-based approach for providing port-based network access. Specifically, 802.1x is a Layer 2 protocol that defines how Extensible Authentication Protocol (EAP) frames are encapsulated—typically between a user's network device (such as a PC) and a switch or wireless access point.

The 802.1x standard also defines hardware components, as shown in Figure 6-15 and defined in Table 6-4.

Figure 6-15   *IEEE 802.1x Hardware Components*

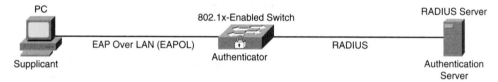

Key Topic

Table 6-4   *IEEE 802.1x Hardware Components*

Component	Description
Supplicant	The supplicant is the user device (for example, a PC) that requests permission to access the network. This device must support the 802.1x standard. For example, a PC running the Microsoft Windows Vista operating system, which supports 802.1x, could act as a supplicant.
Authenticator	A Cisco Catalyst switch is an example of an authenticator, because the authenticator is a device that provides access to the network. However, the authenticator typically does not authenticate the supplicant. Rather, the authenticator acts as a gateway, relaying authentication messages between the supplicant and an external authentication server. The authenticator receives EAPOL frames encapsulated in the 802.1x format, reencapsulates the authentication messages in the RADIUS format, and forwards them to the authentication server. Similarly, authentication messages traveling from the authentication server to the supplicant are encapsulated in a RADIUS format. Those messages are received by the authenticator, reencapsulated in the 802.1x format, and sent to the supplicant.
Authentication server	The authentication server is a RADIUS server (for example, Cisco Secure ACS) that validates a client's credentials against its user database.

During the previous authentication scenario, the PC could send traffic to the RADIUS server, which is part of the protected LAN. However, this does not mean that the PC could send user data to other devices in the protected LAN. Interestingly, the physical switch port that the PC connects to contains two logical ports, a *controlled port* and an *uncontrolled port*. The uncontrolled port is the only port over which the PC (that is, the supplicant) can send traffic until it is authenticated. This uncontrolled port passes only EAPOL, CDP, and STP traffic. However, after the PC is authenticated, the physical switch port opens its logical controlled port, over which the PC then sends its user data.

If the PC is configured for 802.1x, but the switch is not configured for 802.1x, after the PC fails to receive the expected EAP traffic, the PC acts as if it has been authenticated and transmits its user data. Conversely, if the PC is not configured for 802.1x, but the switch is configured for 802.1x, the switch does not grant network access to the client, because the client did not respond to the switch's EAP messages.

The **dot1x port-control** interface configuration mode command can be issued for a switch port to specify the port's 802.1x behavior. This command has three options, as defined in Table 6-5.

Table 6-5 *IEEE 802.1x Port Authorization Options*

Key Topic

Component	Description
forced-authorized	This option, which is the default setting, causes the port to immediately go into the authorized state, without participating in 802.1x.
forced-unauthorized	This option causes a switch port to remain in the unauthorized state, regardless of a supplicant's attempts to authenticate.
auto	This option causes a switch port to be in the unauthorized state by default. In this unauthorized state, the switch port does not pass user data. However, in this mode, as soon as a switch port's link state transitions to up, the port sends an EAP message to the attached device, requesting the identity of the device. The switch uniquely identifies this attached device by the device's MAC address and forwards authentication messages sent from the attached device to the RADIUS server. As soon as the attached device logs off, the port returns to the unauthorized state.

This section has used the example of a single client connecting to an 802.1x-enabled switch port and the port granting or denying access to that single client. Such an implementation is called *single-host mode*.

However, Cisco Catalyst switches support another mode, *multiple-host mode*. In multiple-host mode, multiple clients (that is, multiple MAC addresses) can exist off a single port. The port security commands discussed in the preceding section can be used to limit the MAC addresses that are permissible on this port. With multiple-host mode, if a single attached client authenticates, the port transitions to the authorized state, allowing all the network clients access to the network.

Extensible Authentication Protocols

The specific authentication messages transported by 802.1x and RADIUS protocols are dictated by the EAP in use. Multiple EAP types exist. The following discusses some of the more prevalent ones.

EAP-MD5

EAP-MD5 is a standards-based EAP type. This EAP type uses an MD5-Challenge message. This is much like the challenge message used in PPP CHAP (Point-to-Point Protocol Challenge Handshake Authentication Protocol), which uses MD5 (Message Digest 5) as its hashing algorithm.

Figure 6-16 shows the messages exchanged in an EAP-MD5 authentication. Notice that the authentication begins when the PC (the supplicant) sends an EAP over LAN (EAPOL) message (specifically, an EAPOL-start message) to the switch, which acts as the authenticator. The authenticator responds by sending an EAP Request/Identity message back to the supplicant, requesting credentials (for example, a username/password combination). After the supplicant responds, the authenticator forwards those credentials to the RADIUS server (the authentication server). The authentication server then sends an EAP Request/Challenge to the supplicant, and the supplicant responds to this challenge. If the challenge is successful, the authentication server tells the authenticator (the switch) to enable its port, and the supplicant is informed that its request for network admission is granted. The supplicant can now send traffic into the network via the switch.

Figure 6-16   *EAP-MD5*

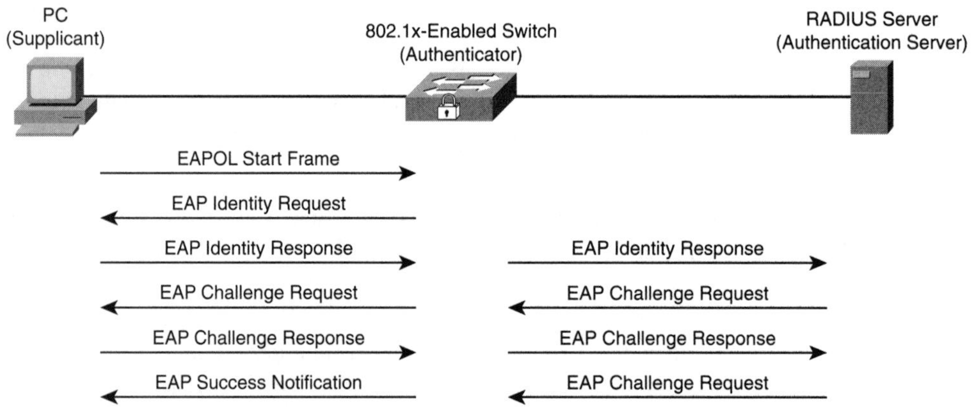

EAP-TLS

Microsoft developed EAP-TLS (Extensible Authentication Protocol Transport Layer Security). EAP-TLS was designed to address weaknesses found in other EAP types (such as the one-way authentication used by EAP-MD5). However, the trade-off for addressing these weaknesses is increased complexity in the deployment of EAP-TLS. Specifically, EAP-TLS uses certificate-based (that is, X.509 certificate-based) authentication. Therefore, to perform mutual authentication between the supplicant and the authentication server, both the supplicant and the authentication server must possess a digital certificate.

The benefits of the EAP-TLS EAP type are as follows:

■ EAP-TLS can provide encryption and authentication for each packet.

■ Keys are exchanged using a standards-based approach.

■ Because EAP-TLS is an extension of PPP, EAP-TLS integrates support for fragmentation and reassembly of frames.

■ EAP-TLS provides acknowledgments for both success and failure conditions.

As a reference, Figure 6-17 illustrates the messages exchanged in an EAP-TLS authentication. One of most unique characteristics of this authentication is the creation of a secure TLS tunnel between the supplicant and the authentication server.

Figure 6-17   *EAP-TLS*

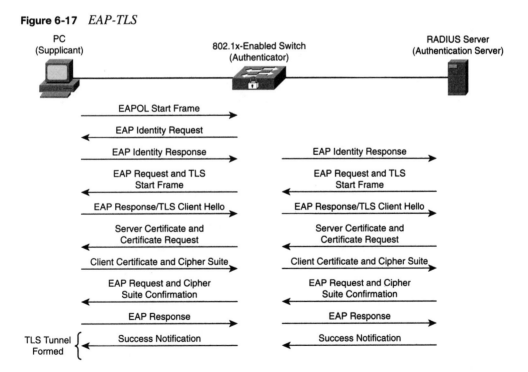

PEAP (MS-CHAPv2)

Protected Extensible Authentication Protocol (PEAP) comes in a couple of variations. PEAP version 0 uses MS-CHAPv2 (Microsoft Challenge Handshake Authentication Protocol version 2). PEAP version 1 uses GTC (generic token card). However, PEAP using MS-CHAPv2 is far more widely deployed than PEAP using a generic token card.

Cisco Systems, Microsoft, and RSA Security collaborated on the development of PEAP with MS-CHAPv2. PEAP increases protection of authentication messages by creating a protected TLS tunnel. Then, within the protection of the TLS tunnel, an authentication protocol, such as MS-CHAPv2, can be used. Specifically, even though an authentication protocol might be susceptible to attacks (such as a dictionary attack) when used independently, even a "vulnerable" authentication protocol can be used. This is because those authentication messages are sent securely within a TLS tunnel.

Notice in Figure 6-18 that MS-CHAPv2 challenge and response messages are exchanged between the supplicant and the authentication server within the protection of a TLS tunnel. This approach allows the supplicant and authentication server to mutually authenticate, without requiring the supplicant to have a digital certification. This was a requirement for EAP-TLS.

Figure 6-18   *EAP with MS-CHAPv2*

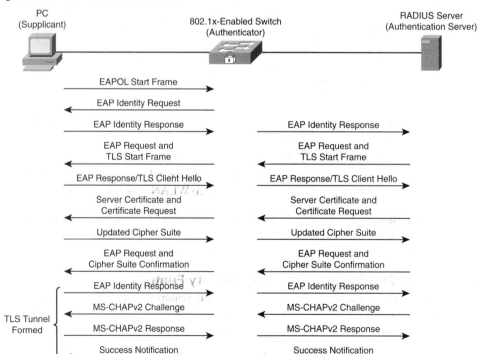

EAP-FAST

Extensible Authentication Protocol Flexible Authentication via Secure Tunneling (EAP-FAST) was developed by Cisco. Similar to EAP with MS-CHAPv2, EAP-FAST protects authentication messages within a secure TLS tunnel. However, EAP-FAST uses shared secret keys. These keys, which are unique to each user, are called *protected access credentials* (PAC). PACs, which can be automatically or manually distributed to the supplicants, cause authentication to happen much faster than using digital certificates. As a reference, the authentication messages exchanged in an EAP-FAST authentication are provided in Figure 6-19.

Figure 6-19 *EAP-FAST*

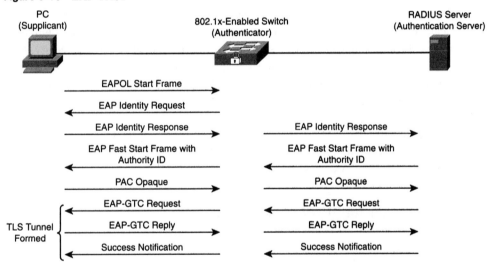

In addition to the EAP methods just described, the Cisco Secure Access Control Server supports the following EAP types:

■ **Lightweight EAP (LEAP)** uses a username/password combination to perform authentication. Typically it is found in a Cisco WLAN implementation.

■ **EAP Tunneled TLS (EAP-TTLS)** uses a secured TLS tunnel to send other EAP authentication messages.

Combining IEEE 802.1x with Port Security Features

Earlier in this chapter you read about port security features supported on Cisco Catalyst switches. Interestingly, these port security features can be used in conjunction with 802.1x authentication to provide enhanced port security.

For example, suppose a client authenticates via 802.1x, and the switch's port security table is not full (or the client's MAC address has been statically configured in the CAM table). The client is permitted to transmit data to the network. However, suppose the client authenticates, but a port security violation occurs (for example, because the configured number of allowable MAC addresses on the port has been reached). The client is not allowed to transmit data to the network.

Also, consider a situation in which a client successfully authenticates via 802.1x and is allowed to transmit on the network based on the port's port security configuration but later logs off. After the client logs off, the port returns to an unauthenticated state.

If you have statically configured a MAC address for a switch port and then remove that statically configured MAC address from the switch's port security table, you should then allow the client to reauthenticate by issuing the **dot1x re-authenticate interface** *interface-identifier* command. Also, if you administratively shut down a port, the port removes all dynamically learned MAC addresses from its port security table and transitions to the unauthenticated state.

Cisco Catalyst switches support using 802.1x authentication together with port security in either single-host or multiple-host mode. A Cisco IP Phone, which uses an *auxiliary VLAN*, can also be connected to such a port.

Using IEEE 802.1x for VLAN Assignment

The authentication server component of an 802.1x topology can also help restrict user access to network resources—specifically, VLANs. In addition to configuration on the RADIUS server (that is, the authentication server), the Cisco Catalyst switch is configured with appropriate AAA commands.

After a client (that is, a supplicant) successfully authenticates by providing a username and password, the RADIUS server, which maintains the username-to-VLAN mappings, sends the client's VLAN information to the switch. This is shown in Figure 6-20. Notice that User A and User B are mapped to separate VLANs, and the nonauthenticated user's port is blocked. However, if the RADIUS server is unable to specify a VLAN, or if the port is not performing 802.1x authentication, the client can use the port's access VLAN.

Figure 6-20 *Combining 802.1x with Port Security*

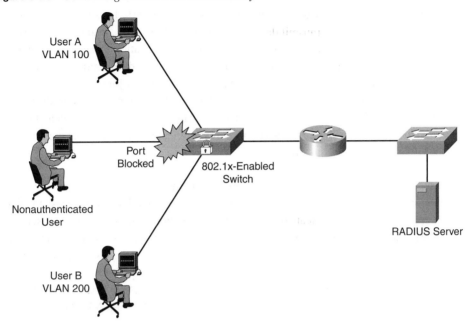

Suppose the switch port is configured for multiple-host mode, in which any attached host can authenticate on behalf of all the clients available off the port. All hosts are placed in the VLAN of the authenticated host based on the RADIUS server's username-to-VLAN mappings. Interestingly, if the port is configured for the forced-authorized, unauthorized, or shutdown state, the port is considered to be in its configured access VLAN.

Follow these steps to configure username-to-VLAN assignments:

- Configure AAA-based authorization on both the Cisco ACS server and the Cisco Catalyst switch.

- Configure the switch port for 802.1x.

- Configure appropriate tunnel parameters on the Cisco ACS server. Specifically, the ACS needs to be able to send the following attributes to the switch (that is, the authenticator):

    — Attribute 64 (contains the VLAN type)

    — Attribute 65 (contains the IEEE 802 value)

    — Attribute 81 (contains either the VLAN name or VLAN ID associated with the authenticated user

Cisco Catalyst switches also support the concept of a *guest VLAN*. Specifically, when a client that is not enabled for 802.1x (or that does not support 802.1x, such as Microsoft Windows 98) is attached to a port, the client does not send EAPOL frames. Nor does the client respond to an EAPOL frame coming from the authentication server, which requests the client's identity. When either of these conditions is observed, the authenticator (the Cisco Catalyst switch) can cause the client's port to dynamically join a guest VLAN. This VLAN typically would have limited access to resources (for example, access to the Internet or access to downloadable IEEE 802.1x software). This guest VLAN feature can be configured with the **dot1x guest-vlan supplicant** command issued in global configuration mode.

Unlike a guest VLAN, which supports clients that are not enabled for 802.1x authentication, a *restricted VLAN* can be used to provide limited network access to clients that support 802.1x but that have failed authentication. For example, suppose a user attempts to log onto the network from her 802.1x-compliant laptop, but her authentication fails. Instead of preventing the user from accessing any resources, you can configure your Cisco Catalyst switch to place the laptop's port into a restricted VLAN that has limited access to network resources. If you want users in the guest VLAN and the restricted VLAN to have the same level of access, be aware that these can be the same VLAN.

A switch configured for a restricted VLAN can place a port into the restricted VLAN after a connected client fails to authenticate after a certain number of attempts. This can be configured with the **dot1x auth-fail max-attempts** command issued in interface configuration mode (with a default of three attempts). After a client is placed in the restricted VLAN, it can attempt to reauthenticate after a certain period of time (with a default time of 1 minute). Even though this reauthentication can be disabled, Cisco recommends that you have reauthentication enabled if the client does not connect directly to the switch port (for example, via a hub connection). The reasoning is that if reauthentication is disabled, and the client disconnects from the hub (or powers down), the switch would not detect a change in the link state and would treat the port as if the unauthenticated client were still connected.

If you choose to use restricted VLANs, be aware of the following caveats:

- Restricted VLANs are supported only on access ports.

- Restricted VLANs are compatible with only a switch port running in single-host mode, as opposed to multiple-host mode.

- A restricted VLAN cannot be a VLAN used for Remote Switch Port Analyzer (RSPAN) purposes.

- A restricted VLAN cannot be used as an auxiliary VLAN (that is, a voice VLAN).

Configuring and Monitoring IEEE 802.1x

Regardless of the EAP in use on the supplicant and authentication server, the 802.1x configuration on the authenticator (that is, the Cisco Catalyst switch) remains the same. Following are the general steps required to configure 802.1x authentication on a Cisco Catalyst switch:

Step 1 Globally enable authentication, authorization, and accounting (AAA) on the Cisco Catalyst switch.

Just as you would enable AAA on a Cisco router, you can enable AAA on a Cisco Catalyst switch by issuing the **aaa new-model** command in global configuration mode.

Step 2 Enable IEEE 802.1x authentication.

After globally enabling AAA on the switch, you specify how the switch will authenticate a user using 802.1x by defining a *method list*. The method list, as the name suggests, is a list of one or more authentication methods. Available methods include the following:

- **enable** performs authentication based on the switch's enable password.

- **group radius** offloads the authentication process to a list of one or more RADIUS servers.

- **line** performs authentication based on a line password (such as the console line or a vty line).

- **local** references a locally configured user database for authentication.

- **local-case** performs case-sensitive authentication based on the local user database.

- **none** authenticates the supplicant without referencing any of the client's credentials.

For 802.1x authentication, you probably will use **group radius** as your preferred method in your method list. Also, instead of creating a custom method list, you could use the **default** keyword to specify that the list of authentication methods you provide is the default list to use, if a method list is not specified.

The global configuration mode syntax to create an 802.1x authentication method list is **aaa authentication dot1x** [*list-name* | **default**] *method*.

Step 3 Optionally configure authorization.

The global configuration mode command **aaa authorization network {default} group radius** can optionally be used to instruct the Cisco Catalyst switch to consult the defined RADIUS server(s) for VLAN assignment or other such requests for network services.

Step 4   Configure the Cisco Catalyst switch to communicate with the
authentication server (that is, the RADIUS server).

Table 6-6 describes the commands used to configure the Cisco Catalyst switch to
communicate with a RADIUS server.

Table 6-6   *Configuring a Cisco Catalyst Switch to Communicate with a RADIUS Server*

Command	Description
Switch(config)# **radius-server host** [*host-name* | *IP-address*]	Identifies the RADIUS server by hostname or IP address
Switch(config)# **radius-server key** [*string*]	Specifies the shared secret key used for authentication and encryption between the switch and RADIUS server
Switch(config)# **radius-server vsa send** [**accounting** | **authentication**]	Optionally used to configure a Cisco Catalyst switch to use vendor-specific attributes (VSA)

Step 5   Globally enable IEEE 802.1x on the Cisco Catalyst switch.

The **dot1x system-auth-control** global configuration mode command enables
802.1x authentication on a Cisco Catalyst switch. If you want to configure your
switch to support the previously described guest VLAN feature, issue the **dot1x
guest-vlan supplicant** command in global configuration mode.

Step 6   Configure IEEE 802.1x on an interface.

Table 6-7 describes the commands used to configure 802.1x on an interface.

Table 6-7   *Configuring IEEE 802.1x at the Interface Level*

Command	Description
Switch(config-if)# **switchport mode access**	Causes a switch port to act as an access port
Switch(config-if)# **dot1x port-control** [**force-authorized** | **force-unauthorized** | **auto**]	Configures the port's 802.1x authentication mode
Switch(config-if)# **dot1x host-mode multi-host**	Optionally configures 802.1x to operate in multiple-host mode, as opposed to single-host mode
Switch(config-if)# **dot1x guest-vlan** *vlan-id*	Optionally identifies the VLAN to be used as an 802.1x guest VLAN
Switch(config-if)# **dot1x auth-fail vlan** *vlan-id*	Optionally identifies the VLAN to be used as an 802.1x restricted VLAN

Step 7 Verify and monitor the IEEE 802.1x configuration.

After you complete your 802.1x configuration on a Cisco Catalyst switch, you can use the commands described in Table 6-8 to verify and monitor your configuration.

Table 6-8 *Monitoring an IEEE 802.1x Configuration*

Command	Description
Switch# **show dot1x**	Displays 802.1x status information
Switch# **show dot1x [all |** *interface-identifier*]	Displays port-level 802.1x status information for all interfaces or for a specified interface
Switch# **show dot1x statistics interface** [*interface-identifier*]	Displays 802.1x statistical information for all ports or a specified port
Switch# **show aaa servers**	Displays operation status for the configured RADIUS server(s)

Exam Preparation Tasks

Review All the Key Topics

Key Topic

Review the most important topics from this chapter, denoted with the Key Topic icon. Table 6-9 lists these key topics and the page where each is found.

Table 6-9 *Key Topics for Chapter 6*

Key Topic Element	Description	Page Number
List	Basic approaches to Layer 2 protection	212
Example 6-1	Disabling trunking	214
Example 6-2	Preventing the use of DTP	214
Example 6-3	Setting the native VLAN	215
Table 6-2	Root Guard versus BPDU Guard	218
Figure 6-5	DHCP server spoofing	219
Figure 6-6	ARP spoofing	221
Figure 6-8	Flooding behavior after a CAM table overflow attack	223
Figure 6-10	MAC address spoofing attack	224
List	Categories of secondary VLANs	227
Table 6-3	PVLAN ports	227
List	Responses to port security violations	228
List	Types of secure MAC addresses	229
List	Recommendations for securing Layer 2 networks	231
Table 6-4	IEEE 802.1x hardware components	234
Table 6-5	IEEE 802.1x port authorization options	235
List	IEEE 802.1x configuration steps	243

Complete the Tables and Lists from Memory

Print a copy of Appendix D, "Memory Tables," (found on the CD) or at least the section for this chapter, and complete the tables and lists from memory. Appendix E, "Memory Tables Answer Key," also on the CD, includes completed tables and lists so that you can check your work.

Definition of Key Terms

Define the following key terms from this chapter, and check your answers in the glossary:

authentication server, authenticator, DHCP snooping, Dynamic ARP Inspection, EAP, IEEE 802.1x, supplicant, Switch Port Analyzer (SPAN) port, VACL, VLAN hopping

Command Reference to Check Your Memory

This section includes the most important configuration and EXEC commands covered in this chapter. To see how well you have memorized the commands as a side effect of your other studies, cover the left side of the table with a piece of paper, read the descriptions on the right side, and see whether you remember the commands.

Table 6-10 *Chapter 6 Configuration Command Reference*

Command	Description
switchport mode access	An interface configuration mode command that disables trunking by setting a Cisco Catalyst switch port to operate as an access port
switchport nonegotiate	An interface configuration mode command that prevents the use of Dynamic Trunking Protocol (DTP) to form an Ethernet trunk
switchport trunk native vlan *vlan-id*	An interface configuration mode command that defines which VLAN on an IEEE 802.1Q trunk will serve as the trunk's native VLAN
spanning-tree guard root	An interface configuration mode command that enables the Root Guard feature on a Cisco Catalyst switch port
spanning-tree portfast bpduguard	An interface configuration mode command that enables the BPDU Guard feature on a Cisco Catalyst switch port
ip dhcp snooping	A global configuration mode command that globally enables the DHCP snooping feature
ip dhcp snooping vlan *vlan-id(s)*	A global configuration mode command that enables the DHCP snooping feature for specified VLANs
ip dhcp snooping trust	An interface configuration mode command that configures a Cisco Catalyst switch port as a trusted DHCP snooping port
ip dhcp snooping limit rate *number*	An interface configuration mode command that limits the number of DHCP messages on a port to a certain number of messages per second

continues

Table 6-10 *Chapter 6 Configuration Command Reference (Continued)*

Command	Description
ip arp inspection trust	An interface configuration mode command that configures a Cisco Catalyst switch port to be a trusted Dynamic ARP Inspection (DAI) port
switchport port-security	An interface configuration mode command that enables port security on a Cisco Catalyst switch port
switchport port-security violation *response*	An interface configuration mode command that specifies a Cisco Catalyst switch port's response to a port security violation
dot1x port-control [forced-authorized | forced-unauthorized | auto]	An interface configuration mode command that specifies the IEEE 802.1x behavior of a Cisco Catalyst switch port
dot1x guest-vlan *vlan-id*	An interface configuration mode command that optionally identifies the VLAN to be used as an 802.1x guest VLAN
dot1x auth-fail vlan *vlan-id*	An interface configuration mode command that optionally identifies the VLAN to be used as an 802.1x restricted VLAN

Table 6-11 *Chapter 6 EXEC Command Reference*

Command	Description
show port-security	Displays Cisco Catalyst switch ports configured for port security, the maximum number of secure MAC addresses configured for those ports, the current number of secure MAC addresses on those ports, the number of security violations that have occurred on those ports, and the actions those ports will take in response to a port security violation
show port-security address	Displays the MAC address(es) learned from Cisco Catalyst switch ports enabled for port security
show port-security interface *interface-id*	Displays port security statistics for the specified Cisco Catalyst switch interface
show dot1x	Displays IEEE 802.1x status information
show dot1x [all | *interface-identifier*]	Displays port-level IEEE 802.1x status information for all interfaces or for a specified interface

Table 6-11   *Chapter 6 EXEC Command Reference (Continued)*

Command	Description
show dot1x statistics interface [*interface-identifier*]	Displays IEEE 802.1x statistical information for all ports or a specified port
show aaa servers	Displays operation status for the configured RADIUS servers

This chapter covers the following topics:

Examining endpoint security: This section begins the discussion by examining a variety of threats faced by endpoints in a network environment. It also introduces a series of techniques that can help safeguard your systems from common operating system vulnerabilities. Furthermore, this chapter examines the destructive nature of buffer overflows, viruses, worms, and Trojan horses and discusses why it is important to guard against each of these.

Securing endpoints with Cisco technologies: Cisco has developed specific technologies to help you defend your endpoints against the forms of attack introduced in the first section, as well as against other threats. This section examines such technologies as IronPort, the Cisco NAC Appliance, and the Cisco Security Agent. It also discusses best practices for endpoint security.

CHAPTER 7

Implementing Endpoint Security

In the network world, the term "endpoint" can mean a myriad of devices—everything from workstations to PDAs, laptops to smart phones. This chapter uses "endpoint" to mean an individual computer or device that acts as a network client. In addition to common endpoints such as laptops, desktop systems, and PDAs, servers may also be considered endpoints in a networked environment. This chapter looks at the variety of threats faced by endpoint devices. It also discusses specific Cisco technologies that have been designed to help defend endpoints.

"Do I Know This Already?" Quiz

The "Do I Know This Already?" quiz helps you determine your level of knowledge of this chapter's topics before you begin. Table 7-1 details the major topics discussed in this chapter and their corresponding quiz questions.

Table 7-1 *"Do I Know This Already?" Section-to-Question Mapping*

Foundation Topics Section	Questions
Examining Endpoint Security	1 to 5
Securing Endpoints with Cisco Technologies	6 to 10

1. Network containment is provided by which of the following Cisco Self-Defending Network elements? (Choose all that apply.)

   a. IPS

   b. NAC

   c. SDN

   d. CSA

   e. HNS

2. Which of the following is not a phase in a worm attack?

   a. Paralyze

   b. Propagate

   c. Eradicate

   d. Persist

3. During the probe phase of a worm attack, which of the following might be used?

   a. Ping scans

   b. File copy

   c. Exploit code

   d. E-mail

4. The great majority of software vulnerabilities that have been discovered are which of the following?

   a. Software overflows

   b. Heap overflows

   c. Stack vulnerabilities

   d. Buffer overflows

5. Hardening your application software involves what? (Choose all that apply.)

   a. Applying patches

   b. Applying virus software

   c. Applying security fixes

   d. Upgrading firmware

6. The Dynamic Vector Streaming (DVS) engine is a scanning technology that enables what?

   a. Layer 4 virus detection

   b. Signature-based virus filtering

   c. Signature-based spyware filtering

   d. Firmware-level virus detection

7. Which of the following are features provided by the Cisco NAC device to help secure enterprise and endpoint systems? (Choose all that apply.)

    a. Authentication and authorization

    b. Posture assignment

    c. Remediation of noncompliant systems

    d. Quarantining of noncompliant applications

8. Which Cisco Security Agent Interceptor is responsible for intercepting all read/write requests to the rc files in UNIX?

    a. File system interceptor

    b. Configuration interceptor

    c. Network interceptor

    d. Execution space interceptor

9. What does the Cisco Security Agent do when an operating system call to the kernel by an application violates the security policy? (Choose all that apply.)

    a. An appropriate error message is passed back to the operating system.

    b. An alert is generated and sent to the Management Center for Cisco Security Agent.

    c. An appropriate error message is passed back to the application.

    d. An alert is generated and sent to the Cisco Security Agent.

10. What is the name of the e-mail traffic monitoring service that underlies that architecture of IronPort?

    a. E-Base

    b. TrafMon

    c. IronPort M-Series

    d. SenderBase

Foundation Topics

Examining Endpoint Security

To devise a successful strategy to defend your endpoints, you must begin with knowledge of the defenses that are available. This section describes the current endpoint protection methods, such as Host-based Intrusion Prevention System (HIPS), integrity checkers, operating system protection, and the Cisco NAC Appliance.

As part of our discussion, we will cover endpoint security and explore the fundamental principles involved in host security. We will also examine specific threats to endpoints, such as buffer overflows, and help you understand how to defend against these, as well as other common threats such as viruses, worms, and Trojan horses.

Defining Endpoint Security

Before you can take steps to defend your endpoints, you must better understand what endpoint security is and what it consists of. We will begin by exploring the fundamental principles involved in host security, as well as discuss the need to defend endpoints from viruses, worms, Trojan horses, and other security threats.

Cisco bases its strategy for securing hosts, as well as the more overarching network and enterprise security needs, on three broad elements (see Table 7-2).

Key
Topic

Table 7-2 *Cisco Security Elements*

Cisco Security Element	Description
Endpoint protection	The Cisco Security Agent provides a new behavior-based technology that is designed to protect endpoints from the threat posed by viruses, Trojan horses, and worms.
Cisco Network Admission Control (NAC)	To ensure that every endpoint complies with network security policies before being granted access to the network, organizations can employ the Cisco NAC framework. Having NAC in place ensures that compliant devices are provided access. Noncompliant devices are either denied access, placed in quarantine, or given restricted access to resources.
Network infection containment	Cisco has introduced network infection containment to address the newest attack methods that can compromise a network. The focus of containment is to automate key elements of the infection response process. This service is provided through various Cisco Self-Defending Network (SDN) elements such as NAC, Cisco Security Agent, and intrusion prevention system (IPS).

You might be wondering why, if you are securing your network borders, an endpoint security strategy is necessary. Endpoints in your environment run various pieces of software, as well as potentially various operating systems. Having an endpoint security strategy is central to securing your environment, because the software that these systems run has historically had weaknesses that attackers have often exploited.

One approach to this is to use "secure" (trustworthy) software that is specifically designed to protect data and withstand attack attempts. In practice, however, "secure" software has generally been used only with the military and in critical commercial systems. This type of software typically is custom-written and is not commercially available. This being the case, what are you to do when your endpoints are running less secure commercial software to meet your business needs?

One step you can take is to "harden" the software. Hardening is the process of making sure that all known patches and security fixes have been applied to the software, as well as adjusting recommended settings to lock down known vulnerabilities. To successfully do this, you need extensive documentation of the software's internals, which often is not provided by vendors.

Secure software has two main areas of focus:

- Security of operating systems

- Security of applications that run on top of the operating system

Examining Operating System Vulnerabilities

The various endpoints that we support on our networks each support some form of endpoint, whether it is a desktop operating system (OS) or Network Operating System (NOS). These operating systems provide a set of basic security services to all applications that run on them. Table 7-3 lists the basic security services.

Table 7-3 *Basic Security Services Provided to Applications by Operating Systems*

Key
Topic

Basic Security Service	Description
Trusted code	This is the assurance that the operating system code is not compromised. This assurance might be provided through a process of integrity checking of all running code using keyed Hash-based Message Authentication Code (HMAC) or digital signatures. A further assurance might be the requirement for integrity verification of add-on software at installation. Digital signatures might also be used here to provide a level of assurance that the code is authentic and uncompromised.

continues

Table 7-3 *Basic Security Services Provided to Applications by Operating Systems (Continued)*

Basic Security Service	Description
Trusted path	A trusted path is a facility that helps ensure that a user is using a genuine system and not a Trojan horse. An example of this is the Ctrl-Alt-Delete key sequence used to log into various Windows operating systems, such as Windows NT, Windows Server 2003, and Windows XP.
Privileged context of execution	Provides a degree of identity authentication and certain privileges based on the identity.
Process memory protection and isolation	Provides separation from other users and their data.
Access control to resources	Ensures confidentiality and integrity of data.

Even with these basic security services in place, an attacker could still unleash an attack. Should either the trusted code or a trusted path not present or become compromised, the operating system and all applications could easily fall victim to hostile code. Adding to your challenge in defending these endpoints is the fact that an operating system might be made more vulnerable if there is a need to provide support for legacy protocols. Standardizing on a proven, modern operating system may help decrease the need for such legacy support.

One of the benefits offered by modern operating systems is that they provide each process with an identity and privileges. During program operation, privilege switching is possible, or this may occur during a single login session. The UNIX world has the suid (set-UID) facility to provide this capability, whereas modern Microsoft Windows operating systems have the runas utility.

Whether you are working with a UNIX OS or one of the versions of Windows, several techniques can help protect your endpoints from common operating system vulnerabilities. These are examined in Table 7-4.

Table 7-4 *Techniques for Protecting Endpoints from Operating System Vulnerabilities*

Protection Technique	Description
Least-privilege concept	The least-privilege concept is fairly straightforward: a process should never be given more privilege than is necessary to perform a job. Unfortunately, this concept is easier to understand than it is to follow sometimes, leading to many forms of vulnerabilities.

Table 7-4 *Techniques for Protecting Endpoints from Operating System Vulnerabilities (Continued)*

Key
Topic

Protection Technique	Description
Isolation between processes	Isolation between processes should be provided by the operating system and may be either physical or virtual. An example of this isolation is using hardware to provide memory protection. Another means used by some trusted operating systems is to provide "logical execution compartments."
Reference monitor	This is an access control concept that refers to a mechanism or process that mediates all access to objects. A central point for all policy decisions is provided by the reference monitor, which typically implements auditing functions to keep track of access as well. Most operating systems provide a form of reference monitor. Additionally, for organizations working with the Cisco Security Agent, it also functions essentially as a reference monitor.
Small, verifiable pieces of code	Providing small, verifiable pieces of code is essential for all security functionality. These may then be managed and monitored by a reference monitor.

By working with both Cisco NAC and Cisco Security Agent, you can effectively provide protection against operating system vulnerabilities.

Examining Application Vulnerabilities

It is important to take the proper steps to address the vulnerabilities faced by your operating system, such as applying service packs and hot fixes and tuning it for secure operation. However, the majority of attacks target applications or, perhaps more specifically, the data they are protecting (or both). These attacks against applications can be categorized as either direct or indirect:

■ **Direct**: An attacker "tricks" the application into performing a task using the application's privileges.

■ **Indirect**: An attacker compromises another subsystem and then, through this compromised subsystem, attacks the application (this is called privilege escalation).

Ultimately, attacks like these seek to use the application's privileges. Hence, the more privileges an application has, the more damage an attacker can do to the application's sensitive data and the system as a whole with this form of attack. The Cisco Security Agent is designed to help you prevent both direct and indirect attacks. The next section examines the Cisco Security Agent in greater detail as we look at a variety of Cisco technologies that can be used to help defend endpoints from attack.

The goal of most attackers is to gain access to an application running on a host that processes sensitive data. By gaining access to an application running on such a host, the attacker can penetrate the sensitive data he wants to obtain. If the application hosting sensitive data is running in such a manner that an attacker has the option of communicating directly with the application, you must ensure that the application is suitably protected from this potential threat. If an attacker's goal is to compromise the confidentiality of the sensitive data, attacks will focus on allowing him to gain read or write access to the data via the application. Another form of attack, a denial-of-service (DoS) attack in a specific application, may seek to make the application and its data unavailable to legitimate users. An example of this might be an attack launched against a database that supports a large e-commerce application.

A common method used in attacks of this nature involves saturating the target (victim) machine with external communication requests. As these communication requests increase, the system is overwhelmed and cannot respond to legitimate traffic, or its responses are so slow that it is rendered effectively unavailable. These DoS attacks may be implemented by two primary means:

- Forcing the targeted computer(s) to reset, or consume its resources so that it can no longer provide the intended service

- Obstructing the communication media between the intended users and the victim machine so that they can no longer communicate

Attacks can occur in a variety of ways. An attacker may attack an application directly by exploiting a known flow or vulnerability in the application itself. He might also attack the application by bypassing its access controls and, in doing so, gain read or write access to sensitive data. As commercial business and personal applications grow more complex, the likelihood of flaws and vulnerabilities has grown. For many organizations, the cost and time involved to develop secure custom applications make it a less-than-feasible option.

Another form of attack at the application level is "elevation of privileges." In this kind of attack, an attacker gains access to sensitive data by using a series of compromises of other system components. An attacker might initially obtain basic user-level access to the system where the sensitive data is stored. Having gained this basic access, the attacker could exploit a given flaw in any local application, using this to attain system administration privileges. Now, with administrative privileges, the attacker may be able to read or write to most objects on the system, including the sensitive data held by the target application.

Understanding the Threat of Buffer Overflows

To understand the threat that buffer overflows present when defending endpoints, you must first understand what a buffer overflow actually is and how applications operate. When a user or other source interacts with an application, it has to carefully verify all input, because the input might contain improperly formatted data, control sequences, or simply too much data for the application to work with. When these things occur, a buffer overflow condition can arise. Attackers realize this and try to exploit this vulnerability. In fact, buffer overflows are a very common type of exploitation used by attackers.

An attacker who unleashes a buffer overflow exploit essentially tries to overwrite memory on an application stack by supplying too much data to the input buffer. Because this form of attack uses the application's very nature against itself, it can be hard to stop. Of course, it is not easy to discover how to initiate a buffer flow and use it to exploit a system. However, as soon as an attacker discovers the vulnerabilities that lead to this condition, he or she can prepackage exploit code for widespread use.

Buffer Overflow Defined

With a buffer overflow, a program writes data beyond the allocated end of a buffer in memory. Often buffer overflows arise from a bug in the application or from improper use of languages such as C or C++ that are not memory-safe. When these overflows occur, valid data may be overwritten as well, making these threats particularly dangerous.

Buffer overflows are one of the most commonly exploited computer security risks because of the structure of how computers handle data. Program control data generally sits in the memory areas next to data buffers. An attacker might initiate a buffer overflow condition to make the computer execute arbitrary, potentially malicious code that is then fed back to the program as data.

A very similar attack is a heap overflow. Applications dynamically allocate a stack known as the heap. This is done at runtime, and it generally contains program data. Attackers can target this as well and exploit it in a similar manner.

The Anatomy of a Buffer Overflow Exploit

Because buffer overflows are one of the most common methods of application subversion in use today on the Internet, it is important that you understand these attacks and how to stop them. Let's take a look at the anatomy of a buffer overflow attack in detail.

In most buffer overflow attacks, the attacker tries to subvert a program function that reads input and calls a subroutine (see Figure 7-1). What makes this possible is that the exploitable program function does not perform input length checks and allocates a fixed amount of memory for data.

Figure 7-1 *Buffer Overflow*

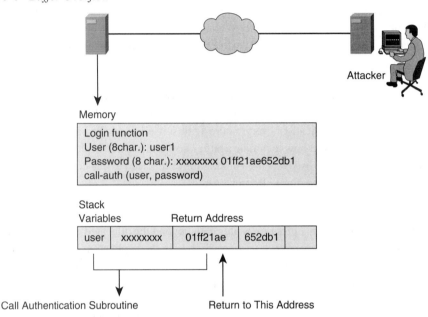

- When an application makes a subroutine call, it places all input parameters on the stack.
- To return from the subroutine, the return address is also placed on the stack by the calling function.
- An attacker-supplied parameter can overwrite the return address, being too long to fit on its place on the stack.

The way applications work is that when an application makes a subroutine call, it places all input parameters on the stack. To return from the subroutine, the return address is also placed on the stack by the calling function. An attacker overwrites the return address by sending data that is longer than the fixed memory space on the stack that the application allocated. After this overwrite occurs, the application returns to an attacker-supplied address, pointing to the attacker's malicious code. In essence, the attacker has hijacked this application communication and now can insert his own malicious code. This code is supplied by the attacker as part of the excessively large input. The end result of this attack is that arbitrary code may now be executed with the privileges of the legitimate application.

Understanding the Types of Buffer Overflows

Most buffer overflow attacks are used to either root a system or cause a DoS attack. We will look at each of these types of attacks.

The phrase "rooting a system" comes from the UNIX world. It means that a system has been hacked so that the attacker has root, or superuser, privileges. Rooting a system is most easily accomplished with either remote root or local root buffer overflows. Of these two, remote root buffer overflows are the more dangerous. This is because an attacker can "own" your system in a matter of seconds if the system is unprotected and vulnerable. If you think in terms of worms, the most dangerous of these have exploited remote root buffer overflows.

Local root buffer overflows work a bit differently. This form of attack generally requires some kind of assistance in distributing the exploit. This is typically done via a virus that is transported by e-mail, or it could be done using a Trojan horse-infected executable. Regardless of the mechanism, the attacker's goal remains the same.

The great majority of software vulnerabilities that have been discovered are buffer overflows. That is why this is such an important area to understand and defend against. In fact, some research suggests that two out of every three software vulnerabilities found by CERT are buffer overflows. As discussed in a later section, Cisco offers technologies that can defend against buffer overflows, such as the Cisco Security Agent, which can actually prevent buffer overflows.

Additional Forms of Attack

Buffer overflows are not the only concern. The larger issue is that a buffer overflow may be used to initiate malicious code such as viruses, worms, and Trojan horses so that they may gain access to your system and begin to do their damage. Two of the most destructive worms that have been unleashed on the Internet are SQL Slammer and Code Red. The destruction these worms caused was made possible by remote root buffer overflows. In contrast to worms, viruses are more likely to take advantage of local root buffer overflows to unleash their exploits. Trojan horses, the third major threat we will examine in this section, generally resemble viruses in that they exploit local root buffer overflows. Let's examine each of these in more detail:

- **Worms**: Worms are a form of malicious code that can replicate themselves without a host over networks by independently exploiting vulnerabilities. In other words, they can replicate themselves without the need to infect a file, as a virus might. Also, because they live in RAM (and because of their capacity for replication), they are incredibly hard to defeat and quite destructive. Although it might seem that the best way to defeat something that lives in memory is to simply reboot the system, effectively clearing out the RAM, this does not address the underlying vulnerability that made the system vulnerable to attack. In a case such as this, the system would be easily reinfected after the reboot if no additional steps are taken to address the vulnerability. Adding to the issue is that worms typically do not require user participation and can spread extremely fast.

Key Topic

- **Viruses**: In contrast to worms, which can replicate themselves independently, viruses are pieces of malicious code that must have a host to unleash their attack. In some cases, viruses piggyback on legitimate programs or content to deliver their malicious payload. In other instances, such as with the ILOVEYOU virus (which was ILOVEYOU.txt.vbs), the payload was delivered independent of any useful application. Replication occurs when the virus attaches itself to other software. For instance, in the case of a macro virus, a word.doc may be used. Unlike worms, viruses typically require some form of end-user activation, such as opening a file or clicking an executable. One thing that makes them particularly sneaky is that they can lie dormant for an extended period and then activate at a specific time or date. Viruses also vary in nature. Some are benign, and others are extremely destructive and can destroy programs, files, or entire systems with their exploits. Another aspect that makes them hard to contain is that they can be programmed to mutate to avoid detection and survive attempts to eradicate them.

  It is not uncommon for a malicious virus to be packaged with the code of a freeware or shareware program that purports to be something useful, such as a screensaver or game. The host program is something that has a degree of merit, so it is shared among users. It is in this sharing of the executable file that the virus is passed from system to system on CD, via FTP, or as an e-mail attachment. When the file's recipient executes the program (the infected executable), the virus becomes loaded into memory on that person's system and can infect other executables on that computer.

  Each virus is unique, as are their behaviors. Some install themselves at the first line of code for the executable so that when the user starts the executable, the code for the virus is immediately run. Other viruses are programmed to first check the local hard disk in search of files that have yet to be infected so that they may infect these files. As soon as the code is run, the behavior may be as harmless as displaying a picture or changing the color of text in a given application, or it may be far more destructive.

- **Trojan horses**: A Trojan horse is different from viruses and worms in that it appears to be a normal and useful program but actually contains hidden, malicious code. When the program is executed, it exploits the privileges of the user who runs it. This can be particularly dangerous if a program such as this is executed by someone with administrative privileges. Often games are used to disguise this malicious code. While the user plays the game, all seems normal, but behind the scenes, the Trojan horse has been installed on the victim's system. After it is installed, the Trojan horse program continues to run after the game has been closed, unleashing whatever form of attack the programmer intended.

Because the purpose of a Trojan horse is to load a program on a user's system without his or her knowledge, the nature of the attacks it unleashes can be quite varied. Some Trojan horses may cause immediate damage, and others might be designed to provide remote access to the system via a "back door." Or the Trojan horse might sit and wait to perform actions as instructed remotely, such as collecting and sending keystrokes captured by a keylogger program running in the background on the machine.

Trojan horses can be hard to defend against. Custom-written Trojan horses, such as those with a specific target, are extremely hard to automatically detect. In addition to taking the proper steps with regard to technology, end-user education is also quite important. A tool such as the Cisco Security Agent is very effective at defeating viruses, worms, and Trojan horses.

Having discussed these three kinds of attacks, let's take a closer look at worms. Table 7-5 breaks down a worm attack piece by piece.

Table 7-5   *Anatomy of a Worm Attack*

Facet of the Worm Attack	Description
Enabling vulnerability	Using an exploit vector such as an e-mail attachment, Trojan horse, or remote buffer overflow, the worm installs itself on a vulnerable system.
Propagation mechanism	The worm replicates itself after it gains access to a device and then chooses new targets.
Payload	Infecting a device with the worm gives the attacker access to the host, usually privileged access. As soon as the attacker has this level of access, he can use a local exploit to escalate his privilege level. The "payload" itself varies, depending on the worm and the attack. However, this generally can be thought of as the intended "action" produced by the worm. For instance, a file might be altered, as with the infamous NIMDA worm, which modified the Host file, placing static entries of 0.0.0.0 for common update sites. This kept systems from getting the latest antivirus signature or Windows update, for instance, because the infected system could no longer resolve the domain name. A worm attempts to exploit system vulnerabilities. Upon successful exploitation, it copies itself from the attacking host to the newly exploited system and restarts the cycle.

continues

Table 7-5 *Anatomy of a Worm Attack (Continued)*

Facet of the Worm Attack	Description
Probe phase	In this phase, vulnerable targets are identified, with the goal being to find computers that can be subverted. Ping scans using Internet Control Message Protocol (ICMP) are used to map networks. In these, the application scans and identifies operating systems and vulnerable software. Also in this phase, attackers may attempt to gain passwords through social engineering, dictionary attacks, brute-force attacks, or network sniffing. Other common scans that may occur during this phase are port scans and vulnerability scans. A port scan seeks to identify all listening ports on an identified host. This information can then be used to shape the attack. A vulnerability scan seeks to identify devices on the network that are open to known vulnerabilities. Each of these types of scans can further shape an attacker's exploit by giving him information that he needs to be most successful against your systems.
Penetration phase	During this phase, exploit code is transferred to the vulnerable target. The goal is to get the target to execute the exploit code through an attack vector such as a buffer overflow, ActiveX or Common Gateway Interface (CGI) vulnerabilities, or an e-mail virus.
Persist phase	After an attack has been successfully launched in memory, its code tries to persist on the target system. In this phase, the goal is to ensure that the attacker code is running and available to the attacker even if the system reboots. This can be achieved by modifying system files, making registry changes, and installing new code.
Propagate phase	In this phase the attacker looks to extend the reach of the attack by finding vulnerable neighboring machines. A number of propagation vectors exist, including e-mailing copies of the attack to other systems, uploading files to other systems using file shares or FTP services, active web connections, and file transfers through Internet Relay Chat (IRC).
Paralyze phase	In this phase the actual damage is done. This is where files may be erased, systems crashed, information stolen, or distributed DoS (DDoS) attacks launched.

Table 7-6 compares worm and virus attacks over the past 20 years. It also highlights some of the differences in how the attacks accomplished the various phases of attack that hackers employ. As you review this table, also note how often worms and viruses use similar methods.

Table 7-6 *Exploit Comparison*

Phase	Morris (1988)	Love Bug (2000)	Code Red (2001)	Slammer (2003)	MyDoom (2004)	Zolob (2005)
Probe	Scan for Fingerd	—	Scan for Internet Information Server (IIS)	—	—	Scan for Microsoft Directory Services
Penetrate	Buffer overflow in Fingerd	Arrive as e-mail attachment	Buffer overflow in IIS	Buffer overflow in SQL and MSDE	Arrive as e-mail attachment	Buffer overflow in Upnp service
Persist	Execute script to download code	Create executable and edit the registry	Execute script to download code	—	Create executables and edit the registry	Create executable, edit the registry, download code
Propagate	Look for addresses to spread to new victims	Open address book and e-mail copies	Pick new addresses and spread to new victim	Pick new addresses and spread to new victim	Open address book and e-mail copies	Start FTP and TFTP services
Paralyze	Many processes slow the system	Worm spreads	Lots of threads slow system	Lots of packets slow network	Worm spreads	Delete registry keys and files and terminate processes

Securing Endpoints with Cisco Technologies

With new and emerging threats to endpoint devices, it is important as a security administrator to put in place the right technologies to defend against these threats. Cisco offers a wide range of technologies that can help you protect your endpoints from these threats. This section explores these technologies and discusses how they complement your overall security strategy.

Understanding IronPort

IronPort is designed to protect an enterprise from various Internet threats that target e-mail and web security. IronPort's e-mail security capabilities are readily used by 20 percent of the largest enterprise organizations in the world. IronPort has a strong history of providing security and reliability. This same code base that protects eight of the ten largest ISPs is built into all of IronPort's e-mail security appliances for enterprises of any size.

In addition to enterprise-level e-mail protection, the IronPort S-Series is the industry's fastest web security appliance. This appliance combines a high-performance security platform with Web Reputation technology and a Dynamic Vectoring and Streaming (DVS) engine. The DVS engine is a new scanning technology that enables signature-based spyware filtering. This solution is complemented by a comprehensive set of management and reporting tools that provide ease of administration and complete visibility into threat-related activities.

IronPort's M-Series security management appliance is designed to complement IronPort's e-mail and web security appliances by providing top performance for all your application security gateways. The IronPort M-Series provides a single location where you can effectively manage, store, and monitor all corporate security policy settings and audit information. This flexible management tool was built to centralize and consolidate policy and runtime data, giving administrators a single interface to manage all their application layer security systems.

The Architecture Behind IronPort

SenderBase represents the first and largest e-mail traffic monitoring service, collecting data from more than 100,000 ISPs, universities, and corporations around the world. More than 120 parameters can be measured and scrutinized with SenderBase. The massive SenderBase database handles more than five billion queries per day. Real-time data is provided from every continent, from both small and large network providers. With this massive amount of data, SenderBase can develop the most accurate view of the sending patterns of any given mail sender. This accuracy has helped SenderBase remain the largest database of its kind in the world. SenderBase is licensed to the open-source community, as well as to other institutions that are working to fight spam.

Examining the Cisco NAC Appliance

Several technologies can defend endpoints from the common threats they face. The Cisco NAC Appliance is one device that can be used to enhance and complement other endpoint security measures. Effectively the Cisco NAC comes in two "flavors." The first is the Cisco NAC framework, which is a software module embedded within NAC-enabled devices. In this framework a number of both Cisco and other NAC-aware vendor products may be used to provide security. The second flavor is the Cisco NAC Appliance. This is an in-band solution that can be used on any switch or router platform to provide a self-contained turnkey solution. This section explores both of these options in greater depth.

The Cisco NAC device enables you to allow only authorized and compliant systems to access the network and allows you to enforce network security policy. This may be done whether the systems are managed or unmanaged. By enabling this enforcement of network security policy, Cisco NAC helps organizations maintain network stability.

The Cisco NAC device provides four key features to help further secure the enterprise and endpoint systems:

■ Authentication and authorization

■ Posture assessment (evaluating an incoming device against the network's policies)

■ Quarantining of noncompliant systems

■ Remediation of noncompliant systems

Table 7-7 covers the two general categories of the Cisco NAC product.

Table 7-7   *General Categories of the Cisco NAC Product*

NAC Category	Description
NAC framework	The NAC framework combines the existing Cisco network infrastructure with third-party software to enforce security policy compliance across endpoints. The NAC framework is built to serve high-performance network environments that include diverse endpoints. Such environments require a consistent LAN, WAN, wireless, extranet, and remote-access solution—one that integrates into the existing security and patch software, tools, and processes. Rather than a single device providing the four key NAC features, different devices in the network may do so.
Cisco NAC Appliance (Cisco Clean Access)	The four key NAC functions are centralized in the Cisco NAC Appliance solution. This appliance provides a turnkey solution to control network access. It is ideally suited for medium-scaled networks requiring a self-contained turnkey solution. For organizations that require simplified yet integrated tracking of operating system and antivirus patches, as well as vulnerability updates, the Cisco NAC Appliance is an excellent choice. It does not require a Cisco network for implementation.

Figure 7-2 shows the components involved when deploying the Cisco NAC Framework. These various components work together to provide compliance-based access control. In this deployment, various NAC functions, such as authentication, authorization, and accounting (AAA), scanning, and remediation, are performed by other Cisco products. As shown in Figure 7-2, the Cisco Secure Access Control Server (ACS) or other partner products such as TrendMicro may be used to provide various functionality.

Figure 7-2 *NAC Framework*

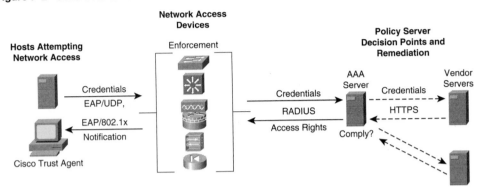

Figure 7-3 shows the Cisco NAC Appliance, which is a standalone NAC appliance that may be incorporated in both Cisco and non-Cisco networks. This device can provide all the key NAC functionality, including authentication and posture assessment, as well as quarantining and remediation of noncompliant systems without the need for additional products. The Cisco NAC Appliance also comes with preconfigured checks for Windows updates and most major antivirus software packages.

Figure 7-3 *NAC Appliance*

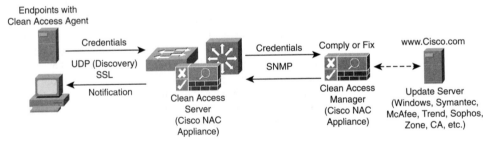

Working with the Cisco Security Agent

In today's computing environment, endpoint protection must encompass more than simple desktop systems. The Cisco Security Agent software provides full-featured endpoint protection with threat protection capabilities for server, desktop, and point-of-service (POS) computing systems. This highly scalable solution can support as many as 100,000 agents from a single management console. Figure 7-4 shows the architecture of the Cisco Security Agent, which can grow with an organization's changing needs.

Figure 7-4   *Architecture of the Cisco Security Agent*

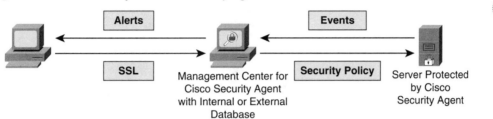

Alerts   Events

SSL   Management Center for   Security Policy   Server Protected
      Cisco Security Agent   by Cisco
      with Internal or External   Security Agent
      Database

Table 7-8 explores the underlying architectural model for the Cisco Security Agent and the two components that make it up.

Table 7-8   *Architectural Components of the Cisco Security Agent*

Component	Description
Management Center for Cisco Security Agents	Using the Management Center for Cisco Security Agent, you can divide network hosts into groups based on function and security requirements. You may then configure security policies for those groups. The Management Center for Cisco Security Agent also supports logging of security violations and can send alerts by e-mail or pager.
Cisco Security Agent	The Cisco Security Agent component is installed on the host system and continuously monitors local system activity and analyzes that system's operations. Cisco Security Agent takes proactive action to block attempted malicious activity and polls the Management Center for Cisco Security Agent at configurable intervals for policy updates.

Secure administration is another key aspect of this solution. An administration workstation may be configured to securely connect to the Management Center for Cisco Security Agent by using a Secure Socket Layer (SSL)-enabled web interface. This allows for flexibility in administration while providing security.

Understanding Cisco Security Agent Interceptors

To help you understand how Cisco Security Agent interceptors work, we must first explore how applications access system resources. Each time an application needs access to system resources, it has to make an operating system call to the kernel. When this occurs, the Cisco Security Agent intercepts these operating system calls and compares them to the cached security policy. Figure 7-5 shows this process.

Figure 7-5   *Cisco Security Agent Interceptors*

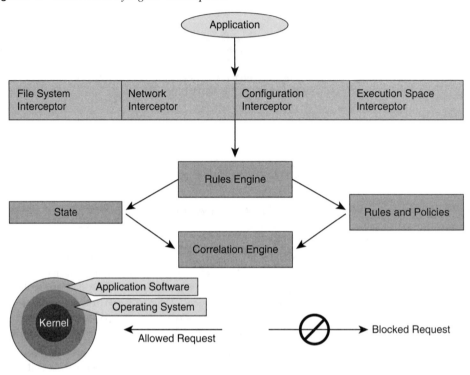

As long as the request does not violate the policy, it is passed to the kernel for execution. However, should the request violate the security policy, the Cisco Security Agent blocks the request and takes one of the following actions:

■   An appropriate error message is passed back to the application.

■   An alert is generated and sent to the Management Center for Cisco Security Agent.

To detect malicious activity, the Cisco Security Agent correlates the particular operating system call with the other calls made by that application or process. By correlating these events, it can see irregularities that denote malicious activity. This "behavior-based" manner of detection adds flexibility and removes the need to rely on signatures and signature updates.

Endpoint protection is provided by the Cisco Security Agent through the deployment of four interceptors, as described in Table 7-9.

Table 7-9 *Cisco Security Agent Interceptors*

Interceptor	Description
File System Interceptor	Responsible for intercepting all file read or write requests and either allowing or denying them based on the security policy.
Network Interceptor	Responsible for controlling Network Driver Interface Specification (NDIS) changes and for clearing network connections through the security policy. This also limits how many network connections are allowed within a specified time period to help prevent DoS attacks. Central to its role is providing hardening features such as SYN flood protection and port scan detection.
Configuration Interceptor	Responsible for intercepting read/write requests to the registry in Windows or to rc files on UNIX. Interception occurs because modifying the operating system configuration can have serious consequences. All read/write requests to the registry are tightly controlled for security by the Cisco Security Agent.
Execution Space Interceptor	It is the responsibility of this interceptor to deal with maintaining the integrity of the dynamic runtime environment of each application. It does this by detecting and blocking requests to write to memory not owned by the requesting application.

In terms of practical application, when this form of attack occurs, the targeted service, such as SMTP, FTP, or TFTP, crashes. More importantly, the attacker's shell code is not launched successfully.

This also blocks attempts by an application to inject code (such as a shared library or dynamic link library [DLL]) into another. Buffer overflows attacks are also detected, helping maintain the integrity of dynamic resources such as the file system and configuration of web services. This also helps preserve the integrity of highly dynamic resources such as memory and network I/O. |

The Cisco Security Agent, by intercepting communication between applications and the underlying system, combines the functionality of a number of traditional security approaches:

- **Distributed firewall**: Through the network interceptor, the CSA performs the functions of a host firewall.

- **HIPS**: The network interceptor and the execution space interceptor combine to provide the alerting capability of a HIPS with the proactive enforcement of a security policy.

■ **Application sandbox**: The file system, configuration, and execution space interceptors act together to provide an application sandbox. Here you can run suspect programs with less than normal access to system resources for security purposes.

■ **Network worm prevention**: Worm protection is provided by the network and execution space interceptors without a need for updates.

■ **File integrity monitor**: The file system and the configuration interceptors work together to act as a file integrity monitor.

The Cisco Security agent is designed with a series of preconfigured policies that implement all these levels of protection without additional configuration. With the Cisco Security Agent, organizations have the flexibility to create or change policies if they like, to tailor them to their specific needs.

Examining Attack Response with the Cisco Security Agent

It seems that each year a number of new software programs and technologies are released. Coming quickly on their heels are malicious attacks that attempt to discover and exploit their vulnerabilities. Although literally thousands of varieties of attacks exist, with new ones constantly being devised, in general almost all of them have the same ultimate goal. With each, the goal is to gain control of the core mechanisms of the system being targeted.

However, significant differences exist between the attack mechanisms used in the different phases of an attack. For instance, the mechanisms used in the probe and penetrate phases are much different from the attack mechanisms used in the persist phase.

With the proliferation of new software and new technologies, attackers are constantly uncovering new vulnerabilities and creating custom exploits to take advantage of them. It is because of this ever-changing nature that the first two phases of an attack are constantly evolving. Effectively combating attacks at the probe and penetrate phases requires an administrator to stay current with malicious IPS signatures and firewall defenses.

Unicode encoding of web strings or overlapping packet fragments are just a couple of the ways that attacks during these early phases may evade detection. A significant amount of interpretation is needed because of the mutability of attacks at the penetrate stage. The false alarms that can be generated at this stage require time-consuming review by a security administrator.

The attack mechanisms generally used in the persist phase and the later phases are much more stable than those employed early on. At these later phases, the malicious activities of an attacker are more limited. Typically, an attack involves making a system call to the kernel to access the system resources. When this occurs, the malicious code may attempt to modify the operating system, modify files, create or alter network connections, or violate the memory space of active processes. These potential attacks on systems resources are much more stable in nature than what we see in earlier phases. Such attacks also use different vectors to access the target systems when compared to attacks launched in earlier phases. In general, local exploits are much more stable and predictable than remote exploits, which are platform-specific because of their use of assembly code.

Because identifying attacks in their early phases is nearly impossible, Cisco Security Agent instead focuses on providing proactive security through controlling access to system resources. Unlike security measures that require almost constant updating of defenses to keep up with the latest attacks, the Cisco Security Agent provides protection that is much more easily managed. The Nimda and Slammer worms caused millions of dollars of damage to enterprises on the first day of their release on the Internet, before updates were readily available. However, the Cisco Security Agent stopped these attacks because it identified their malicious behavior without the need for any updates.

Best Practices for Securing Endpoints

As mentioned earlier, trusted operating systems exist, but they are expensive and can be cumbersome to support. For the most part these are used for military or government purposes, acting as critical servers or workstations. For most modern operating systems, regardless of vendor, the default configuration is still quite untrustworthy. Significant improvements have occurred in the last ten years, but the sophistication of attacks has also greatly improved. As an administrator, you should consider operating system hardening as a mandatory step you must take in sensitive environments. A hardened system can resist an attacker's attempts at exploitation when alternative paths to sensitive data are attempted.

One way to stay current with vulnerabilities that might plague your systems is to visit your vendor's website often. Another way to stay up to date on critical issues is to become familiar with industry organizations that track and categorize vulnerabilities. The SANS Institute is one such organization. Each year it compiles its Top 20 list of vulnerabilities. It breaks them into a variety of areas, such as client-side vulnerabilities, server-side vulnerabilities, application abuse, and the like. It is important to familiarize yourself with these vulnerabilities and to stay current as new vulnerabilities emerge. You may view the SANS Institute's Top 20 list for 2007 at http://www.sans.org/top20.

In addition to performing proper operating system hardening, you should employ network access controls (firewalls) to limit the exposure of hosts to external threats. Only necessary traffic should be allowed to reach internal devices and sensitive machines. A number of security add-ons also should be considered. Tools such as integrity checkers, IPSs, and host firewalls should be put in place for systems that perform important services to help prevent attacks. Additionally, third-party preprocessors may be installed on the host to filter HTTP requests that are received at the web service. Deep packet inspection may also be enabled on routers and ASAs to filter certain request types and protocol-specific parameters before these requests reach the server.

Application Guidelines

When it comes to application design, security should not be an afterthought. It is best to approach application design with a focus on two key ideas. First, be sure to apply the least-privilege principle, limiting access where possible. Second, applications should employ modularization and multiple tiers of application functionality, spread over multiple servers. By following these two steps in your design, you can create a much more secure application.

Even the best single security mechanism cannot stop all threats. That is why it is important to use multiple defenses together to form a multilayered security system to manage host and application risks. Any single security mechanism might be compromised; that is why a multilayered security system does not rely on just one thing. Rather, a multilayered approach employs a number of different security mechanisms to provide a similar protection function while acting as layers so that if one mechanism becomes compromised, another can halt the attack. Although we are discussing this in terms of host and application defense, this principle applies universally to any security system, making it a best practice in any security design.

Apply Application Protection Methods

To conclude our discussion of best practices, it is important that we review four key application protection methods that can help make your environment more secure:

Key Topic

- Using application access controls to enforce least privilege and using secure programming practices are the most significant steps you can take toward application security. The creation of safer, high-level languages, along with the growing awareness of the need for application security among developers, has led to increased security in many current systems. However, most off-the-shelf software used by consumers and businesses is still quite vulnerable to simple attacks that can defeat its security.

- Cryptography is another area of application protection that, when used properly, can provide confidentiality, integrity, and authenticity guarantees for data. These cryptographic methods often are used to protect data when it is no longer under the control of the application. For instance, cryptography might be used to encrypt data on a hard drive so that it can be read only by the application. Another common application of cryptography is to use it to encrypt all data as it flows over the network between the client and the server. This can provide confidentiality in an unsafe network or when communicating using a virtual private network across the Internet.

■   Never trust data from outside sources. This code could be malicious and could harm your application. It is also important to perform rigid input validation to be sure that all information entered into that application meets your expectations. Malformed input from a malicious source could damage your system or crash the application.

■   Unfortunately, you have to assume that some of the users who work with a given application may be malicious. Users may grow disgruntled and use their access to your corporate network to carry out various malicious acts using your own applications and network access. You need to defend against this, as well as against users who might inadvertently do harm. They can do this by introducing threats into your network and applications either through misuse or through lack of knowledge when faced with such things as infected attachments and malicious programs posing as benign freeware.

Exam Preparation Tasks

Review All the Key Topics

Review the most important topics from this chapter, denoted with the Key Topic icon. Table 7-10 lists these key topics and the page where each is found.

Table 7-10 *Key Topics for Chapter 7*

Key Topic Element	Description	Page Number
Table 7-2	Cisco security elements	254
Table 7-3	Basic security services provided to applications by operating systems	255-256
Table 7-4	Techniques for protecting endpoints from operating system vulnerabilities	256-257
List	Various forms of attacks	261
Table 7-5	Anatomy of a worm attack	263-264
List	Key features of the Cisco NAC device	267
Table 7-7	General categories of the Cisco NAC product	267
Figure 7-2	NAC Framework	268
Figure 7-3	NAC Appliance	268
Figure 7-4	Architecture of the Cisco Security Agent	269
Table 7-8	Architectural components of the Cisco Security Agent	269
Figure 7-5	Cisco Security Agent interceptors	270
Table 7-9	Cisco Security Agent interceptors	271
List	Cisco Security Agent functionality	271
List	Key application protection methods	274

Complete the Tables and Lists from Memory

Print a copy of Appendix D, "Memory Tables," (found on the CD) or at least the section for this chapter, and complete the tables and lists from memory. Appendix E, "Memory Tables Answer Key," also on the CD, includes completed tables and lists so that you can check your work.

Definition of Key Terms

Define the following key terms from this chapter, and check your answers in the glossary:

endpoint; Network Admission Control (NAC); host-based intrusion prevention system (HIPS); worm; virus; Trojan horse; denial-of-service attack; elevation of privileges; buffer overflow; heap overflow; authentication, authorization, and accounting (AAA); cryptography

This chapter covers the following topics:

Overview of SAN operations: This section examines the basics of storage-area network (SAN) operation. It looks at the benefits a SAN brings to the enterprise as a whole and explores the underlying technologies that make this an efficient solution for a large number of organizations with growing storage needs. This section also covers how to identify attacks focused on the SAN.

Implementing SAN security techniques: With ever-increasing data storage needs, organizations also have to face the reality of securing this information both on the hard disk and in transit over the network. This section examines a variety of security mechanisms, such as Logical Unit Number (LUN) masking, SAN zoning, and port authentication, to explore what steps may be taken to safeguard data in a SAN environment.

CHAPTER 8

Providing SAN Security

It seems that every year organizations create more and more critical data—data that needs to be stored securely for future reference. Storage-area networks (SAN) offer these organizations a targeted solution to meet this need in a cost-effective manner. With so much crucial data now residing on a SAN, securing this data effectively is a prime concern for these businesses. This chapter explores the fundamentals of SAN operations as well as the steps to take to effectively implement SAN security.

"Do I Know This Already?" Quiz

The "Do I Know This Already?" quiz helps you determine your level of knowledge of this chapter's topics before you begin. Table 8-1 details the major topics discussed in this chapter and their corresponding quiz questions.

Table 8-1 *"Do I Know This Already?" Section-to-Question Mapping*

Foundation Topics Section	Questions
Overview of SAN Operations	1 to 5
Implementing SAN Security Techniques	6 to 10

1. Which of the following is not a reason for an organization to incorporate a SAN in its enterprise infrastructure?

   a. To meet changing business priorities, applications, and revenue growth

   b. To decrease the threat of viruses and worm attacks against data storage devices

   c. To increase the performance of long-distance replication, backup, and recovery

   d. To decrease both capital and operating expenses associated with data storage

2. Which of the following is the basis of all the major SAN transport technologies?

   a. ATA

   b. IDE

   c. EIDE

   d. SCSI

3. Which of the following represent SAN transport technologies? (Choose all that apply.)

   a. Fibre Channel

   b. SCSI

   c. FCIP

   d. iSCSI

   e. RAID

4. Which of the following are classes of SAN attacks? (Choose all that apply.)

   a. Viruses

   b. Snooping

   c. Worms

   d. Spoofing

   e. Denial of service (DoS)

5. Spoofing represents an attack against data _____.

   a. Confidentiality

   b. Availability

   c. Accuracy

   d. Integration

6. A LUN is used by which of the following protocols as a way to differentiate the individual disk drives that comprise a target device?

   a. HBA

   b. iSCSI

   c. SCSI

   d. ATA

7. At what level is LUN masking implemented?

   a. Drive

   b. Disk

   c. Controller

   d. Host Bus Adapter

8. Which of the following statements correctly describes Fibre Channel zoning?

   a. Combining a Fibre Channel fabric into larger subsets

   b. Partitioning a Fibre Channel fabric into smaller subsets

   c. Segmenting a Fibre Channel fabric through the use of a LUN mask into smaller subsets

   d. Combining the Fibre Channel fabric, through the use of LUN masks, into larger sections

9. Which of the following is perceived as a drawback of implementing Fibre Channel Authentication Protocol (FCAP)?

   a. It requires the use of netBT as the network protocol.

   b. It is restricted in size to only three segments.

   c. It relies on an underlying Public Key Infrastructure (PKI).

   d. It requires the implementation of IKE.

10. Which of the following are the two primary port authentication protocols used with VSANs? (Choose two.)

   a. SPAP

   b. CHAP

   c. DHCHAP

   d. ESP

   e. MSCHAP v2

Foundation Topics

Overview of SAN Operations

Organizations are producing ever-increasing amounts of data. A storage-area network (SAN) is an effective means to allow them to store and access this data in a secure fashion. This section examines the fundamentals of SAN operation and describes the technology behind these focused networks. It also examines attacks focused on SANs and discusses their defense.

Fundamentals of SANs

With ever-increasing storage needs, many organizations are moving away from traditional file servers to more sophisticated SAN solutions that are made up of a specialized network that enables fast, reliable access among servers and external storage resources. No longer is the storage device the exclusive property of a given server; instead, in a SAN solution, storage devices are shared among all networked servers as peer resources. In much the same way that a LAN is used to connect clients to servers, a SAN may be used to connect servers to storage, servers to each other, and storage to storage. Figure 8-1 shows a SAN in a basic network topology.

Figure 8-1 *Storage-Area Network (SAN)*

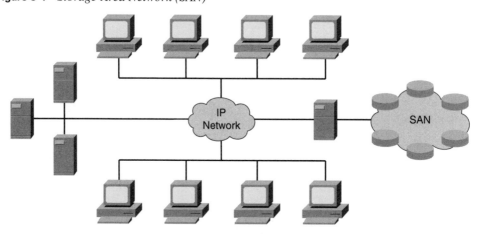

A SAN doesn't need to be a physically separate network. The SAN can be implemented on a dedicated subnet built to carry only business-critical I/O traffic between servers and storage devices. The subnet where the SAN resides would not be burdened with general-purpose traffic such as e-mail or database access. Instead, it would be limited to I/O traffic, such as reading a file from a disk or writing a file to a disk.

Traditional LANs with file servers suffer performance hits as they share the network with general network traffic. Taking the approach described here allows you to increase efficiency and drive down access time for clients. These areas are compromised when you use a single network for all applications.

Organizational Benefits of SAN Usage

Whenever a network or server is unavailable, companies suffer a loss both in terms of productivity and potentially in revenue. This makes it critical that data storage be highly available. At the same time, the amount of data that needs to be managed and stored is increasing significantly each year.

Compared to traditional file server solutions, SANs offer an effective means to deal with this ever-increasing amount of data, while helping ensure its ongoing availability. An added benefit of implementing a SAN is that you can offload storage-related data traffic from your daily network operations. By establishing a direct connection between your storage media and servers, you see an increase in performance as well.

For many organizations, incorporating SANs in their enterprise infrastructure allows them to meet three primary business requirements:

- Effectively meet changing business priorities, application requirements, and revenue growth

- Increase performance of long-distance replication, backup, and recovery to meet regulatory requirements as well as industry best practices

- Decrease both capital and operating expenses associated with data storage

Cisco offers an enterprise-wide approach to deploying scalable, highly available, and more easily administered SANs to meet these requirements for the enterprise. Figure 8-2 shows SAN usage in the enterprise.

Figure 8-2 *SAN in the Enterprise*

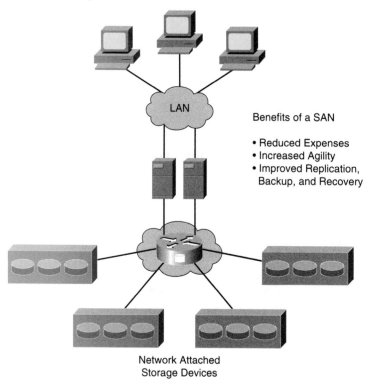

Benefits of a SAN

• Reduced Expenses
• Increased Agility
• Improved Replication,
  Backup, and Recovery

Network Attached
Storage Devices

Cisco offers solutions for intelligent SANs that are designed to be an integral part of an enterprise data center architecture. This provides a better way to access, manage, and protect growing information resources. The Cisco SAN solution provides access across a consolidated Fibre Channel, Fibre Channel over IP (FCIP), Internet Small Computer Systems Interface (iSCSI), Gigabit Ethernet, or optical network for improved performance and access.

Understanding SAN Basics

The Small Computer Systems Interface (SCSI) communications model serves as the basis for all the major SAN transport technologies. In fact, many might say that a SAN can best be described as the merging of SCSI and networking. This combination makes for the fast, reliable data access and storage that today's enterprise networks need. Table 8-2 describes the three major SAN transport technologies.

Table 8-2   *SAN Transport Technologies*

SAN Transport Technology	Description
Fibre Channel	Represents the primary SAN transport used for host-to-SAN connectivity.
iSCSI	A host-to-SAN connectivity model generally employed in the LAN to map SCSI over TCP/IP.
FCIP	Represents a SAN-to-SAN connectivity model frequently used in WAN or metropolitan-area network (MAN) implementations.

Fundamentals of SAN Security

With more and more critical data created each business day, and that data now residing on a SAN, security is a top concern. Securing your SAN solution calls on the processes and solution features that protect the integrity and availability of data stored on storage networks. Providing a comprehensive SAN security solution involves four key aspects:

■ Centralized authentication, authorization, and logging of all changes via secure roles-based management

■ Centralized authentication of devices connected to the network, ensuring that only authorized devices may be connected

■ Secure transmission and receipt of data through traffic isolation and access controls, which ensure protection from activities of other devices in the network

■ Full encryption of all data leaving the storage network for business continuance, remote vaulting, and backup. Figure 8-3 shows aspects of SAN security.

Figure 8-3   *Securing the SAN*

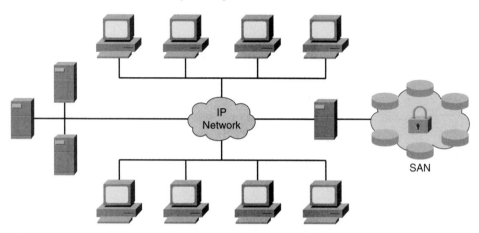

Securing a Storage Area Network

SAN

- Roles-based management with centralized authentication, authorization, and logging.
- Centralized authentication of devices connected to the network.
- Traffic isolation and access controls.
- Encryption of all data leaving the storage network for business continuance, remote vaulting, and backup.

The Cisco MDS 9000 family of products is designed to allow storage professionals to achieve optimal security for their SANs. The security features of this product line make it well suited for data-critical environments that require the highest levels of security, such as government, banking, and patient records in healthcare environments.

The MDS 9000 SAN-OS from Cisco provides a comprehensive approach to network security. In addition to providing services such as virtual storage-area networks (VSAN), aimed at providing true isolation of SAN-attached devices, Cisco's SAN-OS offers a myriad of additional security features to provide secure local and remote SAN deployments. These features include such things as switch and host authentication using Fibre Channel Security Protocol (FC-SP), IP security for FCIP and iSCSI, role-based access control, port security and fabric binding, and zoning.

Classes of SAN Attacks

As with other areas of your LAN, your SAN is not immune to attacks. There are several types of attacks against SANs. In general, they all fall into one of three classes of attack, as shown in Table 8-3.

Table 8-3   *Classes of SAN Attacks*

Class of SAN Attack	Description
Snooping	Attacks against the confidentiality of data
Spoofing	Attacks against the confidentiality and possibly also integrity of data
Denial of service (DoS)	Attacks against the availability of data

Implementing SAN Security Techniques

With the ever-increasing importance of data storage in enterprise environments, we must also be concerned about securing this data—as it resides on the disk and when it is in transit on the network. This section explores a number of technologies you can use to secure your SAN environment to better protect your valuable data.

Using LUN Masking to Defend Against Attacks

A Logical Unit Number (LUN) is an address for an individual disk drive and, by extension, the disk device itself. The SCSI protocol uses the term LUN as a way to differentiate the individual disk drives that comprise a common SCSI target device, such as a SCSI disk array.

To defend against attacks, LUN masking may be employed. In this authorization process, a LUN is made available to some hosts and unavailable to other hosts. Generally, this technique of LUN masking is implemented at the host bus adapter (HBA) level. Unfortunately, when LUN masking is implemented at this level, it is vulnerable to any attack that compromises the HBA.

Benefits, with regard to security, are limited with the implementation of LUN masking. This is because with many HBAs it is possible for an attacker to forge source addresses. For this reason, LUN masking is implemented mainly as a way to protect against malfunctioning servers corrupting disks belonging to other servers.

An example of where LUN masking might be useful is in the case of Windows servers attached to a SAN. In some instances these corrupt non-Windows volumes by attempting to write Windows volume labels to them. In these cases, hiding the LUNs of the non-Windows volumes from the Windows server can prevent this behavior. With the LUNs masked, the Windows server is unaware of the non-Windows volumes and thereby makes no attempt to write Windows volume labels to them. In today's implementations, typically LUNs are not individual disk drives but rather virtual partitions (or volumes) within a RAID array.

Examining SAN Zoning Strategies

It is not uncommon for a SAN to contain a number of different storage devices. In these instances, for security purposes, one device should not necessarily be allowed to interact with all other devices in the SAN. To prevent this behavior, Fibre Channel zoning may be employed. Fibre Channel zoning is the partitioning of a Fibre Channel fabric into smaller subsets. Figure 8-4 shows an example of Fibre Channel zoning.

Figure 8-4   *Fibre Channel Fabric Zoning*

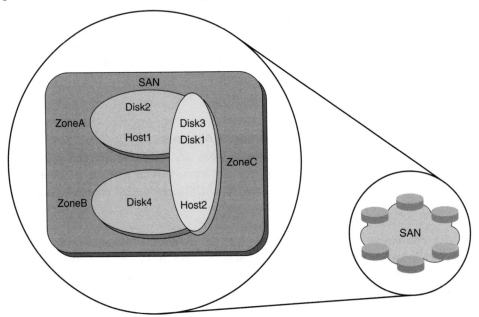

Examining Soft and Hard Zoning

Although both zoning and LUN masking have the same objectives, zoning is implemented on fabric switches, and LUN masking is performed on endpoint devices. Because zoning is implemented at the switch level, rather than on the individual endpoints, when compared with LUN masking, zoning may also be a more secure measure. The Cisco MDS 9100 series fabric switch, shown in Figure 8-5, represents a cost-effective, intelligent SAN solution that allows for the implementation of zoning.

Figure 8-5 *Cisco MDS 9100 Series Fabric Switch*

Cisco MDS 9124

The two main zoning methods are hard zoning and soft zoning. With soft zoning, you restrict only the fabric name services. In other words, soft zoning shows a device only an allowed subset of devices. So, with soft zoning in place, when a server looks at the fabric's content, it sees only the devices it is allowed to see. However, this does not prevent the fact that any server can attempt to contact other devices based on their addresses.

Compared to soft zoning, hard zoning truly restricts communication across a fabric by using access control lists (ACL) that are applied by the switch port ASIC to every Fibre Channel frame that is switched. This approach is more secure than soft zoning and is more commonly used. Whether you choose to apply hard or soft zoning, be aware that these security measures apply only to the switched fabric topology.

Understanding World Wide Names

Fibre Channel networks use 64-bit addresses known as World Wide Names (WWN) to uniquely identify each element in a Fibre Channel network. These WWNs may be used in zoning to assign security permissions.

Figure 8-6 shows a Cisco MDS 9100 series switch with a sample WWN assigned.

Figure 8-6 *World Wide Name*

Key
Topic

16:8A:EE:31:9D:54:8C:FF
WWN

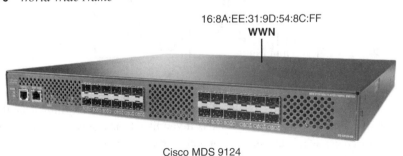

Cisco MDS 9124

Name servers in the switches may also be used to either allow or block access to particular WWNs in the fabric. However, using WWNs for security purposes is inadvisable. WWNs are inherently insecure because a device's WWN is a user-configurable parameter. Using WWNs for zoning is susceptible to unauthorized access, because the zone can be bypassed through an attacker spoofing the WWN of an authorized HBA.

Defining Virtual SANs

In addition to traditional SANs, you may create a virtual storage-area network (VSAN). VSANs were originally invented by Cisco, but they are now an ANSI standard. Figure 8-7 shows the construction of a VSAN.

Figure 8-7 *Constructing VSANs*

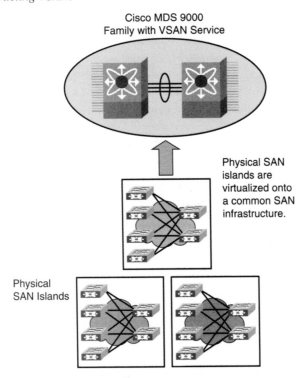

A VSAN is created from a collection of ports that are part of a set of connected Fibre Channel switches. These ports together form a virtual fabric. Ports within a single switch can be partitioned to form multiple VSANs if you like. Conversely, you can use multiple switches together and join any number of their ports to form a single VSAN. If this sounds familiar, VSANs when put together in this manner strongly resemble VLANs. Like

VLANs, all traffic is tagged as it crosses interswitch links with the VSAN ID. Another commonality with VLANs is that through the construction of VSANs we can add a layer of security at the port level.

Combining VSANs and Zones

Combining VSANs and zones is an effective means of providing security control for your VSAN. To combine these complementary protocols, you first must associate the physical ports with a VSAN. This step is quite similar to associating switch ports with VLANs. Next you need to logically divide the VSANs into zones. With these actions complete, you can effectively provide a security control for your VSAN. Figure 8-8 shows how VSANs work with zones.

Figure 8-8 *Relating VSANs to Zones*

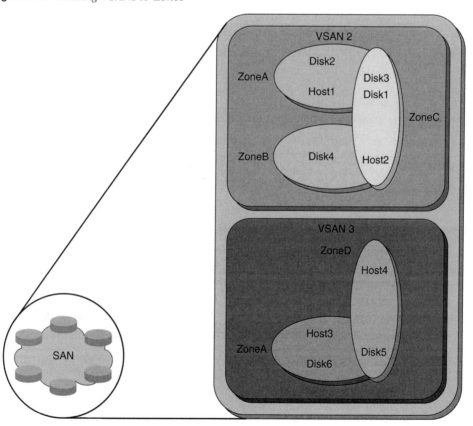

Identifying Port Authentication Protocols

You need to be aware of two primary port authentication protocols when working with VSANs:

- Diffie-Hellman Challenge Handshake Authentication Protocol (DHCHAP)

- Challenge Handshake Authentication Protocol (CHAP)

Understanding DHCHAP

DHCHAP may be used to authenticate devices connecting to a Fibre Channel switch. By using Fibre Channel authentication, you allow only trusted devices to be added to a fabric. This prevents unauthorized devices from accessing the Fibre Channel switch.

DHCHAP supports both switch-to-switch and host-to-switch authentication. It's a mandatory password-based, key-exchange authentication protocol. Before any authentication may be performed, DHCHAP negotiates hash algorithms and Diffie-Hellman (DH) groups. In addition, it supports Message Digest 5 (MD5) and Secure Hash Algorithm 1 (SHA-1)-based authentication.

CHAP in Securing SAN Devices

CHAP is the mandatory protocol for iSCCI, as chosen by the Internet Engineering Task Force (IETF). CHAP has been around for quite some time and is based on shared secrets. To strengthen CHAP, DHCHAP adds a DH exchange that both strengthens CHAP and provides an agreed-upon secret key. The goal of DHCHAP is to be a simple, easy-to-implement protocol.

Working with Fibre Channel Authentication Protocol

If your organization needs a stronger means of securing the SAN than the password-based mechanism used in CHAP, Fibre Channel Authentication Protocol (FCAP) is available. FCAP, shown in Figure 8-9, was born from Switch Link Authentication Protocol (SLAP), the first authentication protocol proposed for Fibre Channel. With changes over time, this protocol was generalized and renamed FCAP. This optional authentication mechanism may be employed between any two devices or entities on a Fibre Channel network. It uses certificates or optional keys to provide a stronger level of security.

Figure 8-9 *Fibre Channel Authentication Protocol*

Application of Fibre Channel Authentication Protocol

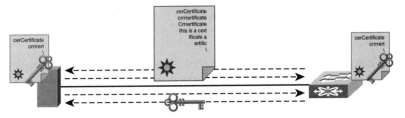

- FCAP is an optional authentication mechanism.
- Works with certificates or optional keys.

FCAP relies on an underlying public key infrastructure (PKI) to provide enterprise-class security. By using PKI, often present in more security-conscious organizations, as a foundational element, along with a certificate-based protocol, FCAP provides numerous advantages. Central among these are strong authentication and management data integrity. For some organizations, the complexities associated with a PKI can be daunting. This is the only significant argument against FCAP.

Understanding Fibre Channel Password Authentication Protocol

Fibre Channel Password Authentication Protocol (FCPAP) is an optional password-based authentication key-exchange protocol. It may be used in Fibre Channel networks to provide mutual authentication between Fibre Channel ports. FCPAP, which is based on passwords, was proposed as an alternative to FCAP. It has its roots in another protocol called Secure Remote Password (SRP).

As compared to FCAP, FCPAP does not require a PKI to operate. This was one of the main drivers behind its proposal. Although FCPAP does not require PKI, complexities are still associated with managing the passwords and other aspects of FCPAP.

Assuring Data Confidentiality in SANs

SANs provide an effective way for organizations to meet the ever-expanding need to store data. Because organizations store everything from social security records to client records to proprietary information on SANs, it is extremely important that this storage medium be secure and that the data be secure while in transit. This section examines the benefits of incorporating Encapsulating Security Payload (ESP) in your SAN solution. As an Internet standard, ESP can provide both encryption and authentication to further secure an organization's crucial data. We will also discuss the use of Fibre Channel Security Protocol (FC-SP) to provide both host-to-switch and switch-to-switch authentication to further secure enterprise-wide fabrics.

Incorporating Encapsulating Security Payload (ESP)

SANs are designed to provide fast access and expandable storage for your data needs. However, that access must also be secure. ESP represents a means of providing this security. ESP is an Internet standard that allows IP packets to be authenticated and encrypted.

ESP is a common security standard in many IP networks, but it also has been adapted for use in Fibre Channel networks. In fact, the IETF iSCSI proposal specifies ESP link authentication and optional encryption. ESP over Fibre Channel provides a means of protecting data in transit throughout the Fibre Channel network. Although ESP over Fibre Channel is an effective means to secure data while it is in transit, it does not address the need to secure data while it is stored on the Fibre Channel network.

Providing Security with Fibre Channel Security Protocol

FC-SP is designed to overcome the security challenges for enterprise-wide fabrics by providing switch-to-switch and host-to-switch authentication. FC-SP is a project of Technical Committee T11 of the International Committee for Information Technology Standards (INCITS). It focuses on protecting data in transit throughout the Fibre Channel network. Much like ESP, FC-SP does not address the security of data stored on the Fibre Channel network.

FC-SP is a security framework that includes a number of protocols to enhance Fibre Channel security in several areas. For instance, FC-SP addresses the authentication of Fibre Channel devices. It also provides cryptographically secure key exchange and cryptographically secure communication between Fibre Channel devices.

Exam Preparation Tasks

Review All the Key Topics

Review the most important topics from this chapter, denoted with the Key Topic icon. Table 8-4 lists these key topics and the page where each is found.

Table 8-4 *Key Topics for Chapter 8*

Key Topic Element	Description	Page Number
List	Business requirements met by a SAN	283
Table 8-2	SAN transport technologies	285
List	Key aspects of a comprehensive SAN security solution	285
Table 8-3	Classes of SAN attacks	287
Figure 8-4	Fibre Channel fabric zoning	288
Figure 8-6	World Wide Names (WWN)	289
Figure 8-7	Constructing virtual SANs (VSAN)	290
Figure 8-8	Relating VSANs to zones	291
List	Primary port authentication protocols used with VSANs	292
Figure 8-9	Fibre Channel Authentication Protocol (FCAP)	293

Complete the Tables and Lists from Memory

Print a copy of Appendix D, Memory Tables," (found on the CD) or at least the section for this chapter, and complete the tables and lists from memory. Appendix E, "Memory Tables Answer Key," also on the CD, includes completed tables and lists so that you can check your work.

Definition of Key Terms

Define the following key terms from this chapter, and check your answers in the glossary:

storage-area network (SAN), Fibre Channel, Small Computer Systems Interface (SCSI), Fibre Channel over IP (FCIP), snooping, spoofing, denial of service (DoS), LUN masking, Host Bus Adapter (HBA), Fibre Channel zoning, World Wide Name (WWN), virtual SAN (VSAN), Diffie-Hellman Challenge Handshake Authentication Protocol (DHCHAP), Challenge Handshake Authentication Protocol (CHAP), Fibre Channel Authentication Protocol (FCAP), Fibre Channel Password Authentication Protocol (FCPAP), Encapsulating Security Payload (ESP), Fibre Channel Security Protocol (FC-SP)

This chapter covers the following topics:

Defining voice fundamentals: This section introduces voice over IP (VoIP) networks. You learn what business benefits VoIP offers, as well as the components and protocols that support the transmission of packetized voice across a data network.

Identifying common voice vulnerabilities: This section makes you aware of specific threats targeting a VoIP network. Although some threats (such as toll fraud) are found in traditional telephony networks, other threats are specific to VoIP.

Securing a VoIP network: This section identifies specific actions you can take to increase the security of VoIP networks. For example, you will consider how to use firewalls and VPNs to protect voice networks and how to harden the security of Cisco IP Phones and voice servers.

CHAPTER 9

Exploring Secure Voice Solutions

In the past, large companies used privately owned telephone systems (such as private branch exchanges [PBX]) to provide voice services to their employees. As data networks began to emerge, most companies maintained separate voice and data networks, and perhaps even a separate video network.

However, with the performance and reliability offered by modern data networks, many network administrators began to see the wisdom of consolidating voice, data, and video traffic on the same network. This *converged network* approach offers cost benefits, such as toll bypass, achieved by sending voice calls across a WAN link, and reduced recurring expenses for separate voice, data, and video connections between offices. Also, sending voice traffic over an IP network, known as voice over IP (VoIP), adds multiple features to traditional voice networks.

For example, VoIP networks might offer a converged messaging solution to provide a single repository for voice mail, e-mail, and fax messages. Also, a *presence* feature can allow a caller to see the status of a destination number (for example, idle or in a call) before he or she calls that number.

The addition of voice devices to a network, however, introduces potential security threats. Therefore, after reviewing VoIP technology, this chapter examines various attacks that could be launched against a VoIP network and recommends steps for securing a VoIP network.

"Do I Know This Already?" Quiz

The "Do I Know This Already?" quiz helps you determine your level of knowledge of this chapter's topics before you begin. Table 9-1 details the major topics discussed in this chapter and their corresponding quiz questions.

Table 9-1   *"Do I Know This Already?" Section-to-Question Mapping*

Foundation Topics Section	Questions
Defining Voice Fundamentals	1 to 4
Identifying Common Voice Vulnerabilities	5 to 8
Securing a VoIP Network	9 to 11

1. You administer a network that contains analog telephony devices connected to voice gateways. These voice gateways connect to the Public Switched Telephone Network (PSTN). Which of the following best describes this type of network?

   a. VoIP

   b. IP telephony

   c. Converged communications

   d. Unified communications

2. Which of the following are justifications for migrating from a traditional telephony network to a VoIP network? (Choose all that apply.)

   a. Reduced recurring expenses

   b. Reduced end-to-end delay

   c. Advanced functionality

   d. Adaptability

3. Which of the following VoIP components can permit or deny a call attempt based on a network's available bandwidth?

   a. Gateway

   b. Gatekeeper

   c. MCU

   d. Application server

4. Which two protocols can be used to carry voice media packets? (Choose two.)

   a. RTCP

   b. RTP

   c. SRTP

   d. SIP

   e. SRTCP

5. Which of the following attacks against a VoIP network attempts to deplete the resources available on a server (for example, processing resources)?

   a. Accessing VoIP resources without appropriate credentials

   b. Gleaning information from unsecured VoIP network resources

   c. Launching a denial-of-service (DoS) attack

   d. Capturing telephone conversations

6. VoIP spam is also known by which of the following acronyms?

   a. CAPF

   b. cRTP

   c. GARP

   d. SPIT

7. Which of the following best describes vishing?

   a. Influencing users to provide personal information over a web page

   b. Influencing users to provide personal information over the phone

   c. Influencing users to forward a call to a toll number (for example, a long distance or international number)

   d. Using an inside facilitator to intentionally forward a call to a toll number (for example, a long distance or international number)

8. Which of the following Cisco Catalyst switch mechanisms can be used to prevent a man-in-the-middle attack launched against a SIP network?

   a. RSTP

   b. DAI

   c. PAgP

   d. DTP

9. A Cisco IP phone can send traffic from an attached PC in a data VLAN while sending voice packets in a separate VLAN. What is the name given to this separate voice VLAN?

   a. PVID

   b. Auxiliary VLAN

   c. Native VLAN

   d. Access VLAN

10. What type of firewall is required to open appropriate UDP ports required for RTP streams?

    a.   Stateless firewall

    b.   Proxy firewall

    c.   Stateful firewall

    d.   Packet filtering firewall

11. Which two of the following statements are true about a Cisco IP phone's web access feature? (Choose two.)

    a.   It is enabled by default.

    b.   It requires login credentials, based on the UCM user database.

    c.   It can provide IP address information about other servers in the network.

    d.   It uses HTTPS.

Foundation Topics

Defining Voice Fundamentals

This section begins by defining voice over IP and considering why it is needed in today's corporate environment. Because voice packets are flowing across a data infrastructure, various protocols are required to set up, maintain, and tear down a call. This section defines several popular voice protocols, in addition to hardware components that make up a voice over IP network.

Defining VoIP

VoIP sends packetized voice over an IP network. Typically, the IP network serves as a data network as well, resulting in potential quality and security issues. Fortunately, Cisco offers a collection of quality of service (QoS) and security features to ensure the quality and security of voice transmissions.

The ability to transmit voice over an IP network (for example, the Internet) allows many corporate networks to readily interconnect their sites without purchasing dedicated leased lines between their sites or relying on the public switched telephone network (PSTN), which imposes charges for certain call types (for example, long distance and international calls).

With the advent of VoIP technology, some confusion has arisen around its associated nomenclature. For example, consider the terms *VoIP* and *IP telephony*. Both refer to sending voice across an IP network. However, the primary distinction revolves around the endpoints in use. For example, in a VoIP network, traditional analog or digital circuits connect into an IP network, typically through some sort of *gateway*. However, an IP telephony environment contains endpoints that natively communicate using IP.

To further illustrate the distinction between VoIP and IP telephony, consider Figure 9-1. In the top portion of the figure, the endpoints in the VoIP network are an analog phone (connected to an analog port on a gateway) and a private branch exchange (PBX) (connected to a digital port on a different gateway). Because neither of these endpoints natively speaks IP, the topology is considered a VoIP network. The bottom portion of Figure 9-1 shows a Cisco IP phone, which does natively communicate using IP. The Cisco IP phone registers with a Cisco Unified Communications Manager server, which makes call routing decisions on behalf of the Cisco IP phone. Therefore, the bottom topology in the figure is considered an IP telephony network. Realize, however, that some literature might use the terms VoIP and IP telephony interchangeably.

Figure 9-1 *VoIP Versus IP Telephony*

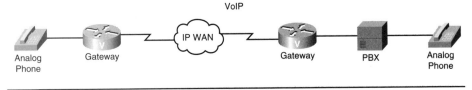

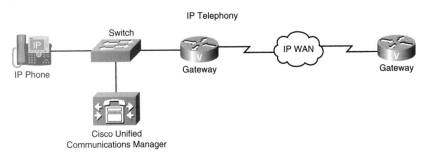

The Need for VoIP

Originally, one of the primary business drivers for the adoption of VoIP was saving money on long distance calls. However, increased competition in the industry drove down the cost of long distance calls to the point that cost savings alone was insufficient motivation for migrating a PBX-centric telephony solution to a VoIP network. However, several other justifications exist for purchasing VoIP technology:

- **Reduced recurring expenses**: In many traditional PBX-centric networks, a digital T1 circuit typically could carry either 23 or 24 simultaneous voice calls (based on the type of signaling being used). Specifically, a T1 usually had 23 or 24 *channels* available. Each channel had a bandwidth of 64 kbps and could handle one, and only one, phone call. However, VoIP networks often leverage *coder/decoders* (codecs) to compress voice. Each voice call consumes less than 64 kbps of bandwidth per call, thereby allowing additional simultaneous calls, as compared to traditional technology.

- **Adaptability**: Because VoIP networks send voice traffic over an IP network, administrators have a high level of control over the voice traffic. Different customers could be granted access to different voice applications (for example, a messaging application or an interactive voice response [IVR] application).

- **Advanced functionality**: VoIP and IP telephony networks can also offer advanced features, such as the following:

— **Call routing**: Existing routing protocols (for example, EIGRP and OSPF) could be used to provide rapid failover to a backup link if a primary network link failed. Additionally, calls could be routed over different network links based on link quality or the link's current traffic load.

— **Messaging**: A solution such as Cisco Unity could be used to provide a single repository for a variety of messaging types. For example, a Microsoft Exchange message store could be used to consolidate the storage of fax transmissions, e-mail messages, and voice mail. Then a user could, for example, call into a Cisco Unity system and have her e-mail read to her via text-to-speech conversion.

— **Call center solutions**: Cisco offers a variety of solutions for call centers. For example, Cisco's Contact Center and Contact Center Express solutions can intelligently route incoming calls to appropriate call center agents. Also, because the call center would be using Cisco IP Phones, the phones can be geographically separated (for example, call center agents working from home).

— **Security**: If an attacker were to intercept and capture VoIP packets, he could potentially play them back to eavesdrop on a conversation. As another example, a user might enter her personal identification number (PIN) into a bank's IVR system, and the attacker might capture those packets. Attackers might also introduce rogue devices (for example, IP phones or call agent servers) into the network. Fortunately, Cisco offers a variety of technologies and best practices for hardening the security of a VoIP network.

— **Customer-facing solutions**: Some customers might prefer to interact via a chat interface or e-mail, as opposed to talking with a company's customer service representative. Because a VoIP network works over a data network, data network features such as chat and e-mail can be integrated into a customer's selection of contact options, thereby increasing the customer's level of satisfaction.

VoIP Network Components

Figure 9-2 illustrates components commonly found in a VoIP network. They are described in Table 9-2.

Figure 9-2   *VoIP Network Components*

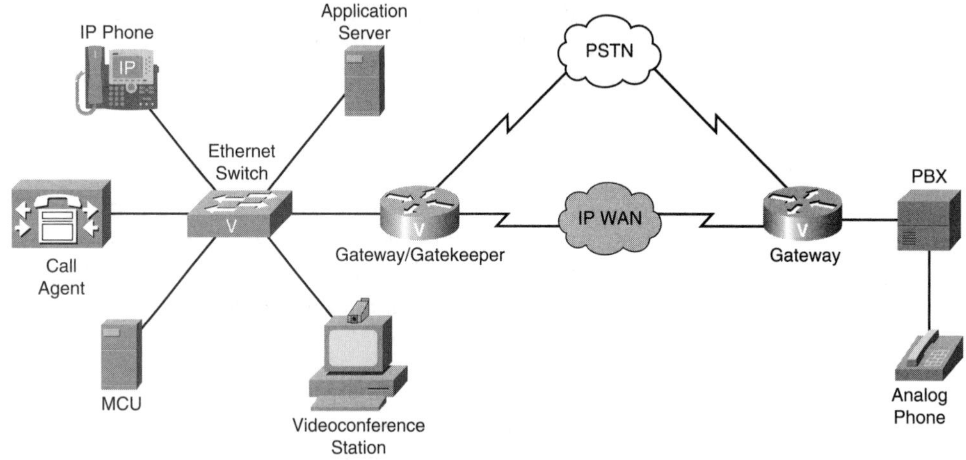

IP Phone

Application Server

PSTN

Ethernet Switch

PBX

Call Agent

Gateway/Gatekeeper

IP WAN

Gateway

MCU

Videoconference Station

Analog Phone

Table 9-2   *VoIP Components*

Component	Description
IP phone	IP phones use an Ethernet network connection to send and receive voice calls. Figure 9-3 shows an example of a Cisco IP Phone, the Cisco 7970G.
Call agent	Call agents replace many of the features previously provided by PBXs. For example, a call agent can be configured with rules that determine how calls are routed. Cisco Unified Communications Manager (UCM) is an example of a call agent.
Gateway	Gateways can forward calls between different types of networks. For example, you could place a call from an IP phone in your office, through a gateway, and to the PSTN to call your home.
Gatekeeper	Gatekeepers can be thought of as the traffic cops of the WAN. For example, because bandwidth on a WAN typically is somewhat limited, a gatekeeper can monitor the available bandwidth. Then, when there is not enough bandwidth to support another voice call, the gatekeeper can deny future call attempts.
Multipoint Control Unit (MCU)	MCUs are useful for conference calling. In a conference call, you might have multiple people talking at the same time, and everyone on that conference call can hear them. It takes processing power to mix together these audio streams. MCUs provide that processing power. MCUs might contain digital signal processors (DSP), which are dedicated pieces of computer circuitry that can mix together those audio streams.
Application server	Application servers offer additional services, such as voice mail, to a VoIP environment.

Table 9-2 *VoIP Components (Continued)*

Key Topic

Component	Description
Videoconference station	Videoconference stations are devices and/or software (such as Cisco Unified Video Advantage) that allow a calling or called party to view and/or transmit video as part of their telephone conversation.
Voice-enabled switch	A voice-enabled Cisco Catalyst switch can provide inline power to an attached Cisco IP Phone, eliminating the need for an external power supply connected to the IP Phone. Also, a voice-enabled switch can recognize voice frames arriving from the attached IP Phone and give those frames higher priority than other frames.

Figure 9-3 *Cisco 7970G IP Phone*

VoIP Protocols

To support communication among Cisco IP Phones, analog telephones, traditional PBXs, and the PSTN (as just a few examples), VoIP networks require a collection of protocols. Some protocols are signaling protocols (for example, H.323, MGCP, H.248, SIP, and SCCP) used to set up, maintain, and tear down a call. Other protocols are targeted at the actual voice packets (for example, RTP, SRTP, and RTCP) rather than signaling information. Table 9-3 describes some of the more common VoIP protocols.

**Key
Topic**

Table 9-3   *VoIP Protocols*

Protocol	Description
H.323	H.323 is an ITU standard. Rather than being a single protocol, it is a suite of protocols. Beyond protocols, the H.323 standard also defines certain devices, such as VoIP gateways and gatekeepers. H.323 is considered a peer-to-peer protocol, because some H.323 devices can make their own call-routing decisions, as opposed to relying on an external database.
MGCP	Originally developed by Cisco, Media Gateway Control Protocol (MGCP) is considered a client/server protocol. The client (for example, an analog port in a voice-enabled router) can communicate with a server (for example, a Cisco Unified Communications server) via a series of events and signals. The server could tell the client that in the *event* of an attached phone going off-hook, play the *signal* of dial tone to that phone.
H.248	Based on MGCP, the H.248 standard is also known as *Megaco*. Specifically, H.248 is a joint IETF and ITU standard. Although H.248 is similar to MGCP, it is more flexible in its support for gateways and applications.
SIP	Session Initiation Protocol (SIP), like H.323, is considered a peer-to-peer protocol. SIP is a very popular protocol to use in mixed-vendor environments, perhaps because of SIP's use of existing protocols, such as HTTP and SMTP.
SCCP	Skinny Client Control Protocol (SCCP), which is often called *skinny protocol*, is a Cisco-proprietary signaling protocol. SCCP is often used for signaling between Cisco IP Phones and Cisco Unified Communications Manager servers. However, some Cisco gateways also support SCCP. SCCP is considered a client/server protocol, like MGCP and H.248.
RTP	Real-time Transport Protocol (RTP) carries the voice payload. Interestingly, although RTP is a Layer 4 protocol, it is encapsulated inside UDP (also a Layer 4 protocol). Although the UDP port numbers used can vary by vendor, in Cisco environments, RTP typically uses even UDP ports in the range 16,384 to 32,767.
RTCP	RTP Control Protocol (RTCP) provides information about an RTP flow (for example, information about the quality of the call). In a Cisco environment, RTCP typically uses odd UDP ports in the range 16,384 to 32,767.
SRTP	Secure RTP (SRTP) secures the transmission of voice via RTP. Specifically, SRTP adds encryption, authentication, integrity, and anti-replay mechanisms to voice traffic.

Identifying Common Voice Vulnerabilities

Because IP phones are readily accessible and plentiful in many corporate environments, they become attractive targets for attackers. Also, VoIP administrators should be on guard against VoIP variations of spam and fishing (both common in e-mail environments), as well as toll fraud (common in PBX environments). This section details these common attack targets for a VoIP network.

Attacks Targeting Endpoints

Table 9-4 describes a few common VoIP attacks targeting endpoints.

Table 9-4 *Common VoIP Attack Targets*

Attack	Description
Accessing VoIP resources without appropriate credentials	Attackers can attempt to maliciously modify VoIP network devices and settings, in addition to intercepting voice streams. For example, an attacker might access or manipulate users in the LDAP directory used by Cisco Unified Communications Manager. This could prevent a user from logging into a Cisco IP Phone (for example, when using the Extension Mobility feature, which allows users to log into a phone and have their profiles applied to that phone). As another example, an attacker might try to gain administrative access to a voice mail system (such as Cisco Unity) and manipulate parameters, such as the voice mail greeting that callers hear.
Gleaning information from unsecured VoIP network resources	Because VoIP networks typically rely on well-known protocols (as described in the preceding section), attackers can leverage their knowledge of these protocols to gather information about VoIP network resources. For example, an attacker could use a known vulnerability in a signaling protocol to disrupt a VoIP network or to gather information about the VoIP infrastructure by monitoring a signaling protocol.
Launching a denial-of-service (DoS) attack	A common attack on a data network is a denial-of-service (DoS) attack, in which an attacker consumes too many resources on a target system, resulting in a failure of that target system. Variations of DoS attacks also exist in a VoIP environment. For example, an attacker could attempt to consume too much bandwidth on a VoIP link, resulting in failed calls or poor-quality calls. Alternatively, an attacker could target a VoIP server (for example, a Cisco Unified Communications Manager server) in an attempt to consume the server's resources (for example, processor and/or memory resources). Also, attackers could exploit known protocol vulnerabilities (for example, a particular packet structure that could cause a specific system to crash).

continues

Table 9-4   *Common VoIP Attack Targets (Continued)*

Attack	Description
Capturing telephone conversations	The concept of *wire tapping* is nothing new to the telephony world. However, in the VoIP world, wire tapping (that is, eavesdropping) can be accomplished by capturing voice packets (that is, RTP packets) and then converting those captured packets into an audio file that the attacker can listen to.

VoIP Spam

Unless your e-mail account is well protected by a spam filter, you probably occasionally receive unsolicited e-mails. Spam can be an annoyance for an e-mail user. VoIP administrators should be aware of VoIP spam, more commonly called *spam over IP telephony* (SPIT). A SPIT attack on your Cisco IP Phone could, for example, make unsolicited messages periodically appear on a phone's LCD screen or make the phone periodically ring, resulting in lost employee productivity. SPIT can also be used for fraud. For example, a SPIT attack could make incorrect caller ID information appear on your phone.

Unfortunately, common methods of mitigating e-mail spam are ineffective against SPIT. For example, a SPIT attack launched against your phone might cause your phone to ring every ten minutes. Although this behavior is certainly annoying and affects your productivity, the frequency of the calls is probably too low to be detected as malicious traffic (for example, by an Intrusion Prevention System [IPS] sensor).

However, modern Cisco IP Phones can be configured for authentication using Transport Layer Security (TLS). This approach allows a Cisco IP Phone to authorize any other device attempting to communicate directly with the phone. As a result, the nonauthenticated devices that source the SPIT would not be allowed to communicate with the Cisco IP Phone.

Vishing and Toll Fraud

The term *phishing* recently entered the technical vernacular. The basic concept of phishing is an attacker sending an e-mail to a user. The e-mail appears to be from a legitimate business. The user is asked to confirm her information by entering data on a web page, such as her social security number, bank or credit card account number, birth date, or mother's maiden name. The attacker can then take this user-provided data and use it for fraudulent purposes.

Similar to phishing, the term *vishing* refers to maliciously collecting such information over the phone. Because many users tend to trust the security of a telephone versus the security of the web, some users are more likely to provide confidential information over the telephone. User education is the most effective method to combat vishing attacks.

Another type of fraud committed against telephony systems is *toll fraud*. The basic concept of toll fraud is an attacker using a telephony system to place calls he should not be allowed to place. For example, a corporate telephony use policy might state that long distance personal calls are not allowed. If an employee ignored that directive and placed a personal long distance call, that would be a simple example of toll fraud.

More advanced forms of toll fraud involve taking advantage of a weakness in the telephony system to place calls. Cisco Unified Communications Manager includes several features that help combat toll fraud. For example, *partitions* and *calling search spaces* can be used to identify which phone numbers can be called from specific Cisco IP Phones. As another example, a *Forced Authorization Code* (FAC) could be used to require a user to enter a code to call a particular destination.

SIP Attack Targets

The previously described Session Initiation Protocol (SIP) is gaining rapid acceptance in mixed-vendor VoIP networks. One of the most attractive characteristics of SIP is its use of existing protocols. Also, by default, SIP messages are sent in plain text.

Unfortunately, the very characteristics that make SIP attractive can also be leveraged by attackers to compromise the security of a SIP network. For example, an attacker could launch a *man-in-the-middle* attack, in which the attacker convinces a router, phone, or SIP server to send SIP and/or RTP packets to the attacker's PC. The attacker could then perform *registration hijacking*, which allows the attacker to intercept incoming calls and determine how those calls are routed.

Also, because SIP messages are transmitted in plain text by default, an attacker could manipulate the SIP messages. For example, the attacker could change the SIP addresses in the messages. This type of attack is known as *message tampering*.

Because SIP networks often rely on SIP servers (for example, SIP registrar, location, proxy, and/or redirect servers), an attacker could also launch a DoS attack against one of those servers. For example, if a DoS attack made a SIP registrar server unusable, new SIP phones would be unable to register with the network.

Cisco offers several solutions for combating such attempts to attack a SIP network. For example, a secure tunnel, such as IPsec, could be used to encrypt SIP messages traveling between routers. In fact, a Cisco Unified Communications Manager server could act as a peer in an IPsec tunnel. Also, a firewall or IPS sensor could be used to detect and mitigate common DoS attacks. Cisco Catalyst switches could be used to help prevent a man-in-the-middle attack (for example, using Dynamic ARP Inspection [DAI]).

Table 9-5 summarizes some of the attacks described in this section.

Table 9-5 *Examples of Attacks Targeting Voice Networks*

Attack	Description
SPIT	Spam over IP telephony (SPIT) involves, for example, sending unsolicited messages to an IP phone's display or causing the IP phone to periodically ring.
Vishing	Vishing is similar to phishing, except that the victim provides her confidential information over the telephone instead of a website.
Toll fraud	Toll fraud occurs when users inappropriately use a telephone system to make toll calls (for example, long distance and/or international calls) that they do not have permission to make.
SIP attacks	SIP attacks attempt to exploit SIP's use of well-known protocols to intercept or manipulate SIP messages. Also, an attacker might launch a DoS attack against a SIP server.

Securing a VoIP Network

Now that you have a foundational understanding of the myriad attacks that can target a VoIP network, this section addresses specific VoIP attack mitigations. Specifically, it covers separating voice traffic from data traffic using voice VLANs, using firewalls and VPNs to protect voice traffic, and approaches to harden the security of voice endpoints and servers.

Protecting a VoIP Network with Auxiliary VLANs

A fundamental approach to protecting voice traffic from attackers is to place it in a VLAN separated from data traffic. This voice VLAN is often called an *auxiliary VLAN*. VLAN separation alone protects voice traffic from a variety of Layer 2 attacks. For example, an attacker would be unable to launch a *man-in-the-middle attack* against an IP Phone, where the attacker's MAC address claimed to be the MAC address of the IP Phone's next-hop gateway. Such an attack would be mitigated, because the attacker's PC would be connected to a data VLAN while the IP Phone was connected to the auxiliary VLAN.

Many models of Cisco IP Phones include an extra Ethernet port to which a PC can attach. The attached PC communicates through the Cisco IP Phone into a Cisco Catalyst switch at the access layer. Fortunately, the PC and the Cisco IP Phone can transmit traffic in separate VLANs (that is, a data VLAN for the PC's traffic and an auxiliary VLAN for the phone's voice traffic) while still connecting to a single Cisco Catalyst switch port.

In Figure 9-4, notice that the PC communicates on VLAN 110, while the Cisco IP Phone sends voice traffic on VLAN 210. Traffic from both VLANs enters Switch1 on port Gigabit 0/1. A single Cisco Catalyst switch port accommodating traffic from two VLANs might seem like a trunk port. Interestingly, Cisco makes an exception on many Cisco Catalyst switch models, allowing the port that accepts traffic from the data VLAN and the auxiliary VLAN to be an access port.

Figure 9-4 *Auxiliary VLAN*

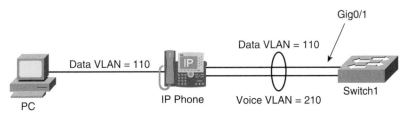

Protecting a VoIP Network with Security Appliances

Security appliances such as firewalls and VPN termination devices also can be used to protect voice networks. However, one challenge of protecting voice networks with a firewall is that the administrator is unsure what UDP ports will be used to transmit the RTP voice packets. For example, in a Cisco environment, a UDP port for an RTP stream typically is an even-numbered port selected from the range of 16,384 to 32,767. Opening this entire range of potential ports could open unnecessary security holes.

Fortunately, Cisco firewalls (that is, the PIX and Adaptive Security Appliance [ASA] firewalls) can dynamically *inspect* call setup protocol traffic (for example, H.323 traffic) to learn the UDP ports to be used for RTP flows. The firewall then temporarily opens those UDP ports for the duration of the RTP connection.

To understand this concept, consider Figure 9-5. In the first step, the Cisco IP Phone uses SCCP to initiate a call to the PSTN. SCCP, which uses TCP port 2000, is used to communicate between the Cisco IP Phone and the UCM server. UCM determines, based on the dialed digits, that the call needs to be sent out the H.323 gateway. In the second step, using TCP port 1720, UCM initiates a call setup with the H.323 gateway. The firewall between these devices is configured to permit the H.323 protocol. The firewall is also instructed to inspect H.323 traffic, to dynamically determine which UDP ports are selected for the voice path. In the third step, UDP ports 20,548 and 28,642 were randomly selected. Because an RTP flow is unidirectional, two UDP ports are selected to support bidirectional communication. Because the firewall inspected H.323 and dynamically learned the UDP ports to be used, the firewall permits the bidirectional RTP flow for the duration of the conversation.

Figure 9-5 *RTP Inspection*

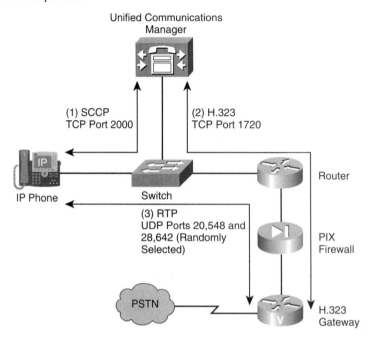

Aside from permitting or denying specific ports, a firewall can also provide additional protection to a voice network. For example, a firewall can be configured to enforce specific policies, which might block specific phones. As another example, a firewall can determine if too many messages (as configured with a threshold value) of a certain type (for example, SIP requests) occur within a certain period of time.

Although many Cisco IP Phones can encrypt and authenticate traffic within the phone itself, many other IP telephony and VoIP devices lack this capability. To add encryption and authentication support for these devices, consider sending their voice packets over an IPsec-protected VPN tunnel. A variety of devices could be used for VPN termination, including Cisco Unified Communications Manager (version 5.0 and later). Figure 9-6 shows an IPsec tunnel encrypting traffic between a Cisco Unified Communications Manager server and an H.323 gateway.

Figure 9-6 *Protecting Voice with an IPSec Tunnel*

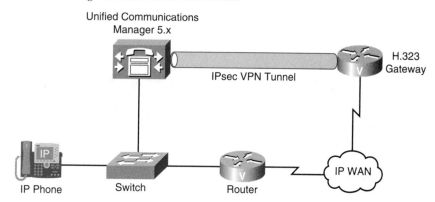

Hardening Voice Endpoints and Application Servers

Endpoints, such as Cisco IP Phones, tend to be less protected than other strategic devices (for example, servers) in a voice network. Therefore, attackers often try to gain control of an endpoint and use that as a jumping-off point to attack other systems. An attacker might be able to gain control of a Cisco IP Phone by modifying the image or configuration file used by the phone.

Alternatively, the attacker could capture packets from the PC switch port on the Cisco IP Phone, or from the network (in a man-in-the-middle attack). Interestingly, an attacker could get the IP addresses of other servers (for example, DNS, DHCP, and TFTP servers) by simply pointing a web browser to the Cisco IP Phone's IP address.

Figure 9-7 shows some of the information that can be gleaned by pointing a web browser to the IP address of a Cisco IP Phone. Access to this web page, made possible by the web access feature enabled on the phone (which is a default setting), does not require any login credentials. The information is freely available.

Figure 9-7   *Web Access to Cisco IP Phone Configuration Information*

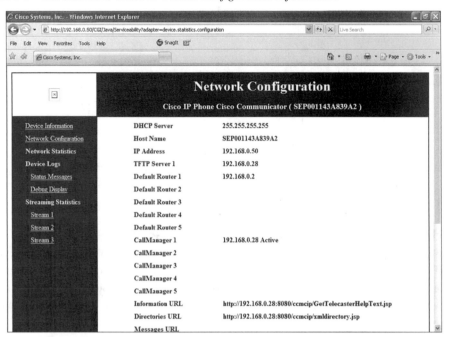

To help tighten the security of a Cisco IP Phone, beginning in Cisco Unified Communications Manager (UCM) 3.3(3), Cisco introduced support for phone image authentication, in which Cisco Manufacturing digitally signs the image file. As of UCM 4.0 and later, Cisco supports configuration file authentication in addition to image file authentication.

Several proactive steps can be taken by navigating to a phone's configuration page within the Cisco Unified Communications Manager Administration interface, as shown in Figure 9-8, and changing some of the default settings.

Recall that a Cisco IP Phone makes a collection of configuration information freely available by pointing a web browser to the IP address of the Cisco IP Phone. This potential weakness can be mitigated by changing the **Web Access** parameter from **Enabled** to **Disabled**. Also, to prevent a man-in-the-middle attack, you could change the **Gratuitous ARP** setting from **Enabled** to **Disabled**. By disabling the gratuitous ARP feature, you are preventing a Cisco IP Phone from believing unsolicited Address Resolution Protocol (ARP) replies, which potentially could have come from an attacker claiming to be the next-hop gateway for the Cisco IP Phone.

Figure 9-8 *Cisco IP Phone Configuration Screen*

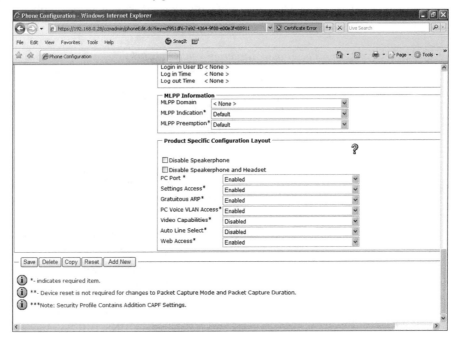

Aside from voice endpoints, other popular attack targets on voice networks include application servers, such as a Cisco UCM server. Fortunately, Cisco provides an already hardened version of the operating system that runs on a UCM server.

> **NOTE**   In UCM versions 3.x and 4.x, the underlying operating system is Microsoft Windows 2000. In UCM versions 5.x and 6.x, the underlying operating system is based on RedHat Linux.

The UCM server's operating system already has several unneeded services disabled. Depending on the UCM version, many default usernames (such as "root") are disabled, and the Cisco Security Agent (CSA) Host-based Intrusion Prevention System (HIPS) product is installed. Also, beginning in UCM 5.0, UCM supports IPsec.

However, depending on the role of a particular application server, you might decide to turn off additional services that are unneeded. Therefore, by effectively combining a collection of security solutions Cisco makes available for IP telephony networks, you can prevent and/ or defeat the vast majority of attacks that could be launched against your voice network.

Summary of Voice Attack Mitigation Techniques

Table 9-6 summarizes some of the methods of mitigating attacks that were described in this section.

Table 9-6   *Methods of Mitigating Attacks Targeting Voice Networks*

Attack	Description
Using auxiliary VLANs	Auxiliary VLANs carry voice traffic in a different VLAN from data traffic. This helps improve the quality of the voice transmission and helps secure the voice traffic from Layer 2 attacks.
Using firewalls	Firewalls can be used to prevent potentially malicious traffic from entering a voice network while dynamically opening appropriate UDP port numbers for individual RTP flows.
Using IPsec-protected VPNs	IPsec-protected VPNs can be used to secure the transmission of voice signaling and media packets, which might otherwise be intercepted and interpreted or modified by an attacker.
Disabling web access	Disabling web access to a Cisco IP Phone, which is enabled by default, prevents an attacker from pointing his web browser to the IP address of a Cisco IP Phone. If the attacker did this, he could learn the IP addresses of other servers, which could become potential attack targets (for example, DNS, DHCP, or Unified Communications Manager servers).
Disabling gratuitous ARP	Disabling gratuitous ARP (GARP) can mitigate a man-in-the-middle attack. In this kind of attack, the attacker sends unsolicited ARP replies to a Cisco IP Phone, claiming that the MAC address of the Cisco IP Phone's next-hop gateway is the MAC address of the attacker's PC.
Disabling unneeded services	Disabling unneeded services (for example, the TFTP service on a UCM server not acting as a TFTP server) can close potential security holes in a system.

Exam Preparation Tasks

Review All the Key Topics

Review the most important topics from this chapter, denoted with the Key Topic icon. Table 9-7 lists these key topics and the page where each is found.

Key
Topic

Table 9-7 *Key Topics for Chapter 9*

Key Topic Element	Description	Page Number
Figure 9-1	VoIP versus IP telephony	302
List	Justifications for the purchase of VoIP technology	302
Table 9-2	VoIP components	304-305
Table 9-3	VoIP protocols	306
Table 9-4	Common VoIP attack targets	307-308
Table 9-5	Examples of attacks targeting voice networks	310
Figure 9-5	RTP inspection	312
Table 9-6	Methods of mitigating attacks targeting voice networks	316

Complete the Tables and Lists from Memory

Print a copy of Appendix D, "Memory Tables," (found on the CD) or at least the section for this chapter, and complete the tables and lists from memory. Appendix E, "Memory Tables Answer Key," also on the CD, includes completed tables and lists so that you can check your work.

Definition of Key Terms

Define the following key terms from this chapter, and check your answers in the glossary:

voice over IP (VoIP), public switched telephone network (PSTN), IP telephony, call agent, gateway, gatekeeper, Multipoint Control Unit (MCU), Media Gateway Control Protocol (MGCP), Skinny Client Control Protocol (SCCP), Session Initiation Protocol (SIP), Real-time Transport Protocol (RTP), RTP Control Protocol (RTCP), Secure RTP (SRTP), spam over IP telephony (SPIT), vishing, auxiliary VLAN

This chapter covers the following topics:

Exploring firewall technology: This section explores the evolution of firewall technology. It also examines the use of firewalls to construct an overall network defense.

Using ACLs to construct static packet filters: This section examines access control lists (ACL) and how they can be used to construct a static packet-filtering mechanism for your environment. This section also looks at the construction of ACLs and examines how to place them on router interfaces to achieve the desired results.

Implementing a Cisco IOS zone-based firewall: Zone-based firewalls represent a significant advance in firewall technology. This section explores this new technology and describes working with zone pairs.

CHAPTER 10

Using Cisco IOS Firewalls to Defend the Network

Because of the prevalence of Internet usage in business today, it has become increasingly important for growing businesses to look more closely at the security of their networks. As more and more business functions move to the public network, organizations need to take steps to ensure that their data and private information is not compromised or that this information does not end up in front of the wrong individuals.

If a network were to experience unauthorized network access on the part of an outside hacker or disgruntled employee, this could wreak havoc on an organization. This could potentially expose proprietary data, negatively impact the corporation's image and reputation in the marketplace, decrease company productivity, and potentially cause the business to close if the impact is great enough. Even if the unauthorized access does not reach this critical level, it can at the very least harm relationships with customers and business partners, who might question the company's ability to safeguard confidential information.

For these reasons, it is critical that an organization take steps to safeguard its network and confidential information—from both outside attackers and those within the organization who should not gain access to classified information. This chapter examines the Cisco IOS Firewall, looking at its historical function and introducing you to the latest advances so that you can effectively defend your network.

"Do I Know This Already?" Quiz

The "Do I Know This Already?" quiz helps you determine your level of knowledge of this chapter's topics before you begin. Table 10-1 details the major topics discussed in this chapter and their corresponding quiz questions.

Table 10-1 *"Do I Know This Already?" Section-to-Question Mapping*

Foundation Topics Section	Questions
Exploring Firewall Technology	1 to 5
Using ACLs to Construct Static Packet Filters	6 to 10
Implementing a Cisco IOS Zone-Based Firewall	11 to 15

1. A static packet-filtering firewall does which of the following?

    a.   It analyzes network traffic at the network and transport protocol layers.

    b.   It evaluates network packets for valid data at the application layer before allow-
         ing connections.

    c.   It validates the fact that a packet is either a connection request or a data packet
         belonging to a connection.

    d.   It keeps track of the actual communication process through the use of a state
         table.

2. Which of the following are advantages of an application layer firewall? (Choose all that
   apply.)

    a.   It authenticates individuals, not devices.

    b.   It makes it more difficult to spoof and implement DoS attacks.

    c.   It allows monitoring and filtering transport data.

    d.   It provides verbose auditing.

3. Application inspection firewalls are aware of the state of which layers? (Choose all that
   apply.)

    a.   Layer 2 connections

    b.   Layer 3 connections

    c.   Layer 4 connections

    d.   Layer 5 connections

4. Which of the following is not a limitation of a stateful firewall?

    a.   It does not work well with applications that open multiple connections.

    b.   It cannot defend against spoofing and DoS attacks.

    c.   User authentication is not supported.

    d.   It does not prevent application layer attacks.

5. Which of the following firewall best practices can help mitigate worm and other
   automated attacks?

    a.   Segment security zones

    b.   Use logs and alerts

    c.   Restrict access to firewalls

    d.   Set connection limits

6. When creating an extended ACL, which of the following number ranges may be used? (Choose all that apply.)

    a. 1 to 99

    b. 100 to 199

    c. 1300 to 1999

    d. 2000 to 2699

7. Each Cisco ACL ends with which of the following?

    a. An explicit allow all

    b. An implicit deny all

    c. An implicit allow all

    d. An explicit deny all

8. To view the status of your Turbo ACLs, which command would you use?

    a. **show access-list status**

    b. **show access-list turbo compiled**

    c. **show access-list compiled**

    d. **show access-list complete**

9. Which of the following are true of the Turbo ACL feature? (Choose all that apply.)

    a. The Turbo ACL feature processes ACLs into lookup tables for greater efficiency.

    b. Turbo ACLs increase the CPU load by matching the packet to a predetermined list.

    c. The Turbo ACL feature leads to reduced latency, because the time it takes to match the packet is fixed and consistent.

    d. The Turbo ACL feature leads to increased latency, because the time it takes to match the packet is variable.

10. You examine your IDS Event Viewer and find that the IP address 192.168.15.10 keeps appearing. You determine that your web server is under attack from this IP and would like to resolve this permanently. What happens if you place this address at the bottom of the ACL?

    a. Attacks from this IP address will be blocked because of the line you have added.

    b. Attacks will continue. This line will never be reached, because above this line is a **permit any** statement.

    c. ACLs may not be used to block traffic originating outside your network address range.

    d. ACLs may not be modified after they are created.

11. Cisco IOS classic firewall can provide network protection on multiple levels using all of the following except which item?

a. Traffic zoning

b. Traffic filtering

c. Traffic inspection

d. Intrusion prevention

12. Cisco IOS Release 12.4(6)T added which of the following capabilities to the Cisco IOS Firewall? (Choose all that apply.)

a. Application inspection

b. A default deny-all policy

c. URL filtering

d. Subnet and host inspection policies

13. Interfaces may be assigned to how many security zones?

a. Four

b. One

c. Two

d. Subnets are assigned to zones, not interfaces.

14. Which two actions can be configured to permit traffic to traverse an interface when zone-based security is being employed? (Choose two.)

a. Allow

b. Inspect

c. Pass

d. Flow

15. Creating Cisco IOS zone-based firewall policies involve which of the following constructs? (Choose all that apply.)

a. Class map

b. Class policy

c. Policy map

d. Parameter map

e. Policy action

Foundation Topics

Exploring Firewall Technology

Securing all aspects of your network can be a daunting task. For an organization with e-commerce, intranet, and extranet sites, as well as e-mail, this only adds to the complexity of the task. Of course, there are costs to providing a high level of security, in terms of both staff and equipment needed to implement a network security policy. These costs must be weighed against the possibility of network security breaches.

For many organizations, the Cisco IOS Firewall meets their need to provide security if they choose not to use a firewall appliance because of financial constraints or technical complexity. For these organizations, the Cisco IOS Firewall provides a full-featured firewall implemented on Cisco routers using Cisco IOS software. This section explores the Cisco IOS Firewall and discusses various firewall technologies.

The Role of Firewalls in Defending Networks

Have you ever wondered where we get the term "firewall"? It originally described the segment that separated the engine compartment from the interior of an automobile. In the network world, this term has been used as a metaphor for how we separate our internal network from the dangers of the outside world. Firewalls allow us to segment our networks into different physical subnetworks, thereby helping limit the potential damage that could spread from one subnet to another. This is much like how original firewalls worked to limit the spread of a fire.

In our world of network security, a firewall may be a piece of software or hardware that acts as a barrier between our internal (trusted) network and the external (untrusted) network, such as the Internet. In practical terms, a firewall is a set of related programs that enforce an access control policy between two or more networks.

Firewalls consist of a pair of mechanisms that perform two separate functions, as shown in Figure 10-1:

■ One mechanism blocks traffic.

■ The second mechanism permits traffic.

A firewall is a set of related programs located at a network gateway server that protects the resources of a private network from users on other networks. As shown in Figure 10-1, basic firewall services may be provided through several means:

■ Static packet filtering

■ Circuit-level firewalls

■ Proxy server

■ Application server

Figure 10-1 *Basic Firewall*

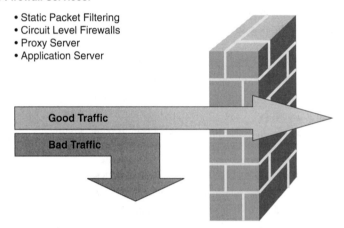

Basic Firewall Services:

• Static Packet Filtering
• Circuit Level Firewalls
• Proxy Server
• Application Server

Good Traffic

Bad Traffic

By placing greater emphasis on either blocking traffic or permitting it based on the specifications you determine, modern firewall designs attempt to balance these two functions. Before implementing a given firewall solution, you must define an access control policy. Upon deployment, the firewall enforces access to and from your network via the firewall. Firewall designs can range from a simple single firewall solution in a small network to multiple firewall designs used to protect multiple network segments in large network implementations.

If you are hosting an application for use over the network, firewalls can be used to manage public access to private network resources such as this. Firewalls can log all attempts to enter the private network, and some can trigger alarms when unauthorized or hostile entry is attempted.

Firewalls filter packets based on a variety of parameters, such as their source or destination address and port number. Network traffic can also be filtered based on the protocol used (HTTP, FTP, or Telnet). The result is that the traffic is either forwarded or rejected. Firewalls also can use packet attribute or state to filter traffic.

The Advance of Firewall Technology

Firewall technology has been available to defend networks for quite some time. This section describes four generations of firewall technologies developed between 1983 and 1995. As shown in Figure 10-2, these four generations include static packet-filtering firewalls, circuit-level firewalls, application layer firewalls, and dynamic packet-filtering firewalls. Taken together, these form the foundation of the current technology employed in Cisco firewalls. Figure 10-2 also notes when Cisco acquired PIX technology.

Figure 10-2 *Firewall Technologies Through the Years*

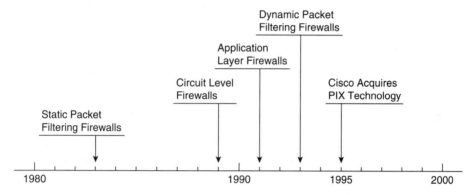

Initial firewalls inspected network traffic using one of four architectural models defined by the information they examine. They used this information to make security-related decisions, determining what to block and what to allow. Today's firewalls have more-advanced capabilities, as we can see in the Cisco PIX Security Appliance and Cisco IOS Firewall.

Table 10-2 lists additional details of the four initial firewall technologies.

Table 10-2 *Initial Firewall Technologies*

Firewall Technology	Description
Static packet-filtering firewall	This first-generation firewall technology is a Layer 3 device that analyzes network traffic. IP packets are examined to see if they match one of a set of rules defining which data flows are allowed. These rules specify whether communication is allowed based on information contained in the network and transport layer headers, as well as the direction of the packet flow.
Circuit-level firewall	This second-generation firewall technology validates the fact that a packet is either a connection request or a data packet belonging to a connection, or virtual circuit, between two peer transport layers.

continues

Table 10-2 *Initial Firewall Technologies (Continued)*

Firewall Technology	Description
Application layer firewall	This third-generation firewall technology evaluates network packets for valid data at the application layer before allowing a connection. Data in all network packets is examined at the application layer and maintains complete connection state and sequencing information. Application layer firewalls also can validate other security items that appear only within the application layer data, such as user passwords and service requests.
Dynamic packet-filtering firewall	This fourth-generation firewall technology, sometimes called stateful firewalls, keeps track of the actual communication process through the use of a state table. These firewalls operate at Layers 3, 4, and 5.

These various firewall technologies each have advantages and disadvantages, and each has a role to play, depending on the needs of your organization.

The Cisco advances in firewall technologies include the acquisition of the original Private Internet Exchange (PIX) technology in 1995. Today Cisco continues to develop PIX capabilities. The Cisco PIX appliances represent network layer firewalls that employ stateful inspection. These firewalls allow internal connections out (outbound traffic) and only allow inbound traffic that is a response to a valid request or that is explicitly allowed by an access control list (ACL). Cisco PIX technology may be configured to perform a variety of critical network functions, including Network Address Translation (NAT) and Port Address Translation (PAT).

In addition to working with Cisco PIX appliances, you may choose to use the features of the Cisco IOS Firewall embedded in Cisco IOS software. This allows you to turn your router into an effective, robust firewall with many of the capabilities of the Cisco PIX Security Appliance. In addition, Cisco offers the Adaptive Security Appliance (ASA), which provides an easy-to-deploy solution that integrates firewall, Unified Communications (voice/video) security, SSL and IPsec VPN, intrusion prevention system (IPS), and content security services.

Transparent Firewalls

In traditional network configurations, a firewall acts as a default gateway for hosts that connect to one of its screened subnets. A transparent firewall is a Layer 2 firewall and behaves like a "stealth firewall." In other words, it is not seen as a router hop to connected devices. In this implementation, the security appliance connects the same network on its inside and outside ports. However, each interface resides on a separate VLAN.

The characteristics of transparent firewall mode are as follows:

- Transparent firewall mode supports two interfaces, usually an inside interface and an outside interface.

- Transparent firewall mode can run in single as well as multiple context mode.

- Packets are bridged by the security appliance from one VLAN to the other instead of being routed.

- MAC lookups are performed rather than routing table lookups.

A transparent firewall can be easily introduced into an existing network. Because it is not a routed hop, IP readdressing is unnecessary. Maintenance is also easy, because there are no routing patterns that might require troubleshooting and no NAT configuration to be done.

Even though transparent mode acts as a bridge, there is no need to be concerned that Layer 3 traffic (IP traffic) will pass through the security appliance from a lower security level interface to a higher security level interface.

You can configure transparent firewalls to allow any traffic through using either an extended ACL (for IP traffic) or an EtherType ACL (for non-IP traffic) if you want. Without a specific ACL, the only traffic allowed to pass through the transparent firewall is Address Resolution Protocol (ARP) traffic; this can be controlled by ARP inspection. Note also that transparent firewalls do not pass CDP packets or any packets that do not have a valid EtherType greater than or equal to 0x600. For example, it is not possible to pass IS-IS packets. One exception is BPDUs, which are supported.

Because the security appliance acts as a bridge device in this configuration, IP addressing should be configured as if the security appliance is not in the network. Note, however, that a management IP address is required for connectivity to and from the security appliance itself and that this address must be on the same subnet as the connected network. A further consideration is that as a Layer 2 device, the security appliance interfaces must be on different VLANs to differentiate the traffic flow.

Application Layer Firewalls

If you are looking to provide a higher level of security than what is offered via circuit-level firewalls, application layer firewalls may be the right choice. Application layer firewalls, sometimes called proxy firewalls or application gateways, allow the greatest level of control and work across all seven layers of the OSI model, as shown in Figure 10-3. These firewalls filter traffic at Layers 3, 4, 5, and 7 of the OSI model.

Figure 10-3 *Mapping the Application Layer Firewall to the OSI Model*

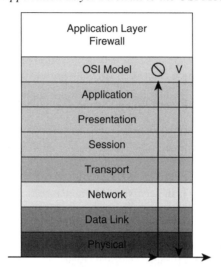

Many application layer firewalls include specialized application software and proxy servers. Proxy services manage traffic through a firewall for a specific service, such as HTTP or FTP. The proxy services provided are specific to the protocols that they are designed to forward. These can also provide increased access control along with detailed checks for valid data and can even be used to generate audit records of the traffic that they transfer.

Proxy firewalls serve as an intermediary between networks, often your internal network and the Internet at large, determining whether to allow communication to proceed. In a configuration that employs proxy firewalls, there is no direct connection between an outside user and internal network resources. The proxy server provides the only visible IP address on the Internet. Clients connect to the proxy server to submit their application layer requests. These requests include the actual destination as well as the data request itself. Based on the proxy server settings, the proxy server analyzes the request and may even filter or change the packet contents before proceeding. The proxy server also makes a copy of all the incoming packets and then changes the source address. It does this to hide the internal address from the outside world before it sends the packet to the destination address.

The proxy server receives a reply from the destination server, and then the proxy server is responsible for passing the response to the client.

Benefits of Using Application Layer Firewalls

The proxy server monitors and controls outbound traffic. Doing so helps protect the private network servers inside the network. Access to the network is provided by the proxy server. The proxy server establishes the session state, user authentication, and authorized policy. In this way, users connect to services through application programs or "proxies" running on the gateway that connects to the outside or unprotected zone. Figure 10-4 shows the application layer proxy firewall and the layers at which it may be used to filter traffic based on the OSI model.

Figure 10-4 *Application Layer Proxy Firewall and the OSI Model*

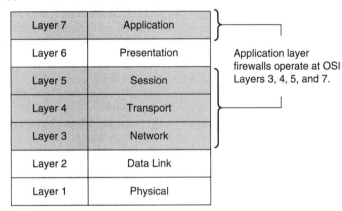

Key
Topic

Application layer firewalls are responsible for filtering at Layers 3, 4, 5, and 7 of the OSI reference model. Because they process information at the application layer, most firewall control and filtering is performed in the software. By locating the firewall at the application layer, you gain greater control over traffic compared to packet-filtering, stateful, or application inspection firewalls.

Application support can vary based on the application layer firewall. Some support only a limited number of applications, and others are designed to support only a single application. Typically, application layer firewalls might support such applications as e-mail, web services, DNS, Telnet, FTP, Usenet news, Lightweight Directory Access Protocol (LDAP), and finger.

Table 10-3 describes some of the advantages of application layer firewalls.

Key Topic

Table 10-3 *Advantages of Application Layer Firewalls*

Advantage	Description
Authenticate individuals, not devices	Typically, connection requests can be authenticated before traffic is allowed to pass to an internal or external resource. This allows you to authenticate the user requesting the connection instead of authenticating the device.
It's more difficult to spoof and implement DoS attacks	Application layer firewalls can help prevent most spoofing attacks, and DoS attacks are limited to the application firewall itself. Application firewalls can detect DoS attacks, thereby reducing the burden on your internal resources.
Can monitor and filter application data	Application attacks such as malformed URLs, buffer overflow attempts, unauthorized access, and others can be quickly detected, because you can monitor all data on a connection. Application layer firewalls also allow you to control what commands or functions you allow an individual to perform based on the authentication and authorization information.
Can provide detailed logging	Detailed logs may be generated, and you can monitor the actual data that the individual is sending across a connection. This capacity is useful in tracking new types of attacks, because you can monitor what the hacker does and how the machine does it, allowing you to address the attack. Logging may also be used for management purposes, helping you track who is accessing what resources, how much bandwidth is used, and how often a user accesses the resources.

Working with Application Layer Firewalls

Application level proxy firewalls control how internal users access the outside world of the Internet and how Internet users access the internal network. They do this by running at the application level of the network protocol stack for each type of service that they want to provide (such as FTP or HTTP). In some configurations, proxy servers are used to block all incoming traffic and only allow internal users to access the Internet. In these implementations, the only packets allowed back through the proxy server are return responses to requests from inside the firewall. Other implementations allow closely controlled traffic to pass onto the internal network, as well as allow for outbound traffic to the Internet.

Figure 10-5 shows the operation of an application level proxy server as it sits between the internal network and the Internet.

Figure 10-5 *Application Level Proxy Server*

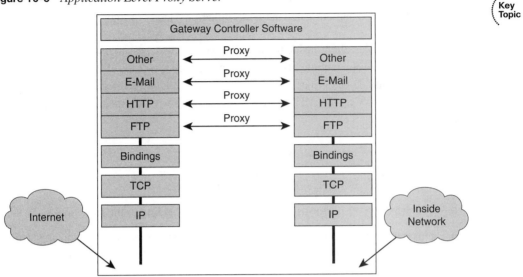

The topology shown in Figure 10-6 represents a typical proxy server deployment. In this configuration, the application layer firewall usually has two network interfaces. One is used for the client connections, and the other is used to access the website from the Internet.

Figure 10-6 *Typical Proxy Server Deployment*

Proxy Server: Dedicated
Application Layer Filter
(Proxy) for HTTP

2. Repackaged Request

1. Request

3. Response

4. Repackaged Response

Internet

Client

Web Server

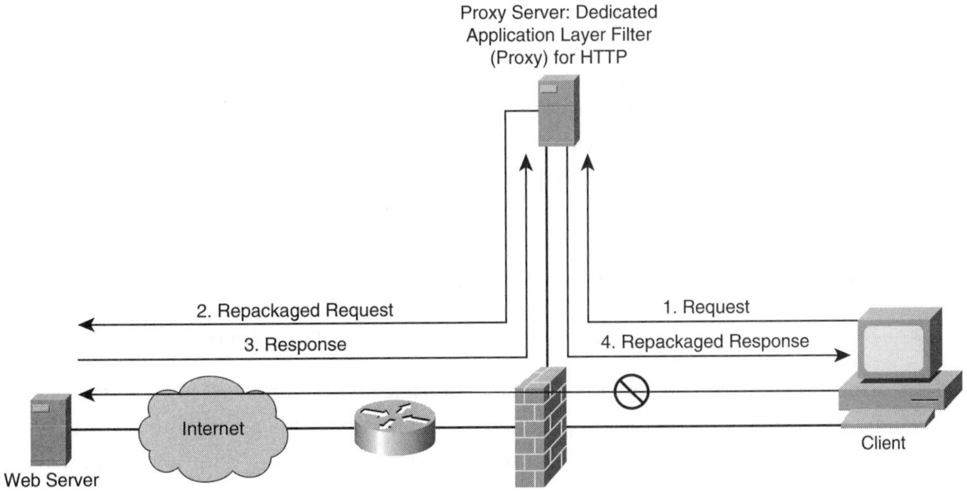

• The proxy server requests connections between a client on the inside of the firewall and the Internet.
• Client requests are filtered on the basis of Layer 5 and Layer 7 information.

By standing in the gap between the internal and external networks, application proxies separate the trusted and untrusted networks either physically or logically.

Figure 10-6 shows a client inside the network requesting access to a website. When the client attempts the connection, his browser uses a proxy server to fulfill all HTTP requests. Note that client-side DNS queries and client-side routing to the Internet are not needed when using a proxy server. All the client needs to be able to do is reach the proxy server to make the request.

Let's examine how the process works:

1. The proxy server receives the request from a client.

2. The proxy server performs user authentication according to the rules applied to it.

3. It uses its Internet connection to access the requested website. In accessing the website, it forwards only Layer 3 and Layer 4 packets that match the firewall rules.

4. When returning content to the requesting client, the proxy server forwards only Layer 5 and Layer 7 messages and content that the server allows (such as nonmalicious traffic) according to the firewall rules.

Application layer firewalls are designed for a single task—to provide the highest level of filtering for a specific protocol. Despite this benefit, a proxy server slows network performance because it must evaluate a significant amount of information embedded in a large number of packets.

Application Firewall Limitations

Application layer firewalls are very processor-intensive, requiring many CPU cycles and a lot of memory to process every packet that needs inspection. Sometimes this leads to issues with throughput. The detailed logging that they can provide, although beneficial, may also lead to significant consumption of disk space. Two solutions can address these issues:

■ Use a Context Transfer Protocol (CXTP)

■ Have the application layer firewall monitor only key applications

By using a CXTP, you can perform authentication and authorization exclusively, rather than adding the overhead of monitoring data on the connection. This greatly improves performance, although without monitoring, you are reducing your ability to be alerted to and track new attack types.

In the second solution, you limit the application layer firewall to processing only certain application types (such as e-mail, Telnet, FTP, or web services). To further reduce process usage, you could process only connections to specific internal resources. The downside of this approach is that you are not monitoring all applications and connections, and this creates a security weakness.

Another limitation of application layer firewalls is that because generally they do not support all applications, you cannot monitor data on all connections. Remember, generally they are limited to one or a small number of connection types, such as e-mail, Telnet, FTP, or web services.

Finally, some application layer firewalls require the installation of vendor-specific software on the client, which the firewall then uses to handle the authentication process and any connection redirection. This can greatly limit scalability and may create management problems if support for thousands of clients is required.

Static Packet-Filtering Firewalls

Packet-filtering firewalls, which typically are part of a router firewall solution, work by filtering traffic at the network layer of the OSI model (the IP layer of TCP/IP). Figure 10-7 shows how static packet-filtering firewalls map to the layers of the OSI model.

Figure 10-7 *Packet-Filtering Firewalls and the OSI Model*

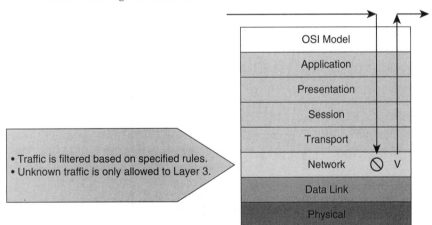

Static packet-filtering firewalls act as Layer 3 devices and use filtering rules and ACLs to determine whether to permit or deny traffic based on source and destination IP addresses, as well as source and destination port numbers, and packet type. Rules may also be used to help these firewalls decide whether to reject any packet from the outside that claims to come from an address inside the network.

You will recall that each service relies on specific ports. Static packet-filtering firewalls can also control traffic flow based on ports. Therefore, by restricting certain ports, you can restrict the services that rely on those ports. For instance, if you wanted to block web traffic from a given host, you could block port 80, preventing the host from gaining access to websites.

Packet-filtering firewalls are similar to packet-filtering routers but offer additional benefits. For instance, packet filters are very scalable and application-independent and have high performance standards. The downside is that they do not offer the full range of security solutions required in today's networks.

Packet filtering may be performed by any device that uses ACLs. For instance, Cisco IOS router configurations frequently use ACLs, not only as packet-filtering firewalls, but also to select specified types of traffic to be analyzed, forwarded, or influenced in some way.

Figure 10-8 shows packet filtering using a Cisco router.

Figure 10-8   *Static Packet Filtering Using a Cisco Router*

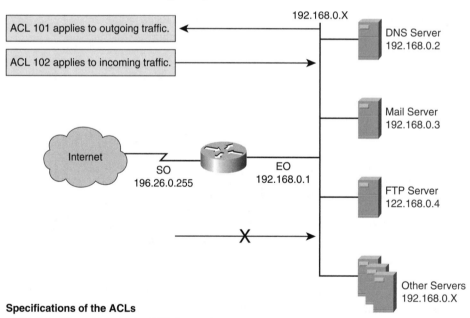

Specifications of the ACLs

- ACL 101- Allows All Outgoing TCP Connections
- ACL 102- Allows Incoming DNS, SMTP, and FTP Connections and Return Traffic
- ACL 102- Denies All Other Services

In most implementations, we seek to protect the Ethernet interface connecting to the internal (inside) network, while the serial interface that connects to the Internet (outside) is unprotected. In the example, our internal addresses that the firewall must protect are in the 192.168.0.x range (on the Ethernet interface). Our subnet mask is set to 255.255.255.0, making the IP address of the Ethernet 0 interface 192.168.0.1 255.255.255.0.

As you examine the network security policy shown in Figure 10-8, you see that ACL 101 allows all users from the inside to access Internet services on the outside. In this case, all outgoing connections are accepted. Our router, as configured, checks only packets coming from the Internet (security policy ACL 102).

As you can see, ACL 101 allows Domain Name System (DNS), mail, FTP services, and the return of traffic initiated from the inside, whereas ACL 102 denies access to all other services.

Stateful Packet-Filtering Firewalls

The most common firewall technology is stateful packet filters, or stateful firewalls. This is in no small part related to the fact that they are the most versatile firewall technology. The ability to dynamically filter packets is provided through stateful filtering. This stateful inspection is a firewall architecture that works at the network layer. Unlike static packet filtering, which examines a packet based on the information in its header, stateful inspection can track each connection traversing all interfaces of the firewall and confirm that they are valid.

Stateful Packet Filtering and the State Table

Stateful packet filtering maintains a state table that is part of the firewall's internal structure. It tracks all sessions and inspects all packets passing through the firewall. If a packet has properties matching those listed in the state table, the firewall allows the packet to pass. Depending on the traffic flow, the state table changes dynamically. Figure 10-9 shows how stateful packet filtering maps to the OSI model.

Figure 10-9   *Stateful Packet Filtering and the OSI Model*

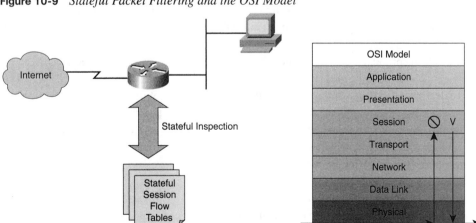

Stateful firewalls use the state table to keep track of the actual communication process. These firewalls operate at Layers 3, 4, and 5 of the OSI model. At the transport layer, the firewall examines information in the headers of Layer 3 packets and Layer 4 segments. The stateful firewall would examine the TCP header for SYN, RST, ACK, FIN, and other control codes to determine the state of the connection. In our example, the session layer is responsible for both establishing and tearing down the connection.

Whenever an outside service is accessed, the stateful packet filter firewall "remembers" certain details. In other words, it saves the details of the request in the state table. When a TCP or UDP connection is established, either inbound or outbound, the firewall logs the information in a stateful session flow table. This information is then used when the outside system responds to the request. The firewall compares the received packets with the saved state to allow or deny network access.

Source and destination addresses, port numbers, TCP sequencing information, and additional flags for each TCP or UDP connection associated with that particular session are contained in the stateful session flow table, or "state table." Together, this information creates a connection object. The firewall uses this connection object to compare all inbound and outbound packets against session flows in the stateful session flow table. The firewall permits data only if an appropriate connection exists to validate the passage of that data.

Features vary by firewall. Some of the more advanced stateful firewalls can parse FTP port commands to update the state table to allow FTP to work transparently through the firewall. To ensure that the only packets that are allowed back through the firewall are in response to queries that originate inside the network, TCP sequence number interpretation and DNS query and response matching are used. The threat of TCP RST flood attacks and DNS cache poisoning is greatly reduced through the use of these features.

Disadvantages of Stateful Filtering

Although stateful packet filtering offers speed and transparency, it has a potential disadvantage. Remember, packets must make their way to the outside network. In doing so, internal IP addresses might be exposed to potential hackers. To guard against this, most firewalls incorporate stateful inspection, NAT, and proxy servers together for added security.

To deal with this disadvantage, stateful firewalls keep track of the state of a connection and whether the connection is in an initiation, data transfer, or termination state. This information may be used when you want to deny the initiation of connections from external devices while still allowing users to establish connections to these devices and permit the responses to come back through the stateful firewall.

Figure 10-10 shows a successfully established HTTP TCP session. This session leads to a dynamic ACL rule entry on the outside interface and permits response packets from the web server to the client.

Figure 10-10 *Stateful Firewall*

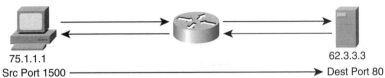

75.1.1.1
Src Port 1500 ──────────────────────────────────────→ Dest Port 80

62.3.3.3

Inside ACL (Incoming Traffic)	Outside ACL (Incoming Traffic)
permit ip 75.0.0.0 0.0.0.255 any	Dynamic: permit tcp host 62.3.3.3 eq 80 host 75.1.1.1 eq 1500 permit esp any any permit udp any any eq 500 deny ip any any

Uses of Stateful Packet-Filtering Firewalls

Stateful packet-filtering firewalls may be used in a number of applications, as described in Table 10-4.

Table 10-4 *Uses of Stateful Packet-Filtering Firewalls*

Use of Firewall	Description
A primary means of defense	Stateful firewalls may be used as a primary means of defense by filtering unwanted, unnecessary, or undesirable network traffic.
An intelligent first line of defense	Routing devices that support a stateful function may be used as a primary line of defense or as an added layer of security on perimeter routers.
To strengthen packet filtering	Stateful filtering provides a cost-effective means to gain greater control over security than does packet filtering.
Improve routing performance	Stateful packet-filtering devices provide better performance than packet filters or proxy servers and do not require a large range of port numbers to allow returning traffic back into the network. By using the state table, the device can quickly determine whether a packet is returning traffic. If it is not, the filtering table filters the traffic.
Defend against spoofing and DoS attacks	Stateful packet-filtering firewalls track the state of the connection in the state table, listing every connection or connectionless transaction. Tracking whether packets belong to an existing connection or are from an unauthorized source lets these firewalls allow only traffic from connections listed in the table. After the connection is removed from the state table, the firewall does not allow any more traffic from that device. Stateful firewalls can log more information than a packet-filtering firewall can, allowing them to track when a connection was set up, how long it was up, and when it was torn down, making connections harder to spoof.

Stateful firewalls also have their limitations, as outlined in Table 10-5.

Table 10-5   *Limitations of Stateful Packet-Filtering Firewalls*

Stateful Firewall Limitation	Description
No prevention of application layer attacks	For example, a network might permit traffic to port 80 to a web server. A stateful firewall will examine the destination address in the Layer 3 packet and the destination port number in the segment. If a match occurs, the stateful firewall allows the incoming and outgoing traffic. The issue here is that the stateful firewall does not examine the actual contents of the HTTP connection, potentially allowing a malicious threat.
Not all protocols are stateful	Stateful firewalls cannot monitor protocols such as UDP and Internet Control Message Protocol (ICMP), which are not stateful.
Applications that open multiple connections	In an application such as FTP, if the client is inside the network and the server is outside the network, both stateful and packet-filtering firewalls have an issue dealing with the data connection that the FTP server establishes to the client. In this case a whole range of ports would need to be opened to allow this second connection.
User authentication is not supported	User authentication is not supported by stateful firewall technology when used alone.

Application Inspection Firewalls

Application inspection firewalls, sometimes called deep inspection firewalls, are used to provide for the security of applications and services. Of course, certain applications require special handling by the firewall application inspection function. Applications that embed IP addressing information in the user data packet or that open secondary channels on dynamically assigned ports require special application inspection functions.

Figure 10-11 shows an application layer firewall. Application inspection firewalls are essentially stateful firewalls with intrusion detection system capabilities. Specifically, application inspection firewalls

■   Are aware of the Layer 5 state of a connection.

■   Check the conformity of application commands on Layer 5.

■   Can check and affect Layer 7 (such as Java applet or peer-to-peer filtering).

■   Prevent more kinds of attacks than stateful firewalls.

Figure 10-11   *Application Layer Firewall*

An application inspection firewall operates
on OSI Layers 3, 4, 5, and 7.

Layer 7	Application
Layer 6	Presentation
Layer 5	Session
Layer 4	Transport
Layer 3	Network
Layer 2	Data Link
Layer 1	Physical

The application inspection function uses NAT to help identify the location of embedded addressing information. NAT is used to translate embedded addresses and to update any checksum or other fields that are affected by the translation.

The application inspection function also actively monitors sessions to determine the port numbers for secondary channels. A number of protocols open secondary TCP or UDP ports. The initial session, which takes place on a well-known port, is then used to negotiate dynamically assigned port numbers. These sessions are monitored by the application inspection function. It can identify the dynamic port assignments, and it permits data exchange on these ports for the duration of the specific session. Let's see an example of how this is done.

We begin with an FTP client that opens a control channel between its port 2010 and the FTP server port 21. As data is to be exchanged, our FTP client alerts the FTP server through the control channel where it expects the data to be delivered. In this case it expects data from FTP server port 20 to its port 2012. If FTP inspection is not enabled, the return data from FTP server's port 20 to FTP client port 2010 is blocked by the stateful firewall. If FTP inspection is enabled, the stateful firewall inspects the FTP control channel to recognize that the data channel will be established to the new FTP client port 2012. Based on this, the firewall temporarily creates an opening for the data channel traffic for the life of the session.

An application inspection firewall behaves in different ways according to each layer, as described in Table 10-6.

Table 10-6 *Inspection Firewall Behavior*

OSI Layer	Behavior
Transport layer	With the transport layer, the application inspection firewall acts like a stateful firewall by examining information in the headers of Layer 3 packets and Layer 4 segments. The application inspection firewall looks at the TCP header for SYN, RST, ACK, FIN, and other control codes to determine the state of the connection, for example.
Session layer	With the session layer, the application inspection firewall checks the conformity of commands within a known protocol. For example, when it checks Simple Mail Transfer Protocol (SMTP), only acceptable message types on Layer 5 are allowed (DATA, HELO, MAIL, NOOP, QUIT, RCPT, RSET). It also checks whether the command attributes that are used conform to the internal rules.
Application layer	With the application layer, the application inspection firewall protocol is rarely supported. Application layer firewalls may provide protocol support for HTTP, and they can determine whether the content is really an HTML website or a tunneled application. If it were a tunneled application, the application inspection firewall would block the content or terminate the connection.

Application inspection firewalls also offer a number of advantages:

- Application inspection firewalls are aware of the state of Layer 4 and Layer 5 connections. For example, they know that a Layer 5 SMTP **mail-from** command always follows a **HELO** command.

- Application inspection firewalls check the conformity of application commands on Layer 5.

- Application inspection firewalls can check and affect Layer 7, as previously discussed.

- Application inspection firewalls can prevent more kinds of attacks than stateful firewalls.

Application Inspection Firewall Operation

Figure 10-12 shows inspection engines, a subset of the application inspection firewall. As you can see, one inspection engine is responsible for checking a specific protocol.

Figure 10-12 *Application Inspection Firewall Operation*

Inspection Engines:
- Protocol Support Through Firewalls
- Conformity of Commands Through Checks

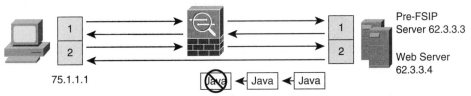

75.1.1.1

Pre-FSIP
Server 62.3.3.3

Web Server
62.3.3.4

Inspect Outgoing Traffic	Inspect Incoming Traffic			
Session Initiation Protocol To: INVITE sip:cch@62.3.3.3 SIP/2.0 From: <sip:bill@75.1.1.1>;tag=4c101d Media Port: 33005	Source	Destination	Protocol	Action
	62.3.3.3	75.1.1.1	TCP 5060	Permit
	Source	Destination	Protocol	Action
	62.3.3.3	75.1.1.1	UDP 33005	Permit

HTTP
  GET/HTTP/1.1\r\n
  Host: www.magazin.com\r\n
	Filtered Java Applet
	<applet code="fbun.class" width=550 height=300 align="left">
	</applet>			

The first example shows how a client establishes a pre-Fast Serial Interface Processor (pre-FSIP) session to the pre-FSIP server and then a voice call controlled by pre-FSIP. You can see that the application inspection firewall dynamically inspects and allows response traffic from the pre-FSIP server. In addition, the Layer 5 traffic is being inspected, and the pre-FSIP inspection engine recognizes a pre-FSIP call setup by understanding the pre-FSIP protocol INVITE message on this layer. Notice that the inspection engine dynamically reads the used media port for the Real-time Transport Protocol (RTP) data stream and dynamically allows that traffic to pass through the firewall.

The next example shows a user opening a website on a web server. The HTTP inspection engine recognizes on Layer 7 that the site contains a Java applet and filters the applet because of filtering rules.

Effective Use of an Application Inspection Firewall

Although application inspection firewalls have their place, they are not without disadvantages:

- Only a few inspection engines currently are available that support Layer 7 content because it is so complex.

- Alone, application inspection firewall technology does not support user authentication.

- An extra load is placed on the firewall's processing capacity as the application inspection firewall is busy building and maintaining the state table. As monitored connections increase, the more processing power your application inspection firewall needs to maintain the table, driving up operation cost.

Application inspection firewalls are appropriate for specific situations. Table 10-7 describes these possible scenarios.

Key Topic

Table 10-7   *Uses of an Application Inspection Firewall*

Use of Firewall	Description
Secondary means of defense	By filtering unwanted, malicious, or undesirable traffic, an application inspection firewall is used as a secondary means of defense.
To provide more stringent controls over security than stateful filtering provides	Without adding significant cost, application inspection firewalls provide a more stringent means of examining traffic compared to a stateful firewall. They also provide more control than stateful filtering firewalls do, at a minimal increase in cost.

Overview of the Cisco ASA Adaptive Security Appliance

The Cisco ASA 5500 Series Adaptive Security Appliance can scale to meet a range of requirements and network sizes. Currently the ASA 5500 Security Appliance family has six models: the ASA 5505, 5510, 5520, 5540, 5550, and 5580. This section explores the Cisco ASA adaptive security appliance and its role in securing the network. Figure 10-13 shows these various ASA appliances and their roles in meeting business needs.

The ASA 5505 has a number of features, including a built-in Layer 2 switch with eight Fast Ethernet ports that can be divided into VLANs. The ASA 5510, another in the family, can support three integrated Fast Ethernet ports as well as one out-of-band management port. If you have an upgrade license, the ASA 5510 can support five Fast Ethernet ports. Other members of the product line support a single management 10/100 Fast Ethernet port and four Gigabit Ethernet ports (ASA 5520 and 5540). The ASA 5550 supports a single management 10/100 Fast Ethernet port and 12 Gigabit Ethernet ports. Of these, only eight can be used at any given time. Four of these can be used for copper Gigabit Ethernet termination only; the other four may be used for either copper or fiber Gigabit Ethernet termination. The ASA 5580-20 and 5580-40 round out the Cisco ASA family of products. These systems provide service provider level capabilities, including 1-Gbps VPN throughput, the ability to support up to 10,000 concurrent SSL or IPsec VPN sessions, and a 4-RU profile, stateful failover, and VPN load balancing. These 5580 ASAs also offer the largest number of interfaces with two USB ports, two RJ-45 management ports, and two gigabit Ethernet management ports.

Figure 10-13 *Cisco ASA 5500 Series Adaptive Security Appliance Family*

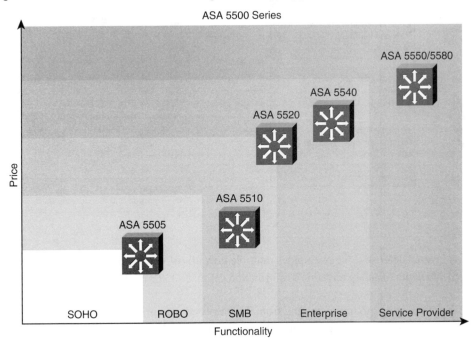

Secure Socket Layer (SSL) VPNs are also supported by the ASA 5500 family of products. An optional Security Services Module (SSM) also is supported on selected units (ASA 5510, 5520, 5540). Even without these added features, the Adaptive Security Appliance is secure right out of the box. With only a few installation procedures and a brief initial configuration, the ASA is operational and can begin protecting your network.

The Role of Firewalls in a Layered Defense Strategy

Firewalls provide perimeter security for the entire network and for internal network segments in the core in a layered defense strategy. Firewalls can be used to separate an organization's human resources or sales networks from other networks or network segments within the organization, adding a layer of security. Figure 10-14 explores the role of firewalls in the layered defense strategy.

Key Topic

Figure 10-14   *Role of Firewalls in the Layered Defense Strategy*

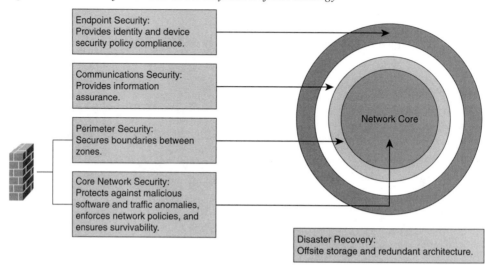

A layered defense strategy employs multiple firewalls of varying types, combined in layers to add depth to an organization's information defenses. Let's examine how this might work.

We will begin with traffic coming from the untrusted network. In a layered defense, the traffic first encounters a packet filter on the outer router. Next, the traffic goes to either a screened host firewall or a bastion host system. This system applies more rules to the traffic and discards any suspect packets. If the traffic is not discarded, it goes to an interior screening router. Only after this series of steps does the traffic pass to the internal host that is the destination. This multilayer approach is called a demilitarized zone (DMZ) or a screened subnet configuration.

Even with the benefits of a layered firewall topology, you cannot implement this and then declare your internal network to be safe. Although some firewall manufacturers may encourage this mentality, you still need to consider a number of factors to build a complete defense in depth:

Key Topic

■   Firewalls do not protect you from the significant number of intrusions that come from hosts within the network. One example of this is that firewalls do little to protect against viruses downloaded through e-mail.

■   Firewalls cannot protect against rogue modem installations.

■ Firewalls are not a substitute for well-planned backup and disaster recovery mechanisms that may need to be implemented because of attack or hardware failure. An in-depth defense helps in these situations by implementing offsite storage and redundant hardware topologies.

Creating an Effective Firewall Policy

Some organizations are quick to put technology in place without first taking the time to develop a sound security policy. Remember, the firewall(s) that you implement should be in accordance with your policies. Your policies should not be solely driven by your technologies. Having said this, your firewall policy should be developed before you approach implementation. It should detail what traffic the firewall will filter and the nature of network connectivity needed before you begin any implementation efforts.

If you don't take the time to develop a well-thought-out firewall policy, one that takes into account your business needs, you can end up making what seem to be good decisions, only to find out that you have impaired your organization's ability to conduct business. For example, suppose you have configured your firewall to block Microsoft Remote Procedure Call (RPC)-based traffic from entering or leaving a protected subnet. On the surface this might seem like a good idea. However, later you learn that users in that subnet need RPC services to contact hosts on the outside. If you have not defined appropriate RPC filtering rules, it will be difficult to deny access to these workers, particularly if this means that you will impair their productivity or, worse, cause them to be unable to work at all. Decisions like this, made without a full understanding of the impact, often cause administrators to have to make an exception. After one exception is made, more exceptions are likely to come into practice, leading to the construction of filtering rules that are complex and ultimately unmanageable.

Always be mindful that your filtering and connectivity policies incorporate a clear understanding of the organization's security and business needs. In the example just discussed, a better solution would be to locate the firewall at the Internet gateway, rather than at the subnet. This would give users the RPC access they need without compromising overall security. Most situations can be handled with careful planning and a solid understanding of your business needs.

Cisco offers a number of best-practice lists to guide you in developing a sound firewall policy. Table 10-8 summarizes a number of key points to add to what we have discussed so far.

Key
Topic

Table 10-8 *Best Practices When Developing a Firewall Policy*

Best Practice	Description
Trust no one	It is best to deny all traffic by default and enable only those services absolutely necessary to conduct business. Understand what information users need, and give them access to only that information. Employ the least-privilege principle to grant no more privilege than is necessary for a user to perform his or her job successfully. When configuring the firewall, eliminate unneeded or redundant rules to ensure that your configuration supports your specific needs.
Deny physical access to firewall devices	Be sure that physical access to the firewall is controlled.
Allow only necessary protocols	Develop a list of the protocols you need to support to allow business operations to connect to other networks and subnetworks, and allow only these necessary protocols. For instance, you might want to disable protocol inspection for traffic types that are not on your network.
Use logs and alerts	Develop a logging strategy that takes into account the level and type of logging needed, and be sure to monitor logs on all firewalls regularly. To make log modifications and manipulation difficult for an attacker, use a secure remote syslog server.
Segment security zones	Firewalls can be used to protect internal systems from internal misuse as well as their traditional role of protecting public servers from being accessed by malicious attacks from the Internet. Firewalls can be used to create DMZs to limit access to defined security zones within your organization.
Do not use a firewall as a server	Firewalls should never be included in server consolidation plans. You should, however, disable or uninstall any unnecessary services and software on the firewall. Also, be sure to remove management tools from firewalls to prevent hackers from installing Trojan horse software or back doors. Programs such as antivirus, content filtering, VPN, DHCP, and authentication software should be run on other dedicated systems behind the firewall.
Never use a firewall as a workstation for a user	Workstations rely on a variety of client applications (Microsoft Internet Explorer, Microsoft Outlook Express, FTP, and so on) that can expose a firewall to viruses, worms, and other exploits.
Set connection limits	Enforcing connection limits on Cisco security appliance firewalls can mitigate worms and other automated attacks. Default connection limits can be changed in the global settings.

Table 10-8 *Best Practices When Developing a Firewall Policy (Continued)*

Key
Topic

Best Practice	Description
Restrict access to firewalls	Firewall accounts should be restricted to administrator use. No network logins should be allowed. Use strong passwords or challenge-response and OTP cards. A unique user ID should be used instead of "administrator" or "root." Each firewall should have a different user ID and password.
Combine firewall technology	Packet filtering alone should not be your sole line of defense. Combine this with stateful inspection, protocol inspection, and application inspection, as applicable.
Use firewalls as part of a comprehensive security solution	Firewalls should be used in conjunction with other devices to build a full security solution. They should be integrated with other technologies, including these possibilities: • Network intrusion detection system (IDS) and IPS • Host IPS (HIPS) • Personal firewalls • Antivirus software • E-mail and web content filtering software • URL filtering software • Third-party authentication systems
Maintain your installation	Software patches and updates should be kept current. Be sure to perform system maintenance in a regular and timely fashion. Take care to patch your network operating system and application software with the latest code on a regular basis. Be sure to test these updates in a controlled, nonproduction environment whenever possible before application. Update your firewall configuration as application requirements change.

Using ACLs to Construct Static Packet Filters

Access control lists (ACL) can be used to provide basic traffic filtering capabilities on Cisco routers. ACLs can be configured for all routed network protocols to filter packets as they pass through a router or security appliance. There are a number of reasons why you might configure these. For instance, you might want to use an ACL to restrict the contents of routing updates or to provide traffic flow control. Perhaps the most important reason to configure ACLs is to provide security for your network, and that is what you will consider in this section. This section describes the different types of ACLs that are available and gives you guidelines to help you better create ACLs to provide network security.

The Basics of ACLs

An ACL may be used for packet filtering (a type of firewall), as well as for selecting types of traffic to be analyzed, forwarded, or influenced in some manner. It is because of this flexibility that the ACL is one of the most commonly used objects in Cisco IOS software.

Now that you understand the flexibility and the power of an ACL, let's consider its makeup. An ACL is a group of statements wherein each statement defines a pattern in an IP packet or UDP/TCP packet. If it is an extended ACL, you can include the port number and established bit if you like. As packets pass through an interface where an ACL has been associated, the router scans the list from top to bottom in the exact order in which it appears, looking for a pattern that matches the incoming packet. Each pattern has an associated permit or deny rule that determines whether the packet is allowed or denied entry to the network.

ACLs are used as packet filters to determine which packets can access a router service or cross an interface. Packets that are allowed across an interface are called "permitted" packets. Those that are not allowed across an interface are called "denied" packets.

You may use an ACL to enforce one or more of your corporate security policies. For instance, you might have a corporate security policy that states that you may allow packets only using source addresses from within the trusted network to access the Internet. With a written security policy such as this, you can develop an ACL that includes certain statements that, when applied to a router interface, can enforce this corporate security policy.

Well-written ACLs are central to Cisco router security. They are used to restrict access to router network services and to filter packets as they pass through the router.

Cisco routers support two types of ACLs—standard IP ACLs and extended IP ACLs:

■ **Standard ACLs** allow you to permit or deny traffic from only specific IP addresses. With these ACLs, the destination of the packet and the ports involved are not taken into account. In the following example, this ACL allows traffic from all addresses in the range 192.168.3.0 to 192.168.3.255:

```
access-list 10 permit 192.168.3.0
```

- **Extended ACLs** are made up of a series of statements created in global mode. With extended ACLs you can filter IP packets based on a number of attributes. Extended ACLs can filter packets according to protocol type, source and IP address, destination IP address, source TCP or UDP ports, destination TCP or UDP ports, and optional protocol type information if you require finer granularity of control. The following example shows ACL 101, which has been configured to permit traffic originating from any address on the 63.36.9.0/24 network to any destination host port 80 (HTTP):

```
access-list 101 permit tcp 63.36.9.0 0.0.0.255 any eq 80
```

Cisco ACL Configuration

In versions of the Cisco IOS before Release 11.2, a number had to be assigned to each ACL when it was created. Since this release, you may now use either a number or a name to identify Cisco ACLs and the protocols that they are being used to filter.

Numbered ACLs can be effective when working with smaller networks with more homogeneously defined traffic. Each ACL type is limited to an assigned range of numbers, so it is easy to determine the type of ACL that you are using. There can be up to 99 standard IP ACLs, numbered from 1 to 99. Additionally, the expanded range for standard ACLs range from 1300 to 1999. Extended IP ACLs may range from 100 to 199, with an expanded range from 2000 to 2699. Table 10-9 lists the number ranges and the types of associated ACL.

Table 10-9 *ACL Numbers and Types*

ACL Number Range	Description
1 to 99	IP standard ACL
100 to 199	IP extended ACL
200 to 299	Protocol type code ACL
300 to 399	DECnet (developed by Digital Equipment Corporation) ACL
400 to 499	Xerox Network Systems (XNS) standard ACL
500 to 599	XNS extended ACL
600 to 699	AppleTalk ACL
700 to 799	48-bit MAC address ACL
800 to 899	Internetwork Packet Exchange (IPX) standard ACL
900 to 999	IPX extended ACL
1000 to 1099	IPX Service Advertisement Protocol (SAP) ACL
1100 to 1199	Extended 48-bit MAC address ACL
1200 to 1299	IPX summary address ACL
1300 to 1999	IP standard ACL (expanded range)
2000 to 2699	IP extended ACL (expanded range)

As mentioned, with Cisco IOS Release 11.2, you can now identify ACLs with a name rather than a number. If you're working with a release earlier than IOS 11.2, it will not recognize named ACLs. Named ACLs give you greater flexibility and allow you to configure more ACLs in a router than you could with numbered ACLs. Note, however, that if you identify your ACL with a name instead of a number, the mode and command syntax you will use are different. Also be aware that for now, only packet and route filters can use a named list.

Working with Turbo ACLs

As discussed earlier, routers work with ACLs by searching the ACL sequentially, looking for a matching rule. However, because of increasing needs and requirements for security filtering, along with packet classification, ACLs are getting longer and longer. ACLs can expand to the point that searching them can require a significant amount of time and can impact the memory used when the router is forwarding packets. Another issue is that the time it takes the router to search the list is not always consistent. Unfortunately, this adds variable latency to the packet forwarding. ACLs with several entries can impact your router, causing a high CPU load as well.

The Cisco 7200 series, Cisco 7500 series, and Cisco 12000 series routers support the Turbo ACL feature, which processes ACLs into lookup tables for greater efficiency. Turbo ACLs use the packet header to access these tables in a small, fixed number of lookups, independent of the existing number of ACL entries. The Turbo ACL feature has a number of benefits:

- For ACLs with more than three entries, the CPU load is lower when matching the packet to the predetermined packet matching. The Turbo ACL feature fixes the CPU load, regardless of the size of the ACL, allowing the use of larger ACLs without adding CPU overhead.

- The Turbo ACL feature leads to much reduced latency because the time it takes to match the packet is fixed. More importantly, the time taken to match is consistent, allowing for better network stability and more accurate transit times.

Figure 10-15 shows a sample topology with Turbo ACLs.

Figure 10-15 *Turbo ACLs*

If the routers you are working with support Turbo ACLs, you should use the **access-list compiled** command in global configuration mode whenever you develop ACLs with more than three statements. This command supports no keywords or arguments.

If you want to view the status of your Turbo ACLs, you may use the **show access-list compiled** command in privileged EXEC mode. This command does not support any keywords or arguments.

```
R2(config)# access-list compiled
R2(config)# exit
R2# show access-list compiled
```

Developing ACLs

You must consider a number of things before you begin developing any ACLs. Table 10-10 summarizes some of the key considerations.

Table 10-10 *Guidelines for Developing ACLs*

Key Topic

Guideline	Description
Create ACLs based on your security policy	The ACLs you create should be based on a comprehensive security policy so that you can be sure that they will control access in the way that you intended.
Write out your ACLs	Always map out your ACLs in writing before sitting down at a router to implement them. It is a best practice to write out a list of things that you want the ACL to accomplish before you begin. You can begin with a simple statement such as this: "This ACL must block all Internet Control Message Protocol (ICMP) traffic to the router except for traffic from the host at 18.1.1.10."
Set up a development system	Develop and store your ACLs on a specific secured machine. You can use any word processor or text editor you like, so long as you can save the files in ASCII text format. It is a good idea to create a library of commonly used ACLs and use them as a source when creating new files. After they are developed, your ACLs can be pasted into the router running configuration, or they may be stored in a router configuration file. Whatever system you choose should support TFTP to make it possible for you to transfer any resulting configuration files to the router.
Test your ACLs	Whenever possible, be sure to test your ACLs in a secure environment before putting them onto a production router. Some organizations might view testing as an unnecessary cost, but over time it can save both time and money.

Using the CLI to Apply ACLs to the Router Interface

For the ACL to take effect, you must first apply packet-filtering ACLs to a router interface. These ACLs are applied based on the direction of the data flow.

Figure 10-16 shows the directional nature of ACL application to router interfaces. The ACL may be applied to either incoming packets (an "in ACL") or outgoing packets (an "out ACL"):

- **Inbound (in)**: Applies to packets received on the router interface.

- **Outbound (out)**: Applies to packets transmitted outbound on the router interface. When configuring out ACLs, you set up the filter only on the one outgoing interface instead of on each individual incoming interface.

Figure 10-16   *Applying ACLs to Router Interfaces*

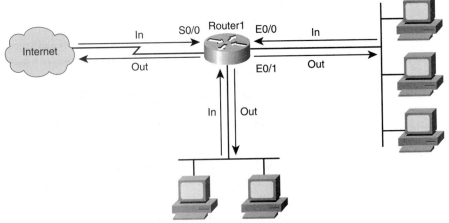

- Inbound ("in ACL"): Data flows toward the router interface.
- Outbound ("out ACL"): Data flows away from the router interface.

One of the more challenging aspects of applying an ACL is making sure that it is applied in the right direction. Before you apply a packet-filtering ACL to a router interface, be sure that you understand in which direction it will filter.

To apply an ACL to a router's interface, use the **ip access-group** command in interface configuration mode:

```
ip access-group {access-list-number | access-list-name} {in | out}
```

Table 10-11 describes this syntax.

Table 10-11   **ip access-group** *Command Syntax*

Command Element	Description
access-list-number	The number of the IP standard numbered or IP extended numbered ACL. This is a decimal number from 1 to 199 or from 1300 to 2699.
access-list-name	The name of the IP standard named or IP extended named ACL as specified in the **ip access-list** command.
In	Used to filter on inbound (flowing toward the router interface) packets.
Out	Used to filter on outbound (flowing away from the router interface) packets.

Considerations When Creating ACLs

Table 10-12 describes some of the caveats that you need to consider when creating ACLs.

Table 10-12   *Caveats to Consider When Creating ACLs*

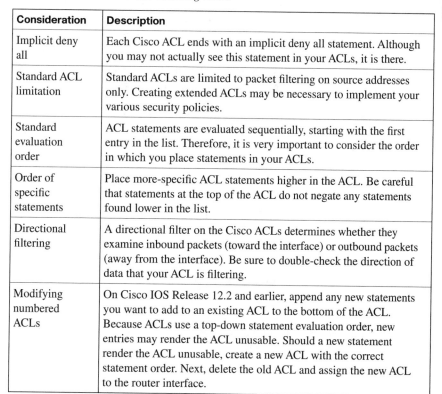

Consideration	Description
Implicit deny all	Each Cisco ACL ends with an implicit deny all statement. Although you may not actually see this statement in your ACLs, it is there.
Standard ACL limitation	Standard ACLs are limited to packet filtering on source addresses only. Creating extended ACLs may be necessary to implement your various security policies.
Standard evaluation order	ACL statements are evaluated sequentially, starting with the first entry in the list. Therefore, it is very important to consider the order in which you place statements in your ACLs.
Order of specific statements	Place more-specific ACL statements higher in the ACL. Be careful that statements at the top of the ACL do not negate any statements found lower in the list.
Directional filtering	A directional filter on the Cisco ACLs determines whether they examine inbound packets (toward the interface) or outbound packets (away from the interface). Be sure to double-check the direction of data that your ACL is filtering.
Modifying numbered ACLs	On Cisco IOS Release 12.2 and earlier, append any new statements you want to add to an existing ACL to the bottom of the ACL. Because ACLs use a top-down statement evaluation order, new entries may render the ACL unusable. Should a new statement render the ACL unusable, create a new ACL with the correct statement order. Next, delete the old ACL and assign the new ACL to the router interface.

continues

Key Topic

Table 10-12   *Caveats to Consider When Creating ACLs (Continued)*

Consideration	Description
Special packets	Router-generated packets (routing table updates) are not subject to outbound ACL statements on the source router. Inbound ACLs on adjacent routers or other router filter mechanisms using ACLs must be used to do the filtering task if your security policy requires filtering these types of packets.
Extended ACL placement	Using extended ACLs on routers too far from the source that you need to filter might adversely affect packets flowing to other routers and interfaces. It is best to place extended ACLs on routers as close as possible to the source that you are filtering.
Standard ACL placement	Placing standard ACLs too close to the source can adversely affect packets destined for other destinations, because these filter packets are based on the source address. It is best to place standard ACLs as close to the destination as possible.

Filtering Traffic with ACLs

You should filter traffic with ACLs to block services that hackers use to gather information about your network. This is an effective way to decrease the likelihood that an attacker will be able to develop an effective footprint of your organization's services. Always apply these general rules when considering how to handle router services, ports, and protocols:

- **Disable unused services, ports, or protocols**: If you find that there is no need to use an enabled service, port, or protocol, disable it immediately.

- **Limit access to services, ports, or protocols**: If a limited number of users or systems need access to an enabled router service, port, or protocol, limit access to it using ACLs.

ACLs act as traffic filters between your corporate (trusted) network and the Internet (untrusted network), as shown in Figure 10-17. The router uses these ACLs to enforce corporate security policies by rejecting protocols and restricting port usage.

The "Blocked Services" table lists common router services attackers use to gather information about your network and that might lead to an attack. Unless your specific network configuration requires one of these services to operate properly, do not allow them to traverse the router. ACLs should be used to block these services inbound to the protected network and outbound to the Internet. Table 10-13 lists blocked services, along with the port and transport protocol that they use.

Figure 10-17 *Filtering Traffic with ACLs*

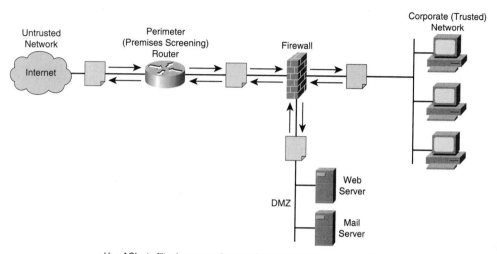

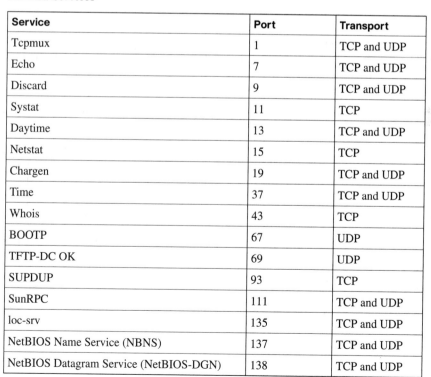

- Use ACLs to filter ingress and egress from routers and firewall appliances.
- Use ACLs to disable and limit services, ports, and protocols.

Table 10-13 *Blocked Services*

Service	Port	Transport
Tcpmux	1	TCP and UDP
Echo	7	TCP and UDP
Discard	9	TCP and UDP
Systat	11	TCP
Daytime	13	TCP and UDP
Netstat	15	TCP
Chargen	19	TCP and UDP
Time	37	TCP and UDP
Whois	43	TCP
BOOTP	67	UDP
TFTP-DC OK	69	UDP
SUPDUP	93	TCP
SunRPC	111	TCP and UDP
loc-srv	135	TCP and UDP
NetBIOS Name Service (NBNS)	137	TCP and UDP
NetBIOS Datagram Service (NetBIOS-DGN)	138	TCP and UDP

continues

Table 10-13 *Blocked Services (Continued)*

Service	Port	Transport
NetBIOS Session Service (NetBIOS-SSN)	139	TCP and UDP
X-Display Manager Client Protocol (XDMCP)	177	UDP
NetBIOS	445	TCP
Rexec	512	TCP
Line printer remote (LPR)	515	TCP
Talk	517	UDP
Ntalk	518	UDP
UNIX-to-UNIX Copy Program (UUCP)	540	TCP
Internet Relay Chat (IRC)	667	TCP
Microsoft UPnP SSDP	1900, 5000	TCP and UDP
Network File System (NFS)	2049	UDP
X Window System	6000 to 6063	TCP
NetBus	12345, 12346	TCP
Back Orifice	31337	TCP and UDP

Table 10-14 lists common services that reside on either the corporate protected network or the router itself. ACLs should be used to deny these services to untrusted clients.

Table 10-14 *Services to Deny*

Service	Port	Transport
Finger	79	TCP
SNMP	161	TCP and UDP
SNMP trap	162	TCP and UDP
rlogin	513	UDP
Who	513	UDP
Remote Shell Protocol (rsh), Remote Copy Protocol (rcp), rdist, rdump	514	TCP
Syslog	514	UDP
new-who	550	TCP and UDP

Access to router services can be controlled in two ways:

- **Disable the service**: Disabling a router service makes it impossible for anyone to use that service. This is a safer and more reliable action than attempting to block all access to the service using an ACL.

- **Restrict access to the service using ACLs**: If limited access to a service is required, it is best to build and test appropriate ACLs to apply to the service.

Preventing IP Spoofing with ACLs

You may implement ACLs to mitigate a wide range of threats. This section looks at how you can use ACLs to mitigate IP spoofing:

- IP address spoofing: inbound

- IP address spoofing: outbound

To mitigate IP address spoofing, do not allow any IP packets containing the source address of any internal hosts or networks inbound to a private network. Figure 10-18 shows the topology referenced in the ACL application shown in Example 10-1, where ACL 150 is applied to router R2.

Figure 10-18 *Mitigating IP Address Spoofing*

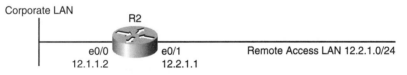

Example 10-1 *Mitigating IP Address Spoofing with an ACL*

```
R2(config)# access-list 150 deny ip 12.1.1.0 0.0.0.255 any log
R2(config)# access-list 150 deny ip 127.0.0.0 0.255.255.255 any log
R2(config)# access-list 150 deny ip 0.0.0.0 0.255.255.255 any log
R2(config)# access-list 150 deny ip 12.0.0.0 0.255.255.255 any log
R2(config)# access-list 150 deny ip 172.16.0.0 0.15.255.255 any log
R2(config)# access-list 150 deny ip 224.0.0.0 15.255.255.255 any log
R2(config)# access-list 150 deny ip host 255.255.255.255 any log
R2(config)# access-list 150 permit ip any 12.1.1.0 0.0.0.255
R2(config)# interface e0/1
R2(config-if)# ip access-group 150 in
R2(config-if)# exit
```

This ACL denies all packets containing these IP addresses in their source field:

■ Any addresses from the internal 12.1.1.0 network

■ Any local host addresses (127.0.0.0/8)

■ Any reserved private addresses (RFC 1918)

■ Any addresses in the IP multicast address range (224.0.0.0/4)

You will want to apply this ACL inbound to the external interface (e0/1) of router R2 to help mitigate IP spoofing attacks.

Also, you should not allow any outbound IP packets with a source address other than a valid IP address of the internal network. Example 10-2 shows the application of an ACL to do this.

Example 10-2   *Applying an ACL to Disallow Any Outbound Packets with a Nonvalid Source Address*

```
R2(config)# access-list 105 permit ip 12.1.1.0 0.0.0.255 any
R2(config)# access-list 105 deny ip any any log
R2(config)# interface e0/1
R2(config-if)# ip access-group 105 in
R2(config-if)# end
```

ACL 105 is on router R2. This ACL permits only packets that contain source addresses from the 12.2.1.0/24 network and denies all others.

Note that this ACL is applied inbound to the inside interface (e0/0) of router R2.

If you are working with Cisco routers running Cisco IOS Release 12.0 and later, they may use IP Unicast Reverse Path Forwarding (RPF) verification. This would provide an alternative IP address spoof mitigation mechanism.

Restricting ICMP Traffic with ACLs

Unfortunately, hackers can use a number of ICMP message types to attack a network. Many legitimate ICMP messages exist, so deciding what to permit and what to deny can be challenging. For instance, various management applications use ICMP messages, and network management uses ICMP messages automatically generated by the router.

One favorite of hackers are ICMP echo packets. Hackers use ICMP echo packets to discover subnets and hosts on the protected network as well as to generate DoS floods. Hackers can also use ICMP redirect messages to alter host routing tables. Because hackers can use both ICMP echo and redirect messages maliciously, the router should block them inbound.

Example 10-3 shows ACL 112. This ACL statement is used to block all ICMP echo and redirect messages.

Example 10-3 *Blocking ICMP Echo and Redirect Messages with an ACL*

```
R2(config)# access-list 112 deny icmp any any echo log
R2(config)# access-list 112 deny icmp any any redirect log
R2(config)# access-list 112 deny icmp any any mask-request log
R2(config)# access-list 112 permit icmp any 12.2.1.0 0.0.0.255
R2(config)# interface e0/0
R2(config-if)# ip access-group 112 in
R2(config-if)# end
```

For even greater security, this ACL also blocks ICMP mask request messages. Note that this ACL allows all other ICMP messages inbound to the 12.2.1.0/24 network.

The following ICMP messages are required for proper network operation; they should be allowed outbound:

- **Echo** allows users to ping external hosts.

- **Parameter problem** tells the host about packet header problems.

- **Packet too big** is required for packet maximum transmission unit (MTU) discovery.

- **Source quench** throttles down traffic as needed.

As a best practice, all other ICMP message types should be blocked outbound. Example 10-4 shows how you can use an ACL to properly handle ICMP messages.

Example 10-4 *Applying an ACL to Properly Handle ICMP Messages*

```
R2(config)# access-list 114 permit icmp 12.2.1.0 0.0.0.255 any echo
R2(config)# access-list 114 permit icmp 12.2.1.0 0.0.0.255 any parameter-problem
R2(config)# access-list 114 permit icmp 12.2.1.0 0.0.0.255 any packet-too-big
R2(config)# access-list 114 permit icmp 12.2.1.0 0.0.0.255 any source-quench
R2(config)# access-list 114 deny icmp any any log
R2(config)# interface e0/1
R2(config-if)# ip access-group 114 out
R2(config-if)# end
```

ACL 114 permits all the required ICMP messages outbound to the e0/1 interface while denying all others.

Configuring ACLs to Filter Router Service Traffic

ACLs are an effective means of filtering router service traffic. This section examines how to use ACLs to filter IP traffic destined for Telnet, SNMP, and Routing Information Protocol (RIP).

Typically when constructing an ACL, you would not build a succession of small ACLs, as we will here. However, for clarity it is best to initially examine each of these individually. In practice, you might want to build at least one ACL for the outside router interface, one for the inside router interface, and one or more ACLs for general router use.

vty Filtering

Systems administrators use Secure Shell (SSH) to remotely access the router console to perform configuration and maintenance. Because of the power this solution provides, you should restrict which hosts have access to the router's vty lines by using an ACL statement.

Figure 10-19 shows an example of vty filtering with an ACL. Example 10-5 shows how to create an ACL to perform vty filtering.

Figure 10-19 *vty Filtering with an ACL*

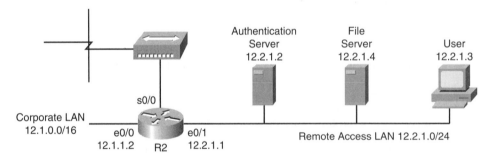

Example 10-5 *Performing vty Filtering with an ACL*

```
R2(config)# access-list 90 permit host 12.2.1.3 log
R2(config)# access-list 90 deny any log
R2(config)# line vty 0 4
R2(config-line)# login authentication vty-sysadmin
R2(config-line)# transport input ssh
R2(config-line)# access-class 90 in
R2(config-line)# end
```

The IP standard ACL 90 shown here allows only host 12.2.1.3 to access router R2 using SSH (port 22). The command **transport input ssh** also denies SSH access to R2 from any other hosts. As configured, this ACL also logs all successful and unsuccessful attempts to access R2 using SSH. This log provides a record for future reference and can serve as a means to help detect attempted unauthorized access.

SNMP Service Filtering

SNMP version 2c (SNMPv2c) lacks authentication, so you should use it only on protected internal networks. It is also a best practice to limit access to a router SNMP agent using an ACL statement.

Figure 10-20 shows a topology in which SNMP service filtering with an ACL occurs. Example 10-6 shows the syntax necessary to perform SNMP service filtering with an ACL.

Figure 10-20   *SNMP Service Filtering with an ACL*

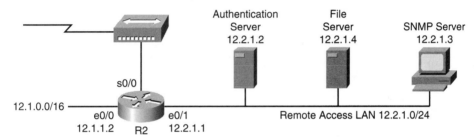

Example 10-6   *Using an ACL to Provide SNMP Service Filtering*

```
R2(config)# access-list 80 permit host 12.2.1.3
R2(config)# snmp-server community snmp-host1 ro 80
```

Here only the SNMP server with an IP address of 12.2.1.3 may access the router R2 SNMP agent. The **snmp-server** command specifies that the SNMP server must use a community string of snmp-host1.

SNMP version 3 (SNMPv3) is supported in the latest Cisco IOS software versions. This version offers more-secure SNMP operations and should be implemented rather than older SNMP versions whenever possible.

RIPv2 Route Filtering

To provide directions on where to route traffic, Cisco routers share routing table update information. You can use ACLs to limit which routes a router accepts or advertises to its counterparts. Figure 10-21 shows a sample topology using RIPv2. Example 10-7 shows the syntax necessary to provide RIPv2 filtering with an ACL.

Figure 10-21 *RIPv2 Route Filtering with an ACL*

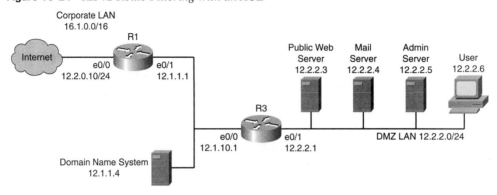

Example 10-7 *Using an ACL to Provide RIPv2 Route Filtering*

```
R1(config)# access-list 12 deny 12.2.2.0 0.0.0.255
R1(config)# access-list 12 permit any
R1(config)# router rip
R1(config-router)# distribute-list 12 out
R1(config-router)# version 2
R1(config-router)# no auto-summary
R1(config-router)# network 12.0.0.0
R1(config-router)# end
```

Here a standard IP ACL is applied to RIP. Access list 12 is used to prevent R1 from advertising any routes of the 12.2.2.0 DMZ network out of interface e0/0.

Grouping ACL Functions

To this point we have looked at a number of discrete ACLs that are designed for a specific function. Although this has worked well for the purposes of our discussion, it is not a realistic application of how ACLs typically are used. It is far more common to combine many ACL functions into two or three larger ACLs.

This section examines a possible configuration for a typical router. Example 10-8 shows a partial configuration file that contains several ACLs made up of most of the ACL features we have discussed. This is presented as an example of how to integrate multiple ACL policies into a few main router ACLs.

Example 10-8 *Integrating Multiple ACL Policies*

```
hostname R2
!
interface Ethernet0/0
ip address 12.1.1.2 255.255.0.0
ip access-group 126 in
!
interface Ethernet0/1
ip address 12.2.1.1 255.255.255.0
ip access-group 128 in
!
router ospf 44
network 12.1.0.0 0.0.255.255 area 0
network 12.2.1.0 0.0.0.255 area 1
!
no access-list 80
access-list 80 permit host 12.2.1.2
access-list 80 permit host 12.2.1.3
!
!snmp-server community snmp-host1 ro 80
no access-list 126
! comment - the entry below prevents any IP packets containing the
! source address of any internal hosts or networks, inbound to the
! private network.
access-list 126 deny ip 12.2.1.0 0.0.0.255 any log
! comment - the set of entries below prevent any IP packets
! containing the invalid source address such as the local loopback
access-list 126 deny ip 127.0.0.0 0.255.255.255 any log
access-list 126 deny ip 0.0.0.0 0.255.255.255 any log
access-list 126 deny ip 12.0.0.0 0.255.255.255 any log
access-list 126 deny ip 172.16.0.0 0.15.255.255 any log
access-list 126 deny ip 192.168.0.0 0.0.255.255 any log
access-list 126 deny ip 224.0.0.0 15.255.255.255 any log
access-list 126 deny ip any host 12.2.1.255 log
access-list 126 deny ip any host 12.2.1.0 log
access-list 126 permit tcp any 12.2.1.0 0.0.0.255 established
access-list 126 deny icmp any any echo log
access-list 126 deny icmp any any redirect log
access-list 126 deny icmp any any mask-request log
access-list 126 permit icmp any 12.2.1.0 0.0.0.255
access-list 126 permit ospf 12.1.0.0 0.0.255.255 host 16.1.1.2
access-list 126 deny tcp any any range 6000 6063 log
access-list 126 deny tcp any any eq 6667 log
access-list 126 deny tcp any any range 12345 12346 log
```

continues

Example 10-8   *Integrating Multiple ACL Policies (Continued)*

```
access-list 126 deny tcp any any eq 31337 log
access-list 126 permit tcp any eq 20 12.2.1.0 0.0.0.255 gt 1023
access-list 126 deny udp any any eq 2049 log
access-list 126 deny udp any any eq 31337 log
access-list 126 deny udp any any range 33400 34400 log
access-list 126 permit udp any eq 53 12.2.1.0 0.0.0.255 gt 1023
access-list 126 deny tcp any range 0 65535 any range 0 65535 log
access-list 126 deny udp any range 0 65535 any range 0 65535 log
access-list 126 deny ip any any log
!
no access-list 128
access-list 128 permit icmp 12.2.1.0 0.0.0.255 any echo
access-list 128 permit icmp 12.2.1.0 0.0.0.255 any parameter-problem
access-list 128 permit icmp 12.2.1.0 0.0.0.255 any packet-too-big
access-list 128 permit icmp 12.2.1.0 0.0.0.255 any source-quench
access-list 128 deny tcp any any range 1 19 log
access-list 128 deny tcp any any eq 43 log
access-list 128 deny tcp any any eq 93 log
access-list 128 deny tcp any any range 135 139 log
access-list 128 deny tcp any any eq 445 log
access-list 128 deny tcp any any range 512 518 log
access-list 128 deny tcp any any eq 540 log
access-list 128 permit tcp 12.2.1.0 0.0.0.255 gt 1023 any lt 1024
access-list 128 permit udp 12.2.1.0 0.0.0.255 gt 1023 any eq 53
access-list 128 permit udp 12.2.1.0 0.0.0.255 any range 33400 34400
log
access-list 128 deny tcp any range 0 65535 any range 0 65535 log
access-list 128 deny udp any range 0 65535 any range 0 65535 log
access-list 128 deny ip any any log
!
snmp-server community snmp-host1 ro 80
!
```

Implementing a Cisco IOS Zone-Based Firewall

Traditionally, Cisco IOS Firewalls were configured as an inspection rule only on interfaces. This has changed, however, with the introduction of zone-based firewalls. This section examines the Cisco IOS unidirectional firewall policy between groups of interfaces known as zones and shows you how to configure a Cisco IOS zone-based policy firewall.

Understanding Cisco IOS Firewalls

The Cisco IOS classic firewall, formerly known as Context-Based Access Control (CBAC), is one of the key feature sets of the Cisco IOS Firewall. This section explores how to configure the Cisco IOS classic firewall, including how to configure Granular Protocol Inspection (GPI) and an application firewall.

The Cisco IOS classic firewall can provide network protection on multiple levels using a variety of functions:

- Traffic filtering

- Traffic inspection

- Alerts and audit trails

- Intrusion prevention

Traffic Filtering

The Cisco IOS classic firewall can intelligently filter TCP and UDP packets based on application layer protocol session information. The Cisco IOS classic firewall can be configured to permit specified TCP and UDP traffic through the firewall only when the connection is initiated from within the network that you want to protect. Traffic inspection for sessions that originate from either side of the firewall is an added capability. The Cisco IOS classic firewall also offers the flexibility to be used for intranet, extranet, and Internet perimeters of your network.

If not for the Cisco IOS classic firewall, traffic filtering would be limited to ACL implementations. Such implementations only examine packets at the network layer or, at most, the transport layer.

An advantage of the Cisco IOS classic firewall is that it examines not only network and transport layer information but also the application layer protocol information in an effort to learn about the state of the session. This enables the Cisco IOS classic firewall to support protocols that involve multiple channels created as a result of negotiations in the control channel. This is essential in supporting most of the multimedia protocols as well as some other protocols (such as FTP, RPC, and SQL*Net) that involve multiple channels.

The Cisco IOS classic firewall offers Java blocking. This blocking can be configured to filter HTTP traffic based on the server address or to deny access to Java applets not embedded in an archived or compressed file. An issue with Java is the potential for a user to inadvertently download destructive applets into your network.

One way to protect against this risk is to require all users to disable Java in their browsers. This may be too limiting, though, and it might not be possible for your organization. If this is the case, you should create a Cisco IOS classic firewall inspection rule and use this to filter Java applets. Taking this step will allow users to download only applets residing within the firewall and trusted applets from outside the firewall. If you require more robust content filtering of Java, ActiveX, or virus scanning, you might want to consider purchasing a dedicated content-filtering product.

Traffic Inspection

One of the key responsibilities of the Cisco IOS classic firewall is to inspect traffic as it travels through the firewall to discover and manage state information for the various TCP and UDP sessions. Using this state information, temporary openings are created in the firewall to allow return traffic as well as additional data connections for sessions that are permitted.

The Cisco IOS classic firewall uses packet inspection at the application layer, and maintenance of TCP and UDP session information, to provide the ability to detect and prevent certain types of network attacks such as TCP SYN flooding attacks. In a TCP SYN flooding attack, an attacker floods a server with a barrage of requests for connection but does not complete the connection. As a result, the volume of half-open connections overwhelms the server, causing it to deny service to valid requests. Attacks such as this, which deny access to a network device or service, are called denial-of-service (DoS) attacks.

The Cisco IOS classic firewall helps protect against attacks in a number of ways. For instance, it inspects packet sequence numbers in TCP connections to see if they are within expected ranges and drops any suspicious packets. Cisco IOS classic firewall also may be configured to drop half-open connections. It also can detect unusually high rates of new connections and issue alert messages.

Cisco IOS classic firewall also can help prevent certain DoS attacks involving fragmented IP packets. For instance, an attacker can overwrite the fragment offset in the noninitial IP fragment packets. If this occurs, when the firewall reassembles the IP fragments, it might create wrong IP packets, causing the memory to overflow or your system to crash. Another form of attack can occur when an attacker makes the fragment size small enough to force Layer 4 (TCP and UDP) header fields into the second fragment. When this occurs, the ACL rules that have been configured for those fields do not match.

In another form of attack, the attacker might send a continuous stream of incomplete IP fragments, causing the firewall to lose CPU processing power and memory while trying to reassemble the bad packets. As you can see, even when the firewall prevents an attacker from making an actual connection to a given host, an attacker can still disrupt services provided by that host.

The Role of Alerts and Audit Trails

Real-time alerts and audit trails generated by the Cisco IOS classic firewall provide a means for you to gain insight into what is happening on your firewall. Syslog provides a means to track all network transactions. With this, you can capture such information as recording time stamps, source host, destination host, ports used, and the total number of transmitted bytes. This allows you to create advanced, session-based reporting. The real-time alert capability sends syslog error messages to central management consoles as soon as suspicious activity is detected. You can also configure alerts and audit trail information on a per-application protocol basis using Cisco IOS classic firewall inspection rules. For example, if you want to generate audit trail information for HTTP traffic, you can specify this in the rule covering HTTP inspection.

Classic Firewall Process

The Cisco IOS classic firewall provides Stateful Packet Inspection (SPI) to inspect traffic and create temporary openings at firewall interfaces. When specified traffic exits your internal network through the firewall, the Cisco IOS classic firewall creates these openings. They allow returning traffic (that would normally be blocked) and additional data channels to enter your internal network through the firewall. This traffic is managed by the firewall and is allowed only if it is part of the same session as the original traffic that triggered Cisco IOS classic firewall when exiting through the firewall.

Figure 10-22 shows the operation of a classic firewall and the flow of traffic as a user connects with a web server on the Internet. The ACL shown in Example 10-9 makes this traffic flow possible from the internal network while blocking traffic from an outside attacker, as shown in Figure 10-22. In this figure and example, traffic is inspected, and a temporary opening is created in the firewall interfaces to permit allowed traffic to pass. Return traffic from sessions initiated inside the internal network is also allowed to enter the internal network through the firewall. All other traffic from the outside is denied in this example.

Figure 10-22 *Operation of a Classic Firewall*

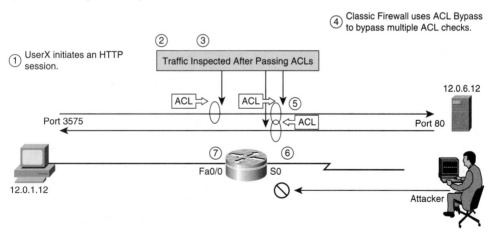

Example 10-9 *Applying ACLs for Classic Firewall Operation*

```
router(config)# ip access-list 104 deny ip any any
router(config)# ip access-list 103 permit http any any
router(config)# ip inspect name FWRULE tcp
router(config)# interface S0
router(config-if)# ip access-group 103 out
router(config-if)# ip access-group 104 in
router(config-if)# ip inspect FWRULE out
router# show ip inspect sessions

Established Sessions
 Session 641721A8 (12.0.1.12:3575)=>(12.0.6.12:80) http SIS_OPEN
```

SPI and CBAC

Stateful Packet Inspection (SPI) was introduced as a feature called Context-Based Access Control (CBAC). Before this, the ACL was the only packet-filtering mechanism offered by Cisco IOS software. CBAC represented a significant advance over ACLs in that it provided stateful packet-filtering capability.

CBAC can monitor several attributes in TCP connections, UDP sessions, and ICMP. This monitoring is done in an effort to be sure that the only traffic allowed through a firewall ACL is the return traffic for a dialogue that was originated on the private side of the firewall.

Cisco IOS SPI provides a mechanism to discover connections that originate on the secure (trusted) side of the firewall, and watch for and allow the return traffic that corresponds with these connections. Connections originating on the unsecure (untrusted) side of the firewall are not allowed to reach the secure network. This is controlled by an ACL facing the unsecure network.

CBAC has undergone a number of changes over the years to enhance its capabilities and increase performance. For instance, inspection of some protocols has been enhanced to ensure protocol compliance or to offer application-level service filtering.

In Cisco IOS software Release 12.3(4)T and continuing forward, substantial improvements in performance and significant changes to the stateful inspection architecture were added through the ACL Bypass feature. Over the years, as CBAC developed and its functionality increased, it was renamed Cisco IOS Stateful Packet Inspection to more accurately reflect its capabilities. You may still hear the term CBAC used, because it is frequently used synonymously with Stateful Packet Inspection, but the CBAC name does not reflect the complete feature set offered by Cisco IOS SPI.

SPI works by inspecting the packet after it passes the inbound ACL of an input interface if the **ip inspect in** command is applied, or after the outbound ACL of the output interface if the **ip inspect out** command is used. In this way, outbound traffic must be permitted by input ACLs facing the source and outbound ACLs facing the destination.

Examining the Principles Behind Zone-Based Firewalls

Cisco IOS Release 12.4(6)T introduced a new configuration model for the Cisco IOS Firewall feature set. This new model presented the Cisco IOS zone-based policy. It provides intuitive policies for multiple interface routers, a greater level of granularity with regard to firewall policy application, and the ability to prohibit traffic between firewall zones until an explicit policy is applied to allow desirable traffic via a default deny-all policy.

The new zone-based policy inspection interface supports almost all the firewall features implemented in prior releases:

- Stateful packet inspection

- Application inspection

- Virtual private network (VPN) virtual routing and forwarding (VRF)-aware Cisco IOS Firewall

- URL filtering

- Denial-of-service (DoS) mitigation

Cisco IOS Release 12.4(6)T also adds a number of new capabilities and characteristics:

- Policies are applied between zones

- Default deny-all policy

- Subnet- and host-specific policies

- Combining service lists with network and host address lists is allowed

- Clearer statement of firewall policies

- Unidirectional policy between zones

- Multiple traffic classes and actions are applied per zone pair

- All connection parameters are global unless a parameter map is specified

Policies may be made up of combinations of the following:

- IP addresses or subnets using ACLs

- Protocols

- Application services

- Application-specific policies

This move to the Cisco IOS zone-based policy firewall changes the firewall from an interface-based model to a more flexible, easier-to-understand, zone-based configuration model that helps improve performance as well. Under this new model, interfaces are assigned to zones, and then an inspection policy is applied to traffic moving between the zones.

Considerable flexibility and granularity are provided through interzone policies, allowing different inspection policies to be applied to multiple host groups connected to the same router interface. Firewall policies are configured through the Cisco Policy Language, which employs a hierarchical structure to define inspection for network protocols and allows the grouping of hosts to which the inspection policy will be applied.

Changes to Firewall Configuration

Configuration of the Cisco IOS Firewall has completely changed with the new Cisco IOS zone-based policy firewall. Let's examine some of these changes.

First and perhaps most notable is the introduction of zone-based configuration. The Cisco IOS Firewall is the first Cisco IOS software threat defense feature to implement a zone configuration model, but other features may adopt the zone model in the future.

Prior versions of the Cisco IOS Firewall employed stateful inspection and the CBAC interface-based configuration model. This model employed the **ip inspect** command set, and it will be maintained for a period of time. But few, if any, new features can be configured with the classic command-line interface (CLI). This is because the Cisco IOS zone-based policy firewall does not use the stateful inspection or CBAC commands. Even though this is the case, you may use the two configuration models concurrently on routers, but you may not combine them on interfaces. For instance, an interface cannot be configured as a security zone member and configured for IP inspection simultaneously.

As introduced with Cisco IOS Release 12.4(6)T, zones establish the security borders of your network. The zone itself defines a boundary where traffic is subjected to policy restrictions as it crosses over into another region of your network. The default policy between zones is deny all. This means that if no policy is explicitly configured, all traffic moving between zones is blocked. If you are familiar with the earlier stateful inspection model, you will recognize this as a significant departure. In the former model, traffic was implicitly allowed until it was explicitly blocked with an ACL.

A second significant change with Cisco IOS Release 12.4(6)T is the introduction of a new configuration policy language known as Cisco Policy Language. If you're familiar with the Cisco IOS software modular quality-of-service CLI (MQC), you might recognize the format as similar to how QoS specifies which traffic will be affected by the action applied in a policy map.

Zone Membership Rules

Several rules govern the membership of router network interfaces in zones. These rules pertain to interface behavior as the traffic moves between zone member interfaces. These rules are as follows:

- Before interfaces can be assigned to the zone, a zone must be configured.

- Interfaces may be assigned to only one security zone.

- When an interface is assigned to a zone, all traffic to and from the given interface is implicitly blocked when the interface is assigned to a zone. The exception is traffic to and from other interfaces in the same zone, and traffic to any interface on the router.

- Among interfaces that are members of the same zone, traffic is implicitly allowed to flow by default.

- To permit traffic to and from a zone member interface, a policy allowing or inspecting traffic must be configured between that zone and any other zone.

- The only exception to the default deny-all policy is the self zone. Traffic to any router interface is allowed until traffic is explicitly denied.

- Traffic may not flow between a zone member interface and any other interface that is not a zone member. Pass, inspect, and drop actions can be applied only between two zones.

- If an interface has not been assigned to a zone, it functions as a classical router port and might still use classical stateful inspection or CBAC configuration.

- You may still need to put an interface in a zone and configure a pass-all policy (sort of a dummy policy) between that zone and any other zone to which traffic flow is desired, even if it is required that an interface on the box not be part of the zoning or firewall policy.

- If traffic is to flow among all the interfaces in a router, all the interfaces must be part of the zoning model.

■ The one exception to the preceding deny-by-default approach is traffic to and from the router, which is permitted by default. However, an explicit policy can be configured to restrict such traffic.

To ensure that all interfaces that are assigned to the same zone are protected with a similar level of security, a security zone should be configured for each region of relative security within the network. Figure 10-23 shows a basic firewall topology.

Figure 10-23 *Basic Firewall Topology*

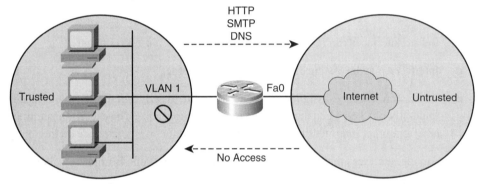

• The private zone must reach the Internet, with access to HTTP, SMTP, and DNS services.
• The Internet should not have any inbound access.

Figure 10-23 shows an access router with two interfaces:

■ One interface connected to the public Internet

■ One interface connected to a private LAN that must be able to reach the public Internet

Both interfaces in this network are assigned to their own zone.

In this example, each zone holds only one interface. If an additional interface were to be added to the private zone, the hosts connected to the new interface in the zone would be able to pass traffic to all hosts on the existing interface in the same zone. The existing policies would also affect the traffic of local hosts to hosts in other zones in a similar manner.

The network generally has two main policies:

■ Private zone connectivity to the Internet

■ Internet zone connectivity to the private zone

Understanding Security Zones

A security zone consists of a group of interfaces to which a policy can be applied. Two steps are involved when grouping interfaces into zones:

■ Creating a zone so that interfaces can be attached to it

■ Configuring an interface to be a member of a given zone

All traffic to and from an interface (except traffic going to the router or initiated by the router) is dropped when an interface is a member of a security zone. If you want to permit traffic to and from a zone member interface, you must make that zone part of a zone pair and then apply a policy to that zone pair. If the policy has been configured to permit traffic (via inspect or pass actions), traffic can flow through the interface. The default behavior is for traffic to be allowed to flow among interfaces that are members of the same zone. If you want traffic to flow among all the interfaces in a router, each interface must be a member of one security zone or another. However, it is not a requirement for all router interfaces to be members of security zones.

Zones and Inspection

Zone-based policy firewalls examine the source and destination zones from the ingress and egress interfaces for a firewall policy. In this configuration it is not necessary that all traffic flowing to or from an interface be inspected. You can specify that individual flows in a zone pair be inspected through the policy map that is applied across the zone pair. The policy map that you apply will contain class maps that specify the individual flows.

Let's consider an example. We can specify a policy map that performs HTTP URL filtering for hosts on 192.168.1.0/24 (salespeople) but that only does plain HTTP inspection for 192.168.2.0/24 (sales managers) for your inside-to-outside traffic.

This results in two flows (192.168.1.0/24 to any, 192.168.2.0/24 to any), and we can apply different inspection parameters to these flows to configure the different behaviors. Zone-based policy firewalls allow inside-to-Internet traffic (the source zone inside and the destination zone outside).

Security Zone Restrictions

The following are important security zone restrictions:

■ Interfaces may not be part of a zone and a legacy inspection policy at the same time.

■ An interface may be a member of only one security zone.

■ If an interface is a member of a security zone, all traffic to and from that interface is blocked unless you configure an explicit interzone policy on a zone pair involving that zone.

■ It is not possible for traffic to flow between an interface that is a member of a security zone and one that is not a member of a security zone, because a policy can be applied only between two zones.

■ For traffic to flow among all the interfaces on a router, each interface must be a member of one security zone or another. This is key, because after you make an interface a member of a security zone, a policy action (such as inspect or pass) is needed to explicitly allow packets. Without this policy action, all packets are dropped.

■ If an interface on a router cannot be part of a security zone or firewall policy, it may be necessary to put that interface in a security zone and configure a "pass all" policy between that zone and other zones where traffic should flow.

■ An ACL may not be applied between security zones or on a zone pair unless defined within a class map.

■ ACLs may not be applied between security zones and zone pairs. A better means to accomplish this is to include the ACL configuration in a class map and to use policy maps to drop traffic.

■ An ACL on an interface that is a zone member should not be restrictive.

■ Each interface in a given security zone must belong to the same VRF.

■ Policies may be configured between security zones whose member interfaces are in separate VRFs. Traffic may not flow between these VRFs unless the configuration allows it.

■ If traffic does not flow between VRFs, the policy across the VRFs is not executed. This represents a misconfiguration on the routing side, rather than on the policy side.

■ Traffic passes freely between interfaces in the same security zone and is not subjected to any policy.

■ Both the source and destination zones in a zone pair must be members of a security zone.

■ You should not define the same zone as both the source and the destination.

Working with Zone Pairs

Zone pairs are used to allow you to specify a unidirectional firewall policy between two security zones.

To define the zone pair, you need to use the **zone-pair security** command. We define the direction of the traffic flow by specifying a source and destination zone. These must be security zones. As mentioned previously, remember that the same zone cannot be defined as both the source and the destination.

Let's take a closer look at how this works. If we have an interface that is configured to be a zone member, all the hosts connected to that interface are included in the zone. However, the traffic flowing to and from this router interface is not controlled by the zone policies. Instead, each IP interface on the router is automatically made part of the self zone when the Cisco IOS zone-based policy firewall is configured. If you want to control IP traffic moving to the router interfaces from the various zones on a router, you must apply policies to block or allow traffic, as well as to inspect traffic between the zone and the router self zone, and vice versa.

You may also select the default self zone as either the source or the destination zone if you want to. This zone, the self zone, is a system-defined zone that does not have any interfaces as members. When a zone pair includes the self zone, along with the associated policy, this applies to traffic directed to the router or traffic generated by the router. However, it does not apply to traffic through the router.

A more common usage of firewalls is to apply them to traffic through a router. This means that you usually need at least two zones rather than working with the self zone.

If you want to permit traffic between zone member interfaces, you must first configure a policy permitting (or inspecting) traffic between that zone and another zone.

To attach a firewall policy map to the target zone pair, you use the **service-policy type inspect** command.

Figure 10-24 shows the application of a firewall policy to traffic flowing from zone Z1 to zone Z2. In this case, the ingress interface for the traffic is a member of zone Z1, and the egress interface is a member of zone Z2.

Figure 10-24 *Security Zone Pairs*

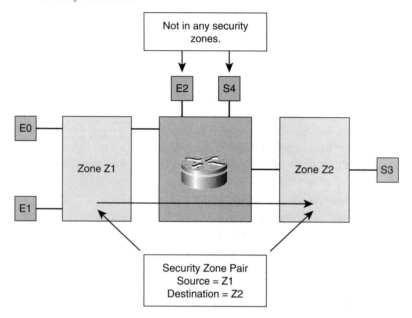

If you are working with a topology such as this, and there are two zones, and you require policies for traffic going in both directions (from Z1 to Z2 and Z2 to Z1), you must configure two zone pairs (one for each direction).

Traffic is dropped if a policy is not configured between a pair of zones. Even though this is the case, it is not necessary to configure a zone pair and a service policy solely for return traffic. Recall that return traffic is allowed by default, so long as a service policy permits the traffic in the forward direction.

In the example that we have been considering, it would not be mandatory for you to configure a zone pair source Z2 destination Z1 solely to allow return traffic from Z2 to Z1. This is taken care of by the service policy on the Z1-Z2 zone pair.

Security Zone Firewall Policies

To build Cisco IOS zone-based policy firewall policies, you use the Cisco Policy Language framework. Creating Cisco IOS zone-based policy firewall policies involves three main constructs:

- Class map

- Policy map

- Parameter map

Let's examine each of these in greater detail.

A class map is a way to identify a set of packets based on its contents using "match" conditions. Classes generally are defined so that you can apply an action on the identified traffic that reflects a policy. The class itself is designated via the class map.

To create a class map, you use the **class-map** command. After it is created, the class map is used to match packets to a specified class. When packets arrive at the targets (for instance, the input interface, output interface, or zone pair), determined by how the **service-policy** command is configured, they are checked against the match criteria that have been configured for a class map to determine if the packet belongs to that class.

Actions are associated with traffic classified by class maps using policy maps. An action is defined as a specific functionality and typically is associated with a traffic class. Some common actions are inspect, drop, and pass.

You can use the **policy-map** command to either create or modify a policy map that can then be attached to one or more targets. This is done to specify a service policy. The **policy-map** command is used to specify the name of the policy map to be created, added to, or modified. This must be done before you can configure policies for classes whose match criteria are defined in a class map.

Parameter maps are used to specify parameters to be applied to classified traffic.

Using the **parameter-map** *type* command, you may specify parameters that control the behavior of actions and match criteria specified under a policy map and a class map.

Table 10-15 defines the three types of parameter maps that are currently available.

Table 10-15   *Types of Parameter Maps*

Key
Topic

Type of Parameter Map	Description
Inspect parameter map	This is an optional map. If a parameter map is not configured, the software uses default parameters. Any parameters associated with the inspect action apply to all nested actions, if any exist. If parameters are specified in both the top and lower levels, any parameters specified in the lower levels override those in the top levels.
URL filter parameter map	For URL filtering (via the URL filter action in a Layer 3 or Layer 4 policy map and the URL filter parameter map), a parameter map is required.
Protocol-specific parameter map	A parameter map is required for an IM application (Layer 7) policy map.

Class Maps

If you are familiar with MQC class maps, you will recall that they have numerous match criteria. In contrast, firewalls have fewer match criteria. Firewall class maps also have the type of "inspect." This information controls what shows up under firewall class maps. The class map defines the traffic that the firewall selects for the policy application.

The class map uses the logical qualifiers match any or match all to determine how a particular packet is matched against the filters in the class map. Table 10-16 describes the three types of filters you will use.

Table 10-16   *Class Map Filters*

Class Map Filter	Description
match *protocol-name*	Used to match Layer 4 protocols (TCP, UDP, and ICMP) and application services such as HTTP, SMTP, and DNS. Any well-known or user-defined service known to Port-to-Application Mapping (PAM) may be specified.
match access-group {*number* | *name*}	The source and destination IP address and source and destination port may be used by a standard, extended, or named ACL to filter traffic.
match *class-map-name*	Used with a subordinate class map nested inside another class map that provides additional match criteria.

The **match-any** or **match-all** operators may be applied by class maps to determine how to apply the match criteria. If **match-any** is specified, traffic must meet only one of the match criteria in the class map. In contrast, if **match-all** is specified, traffic must match all the class map criteria to belong to that particular class.

In cases in which traffic might meet multiple criteria, you should apply match criteria in order from more specific to less specific. Example 10-10 shows a sample class map.

Example 10-10   *Sample Class Map*

```
class-map type inspect match-any my-test-cmap
match protocol http
match protocol tcp
```

In this case, HTTP traffic must encounter the **match protocol http** statement first so that the traffic will be handled by the service-specific capabilities of HTTP inspection. What would happen if we reversed the "match" lines so that traffic encounters the **match protocol tcp** statement before it is compared to the **match protocol http** statement? If this were the case, the traffic would be classified as TCP traffic and would be inspected according to the capabilities of the TCP inspection component of the firewall. This would create a problem for certain services such as FTP and TFTP, as well as various multimedia and voice signaling services such as H.323, session initiation protocol (SIP), Skinny, Real-Time Streaming Protocol (RTSP), and others. It is important that additional inspection capabilities be used to recognize the more complex activities of these services.

An ACL may be applied by class maps as one of the match criteria for policy application. In the case where the only match criteria of a class map is an ACL and the class map is associated with a policy map applying the inspect action, the router applies inspection for all known services (according to the **show ip port-map** command). In this case, the ACL must apply the restriction to limit traffic to specific desired types. Be aware that the PAM list includes only application services such as HTTP, NetBIOS, H.323, DNS, and so on. A service that is not known to PAM will not be inspected. Because the PAM list tends to include more services with each Cisco IOS software release, be sure to check the port map list to be certain that your services are known to the firewall software.

Verifying Zone-Based Firewall Configuration

When your zone-based firewall is in place, it is important to verify your Cisco IOS zone-based policy firewall configuration and operation. With the Cisco IOS zone-based policy firewall, new commands have been introduced that will enable you to view policy configuration as well as monitor firewall activity. Let's take a look at some of the commands that you might want to use.

You can display zone descriptions along with the interfaces contained in a specified zone using the **show zone security** [*zone-name*] command. If the zone name is not included, this command displays information for all the zones that are configured.

If you would like to display the source zone and the destination zone, as well as the policy attached to the zone pair, you can use the **show zone-pair security** [**source** *source-zone-name*] [**destination** *destination-zone-name*] command. If no source or destination is specified, all the zone pairs with source, destination, and the associated policy are displayed. In cases in which only the source or destination zone is mentioned, any of the zone pairs that contain this zone as the source or destination are displayed.

To display a specified policy map, you can use the **show policy-map type inspect** [*policy-map-name* [**class** *class-map-name*]] command. Should the name of a policy map not be specified, this command displays all policy maps of type inspect, including any Layer 7 policy maps that contain a subtype.

Using these commands, you can view configuration details for your Cisco IOS zone-based policy firewall configuration. These commands can also help you verify proper operation and are a good first step in resolving issues that might arise.

Exam Preparation Tasks

Review All the Key Topics

Review the most important topics from this chapter, denoted with the Key Topic icon. Table 10-17 lists these key topics and the page where each is found.

Table 10-17 *Key Topics for Chapter 10*

Key Topic Element	Description	Page Number
Table 10-2	Initial firewall technologies	325-326
List	Understanding transparent firewalls	326
Figure 10-4	Application layer firewall and the OSI model	329
Table 10-3	Advantages of application layer firewalls	330
Figure 10-5	Application level proxy server	331
Figure 10-6	Typical proxy server deployment	331
Figure 10-8	Static packet filtering using a Cisco router	334
Figure 10-10	Example of a stateful firewall	337
Table 10-4	Uses of stateful packet-filtering firewalls	337
Table 10-5	Limitations of stateful packet-filtering firewalls	338
Table 10-6	Inspection firewall behavior	340
List	Application inspection firewall advantages	340
Figure 10-12	Example of application inspection firewall operation	341
Table 10-7	Uses of an application inspection firewall	342
Figure 10-14	The role of firewalls in the layered defense strategy	344
List	Factors to consider when building a complete defense in depth	344
Table 10-8	Best practices when developing a firewall policy	346-347
List	Types of ACLs	348
Table 10-9	ACL numbers and types	349
Table 10-10	Guidelines for developing ACLs	351

Table 10-17 *Key Topics for Chapter 10 (Continued)*

Key Topic Element	Description	Page Number
Figure 10-16	Applying ACLs to router interfaces	352
Table 10-11	**ip access-group** command syntax	353
Table 10-12	Caveats to consider when creating ACLs	353-354
Figure 10-17	Filtering traffic with ACLs	355
Table 10-13	Blocked services	355-356
Table 10-14	Services to deny	356
Figure 10-22	Operation of classic firewall	367
List	New capabilities with Cisco IOS Release 12.4(6)T	369
List	Zone membership rules	371
List	Security zone restrictions	373
Figure 10-24	Security zone pairs	376
Table 10-15	Types of parameter maps	377
Table 10-16	Class map filters	378

Complete the Tables and Lists from Memory

Print a copy of Appendix D, "Memory Tables," (found on the CD) or at least the section for this chapter, and complete the tables and lists from memory. Appendix E, "Memory Tables Answer Key," also on the CD, includes completed tables and lists so that you can check your work.

Definition of Key Terms

Define the following key terms from this chapter, and check your answers in the glossary:

firewall, access control list (ACL), transparent firewall, static firewall, dynamic firewall, application layer firewall, proxy server, network address translation (NAT), demilitarized zone (DMZ), standard access control list (ACL), extended access control list (ACL), Turbo access control list (ACL), zone-based firewall, zone pairs, Context-Based Access Control (CBAC), security zone, class map, policy map, parameter map

Command Reference to Check Your Memory

This section includes the most important configuration and EXEC commands covered in this chapter. To see how well you have memorized the commands as a side effect of your other studies, cover the left side of the table with a piece of paper, read the descriptions on the right side, and see whether you remember the commands.

Table 10-18   *Chapter 10 Configuration Command Reference*

Command	Description
access-list compiled	Used whenever you develop ACLs with more than three statements
ip access-group {*access-list-number* | *access-list-name*} {**in** | **out**}	Applies an ACL to a router's interface in the desired direction
access-list {*access-list-number* | *access-list-name*} {**in** | **out**}	Defines an ACL by number or name in the desired direction
zone-pair security	Defines a zone pair
service-policy type inspect	Attaches a firewall policy map to a target zone pair
class-map	Creates a class map as used with a zone-based firewall
policy-map	Associates an action with traffic classified by a class map
parameter-map type	Specifies parameters that control the behavior of actions and match criteria specified under a policy map or a class map

Table 10-19   *Chapter 10 EXEC Command Reference*

Command	Description
show access-list compiled	Shows the status of your Turbo ACLs
show zone security	Displays zone descriptions along with the interfaces contained in a specified zone
show zone-pair security [**source** *source-zone-name*] [**destination** *destination-zone-name*]	Displays source zone and destination zone, as well as the policy attached to the zone pair
show policy-map type inspect [*policy-map-name* [**class** *class-map-name*]]	Displays a specified policy map

This chapter covers the following topics:

Examining IPS technologies: This section distinguishes between intrusion detection and intrusion prevention. Various intrusion prevention system (IPS) appliances are introduced, and the concept of signatures is discussed.

Using SDM to configure Cisco IOS IPS: This section examines how to configure a Cisco IOS router to act as an IPS sensor, as opposed to using, for example, a dedicated IPS appliance. Specifically, the configuration discussed uses a wizard available in the Cisco Security Device Manager (SDM) interface.

CHAPTER 11

Using Cisco IOS IPS to Secure the Network

When an attacker launches an attack against a network, intrusion detection system (IDS) and intrusion prevention system (IPS) technologies might be able to recognize the attack and respond appropriately. Attacks might be recognizable by comparing incoming data streams against a database of well-known attack signatures. Other mechanisms for detecting attacks include policy-based and anomaly-based approaches.

IDS and IPS solutions can be found in Cisco's 4200 series of sensor appliances. However, other IDS and IPS options are available. For example, IPS software can be installed on a host to provide a host-based intrusion prevention system (HIPS), and many Cisco IOS routers can be configured to provide IPS services.

This chapter contrasts IDS and IPS operation, in addition to contrasting host- and network-based IPS. Obviously, different IDS and/or IPS platforms offer different approaches to configuration. However, the configuration discussed in this chapter focuses on using Cisco's SDM to configure IPS support on a Cisco IOS router platform.

"Do I Know This Already?" Quiz

The "Do I Know This Already?" quiz helps you determine your level of knowledge of this chapter's topics before you begin. Table 11-1 details the major topics discussed in this chapter and their corresponding quiz questions.

Table 11-1 *"Do I Know This Already?" Section-to-Question Mapping*

Foundation Topics Section	Questions
Examining IPS Technologies	1 to 6
Using SDM to Configure Cisco IOS IPS	7 to 11

1. Which two statements are true about the differences between IDS and IPS? (Choose two.)

    a.   IPS operates in promiscuous mode.

    b.   IPS receives a copy of the traffic to be analyzed.

    c.   IPS operates in inline mode.

    d.   IDS receives a copy of the traffic to be analyzed.

2. What is the primary method used to detect and prevent attacks using IDS and/or IPS technologies?

    a.   Signature-based detection

    b.   Policy-based detection

    c.   Anomaly-based detection

    d.   Honey pot detection

3. What two types of interfaces are found on all network-based IPS sensors? (Choose two.)

    a.   Management interface

    b.   Monitoring interface

    c.   Command and control interface

    d.   Loopback interface

4. Which type of signatures use a set of rules that state how certain protocols should behave on the network?

    a.   String signatures

    b.   DoS signatures

    c.   Exploit signatures

    d.   Connection signatures

5. Which protocol used by IPS is preferred over syslog, because it provides a secure communications channel, and it can be used to communicate between IPS clients and servers (for example, a management workstation that collects and correlates events from multiple IPS sensors in the network)?

    a.   CTIQBE

    b.   SDEE

    c.   TLS

    d.   SRTP

6. Which four of the following are configurable responses to an IPS alarm being triggered? (Choose four.)

    a.   Create a log entry

    b.   Drop the offending packet

   c.   Reset the TCP connection

   d.   Send an ICMP Source Quench to the attacker's IP address

   e.   Block the attacker's IP address

7. The Intrusion Prevention Wizard is launched from within which administrative utility?

   a.   SMS

   b.   QPM

   c.   SDM

   d.   IPM

8. The IPS Policies Wizard helps you with which three of the following tasks? (Choose three.)

   a.   Selecting the interface to which the IPS rule will be applied

   b.   Selecting the direction of traffic that will be inspected

   c.   Selecting the inspection policy that will be applied to the interface

   d.   Selecting the Signature Definition File (SDF) that the router will use

9. Which of the following is an implicit command that is the last rule in a list of IPS rules?

   a.   **permit ip any any**

   b.   **deny ip any any**

   c.   **permit tcp 127.0.0.1 any**

   d.   **deny tcp any 255.255.255.255**

10. When editing global IPS settings, which option determines if the IOS-based IPS feature will drop or permit traffic for a particular IPS signature engine while a new signature for that engine is being compiled?

   a.   Enable Engine Fail Closed

   b.   Enable Default IOS Signature

   c.   Enable Fail Opened

   d.   Enable Signature Default

11. In SDM's Edit Signature window, you click a green square next to the parameter you want to configure to make it editable. What color and symbol does the green square change into after you click it?

   a.   Blue circle

   b.   Yellow triangle

   c.   Red diamond

   d.   Orange oval

Foundation Topics

Examining IPS Technologies

Although IDS and IPS perform similar functions, this section explores how these network security solutions differ. Various approaches to detecting and preventing an intrusion are discussed. This section also explores signatures and how they can trigger an alarm. This section concludes by discussing best practices for IPS network design.

IDS Versus IPS

Although both IDS and IPS devices can recognize network attacks, they differ primarily in their network placement. Specifically, although an IDS device receives a copy of traffic to be analyzed, an IPS device resides inline with the traffic, as illustrated in Figure 11-1.

Figure 11-1 *IDS and IPS Network Placement*

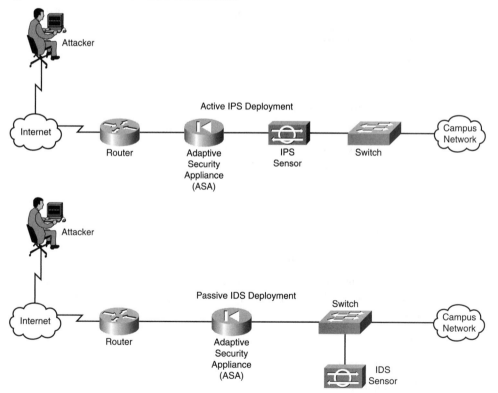

Because the analyzed traffic does not flow through the IDS device, the IDS device is considered *passive*, whereas the IPS device is considered *active*. Both the IDS and IPS devices can send alerts to, for example, a management station. Although an IDS device can also communicate with a security appliance or router to prevent subsequent attack packets, the initially offending traffic reaches its destination. Conversely, an IPS device can drop the traffic inline, thus preventing even the first malicious packet from reaching its intended target.

This discussion of IDS versus IPS devices might seem to suggest that IPS devices should always be used instead of IDS devices. However, in some network environments, these two solutions complement one another. For example, an IDS device can add value to a network that already employs an IPS device by verifying that the IPS device is still operational. The IDS device might also identify suspicious traffic and send alerts about that traffic, without having the IPS device drop the traffic.

IDS and IPS Device Categories

IDS and IPS devices can be categorized based on how they detect malicious traffic. Alternatively, IPS devices can be categorized based on whether they run on a network device or on a host.

Detection Methods

Consider the following approaches for detecting malicious traffic:

- Signature-based detection

- Policy-based detection

- Anomaly-based detection

- Honey pot detection

The following sections discuss each of these in detail.

Signature-Based Detection

The primary method used to detect and prevent attacks using IDS and/or IPS technologies is signature-based. A signature can recognize a string of bytes, in a certain context, that triggers detection.

For example, attacks against a web server typically take the form of URLs. Therefore, URLs could be searched for a certain string that would identify an attack against a web server.

As another example, the IDS and/or IPS device could search for a pattern in the MIME header of an e-mail message. However, because signature-based IDS/IPS is, as the name suggests, based on signatures, the administrator needs to routinely update those signature files. This routine update is similar in nature to regular antivirus updates that you might perform on your computer to make sure the antivirus program is up-to-date.

Policy-Based Detection

Another approach to IDS/IPS is policy-based. With a policy-based approach, the IDS/IPS device needs a very specific declaration of the security policy. For example, you could write a network access policy that identified which networks could communicate with specific hosts. The IDS/IPS device could then recognize "out of profile" traffic that does not conform to the policy and then report that activity.

Anomaly-Based Detection

A third approach to detecting and/or preventing malicious traffic is anomaly-based. This approach is prone to false positives, because a "normal" condition is difficult to measurably define. However, you have a couple of options when detecting anomalies:

- **Statistical anomaly detection**: This approach watches network traffic patterns over a period of time and dynamically builds a baseline. Then, if traffic patterns significantly vary from the baseline, an alarm can be triggered.

- **Nonstatistical anomaly detection**: This approach allows an administrator to define what traffic patterns are supposed to look like. However, imagine that Microsoft released a large service pack for its Vista operating system, and your company has hundreds of computers that are configured to automatically download that service pack. If multiple employees turn on their computers at approximately the same time tomorrow morning, and multiple copies of the service pack simultaneously start to download from microsoft.com, the IDS/IPS device might consider that traffic pattern to be significantly outside of the baseline. As a result, the nonstatistical anomaly detection approach could lead to a false positive (that is, an alarm being triggered in the absence of malicious traffic).

Honey Pot Detection

Finally, the "honey pot" acts as a distracter. Specifically, a system designated as the honey pot appears to be an attractive attack target. One school of thought on the use of a honey pot is to place one or more honey pot systems in the network to entice attackers into thinking the system is real. The attackers then use their resources attacking the honey pot, resulting in their leaving the real servers alone.

Another use of a honey pot is to use it as a system that is extensively monitored, to learn the attacker's identity and what he is attempting to do on the system. For example, a honey pot could be a UNIX system configured with a weak password. After an attacker logs in, surveillance software could log what the attacker does to the system. This knowledge could then be used to protect real servers in the network.

Summary of IDS/IPS Detection Methods

Table 11-2 summarizes these IDS/IPS detection methods.

Table 11-2 *IDS/IPS Detection Methods*

Key Topic

Detection Method	Description
Signature-based detection	The primary method used to detect and prevent attacks using IDS and/or IPS technologies is signature-based. A signature could be a string of bytes, in a certain context, that triggers detection.
Policy-based detection	With a policy-based approach, the IDS/IPS device needs a very specific declaration of the security policy. The IDS/IPS device could recognize "out of profile" traffic that does not conform to the policy and then report that activity.
Anomaly-based detection	This approach is prone to false positives, because a "normal" condition is difficult to measurably define. However, you have a couple of options when detecting anomalies: • Statistical anomaly detection watches network traffic patterns over a period of time and dynamically builds a baseline. Then, if traffic patterns significantly vary from the baseline, an alarm can be triggered. • Nonstatistical anomaly detection allows an administrator to define what traffic patterns are supposed to look like.
Honey pot detection	The "honey pot" acts as a distracter. A system designated as the honey pot appears to be an attractive attack target. One use of a honey pot is to place one or more honey pot systems in the network to entice attackers into thinking the system is real. The attackers then use their resources attacking the honey pot, resulting in their leaving the real servers alone. Another use of a honey pot is to use it as a system that is extensively monitored to learn what the attacker is attempting to do on the system.

Network-Based Versus Host-Based IPS

As previously mentioned, IPS solutions can be either network-based or host-based. Often network-based and host-based solutions can be used together to protect against a wider range of potential attacks.

Network-Based Sensors

A Cisco IOS router configured for the IPS feature could serve as a network-based IP device. Alternatively, a network-based IPS device could be a dedicated appliance such as Cisco's 4200 series of IDS/IPS sensors, as shown in Figure 11-2.

Figure 11-2 *Cisco 4200 Series IDS/IPS Sensor Appliance*

Cisco also supports other hardware modules that can be inserted in a variety of network devices:

- **AIP-SSM**: The Advanced Inspection and Prevention Security Services Module (AIP-SSM), shown in Figure 11-3, installs in a Cisco Adaptive Security Appliance (ASA) to add IPS and/or IDS features to the ASA. Interestingly, even though the module resides in an ASA, the AIP-SSM runs its own software (with its own CPU, RAM, and storage), which is the same software found on other sensor appliances.

Figure 11-3 *AIP-SSM*

■ **IDSM-2**: The Cisco Catalyst 6500 Intrusion Detection System Module 2 (IDSM-2), shown in Figure 11-4, inserts into a slot in a Cisco Catalyst 6500 chassis. Because the module has direct access to the switch's backplane, it can monitor any or all of the VLANs configured on the switch. Like the AIP-SSM, the IDSM-2 supports IDS and/or IPS services and runs the same sensor software found on dedicated IDS/IPS appliances.

Figure 11-4 *IDSM-2*

■ **NM-CIDS**: The Cisco IDS Network Module (NM-CIDS), shown in Figure 11-5, is supported on a variety of router platforms. The module installs in a router's network module bay, and the NM-IDS can monitor traffic from all the router's interfaces. Although the NM-CIDS does run the same sensor software as the previously mentioned appliances and modules, the NM-CIDS module performs only the IDS function, as opposed to both IDS and IPS functions. However, an NM-CIDS does allow a network administrator to implement full signature protection without negatively impacting router performance.

Figure 11-5 *NM-CIDS*

Although http://www.cisco.com provides up-to-date information about which router platforms support the NM-CIDS, as a few examples, the following Cisco router platforms support the NM-CIDS:

— Cisco 2600XM series router

— Cisco 2691 router

— Cisco 3660 router

— Cisco 3725 router

— Cisco 3745 router

— Cisco 2811 ISR

— Cisco 2821 ISR

— Cisco 2851 ISR

— Cisco 3825 ISR

— Cisco 3845 ISR

The operating system running on network-based IPS (NIPS) sensors is considered to be "hardened" against network attacks. A NIPS solution also offers flexibility and scalability in a network design, because additional network devices can be added without necessarily necessitating the addition of new sensor appliances. However, if network patterns grow beyond the capacity of the existing sensor(s), new sensors can easily be added to the network.

Host-Based IPS Software

In addition to the previous examples of network-based IDS/IPS sensors, Cisco offers the Cisco Security Agent (CSA) as a HIPS solution. The CSA software can be installed on selected host systems and optionally report suspicious activity to a centralized management server.

Deploying Network-Based and Host-Based Solutions

NIPS and HIPS solutions can work in tandem. For example, although a NIPS solution can inspect traffic flowing through the network, what if a host had a Secure Socket Layer (SSL) connection to a server, and the malicious traffic traveled over the SSL connection? In that instance, the NIPS hardware would be unable to analyze the malicious traffic, because it would be encrypted inside the SSL connection. However, a HIPS software solution could analyze the malicious traffic after the traffic was decrypted on the host. Similarly, a NIPS device might be able to prevent a denial-of-service (DoS) attack or recognize network reconnaissance patterns. A HIPS solution could focus on protecting applications and host resources.

Figure 11-6 illustrates the deployment of network-based IDS (NIDS), NIPS, and HIPS technologies in the same network. Notice that the sensors are strategically deployed at network boundaries (that is, coming into the network from the Internet and going into the demilitarized zone [DMZ]). As previously discussed, NIDS and NIPS devices are used to complement each other's functions. Additionally, HIPS software (for example, Cisco Security Agent [CSA]) is deployed on strategic hosts—the HTTP, DNS, and e-mail hosts in this example. The NIDS, NIPS, and HIPS devices can all send any alarms triggered on their respective devices to the management console. Using input from these diverse sources, the management console software might be able to perform *event correlation* to recognize broader network attack patterns, rather than just examining a single attack against a single device.

Figure 11-6 *NIDS, NIPS, and HIPS Deployment Example*

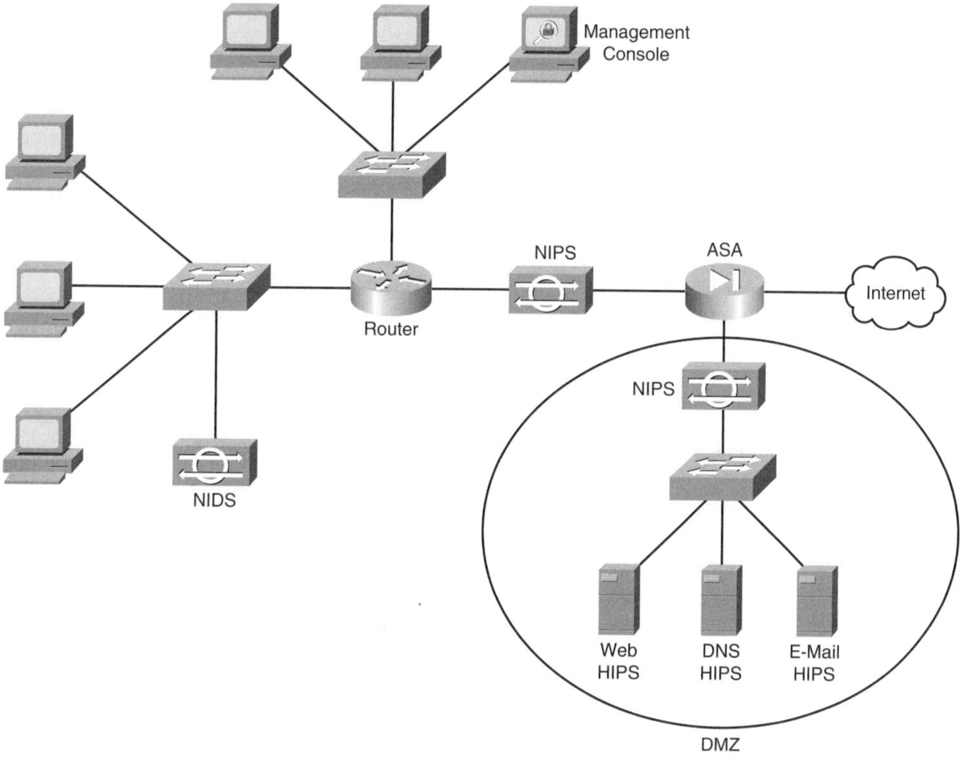

IDS and IPS Appliances

Cisco offers a series of IDS/IPS sensors—specifically, the Cisco 4200 series of IDS/IPS sensors. All sensors contain at least two interfaces:

- **Command and control interface**: A sensor's command and control interface is configured with an IP address and is used to communicate with other network devices (for example, a security appliance or a management workstation) for management purposes.

- **Monitoring interface(s)**: All sensors have at least one monitoring interface, which is used to monitor network traffic.

Depending on the number of available interfaces, sensors can operate in one of two modes, as described in Table 11-3.

Table 11-3 *Sensor Operating Modes*

Operating Mode	Description
Promiscuous mode	Promiscuous mode operation requires only a single monitoring interface. Therefore, all Cisco 4200 sensors support promiscuous mode operation. When running in promiscuous mode, a sensor receives a copy of selected network traffic. If the sensor detects malicious traffic, it can take a variety of actions (for example, triggering an alarm or instructing a security appliance to drop traffic coming from a specific source). Because a sensor running in promiscuous mode is not inline with the traffic, IDS operation is supported, but not IPS operation.
Inline mode	Inline mode operation requires a least two monitoring interfaces (either virtual or physical), because the sensor resides inline with the traffic. (In other words, traffic enters the sensor on one monitoring interface and exits the sensor on another monitoring interface.) Therefore, a sensor running in inline mode supports IPS operation and can drop malicious traffic before the traffic reaches its intended target.

Cisco IDS 4215 Sensor

The Cisco IDS 4215 Sensor, shown in Figure 11-7, has the following specifications:

- **Performance**: 65 Mbps

- **Command and control interface speed**: 10/100 Mbps

- **Maximum number of monitoring interfaces**: Five

Figure 11-7   *Cisco IDS 4215 Sensor*

Cisco IPS 4240 Sensor

The Cisco IPS 4240 Sensor, shown in Figure 11-8, has the following specifications:

- **Performance**: 250 Mbps

- **Command and control interface speed**: 10/100/1000 Mbps

- **Maximum number of monitoring interfaces**: Four

Figure 11-8   *Cisco IPS 4240 Sensor*

Cisco IPS 4255 Sensor

The Cisco IPS 4255 Sensor, shown in Figure 11-9, has the following specifications:

- **Performance**: 500 Mbps

- **Command and control interface speed**: 10/100/1000 Mbps

- **Maximum number of monitoring interfaces**: Four

Figure 11-9   *Cisco IPS 4255 Sensor*

Cisco IPS 4260 Sensor

The Cisco IPS 4260 Sensor, shown in Figure 11-10, has the following specifications:

- **Performance**: 1 Gbps

- **Command and control interface speed**: 10/100/1000 Mbps

- **Maximum number of monitoring interfaces**: Nine

Figure 11-10 *Cisco IPS 4260 Sensor*

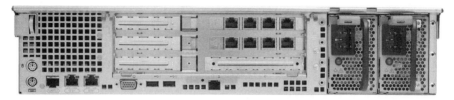

Signatures

Now that you posses a basic understanding of the roles of IDS and IPS sensors in a network and are acquainted with various IDS and IPS hardware solutions, next consider how a sensor detects an attack. The sensor uses a collection of signatures to detect potentially malicious network traffic. If the observed traffic matches a signature, the sensor can trigger an alarm (or perform a variety of other actions).

Because of the diversity of a sensor's signature collection, groups of similar signatures are handled by *microengines*. A sensor contains multiple microengines. The sensor decides which microengine(s) it will use to analyze traffic based on criteria such as the network protocol being used by the traffic, the signature's associated operating system, the port number being used by the session, and the type of attack the sensor is looking for. However, at a more macro level, you can categorize signatures into one of four broad categories, as described next.

Exploit Signatures

An exploit attempts to leverage a weakness in the network. That weakness could, for example, be associated with a network application at the application layer of the OSI model. Alternatively, exploit attacks could target the transport and/or network OSI layers. Following are examples of potential attacker exploits at these OSI layers:

■ **Application layer**: As an attacker is preparing to attack a network, he might perform network reconnaissance, in which he attempts to learn more about the network. One form of network reconnaissance involves performing Domain Name System (DNS) queries to learn more about a target domain. For example, the http://www.betterwhois.com website provides, for free, detailed information about a domain, including contact information for the domain administrator. Other examples of application layer exploits include launching DoS attacks (attempts to deplete system resources), directory traversal attacks, viruses, Trojan horses, and worms.

■ **Transport layer**: Protocols such as TCP and UDP reside at the transport layer of the OSI model. Both TCP and UDP communicate on various ports. For example, the Telnet application communicates on TCP port 23, and Simple Mail Transfer Protocol (SMTP) communicates on TCP port 25. An attacker might perform a *port scan* to determine what services (for example, Telnet or SMTP) are available at specific IP addresses. Another example of a transport layer exploit floods a device with a series of TCP synchronization (SYN) segments, which is part of TCP's three-way handshake process. However, this TCP SYN flood attack never completes the three-way handshake. Rather, the attacker creates multiple partially open connections (that is, *embryonic* connections) to exhaust resources on the attack target.

- **Network layer:** Similar to the transport layer's port scan attack, at the network layer an attacker might perform a *ping sweep*. Here the attacker attempts to ping a range of IP addresses to determine which ones respond to the ping. After the attacker compiles a list of IP addresses that responded to his pings, he can further investigate those systems using, for example, the previously mentioned port scan.

Connection Signatures

Connection signatures use a set of rules that state how certain protocols should behave on the network. For example, administrators can configure policies that dictate what types of network connections or network traffic are allowed.

String Signatures

Some attacks can be recognized by a series of bytes contained in the malicious packet. This series of bytes is called a *string*. Other than the strings already known to a sensor's signature database, administrators can use *regular expressions* to match known strings. Regular expressions leverage a series of wildcards, called *metacharacters*, to allow a single expression to match multiple strings.

Denial-of-Service Signatures

The purpose of a DoS attack is to consume the resources of the attack target, such as the memory or processor resources of a mission-critical server. DoS signatures can recognize multiple types of DoS attacks. By consuming system resources, an attacker can prevent legitimate users from accessing those resources. A distributed denial-of-service (DDoS) attack distributes a DoS attack, such that multiple devices attempt to consume resources on a target system.

Signature Definition Files

As mentioned earlier in this chapter, in addition to sensor appliances, a Cisco IOS router, with an appropriate version IOS, can act as an IPS sensor, thus allowing an IOS router to drop malicious traffic before the traffic reaches its intended target. In addition to dropping the offending traffic, the router can log the activity using either the syslog or Security Device Event Exchange (SDEE) protocol. The SDEE protocol is preferred over syslog. SDEE provides a secure communications channel, and it can be used to communicate between IPS clients and servers (for example, a management workstation that collects and correlates events from multiple IPS sensors in the network).

The IOS router acting as an IPS device needs a database of signatures to identify malicious traffic. The router's signature database is in the form of a Signature Definition File (SDF). Modern routers typically ship with an SDF installed in flash memory. However, the administrator usually needs to periodically update the router's SDF, because Cisco routinely updates these files to address emerging threats. A router can also reference multiple SDFs for increased signature coverage.

SDFs vary in their number of signatures, and the SDF used by a particular router platform is largely determined by the router's RAM. For example, if a router contains 128 MB of RAM, it might use the 128MB.sdf, which contains approximately 300 signatures. Alternatively, a router with 256 MB of RAM might use the 256MB.sdf, which contains approximately 500 signatures.

The collection of signatures contained in an SDF might not be appropriate for a specific network. Fortunately, network administrators can tune individual signatures, or even disable a signature, to better meet the needs of their network.

Alarms

After an IPS sensor triggers an alarm, which is sometimes called a "signature firing," one or more events can occur. These events are described in Table 11-4.

Table 11-4 *Responses to a Signature Firing*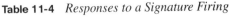

Response	Description
Create a log entry	The triggering of an alarm can cause the IPS sensor to create a log message indicating that a particular signature was matched. The log message can be written using syslog or SDEE.
Drop the offending packet	When a packet triggers an alarm, the IPS sensor can be configured to drop the offending packet, thus preventing the potentially malicious traffic from reaching its intended target.
Reset the TCP connection	In a TCP-based connection, the IPS sensor can reset the connection when a signature is matched. Specifically, the sensor sends a TCP RST message to both parties involved in the TCP conversation.
Block the attacker's IP address	A signature firing can also cause the IPS sensor to drop all traffic sourced from the attacker's IP address. Typically, this blocking behavior occurs for only a specific period of time. However, if you configure this response using IOS-based IOS, be aware that you might block one of your own users, whose IP address is being spoofed by the attacker.

Table 11-4 *Responses to a Signature Firing*

Response	Description
Block traffic associated with the offending connection	Perhaps you do not want a signature firing to block all traffic from the attacker's IP address, but you do want to block all traffic associated with a particular connection (such as an HTTP session). Such an action is possible with an IPS sensor. Like the action of blocking an attacker's IP address, this action of blocking a connection's traffic can be configured to remain in effect for a specified period of time. This approach reduces the likelihood that you will inadvertently block one of your network users because of the attacker spoofing the user's IP address. However, because only a single connection is being blocked, the attacker could relaunch his attack using a different protocol and/or port number.

Sometimes a network administrator wants a signature firing to result in more than one of the previous actions. For example, you might want to generate a log entry and block all traffic sourced from the attacker's IP address. Changing these signature responses is called *signature tuning*.

Using SDM to Configure Cisco IOS IPS

Although Cisco offers IPS services on a wide variety of platforms, this section focuses on configuring IOS-based IPS using Cisco's Security Device Manager (SDM). Cisco's SDM is a graphical interface that supports a wizard-like configuration tool for configuring a variety of IOS features, including IOS-based IPS.

Launching the Intrusion Prevention Wizard

To begin configuring IPS on a Cisco IOS router using SDM, launch the SDM interface. The SDM home page, shown in Figure 11-11, provides summary information about the router.

To begin a configuration task using SDM, click the **Configure** button at the top of the SDM home page. The configuration screen, as shown in Figure 11-12, has a column of tasks along the left side of the page.

Figure 11-11 *SDM Home Page*

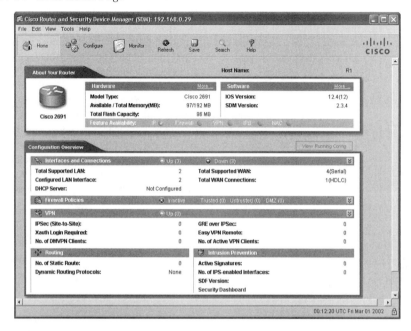

Figure 11-12 *SDM Configuration Page*

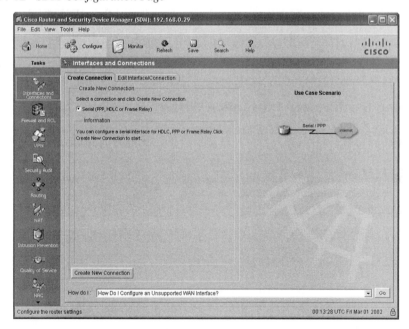

A wide range of tasks, including configuring an IOS-based firewall or a virtual private network (VPN), is available. To configure an IOS-based IPS, click the **Intrusion Prevention** option in the Tasks column. The Intrusion Prevention System (IPS) configuration screen appears, as shown in Figure 11-13. This screen has three tabs: **Create IPS**, **Edit IPS**, and **Security Dashboard**.

Figure 11-13 *Intrusion Prevention System (IPS) Configuration Page*

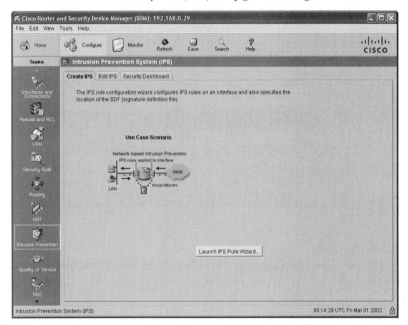

The default tab is **Create IPS**; notice the **Launch IPS Rule Wizard** button. Click this button to begin the wizard.

An Information window appears, similar to the one shown in Figure 11-14, indicating that the router does not currently have SDEE notification enabled. By clicking **OK** in this window, you allow SDM to enable SDEE notification on the router.

Figure 11-14   *SDEE Notification Window*

Another information window appears, like the one shown in Figure 11-15. It lets you know that SDM will open a subscription with the router to get the SDEE events.

Figure 11-15   *SDEE Subscription Window*

IPS Policies Wizard

After you confirm the SDEE messages, the IPS Policies Wizard window appears, as shown in Figure 11-16.

The initial screen explains that the IPS Policies Wizard helps you with the following tasks:

- Selecting the interface to which the IPS rule will be applied

- Selecting the direction of traffic that will be inspected

- Selecting the SDF file to be used by the router

After you click **Next**, the IPS Wizard prompts you to select the interface(s) to which the IPS rule should be applied, in addition to the direction of traffic (that is, inbound or outbound). In the example shown in Figure 11-17, the IPS Wizard has been instructed to apply the IPS rule to inbound traffic for interface Serial 1/0.

Figure 11-16   *IPS Wizard Welcome Screen*

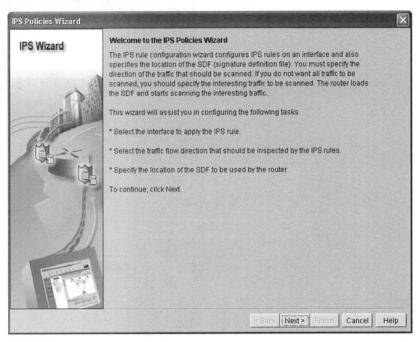

Figure 11-17   *Interface Selection Screen*

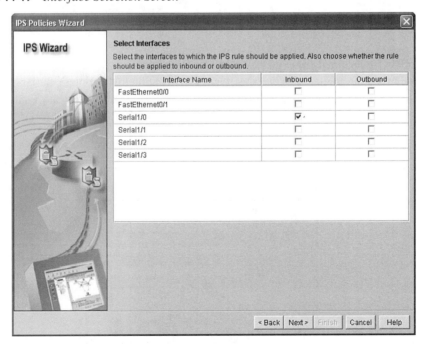

After you click **Next** again, the SDF Locations screen appears, as shown in Figure 11-18. It allows you to specify one or more locations for the router to retrieve an SDF file. You can set the order of the locations using the **Move Up** and **Move Down** buttons.

Figure 11-18 *SDF Locations Screen*

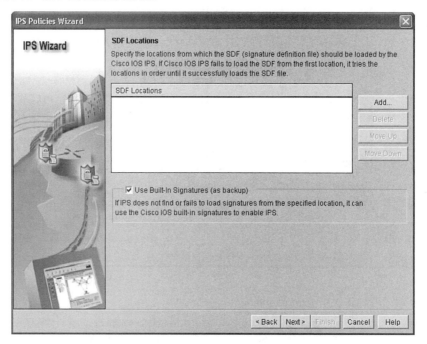

Click the **Add** button to bring up the Add a Signature Location window, as shown in Figure 11-19. From this window you can specify an SDF location in the router's flash or at a specific URL. Also, notice the **autosave** checkbox. Checking this option allows the router to save the SDF file in the event of a router crash, eliminating the need to reconfigure the SDF location after the router comes back up.

Figure 11-19 *Specifying a Signature Location*

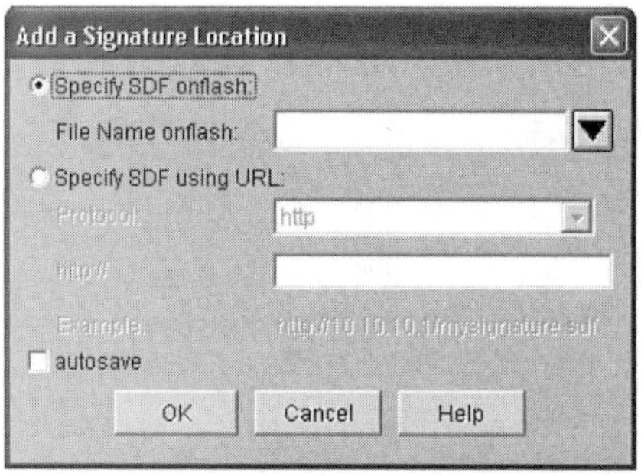

In Figure 11-20, the 128MB.sdf SDF file stored in flash is specified. This particular file was selected because of the router's memory. If the router contained 256 MB of RAM, the 256MB.sdf file could have been used instead, to provide a larger signature database.

Figure 11-20   *Flash Selected as the SDF Location*

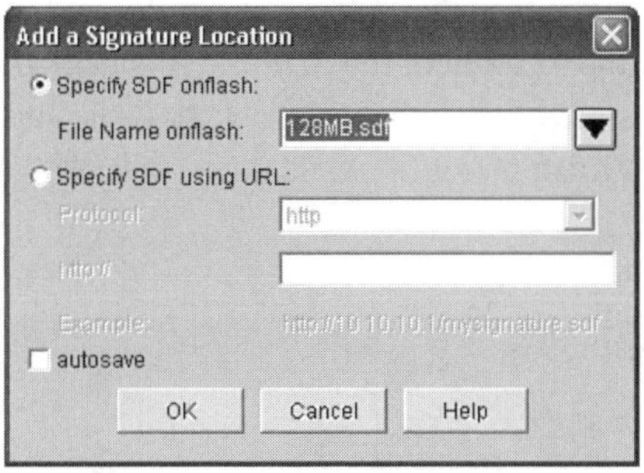

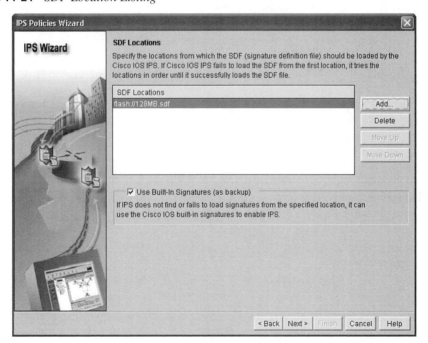

The newly configured SDF location then appears in the SDF Locations pane, as shown in Figure 11-21. Multiple SDF locations could be specified, and the router would attempt to load the SDF from the first location in the list. If it failed, the next SDF location would be attempted. However, in this example, only a single SDF location is specified.

Figure 11-21   *SDF Location Listing*

Also notice the **Use Built-In Signatures (as backup)** checkbox. Checking this box allows IPS to use the Cisco IOS built-in signatures if a signature definition file cannot be found. After you add one or more SDF locations, click the **Next** button to continue.

A Summary window appears, as shown in Figure 11-22. It identifies the interface(s) on which IPS will be applied and in what direction(s) traffic will be analyzed as it crosses the interface. Additionally, the location of the SDF file is specified, and you can see if the **Use Built-In Signatures (as back)** checkbox is checked. If the summary information appears to be correct, click the **Finish** button.

Figure 11-22 *Summary Window*

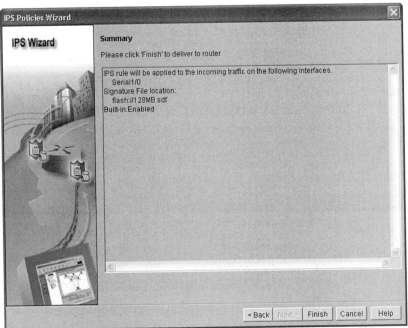

The commands required to configure IOS-based IPS are then sent from SDM to the router. After the commands are delivered, click the **OK** button in the Commands Delivery Status window, shown in Figure 11-23.

Figure 11-23 *Commands Delivery Status Window*

When the Intrusion Prevention Wizard is finished, your view changes in the **Edit IPS** tab, as shown in Figure 11-24. From this tab, you can edit IPS rules, set global IPS settings, and configure IPS signatures.

Figure 11-24 *Edit IPS Tab*

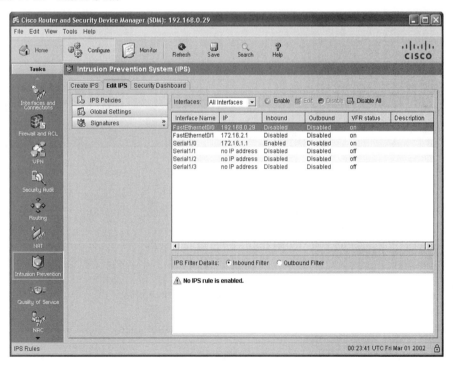

Creating IPS Rules

The previously described configuration enabled IOS-based IPS for interface Serial 0/1. If you click the interface, the IPS Filter Details pane, as shown in Figure 11-25, reveals that although the IPS rule is enabled, no filtering is associated with this rule.

Figure 11-25 *IPS Filter Details Pane*

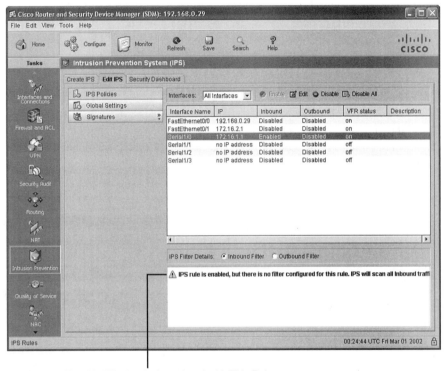

Warning That No Filtering Is Associated with This Rule

To see how to add an associated rule, consider the following scenario:

You want to block inbound Telnet traffic on interface Serial 0/1 while permitting all other traffic.

The following steps illustrate how to accomplish this objective:

Step 1   With the desired interface selected (that is, highlighted), click the **Edit** button. This action displays the Edit IPS on an Interface window, as shown in Figure 11-26.

Figure 11-26   *Edit IPS on an Interface Window*

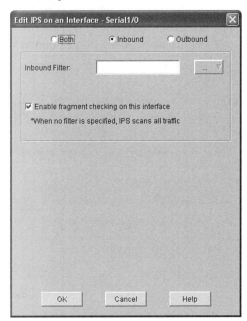

Step 2   Verify that **Inbound** is the selected direction, and click the drop-down menu to the right of the **Inbound Filter** box. From the drop-down menu, choose **Create a new rule(ACL) and select**, as shown in Figure 11-27.

Figure 11-27   *Edit IPS on an Interface Window Drop-Down Menu*

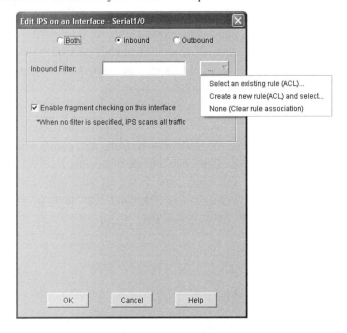

Step 3   When the Add a Rule window appears, as shown in Figure 11-28, enter a name or number for the rule. Also select the type of rule (that is, standard or extended) from the **Type** drop-down menu. Optionally, you can document the rule's purpose in the **Description** field.

Figure 11-28   *Add a Rule Window*

Step 4   Click the **Add** button in the Add a Rule window to bring up the Add an Extended Rule Entry window (assuming that you selected Extended Rule as the type of rule). In this window, shown in Figure 11-29, using a series of drop-down menus and ... buttons, you can specify what traffic you want to permit or deny. In this example, the rule is configured to deny all traffic destined for the TCP Telnet service.

Step 5   Click **OK** to add the rule. You are returned to the Add a Rule window, as shown in Figure 11-30. Notice that the rule that denies inbound Telnet traffic appears in the Rule Entry pane. However, these rules contain an implicit **deny ip any any** statement. Therefore, if another rule to permit traffic is not added, all traffic will be denied.

Figure 11-29 *Add an Extended Rule Entry Window*

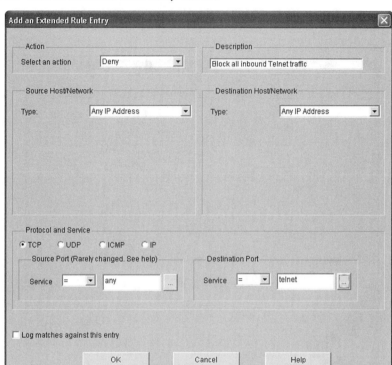

Figure 11-30 *Confirmation of Rule Entry*

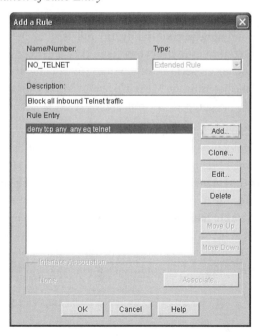

Step 6   Click the **Add** button again to add a rule that permits any traffic to any destination, as shown in Figure 11-31.

Figure 11-31   *Creating a Rule to Permit All Other Traffic*

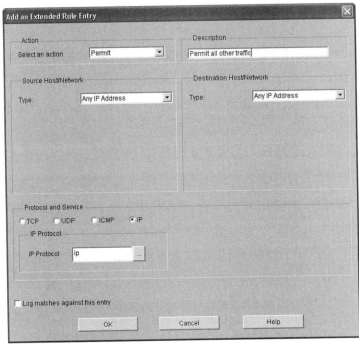

Step 7   You are returned to the Add a Rule window. Notice, in Figure 11-32, that the newly configured **permit ip any any** rule is at the bottom of the rule list. The order of rules is critical, because they are processed top-down. You can optionally select one of the rules (by clicking it) and changing its order in the list using the **Move Up** and/or **Move Down** buttons. Click the **OK** button to complete the rule entry.

Step 8   The Edit IPS on an Interface window appears, as shown in Figure 11-33. From this window, you can specify whether you want the IOS router to perform Virtual Fragment Reassembly (VFR). Specifically, IOS-based IPS cannot thoroughly scan the contents of IP fragments, thus allowing fragmented traffic to pass through the router without being analyzed. When the **Enable fragment checking on this interface** checkbox is checked, the router uses the VFR feature to dynamically create access control lists to protect the network from fragmentation attacks. Click **OK** to deliver the configuration commands to the router.

Figure 11-32 *Ordered List of Rules*

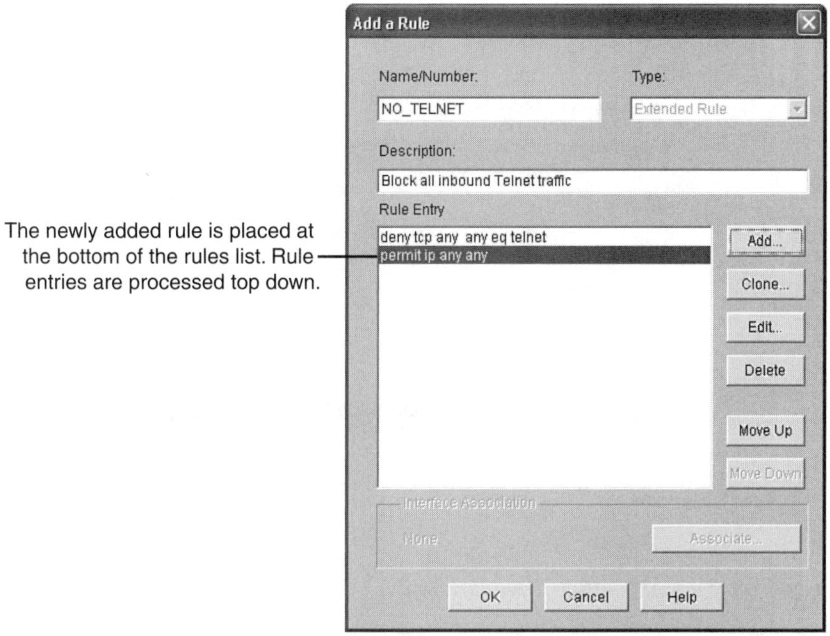

The newly added rule is placed at the bottom of the rules list. Rule entries are processed top down.

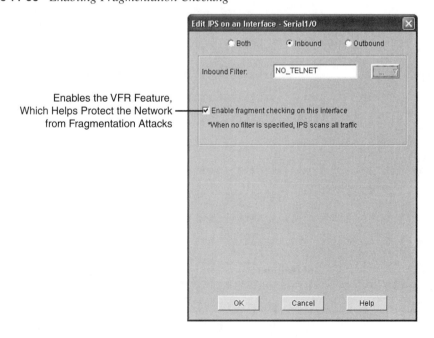

Figure 11-33 *Enabling Fragmentation Checking*

Enables the VFR Feature, Which Helps Protect the Network from Fragmentation Attacks

Step 9   The Commands Delivery Status window, shown in Figure 11-34, informs
you when the IPS rule configuration commands have been delivered to
the router. After the delivery is complete, click the **OK** button.

Figure 11-34   *Delivering Commands to the Router*

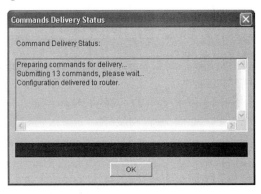

Figure 11-35   *Verifying IPS Filter Configuration*

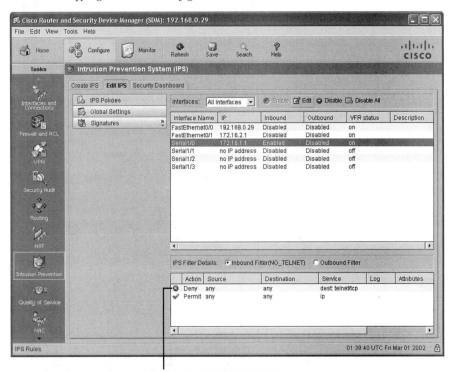

Details the Rules Contained in the NO_TELNET ACL

After the rules have been added to the interface, the rules appear in the IPS Filter Details pane. Figure 11-35 shows that the NO_TELNET inbound filter has been applied to the selected interface (Serial 1/0).

Manipulating Global IPS Settings

The **Edit IPS** tab also allows administrators to configure global IPS settings. Clicking the **Global Settings** button displays a screen similar to the one shown in Figure 11-36.

Figure 11-36   *Global IPS Settings*

Global Settings Include syslog, SDEE, and Engine Options

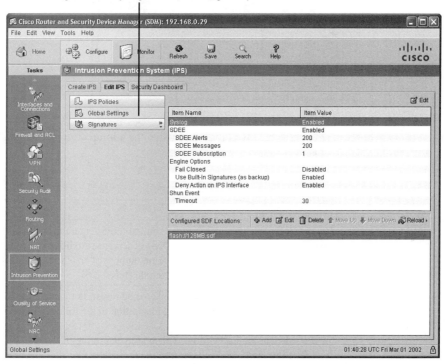

To configure these global settings, an administrator can double-click one of the shown parameters (**Syslog**, **SDEE**, or **Engine Options**). The Edit Global settings window appears, as shown in Figure 11-37.

Figure 11-37 *Edit Global Settings Window: Syslog and SDEE Tab*

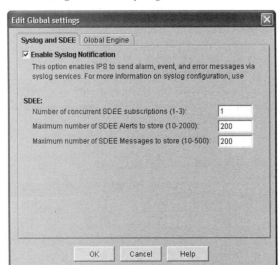

The Edit Global settings window has two tabs from which the administrator can configure global settings, as described in Table 11-5.

Table 11-5 *Tabs in the Edit Global Settings Window*

Tab	Description
Syslog and SDEE	With this tab, an administrator can cause the IPS feature to send alarm, event, and error information using syslog services. Additionally, SDEE parameters (for example, the maximum number of concurrent SDEE subscriptions) can be configured from this tab.
Global Engine	With this tab, shown in Figure 11-38, the administrator can configure a timeout for loading IPS signatures, in addition to the following options: • **Enable Engine Fail Closed**: This option determines if the IOS-based IPS feature will drop or permit traffic for a particular IPS signature engine while a new signature for that engine is being compiled. If this option is enabled, traffic is dropped if IPS services are unavailable. If this option were disabled (which would be known as a *fail open* configuration), traffic would be passed when IPS services are unavailable. • **Use Built-In Signatures (as backup)**: This option, which is enabled by default, allows the IPS feature to use built-in IOS signatures if the configured signature fails to load. • **Enable deny action on IPS interface**: This option allows an access control list to be configured on an interface that has IPS rules applied.

Figure 11-38   *Edit Global Settings Window: Global Engine Tab*

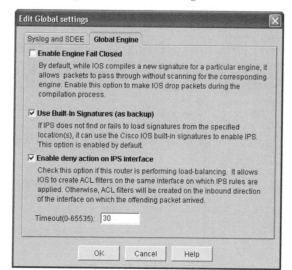

Signature Configuration

After enabling the IPS feature on a router, you might want to manipulate the default signature settings. For example, you might want to disable some of the signatures that are enabled by default, and vice versa. Also, you might want to alter the action or actions taken in response to a signature being triggered.

To configure such signature parameters, click the **Signatures** button on the **Edit IPS** tab. This displays a listing of signatures, as shown in Figure 11-39.

Notice that all known IPS signatures are listed in the right pane. If you know the name of the signature you are attempting to find, you can scroll through the list to locate it. Alternatively, notice that the signatures are categorized in a hierarchical fashion, under the **OS**, **Attack**, **Service**, **L2/L3/L4 Protocol**, and **Releases** categories.

Figure 11-39   *Signature Listing*

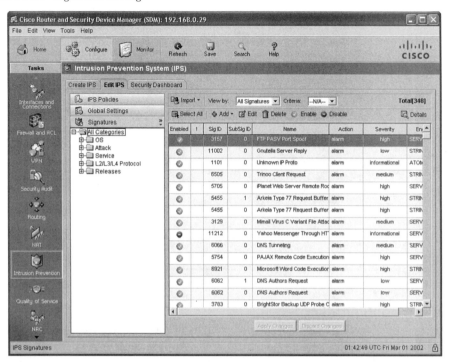

To understand the editing of a signature, consider the following scenario:

You want to change the action taken in response to the POP Overflow signature being fired, such that an alarm is generated and the offending packet is dropped.

The following steps illustrate how to accomplish this objective:

Step 1   Scroll down in the right pane, and locate the desired signature, as shown in Figure 11-40.

Figure 11-40 *Locating the Desired Signature*

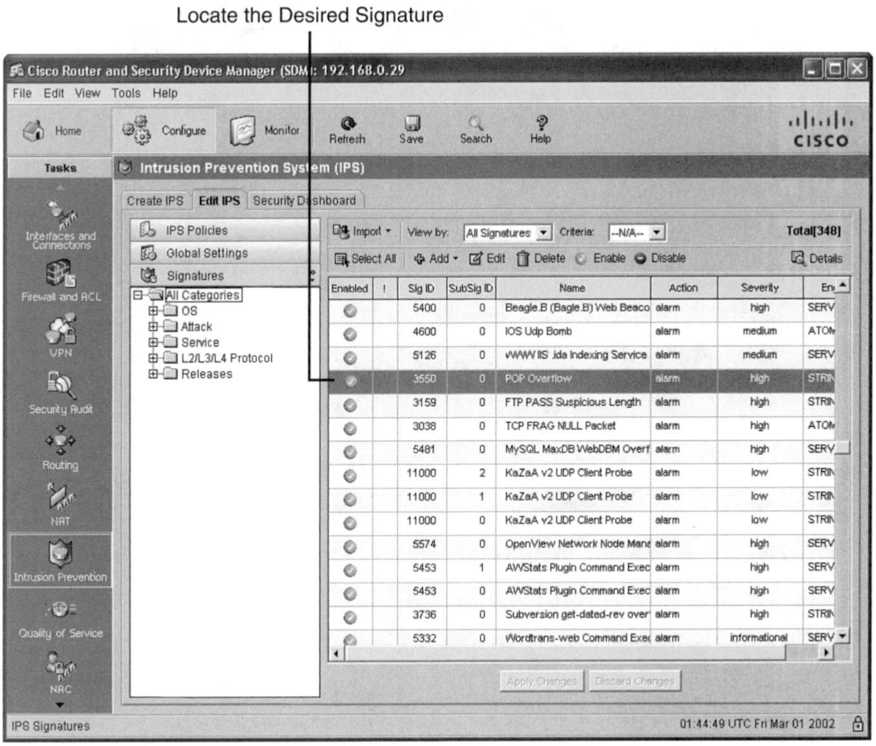

Step 2   Double-click the signature to open the Edit Signature window, as shown in Figure 11-41.

Figure 11-41   *Edit Signature Window*

Step 3   Notice that the configurable values are currently dimmed. To make one
of the fields editable, click the green square to the left of the field. The
green square changes into a red diamond after you click it, and the field
can now be edited. In this example, you click the green square adjacent
to the **EventAction** field, as shown in Figure 11-42. To meet the scenario
objective, both the **alarm** and **drop** actions must be selected (that is,
highlighted). To select more than one action, click the first action, hold
down the **Ctrl** key, and click the subsequent action(s).

Figure 11-42 *Configuring Signature Parameters*

When editing a signature, click on the green square next to a signature property you want to change. The green square changes to a red diamond, indicating that you can edit the property.

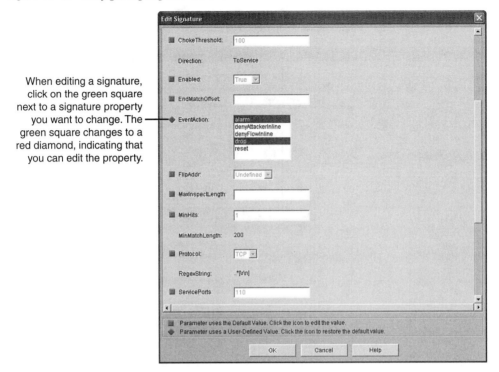

After the parameters are configured as desired, click the **OK** button at the bottom of the Edit Signature window. You are returned to the **Edit IPS** tab. Notice that the signature you edited now has a yellow octagon symbol with a minus sign in it, in the **!** column, as shown in Figure 11-43. This symbol indicates that the changes you made have not yet been delivered to the router. Click the **Apply Changes** button, which is just below the signatures pane, to deliver the commands to the router and make the specified changes.

Figure 11-43 *Changes Not Delivered to the Router*

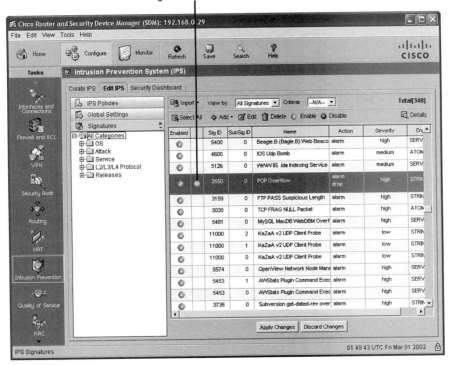

Exam Preparation Tasks

Review All the Key Topics

Review the most important topics from this chapter, denoted with the Key Topic icon. Table 11-6 lists these key topics and the page where each is found.

Key
Topic

Table 11-6   *Key Topics for Chapter 11*

Key Topic Element	Description	Page Number
Table 11-2	IDS/IPS detection methods	391
List	Sensor interface types	396
Table 11-3	Sensor operating modes	396
List	Exploits at various OSI layers	398
Table 11-4	Responses to a signature firing	400-401
List	Tasks performed by the IPS Policies Wizard	404
Table 11-5	Tabs in the Edit Global Settings window	418
List	Signature editing steps	420

Complete the Tables and Lists from Memory

Print a copy of Appendix D, "Memory Tables," (found on the CD) or at least the section for this chapter, and complete the tables and lists from memory. Appendix E, "Memory Tables Answer Key," also on the CD, includes completed tables and lists so that you can check your work.

Definition of Key Terms

Define the following key terms from this chapter, and check your answers in the glossary:

intrusion detection system (IDS), intrusion prevention system (IPS), Cisco Security Agent (CSA), promiscuous mode, inline mode, microengine, signature definition file (SDF)

IINS exam topics covered in this part:

- Describe the Cisco security family of products and their interactions

- Explain the different methods used in cryptography

- Explain IKE protocol functionality and phases

- Describe the building blocks of IPsec and the security functions it provides

- Configure and verify an IPsec site-to-site VPN with pre-shared key authentication using SDM

Part III: Extending Security and Availability with Cryptography and VPNs

This chapter covers the following topics:

Introducing cryptographic services:
Cryptographic services can be divided into two halves: the construction of codes and the breaking of codes. This section explores the interworking of cryptographic services and examines symmetric and asymmetric algorithms. It also discusses the use of block and stream ciphers, because these are used to manipulate and secure data by various algorithms.

Exploring symmetric encryption: This section focuses on symmetric encryption to help you better understand their nature and uses. It looks at a variety of symmetric algorithms, including DES, 3DES, AES, SEAL, and various Rivest ciphers (RC). As we explore these algorithms, you will gain an understanding of their use and the benefits they provide to modern computing environments.

Understanding security algorithms: This section examines the characteristics of encryption algorithms, discusses cryptographic hashes, and explores the role of key management in securing the encryption process. This section also looks at implementing encryption by examining its use in an SSL VPN.

CHAPTER 12

Designing a Cryptographic Solution

The mention of cryptography may conjure up images of intrigue and cloak-and-dagger spy movies, but in the real world, cryptography is at the heart of many security implementations. Cryptographic solutions provide confidentiality and integrity of data in circumstances where data might be exposed to threats from untrusted individuals. To create a successful security policy, you must understand the basic functionality of cryptography and how you can use encryption and hashing to provide confidentiality and integrity for your data. Along with this, you must understand the importance of key management to keep your solution secure.

"Do I Know This Already?" Quiz

The "Do I Know This Already?" quiz helps you determine your level of knowledge of this chapter's topics before you begin. Table 12-1 details the major topics discussed in this chapter and their corresponding quiz questions.

Table 12-1 *"Do I Know This Already?" Section-to-Question Mapping*

Foundation Topics Section	Questions
Introducing Cryptographic Services	1 to 5
Exploring Symmetric Encryption	6 to 10
Understanding Security Algorithms	11 to 15

1. What form of attack are all algorithms susceptible to?

   a. Meet-in-the-middle

   b. Spoofing

   c. Stream cipher

   d. Brute-force

2. Which type of cipher achieves security by rearranging the letters in a string of text?

    a. Vigenère cipher

    b. Stream cipher

    c. Transposition cipher

    d. Block cipher

3. In terms of constructing a good encryption algorithm, what does it mean to create an avalanche effect?

    a. Changing only a few bits of a plain-text message causes the ciphertext to be completely different.

    b. Altering the key length causes the ciphertext to be completely different.

    c. Changing only a few bits of a ciphertext message causes the plain text to be completely different.

    d. Altering the key length causes the plain text to be completely different.

4. Which of the following are techniques used by symmetric encryption cryptography? (Choose all that apply.)

    a. Block ciphers

    b. Message Authentication Codes (MAC)

    c. One-time pad

    d. Stream ciphers

    e. Vigenère ciphers

5. Which of the following is not a common stream cipher?

    a. RC4

    b. RSA

    c. SEAL

    d. DES

6. Which of the following characteristics accurately describe symmetric encryption algorithms? (Choose all that apply.)

    a. They are faster than asymmetric algorithms.

    b. They have longer key lengths than asymmetric encryption algorithms.

    c. They are stronger than asymmetric algorithms.

    d. They are less complex mathematically than asymmetric algorithms.

    e. They are slower than asymmetric algorithms.

    f. They are weaker than asymmetric algorithms.

7. DES typically operates in block mode, where it encrypts data in what size blocks?

   a. 56-bit blocks

   b. 40-bit blocks

   c. 128-bit blocks

   d. 64-bit blocks

8. Stream ciphers operate on which of the following?

   a. Fixed-length groups of bits called blocks

   b. Individual digits, one at a time, with the transformations varying during the encryption

   c. Individual blocks, one at a time, with the transformations varying during the encryption

   d. Fixed-length groups of digits called blocks

9. Which statement accurately describes ECB mode?

   a. In ECB mode, each 64-bit plain-text block is exclusive ORed (XORed) bitwise with the previous ciphertext block.

   b. ECB mode uses the same 64-bit key to serially encrypt each 56-bit plain-text block.

   c. ECB mode uses the same 56-bit key to serially encrypt each 64-bit plain-text block.

   d. In ECB mode, each 56-bit plain-text block is exclusive ORed (XORed) bitwise with the previous ciphertext block.

10. What method does 3DES use to encrypt plain text?

   a. 3DES-EDE

   b. EDE-3DES

   c. 3DES-AES

   d. AES-3DES

11. Which of the following is not considered a trustworthy symmetric encryption algorithm?

   a. 3DES

   b. IDEA

   c. EDE

   d. AES

12. In a brute-force attack, generally an attacker has to search through what percentage of the keyspace until he or she finds the key that decrypts the data?

    a. Roughly 10 percent

    b. Roughly 75 percent

    c. Roughly 66 percent

    d. Roughly 50 percent

13. How many weak keys are a part of the overall DES keyspace?

    a. Five

    b. One

    c. Four

    d. None

14. Which of the following is not a component of the key management life cycle?

    a. Key verification

    b. Key transposition

    c. Key generation

    d. Key exchange

    e. Key storage

15. Hashing is used to provide which of the following?

    a. Data consistency

    b. Data binding

    c. Data checksums

    d. Data integrity

Foundation Topics

Introducing Cryptographic Services

To understand cryptographic services, first you must understand the science of cryptology, which in essence is the making and breaking of secret codes. Cryptology can be broken into two distinct areas: cryptography and cryptanalysis. Cryptography is the development and use of codes. Cryptanalysis is all about the breaking of these codes. This section explores these two disciplines to give you a better understanding of cryptographic services as a whole.

Understanding Cryptology

Because cryptography is made up of two halves—the creation of codes and the attempted breaking of those codes—a natural give-and-take relationship is at play. Therefore, it is only natural that at times one side will be ahead of the other.

History offers an excellent example of this during the Hundred Years War between France and England. At that time, the cryptanalysts were ahead of the cryptographers. France believed that the Vigenère cipher was unbreakable. The British, however, cracked the code and broke it.

In another historical example, many historians now believe that the outcome of World War II largely turned on the fact that the winning side on both fronts was much more successful than the other at cracking the encryption of its enemy.

Given these examples, you might wonder who presently has the edge in this game of give and take. For the time being, conventional wisdom within the cryptology community holds that cryptographers currently have the edge. Of course, this can, and likely will, change some day.

So exactly how do we make such judgments about who is ahead or what code is unbreakable? In fact, in cryptography, it truly is impossible to prove that any given algorithm is "secure." The best that can be accomplished is to show that the algorithm is not vulnerable to any known cryptanalytic attacks. This limits our certainty to an extent, because there may be methods that have been developed but as of yet are unknown, that could crack the algorithm. The one exception to this rule is a brute-force attack.

All algorithms are vulnerable to brute force. It is simply in the nature of the attack. In other words, if every possible key is tried, one of them will surely work. The issue is time.

Depending on the complexity of the algorithm, a brute-force attack could take an inordinate amount of time to ultimately succeed. But no algorithm is truly unbreakable.

Cryptography Through the Ages

Cryptography has a long and storied past, dating back to the courts of kings, who would use early encryption to secure messages sent to other courts. Even these early times involved a degree of intrigue, because some of the courts involved would attempt to steal any message sent to an opposing kingdom.

From the courts of kings to the tools of military commanders, encryption was quickly adopted as a means of securing communications. Because messengers sometimes were killed as they transported critical military messages, encryption was seen as an indispensable means of securing these communications even if they fell into enemy hands.

Even dating back to the days of Julius Caesar, encryption was used to secure communications. Caesar's simple substitution cipher was used on the battlefield to quickly encrypt messages to his commanders. Thomas Jefferson even invented an encryption system that many historians believe he used while serving as Secretary of State from 1790 to 1793.

One of the great advances in encryption came with a machine invented by Arthur Scherbius in 1918. This machine served as a template for the systems used by each of the major participants in World War II. Scherbius called his machine the Enigma and sold it to Germany. When speaking about the security of his machine, he estimated that if 1000 cryptanalysts tested four keys per minute, all day, every day, it would take 1.8 billion years to try them all.

Throughout World War II, both the Germans and the Allies created machines modeled on the Scherbius machine. Arguably, these were the most sophisticated encryption devices ever developed. To defend against this level of encryption, the British created what most call the world's first computer, the Colossus. The Colossus was then used to break the encryption that was used by Germany's Enigma.

The Substitution Cipher

Put simply, a cipher is an algorithm for performing encryption and decryption. Typically, ciphers represent a series of well-defined steps that you can follow as a procedure. With a substitution cipher, one letter is substituted for another to encrypt a message. Substitution ciphers vary in complexity, but in their simplest form, the letter frequency of the original message is retained when character substitution is done.

As mentioned, Julius Caesar made use of a simple substitution cipher on ancient battlefields. During these times, each day would have a different key, and that key would be used to adjust the alphabet accordingly. Let's look at an example.

Let's say that the key for today is 10. In this case the letter to be substituted for A is the character in the alphabet that is ten spaces forward. In other words, to represent an A, we would substitute a K. If we follow this through the alphabet, a B would be an L, a C would be an M, and so on. To keep the nature of the substitution secret, each day the key might move a random number of places, and the process would begin again.

One of the shortcomings of this simple cipher is its vulnerability to frequency analysis. Let's say that a message has 15 occurrences of the letter B, and B is to be replaced by L. This would mean that although we are substituting the character, there would still be 15 occurrences of the letter L. So if a message were long enough, it would be vulnerable to frequency analysis. This is because the message would retain the frequency patterns found in the language even though the characters might be different.

Analysts trying to crack this cipher might look at the natural occurrence pattern for each letter in the English language. They could then use this to compare the frequency of a certain letter in the encrypted text. For instance, if the letter S appears in 20 percent of all English words, and the letter X appears in 20 percent of all the words that have been encrypted, analysts might conclude that for this cipher, X equals S. To defend against this core weakness of the substitution cipher, polyalphabetic ciphers were invented.

The Vigenère Cipher

Polyalphabetic ciphers were invented to make up for the shortcomings of the substitution cipher. The Vigenère cipher is an excellent example of this kind of cipher. It encrypts text through the use of a series of different Caesar ciphers based on the letters of a particular keyword. Although this is a simple form of polyalphabetic substitution, it still proves invulnerable to frequency analysis.

This form of encryption dates back to a book written in 1553 by Giovan Batista Belaso, although the name of this cipher came from Blaise de Vigenère, a French cryptographer. He was mistakenly credited with its invention, and to this day it carries his name.

Let's take a look at how we might use this cipher to encrypt a message. We begin with a key of SECRET. This key is then used to encode the message X MARKS THE SPOT. We encode the X by looking at the row starting with S for the letter in the X column. In this case, the X is replaced with P. Next we look for the row that begins with E for the letter M. This results in Q as our second character. To encode the full phrase, we would simply map the characters by row and column and continue our substitution.

Transposition Ciphers

If you have ever seen the beginning of the movie *Sneakers*, as the letters on-screen scramble to then become the correct words, you have a slight feel for a transposition cipher. In these ciphers, no letters are replaced; they are just rearranged. A simple form of this might take a phrase like THE QUICK BROWN FOX and simply transpose the letters so that it becomes XOFNWORBKCIUQEHT.

The Rail Fence Cipher is another kind of transposition cipher in which the words are spelled out as if they were a rail fence. The following example uses a key of three to illustrate how this could be done:

```
T...U..B...N...J...E...E...E...Y..
.H.Q.I.K.R.W.F.X.U.P.D.V.R.H.L.Z.D.G.
..E...C...O...O...M...O...T...A...O
```

To read this message, we need to follow the diagonal pattern along the rail fence. Using this form of encoding, the message THE QUICK BROWN FOX JUMPED OVER THE LAZY DOG would be encoded as TUBNJEEEYHQIKRWFXUPDVRHLZDGECOOMOTAO. Much like the earlier example, no letters have been changed; rather, they have merely been transposed.

Working with the One-Time Pad

The one-time pad has been around for more than 90 years. It was invented and patented in 1917 by Gilbert Vernam of AT&T. The idea behind the one-time pad was to have a stream cipher that would apply the exclusive OR (XOR) operation to plain text with a key. Vernam's idea was enhanced with a contribution from Joseph Maubourgne, a captain in the U.S. Army Signal Corps, who suggested the use of random data as a key.

The one-time pad represents such a significant contribution to cryptography that the NSA has called this patent "perhaps the most important in the history of cryptography." However, using this significant idea in a real-world application has a number of difficulties.

One of the more significant challenges is creating random data. On the surface, this sounds simple enough. However, because computers have a mathematical foundation, they cannot create random data. Another significant issue is that should a key be used more than once, it can easily be broken. Adding to these issues, key distribution can also be quite challenging.

One example in which the Vernam cipher has been successfully used is in RC4, which is widely used across the Internet. However, this is not a true one-time pad, because the key used is not random.

The Encryption Process

Uses of encryption are all around us, from secured online purchases to transferring data through a VPN connection. When encryption is used, some form of plain, readable text is converted to ciphertext. Ciphertext represents this text in an unreadable form, whereas decryption is the process of reversing this process. The goal of encryption is to guarantee the confidentiality of data so that only those who have authorization may read the original message. Figure 12-1 shows plain text being transformed into ciphertext.

Figure 12-1   *Plain Text Transformed into Ciphertext*

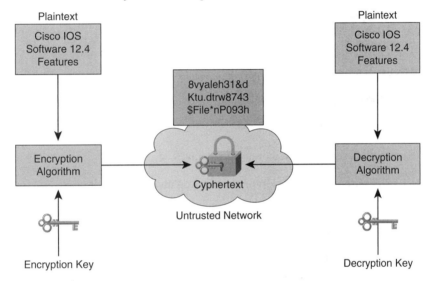

With the various older encryption algorithms we have examined, the key to their success was the secrecy of the algorithm. Today, reverse engineering is often quite simple, making this secrecy less important. Therefore, public-domain algorithms are often used. With these algorithms, successful decryption requires knowledge of the appropriate cryptographic keys. In other words, there has been a shift from the importance of the algorithm's secrecy to ensuring the secrecy of the keys.

Encryption is used to provide confidentiality in terms of the Open Systems Interconnection (OSI) layers in these ways:

■ At the application layer, data encryption is used for secure e-mail, secure database sessions (Oracle SQL*net), and secure messaging (Lotus Notes sessions).

■ At the session layer, data is encrypted using a protocol such as Secure Socket Layer (SSL) or Transport Layer Security (TLS).

- At the network layer, data is encrypted using protocols such as those that make up the IPsec protocol suite.

Cryptanalysis

When we seek to break encoded data, this undertaking is called cryptanalysis. An attacker who is attempting to break an algorithm or encrypted ciphertext may use one of a variety of attacks:

- Chosen plain-text attack

- Chosen ciphertext attack

- Birthday attack

- Meet-in-the-middle attack

- Brute-force attack

- Ciphertext-only attack

- Known plain-text (the usual brute-force) attack

Table 12-2 describes these attack types to help you understand their usage as a form of cryptanalysis.

Table 12-2 *Defining Attack Types*

Type of Attack	Description
Chosen plain-text attack	In this attack the attacker chooses what data the encryption device encrypts and then observes the ciphertext output. This is a more powerful attack than a known plain-text attack, because the attacker gets to choose the plain-text blocks to encrypt. This allows the attacker to choose plain text that could potentially yield more information about the key. However, the practicality of this attack may be called into question. This is because it is often difficult, if not impossible, to capture both the ciphertext and plain text. This would generally require that the trusted network be compromised as well, yielding access to confidential information.
Chosen ciphertext attack	In this attack, the attacker may choose different ciphertexts to be decrypted. The attacker also has access to the decrypted plain text. This combination makes it possible for an attacker to search through the keyspace and determine which key decrypts the chosen ciphertext. This attack is somewhat like the chosen plain-text attack and, like that attack, it may not be too practical. Capturing both the ciphertext and plain text without first breaking into the trusted network would prove nearly impossible.

Table 12-2 *Defining Attack Types*

Type of Attack	Description
Birthday attack	The birthday attack derives its name from the statistical probability involved in two individuals in a group having the same birthday. Statisticians say that in a group of 23 individuals, the likelihood that two people will have the same birthday is greater than 50 percent. This attack is a form of brute-force attack focused on hash functions. If a given function, when supplied with a random input, returns one of k equally likely values, repeating the function with various inputs, the same output would be expected after $1.2k^{1/2}$ times.
Meet-in-the-middle attack	This is a known plain-text attack in which the attacker knows a portion of the plain text and the corresponding ciphertext. The attacker encrypts the plain text with every possible key, and the results are stored. The attacker then decrypts the ciphertext using every key until one of the results matches one of the stored values.
Brute-force attack	All encryption algorithms are vulnerable to a brute-force attack. In this attack, an attacker tries every possible key with the decryption algorithm. Generally, a brute-force attack will succeed about 50 percent of the way through the keyspace. To defend against this form of attack, modern cryptographers have to create a sufficiently large keyspace so that attacking it in this way requires too much time and money to be practical.
Ciphertext-only attack	In this form of attack, the attacker has the ciphertext of several messages. Each of these messages has been encrypted using the same encryption algorithm. However, the attacker has no knowledge of the underlying plain text. To be successful, the attacker must recover the ciphertext of as many messages as possible. Alternatively, the attacker could deduce the key or keys used to encrypt the messages and use this to decrypt other messages encrypted with the same keys. This could be achieved using statistical analysis. Today, however, these attacks are no longer practical, because modern algorithms produce pseudorandom output that is resistant to statistical analysis.
Known plain-text attack	In this attack, like the ciphertext-only attack, the attacker has access to the ciphertext of several messages, and he also knows something about the plain text underlying that ciphertext. Knowing the underlying protocol, file type, and some characteristic strings that may appear in the plain text, an attacker then employs a brute-force attack to try keys until decryption with the correct key succeeds. Compared to other attacks, this may be the most practical attack. Attackers can usually assume the type and some features of the underlying plain text after capturing the ciphertext. Although it is more practical, the enormous keyspaces employed by modern algorithms make it unlikely that this attack will succeed.

Understanding the Features of Encryption Algorithms

Good encryption algorithms have several benefits:

■   They are resistant to cryptographic attacks.

■   They support variable and long key lengths and scalability.

■   They create an avalanche effect.

■   They have no export or import restrictions.

When an attacker sets out to penetrate data protected by a cryptographic algorithm, the best way to do so is to try to decrypt the data using all the possible keys. Of course, the time required to undertake such an attack is determined by the number of possible keys. In practical terms, this process could take quite a long time. In fact, when appropriately long keys are used, this form of attack generally is infeasible.

A couple of other desirable attributes of a good cryptographic algorithm are variable key lengths and scalability. It stands to reason that the longer the key used for encryption, the longer it will take for an attacker to break it. Having the scalability provided by flexible key lengths lets you select the strength and speed of encryption that you need. Let's compare a couple of possible key lengths.

If we were to use a 16-bit key (nowhere near the strongest possible), there would be 65,536 possible keys. This may sound like a large number of keys, but consider that a 56-bit key would yield $7.2 * 10^{16}$ possible keys. As you can see, variable key lengths can provide an ever-increasing number of keys, creating ever-stronger levels of encryption.

Another desirable attribute is called the avalanche effect. It says that changing only a few bits of a plain-text message causes its ciphertext to be completely different. An encryption algorithm that provides the avalanche effect makes it possible for messages that are quite similar to be sent over an untrusted medium, because the encrypted (ciphertext) messages remain completely different.

Export and import restrictions must also be carefully considered when you use encryption internationally. Certain countries prohibit the export of encryption algorithms or allow only the export of algorithms with smaller (more easily broken) keys. Other countries have strict regulations and restrictions governing the import of cryptographic algorithms. Before importing or exporting a cryptographic algorithm internationally, it is best to check with the governments involved to better understand their laws and regulations.

The U.S. has specific restrictions for the export of cryptographic algorithms, but in January 2000 these restrictions were substantially relaxed. At present, any cryptographic product may be exported under a license exception unless the end users are governments outside the U.S. or are among those nations that have an embargo in place. To learn more about current practices for the import and export of cryptographic algorithms in the U.S., visit http://www.commerce.gov.

Symmetric and Asymmetric Encryption Algorithms

This section discusses both symmetric and asymmetric algorithms, noting their differences and uses. Most striking among these two widely used types of encryption algorithms is their differences in key usage. Whereas symmetric encryption algorithms use a single key for both encryption and decryption, asymmetric encryption algorithms employ two separate keys—one for encryption and the other for decryption. Other differences will also be discussed with regard to the algorithms' speed and complexity.

Encryption Algorithms and Keys

Ciphers are two-part mathematical functions that encrypt and decrypt data. Exposure of the algorithm itself could compromise the security of the encryption system if it is based on the algorithm's secrecy. If this should happen, each party working with the algorithm must change it. However, this is a dated view of cryptography. In modern cryptography, all algorithms are public, and complex cryptographic keys are used to ensure the secrecy of the data.

Cryptographic keys are created from sequences of bits that, together with the data that will be encrypted, are input into an encryption algorithm. Table 12-3 describes the two classes of encryption algorithms and details their use of keys.

Table 12-3 *Classes of Encryption Algorithms*

Key
Topic

Class of Algorithm	Description
Symmetric encryption algorithms	This class of algorithm employs the same key to both encrypt and decrypt data.
Asymmetric encryption algorithms	This class of algorithm employs two separate keys. One key is used to encrypt data, and the other key is used to decrypt data.

Symmetric Encryption Algorithms

As shown in Table 12-3, symmetric encryption algorithms use the same key for both encryption and decryption. This means that both the sender and receiver must share the same secret key to transfer data securely. Figure 12-2 shows how symmetric encryption encrypts and decrypts data.

Figure 12-2 *Symmetric Encryption and Decryption Process*

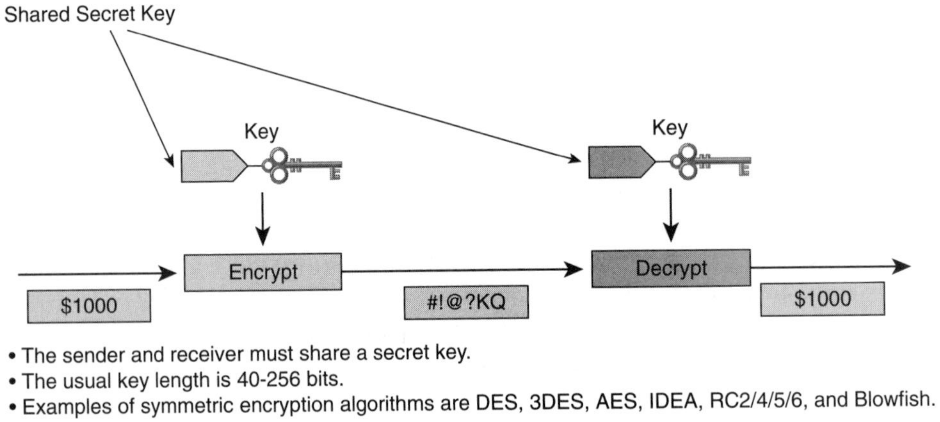

Shared Secret Key

Key   Key

Encrypt   Decrypt

$1000   #!@?KQ $1000

- The sender and receiver must share a secret key.
- The usual key length is 40-256 bits.
- Examples of symmetric encryption algorithms are DES, 3DES, AES, IDEA, RC2/4/5/6, and Blowfish.

For a symmetric algorithm to be secure, the key itself must remain a secret. Should this key become available, anyone holding it could encrypt and decrypt messages. Because of this need for security, symmetric encryption is frequently called secret-key encryption. Symmetric encryption represents the more traditional form of cryptography. It uses key lengths ranging from 40 to 256 bits.

A number of well-known symmetric encryption algorithms exist. Table 12-4 details some of these, along with their key sizes.

Table 12-4 *Popular Symmetric Algorithms*

Symmetric Algorithm	Key Size
DES	56-bit keys
Triple Data Encryption Standard (3DES)	112-bit and 168-bit keys
AES	128-bit, 192-bit, and 256-bit keys
International Data Encryption Algorithm (IDEA)	128-bit keys
RC2	40-bit and 64-bit keys
RC4	1-bit to 256-bit keys
RC5	0-bit to 2040-bit keys
RC6	128-bit, 192-bit, and 256-bit keys
Blowfish	32-bit to 448-bit keys

Symmetric encryption cryptography uses a number of different techniques. The most common are

- Block ciphers

- Stream ciphers

- Message Authentication Codes (MAC)

Symmetric algorithms generally are quite fast and therefore are a frequent choice to provide wire-speed encryption in data networks. Because symmetric algorithms are based on less-complex mathematical operations, they can be readily accelerated through the use of hardware. Due to their speed, symmetric algorithms may be used for bulk encryption when data privacy is required. One common example of their practical usage in this regard is to protect a VPN.

Despite the benefit of their speed, symmetric encryption algorithms do present a challenge with regard to key management. In particular, all parties involved in the communication must exchange the secret key over a secure channel before the encryption process can begin. This means that the security of any cryptographic system hinges on the ability of the key exchange method to protect the keys. Given this need, symmetric algorithms often are used to provide encryption services while additional key management algorithms are used to secure the key exchange.

Asymmetric Encryption Algorithms

Unlike symmetric algorithms, which use the same key for both encryption and decryption, asymmetric algorithms, often called public-key algorithms, use two different keys. One key is used for encryption, and the other is used for decryption. A central facet of this design is that the decryption key cannot feasibly be calculated from the encryption key, and vice versa. Figure 12-3 shows the encryption and decryption process using an asymmetric encryption algorithm.

With asymmetric algorithms, key lengths generally range from 512 to 4096 bits. However, no direct comparison can be made between the key length of asymmetric and symmetric algorithms, because the underlying design of these algorithm classes is quite different. In terms of resistance to brute-force attacks, experts generally agree that an RSA encryption key of 2048 bits generally is equivalent in strength to an RC4 key of only 128 bits.

Figure 12-3 *Encrypting and Decrypting with Asymmetric Algorithms*

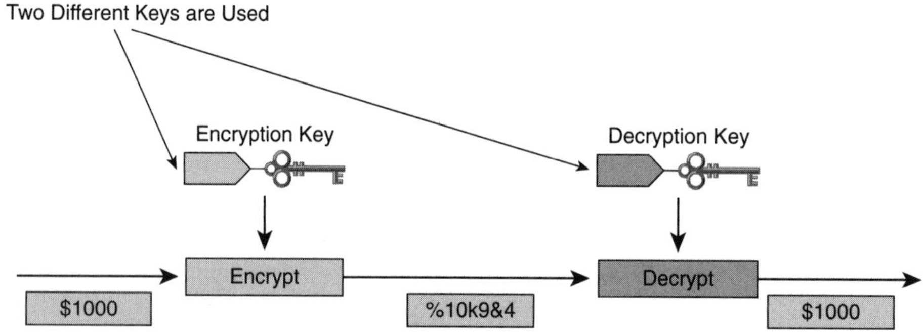

- Asymmetric encryption algorithms are best known as key algorithms.
- The usual key length is 512-4096 bits.
- Examples of asymmetric encryption algorithms are RSA, ElGamal, elliptic curves, and Diffie-Hellman.

One downside of symmetric algorithms is that they can be up to 1000 times slower than symmetric algorithms. This is because their design is based on complex mathematical calculations. Often these designs employ such things as factoring extremely large numbers or computing discrete logarithms of extremely large numbers.

Because of the issues with the speed of these algorithms, they generally are used in low-volume cryptographic mechanisms. For instance, they might be employed in digital signatures or for key exchange. One noted benefit is that key management of these algorithms generally is less complex than for symmetric algorithms. This stems from the fact that typically one of the two keys, either the encryption or decryption key, may be made public.

The Difference Between Block and Stream Ciphers

Both block and stream ciphers have their place in encryption algorithms as a mechanism for generating ciphertext from plain text. This section explores their basic differences and their uses in modern cryptography.

Block Ciphers

Block ciphers derive their name from the fact that they transform a fixed-length "block" of plain text into a "block" of ciphertext. These two blocks are of the same length. When the reverse transformation is applied to the ciphertext block, by using the same secret key, it is decrypted. Block ciphers use a fixed length or block size. Generally this is 128 bits, but they can range in size. For instance, DES has a block size of 64 bits.

The concept of block size determines how much data may be encrypted at a given time. This varies according to key length, because the key length refers to the size of the encryption key. To use the example from earlier, DES encrypts blocks in 64-bit chunks but does so using a 56-bit key length.

Because ciphertext must always be a multiple of the block size, the output data from a block cipher is larger than the input data. Block algorithms work with data one chunk at a time, such as 8 bytes, and then use padding to add artificial data (blanks) should there be less input data than one full block. Here are some of the more common block ciphers:

- DES and 3DES, running in Electronic Code Book (ECB) or Cipher Block Chaining (CBC) mode

- Skipjack

- Blowfish

- RSA

- AES

- IDEA

- Secure and Fast Encryption Routine (SAFER)

Stream Ciphers

Stream ciphers use smaller units of plain text than what are used with block ciphers; typically they work with bits. Transformation of these smaller plain-text units also varies, depending on when during the encryption process they are encountered. One of the great benefits of stream ciphers compared to block ciphers is that they are much faster and generally do not increase the message size. This is because they can encrypt an arbitrary number of bits.

Here are some common stream ciphers:

- RC4

- DES and 3DES, running in output feedback (OFB) or cipher feedback (CFB) mode

- Software Encryption Algorithm (SEAL)

Exploring Symmetric Encryption

Encryption algorithms use encryption keys to provide confidentiality of encrypted data. With symmetric encryption algorithms, the same key is used to encrypt and decrypt data. This section explores the principles that underlie symmetric encryption. It also examines some of the major symmetric encryption algorithms and discusses the means by which they operate, their strengths, and their weaknesses.

Functionality of Symmetric Encryption Algorithms

Because of the simplicity of their mathematics and the speed at which they operate, symmetric algorithms are the most commonly used form of cryptography. Symmetric encryption algorithms are also stronger. Therefore, they can use shorter key lengths compared to asymmetric algorithms. This helps increase their speed of execution in software.

Key Lengths

Key lengths for current symmetric algorithms range from 40 to 256 bits, giving symmetric algorithms keyspaces that range from 2^{40} (1,099,511,627,776) possible keys to 2^{256} (1.5 * 10^{77}) possible keys. As discussed previously, a large key space is central to determining how vulnerable an algorithm will be to a brute-force attack. Figure 12-4 shows a symmetric algorithm with 2^{256} possible keys.

Figure 12-4 *Key Lengths for Symmetric Encryption*

At the low end, a key length of 40 bits may be easily broken using a brute-force attack. On the other hand, if your key length is 256 bits, it is not likely that a brute-force attack will succeed. The keyspace generated with a 256-bit key is simply too large to easily fall victim to a brute-force attack.

Table 12-5 illustrates ongoing expectations for key lengths, assuming that the algorithms are mathematically and cryptographically sound. A further assumption in such calculations is that computing power will continue to keep pace with its present rate of growth and that capacity to perform brute-force attacks will also increase at the same rate. Note that if a method other than brute-force is discovered to crack a given algorithm, the key lengths in the table become obsolete.

Table 12-5 *Key Lengths and Their Continued Protection*

	Symmetric Key	Asymmetric Key	Digital Signature	Hash
Protection up to three years	80	1248	160	160
Protection up to ten years	96	1776	192	192
Protection up to 20 years	112	2432	224	224
Protection up to 30 years	128	3248	256	256
Protection against quantum computers	256	15,424	512	512

Features and Functions of DES

One of the most well-known and most widely used symmetric encryption algorithms is Data Encryption Standard (DES). DES typically operates in block mode, where it encrypts data in 64-bit blocks. Like other symmetric algorithms, DES uses the same algorithm and key for both encryption and decryption. DES has stood the test of time. Cryptography researchers have scrutinized it for nearly 35 years and so far have found no significant flaws. Adding to its appeal, because DES is based on relatively simple mathematical functions, it may be easily implemented and accelerated in hardware.

Working with the DES Key

DES employs a fixed key length of 64 bits, but only 56 of these bits are used for encryption; the other 8 bits are used for parity. The least-significant bit of each key byte indicates odd parity.

This means that each DES key is always 56 bits long. If DES is used with a weaker encryption, such as a 40-bit key, this means that the encryption key is 40 secret bits and 16 known bits, so the key length remains at 56 bits. In this case, however, DES would have a key strength of only 40 bits.

Modes of Operation for DES

DES uses two different types of ciphers to encrypt or decrypt more than 64 bits of data—the block cipher and the stream cipher.

- **Block ciphers** use fixed-length groups of bits known as blocks, with an unvarying transformation.

- **Stream ciphers** operate on individual digits one at a time, with the transformation varying during the encryption.

For block cipher mode, DES uses two standardized modes:

■ Electronic Code Book (ECB)

■ Cipher Block Chaining (CBC)

ECB mode uses the same 56-bit key to serially encrypt each 64-bit plain-text block. Should two identical plain-text blocks be encrypted using the same key, their ciphertext blocks are the same. This means that an attacker could identify similar or identical traffic as it flows across a communications channel. The attacker could use this information to help build a catalogue of messages that have a certain meaning, and then replay them later, without knowing their real meaning. For instance, suppose an attacker captures a login sequence for a user who has administrative privilege and whose traffic is protected by DES-ECB, and then replays it. This sort of risk must be mitigated, and that is why CBC was invented.

With CBC mode, each 64-bit plain-text block is exclusive ORed (XORed) bitwise with the previous ciphertext block. It is then encrypted using the DES key. This means that the encryption of each block depends on previous blocks, and encryption of the same 64-bit plain-text block can result in different ciphertext blocks. Thanks to this, CBC mode can help guard against certain attacks. Of course, it cannot help guard against sophisticated cryptanalysis or if an attacker launches an extended brute-force attack.

Figure 12-5 shows the differences between ECB mode and CBC mode.

Figure 12-5 *DES ECB Mode Versus CBC Mode*

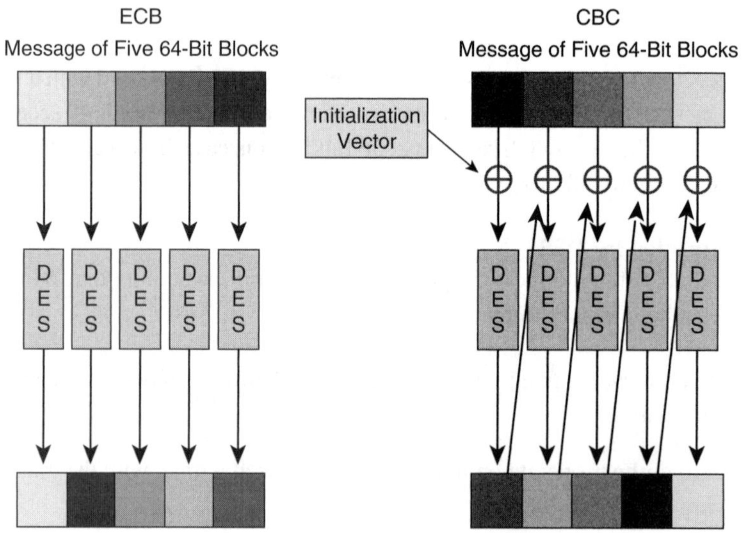

Cisco IP Security (IPsec) implementation currently uses DES and Triple Data Encryption Standard (3DES) in CBC mode.

Working with DES Stream Cipher Modes

When working with DES in stream cipher mode, the cipher uses previous ciphertext along with the secret key to generate a pseudorandom stream of bits. This may only be generated by the secret key.

To encrypt data, it is XORed with the pseudorandom stream on a bit-by-bit basis. Alternatively, this may be done byte by byte to obtain the ciphertext. To decrypt the data, the process is the same. The receiver uses the secret key to generate the same random stream and then XORs the ciphertext with the pseudorandom stream to gain access to the plain text.

If it is necessary to encrypt or decrypt more than 64 bits of data, two common stream cipher modes may be used:

- **Cipher feedback (CFB)** is similar to CBC. It may be used to encrypt any number of bits, even single bits or single characters.

- **Output feedback (OFB)** generates keystream blocks that are then XORed with the plain-text blocks to generate the ciphertext.

Usage Guidelines for Working with DES

You should consider a number of things when seeking to protect the security of DES-encrypted data, as described in Table 12-6.

Table 12-6 *Considerations for Protecting the Security of DES-Encrypted Data*

Consideration	Description
Change keys	Keys should be changed frequently to help prevent brute-force attacks.
Use a secure channel	A secure channel from the sender to the receiver should be used to communicate the DES key.
Use CBC mode	Using DES in CBC mode means that the encryption of each 64-bit block depends on the previous block, making this more secure.
Avoid weak keys	Be sure to test a key before using it to check it for weakness. DES has four weak keys and 12 semiweak keys. Testing will not significantly impact encryption time and can prevent the use of a weak key.

Understanding How 3DES Works

As mentioned, DES, with its original 56-bit key, is too short to withstand even medium-budget attackers. One means of increasing the security of DES without changing the well-analyzed algorithm itself is to use the same algorithm but with different keys multiple times in a row. In essence, that is what 3DES does.

By applying DES three times in a row to a plain-text block, we have what is known as 3DES. This application of DES three times with different keys makes brute-force attacks on 3DES infeasible. This stems from the fact that the basic algorithm has stood the test of time, weathering 35 years in the field and proving quite trustworthy.

Encrypting with 3DES

To encrypt plain text, 3DES uses a method called 3DES-encrypt-decrypt-encrypt (3DES-EDE). Figure 12-6 shows the 3DES-EDE encryption process, described in the following steps:

Step 1 The message to be secured is encrypted using the first 56-bit key (K1).

Step 2 Data is decrypted using the second 56-bit key (K2).

Step 3 Data to be secured is again encrypted using a third 56-bit key (K3).

Figure 12-6 *3DES-EDE Encryption Process*

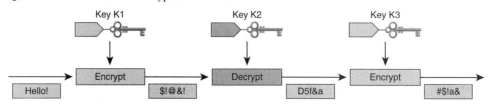

By applying the keys as it does, the 3DES-EDE process provides encryption with an effective key length of 168 bits. Should keys K1 and K3 be equal, a less-secure encryption of 112 bits is achieved.

To decrypt a message that has been encrypted with this process, the following steps, which are the opposite of the 3DES-EDE method, are used:

Step 1 Use key K3 to decrypt the ciphertext.

Step 2 Use key K2 to encrypt the data.

Step 3 Use key K1 to decrypt the data.

Simply encrypting data three times with three different keys does not significantly increase security. To achieve security, the 3DES-EDE method must be employed. In fact, if we were to simply encrypt data three times in a row using three different 56-bit keys, we would generate an effective 58-bit key strength, rather than the full 168-bit key strength we achieve by using 3DES-EDE.

AES

Although DES has withstood the test of time, it has been recognized for some time that DES would eventually reach the end of its usefulness. The Advanced Encryption Standard (AES) initiative was announced in 1997. The public was invited to propose candidate encryption schemes to be evaluated as the encryption standard to replace DES.

The Rijndael Cipher

The Rijndael cipher was selected as the AES algorithm in October 2000 by the U.S. National Institute of Standards and Technology (NIST). In 2002 the U.S. Secretary of Commerce approved the adoption of AES as an official U.S. government standard. Joan Daemen and Vincent Rijmen developed the Rijndael cipher, which employs a variable block length and key length. The algorithm provides nine different combinations of key length and block length. Keys with a length of 128, 192, or 256 bits may be used to encrypt blocks with a length of 128, 192, or 256 bits.

The Rijndael cipher is an iterated block cipher. In this cipher the initial input block and cipher key undergo multiple transformation cycles before producing output. This algorithm can operate over variable-length blocks using variable-length keys. Currently, the AES implementation of Rijndael contains only some of the capabilities of the Rijndael algorithm. One of the key features of this algorithm is that it is written so that the block length or the key length (or both) may be extended easily in multiples of 32 bits. This system was designed for efficient implementation in either hardware or software on a range of processors.

Comparing AES and 3DES

The key length of AES is much stronger than that of DES, and AES runs much faster than 3DES on comparable hardware. With these features, AES was chosen to replace DES and 3DES. AES is also better suited for high-throughput, low-latency environments. This is especially true when pure software encryption is used.

In terms of longevity, AES is a relatively young algorithm. As mentioned previously, a more mature algorithm is always more trusted. That being the case, 3DES represents a more conservative yet more trusted choice in terms of strength, because it has been analyzed for nearly 35 years.

Availability of AES in the Cisco Product Line

Cisco offers AES implementation in a number of virtual private network (VPN) devices as an encryption transform, applied to IPsec-protected traffic:

- Cisco PIX Firewall Software version 6.3 and later

- Cisco ASA Software version 7.0 and later

- Cisco VPN 3000 Software version 3.6 and later

- Cisco IOS Release 12.2(13)T and later

SEAL

For those seeking an alternative algorithm to software-based DES, 3DES, and AES, SEAL encryption uses a 160-bit encryption key. SEAL also offers the benefit of having less impact on the CPU compared to other software-based algorithms. Cisco IOS IPsec implementations feature SEAL encryption and provide support for the SEAL algorithm. The Cisco IOS software Release 12.3(7)T also added support for SEAL.

SEAL Restrictions

SEAL is bound by several restrictions:

- IPsec must be supported by your Cisco router and the other peer.

- The k9 subsystem must be supported by your Cisco router and the other peer.

- Only Cisco equipment supports this feature.

A further restriction is that your router and the other peer must not have hardware IPsec encryption.

The Rivest Ciphers

Many networking applications employ the Rivest cipher (RC) family of algorithms. This is because of their favorable speed and variable key-length capabilities.

Ronald Rivest played a significant role in designing all or at least part of all the RC algorithms. Table 12-7 describes some of the most widely used RC algorithms.

Table 12-7 *Most Widely Used RC Algorithms*

RC Algorithm	Description
RC2	Designed as a drop-in replacement for DES, RC2 is a variable key-sized cipher.
RC4	Often used in file encryption products, as well as for secure communication, such as in Secure Socket Layer (SSL), RC4 is a variable key-size stream cipher.
RC5	This fast block cipher has a variable block size and variable key length. With its 64-bit block size, it may be used as a drop-in replacement for DES.
RC6	Based on RC5, this block cipher had as its main design goal meeting the requirement of AES.

Of the various RC algorithms listed in Table 12-7, the most popular is RC4. RC4 represents a variable key-size stream cipher that employs byte-oriented operations and is based on the use of a random permutation. Via analysis, it has been determined that the period of the cipher is quite large, likely greater than 10^{100}. To give you a better sense of this, each output byte requires from eight to 16 machine operations and can be expected to run very quickly in software.

RC4 is considered a secure algorithm and as such is often used for file encryption. It is also used frequently to encrypt website traffic within the context of the SSL protocol.

Understanding Security Algorithms

It is almost hard to imagine modern computing and networking without also thinking about the mechanisms that provide for the underlying security of the data that resides on these systems or travels across the wire. Security algorithms are central to securing the data created within an organization, as well as securing it in transit. This section examines the characteristics of the encryption process and what makes for a strong, trustworthy encryption algorithm. This section also explores the use of cryptographic hashes and how key management plays an important role in securing the encryption process.

Selecting an Encryption Algorithm

Proper selection of an encryption algorithm is one of the key steps in building a cryptography-based solution. With this selection process, two main criteria should be considered. Table 12-8 details these selection criteria for your consideration.

Table 12-8   *Criteria for Selecting an Encryption Algorithm*

Selection Criteria	Description
Trust in the algorithm by the cryptographic community	Because many new algorithms are often broken very quickly, algorithms that have stood the test of time by resisting attacks for a number of years are the most preferred. Although there is often a great deal of talk about the benefits of a new algorithm, there are truly few or no revolutions in cryptography.
Protection against brute-force attacks	A trusted algorithm has no shortcut to break it. An attacker has to search through the keyspace to guess the correct key. An algorithm also must allow key lengths that satisfy an organization's confidentiality requirements. This is not always the case. For example, DES does not provide enough protection for most organizations because of its short key length.

The following symmetric encryption algorithms are considered trustworthy:

- DES

- 3DES

- IDEA

- RC4

- AES

Each of these algorithms has its place. For instance, because it uses very short key lengths, DES is a good protocol to protect data for a very short period of time. If you need to protect data with an algorithm that is very trusted and has much greater security strength, 3DES would be a much better choice.

AES, although not proven to the degree that 3DES has been, is still a good choice, because it is more efficient. This makes it ideal in high-throughput, low-latency environments. This is particularly the case when 3DES cannot handle the throughput or latency requirements. Over time, AES will likely gain even greater trust as more attacks are attempted against it.

Symmetric encryption algorithms such as RSA and Diffie-Hellman (DH) are considered trustworthy for confidentiality. But many others, like ECC, generally are considered immature in cryptographic terms.

Understanding Cryptographic Hashes

Hashing is used to provide data integrity. Hashes are based on one-way mathematical functions. These can be easy to compute but extremely challenging to reverse. The process of hashing and the difficulty of reversing the hash is akin to scrambling an egg and then trying to put it back together again.

Working with Hashing

The way that hashing works in practice is that data of arbitrary length is input into the hash function and then is processed through the function, resulting in a fixed-length hash. The resultant fixed-length hash is called a digest or fingerprint. Figure 12-7 shows the hashing process.

Figure 12-7 *Hashing Process*

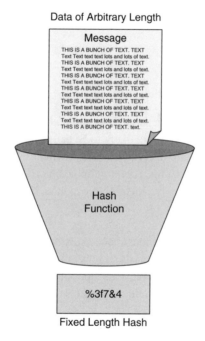

Data of Arbitrary Length

Message

THIS IS A BUNCH OF TEXT. TEXT
Text Text text text lots and lots of text.
THIS IS A BUNCH OF TEXT. TEXT
Text Text text text lots and lots of text.
THIS IS A BUNCH OF TEXT. TEXT
Text Text text text lots and lots of text.
THIS IS A BUNCH OF TEXT. TEXT
Text Text text text lots and lots of text.
THIS IS A BUNCH OF TEXT. TEXT
Text Text text text lots and lots of text.
THIS IS A BUNCH OF TEXT. TEXT
Text Text text text lots and lots of text.
THIS IS A BUNCH OF TEXT. text.

Hash
Function

%3f7&4

Fixed Length Hash

If you are familiar with the calculation of cyclic redundancy check (CRC) checksums, hashes are quite similar to this but are cryptographically much stronger. If you're not too familiar with CRC, if you have the CRC value, it is relatively easy to generate data with the same CRC. Because of the strength of hash functions, it is computationally infeasible for an attacker to possess two separate sets of data that would come up with the same fingerprint.

Designing Key Management

One of the most challenging aspects of designing a cryptosystem is planning for key management. In fact, cryptosystem failures have occurred because of shortcomings in key management. Each of the current cryptographic algorithms requires the services of key management procedures, making this an extremely important area to consider. For an attacker, the general target when seeking to attack a cryptographic system is the key management system, rather than the algorithm itself.

Components of Key Management

When considering key management, you must consider several components that address the life cycle of key management from generation to destruction:

- Key generation

- Key verification

- Key storage

- Key exchange

- Key revocation and destruction

Modern cryptographic systems generate keys automatically, rather than leaving it to the end user. To help ensure that all keys are likely to be equally generated, so that the attacker cannot predict which keys are likely to be used, quality random-number generators are necessary. It is not uncommon for a cryptographic algorithm to have some weak keys that should not be used. Proper key verification procedures should be used to regenerate these keys when they occur.

Key storage is another factor that must be considered. With today's modern multiuser operating systems that work with cryptography, a key can be stored in memory. When memory is swapped to the disk, it presents a possible problem, because a Trojan horse program, if installed on the PC, could then gain access to that user's private keys.

A secure key exchange mechanism is also necessary. It should allow secure agreement on the keying material with the other party, likely over an untrusted medium.

The final element of good key management to consider is key revocation and destruction. The process of key revocation notifies all the parties involved that a given key has been compromised and should not be used. Key destruction goes beyond this by erasing old keys so that a malicious attacker cannot recover them.

Understanding Keyspaces

The keyspace of an algorithm represents a defined set of all possible key values. For each key of n bits, a keyspace is produced that has 2^n possible key values. This means that adding 1 bit to the key would effectively double the size of the keyspace.

Let's look at DES by way of an example. DES employs a 56-bit key and with this produces a keyspace of more than 72,000,000,000,000,000 (2^{56}) potential keys. If we were to add 1 bit to the key length, the keyspace would double. That means that an attacker would need twice as much time to search the keyspace.

No algorithm is without some weak keys in its keyspace, as discussed previously. These weak keys may enable an attacker to break the encryption via a shortcut. So what exactly constitutes a weak key?

A key is said to be weak when it shows regularities in encryption or poor encryption. A good example is DES. DES has four keys for which encryption is exactly the same as decryption. Should one of these weak keys be encrypted twice, the original plain text would be recovered.

The chance that such keys would be chosen is almost unimaginable. However, each implementation should still verify all keys and take steps to prevent weak keys from being used. This is particularly the case with manual key generation, so you should take special care to avoid defining weak keys.

Issues Related to Key Length

As we have discussed, the only way to break a proven cryptographic system is with a brute-force attack. These attacks search the entire keyspace, trying all possible keys, until the key that decrypts the data is found. To defend against this form of attack, the keyspace must be sufficiently large enough that such a search would require an enormous amount of time, rendering this form of attack impractical.

Even for successful brute-force attacks, generally an attacker has to search half the keyspace to find the correct key. Of course, the time required for such a search depends on the computer resources available to the attacker. With key lengths of significant size, such an attack could take many millions, if not billions, of years to yield success.

The protection strength of modern trusted algorithms depends exclusively on the length of the key. You should select a key length so that it protects data confidentiality or integrity for an adequate period of time. The more sensitive the data, and the longer the period required for secrecy, the longer the key that must be used.

When considering the level of protection required, you must also take into account the characteristics of those likely to attack your data. For instance, you must estimate the attacker's resources and how long you must protect the data.

For example, suppose a would-be attacker has $1 million of funding that can be used toward the attack, and the data must be protected for a period of no less than one year. What form of encryption should we choose? Classic DES would not be a good choice, because it can be broken by a $1 million machine in only a couple of minutes. If instead we employed 168-bit 3DES or even 128-bit RC4, it would take that same attacker, funded with that same $1 million, a million years or more to crack into your data. Considering our attacker, his funding and our need for security are both important in selecting the proper key length.

Another issue impacting the choice of key length is performance. It is important to strive to balance speed and protection strength for the selected algorithm. Certain algorithms, such as RSA, take much longer to run with large key sizes. We should strive for adequate protection, without hindering communication over untrusted networks.

Finally, you also need to be aware that because of rapid advances in technology and cryptanalytic methods, what may be an adequate key size today may quickly no longer be appropriate. The National Institute of Standards and Technology (NIST) offers recommendations on adequate key lengths for various applications. You may review these on the NIST website at http://www.keylength.com/en/4/.

SSL VPNs

Security on the Internet for such applications as web browsing, e-mail, Internet faxing, instant messaging, and other forms of data transfer is provided by cryptographic protocols. Among the most popular choices to support these applications are Transport Layer Security (TLS) and its predecessor, Secure Socket Layer (SSL). Although there are subtle differences between SSL and TLS, the actual protocol remains quite similar.

Both SSL and TLS support a variety of cryptographic algorithms, or ciphers, to help provide such functions as authenticating the server and client to each other, transmitting certificates, and establishing session keys. For bulk encryption, symmetric algorithms are used. Asymmetric algorithms are used for authentication and key exchange. Hashing is used as part of the authentication process.

With an SSL-based VPN, you can easily provide remote-access connectivity from almost any Internet-enabled location. All that is needed is a standard web browser and its native SSL encryption. There is no need for special-purpose client software on the remote system. This flexibility allows SSL VPNs to provide "anywhere" connectivity from corporate desktops, as well as from noncompany-managed desktops. Employees may use the SSL-based VPN to connect from home on their own PCs, contractor or business partner desktops can also be easily connected, and users can even connect via Internet kiosks. Through dynamic download, clients are supplied with all the software needed for application access across the SSL VPN connection. This feature dramatically minimizes the maintenance of desktop software.

If you need to support the remote resource needs of a diverse user base, SSL VPNs and IPsec VPNs provide complementary technologies that can be deployed together to meet these needs. Each of these VPN solutions offers access to virtually any network application or resource from a remote location. However, SSL VPNs do offer some additional features, allowing for easy connectivity from desktops outside your company's management, as well as little or no desktop software maintenance, and user-customized web portals upon login.

Establishing an SSL Tunnel

Let's examine the steps involved in establishing an SSL tunnel (see Figure 12-8):

Step 1 The user makes an outbound connection to TCP port 443.

Step 2 The router presents a digital certificate that contains a public key that is digitally signed by a trusted certificate authority (CA).

Step 3 The user's computer generates a shared-secret symmetric key that will be used by both parties.

Step 4 The router's public key is used to encrypt the shared secret and is transmitted to the router. The router's software uses the private key to decrypt the packet. When this is complete, both parties in the session know the secret key.

Step 5 The key encrypts the SSL session.

Figure 12-8 *Establishing an SSL Tunnel*

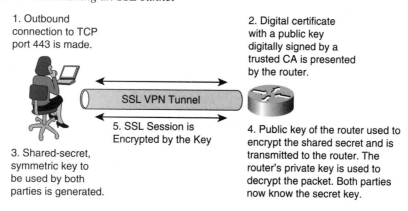

With the SSL tunnel established, two parties may securely transmit data. By using the mechanisms discussed here, you can effectively extend the reach of your corporate network, allowing users to easily and securely gain access to corporate resources from wherever they may be.

Exam Preparation Tasks

Review All the Key Topics

Key
Topic

Review the most important topics from this chapter, denoted with the Key Topic icon. Table 12-9 lists these key topics and the page where each is found.

Table 12-9 *Key Topics for Chapter 12*

Key Topic Element	Description	Page Number
List	How encryption works in terms of the OSI model	437
List	Various cryptographic attacks	438
Table 12-2	Defining attack types	438–439
List	Features of quality encryption algorithms	440
Table 12-3	Classes of encryption algorithms	441
Table 12-4	Popular symmetric algorithms	442
List	Symmetric encryption techniques	443
List	Common block ciphers	445
List	Common stream ciphers	445
Table 12-5	Key lengths and their continued protection	447
List	DES ciphers	447
List	Standardizing block cipher modes with DES	448
List	Common stream cipher modes	449
Table 12-6	Considerations for protecting the security of DES-encrypted data	449
Steps	Detailed steps used in the 3DES-EDE encryption process	450
List	The Cisco AES implementation for VPN devices	452
List	SEAL restrictions	452
Table 12-7	Most widely used RC algorithms	453
Table 12-8	Criteria for selecting an encryption algorithm	454
List	Trustworthy symmetric encryption algorithms	454
List	Components of key management	456
Steps	Detailed steps for establishing an SSL tunnel	459

Complete the Tables and Lists from Memory

Print a copy of Appendix D, "Memory Tables," (found on the CD) or at least the section for this chapter, and complete the tables and lists from memory. Appendix E, "Memory Tables Answer Key," also on the CD, includes completed tables and lists so that you can check your work.

Definition of Key Terms

Define the following key terms from this chapter, and check your answers in the glossary:

Advanced Encryption Standard (AES), block cipher, cryptography, ciphertext, Data Encryption Standard (DES), Triple Data Encryption Standard (3DES), hashing, keyspace, Rivest Cipher (RC) algorithms, Software Encryption Algorithm (SEAL), stream cipher

This chapter covers the following topics:

Examining hash algorithms: This section explores the construction and use of hash algorithms. It examines a variety of hash algorithms and discusses their relative strengths and weaknesses in practical application.

Using digital signatures: This section examines the components that make up a digital signature, as well as the application of these as a means of proving the authenticity of a message.

CHAPTER 13

Implementing Digital Signatures

As you examine the security at play in your network and seek to increase your defenses, it is important to have a general understanding of cryptography and digital signatures. In cryptography, a cryptographic hash function is a transformation that takes an input and returns a string, which is called the hash value. Digital signatures are rather like written signatures in that they are used to provide authentication of the associated input, typically called a message. These messages can be anything from an e-mail to a username-and-password combination or even a message sent with an even more sophisticated cryptographic tool. This chapter examines digital signatures so that you can better understand how these may be implemented to secure your network.

"Do I Know This Already?" Quiz

The "Do I Know This Already?" quiz helps you determine your level of knowledge of this chapter's topics before you begin. Table 13-1 details the major topics discussed in this chapter and their corresponding quiz questions.

Table 13-1 *"Do I Know This Already?" Section-to-Question Mapping*

Foundation Topic Section	Questions
Examining Hash Algorithms	1 to 5
Using Digital Signatures	6 to 11

1. Cryptographic hashes can be used to provide which of the following? (Choose all that apply.)

   a. Message integrity

   b. Functional analysis

   c. Security checks

   d. Message lists

   e. Digital signatures

2. Which of the following is an example of a function intended for cryptographic hashing?

   a. MD65

   b. XR12

   c. SHA-135

   d. MD5

3. An HMAC provides which of the following benefits? (Choose all that apply.)

   a. It may be used to verify data integrity.

   b. It may be used to calculate a checksum.

   c. It may be used to verify a message's authenticity.

   d. It may be used to examine a message header.

4. What may be added to a password stored in MD5 to make it more secure?

   a. Cryptotext

   b. Ciphertext

   c. Rainbow table

   d. Salt

5. Which of the following employ SHA-1? (Choose all that apply.)

   a. SMTP

   b. SSL

   c. TLS

   d. IGMP

   e. IPsec

6. A digital signature provides which of the following?

   a. Auditing

   b. Authentication

   c. Authorization

   d. Analysis

7. Digital signatures employ a pair of keys made up of which of the following? (Choose two.)

   a. A personal key

   b. A public key

   c. A private key

   d. A universal key

8. A digital signature scheme is made up of which of the following? (Choose all that apply.)

   a. Authentication algorithm

   b. Key generation algorithm

   c. Encryption algorithm

   d. Signing algorithm

   e. Signature verification algorithm

9. Which of the following algorithms was the first to be found suitable for both digital signing and encryption?

   a. MD5

   b. HMAC

   c. SHA-1

   d. RSA

10. Which of the following attacks focus on RSA? (Choose all that apply.)

    a. Man-in-the-middle attack

    b. BPA attack

    c. Adaptive chosen ciphertext attack

    d. DDoS attack

11. The Digital Signature Standard outlines the use of which of the following algorithms in the creation of digital signatures?

    a. LSA

    b. DSA

    c. PGP

    d. MD5

Foundation Topics

Examining Hash Algorithms

For centuries everyone from kings to generals to college students has wanted to ensure the authenticity of their communications. In this section we will examine the role of hash algorithms in helping provide this assurance through the process of *hashing*. Along the way we will examine hash functions and learn about HMAC, as well as explore MD5 and SHA-1. Let's begin with a brief overview of what a hash function does.

A hash function is a means of turning data into a relatively small number that then may act as a digital fingerprint of the data. The algorithm that is used substitutes or transposes the data to create this unique fingerprint. These fingerprints may be called hash sums, hash values, hash codes, or just hashes. Cryptographic hashes serve a variety of purposes in information security applications. They are used to do message integrity checks and provide digital signatures in various information security applications, such as authentication and message integrity.

Exploring Hash Algorithms and HMACs

Figure 13-1 is an example of how a simple sentence can be transformed using a hash function to yield a cryptographic result. You can see that changing a single word alters the hash output.

Figure 13-1 *Hashing Example*

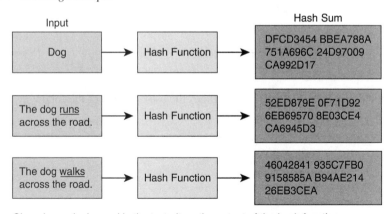

Changing a single word in the text alters the output of the hash function.

Although you might not need to hash a simple sentence like this, many other applications exist in terms of network security. Hashes can be employed to help secure data as it traverses your network, as well as to secure login authentication credentials as a user is validated before accessing network resources.

Anatomy of a Hash Function

A variety of hash functions exist, but they all share the common characteristic that they are built for speed and are designed to yield very few hash collisions in their expected input domains. A hash "collision" (sometimes called a "hash clash") happens when two distinct inputs entered into a hash function produce identical outputs. Each hash function has the potential for collisions, but if you are working with a well-designed hash function, collisions should occur less frequently. In terms of hash functions, collisions inhibit the distinguishing of data, making records more costly to find in hash tables and data processing.

Another characteristic of hash functions is that they must be deterministic. In other words, if a hash function generates two hashes that are different, we can conclude that the two inputs were different in some way.

Hash values that are computed may be the same for different input values. This may seem odd, but it is because of the general requirement that the hash value must be able to be stored in fewer bits than the data that is being hashed. A primary design goal of hash functions is to minimize the likelihood of a hash collision.

One desirable property of a hash function is the mixing property. What this means is that a small change in the input (1 bit) should cause a large change in the output (about half of the bits). This significant change in the outcome is called the avalanche effect.

Most hash functions have what is called an infinite domain. This might be something like byte strings of arbitrary length. They also have a finite range—for instance, bit sequences of a fixed length. In some applications, hash functions may be designed with a one-to-one mapping between an identically sized domain and range. Hash functions such as these, which are one-to-one, are also called permutations. For these hash functions, reversibility is achieved by using a series of reversible "mixing" operations on the function input.

Application of Hash Functions

Hash functions may be used for a variety of applications; therefore, they are often tailored to a given need. Cryptographic hash functions begin with the assumption that an adversary can deliberately try to find inputs with the same hash value. The creation of a well-designed cryptographic hash involves a one-way operation in which no practical way exists to calculate a particular data input that will result in a desired hash value. This one-way nature

Key
Topic

makes the hash very difficult to forge. Message Digest 5 (MD5) is an example of a function intended for cryptographic hashing that is commonly used as a stock hash function.

When a function is used for error detection and correction, it focuses on distinguishing those cases in which data has been disturbed by a random process. One way that a hash function might be employed is as a checksum. Hash functions have a relatively small hash value that can be used to verify that a data file of any size has not been altered, making them valuable in network security implementations.

In terms of real-world application, perhaps an example is in order. One of the most common applications of hash functions is helping prove the authenticity of a message. When a hash function is employed in this manner, it produces a "fingerprint" of the message. This fingerprint is the hash code or message digest, which is the output of the hash function. This is used to create a digital signature for the message to ensure its authenticity. We will explore the concept of digital signatures as well as various hash functions in later sections.

Cryptographic Hash Functions

Put simply, a cryptographic hash function takes an input and returns a fixed-length string, which is called the hash value or hash sum. These hash functions, as mentioned in the preceding section, may be used for a variety of purposes, including cryptography. A hash value, as complex as it may become, is, on the surface, simply a concise representation of a longer message or document from which it was derived. The output of the hash function, often called the message digest, is a sort of "digital fingerprint" of the larger document. Message integrity checks and digital signatures, used for various security applications such as authentication and message integrity, can be provided by cryptographic hash functions.

The way this works is that the hash function accepts a string of variable length, sometimes called a message, as an input and then produces a fixed-length string, called a message digest or digital fingerprint, as an output. A hash value, often called a "digest" or "checksum," is a type of signature that represents the contents of a stream of data.

Put another way, a hash is akin to the seal on certain over-the-counter medications. A plastic film covers the top of the bottle. If it has been disturbed, it is evident that that the medication has been tampered with. The hash serves this same function, only as a digital mechanism.

Two of the most widely used hash functions are MD5 and SHA-1 (Secure Hash Algorithm 1). However, in 2005 security flaws were identified in both of these common algorithms. Although these hash functions are indeed flawed, they are still widely used today. Why is this?

As cryptographic analysts seek to break hash functions, sometimes they are successful. However, this is often after many years and with the aid of computing technology outside of what would be considered the norm. So even though these two hash functions have security flaws, it's very unlikely that an attacker, under normal and reasonable circumstances, could exploit them. Therefore, these two functions are still widely used for a variety of purposes today. We will explore both MD5 and SHA-1 and their application to networking technologies later in this chapter.

When we consider the security of a cryptographic hash function, it should behave as much as possible like a random function while still being efficiently computable and deterministic in nature.

If either of the following statements is computationally feasible, a cryptographic hash function is considered insecure:

- A previously unseen message that matches a given digest

- Two different messages having the same message digest, called a collision

If an attacker can discover either of these things, he may be able to exploit the vulnerability in the hash function. For instance, he might be able to substitute an unauthorized message for one that has been authorized.

With a truly secure cryptographic hash function, it should not be possible to find two messages whose message digests are substantially similar, let alone exactly the same. Likewise, with a secure cryptographic hash, an attacker should not be able to learn anything of value about a message from only its digest. However, if an attacker can compromise security and obtain the digest, this could prove valuable should that same message occur again.

Application of Cryptographic Hashes

Let's examine a cryptographic hash to better understand how it works.

Suppose Anthony presents Tom with a rather difficult math problem that he claims to have solved. Tom wants to try to solve the problem himself, but he also wants to be sure that Anthony is telling the truth about having solved it. Anthony writes down his solution and then appends a random nonce, computes its hash, and tells Tom this hash value. The nonce that Anthony uses in this case is a random or pseudorandom number that is used only once for the purposes of this communication. All Tom has is the hash value; Anthony keeps the solution and the nonce secret. Tom gets to work on the math problem. When Tom finally solves the problem, Anthony can prove that he solved the problem as well by telling Tom the nonce. This example employs what cryptographers call a simple commitment scheme. In the world of computer networking, "Tom" and "Anthony" might very well be two computer programs attempting to prove a message's authenticity.

Secure hashes often provide a mechanism to verify message integrity. Let's say that a file is to be sent across the Internet, and you are concerned that it might be intercepted and altered in transit. Using a secure cryptographic hash would allow you to determine whether any changes have been made to the file. For example, you could do this by comparing message digests calculated before, and after, transmission of the file over the public network.

One means to reliably identify a file is a message digest. For instance, the Git source code management system uses the sha1sum program to examine various types of content such as file content, directory trees, ancestry information, and the like to uniquely identify a file.

Another frequent use of cryptographic hashes is password verification. When we think in terms of passwords, we know that protecting them is of the utmost importance. That is why passwords generally are not stored in clear text but rather in a digest form. When a digest is used, a user is authenticated in the following manner: The user provides her username and password. The password she presents is hashed and then compared to the hash that has been stored. If a match is found, the user is granted access. This type of cryptographic hash generally is called one-way encryption.

SHA-1, MD5, and as RIPEMD-160 are some of the most widely used message digest algorithms. This is true even though in August 2004, researchers found weaknesses in a number of hash functions, including MD5, SHA-0, and RIPEMD. These findings also have called into question the long-term security of later algorithms derived from these hash functions—in particular, SHA-1, which is a strengthened version of SHA-0. As recently as August 2005, an attack against SHA-1 found collisions in 2^{63} operations. An attack in February of that same year found collisions in about 2^{69} hashing operations, rather than the 2^{80} expected for a 160-bit hash function. Findings such as these call into question the security of these common cryptographic hashes. However, in terms of practical applications, these collisions do not warrant stopping the use of these extremely popular hash functions.

HMAC Explained

Keyed Hash-based Message Authentication Code (HMAC) in cryptographic terms is a type of message authentication code (MAC) calculated by using a cryptographic hash function along with a secret key. It may be used to simultaneously verify the data's integrity and the message's authenticity. An iterative cryptographic hash function such as MD5 or SHA-1 may be used to calculate the HMAC. When these are used, the resulting MAC algorithm is called HMAC-MD5 or HMAC-SHA-1, for instance. The cryptographic strength of the underlying hash function, along with the size and quality of the key and the size of the hash output length in bits, define the cryptographic strength of the HMAC. Figure 13-2 illustrates HMAC.

Figure 13-2 *HMAC*

Hash Message Authentication Code (HMAC)

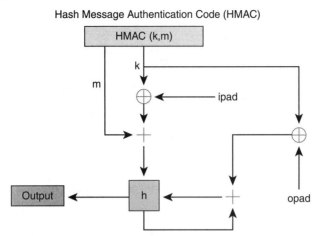

h = Cryptographic hash function.
m = Message to be authenticated.
k = Secret key padded with extra 0's (ipad/opad) to the block size of the hash function.
ipad = Inner padding.
opad = Outer padding.

Iterative hash functions, such as MD5 and SHA-1, break a message into blocks of a fixed size and then iterate over them with a compression function. For instance, MD5 and SHA-1 operate on 512-bit blocks. As mentioned, the size of the HMAC output is the same as that of the underlying hash function (128 or 160 bits in the case of MD5 and SHA-1), but you can truncate this if you want to. When the hash image is truncated, the security of the MAC is reduced.

In 1996 Mihir Bellare, Ran Canetti, and Hugo Krawczyk wrote about the construction and analysis of HMACs. These authors also wrote RFC 2104 in 1997 and FIPS PUB 198, which generalizes and standardizes the use of HMACs. Both the IPsec and TLS protocols use HMAC-SHA-1 and HMAC-MD5.

MD5 Features and Functionality

Defined in RFC 1321, MD5 (Message Digest algorithm 5), with its 128-bit hash value, has been employed in a wide variety of security applications. It is also commonly used to check the integrity of files. An MD5 hash typically is expressed as a 32-character hexadecimal number.

Figure 13-3 shows a single MD5 operation. In practice, MD5 consists of 64 of these operations. These are grouped in four rounds of 16 operations. In this figure, F is a nonlinear function; one function is used in each round. M_i denotes a 32-bit block of the message input, and K_i denotes a 32-bit constant, which is different for each operation.

Key
Topic

Figure 13-3 *MD5 Algorithm*

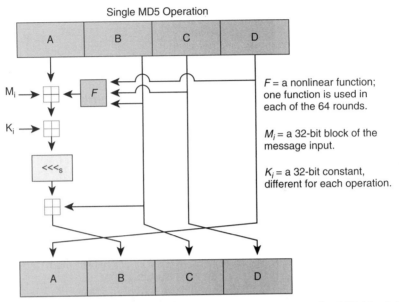

Ronald Rivest designed MD5 in 1991 as a replacement for the earlier MD4 hash function. Five years later, in 1996, a flaw was found in the design of MD5. Although this flaw was not a fatal weakness, the cryptography community began recommending the use of other algorithms, such as SHA-1. Ironically, the widely used SHA-1 algorithm has since been shown to be vulnerable as well, as noted earlier. In 2004, researchers discovered more serious flaws in the algorithm, calling into question the use of the algorithm for certain security purposes.

Origins of MD5

Ronald Rivest of MIT created Message Digest as a series of message digest algorithms. MD5 was designed to be a secure replacement for its predecessor, MD4, when work demonstrated that MD4 was likely unsecure. Security of the MD5 algorithm was initially brought into question in 1993 when researchers found a pseudo-collision of the MD5 compression function. In other words, two different initialization vectors produced an identical digest.

In 1996, a true collision of the MD5 compression function was announced. Although this was not an attack on the full MD5 hash function, it was close enough for cryptographers to recommend switching to a replacement. Among the recommendations were WHIRLPOOL, SHA-1, and RIPEMD-160.

The hash, at only 128 bits, was small enough for cryptographers to fear that it would be vulnerable to a birthday attack. A birthday attack is a type of cryptographic attack that takes advantage of the mathematics behind the birthday paradox. The birthday paradox addresses the probability that, in a set of randomly chosen people, two of them will have the same birthday. If the random group consists of 23 or more people, the probability that two of them will have the same birthday is greater than 50%. If the number of people in the pool grows to 57, the probability of a shared birthday is more than 99%. The probability approaches 100% as the number of individuals grows.

To test this theory, MD5CRK, a distributed project, was started in March 2004. The aim of the project was to demonstrate that MD5 is practically insecure by finding a collision using a birthday attack.

In less than six months, MD5CRK ended in August 2004 when collisions for the full MD5 were announced. The reported attack took only one hour on an IBM p690 cluster.

Further weaknesses were discovered in March 2005. A team of researchers constructed two x.509 certificates with different public keys and the same MD5 hash, a demonstrably practical collision. Within days, additional researchers announced an improved algorithm that could construct MD5 collisions in a few hours on a single notebook computer. Further hardship followed when, on March 18, 2006, an algorithm was published that could find a collision within one minute on a notebook computer using a method called tunneling.

Vulnerabilities of MD5

MD5 makes only a single pass over data. Because of this, if two prefixes with the same hash can be constructed, it is possible to add a common suffix to both to make the collision reasonably more possible.

Currently there exist collision-finding techniques that allow the preceding hash state to be specified arbitrarily. Therefore, a collision can be found for any desired prefix. This means that for any given string of characters X (for instance, a password), two colliding files can be determined that both begin with X.

To generate these two colliding files, all that is needed is a template file, with a 128-byte block of data aligned on a 64-byte boundary, that can be changed freely by the collision-finding algorithm.

Figure 13-4 shows a rainbow table. Attackers can use rainbow tables to try to reverse hashes into strings.

Attackers can use MD5 rainbow tables, which are easily accessible online, to reverse many MD5 hashes into strings that collide with the original input. The general purpose of such attacks is password cracking. One means of defense is to combine passwords with a salt (a series of random bits added to the password) before the MD5 digest is generated. This combination makes rainbow tables much less useful.

Figure 13-4   *Rainbow Table*

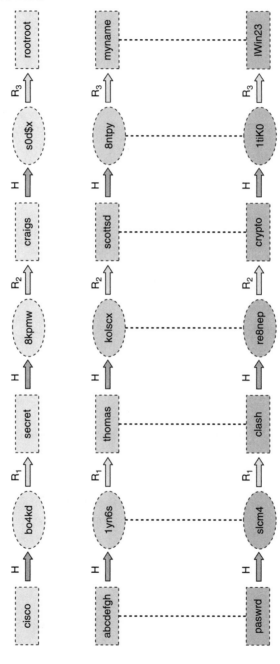

Usage of MD5

One of the most common uses of MD5 digests is to provide some degree of assurance that a transferred file has arrived intact. An example of this is when a file server provides a precomputed MD5 checksum for a file. To ensure that the file has not been tampered with, the user can compare the checksum of the downloaded file to the one provided by the file server. Various UNIX-based operating systems include MD5 checksum utilities. For those working with Windows operating systems, this capability generally is provided by third-party applications.

Recent vulnerabilities that have been discovered with MD5 now make it easy to generate MD5 collisions. That being the case, it is possible for the person who created the file to create a second file with the same checksum, negating the protection against some forms of malicious tampering. At other times, the checksum might not be trustworthy, such as if it was obtained over the same channel as the downloaded file. In a case such as this, MD5 can only provide error checking, allowing it to recognize a corrupt or incomplete download. This is often the case when you download large files.

Another common usage of MD5 is to store passwords. To provide a defense against the vulnerabilities we have discussed, a salt can be added to the password before it is hashed. In fact, some implementations of this technique apply the hashing function multiple times to provide greater security.

SHA-1 Features and Functionality

SHA-1 (Secure Hash Algorithm 1) is one of five cryptographic hash functions referred to as SHA hash functions. They were designed by the National Security Agency (NSA) and published by the National Institute of Standards and Technology (NIST) as a U.S. Federal Information Processing Standard. Much like the MD5 hash algorithm, SHA-1 computes a fixed-length digital representation (a *message digest*) from an input data sequence (the *message*) of any length.

A hash such as this is defined as "secure" when it is computationally infeasible to

■ Find a message that corresponds to a given message digest

■ Find two different messages that produce the same message digest

When working with a secure hash such as this, any change to a message should, with a very high degree of probability, result in a different message digest.

Figure 13-5 shows the SHA-1 hash and how it is used. We will discuss the application of SHA-1 in greater detail in an upcoming section.

Key Topic

Figure 13-5 *SHA-1 Hash*

```
SHA1("The quick brown fox jumps over the lazy dog")
= 2fd4e1c6 7a2d28fc ed849ee1 bb76e739 1b93eb12
```

With SHA-1, a small change in the message will result in a completely different hash due to the avalanche effect. For example, changing *dog* to *log*:

```
SHA1("The quick brown fox jumps over the lazy log")
 = de9f2c7f d25e1b3a fad3e85a 0bd17d9b 100db4b3
```

Overview of SHA-1

The SHA-1 hash produces a message digest that is 160 bits long, as opposed to 128 bits for MD5. A number of widely used security applications and protocols employ SHA-1, including TLS, SSL, PGP, SSH, S/MIME, and IPsec. SHA-1 has been positioned as the successor to MD5, which was one of the most widely used hash functions until SHA-1 was introduced.

Like its predecessor, MD5, researchers have attempted to validate the security of SHA-1. Although it has been somewhat compromised, no attacks have yet been reported on the SHA-2 variants, which are algorithmically similar to SHA-1.

To expand on these SHA-2 variants, NIST has published four additional hash functions in the SHA family. Each has a longer digest. Collectively they are known as SHA-2. Each of these individual variants is named after its digest length (in bits): SHA-224, SHA-256, SHA-384, and SHA-512. The final three were first published in 2001 in the draft Federal Information Processing Standard publication (FIPS PUB) 180-2. This publication (FIPS PUB 180-2) also includes SHA-1 and was released as an official standard in 2002. A change notice was published for FIPS PUB 180-2 in February 2004. This specified an additional variant, SHA-224. These variants have not yet received the degree of scrutiny from the cryptographic community that SHA-1 has, so their cryptographic security is not yet as well-established.

Currently efforts are under way within the cryptography community to develop improved alternative hashing algorithms. In one such effort, NIST is seeking to develop one or more additional hash algorithms through a public competition, similar to the development process used for the Advanced Encryption Standard (AES). It is the hope of NIST that a new standard will be developed and announced in 2012.

Vulnerabilities of SHA-1

Some researchers working with SHA-1 have called into question its use in new cryptosystems. NIST has announced that it plans to phase out the use of SHA-1 by 2010 in favor of the SHA-2 variants. To better understand the vulnerabilities of SHA-1 and why NIST is searching for a replacement, you need to better understand the research that has been done into its weaknesses.

SHA-1 has fallen victim to various attacks that call into question its cryptographic strength. One such attack, published by researchers in early 2005, found collisions when working with a reduced version of SHA-1. In February of that same year, a team of researchers announced an attack that could find collisions in the full version of SHA-1, requiring fewer than 2^{69} operations. To put this in perspective, a brute-force search attack would require 2^{80} operations.

When asked how these attacks were possible, researchers pointed to the exploitation of two weaknesses:

- Weak file processing step

- Certain math operations in the first 20 rounds have unexpected security issues

In the world of research and academic cryptography, an attack that has less computational complexity than a brute-force search is considered a break. However, academic research is sometimes far removed from practical application. The vulnerabilities identified in SHA-1 do not necessarily mean that the attack can be practically exploited. That being said, if an attacker could harness a massive distributed Internet search, theorists believe that finding a collision for SHA-1 would be possible.

In a practical sense, the primary concern about attacks that have been launched against SHA-1 is that they might pave the way to more efficient attacks—ones that might be practically carried out by would-be attackers. It is because of this potential that cryptographers believe that a migration to stronger hashes would be prudent. That is one reason why NIST is working toward a new solution.

A collision attack, as described earlier, does not present the same kinds of risks that a preimage attack does. A preimage attack on a cryptographic hash represents an attempt to find a message with a specific hash value. This type of attack differs from a collision attack in that a fixed hash or message is the focus of the attack.

Current application of cryptographic hashes for such purposes as password storage and document signing is only minimally affected by a collision attack. For instance, where it is used to sign a document, an attacker could not simply fake a signature from an existing document. In a case such as this, the attacker would also have to fool the private key holder into signing a preselected document. Where it has been applied for password usage, practical security threats are also less likely. An attacker would not be able to reverse password encryption to obtain a user's password to use elsewhere using a collision attack. Constructing a password that works for a given account requires a preimage attack, along with access to the hash of the original password (typically held in a *shadow* file).

Usage of SHA-1

SHA-1 and other SHA hash algorithms (SHA-224, SHA-256, SHA-384, and SHA-512) are secure hash algorithms required by law for use in certain U.S. government applications. This includes the use of SHA-1 within other cryptographic algorithms and protocols to protect sensitive yet unclassified information. Adoption and usage of SHA-1 by private and commercial organizations has been encouraged by FIPS PUB 180-1. Central to the publication of SHA was the Digital Signature Standard, in which it is incorporated. We will examine this in the section "Exploring the Digital Signature Standard."

Using Digital Signatures

Much like written signatures, digital signatures may be used to authenticate an associated input. In the written sense, we might find a signature providing authentication on anything from a letter to a legal contract. In the digital sense, a digital signature's input is called a "message." These messages may be anything. They might be an e-mail or a legal contract, or it might even be a message sent in a more complicated cryptographic protocol.

These digital signatures are used to create public key infrastructure (PKI) schemes wherein a user's public key (whether for public key encryption, digital signatures, or another purpose) is linked to a user by a digital identity certificate issued by a certificate authority (CA). These PKI schemes seek to create an unbreakable bond between the user's information (such as name, address, and phone number) and the public key. This relationship allows the user to use these public keys as a form of electronic identification.

Let's look at an example. Figure 13-6 shows the process of using a digital signature to support a PKI scheme in which the user's public key is linked to the user through the digital certificate issued by the CA.

Figure 13-6 *PKI*

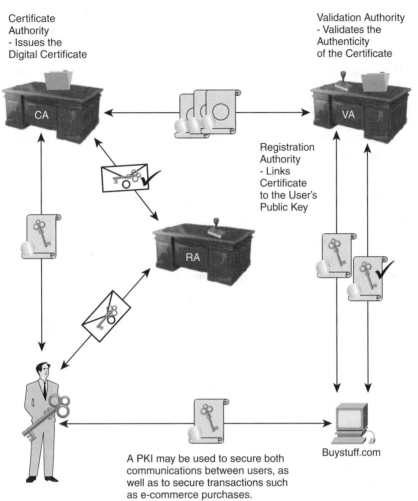

Certificate
Authority
- Issues the
Digital Certificate

Validation Authority
- Validates the
Authenticity
of the Certificate

Registration
Authority
- Links
Certificate
to the User's
Public Key

Buystuff.com

A PKI may be used to secure both
communications between users, as
well as to secure transactions such
as e-commerce purchases.

Here is how the process works:

1. The user's identity is bound to his public key through the CA. This is carried out through the binding and issuance process.

2. The actual binding of the certificate is done by the registration authority (RA).

3. After the binding, the user may use this certificate to represent himself and in the creation of messages.

4. The user may freely distribute his public key to those with whom he wants to communicate.

5. To provide authenticity of a message, the user may sign his message using his private key. Recipients may then validate the message's authenticity by applying the sender's public key.

6. To secure communications with the holder of the public/private key pair, the user can encrypt a message with the recipient's public key. This message then may be decrypted only through the use of the recipient's private key.

A digital signature (or digital signature scheme) is a form of asymmetric cryptography that is used to simulate the security characteristics of a written signature in digital form. Digital signature schemes typically use two algorithms that employ a pair of public and private keys. One algorithm is used for signing, which involves the user's secret or private key. The other is used to verify these signatures. This typically involves the use of the user's public key. The end result of this signature process is called the digital signature. It has widespread use in electronic security.

Understanding Digital Signatures

To understand digital signatures, we need to begin by examining digital signature schemes and their commonalities. All digital signature schemes have a number of prior requirements. Figure 13-7 shows a digital signature.

Figure 13-7 *Digital Signature*

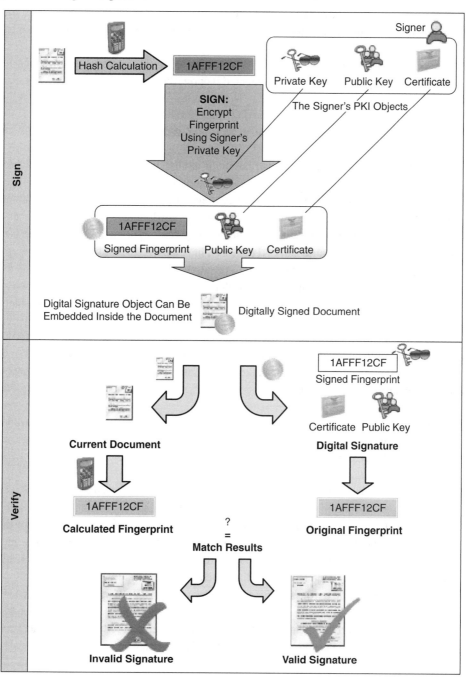

The first requirement is quality algorithms. As we have discussed, some of the available public key algorithms have been called into question with regard to security. Others are known to be insecure based on predictable attacks having been launched against them.

The second requirement is quality implementations. What this means is that even if you have a quality algorithm, if it is implemented incorrectly, it won't help you.

The third requirement is that the private key must remain secret. If this private key is compromised, an attacker can create an exact digital signature of anything he wants.

The fourth requirement is that the distribution of public keys has to be done in a manner that ensures that a public key belonging to a given user actually does belong to that user. Often this is done using a PKI. The public key user association is attested to by the operator of the PKI, the CA. In the case of "open" PKIs—ones in which anyone can request such an attestation—embodied in an identity certificate, the potential for mistaken attestation is not trivial. Unfortunately, commercial PKI providers have suffered a number of publicly known issues. Mistakes such as these could lead to falsely signed, and thus improperly attributed, documents. Maintaining a "closed" PKI system is more costly for organizations but less easily subverted, providing a stronger level of security for those who can take such steps.

Finally, beyond the PKI infrastructure and the steps that administrators must take to provide security, the fifth and final area of concern is users. The users of these PKI systems themselves (and their software) must take care to carry out the signature protocol properly to not compromise the signature.

All the conditions just listed must be met for a digital signature to reliably provide evidence of who sent the message, and therefore of his assent to its contents. Even legal measures cannot alter this reality.

Based on local laws, many countries accord a digital signature the same status as a traditional pen-and-paper signature with regard to its capacity to bind parties in a legal agreement such as a contract. Because of the legally binding nature of digital signatures in some parts of the world, it is generally best to use separate key pairs for encrypting and signing. Use of these key pairs allows an individual to engage in an encrypted conversation about matters that might be legally binding, such as the negotiation of a contract for employment. When the parties involved in the discussion reach an agreement, they can use their signing keys to "sign" the electronic document. At this point they are legally bound by the terms of a specific document. After this signing has taken place, the electronic document can be sent across an encrypted link to complete the transaction.

Digital Signature Scheme

Three algorithms generally make up a digital signature scheme:

- The key generation algorithm, which is used to randomly produce the key pair (public/private keys) used by the signer

- The signing algorithm, which, upon input of a message and a signing key, produces a signature

- The signature verifying algorithm, which, upon input of a message, a verifying key, and a signature, is used to either accept or reject the signature

Authentication and Integrity

One of the more practical uses of a digital signature in today's networks is for authentication and integrity checking. An example of this is the verification of authenticity in a message sent across a network.

Many times messages sent across the network include information about the entity sending the message. However, the authenticity of that information might be called into question. Digital signatures give us a mechanism to authenticate the source of such messages. With digital signatures, it is assumed that the ownership of a digital signature secret key is known to only a specific user. That being the case, a valid signature reflects that the message was sent by that specific user. The need for high levels of confidence in these matters is underscored by their use in financial matters, such as conducting credit card transactions or accessing bank account information.

For example, if a user accesses her bank account online and requests a transfer of funds between accounts, the bank must be certain of the authenticity of this request. If the bank has any question about this, transferring the funds would be a mistake.

In scenarios such as bank transactions, in addition to being assured of the user's authenticity, both the user (the sender) and her bank (the recipient of the message) may require confidence that the message has not been altered during transmission. Although the use of proper encryption can hide the contents of a message in transit, it may be possible to alter an encrypted message without understanding it. Certain nonmalleable encryption algorithms prevent this, but others do not. However, if a message is digitally signed, any change to the message while it is in transit invalidates the signature and alerts the parties that the message has been corrupted.

Examining RSA Signatures

The first algorithm found to be suitable for signing as well as encryption was RSA. RSA is an algorithm for public key cryptography. It represents what many believe to be one of the first great advances in public key cryptography. Today RSA is widely used in a number of electronic commerce protocols. Thanks to its long cryptographic keys and the use of up-to-date implementations, it is believed to be secure.

Exploring the History of RSA

The algorithm that would become RSA was first described in 1977 by Ron Rivest, Adi Shamir, and Leonard Adleman of MIT. A quick look at the first letters of their surnames tells you where the term RSA came from. Today RSA encryption is widely known and widely used for a variety of security needs.

Interestingly, a British mathematician named Clifford Cocks, who worked for the UK intelligence agency GCHQ, described an equivalent system in a top-secret internal document in 1973. However, because of the cost of computing resources to implement it, it was never deployed. This discovery was not revealed until 1997 because of its top-secret classification. Rivest, Shamir, and Adleman devised RSA independently of this initial work. In 1983 MIT was granted U.S. patent 4405829 for a "cryptographic communications system and method" that used the RSA algorithm. The patent expired on September 21, 2000.

Understanding How RSA Works

Key Topic

RSA uses a public key/private key combination. The public key in this pair can be known by anyone and can be distributed widely without issue to encrypt messages. After a message has been encrypted with a specific public key, it may be decrypted only through the use of the matching private key, which is privately held and is never distributed publicly.

If you are ready for some math, let's look at how the keys for the RSA algorithm are generated.

We begin by selecting two distinct large random prime numbers p and q. Next we compute $n=pq$, where n is used as a modulus for both the public and private keys. Then we compute the totient using the formula $\phi(n)=(p-1)(q-1)$.

Next we choose an integer e such that $1<e<\phi(n)$, and e and $\phi(n)$ share no factors other than 1 (coprime). The public key exponent that is released is e. You compute d to satisfy the congruence relation as $de=1(\mod \phi(n))$. The private key exponent is d.

The public key consists of the modulus n and the public (or encryption) exponent e. The private key consists of the modules n and the private (or decryption) exponent d that must always remain secret.

Encrypting and Decrypting Messages with RSA

Based on our earlier discussion, you know that RSA employs a combination of a public and private key to both encrypt and decrypt messages. This means that a user who wants to send and encrypt a message with RSA would transmit her public key (n and e) to another user while keeping her private key to herself. When the recipient of the public key wants to communicate with the sender, he uses the public key he received from the sender. The way this works is that the user (through an application) first turns her message (m) into a number where $m<n$ by using an agreed-upon reversible protocol called a padding scheme. Next, the ciphertext c is computed such that $c=m^e \bmod n$. Finally, the user transmits this ciphertext to the holder of the private key—the only one who can decrypt this message.

Now that you have a sense of how encryption works, let's take a look at the decryption process. From the preceding example, the message recipient (holder of the private key) now must recover the message (m) from the ciphertext by using his private key exponent . He does this by using the computation $m=c^d \bmod n$. Given that the user has the message (m), she may now recover the original message.

Signing Messages with RSA

In addition to encrypting and decrypting messages, RSA can be used to sign messages. To continue our example of two individuals exchanging a message, let's suppose that one of the individuals uses the other's public key to encrypt and send a message. Although the message is encrypted, the sender may not be who we think she is.

In other words, because the public key has been widely distributed, you have no way of verifying that the message is in fact from the individual who claims to have sent it. That's because anyone could use this key to encrypt and send back a message to the recipient, who holds the private key. To be sure of the sender's identity, RSA may also be used to digitally sign the message as well as encrypt it. This ensures both the privacy of the message contents and the validity of its origin.

Let's take a look at the digital signing process with RSA. We can begin with a user who wants to send a signed message to a recipient:

1. The user who wants to send a signed message first must produce a hash value for the message itself and then raise it to the power of $d \bmod n$. (This same process is followed when a message is decrypted.)

2. The hash value is attached to the message as a digital signature.

3. When the message is received, the recipient must raise the signature to a power of e $\bmod n$, just like when the message contents are encrypted.

4. The resulting hash value is compared with the message's actual hash value to make sure they match.

5. If the two hash values are identical, the recipient can be assured that the author of the message does in fact have a secret key, so the message has not been tampered with.

Vulnerabilities of RSA

RSA's strength and security are based on two mathematical problems: the problem of factoring large numbers and the RSA problem. Cryptographers believe that complete decryption of an RSA ciphertext is not feasible based on the assumption that both of these problems are extremely difficult. In other words, currently there exists no efficient algorithm for solving them. Partial decryption is another matter. To provide security against this, it may be necessary to add a secure padding scheme. Even with these factors, a number of specific attacks still focus on RSA. The most common of these are listed in Table 13-2.

Key Topic

Table 13-2 *RSA Attack Vulnerabilities*

Attack	Description
Timing attack	In 1995 an attack against RSA was described wherein if the attacker knew a user's hardware in enough detail, and he could measure the decryption times for several known ciphertexts, he could deduce the decryption key quickly. This same attack could then also be applied against the RSA signature scheme as well. One way to defend against this form of attack is to make sure that a consistent amount of time is required for the decryption operation of each ciphertext. Although this would work, it may not be worth the performance degradation that would result. Most RSA implementations use an alternative approach known as blinding. In this approach, the multiplicative property of RSA is used. The result of applying RSA blinding is that the decryption time is no longer correlated to the value of the input ciphertext, so the timing attack fails.
Adaptive chosen ciphertext attack	The first practical adaptive chosen ciphertext attack against an RSA-encrypted message was described in 1995. This attack used the targeted flaws in the PKCS #1 scheme, which was used in concert with RSA. This attack focused on RSA implementations of the Secure Socket Layer protocol and was used to recover session keys. Because of the success of this attack, it is now recommended that RSA be used with other, more secure padding schemes, such as Optimal Asymmetric Encryption Padding. Additionally, RSA Laboratories has released updated versions of PKCS #1 that are not vulnerable to this form of attack.
Branch prediction analysis (BPA) attack	A number of processors use a branch predictor to determine whether a conditional branch in a program's instruction flow is likely to be taken. Generally speaking, these types of processors also implement simultaneous multithreading (SMT). A branch prediction analysis attack uses a spy process to statistically discover the private key when it is processed by these processors.

Exploring the Digital Signature Standard

NIST created DSS, specified in FIPS 186 [1], and adopted it in 1993. Since its adoption, the standard has been revised in 1996 and in 2000, with a degree of expansion. DSS employs the Digital Signature Algorithm (DSA), which was proposed for use in the standard by NIST.

Using the DSA Algorithm

The DSS outlines the use of the DSA by a signer to generate a digital signature to be applied to data and by a recipient of the data to verify the authenticity of the signature. To create the digital signature, you need both a public key and a private key. The private key is used to generate the signature, and the public key is used to verify the signature. For both signature generation and verification, the data, which is called a message, is reduced through the use of SHA.

If an individual does not know the private key of the message signer, he cannot generate the signer's correct signature. This prevents the digital forgery of these signatures. The signature then can be verified by the message recipient or anyone holding the signer's public key. Of course, for this system to be useful, we need a mechanism for associating public and private key pairs to the corresponding users. In other words, we must bind a user's identity and public key. The binding of this association may be certified by a mutually trusted third party.

We see the application of this in secure e-commerce. In these instances, a certifying authority signs the credentials containing a user's (or company's) public key and identity to form a certificate. The DSS does not go into detail about systems for certifying credentials and distributing certificates, because they are beyond the scope of the standard.

Exam Preparation Tasks

Review All the Key Topics

Review the most important topics from this chapter, denoted with the Key Topic icon. Table 13-3 lists these key topics and the page where each is found.

Table 13-3 *Key Topics for Chapter 13*

Key Topic Element	Description	Page Number
Figure 13-1	Hashing example	466
Explanation	Application of hash functions	467
List	Vulnerability of a hash function	469
Example	Application of a cryptographic hash	469
Figure 13-2	HMAC	471
Figure 13-3	An MD5 algorithm	472
Explanation	Collisions	473
Figure 13-4	An MD5 rainbow table	474
List	Components of a secure hash function	475
Figure 13-5	An SHA-1 hash	476
List	SHA-1 weaknesses	477
Figure 13-6	PKI	479
Figure 13-7	A digital signature	481
List	A digital signature scheme	483
Explanation	How RSA works	484
Explanation	The digital signing process with RSA	485
Table 13-2	RSA attack vulnerabilities	486

Complete the Tables and Lists from Memory

Print a copy of Appendix D, "Memory Tables," (found on the CD) or at least the section for this chapter, and complete the tables and lists from memory. Appendix E, "Memory Tables Answer Key," also on the CD, includes completed tables and lists so that you can check your work.

Definition of Key Terms

Define the following key terms from this chapter, and check your answers in the glossary:

authentication, authorization, certificate authority (CA), checksum, ciphertext, collision, cryptography, cryptographic hash, digital signature, Digital Signature Algorithm (DSA), HMAC, message, Message Digest 5 (MD5), National Institute of Standards and Technology (NIST), private key, public key, Public Key Infrastructure (PKI), rainbow table, RSA, salt, SHA-1

This chapter covers the following subjects:

Understanding asymmetric algorithms: This section explores asymmetric encryption and looks at how this is used in a Public Key Infrastructure (PKI). It also examines the features and capabilities of RSA, as well as its history. This section concludes by delving into the Diffie-Hellman algorithm and how it is used for key exchange.

Working with a PKI: This section examines the principles behind a PKI and discusses the attempts at standardization in this area. It also covers the role of certificate authorities (CA) in support of the PKI and examines the various topologies in which they may be used.

CHAPTER 14

Exploring PKI and Asymmetric Encryption

Asymmetric encryption algorithms accomplish two primary objectives: confidentiality and authentication. Asymmetric algorithms are slower than symmetric algorithms because they are more complex mathematically. Because asymmetric algorithms are slower, they are usually used as key exchange protocols. This chapter discusses the principles behind asymmetric encryption and provides examples of major asymmetric encryption algorithms, including Rivest, Shamir, and Adleman (RSA); Diffie-Hellman (DH); and Public Key Infrastructure (PKI).

"Do I Know This Already?" Quiz

The "Do I Know This Already?" quiz helps you determine your level of knowledge of this chapter's topics before you begin. Table 14-1 details the major topics discussed in this chapter and their corresponding quiz questions.

Table 14-1 *"Do I Know This Already?" Section-to-Question Mapping*

Foundation Topics Section	Questions
Understanding Asymmetric Algorithms	1 to 5
Working with a PKI	6 to 10

1. Which of the following is not a popular public-key encryption algorithm?

   a. Digital Signature Algorithm (DSA)

   b. DAH

   c. RSA

   d. Diffie-Hellman

2. RSA employs keys that generally have what bit length?

   a. 129 to 256 bits

   b. 256 to 512 bits

   c. 512 to 2048 bits

   d. 1024 to 2048 bits

3. Before a Diffie-Hellman exchange may begin, the two parties involved must agree on what?

    a. Two secret numbers

    b. Two secret keys

    c. Two nonsecret keys

    d. Two nonsecret numbers

4. Modern digital signatures generally rely on which of the following? (Choose all that apply.)

    a. A public-key algorithm

    b. A private-key algorithm

    c. An encryption function

    d. A hash function

5. Which of the following are distinctions between asymmetric and symmetric algorithms? (Choose all that apply.)

    a. Asymmetric algorithms are based on more complex mathematical computations.

    b. Only symmetric algorithms have a key exchange technology built in.

    c. Symmetric algorithms are based on more complex computations.

    d. Only asymmetric algorithms have a key exchange technology built in.

    e. Asymmetric algorithms are used quite often as key exchange protocols for symmetric algorithms.

    f. Symmetric algorithms are used quite often as key exchange protocols for asymmetric algorithms.

6. A Public Key Infrastructure serves as a basis for providing which of the following security services? (Choose all that apply.)

    a. Encryption

    b. Virus protection

    c. Intrusion prevention

    d. Authentication

    e. Nonrepudiation

7. Which of the following best describes a certificate authority (CA)?

    a. An agency responsible for granting and revoking public-private key pairs

    b. A trusted third party responsible for signing the public keys of entities in a PKI-based system

    c. A trusted third party responsible for signing the private keys of entities in a PKI-based system

    d. An entity responsible for registering the private key encryption used in a PKI

8. Which of the following are valid certificate authority (CA) architectures? (Choose all that apply.)

    a. Certified CA

    b. Single-root CA

    c. Bidirectional CA

    d. Cross-certified CA

    e. Hierarchical CA

9. Which of the following Public Key Cryptographic Standards (PKCS) defines the syntax for encrypted messages and messages with digital signatures?

    a. PKCS #10

    b. PKCS #8

    c. PKCS #12

    d. PKCS #7

10. Which of the following is not one of the five main areas that constitute a PKI?

    a. Storage and Protocols

    b. User Authentication through Local Registration Authorities (LRA)

    c. CAs to Provide Management of Passwords

    d. Supporting Legal Framework

Foundation Topics

Understanding Asymmetric Algorithms

Asymmetric algorithms support two of the primary objectives of any form of security, because their main objectives are confidentiality and authentication. To meet these objectives, these algorithms are based on much more complex mathematical formulas that require greater time to compute than symmetric algorithms. With their greater security through a more complex computation, asymmetric algorithms are used quite often as key exchange protocols for symmetric algorithms. This is because symmetric algorithms have no inherent key exchange technology built in. This section explores asymmetric algorithms and their usage.

Exploring Asymmetric Encryption Algorithms

Asymmetric algorithms employ a two-key technology: a public key and a private key. Often this is simply called public-key encryption. In this key pair, the "public" key may be distributed freely, whereas the "private" key must be closely guarded. If it is compromised, the system as a whole fails. In fact, calling this just public-key encryption oversimplifies this process, because both keys are required, with the complementary key being used to provide decryption. Figure 14-1 shows the use of asymmetric encryption algorithms.

Figure 14-1 *Asymmetric Encryption Algorithms*

- The typical key length is 512–4096 bits.
- Key lengths greater than or equal to 1024 bits can be trusted.
- Key lengths that are shorter than 1024 bits are considered unreliable for most algorithms.

With public-key encryption, the public key is used to encrypt the data. After it is encrypted, only the private key can decrypt the data. The opposite is also true. If data is encrypted by the private key, the public key may be used to decrypt the data.

A number of public-key encryption algorithms exist. Although each algorithm differs, they all share a common trait in that the mathematics behind them is quite complicated. Here are some of the most popular algorithms:

- RSA

- Digital Signature Algorithm (DSA)

- Diffie-Hellman (DH)

- ElGamal

- Elliptic Curve Cryptography (ECC)

Key
Topic

The design of asymmetric algorithms is such that the key used for encryption is substantially different from the key used for decryption. This is done so that an attacker cannot, in any reasonable amount of time, calculate the decryption key from the encryption key, and vice versa. These keys come in varying lengths, but the general range for a key built using asymmetric algorithms is from 512 to 4096 bits. As another security feature, the key lengths for asymmetric algorithm keys cannot be directly compared to symmetric algorithm key lengths. This is because these two forms of algorithms differ greatly in the structure of their design.

As mentioned, a number of asymmetric cryptographic algorithms exist, but the most widely known and used are RSA, ElGamal, and elliptic curve algorithms. It is generally true, with regard to key length, that an RSA encryption key of 2048 bits is roughly equivalent to a 128-bit key of RC4 in terms of its ability to resist brute-force attacks.

Using Public-Key Encryption to Achieve Confidentiality

To achieve confidentiality, the encryption process begins with the public key. Using the public key to encrypt data ensures that only the private key can decrypt the protected data. Confidentiality is assured in this manner because only one host has the private key necessary for decryption. This process hinges on the integrity of the private key. Should the private key become compromised, this guarantee of confidentiality is lost, and another key pair must be generated to replace the compromised key. It is not possible to re-create the compromised key, so both keys in the pair are replaced.

Let's examine an example in which a public key pair is used, with the goal being to provide confidentiality. This exchange is shown in Figure 14-2 and is detailed in the following steps:

Step 1 Addison gains access to Matthew's public key.

Step 2 Addison uses Matthew's public key to encrypt a message to be sent to Matthew. This process often uses a symmetric key, with an agreed-upon algorithm.

Step 3   Addison sends the encrypted message to Matthew.

Step 4   Matthew uses his private key to decrypt the message and reveal the contents.

Figure 14-2   *Asymmetric Confidentiality Process*

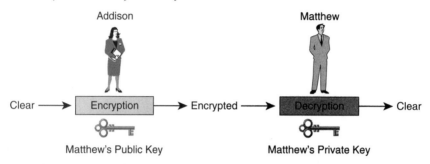

Providing Authentication with a Public Key

Authentication with an asymmetric algorithm is achieved when the encryption process is begun using the private key rather than the public key, as you saw when the goal was confidentiality. In this instance, the private key is used to encrypt the data, and the public key must then be used to decrypt the data. The same rules apply, however, in that only one host has the private key. In this case, this means that only that host can encrypt the message. In addition to providing security, this authenticates the sender, because only that host has the private key.

The public key is just that—public—and generally no attempt is made to preserve the secrecy of this key. That means that any number of hosts may have this public key and, therefore, any or all could decrypt the message. After a message has been successfully decrypted using the host's public key, that host trusts that the message was encrypted by the sender's private key. This serves to verify the identity of the sender, providing a form of authentication.

Much as we discussed with the public key, should the private key become compromised, another key pair needs to be generated to replace the compromised key.

Let's examine an example in which the private key is used to provide authentication as two individuals exchange data. Figure 14-3 illustrates the following steps:

Step 1   Addison encrypts the message to be sent with her private key using an agreed-upon algorithm.

Step 2   Addison sends the encrypted message to Matthew.

Step 3   Matthew acquires Addison's public key.

Step 4   Matthew uses Addison's public key to decrypt the message and reveal its
contents. This also serves to authenticate that the message is indeed from
Addison, because Matthew is the only person with this private key.

Figure 14-3   *Asymmetric Authentication Process*

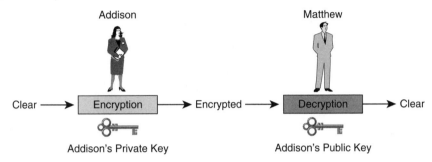

Understanding the Features of the RSA Algorithm

RSA, invented by Ron Rivest, Adi Shamir, and Len Adleman in 1977, is one of the most
common asymmetric algorithms in use today. This public-key algorithm was patented until
September 2000, when the patent expired, making the algorithm part of the public domain.
RSA has been widely embraced over the years, in part because of its ease of implementation and
flexibility. This flexibility is because of RSA's use of a variable key length. This allows
implementers to trade speed for the security of the algorithm if they so choose.

RSA has stood the test of time, having been in existence for 31 years. RSA has withstood
many years of extensive cryptanalysis. Although the security of RSA has been neither
proven nor disproven, its longevity suggests, if nothing more, a strong level of confidence
in the RSA algorithm, whose keys are generally 512 to 2048 bits long. Security provided
by RSA is based on the difficulty of factoring very large numbers. This process breaks these
large numbers into multiplicative factors. Should researchers or attackers derive an easy
method of factoring these large numbers, RSA's effectiveness would cease to exist.

The RSA algorithm is based on the premise that each entity has two keys, a public key and
a private key. As discussed earlier, the public key can readily be published and given away.
The private key, on the other hand, must be kept secret and should be available only to the
owner of the key pair. Determining the makeup of either key based on the other key is not
computationally feasible. Taken together, what one key can encrypt, the other can decrypt.
The nature of these RSA keys is to be long-term. Generally they are either changed or
renewed after several months of usage. Some even stay in use for years.

Working with RSA Digital Signatures

Modern digital signatures rely on more than public-key operations. They actually combine a hash function with a public-key algorithm to create a more secure signature, as shown in Figure 14-4.

Figure 14-4 *RSA Digital Signature Process*

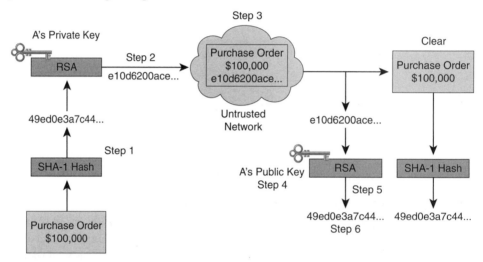

Let's examine the steps involved in the signature process:

Step 1   To uniquely identify the document and its contents, the signer makes a hash or fingerprint of the document.

Step 2   The signer's private key is used to encrypt the hash.

Step 3   The signature (the encrypted hash) is appended to the document.

Continuing the process, the following steps outline verification:

Step 4   The verifier obtains the signer's public key.

Step 5   The signer's public key is used to decrypt the signature. This step reveals the signer's assumed hash value.

Step 6   The verifier makes a hash of the received document, without its signature. This is compared to the decrypted signature hash. If the two hashes match, the document is thought to be authentic. In other words, it was signed by the assumed signer, and it has not been altered since it was signed.

In the exchange just depicted, you can see how both the authenticity and integrity of the message are ensured, even though the actual text is public. To ensure that the message remains private and that it has not been altered, both encryption and digital signatures are required.

Guidelines for Working with RSA

Although RSA is widely accepted and has a long history, it is certainly not the fastest algorithm. When compared to Data Encryption Standard (DES) in software, it is approximately 100 times slower. When compared to DES in a hardware implementation, it is nearly 1000 times slower. Because of these speed issues, RSA generally is used to protect only small amounts of data. In fact, RSA is used for two main reasons:

- To perform encryption to ensure the confidentiality of data

- To generate digital signatures to provide authentication of data, nonrepudiation of data, or both

Examining the Features of the Diffie-Hellman Key Exchange Algorithm

The Diffie-Hellman (DH) Key Exchange Algorithm was invented by Whitfield Diffie and Martin Hellman in 1976. The Diffie-Hellman algorithm derives its strength from the difficulty of calculating the discrete logarithms of very large numbers. The functional usage of this algorithm is to provide secure key exchange over insecure channels such as the Internet. DH is also often used to provide keying material for other symmetric algorithms, such as DES, 3DES, or AES.

The DH algorithm serves as the basis for many of our modern automatic key exchange methods. It is used within the Internet Key Exchange (IKE) protocol in IP Security (IPsec) virtual private networks (VPN). In this role it provides a reliable and trusted method for key exchange over untrusted channels such as the Internet.

Before the DH exchange may begin, the two parties involved must agree on two nonsecret numbers. The first number selected is used as the generator and is termed g, for generator. The second number is called p, and it serves as the modulus. There is no need to keep these numbers secret; generally they are chosen from a table of known values. In most cases g is usually a very small number, a single integer such as 2, 3, or 4, and p is a very large prime number. After these numbers are selected, each party generates its own secret value. Finally, these numbers are used together. Based on the values of g and p, as well as the secret value of each party, each party calculates its public value. The following formula is used to compute the public value:

$Y = g^x \bmod p$

x represents the entity's secret value, and Y is the entity's public value.

After these public values have been computed by both parties, they are exchanged. Then each party exponentiates the public value it received with its own secret value. This step computes a common shared secret value. When the algorithm finishes, each party has the same shared secret.

If an attacker is listening on the channel, he can't compute the secret value, because only g, p, Y_A, and Y_B are known. To calculate the shared secret value, at least one secret value is needed. Given the nature of this process, for an attacker to obtain the shared secret, he would have to be able to compute the discrete algorithm of the equation we discussed to recover X_A or X_B.

Steps of the Diffie-Hellman Key Exchange Algorithm

Let's take a closer look at the steps involved in the DH key exchange:

Step 1 Matthew and Abby agree on generator g and modulus p.

Step 2 Matthew selects a random large integer X_a and sends Abby its public value, Y_A, where $Y_A = g^{x(A)} \bmod p$.

Step 3 Abby selects a random large integer X_B and sends Matthew her public value, Y_B, where $Y_B = g^{x(B)} \bmod p$.

Step 4 Matthew computes $k = Y_B{}^{x(A)} \bmod p$.

Step 5 Abby computes $k' = Y_A{}^{x(B)} \bmod p$.

Step 6 Both k and k' are equal to $g^{x(A)x(B)} \bmod p$.

Now that Matthew and Abby have gone through this process, they have a shared secret ($k=k'$). Even if an attacker has been able to listen in on an untrusted channel, there is no way he could compute the secret from the captured information. As mentioned earlier, computing a discrete logarithm of Y_A or Y_B is nearly unfeasible.

Working with a PKI

By implementing a Public Key Infrastructure (PKI), organizations can provide an underlying basis for a number of security services, such as encryption, authentication, and nonrepudiation. You are likely familiar with encryption and authentication, but nonrepudiation may be somewhat unfamiliar. Nonrepudiation blocks the false denial of a particular action.

PKI is often a central authentication source for corporate VPNs, because it provides a scalable solution to meet the growing needs of today's organizations.

A number of terms are specific to the PKI structure. The following sections explore these and examine how a PKI works.

Examining the Principles Behind a PKI

To understand all that a PKI has to offer, first you must understand its components. A PKI provides organizations with the framework needed to support large-scale public-key-based technologies. Taken as a whole, a PKI is a set of technical, organizational, and legal components that combine to establish a system that enables large-scale use of public-key cryptography. Via a PKI, an organization can provide authenticity, confidentiality, integrity, and nonrepudiation services. This section examines the principles of implementing a PKI.

Understanding PKI Terminology

The following are two very important PKI terms:

- **Certificate authority (CA)**: A trusted third party responsible for signing the public keys of entities in a PKI-based system.

- **Certificate**: A document issued and signed by the CA that binds the name of the entity and its public key.

In a PKI, the certificate issued to a user is always signed by a CA. Each CA also has a certificate of its own. This certificate, called a CA certificate or a root certificate, contains its public key and is signed by the CA itself. This is why it is also called a self-signed CA certificate.

Components of a PKI

Creating a large PKI involves more than simply the CA and users who obtain certificates. It also involves substantial organizational and legal work. When we consider this in its entirety, we see that five main areas constitute the PKI:

- CAs to provide management of keys

- PKI users (people, devices, servers)

- Storage and protocols

- Supporting organizational framework (practices) and user authentication through Local Registration Authorities (LRA)

- Supporting legal framework

A number of vendors provide effective CA servers. These act as a managed service or may be an end-user product; this varies by vendor. The primary providers are as follows:

- Microsoft

- Cybertrust

- VeriSign

- Entrust Technologies

- RSA

- Novell

Classes of Certificates

CAs can issue a number of different classes of certificates. These classes vary, depending on how trusted a certificate is. For instance, an outsourcing vendor such as VeriSign or RSA might run a single CA, issuing certificates of different classes. The customers who obtain these certificates then can use this CA that they need based on their desired level of trust.

Certificate classes are defined by a number, 0 through 4. The higher the number, the more trusted the certificate. So what determines the "trust" in a given certificate?

Trust in the certificate generally is determined by how rigorous the verification process was with regard to the holder's identity at the time the certificate was issued. Let's consider an example.

If an organization wanted a class 0 certificate, it might be issued without any checks. This form of certificate might be used for testing purposes internally. A class 1 certificate, in contrast, would likely require an e-mail reply from the holder to confirm her wish to enroll. This is still a very weak form of authentication for the user, but again, a class 1 certificate is not highly trusted. If an organization requires a higher level of trust for its certificate, it may go through the process to obtain a class 3 or 4 certificate. Before these certificates are issued, the future holder is required to prove her identity. The applicant must authenticate her public key by appearing in person, with a minimum of two official ID documents. As you can see, the various classes of certificates range greatly in their degree of trust to meet an organization's needs.

Examining the PKI Topology of a Single Root CA

In addition to offering a number of different certificates with varying levels of trust, PKIs form different topologies of trust. Here we will examine the most simple of these models, a single CA (see Figure 14-5).

Figure 14-5 *Single-Root CA*

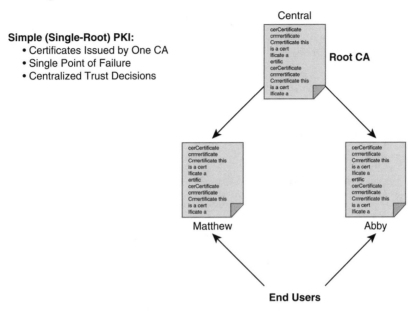

This topology is often called a root CA. This single CA is responsible for issuing all the certificates to the end users. The initial attraction of this PKI topology is its simplicity; however, it also has a number of pitfalls:

■ It is difficult to scale this topology to a large environment.

■ This topology needs a strictly centralized administration.

■ There is a critical vulnerability in using a single signing private key. If it is stolen, the whole PKI falls apart, because the CA can no longer be trusted as a unique signer.

This form of topology may be used to support VPNs. In some cases, this topology may be used when there is not a greater need beyond the VPN for the PKI.

Examining the PKI Topology of Hierarchical CAs

For organizations that want to avoid the pitfalls of the single-root CA, more complex CA structures can be devised and implemented. This section examines the hierarchical CA structure and its application, as shown in Figure 14-6.

Figure 14-6 *Hierarchical CAs*

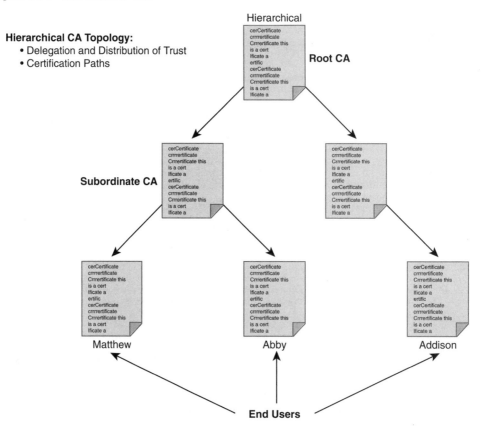

The hierarchical CA structure is a more robust and complicated implementation of the PKI. In this topology, CAs may issue certificates to both end users and subordinate CAs. These subordinate CAs then may issue their certificates to end users, other CAs, or both. This topology creates a tree-like structure of CAs and end users in which each higher-level CA may issue certificates to any lower-level CAs and end users. This structure gets around the issues that we saw with the single-root CA.

For many organizations that implement this topology, the main benefit they achieve is a significant increase in scalability and manageability. In this topology, trust decisions may be hierarchically distributed to smaller branches lower in the tree. This distribution fits well with the structure of many larger enterprise organizations. Let's take a look at an example.

A large enterprise organization may choose to have a root CA in its headquarters that is responsible for issuing certificates to level-2 CAs both locally and in regional locations. It then falls on these level-2 CAs to issue all certificates to the end users.

This solution also addresses security, because the root-signing key, held by the root CA, is seldom used after the subordinate CA certificates are issued. This means that in this topology its exposure is limited and, therefore, more readily trusted. This structure also addresses the threat of having a key stolen from a subordinate CA. Should this occur, only that branch of the PKI is rendered untrusted. All other users simply no longer trust that particular CA.

Even though this hierarchical topology has great benefits, some matters must be considered. Given the complex nature of a structure with numerous branches, one issue can be finding the certification path for a certificate. Finding this path allows you to understand the signing process. If a great number of CAs exist between the root CA and the end user, determining and verifying this certification path can be quite difficult.

Examining the PKI Topology of Cross-Certified CAs

Cross-certifying represents another form of hierarchical PKI topology. This structure has a number of flat, single-root CAs. Each of these CAs establishes a trust relationship horizontally by cross-certifying its own CA certificates, as shown in Figure 14-7.

Figure 14-7   *Cross-Certified CAs*

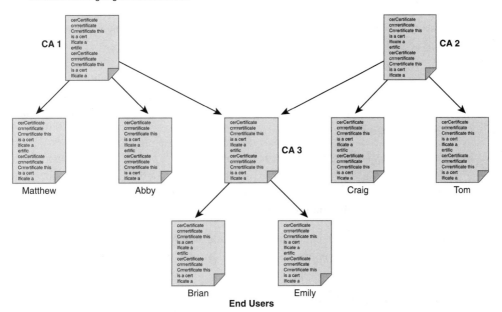

Understanding PKI Usage and Keys

Depending on the PKI's structure and implementation, it may offer or even require the use of two key pairs for each entity involved:

■ The first public and private key pair is used only for encryption. In this combination, the public key encrypts, and the private key decrypts.

■ The second key pair is intended exclusively for signing. In this case, the private key signs, and the public key is used to verify the signature.

These key pair combinations go by different names. You might hear them called "special keys" or "usage keys." In either case, they serve the same purpose. These key pairs may differ in key length. They may also differ in the choice of the public-key algorithm they employ.

If the PKI that is employed requires two key pairs per entity, the user has two certificates as well. These certificates contain the following two components:

■ An encryption certificate containing the user's public key, which encrypts the data

■ A signature certificate containing the user's public key, which verifies the user's digital signature

Usage keys may be employed in a number of situations. Let's examine a few of these situations so that we may look more closely at their application:

■ Where encryption is used more frequently than signing, a certain public and private key pair is more exposed because of this frequent usage. Its lifetime is shortened, and it changes more frequently. The separate signing private and public key pair could have a much longer lifetime.

■ If key recovery is desired, such as when a copy of a user's private key is kept in a central repository for various backup reasons, usage keys allow for backing up only the private key of the encrypting pair. In this instance, the signing private key remains with the user, allowing for true nonrepudiation.

■ When different levels of encryption and digital signing are required because of legal, export, or performance issues, usage keys allow you to assign different key lengths to the pairs.

Working with PKI Server Offload

As we have discussed, the CA plays a central role in the PKI with its private key. Its security is a critical element in making the PKI work successfully. To make the operation of the CA more secure, a great many of the key management tasks may be effectively offloaded to registration authorities (RA). These RAs are PKI servers that are responsible for performing management tasks on behalf of the CA. Having an RA in place allows the CA to focus on the signing process.

Having an RA in place allows for the offloading of three main tasks:

- Authentication of users when they enroll with the PKI

- Key generation for users who cannot generate their own keys

- Distribution of certificates after enrollment

Understanding PKI Standards

As discussed in an earlier section, the market has a number of PKI vendors, making standardization and interoperability an issue when interconnecting PKIs. Some progress has been made in this area by the X.509 standards and the Internet Engineering Task Force (IETF) Public Key Infrastructure X.509 (PKIX) workgroup. Together they have worked toward publishing a common set of standards to be used for PKI protocols and data formats. In addition to striving toward these standards, it is important to understand the supporting services used by a PKI, such as Lightweight Directory Access Protocol (LDAP)-accessible X.500 directories.

One reason that there is such concern about interoperability between a PKI and its supporting services is that many vendors have proposed and implemented proprietary solutions. Currently, interoperability is in the most basic of states, even though it has been ten years since the development of PKI software solutions.

As mentioned, the IETF is one organization working toward standardization in this area. It has formed a working group dedicated to promote and standardize PKI in the Internet. This group has created and published a draft set of standards that detail common data formats and PKI-related protocols to be used in a network. You may review this draft at http:// www.ietf.org/html.charters/pkix-charter.html.

Understanding X.509v3

X.509 is a well-known industry standard that has been incorporated to define basic PKI formats. Areas that are based on this include both the certificate and certificate revocation list (CRL) format. Using this common standard in this manner underlies the basic interoperability we see in the majority of PKIs. Of course, PKI is not the only technology to take advantage of X.509. It is a widely used standard for many Internet applications, including Secure Socket Layer (SSL) and IPsec.

The format of a digital certificate is defined by X.509 version 3 (X.509v3). This format is currently in use throughout the Internet. Table 14-2 lists some of the ways in which it is currently being used.

Key Topic

Table 14-2   *Uses of X.509v3*

Use of X.509v3	Description
Website authentication	Secure web servers use X.509v3 for website authentication in the SSL protocol.
To support S/MIME	User mail agents that support the Secure/Multipurpose Internet Mail Extensions (S/MIME) protocol use X.509v3 to protect e-mail.
In IPsec VPNs	IPsec VPNs that employ certificates use X.509v3 as a public-key distribution mechanism for IKE RSA-based authentication.
To implement client certificates	Web browsers use X.509v3 to support services that implement client certificates in the SSL protocol.

When working with the CA to provide the authentication procedure, when contacting the PKI, the user first securely obtains a copy of the CA's public key. This public key is used to verify all the certificates issued by the CA. This is central to the proper functioning of the PKI.

Recall that certificates contain the binding between the names and public keys of entities to which they are issued. Generally, these are published in a centralized directory. This is done so that other PKI users can easily access them.

The CA also can distribute its public key in the form of a certificate issued by the CA itself. This certificate is called a self-signed certificate, because in this case the signer of the certificate and the holder of the certificate are the same entity. These self-signed certificates are issued only by a root CA.

Understanding Public Key Cryptography Standards (PKCS)

Public Key Cryptography Standards (PKCS) is used to provide basic interoperability for applications that employ public-key cryptography. Taken together, PKCS defines a set of low-level standardized formats for the secure exchange of arbitrary data. For instance, PKCS defines a standard format for an encrypted piece of data, a signed piece of data, and so on.

Table 14-3 outlines a number of PKCS standards.

Table 14-3 *PKCS Standards*

Standard Number	Description
PKCS #1	RSA Cryptography Standard
PKCS #3	DH Key Agreement Standard
PKCS #5	Password-Based Cryptography Standard
PKCS #6	Extended-Certificate Syntax Standard
PKCS #7	Cryptographic Message Syntax Standard
PKCS #8	Private Key Information Syntax Standard
PKCS #10	Certification Request Syntax Standard
PKCS #12	Personal Information Exchange Syntax Standard
PKCS #13	Elliptic Curve Cryptography Standard
PKCS #15	Cryptographic Token Information Format Standard

Now that you have a sense of these standards and the various areas that they address, let's examine a couple of them in greater detail:

- **PKCS #7**: The Cryptographic Message Syntax Standard defines the syntax of several kinds of cryptographically protected messages. This includes defining the standard for encrypted messages and messages with digital signatures. One place that we see PKCS #7 extensively is S/MIME. PKCS #7 is the basis for S/MIME secure e-mail specification and as such has been widely implemented. PKCS #7 is not limited to working with mail messages. It also has become a basis for message security in a number of diverse systems. PKCS #7 provides message security in the Secure Electronic Transaction (SET) specifications for bank card payments, the World Wide Web Consortium (W3C) digital signature initiative, and PKCS #12, the Personal Information Exchange Syntax Standard.

- **PKCS #10**: The Certification Request Syntax Standard defines the syntax for how certification requests will be made in a PKI. Certification requests are made up of various parts: the distinguished name (DN), a public key, and optionally a set of attributes. If included, these attributes are signed by the entity requesting certification.

All certification requests are sent to a CA. The CA must accept the request and verify the authenticity of the information provided by the applicant. After this occurs, the CA transforms each request into an X.509 public-key certificate. When the CA returns the newly signed certificate, it is presented in a specific form; a PKCS #7 message is one possibility.

If this optional set of attributes is provided, other application-specific information about a given entity may be added to enhance security and flexibility. For example, if a "challenge password" is added, the entity can later request certificate revocation. In addition to these electronic means of certificate requests, CAs may require nonelectronic forms of request and may return nonelectronic replies.

Understanding Simple Certificate Enrollment Protocol (SCEP)

As we have discussed, public-key technology is widely used today and is incorporated in various standards-based security protocols. This increasing emphasis on public-key technology makes it all the more important that there be a certificate management protocol that PKI clients and CA servers can rely on to support all certificate life-cycle operations. Simple Certificate Enrollment Protocol (SCEP), illustrated in Figure 14-8, addresses the need for a certificate management protocol to handle certificate enrollment and revocation, as well as certificate and CRL access. The goal of SCEP is to provide a scalable means to support the secure issuance of certificates, while using existing technology wherever possible. One current use of SCEP is in IPSec VPNs, where it is used by IPSec VPN endpoints for certificate enrollment. This represents a significant improvement over manual/file-based enrollment.

Figure 14-8 *SCEP*

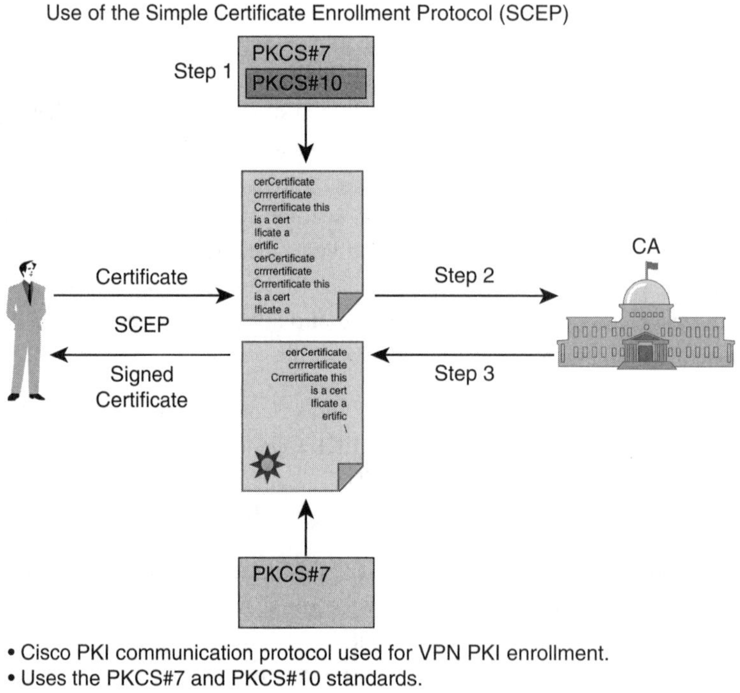

Use of the Simple Certificate Enrollment Protocol (SCEP)

- Cisco PKI communication protocol used for VPN PKI enrollment.
- Uses the PKCS#7 and PKCS#10 standards.

Let's examine the enrollment transaction in greater detail:

1. An end entity creates a certificate request using PKCS #10.

2. The request is enveloped using PKCS #7 and is sent to the CA or RA based on the topology in place.

3. When the CA or RA receives the request, either it is automatically approved and the certificate is sent back, or the end entity has to wait until the operator can manually authenticate the identity of the requesting end entity.

Exploring the Role of Certificate Authorities and Registration Authorities in a PKI

One central tenet behind the use of a PKI and trusted third-party protocols is that all participating parties agree to accept the word of a neutral third party. Should two parties need to validate each other, they turn to this trusted third party, which in turn provides in-depth authentication of the parties involved. This is done rather than having each party perform its own authentication.

These entities rely on the third party (the CA) to conduct an in-depth investigation of each entity before any credentials are issued. Furthermore, these entities rely on this trusted third party to issue credentials that are extremely difficult to forge. With these "assumptions" in place, from this point forward, all individuals who trust the third party agree to readily accept the credentials that it issues. If any of these assumptions are incorrect, the validity of this process is called into question, and the security of all entities is at risk.

Because of networking constraints, processor overhead, and general practicality, it is not reasonable for all parties in a large organization to continuously exchange identification documents for all communications. If you think about it, this is not that different from how your own organization may approach measures of physical security.

For example, you may work for an organization that issues each employee an ID badge. Before someone is given an employee badge, various measures probably are taken in conjunction with general hiring procedures. Perhaps a background check is run, or documentation is collected, such as a copy of the employee's driver's license and birth certificate, to ensure that the employee is who he claims to be. As soon as the employee passes this authentication process, he receives his employee badge. Of course, in addition to these authentication steps, the badge itself is made in such a way that it would be difficult to duplicate or forge. This adds another layer of trust. After the badge is issued, it is accepted as proof of the individual's identity and authority to work within your organization.

You might be wondering what would provide this validation if you did not have a process such as this in place. Let's assume that ten individuals within the organization need to validate each other, and there is no trusted third-party proof of identity, such as company ID badges. What might be involved? If no trusted third party is in place, this process of ten individuals validating each other would result in 90 separate validations before everyone would have validated everyone else. If that sounds messy, consider adding just one more individual to the group. This single addition would require an additional 20 validations, because each of the original group of ten individuals would need to authenticate the new person, and then the new person would need to authenticate the original ten. As you can see, this approach does not scale well. It becomes practically impossible for organizations of considerable size.

Certificate servers act as this trusted third party so that entities can provide the utmost level of trust between themselves, without the time-consuming complexities that would be involved if each individual entity needed to directly validate the others. As the example indicates, this would be impractical.

Examining Identity Management

CA-based solutions give an organization a means of identity management. This is accomplished in two primary ways:

- Through the CA's acting as the trusted third party in PKI implementations.

- Through the use of the X.509 standard, which describes the identity and how to store an authentication key. Information about the format of the X.509 certificate and the syntax of the fields in the certificate is described in Abstract Syntax Notation 1 (ASN.1).

The concept of a trusted third party embodied in the CA is a product of the merger of the X.509 standard with public-key encryption. The CA holds a key pair, a set of asymmetric keys, a private key, and a public key. The X.509 certificate is created to identify the CA, and it contains specific information for this purpose:

- The CA's identity

- The CA's public key

- The signature using the CA's private key

- Parameters such as serial number, algorithms used, and validity

As discussed in earlier sections, the CA's certificate is freely distributed. Therefore, it is incumbent that the recipient of the CA's certificate verify its authenticity out of band.

Retrieving the CA Certificate

Figure 14-9 shows the process that occurs when the CA certificate is retrieved, as described in the following list:

1. Abby and Matt request the CA certificate that contains the CA public key.

2. After the CA certificate is received, Abby and Matt's systems verify the validity of the certificate. This is done using public-key cryptography.

3. Abby and Matt go beyond the technical verification done by their systems by telephoning the CA administrator to verify the public key and the serial number of the certificate. This out-of-band process is a necessary step for true certainty.

Figure 14-9   *Retrieving a CA Certificate*

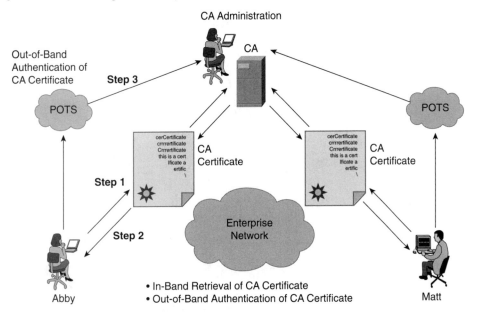

Understanding the Certificate Enrollment Process

After the users have retrieved the CA certificate, they need to submit certificate requests to the CA. This process is shown in Figure 14-10 and described in the following steps:

4. Abby and Matt's systems forward a certificate request that includes their public key along with some identifying information. All of this information is encrypted using the CA's public key.

5. After the certificate request is received, the CA administrator telephones Abby and Matt to confirm that they submitted the request and to verify the public key.

6. The CA administrator adds data to the certificate and then digitally signs it before issuing it.

When this process is complete, one of two things happens. The end user manually retrieves the certificate, or SCEP automatically retrieves it. After it is obtained, the certificate is installed on the system.

Examining Authentication Using Certificates

After the parties involved have installed certificates signed by the same CA, they may authenticate each other, as shown in Figure 14-11. This is done when the two parties exchange certificates. The CA's part in this process is finished, so it is not involved in this exchange.

Figure 14-10 *Certificate Enrollment Process*

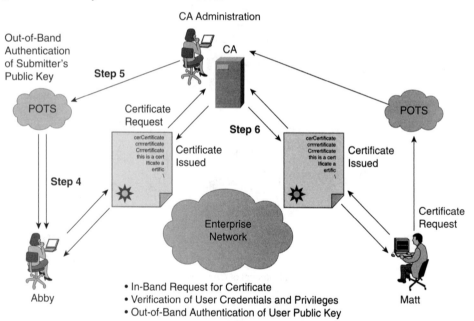

Figure 14-11 *Authentication Using Certificates*

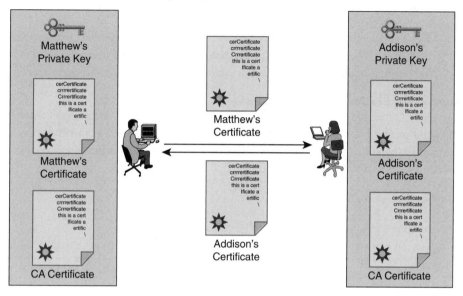

- Authentication no longer requires the presence of the CA server.
- Users exchange their certificates containing public keys.

At this point, each party involved verifies the digital signature on the certificate. This is done by hashing the plain-text portion of the certificate, decrypting the digital signature using the CA's public key, and then comparing the results.

For the certificate to be valid, the results must match when this comparison is conducted. If this is the case, the certificate is verified as being signed by a trusted third party, and the verification by the CA that each party is who it claims to be is accepted.

Examining Features of Digital Certificates and CAs

A number of authentication mechanisms are available to organizations. The following characteristics are unique to the use of a PKI:

■ Authentication of each party involved begins with the parties each obtaining the CA's certificate and their own certificate. To be secure, this process involves out-of-band verification. When it is complete, the presence of the CA is no longer required until the expiration of one of the certificates that is involved.

■ PKI systems use asymmetric keys. One key is public, and the other is private. A feature of these algorithms is that whatever one key encrypts, only the other key may decrypt, providing true nonrepudiation.

- Very long lifetimes, generally in terms of years, may be set for the certificates because of the strength of the algorithms involved.

- Key management is greatly simplified, because two users may freely exchange the certificates. The validity of the received certificates is verified using the CA's public key. Each user has this in his or her possession, making this process easy to undertake.

Understanding the Caveats of Using a PKI

To this point we have discussed the strengths that a PKI can bring to an organization. In addition to these strengths, it is important to understand the caveats involved in implementing a PKI in the enterprise so that you can make an informed decision. Table 14-4 describes some of the caveats.

Table 14-4 *Caveats of Using a PKI*

Caveat	Description
A user certificate is compromised (a private key is stolen)	It is important that no user accept a compromised certificate. To prevent these from being used, it is important to maintain a list of all revoked certificates. This list is called the Certificate Revocation List (CRL). The RLA server, not necessarily the CA server, should be readily accessible to users so that they may periodically download the latest CRL. This list should then be used when authenticating other users. Authentication fails if the received certificate is on the CRL.
The CA's certificate is compromised (the private key is stolen)	A compromised CA invalidates all certificates signed by the CA. In a single CA environment, recovering from this requires the creation of a new CA certificate and new user certificates. Should this occur in a hierarchical CA environment, an Authority Revocation List (ARL) is needed. In this situation, all child certificates of the compromised CA become invalid if the CA is on the ARL.
The CA administrator's process	A further limitation is that the CA administrator must be involved in this process. To lessen the impact, it is important that the CA administrator follow strict rules when issuing certificates. You should define a security policy to address the steps needed to create certificates. This process should include mandatory out-of-band verification of all initial enrollment procedures. It should also detail all steps that the CA administrator should take before approving a certificate request.

Even when certificates are employed in an IP network, they must be combined with another means of authentication. Using public-key authentication alone is not a wholly secure solution. In these instances, you should combine your public-key authentication with another authentication mechanism to provide greater security and more authorization options. An example of combining mechanisms might be something like working with IPsec using certificates for authentication and then combining this with Extended Authentication (XAUTH) that has one-time password hardware tokens. This combination provides a superior authentication scheme over using only certificates. Of course, some limitations exist.

One notable limitation should be mentioned. If an organization moves to digital certificates from Phase Shift Keying (PSK), a data modulation scheme that conveys data by changing or modulating the phase of a reference signal, it can experience an issue with a router. For instance, if it boots with incorrect time information, significant issues could occur. In a similar situation, if an internal battery dies, devices will think the current year is 1998. If you are working with a certificate that was issued in 2008 and it expires in 2010, the VPN will not be functional, and your site-to-site connection will go down. In a case like this, troubleshooting the issue is very hard, because the key areas that normally are examined, such as the routing table, appear normal and without issue, and users on the network can get out to the Internet. Because of this limitation, it is important that you understand that time—the correct time setting on your devices—now plays a critical role in the stability of VPN tunnels.

A second issue to be aware of is that if a router experiences such things as a random reboot, a power supply failure, or the interface going bad, when you replace this router with another one, you cannot simply paste in the former router's configuration and get it back online. This new device must first generate a certificate request and enroll with the CA. After the CA approves the request from the new router, you must install the certificates to bring the VPN tunnels back up. This is a little different than with PSKs. If you are working with PSKs, all the administrator must do is copy over the configuration, and the tunnel is up again.

Understanding How Certificates Are Employed

Certificates first found their use in providing strong authentication for applications. When employed in this manner, each application may have a different implementation of the actual authentication process. They all use a similar type of certificate in the X.509 format.

Secure Socket Layer (SSL) is one of the most widely used and most well known means of certificate-based authentication. With the emergence of e-commerce, SSL's ability to negotiate keys that are used to encrypt the SSL session is readily used to secure everything from online purchases to online banking. Among applications that rely on SSL, one of the most widely used is HTTPS. With the availability of SSL, other applications that previously employed lesser forms of authentication with no encryption were modified to use SSL. Among these are such popular applications as Simple Mail Transfer Protocol (SMTP), LDAP, and Post Office Protocol version 3 (POP3).

One of the most important extensions to secure communications is Multipurpose Internet Mail Extension (MIME). MIME allows arbitrary data to be included in an e-mail. A further enhancement (more properly called an "extension") to e-mail focused on providing greater security to entire mail messages or parts of messages. With Secure MIME (S/MIME) you can authenticate and encrypt e-mail messages.

Certificates may also be used at either the network or application layer by network devices. For instance, Cisco routers, Cisco VPN concentrators, and Cisco PIX firewalls can use certificates to authenticate IPsec peers.

End devices and devices connecting to the LAN may be authenticated by Cisco switches. This authentication process employs 802.1X between the adjacent devices and may be proxied to a central access control server (ACS) via Extensible Authentication Protocol with TLS (EAP-TLS). Cisco routers now can use SSL to establish secure TN3270 sessions rather than providing Telnet 3270 support that does not include encryption or strong authentication.

Figure 14-12 shows certificates being used for various purposes within a network. As you can see, a single CA server may facilitate a number of different applications that require digital certificates for authentication purposes. Using CA servers in these instances provides a solution that simplifies the management of the authentication process. It also provides significant security based on the cryptographic mechanisms used in combination with digital certificates.

Figure 14-12 *Applying Certificates*

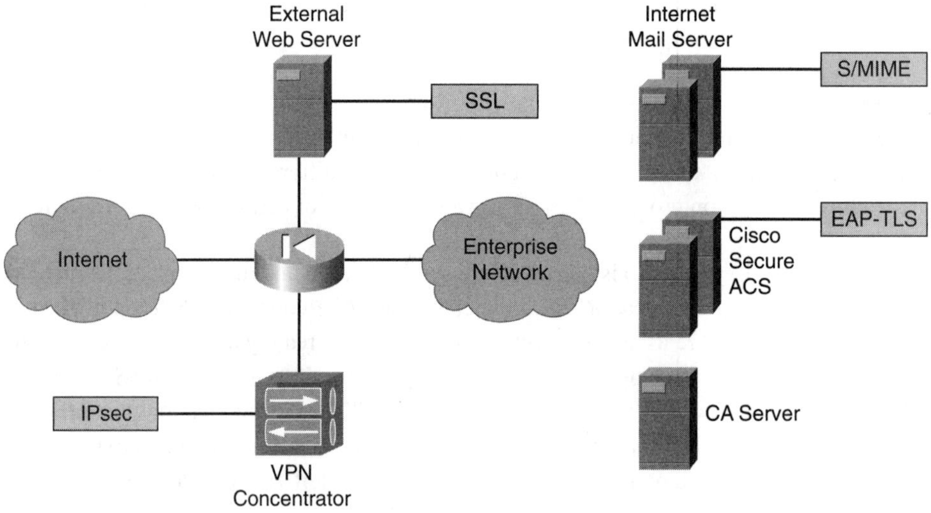

- Certificates can be used for various purposes.
- One CA server can be used for all types of authentication as long as all types support the same PKI procedures.

Exam Preparation Tasks

Review All the Key Topics

Review the most important topics from this chapter, denoted with the Key Topic icon. Table 14-5 lists these key topics and the page where each is found.

Table 14-5 *Key Topics for Chapter 14*

Key Topic Element	Description	Page Number
List	Public-key encryption algorithms	495
Steps	Steps in the signature process	498
Steps	Steps in the verification process	498
List	Key PKI terms	501
List	Main areas that constitute a PKI	501
List	Considerations when selecting a PKI	503
List	Description of the PKI structure with two key pairs	506
List	Certificate components	506
List	Usage key scenarios	506
List	Tasks offloaded with the use of an RA	507
Table 14-2	Uses for X.509v3	508
Table 14-3	PKCS standards	509
List	Identity management	512
List	Information included in a CA certificate	512
List	Characteristics unique to the use of a PKI	515
Table 14-4	Caveats of using a PKI	516

Complete the Tables and Lists from Memory

Print a copy of Appendix D, "Memory Tables," (found on the CD) or at least the section for this chapter, and complete the tables and lists from memory. Appendix E, "Memory Tables Answer Key," also on the CD, includes completed tables and lists so that you can check your work.

Definition of Key Terms

Define the following key terms from this chapter, and check your answers in the glossary:

certificate; certificate authority (CA); asymmetric algorithm; symmetric algorithm; nonrepudiation; Rivest, Shamir, and Adleman (RSA); Diffie-Hellman (DH) Algorithm; Public Key Infrastructure (PKI); key pair; registration authority (RA); X.509v3

This chapter covers the following topics:

Exploring the basics of IPsec: This section introduces an IPsec virtual private network (VPN) and its components. Additionally, you will explore specific devices in the Cisco VPN product family. Finally, you are presented with Cisco best-practice recommendations for VPNs.

Constructing an IPsec site-to-site VPN: This section walks you through the process of configuring an IPsec site-to-site VPN on an IOS router using the command-line interface.

Using Cisco SDM to configure IPsec on a site-to-site VPN: This section walks you through the process of configuring an IPsec site-to-site VPN on an IOS router using the Cisco Security Device Manager (SDM) interface.

CHAPTER 15

Building a Site-to-Site IPsec VPN Solution

Many companies have networks located in different geographic locations, and those networks need to communicate securely with one another. Purchasing dedicated WAN connections (for example, T1 connections using Point-to-Point Protocol [PPP]) or purchasing permanent virtual circuits (PVC) (for example, Frame Relay or Asynchronous Transfer Mode [ATM] PVCs) are options for these interoffice connections. However, these solutions might become cost-prohibitive.

As a more economical solution, consider the use of IPsec VPN connections. Specifically, an IPsec VPN can securely transmit data over an "untrusted" network, such as the Internet. This chapter introduces the protocols and hardware components that comprise an IPsec VPN based on Cisco equipment.

After you gain a foundational understanding of IPsec VPN technologies, this chapter delves into IPsec VPN configuration. First, you learn how to use Cisco IOS commands in the CLI to configure an IPsec site-to-site VPN. Seeing the specific configuration commands helps reinforce the previously presented theory.

Next, you learn how to use Cisco SDM to configure an IPsec site-to-site VPN. The wizard-like Cisco SDM interface can save you a tremendous amount of time if you have multiple site-to-site VPNs to configure.

"Do I Know This Already?" Quiz

The "Do I Know This Already?" quiz helps you determine your level of knowledge of this chapter's topics before you begin. Table 15-1 details the major topics discussed in this chapter and their corresponding quiz questions.

Table 15-1 *"Do I Know This Already?" Section-to-Question Mapping*

Foundation Topics Section	Questions
Exploring the Basics of IPsec	1 to 6
Constructing an IPsec Site-to-Site VPN	7 to 11
Using Cisco SDM to Configure IPsec on a Site-to-Site VPN	12 to 14

1. Which of the following acts as a VPN termination device and is located at a primary network location?

   a. Headend VPN device

   b. VPN access device

   c. Tunnel

   d. Broadband service

2. Which of the following ensures that data is not modified in transit?

   a. Confidentiality

   b. Integrity

   c. Authentication

   d. Authorization

3. What two IKE modes can negotiate an IKE Phase 1 (that is, an ISAKMP) tunnel? (Choose two.)

   a. Main mode

   b. Quick mode

   c. Aggressive mode

   d. Promiscuous mode

4. What are two modes of operation for both Authentication Header (AH) and Encapsulating Security Payload (ESP)? (Choose two.)

   a. Transmission mode

   b. Transport mode

   c. Transparent mode

   d. Tunnel mode

5. Which of the following licenses dictates the number of allowed concurrent connections on an ASA 5500 series appliance?

   a. Feature license

   b. Encryption license

   c. Platform license

   d. Expansion license

6. Which hashing algorithm does Cisco recommend as a best practice because of its increased security and speed?

   a. 3DES

   b. SHA

   c. AES

   d. MD5

7. An IPsec tunnel is negotiated within the protection of which type of tunnel?

   a. L2TP tunnel

   b. L2F tunnel

   c. GRE tunnel

   d. ISAKMP tunnel

8. What component of an IPsec configuration identifies "interesting" traffic—traffic that should be protected within the IPsec tunnel?

   a. Transform set

   b. ISAKMP policy

   c. ACL

   d. Diffie-Hellman group

9. Which command is used to specify Diffie-Hellman group 2 as part of an IKE Phase 1 configuration?

   a. **group 2**

   b. **diffie-hellman 2**

   c. **df group 2**

   d. **pre-share group 2**

10. From what configuration mode would you enter the **set peer** *ip-address* command to specify the IP address of an IPsec peer?

    a. Transform set configuration mode

    b. Crypto map configuration mode

    c. ISAKMP configuration mode

    d. Interface configuration mode

11. To what entity is a crypto map applied to make the crypto map active?

    a. Transform set

    b. Interface

    c. Virtual template

    d. ISAKMP proposal

12. What two site-to-site VPN wizards are available in the Cisco SDM interface? (Choose two.)

    a. Easy VPN Setup

    b. Quick Setup

    c. Step-by-Step

    d. DMVPN Setup

13. What three parameters do you configure when using the Cisco SDM Quick Setup Site-to-Site VPN wizard? (Choose three.)

    a. Interface for the VPN connection

    b. IP address for the remote peer

    c. Transform set for the IPsec tunnel

    d. Source interface where encrypted traffic originates

14. What command displays all existing IPsec security associations (SA)?

    a. **show crypto isakmp sa**

    b. **show crypto ipsec sa**

    c. **show crypto ike active**

    d. **show crypto sa active**

Foundation Topics

Exploring the Basics of IPsec

This section begins by identifying the characteristics of an IPsec VPN. You will learn about various protocols that make IPsec VPNs possible, including IKE protocols and the ESP and AH protocols. Although you can have a Cisco IOS router act as a VPN termination device, Cisco has other network devices that can serve in this capacity, and you will be introduced to the Cisco VPN product family. Finally, you are presented with a collection of Cisco best practices for configuring an IPsec VPN.

Introducing Site-to-Site VPNs

Much of today's workforce (approximately 40 percent according to Cisco) is located outside of a corporate headquarters location. Some employees work in remote offices, and others telecommute. These remote employees could connect to the main corporate network using a variety of WAN technologies (for example, leased lines and PVCs, found in Frame Relay and/or ATM networks). However, these WAN technologies typically cost more than widely available broadband technologies, such as DSL and cable, which might also offer faster speeds.

As illustrated in Figure 15-1, these broadband technologies can be used to support virtual private network (VPN) connections between these geographically dispersed offices. These VPN connections are often called VPN *tunnels*. Even though a VPN tunnel might physically pass through multiple service provider routers, it appears to be a single router hop from the perspective of the routers at each end of the tunnel.

Figure 15-1 *Site-to-Site VPN Connections*

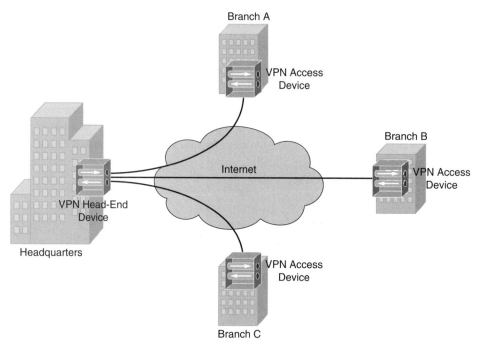

A *remote-access VPN* allows a user, with software on her client computer, to connect to a centralized VPN termination device. A *site-to-site VPN* interconnects two sites without requiring the computers at those sites to have any specialized VPN software installed. Table 15-2 defines the elements of a site-to-site VPN, which is the focus of this chapter.

Table 15-2 *Site-to-Site VPN Elements*

Element	Description
Headend VPN device	Acts as a VPN termination device, located at a primary network location (for example, a headquarters location)
VPN access device	Serves as a VPN termination device, located at a remote office
Tunnel	Provides a logical connection over which traffic flows (for example, an IP Security [IPsec] tunnel and/or a Generic Router Encapsulation [GRE] tunnel)
Broadband service	Transports traffic to and from the Internet (for example, over a cable or DSL connection)

Overview of IPsec

Broadband technologies such as cable and DSL, in addition to other VPN transport mechanisms, often traverse an untrusted network, such as the Internet. Therefore, a primary concern with using a broadband technology as a VPN transport is security.

Different VPN technologies (for example, IPsec, GRE, L2TP, and L2F) offer different features. IPsec VPNs offer security features. Specifically, IPsec offers the following protections for VPN traffic:

- **Confidentiality**: Data confidentiality is provided by encrypting data. If a third party intercepts the encrypted data, he could not interpret it.

- **Integrity**: Data integrity ensures that data is not modified in transit. For example, routers at each end of a tunnel could calculate a checksum value or a hash value for the data. If both routers calculate the same value, the data most likely has not been modified in transit.

- **Authentication**: Data authentication allows parties involved in a conversation to verify that the other party is who he claims to be. Various authentication methods exist:

    — Usernames and passwords

    — One-time passwords (OTP)

    — Biometric technologies (such as fingerprint analysis or retina scan)

    — Preshared keys

    — Signed digital certificates

IPsec not only becomes an attractive VPN technology because of its security enhancements. IPsec also scales to a wide range of networks. It operates at Layer 3 of the OSI model (the Network layer). As a result, IPsec is transparent to applications. That is, applications do not require any sort of integrated IPsec support.

IKE Modes and Phases

IPsec uses a collection of protocols to provide its features. One of the primary protocols it uses is Internet Key Exchange (IKE). Specifically, IPsec can provide encryption between authenticated peers using encryption keys, which are periodically changed. IKE does, however, allow an administrator to manually configure keys.

IKE can use three modes of operation to set up a secure communication path between IPsec peers. These modes are explained in Table 15-3.

Table 15-3 *IKE Modes*

Mode	Description
Main mode	Main mode involves three exchanges of information between the IPsec peers. One peer, called the *initiator*, sends one or more proposals to the other peer, called the *responder*. The proposal(s) include supported encryption and authentication protocols and key lifetimes. Additionally, the proposal(s) indicate whether perfect forward secrecy (PFS) should be used. PFS ensures that a session key remains secure, even if one of the private keys used to derive the session key becomes compromised. The three main mode exchanges can be summarized as follows: Exchange #1: The responder selects a proposal it received from the initiator. Exchange #2: Diffie-Hellman (DH) securely establishes a shared secret key over the unsecured medium. Exchange #3: An Internet Security Association and Key Management Protocol (ISAKMP) session is established. This secure session is then used to negotiate an IPsec session.
Aggressive mode	Aggressive mode more quickly achieves the same results as main mode, using only three packets. The initiator sends the first packet, which contains all information necessary to establish a security association (SA) (an agreement between the two IPsec peers about the cryptographic parameters to be used in the ISAKMP session). The responder sends the second packet, which contains the security parameters selected by the responder (that is, the proposal, keying material, and its ID). This second packet also is used by the responder to authenticate the session. The third and final packet, which is sent by the initiator, finalizes the authentication of the ISAKMP session.
Quick mode	Quick mode negotiates the parameters (that is, the SA) for the IPsec session. This negotiation occurs within the protection of an ISAKMP session.

The IKE modes reflect the two primary phases of establishing an IPsec tunnel. For example, during IKE Phase 1, a secure ISAKMP session is established, using either main mode or aggressive mode. During IKE Phase 1, the IPsec endpoints establish transform sets (that is, a collection of encryption and authentication protocols), hash methods, and other parameters needed to establish a secure ISAKMP session (sometimes called an *ISAKMP tunnel* or an *IKE Phase 1 tunnel*). As a reminder, this collection of parameters is called a *security association* (SA). With IKE Phase 1, the SA is bidirectional, meaning that the same key exchange is used for data flowing across the tunnel in either direction.

IKE Phase 2 occurs within the protection of an IKE Phase 1 tunnel, using the previously described *quick mode* of parameter negotiation. A session formed during IKE Phase 2 is sometimes called an *IKE Phase 2* tunnel, or simply an *IPsec tunnel*. However, unlike IKE Phase 1, IKE Phase 2 performs unidirectional SA negotiations, meaning that each data flow uses a separate key exchange.

Although an IPsec tunnel can be established using just IKE Phase 1 and IKE Phase 2, an optional IKE Phase 1.5 can be used. IKE Phase 1.5 uses the Extended Authentication (XAUTH) protocol to perform user authentication of IPsec tunnels. Like IKE Phase 2, IKE Phase 1.5 is performed within the protection of an IKE Phase 1 tunnel. The user authentication provided by this phase adds a layer of authentication for VPN clients. Also, parameters such as IP, WINS, and DNS server information can be provided to a VPN client during this optional phase.

Authentication Header and Encapsulating Security Payload

In addition to IKE, which establishes the IPsec tunnel, IPsec relies on either the Authentication Header (AH) protocol (IP protocol number 51) or the Encapsulating Security Payload (ESP) protocol (IP protocol number 50). Both AH and ESP offer origin authentication and integrity services, which ensure that IPsec peers are who they claim to be and that the data was not modified in transit.

However, the main distinction between AH and ESP is encryption support. ESP encrypts the original packet, whereas AH does not offer any encryption. As a result, ESP is far more popular on today's networks. In fact, AH is no longer supported in some Cisco implementations.

Both AH and ESP can operate in one of two modes—*transport mode* or *tunnel mode*. Figure 15-2 illustrates the structure of an ESP transport mode packet versus an ESP tunnel mode packet.

Figure 15-2 *Transport Mode Versus Tunnel Mode*

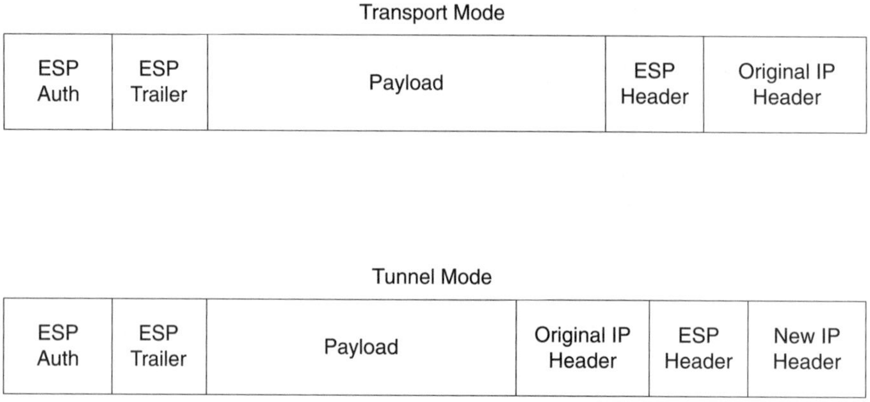

Transport Mode

ESP Auth	ESP Trailer	Payload	ESP Header	Original IP Header

Tunnel Mode

ESP Auth	ESP Trailer	Payload	Original IP Header	ESP Header	New IP Header

The following is a detailed description of the two modes:

Key
Topic

■ **Transport mode**: Transport mode uses a packet's original IP header, as opposed to adding a tunnel header. This approach works well in networks where increasing a packet's size could cause an issue. Also, transport mode is frequently used for remote-access VPNs, where a PC running VPN client software connects to a VPN termination device at a headquarters location.

NOTE   You might be concerned that transport mode allows the IP address of the IPsec peers to remain visible during transit, because the original packet's IP header is used to route a packet. However, IPsec is often used in conjunction with the GRE tunneling protocol. In such a scenario, the original IP packet is encapsulated inside a GRE tunnel packet, which adds a new GRE tunnel header. The GRE packet is then sent over an IPsec tunnel. Even if the IPsec tunnel were running in transport mode, the original packet's IP header would still not be visible. Rather, the GRE packet's header would be visible.

One reason a GRE tunnel might be used with an IPsec tunnel is a limitation on the part of IPsec. Specifically, an IPsec tunnel can transmit only unicast IP packets. The challenge is, large enterprise networks might have a significant amount of broadcast and/or multicast traffic (for example, routing protocol traffic). GRE can be used to take any traffic type and encapsulate the traffic in a GRE tunnel packet, which is a unicast IP packet that can then be sent over an IPsec tunnel. Consider, for example, a multicast packet used by a routing protocol. Even though IPsec cannot directly transport the multicast packet, if the packet is first encapsulated by GRE, the GRE packet can then be sent over an IPsec tunnel, thereby securing the transmission of the multicast packet.

■ **Tunnel mode**: Tunnel mode, unlike transport mode, encapsulates an entire packet. As a result, the encapsulated packet has a new header (that is, an IPsec header). This new header has source and destination IP address information that reflects the two VPN termination devices at different sites. Therefore, tunnel mode is frequently used in an IPsec site-to-site VPN.

Cisco VPN Product Offerings

Cisco offers a wide array of VPN termination hardware:

■ Cisco VPN-enabled routers and switches

■ Cisco VPN 3000 series concentrators (which have reached end-of-sale [EOS] status)

■ Cisco ASA 5500 series appliances

■ Cisco 500 series PIX Security Appliances

■ Hardware acceleration modules

Cisco VPN-Enabled Routers and Switches

Many enterprise networks already contain Cisco IOS routers and/or switches that can serve as VPN termination devices. Examples of these Cisco IOS routers include the Cisco Integrated Services Routers (ISR), shown in Figure 15-3.

Figure 15-3 *Cisco Integrated Services Routers*

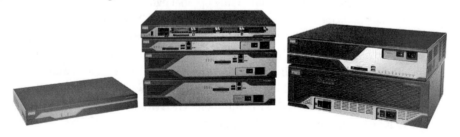

With an appropriate feature set, a Cisco IOS router could act not only as a VPN termination device, but also as a firewall and intrusion prevention system (IPS) device. However, focusing on IOS-based VPN features, a Cisco router with an appropriate IOS offers the following:

■ **Voice and video-enabled VPN**: A voice and video-enabled VPN, sometimes called a *V3PN*, applies quality-of-service (QoS) features to traffic traveling over a VPN to treat different types of traffic with different levels of priority. For example, these QoS features could allow voice traffic to be sent over a VPN before sending less latency-sensitive traffic.

■ **IPsec stateful failover**: Because IPsec site-to-site VPNs can be mission-critical links, failover and redundancy should be considered in their configuration. Fortunately, Cisco IOS supports stateful failover for IPsec VPN connections, meaning that if one IPsec tunnel fails, and another IPsec tunnel takes over as a backup, the backup IPsec tunnel is aware of the previous session's parameters. Therefore, those parameters do not need to be renegotiated. Examples of redundancy and resiliency features supported by Cisco IOS include dead peer detection (DPD), Hot Standby Router Protocol (HSRP), Reverse Route Injection (RRI), and Stateful Switchover (SSO).

■ **Dynamic multipoint VPN**: Consider a hub-and-spoke VPN topology in which multiple remote sites have a site-to-site VPN connection to a headquarters location. In such a topology, if one remote site wanted to communicate securely with another remote site, the traffic would travel between the sites via the headquarters location, rather than directly between the sites. One fix for this suboptimal pathing issue would be to create a full mesh of IPsec site-to-site VPN connections, which would provide a direct IPsec VPN connection between any two remote sites. Such a solution, however, could be complex and expensive to configure and maintain.

A more economical solution to providing optimal pathing without necessitating a full-mesh topology is the *Dynamic Multipoint VPN* (DMVPN) feature. DMVPN allows a VPN tunnel to be dynamically created and torn down between two remote sites on an as-needed basis. Consider Figure 15-4, which shows a hub-and-spoke topology, with the headquarters acting as the hub. Branch B and Branch C want to communicate with one another. Therefore, a DMVPN tunnel is created between these two locations. Next-Hop Resolution Protocol (NHRP), Multipoint GRE (MGRE), and IPsec VPN features are required to support a DMVPN topology.

Figure 15-4 *Dynamic Multipoint VPN*

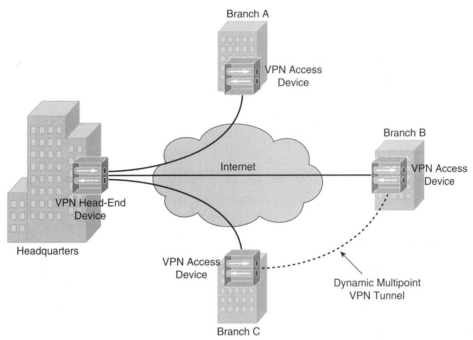

- **Integration of IPsec with MPLS**: Many service providers use Multiprotocol Label Switching (MPLS) to intelligently forward traffic through a service provider's network, as opposed to using less efficient routing tables. Cisco IOS supports the mapping of an IPsec session into an MPLS session, which allows a service provider's VPN service to extend beyond the service provider's boundary.

- **Cisco Easy VPN**: The Cisco Easy VPN feature helps facilitate VPN installations for remote-office and teleworker environments. The two components of Cisco Easy VPN are the Easy VPN Remote and the Easy VPN Server. The Easy VPN Remote component allows a variety of devices (including Cisco IOS routers) to receive security policies from a Cisco Easy VPN Server. The Easy VPN Server allows a variety of devices (including Cisco IOS routers) to push security policies from a central site to remote sites.

Cisco VPN 3000 Series Concentrators

Although Cisco 3000 series concentrators have reached EOS status, you still might encounter existing concentrators in some enterprise networks. A Cisco VPN 3000 series concentrator serves as a dedicated VPN appliance, as opposed to sharing VPN duties with other features, as is the case with a Cisco IOS router.

Consider the following features offered by Cisco VPN 3000 series concentrators:

■ Users can access a VPN via a web browser, as opposed to first installing VPN client software, using the Cisco WebVPN feature. This clientless access is made possible through the downloading of a small Java applet to the user's computer.

■ Robust endpoint security is provided via the Cisco Secure Desktop feature.

■ For terminal service applications, Cisco VPN 3000 series concentrators offer Citrix support. This support does not necessitate the installation of SSL VPN client software on end systems.

■ Cisco VPN 3000 series concentrators can be managed and monitored via a web interface.

■ Groups of Cisco 3000 series concentrators can be combined into a cluster. This clustering provides scalability and load balancing to VPN designs.

■ Cisco VPN 3000 series concentrators allow users to be authenticated using a variety of approaches, including one-time passwords, RADIUS, Microsoft Active Directory (AD), Security Dynamics International (SDI) Secure ID, and digital certificates.

Cisco ASA 5500 Series Appliances

Unlike a dedicated firewall, a dedicated VPN concentrator, or a dedicated IPS sensor, the Cisco Adaptive Security Appliances (ASA) can adapt to a variety of network security needs. For example, a Cisco ASA 5500 series appliance can simultaneously act as a VPN concentrator, a firewall, and an IPS sensor. However, because this chapter focuses on VPNs, consider the following VPN features offered by Cisco ASA 5500 series appliances:

■ Support for both IPsec and SSL tunnels

■ Scalability through clustering

■ Support for Cisco Easy VPN

■ Support for updating user computers with new Cisco VPN Client software

■ Support for Cisco IOS WebVPN

■ QoS support for converged voice, video, and data networks

■ Management via the Cisco Adaptive Security Device Manager (ASDM) graphical interface

Cisco ASA 5500 series appliances are available in a variety of models to meet the needs of a wide range of networks. As an example, Figure 15-5 shows a Cisco ASA 5540 appliance.

Figure 15-5 *Cisco ASA 5540*

A network designer must choose an appropriate ASA model in addition to appropriate ASA licensing. Cisco ASA 5500 series appliances support the following types of licenses:

- **Feature licenses**: Feature licenses allow a security appliance to support security contexts (with the Security Context license) and General Packet Radio Service (GPRS) Tunneling Protocol (GTP) (with the GTP Inspection license).

- **Encryption licenses**: Encryption licenses enhance a security appliance's ability to perform encryption by adding support for 3DES and AES encryption.

- **Platform licenses**: Platform licenses dictate the scalability of a security appliance (for example, by limiting the number of concurrent VPN connections). As the name suggests, these licenses are platform-specific.

Table 15-4 compares various Cisco ASA 5500 series appliance models.

Table 15-4 *Comparison of Cisco ASA 5500 Appliance Models*

Cisco ASA 5500 Series Appliance Model/License	Cisco ASA 5505 Base/Security Plus	Cisco ASA 5510 Base/Security Plus	Cisco ASA 5520	Cisco ASA 5540	Cisco ASA 5550
Target Environment	Small office/home office (SOHO)	Small to medium-sized business/small enterprise	Small enterprise	Medium enterprise	Large enterprise
Maximum 3DES/AES VPN Throughput	100 Mbps	170 Mbps	225 Mbps	325 Mbps	425 Mbps
Maximum Site-to-Site and Remote-Access VPN User Sessions	10/25	250	750	5000	5000
Maximum SSL VPN User Sessions	25	250	750	2500	5000
IPsec and WebVPN Service Support	Yes	Yes	Yes	Yes	Yes

Cisco 500 Series PIX Security Appliances

Traditionally, Cisco PIX appliances performed firewall functions. The current line of Cisco PIX devices is the Cisco 500 series PIX Security Appliances, an example of which is shown in Figure 15-6.

Figure 15-6   *Cisco PIX 535*

Not only do Cisco 500 series PIX Security Appliances offer traditional firewall features, but they also offer a robust set of VPN features:

- Enhanced support for spoke-to-spoke VPNs, allowing encrypted traffic to enter and exit the same interface

- Support for Cisco TCP and UDP NAT traversal

- The ability to enforce the use of security products on an end system (for example, Cisco Security Agent [CSA]) and to verify end-system VPN properties (for example, VPN client version and security policies)

- The ability to block VPN connections based on the type of Cisco VPN client being used

- Support for OSPF routing over an IPsec VPN

- Integrated hardware acceleration on some Cisco 500 series PIX appliance models

Hardware Acceleration Modules

VPN operations, such as encryption, can become processor-intensive. Fortunately, Cisco offers the following hardware acceleration modules to offload much of a device's VPN processing:

- **Advanced Integration Module (AIM):** This is a daughter board that can connect to the motherboard of a Cisco router. The AIM can then be used to offload processor-intensive encryption algorithms from a router's main processor. A variety of AIMs, such as the AIM-VPN 3660, shown in Figure 15-7, are available for several models of Cisco routers.

Figure 15-7 *Cisco AIM-VPN 3660*

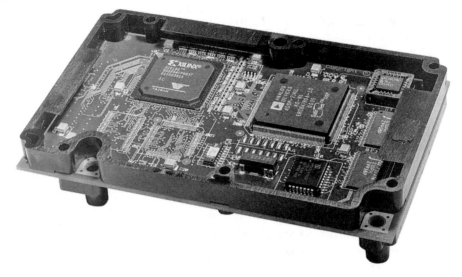

- **Cisco IPsec VPN Shared Port Adapter (SPA)**: This is a module that can be inserted into either a Cisco Catalyst 6500 series switch or a Cisco 7600 series router, offering a scalable VPN solution to these modular devices.

- **Scalable Encryption Processing (SEP)**: This module can be inserted into a Cisco VPN 3000 series concentrator to offload DES, 3DES, and AES encryption processing.

- **Cisco PIX Security Appliance VPN Accelerator Card+ (VAC+)**: This can be installed into a Cisco 500 series PIX Security Appliance to boost the throughput of encrypted traffic. Specifically, the VAC+ supports a throughput of up to 425 Mbps for traffic traversing an IPsec-protected tunnel using DES, 3DES, or AES encryption.

VPN Design Considerations and Recommendations

When designing VPN connectivity for your network, the VPN components of the design should be as transparent as possible to end users and applications while still providing the security, performance, and reliability features expected from a VPN. Network design decisions vary based on specific network requirements. However, consider the following prioritized list of objectives when creating your VPN design:

- Providing secure connectivity

- Meeting reliability, performance, and scalability requirements

- Offering options for availability

Key
Topic

- The ability to authenticate VPN users

- Implementing security features for traffic before and after it passes through the IPsec VPN tunnel

As a reference, consider the following best-practice recommendations for identity and IPsec access control, IPsec, Network Address Translation, and selecting a single-purpose device or multipurpose device.

Best-Practice Recommendations for Identity and IPsec Access Control

A VPN design should provide a mechanism that allows VPN devices to be securely identified. This process of identification is called *authentication*. IPsec VPNs can use either preshared keys or digital certificates for authentication. Consider the following best practices:

- VPN termination devices at each end of a site-to-site VPN tunnel can be configured with preshared keys (or can securely determine a preshared key using the Diffie-Hellman algorithm). Group preshared keys (which are associated with a group name identity) can be used only with remote-access VPNs. Also, wildcard preshared keys (in which all network devices use the same key) should be avoided in site-to-site VPNs.

- Because digital certificates scale better than preshared keys, consider using digital certificates for VPN networks consisting of more than 20 devices. Also, because digital certificates have an associated lifetime, ensure time synchronization for devices using the digital certificates.

- Certificate Revocation Lists (CRL) should be checked to make sure that a certificate appearing in a Certificate Trust List (CTL) has not been revoked (that is, it is still valid). Also, consider using an external certificate authority (CA) to vouch for the validity of a signed certificate when your VPN extends beyond corporate boundaries.

- Evaluate the practicality of protecting digital certificates and preshared keys using a hardware-based solution, as opposed to a (typically less secure) software-based solution.

- To filter unwanted traffic, consider applying inbound access control lists (ACL) on VPN devices.

Best-Practice Recommendations for IPsec

IPsec-protected VPNs offer a collection of features and options to select from. To help you make appropriate design decisions for your environment, consider the following Cisco best practices:

- Use IPsec to provide integrity checking in addition to encryption. You can do this by selecting the previously described ESP option, as opposed to the AH option.

- Use strong encryption algorithms, such as 3DES and AES, as opposed to a weaker standard such as DES.

- Use Secure Hash Algorithm (SHA) instead of Message Digest 5 (MD5) as a hashing algorithm because of SHA's increased security and speed.

NOTE   There are legal limitations on exporting strong encryption algorithms outside the U.S. Consult the following URL for more information: http://www.cisco.com/wwl/export/crypto.

- You can attain an even greater level of security by reducing the lifetime of the Security Association (SA) being used or by enabling Perfect Forward Secrecy (PFS), which helps provide secure key generation. Cisco recommends that you avoid manipulating these parameters unless the data is highly sensitive. The reason for such a counter-intuitive recommendation is the increased processor burden placed on the VPN device.

Best-Practice Recommendations for Network Address Translation

Network Address Translation (NAT) can help preserve a network's limited address space. However, some incompatibilities might arise when you use NAT in conjunction with an IPsec VPN. Therefore, when feasible, Cisco recommends avoiding the use of NAT for VPN traffic.

The only case in which Cisco does recommend the use of NAT for VPN traffic is when the network address spaces at the different ends of the VPN tunnel overlap. In that event, NAT can be used to accommodate the overlapping address spaces.

Best-Practice Recommendations for Selecting a Single-Purpose Versus Multipurpose Device

As previously discussed, VPN termination can be performed by a variety of devices, such as a dedicated VPN concentrator or a Cisco IOS router. A recurring design decision for VPN networks involves selecting a dedicated device to perform VPN functions versus selecting a device that will perform other functions (for example, firewall and/or IPS functions) in addition to its VPN duties.

When deciding between a single-purpose and a multipurpose device, think about the capacity and features offered by each device you are considering. For example, you might determine that a multipurpose device, such as a high-end Cisco IOS router, has more capacity than a single-purpose device, such as a low-end dedicated VPN device. However, the larger the network, the greater the likelihood that a dedicated VPN device will be an appropriate selection.

Constructing an IPsec Site-to-Site VPN

Now that you have a foundational understanding of IPsec site-to-site VPN concepts, this section introduces the configuration of an IPsec site-to-site VPN. Specifically, the next subsection focuses on CLI-based configuration versus the graphical SDM configuration approach, which is covered after the next subsection.

The Five Steps in the Life of an IPsec Site-to-Site VPN

The process of establishing, maintaining, and tearing down an IPsec VPN has five primary steps. These steps are illustrated in Figure 15-8 and described in Table 15-5.

Figure 15-8 *IPsec VPN Steps*

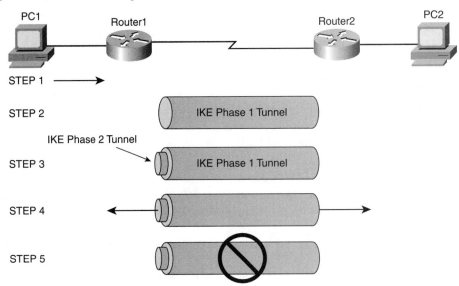

Key
Topic

Table 15-5 *Establishing, Maintaining, and Tearing Down an IPsec Site-to-Site VPN*

Step	Configuration
Step 1	PC1 sends traffic destined for PC2. Router1 classifies the traffic as "interesting," which initiates the creation of an IPsec tunnel.
Step 2	Router1 and Router2 negotiate a Security Association (SA) used to form an IKE Phase 1 tunnel, which is also known as an ISAKMP tunnel.
Step 3	Within the protection of the IKE Phase 1 tunnel, an IKE Phase 2 tunnel is negotiated and set up. An IKE Phase 2 tunnel is also known as an IPsec tunnel.

Table 15-5 *Establishing, Maintaining, and Tearing Down an IPsec Site-to-Site VPN (Continued)*

Step	Configuration
Step 4	After the IPsec tunnel is established, interesting traffic flows through the protected IPsec tunnel. Note that traffic not deemed interesting can still be sent between PC1 and PC2. However, the noninteresting traffic is transmitted outside of the protection of the IPsec tunnel.
Step 5	After no interesting traffic has been seen for a specified amount of time, or if the IPsec SA is deleted, the IPsec tunnel is torn down.

The Five Steps of Configuring an IPsec Site-to-Site VPN

An IPsec site-to-site VPN can be configured by using IOS commands issued from a router's CLI or by using the graphical SDM interface. The CLI approach to configuring an IPsec site-to-site VPN involves five primary steps, as described in Table 15-6.

Table 15-6 *Steps of Configuring an IPsec Site-to-Site VPN*

Step	Configuration
Step 1	Define what parameters will be used for the IKE Phase 1 tunnel (that is, the ISAKMP tunnel). This set of parameters is called an ISAKMP policy.
Step 2	Define what parameters will be used for the IKE Phase 2 tunnel (that is, the IPsec tunnel). This set of parameters is called a transform set.
Step 3	Create an ACL to identify "interesting" traffic, which should be protected and sent over the IPsec tunnel.
Step 4	Create a crypto map, which logically groups the parameters identified in previous steps and points to an IPsec peer. The crypto map should then be applied to the appropriate interface.
Step 5	Optionally, create an additional ACL to block noninteresting traffic from passing between VPN termination devices.

Configuring an IKE Phase 1 Tunnel

To illustrate the CLI configuration of an IPsec site-to-site VPN, consider a scenario using the topology shown in Figure 15-9. The goal of this scenario is to allow all IP traffic to securely flow between network 10.1.1.0/24 (connected to Router1) and network 192.168.0.0/24 (connected to Router2).

Figure 15-9 *IPsec Site-to-Site VPN Configuration*

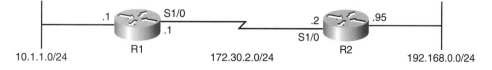

To begin the configuration, you specify the ISAKMP parameters. Example 15-1 shows this initial configuration for Router1, and Example 15-2 provides the configuration for Router2.

Key Topic

Example 15-1   *Router1's IKE Phase 1 Configuration*

```
Router1# conf term
Router1(config)# crypto isakmp policy 1
Router1(config-isakmp)# authentication pre-share
Router1(config-isakmp)# hash sha
Router1(config-isakmp)# encryption aes 128
Router1(config-isakmp)# group 2
Router1(config-isakmp)# lifetime 86400
Router1(config-isakmp)# exit
Router1(config)# crypto isakmp key C1sc0Press address 172.30.2.2
Router1(config)# end
Router1#
```

Example 15-2   *Router2's IKE Phase 1 Configuration*

```
Router2# conf term
Router2(config)# crypto isakmp policy 1
Router2(config-isakmp)# authentication pre-share
Router2(config-isakmp)# hash sha
Router2(config-isakmp)# encryption aes 128
Router2(config-isakmp)# group 2
Router2(config-isakmp)# lifetime 86400
Router2(config-isakmp)# exit
Router2(config)# crypto isakmp key C1sc0Press address 172.30.2.1
Router2(config)# exit
Router2#
```

In the preceding examples, the **crypto isakmp policy 1** command is used to enter ISAKMP configuration mode. From within this mode, the **authentication pre-share** command specifies that preshared keys are to be used for authentication. The **hash sha** command specifies that Secure Hash Algorithm (SHA) will be used as the hashing algorithm for the ISAKMP Security Association (SA). The **encryption aes 128** command causes 128-bit Advanced Encryption Standard (AES) encryption to be used. The **group 2** command specifies that Diffie-Hellman Group 2 be used for the secure exchange of shared keys. Finally in this configuration mode, the lifetime of the SA is set to one day (86,400 seconds) with the **lifetime 86400** command. Then, in global configuration mode, the **crypto isakmp key C1sc0Press address** *peer-IP-address* command sets the shared key to C1sc0Press when communicating with the other router (that is, the peer IP address).

Configuring an IKE Phase 2 Tunnel

Recall that an IKE Phase 2 tunnel (an IPsec tunnel) is negotiated and set up within the protection of an IKE Phase 1 tunnel (an ISAKMP tunnel). Now that you have seen how to configure an IKE Phase 1 tunnel, examine Examples 15-3 and 15-4. They show the syntax to configure an IKE Phase 2 tunnel, building on the topology shown previously in Figure 15-9.

Example 15-3 *Router1's IKE Phase 2 Configuration*

Key
Topic

```
Router1# conf term
Router1(config)# crypto ipsec transform-set MYSET esp-aes esp-sha
Router1(cfg-crypto-trans)# exit
Router1(config)# access-list 101 permit ip 10.1.1.0 0.0.0.255 192.168.0.0 0.0.0.255
Router1(config)# crypto map ROUTER1_TO_ROUTER2 10 ipsec-isakmp
Router1(config-crypto-map)# set peer 172.30.2.2
Router1(config-crypto-map)# match address 101
Router1(config-crypto-map)# set transform-set MYSET
Router1(config-crypto-map)# exit
Router1(config)# exit
Router1#
```

Example 15-4 *Router2's IKE Phase 2 Configuration*

```
Router2# conf term
Router2(config)# crypto ipsec transform-set MYSET esp-aes esp-sha-hmac
Router2(cfg-crypto-trans)# exit
Router2(config)# access-list 101 permit ip 192.168.0.0 0.0.0.255 10.1.1.0 0.0.0.255
Router2(config)# crypto map ROUTER2_TO_ROUTER1 10 ipsec-isakmp
Router2(config-crypto-map)# set peer 172.30.2.1
Router2(config-crypto-map)# match address 101
Router2(config-crypto-map)# set transform-set MYSET
Router2(config-crypto-map)# end
Router2# exit
Router2#
```

In Examples 15-3 and 15-4, a transform set named MYSET is created with the **crypto ipsec transform-set MYSET esp-aes esp-sha-hmac** command. The **esp-aes** parameter specifies the encryption algorithm to be used, and the **esp-sha-hmac** parameter specifies the hashing algorithm (that is, the integrity algorithm) to be used. Each example then contains an ACL numbered 101, which specifies what traffic the IPsec tunnel will protect. By combining these examples, you can see that this scenario configures Router1 and Router2 to protect all IP traffic traveling between the 10.1.1.0/24 network and the 192.168.0.0/24 network. Next, a crypto map is created with the **crypto map** *crypto-map-name* **10 ipsec-isakmp** command. In crypto map configuration mode, the **set peer** *peer-IP-address* command specifies the IP address of the IPsec peer (that is, the IP address of the other router). The

match address 101 address associates the previously created ACL 101 with the crypto map, and the MYSET transform set is linked with the crypto map using the **set transform-set MYSET** command.

Applying Crypto Maps

A crypto map needs to be applied to an interface for an IPsec tunnel to be set up. Continuing with the current scenario, examine Examples 15-5 and 15-6. They illustrate the application of the ROUTER1_TO_ROUTER2 crypto map to Router1 and the application of the ROUTER2_TO_ROUTER1 crypto map to Router 2.

Example 15-5 *Applying a Crypto Map to Router1*

```
Router1# conf term
Router1(config)# interface serial 1/0
Router1(config-if)# crypto map ROUTER1_TO_ROUTER2
Router1(config-if)# end
Router1(config)# ip route 192.168.0.0 255.255.255.0 172.30.2.2
Router1(config)# end
Router1#
```

Example 15-6 *Applying a Crypto Map to Router2*

```
Router2# conf term
Router2(config)# interface serial 1/0
Router2(config-if)# crypto map ROUTER2_TO_ROUTER1
Router2(config-if)# exit
Router2(config)# ip route 10.1.1.0 255.255.255.0 172.30.2.1
Router2(config)# end
Router2#
```

In the preceding examples, notice that you enter interface configuration mode to apply a crypto map. Then you issue the **crypto map** *crypto-map-name* command to apply the previously configured crypto map. Also notice that Examples 5-5 and 5-6 each have an **ip route** command. This command is used to create a static route, pointing to the remote network available off the far-end router.

To test the IPsec configuration, an extended ping can be performed, as shown in Example 15-7. Specifically, Example 15-7 shows an extended ping being initiated from Router1's LAN interface (IP address 10.1.1.1), destined for Router2's LAN interface (IP address 192.168.0.95). Notice that the first ping fails, because the IPsec tunnel is being set up during this time. However, the remaining pings succeed.

Example 15-7 *Testing the IPsec Tunnel with an Extended Ping*

```
Router1# ping

Protocol [ip]:
Target IP address: 192.168.0.95
Repeat count [5]:
Datagram size [100]:
Timeout in seconds [2]:
Extended commands [n]: y
Source address or interface: 10.1.1.1
Type of service [0]:
Set DF bit in IP header? [no]:
Validate reply data? [no]:
Data pattern [0xABCD]:
Loose, Strict, Record, Timestamp, Verbose[none]:
Sweep range of sizes [n]:
Type escape sequence to abort.
Sending 5, 100-byte ICMP Echos to 192.168.0.95, timeout is 2 seconds:
Packet sent with a source address of 10.1.1.1
.!!!!
Success rate is 80 percent (4/5), round-trip min/avg/max = 164/209/296 ms
```

After establishing an IPsec tunnel, you can verify and view the tunnel's parameters by issuing the **show crypto engine connections active** and **show crypto session** commands, as shown in Examples 15-8 and 15-9.

Example 15-8 **show crypto engine connections active** *Command*

```
Router1# show crypto engine connections active

Crypto Engine Connections

   ID Interface  Type  Algorithm       Encrypt  Decrypt IP-Address
    1 Se1/0      IPsec AES+SHA               0        4 172.30.2.1
    2 Se1/0      IPsec AES+SHA               4        0 172.30.2.1
 1001 Se1/0      IKE   SHA+AES               0        0 172.30.2.1
```

Example 15-9 **show crypto session** *Command*

```
Router1# show crypto session

Crypto session current status

Interface: Serial1/0
Session status: UP-ACTIVE
Peer: 172.30.2.2 port 500
  IKE SA: local 172.30.2.1/500 remote 172.30.2.2/500 Active
  IPSEC FLOW: permit ip 10.1.1.0/255.255.255.0 192.168.0.0/255.255.255.0
        Active SAs: 2, origin: crypto map
```

Using Cisco SDM to Configure IPsec on a Site-to-Site VPN

CLI-based IPsec configuration can become a daunting task for network administrators who aren't thoroughly familiar with the myriad of IPsec parameters and options. Fortunately, Cisco SDM offers a Site-to-Site VPN configuration wizard that can help you configure an IPsec site-to-site VPN, as shown in this section.

Introduction to the Cisco SDM VPN Wizard

Cisco SDM makes available both a Quick Setup wizard and a Step-by-Step wizard. These wizards combine administrator input with preconfigured VPN elements to produce VPN configurations. However, a successful VPN configuration requires some VPN elements (such as a PKI) to already be in place.

Figure 15-10 shows how to get started with the Cisco SDM Site-to-Site VPN Configuration Wizard using the following steps:

Step 1 Click the **Configure** button in the Cisco SDM interface.

Figure 15-10 *Invoking the Cisco SDM Site-to-Site VPN Configuration Wizard*

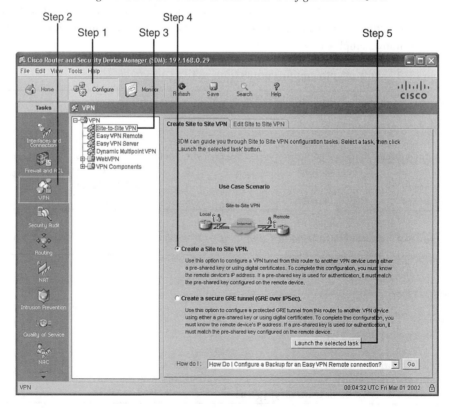

Step 2   Click the **VPN** button in the Tasks pane.

Step 3   Click the **Site to Site VPN** object.

Step 4   Select the **Create a Site to Site VPN.** radio button.

Step 5   Click the **Launch the selected task** button.

Next you are prompted to select either **Quick setup** or **Step by step wizard**, as shown in Figure 15-11.

Figure 15-11   *Selecting a VPN Wizard*

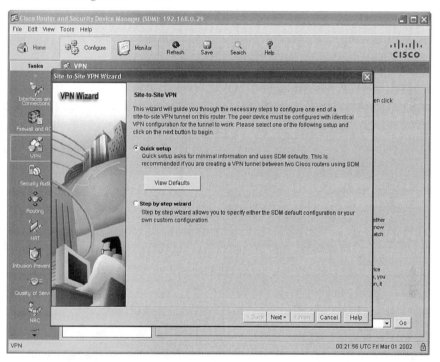

Quick Setup

To demonstrate an IPsec site-to-site VPN configuration using the Quick Setup wizard, consider the topology shown in Figure 15-12.

Figure 15-12   *Quick Setup Wizard Sample Topology*

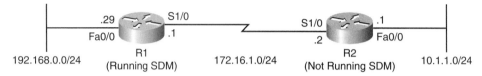

The following steps illustrate how to configure the topology shown in Figure 15-12 to protect traffic traveling between network 192.168.0.0/24 and network 10.1.1.0/24:

Step 1   The Quick Setup wizard offers two default IKE policies and a default IPsec transform set for your use. However, you still need to enter a few parameters into this wizard, as shown in Figure 15-13.

Figure 15-13   *Entering Parameters for the Quick Setup Wizard*

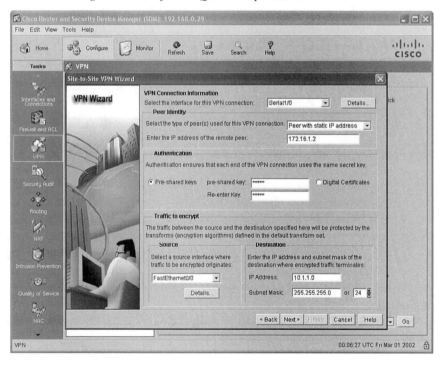

In Figure 15-13, the following parameters are entered:

- Interface for this VPN connection: **Serial 1/0**

- IP address of the remote peer: **172.16.1.2**

- Preshared key: **cisco**

- Source interface where encrypted traffic originates: **FastEthernet0/0**

- Destination IP address (or subnet) where encrypted traffic terminates: **10.1.1.0 255.255.255.0**

Step 2 After entering these parameters, click the **Next** button. You see a configuration summary, as shown in Figure 15-14.

Figure 15-14 *Configuration Summary*

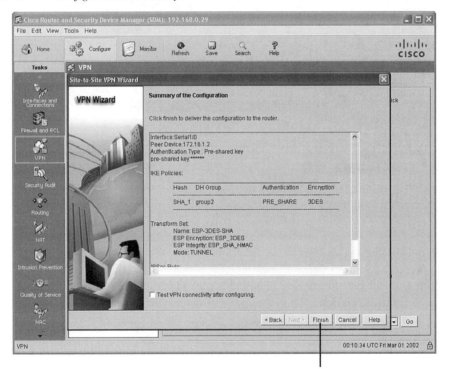

Click to Deliver Commands to the Router

Step 3 After reviewing the summary, click the **Finish** button. The commands are delivered to the router you are configuring. Click the **OK** button, as shown in Figure 15-15, to enter the Edit Site to Site VPN screen.

Figure 15-15 *Command Delivery Confirmation*

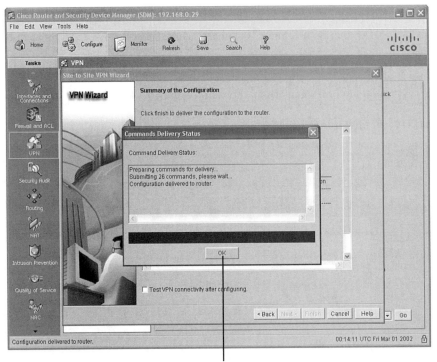

Click to Confirm Delivery Notification

Step 4 In the Edit Site to Site VPN screen, shown in Figure 15-16, notice that
the VPN is down. This is because the router at the other side of the tunnel
has not yet been configured.

Figure 15-16 *Edit Site-to-Site VPN Configuration Screen*

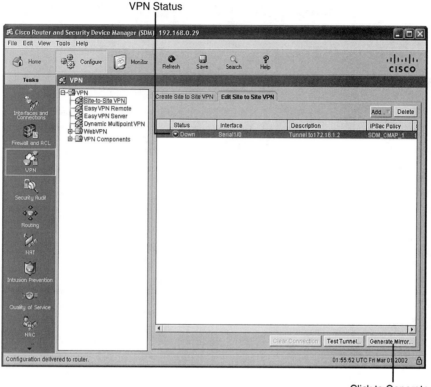

VPN Status

Click to Generate a
Mirrored Configuration

Step 5 Cisco SDM helps you configure the router at the far side of the tunnel,
even if the other router is not running Cisco SDM. Specifically, if you
click the **Generate Mirror** button, the window shown in Figure 15-17
appears, showing a generic form of the configuration to be applied to the
far-end router. The configuration does need some tweaking before being
applied, because you need to specify which interface on the remote router
the generated crypto map should be applied to.

Figure 15-17   *Generated Mirror Configuration*

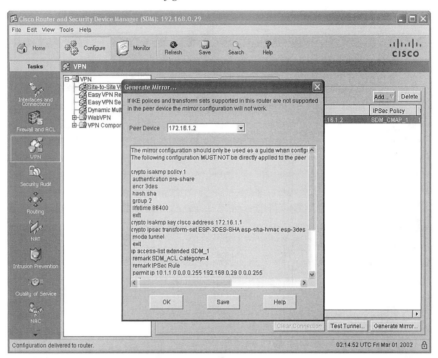

Step 6   Manually apply the generated configuration to the far-end router, and
manually apply the generated crypto map to the appropriate interface on
the far-end router using the **crypto map** *crypto-map-name* command.
Then you can click the **Test Tunnel** button, which opens the VPN
Troubleshooting window, shown in Figure 15-18.

Figure 15-18 *VPN Troubleshooting Window*

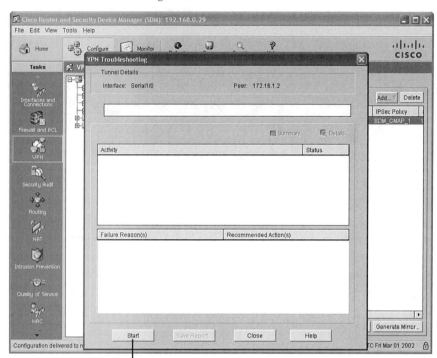

Click to Begin Troubleshooting

Step 7 In the VPN Troubleshooting window, click the **Start** button. The first time you test the connection, you are prompted for a destination IP address available off the far-end router to test. If everything is configured correctly, you receive a message that the VPN tunnel is up, as shown in Figure 15-19.

Figure 15-19   *Tunnel Test Success Message*

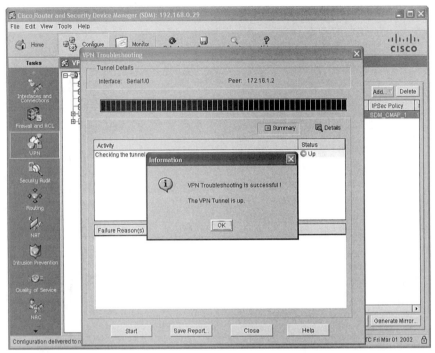

Step 8   After closing the VPN Troubleshooting window, notice that the VPN
tunnel status has changed to up, as shown in Figure 15-20.

Figure 15-20 *Tunnel Status Up*

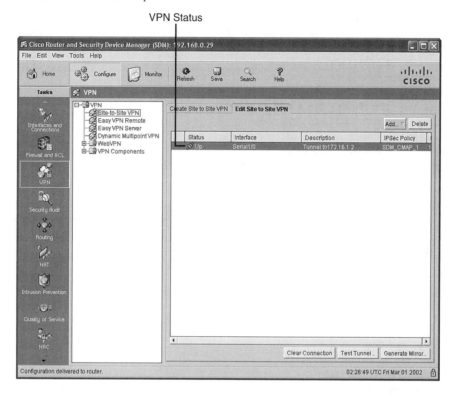

As a reference, Examples 15-10 and 15-11 provide the IPsec-relevant commands entered on routers R1 and R2, with assistance from the Cisco SDM Quick Setup wizard.

Example 15-10 *IPsec-Relevant Configuration Commands on R1*

```
crypto isakmp policy 1
 encr 3des
 authentication pre-share
 group 2
crypto isakmp key cisco address 172.16.1.2
!
crypto ipsec transform-set ESP-3DES-SHA esp-3des esp-sha-hmac
!
crypto map SDM_CMAP_1 1 ipsec-isakmp
 description Tunnel to172.16.1.2
 set peer 172.16.1.2
 set transform-set ESP-3DES-SHA
 match address 100
!
interface FastEthernet0/0
```

continues

Example 15-10 *IPsec-Relevant Configuration Commands on R1 (Continued)*

```
 ip address 192.168.0.29 255.255.255.0
!
interface Serial1/0
 ip address 172.16.1.1 255.255.255.0
 crypto map SDM_CMAP_1
!
ip route 10.1.1.0 255.255.255.0 172.16.1.2
!
access-list 100 remark SDM_ACL Category=4
access-list 100 remark IPSec Rule
access-list 100 permit ip 192.168.0.0 0.0.0.255 10.1.1.0 0.0.0.255
```

Example 15-11 *IPsec-Relevant Configuration Commands on R2*

```
crypto isakmp policy 1
 encr 3des
 authentication pre-share
 group 2
crypto isakmp key cisco address 172.16.1.1
!
crypto ipsec transform-set ESP-3DES-SHA esp-3des esp-sha-hmac
!
crypto map SDM_CMAP_1 1 ipsec-isakmp
 set peer 172.16.1.1
 set transform-set ESP-3DES-SHA
 match address SDM_1
!
interface FastEthernet0/0
 ip address 10.1.1.1 255.255.255.0
!
interface Serial1/0
 ip address 172.16.1.2 255.255.255.0
 crypto map SDM_CMAP_1
!
ip route 192.168.0.0 255.255.255.0 172.16.1.1
!
ip access-list extended SDM_1
 remark SDM_ACL Category=4
 remark IPSec Rule
 permit ip 10.1.1.0 0.0.0.255 192.168.0.0 0.0.0.255
 remark SDM_ACL Category=4
 remark IPSec Rule
```

Step-by-Step Setup

Using the Step-by-Step wizard, as opposed to the Quick Setup wizard, requires additional input from the administrator. Table 15-7 describes parameters required by the Step-by-Step wizard.

Table 15-7   *Step-by-Step Wizard Parameters*

Parameter	Description
Connection settings	The connection settings identify the interface to be used to establish the VPN connection, the IP address of the VPN peer, and the credentials used for authentication.
IKE proposals	The IKE proposals, used to establish the IKE Phase 1 tunnel, include the priority of a specific IKE proposal, the encryption algorithm, the hashing algorithm, the authentication method used for IKE, the Diffie-Hellman group, and the IKE lifetime.
IPsec transform sets	IPsec transform sets identify the encryption algorithms, hashing algorithms, mode of operation (that is, tunnel or transport mode), and compression type used in establishing the IKE Phase 2 tunnel (that is, the IPsec tunnel).
Protected traffic	You can identify the traffic you want to protect over the IPsec VPN by matching traffic with ACLs.

The following sections cover the details of setting these up.

Configuring Connection Settings

If you select **Step by step wizard** from the initial Site-to-Site VPN Wizard screen, as shown earlier in Figure 15-11, you see the connection settings screen, as shown in Figure 15-21.

Figure 15-21 *Connection Parameters*

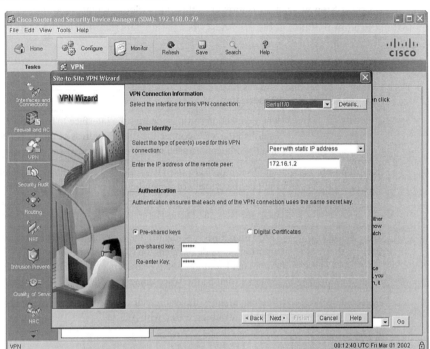

On this initial screen, you are prompted to enter the following information:

■   Interface for this VPN connection

■   Peer IP address type (dynamic or static)

■   IP address of the remote peer (for a peer with a static IP address)

■   Authentication type (preshared keys or digital certificates)

■   Preshared key (for preshared key authentication)

> **NOTE**   When selecting a preshared key, make the key *strong*, just as you would create a strong password. For example, select a key that is long and that is not an actual word. Doing so makes the key more resistant to a brute-force attack or a dictionary attack.

■   After setting the parameters in this initial connection settings screen, click the **Next** button to proceed to the next screen in the wizard. This screen allows you to configure an IKE proposal.

Selecting an IKE Proposal

You can select the default IKE proposal provided by Cisco SDM, as shown in Figure 15-22, or you can click the **Add** button to configure parameters for your own custom IKE policy.

Figure 15-22 *IKE Proposal Parameters*

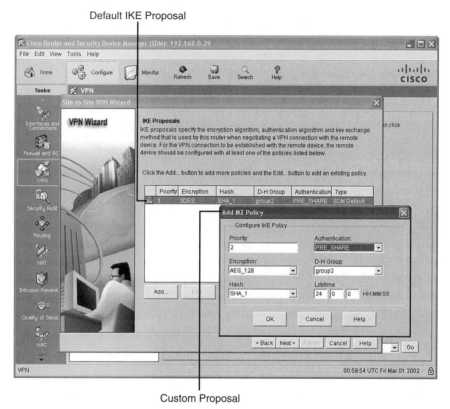

Specifically, you can set the following parameters for an IKE policy:

- Priority (set to 1 in the default policy)

- Encryption (set to 3DES in the default policy)

- Hash (set to SHA_1 in the default policy)

- Diffie-Hellman group (set to group2 in the default policy)

- Authentication (either PRE_SHARE or RSA_SIG)

- Lifetime (the Security Association [SA] lifetime in seconds)

After identifying the IKE proposal(s) you want to use, click the **Next** button to proceed to the next screen in the wizard. This screen allows you to configure a transform set.

Selecting a Transform Set

Whereas an IKE proposal specifies security parameters for an ISAKMP tunnel (an IKE Phase 1 tunnel), a *transform set* specifies security parameters for an IPsec tunnel (an IKE Phase 2 tunnel). The Transform Set configuration screen, shown in Figure 15-23, allows you to either select Cisco SDM's default transform set or click the **Add** button to create a custom transform set.

Figure 15-23 *Transform Set Parameters*

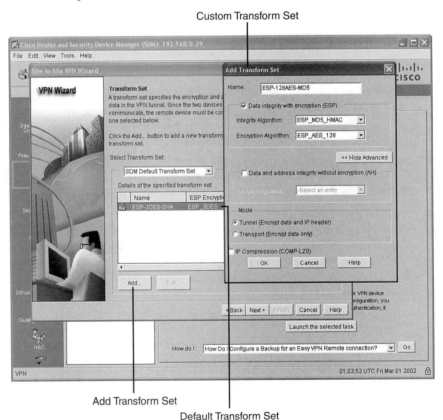

When creating a custom transform set, you can specify the parameters listed in Table 15-8.

After identifying the transform set(s) you want to use, click the **Next** button to proceed to the next screen in the wizard. This screen allows you to identify traffic to protect in the IPsec tunnel.

Table 15-8 *Transform Set Parameters*

Parameter Description	Default Transform Set Value
Transform set name	ESP-3DES-SHA
Encapsulating Security Payload (ESP) or Authentication Header (AH) protocol	Encapsulating Security Payload (ESP)
Integrity algorithm (used to perform hashing)	SHA
Encryption algorithm (if ESP is used, as opposed to AH)	3DES
Mode (tunnel or transport)	Tunnel
IP compression (COMP-LZS)	Not enabled

Selecting Traffic to Protect in the IPsec Tunnel

From the Traffic to protect screen, you can select either **Protect all traffic between the following subnets** or **Create/Select an access-list for IPsec traffic**. Figure 15-24 shows a scenario in which all traffic between two subnets (192.168.0.0/24 and 10.1.1.0/24) is identified.

Figure 15-24 *Protecting All Traffic Between Two Subnets*

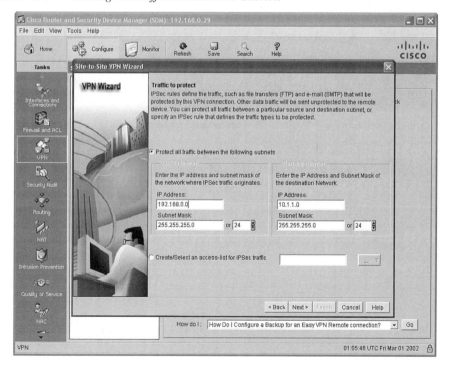

However, if you prefer to protect specific traffic to protect (as identified by an ACL), you can select the **Create/Select an access-list for IPsec traffic** radio button and choose **Create a new rule(ACL) and select** from the adjacent drop-down menu, as shown in Figure 15-25.

Figure 15-25 *Protecting Traffic Identified by an ACL*

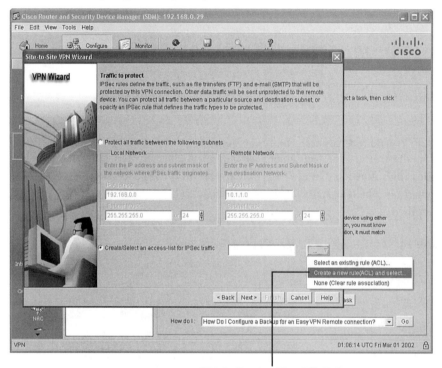

Click to Create a New ACL Rule

After selecting **Create a new rule(ACL) and select**, you see the Add a Rule window, shown in Figure 15-26.

Figure 15-26 *Add a Rule Window*

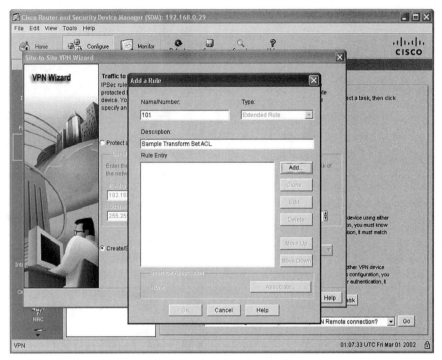

From the Add a Rule window, you can specify a number or name for the ACL you will use to identify traffic to be protected by the IPsec tunnel. Also, you can optionally give a description. To add a rule to the ACL, click the **Add** button.

After you click the **Add** button, the Add an Extended Rule Entry window appears, as shown in Figure 15-27.

Figure 15-27   *Creating an Extended Rule Entry*

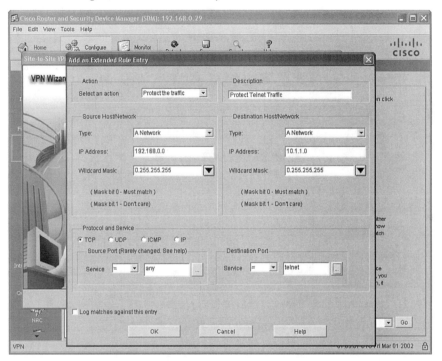

In Figure 15-27, the extended rule matches Telnet traffic sourced from network 192.168.0.0/24 and destined for network 10.1.1.0/24. After creating the rule, click the **OK** button.

Applying the Generated Configuration

After selecting the traffic to protect from the Traffic to protect screen (either all traffic between two subnets or specific traffic identified by an ACL), click the **Next** button to view a summary of the configuration, as shown in Figure 15-28.

Figure 15-28 *Configuration Summary Screen*

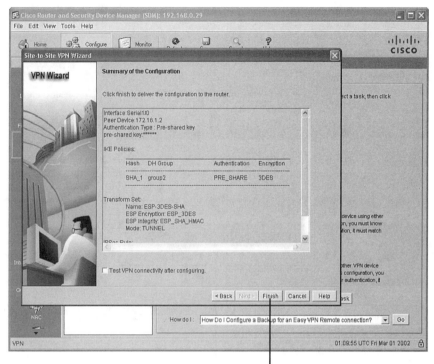

Click to Deliver to Router

After reviewing the configuration summary, click the **Finish** button to send the configuration commands to the router. Click the **OK** button in the Commands Delivery Status window, as shown in Figure 15-29.

Figure 15-29 *Commands Delivery Status Window*

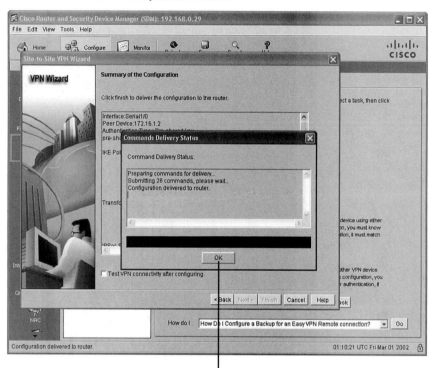

Click to Confirm Delivery

After clicking the **Finish** button, you are sent to the Edit Site to Site VPN screen, as shown in Figure 15-30.

Figure 15-30 *Edit Site-to-Site VPN Screen*

Notice that this screen reports that the tunnel is down. From this screen, as previously described for the Quick Configuration Wizard, you can generate a mirror configuration template to be applied to the router at the other end of the tunnel and then test the VPN tunnel.

Monitoring the Configuration

After the VPN tunnel becomes operational, you can monitor the tunnel status. Click the **Monitor** button (in the button bar at the top of the Cisco SDM screen). Then click the **VPN Status** button (in the Tasks pane, on the left of the Cisco SDM screen). Finally, click the **IPSec Tunnels** option (in the middle pane of the Cisco SDM screen). This monitoring interface, as shown in Figure 15-31, graphically provides traffic statistics for the IPsec VPN tunnel.

Figure 15-31 *IPsec Tunnels Monitoring Screen*

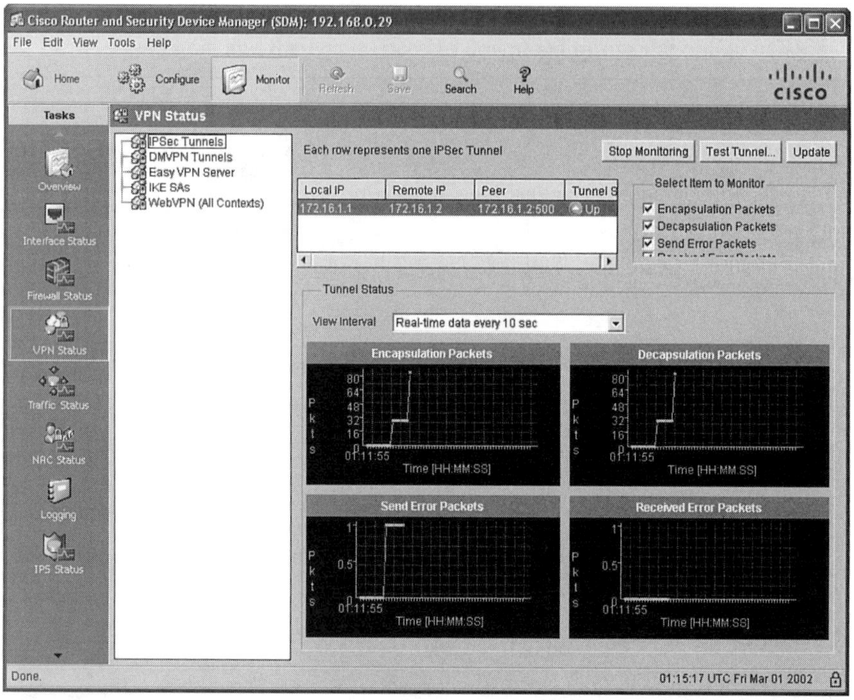

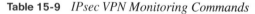

Alternatively, you can issue monitoring and troubleshooting commands from the router's command line. Table 15-9 lists examples of these commands.

Table 15-9 *IPsec VPN Monitoring Commands*

Command	Description
show crypto isakmp sa	Shows all existing IKE Phase 1 (ISAKMP) security associations
show crypto ipsec sa	Shows all existing IKE Phase 2 (IPsec) security associations
debug crypto isakmp	Shows detailed information about the IKE Phase 1 (ISAKMP) and IKE Phase 2 (IPsec) negotiations

Exam Preparation Tasks

Review All the Key Topics

Review the most important topics from this chapter, denoted with the Key Topic icon. Table 15-10 lists these key topics and the page where each is found.

Table 15-10 *Key Topics for Chapter 15*

Key Topic Element	Description	Page Number
Table 15-2	Site-to-site VPN elements	528
List	IPsec protections for VPN traffic	529
Table 15-3	IKE modes	530
List	Transport mode and tunnel mode definitions	532
List	Cisco VPN termination hardware	533
List	ASA licenses	537
List	VPN design objectives	539
List	IPsec best practices	540
Table 15-5	Establishing, maintaining, and tearing down an IPsec site-to-site VPN	542-543
Table 15-6	Steps of configuring an IPsec site-to-site VPN	543
Example 15-1	IKE Phase 1 configuration	544
Example 15-3	IKE Phase 2 configuration	545
Example 15-5	Applying a crypto map	546
Steps	Invoking the Cisco SDM Site-to-Site VPN Configuration Wizard	548
Table 15-7	Step-by-Step Wizard parameters	559
Table 15-8	Transform set parameters	563
Table 15-9	IPsec VPN monitoring commands	570

Complete the Tables and Lists from Memory

Print a copy of Appendix D, "Memory Tables," (found on the CD) or at least the section for this chapter, and complete the tables and lists from memory. Appendix E, "Memory Tables Answer Key," also on the CD, includes completed tables and lists so that you can check your work.

Definition of Key Terms

Define the following key terms from this chapter, and check your answers in the glossary:

> tunnel mode, transport mode, virtual private network (VPN), confidentiality, integrity, authentication, IKE proposal, transform set

Command Reference to Check Your Memory

This section includes the most important configuration and EXEC commands covered in this chapter. To see how well you have memorized the commands as a side effect of your other studies, cover the left side of the table with a piece of paper, read the descriptions on the right side, and see whether you remember the commands.

Table 15-11   *Chapter 15 Configuration Command Reference*

Command	Description
crypto isakmp policy *priority*	A global configuration mode command that defines an IKE policy with a specific priority
authentication pre-share	An ISAKMP configuration mode command that specifies that shared keys will be used for authentication
hash {sha | md5}	An ISAKMP configuration mode command that specifies the hashing method to be used
encryption {des | 3des | aes 128 | aes 192 | aes 256}	An ISAKMP configuration mode command that specifies the encryption algorithm to be used
group {1 | 2 | 5}	An ISAKMP configuration mode command that specifies the Diffie-Hellman group to be used
lifetime *seconds*	An ISAKMP configuration mode command that specifies the lifetime of an IKE Security Association (SA)
crypto isakmp key *key* **address** *peer-IP-address*	A global configuration mode command that configures a preshared key for use with a specified peer
crypto ipsec transform-set *transform-set-name transform1* [*transform2*] [*transform3*] [*transform4*]	A global configuration mode command that associates a collection of security protocols and algorithms with a transform set
crypto map *crypto-map-name sequence-number* **ipsec-isakmp**	A global configuration mode command that creates a crypto map, with a specified sequence number, that uses IKE to establish IPsec SAs
set peer *IP-address*	A crypto map configuration mode command that defines the IP address of an IPsec peer

Table 15-11   *Chapter 15 Configuration Command Reference (Continued)*

Command	Description
match address {*ACL-number* | *ACL-name*}	A crypto map configuration mode command that assigns an ACL to a crypto map entry
set transform-set *transform-set-name* [*transform-set-name2 ... transform-set-name6*]	A crypto map configuration mode command that specifies the transform set(s) that can be used with a crypto map
crypto map *crypto-map-name*	An interface configuration mode command that associates a previously defined crypto map with an interface

Table 15-12   *Chapter 15 EXEC Command Reference*

Command	Description
show crypto engine connections active	Displays a summary of active crypto engine connections
show crypto session	Shows the status for each active crypto session
show crypto isakmp sa	Shows all existing IKE Phase 1 (ISAKMP) security associations
show crypto ipsec sa	Shows all existing IKE Phase 2 (IPsec) security associations
debug crypto isakmp	Shows detailed information about the IKE Phase 1 (ISAKMP) and IKE Phase 2 (IPsec) negotiations

Part IV: Final Preparation

CHAPTER 16

Final Preparation

The first 15 chapters of this book cover the technologies, protocols, commands, and features required for you to be prepared to pass the IINS exam. Although these chapters supply detailed information, most people need more preparation than simply reading the first 15 chapters of this book. This chapter details a set of tools and a study plan to help you complete your preparation for the exams.

This short chapter has two main sections. The first discusses the exam engine and the questions on the CD. The second lists a suggested study plan now that you have completed all the other chapters in this book.

> **NOTE** This chapter refers to many of the chapters and appendixes included with this book, as well as tools available on the CD. Appendixes D and E are included only on the CD that comes with this book. To access those, just insert the CD and make the appropriate selection from the opening interface.

Exam Engine and Questions on the CD

The CD in the back of the book includes exam engine software that displays and grades a set of exam-realistic questions. The question database includes exam-realistic questions, including drag-and-drop and many scenario-based questions that require the same level of analysis as the questions on the IINS exam. Using the exam engine, you can either study by practicing using the questions in Study Mode or take a simulated (timed) IINS exam.

The installation process requires two major steps. The CD in the back of this book has a recent copy of the exam engine software, supplied by Boson Software (http://www.boson.com). The practice exam database of IINS exam questions is not on the CD. Instead, the practice exam resides on the www.boson.com web server, so the second major step is to activate and download the practice exam.

> **NOTE** The cardboard CD case in the back of this book includes the CD and a piece of paper. The paper lists the activation key for the practice exam associated with this book. *Do not lose the activation key.*

Install the Software from the CD

The software installation process is pretty routine as compared with other software installation processes. To be complete, the following steps outline the installation process:

Step 1 Insert the CD into your PC.

Step 2 The software that automatically runs is the Cisco Press software to access and use all CD-based features, including the exam engine, viewing a PDF of this book, and viewing the CD-only appendixes. From the main menu, choose the option to **Install the Exam Engine**.

Step 3 Respond to prompt windows as with any typical software installation process.

The installation process might give you the option to register the software. This process requires that you establish a login at the www.boson.com website. You will need this login to activate the exam, so feel free to register when prompted.

Activate and Download the Practice Exam

After the exam engine is installed, you should activate the exam associated with this book:

Step 1 Start the Boson Exam Engine (BEE) software from the Start menu.

Step 2 The first time you start the software, it should ask you to either log in or register an account. If you do not already have an account with Boson, select the option to register a new account. (You must register to download and use the exam.)

Step 3 After you are registered, the software might prompt you to download the latest version of the software, which you should do. Note that this process updates the exam engine software (formally called the Boson Exam Environment), not the practice exam.

Step 4 To activate and download the exam associated with this book, from the exam engine main window, click the **Exam Wizard** button.

Step 5 From the Exam Wizard pop-up window, select **Activate a purchased exam**, and click the **Next** button. (Although you did not directly purchase the exam, you purchased it indirectly when you purchased this book.)

Step 6 At the next screen, enter the activation key from the paper inside the cardboard CD holder in the back of the book. Then click the **Next** button.

Step 7 The activation process downloads the practice exam. When this is complete, the main exam engine menu should list a new exam, with a name such as "ExSim for Cisco Press IINS ECG." If you do not see the exam, be sure you have selected the **My Exams** tab on the menu. You might need to click the plus sign icon (+) to expand the menu to see the exam.

At this point, the software and practice exam are ready to use.

Activating Other Exams

The exam software installation process, and the registration process, needs to happen only once. Then, for each new exam, only a few steps are required. For instance, if you bought both this book and the *CCENT/CCNA ICND1 Official Exam Certification Guide*, you could follow the steps listed in the last page or so to install the software and activate the exam associated with this book. Then, for the practice exam associated with the ICND1 book, which has about 150 exam-realistic ICND1 questions, you need to follow only a few more steps. All you have to do is start the exam engine (if it's not still up and running), and perform Steps 4 and 5 in the preceding list. If fact, if you purchase other Cisco Press books, or purchase a practice exam from Boson, you just need to activate each new exam as described in Steps 4 and 5.

You can also purchase additional practice exams from Boson directly from its website. When you purchase an exam, you receive an activation key, and then you can activate and download the exam again without requiring any additional software installation.

Study Plan

This section suggests a particular study plan, with a sequence of tasks that may work better than just using the tools randomly. However, feel free to use the tools in any way and at any time that helps you get fully prepared for the exam.

The suggested study plan separates the tasks into two categories:

- **Recall the facts**: Activities that help you remember all the details from the first 15 chapters of the book.

- **Use the exam engine to practice realistic questions**: You can use the exam engine on the CD to study using a bank of unique exam-realistic questions available only with this book.

Recall the Facts

As with most exams, you must recall many facts, concepts, and definitions to do well on the test. This section suggests a couple of tasks that should help you remember all the details:

Step 1   **Review and repeat, as needed, the activities in the Exam Preparation Tasks section at the end of each chapter.** Most of these activities help you refine your knowledge of a topic while also helping you memorize the facts.

Step 2   **Using the exam engine, answer all the questions in the book database.** This question database includes all the questions at the beginning of each chapter. Although some of the questions might be familiar, repeating them will help improve your recall of the topics they cover.

Use the Exam Engine

The exam engine includes two basic modes:

■   **Study mode**: Study mode is most useful when you want to use the questions for a comprehensive review. In study mode, you can randomize the order of the questions, randomize the order of the answers, automatically see the answers, and choose many other options.

■   **Simulation mode**: Simulation mode simulates an actual IINS exam by either requiring or allowing a set number of questions and a set time period. These timed exams not only allow you to study for the actual IINS exam, they also help you simulate the time pressure that can occur on the actual exam.

Choosing Study or Simulation Mode

Both study mode and simulation mode are useful for preparing for the exams. The following steps show how to move to the screen from which to select study or simulation mode:

Step 1   Click the **Choose Exam** button, which should list the exam under the title **ExSim for Cisco Press IINS ECG**.

Step 2   Click the name of the exam, which should highlight the exam name.

Step 3   Click the **Load Exam** button.

The engine should display a window. Here you can choose **Simulation Mode** or **Study Mode** using the radio buttons.

Passing Scores for the IINS Exam

When scoring your simulated exam using this book's exam engine, you should strive to get a score of 85 percent or better. However, the scoring on the book's exam engine does not match how Cisco scores the actual IINS exam. Interestingly, Cisco does not publish many details about how it scores the actual exam. Therefore, you cannot reasonably deduce which questions you got right or wrong and how many points are assigned to each question.

Cisco does publish some specific guidance about how it scores the exam, and other details have been mentioned by Cisco personnel during public presentations about the CCNA exam. Here are some of the key facts about scoring:

■   Cisco does give partial credit on simulation questions. So, complete as much of a simulation question as you can.

■   Cisco might give more weight to some questions.

■   The test does not adapt based on your answers to early questions in the test. For example, if you miss an IPS question, the test does not start giving you more IPS questions.

■   The Cisco scores range from 300 to 1000, with a passing grade usually (but not always) around 849 for the IINS exam.

■   The 849 out of 1000 does not necessarily mean that you got 84.9% of the questions correct.

Part V: Appendixes

Answers to "Do I Know This Already?" Questions

Chapter 1

Q&A

1. B
2. A, C, and D
3. B, C, and D
4. A, B, and C
5. B, C, and D
6. C
7. D
8. C
9. A
10. B
11. A and D
12. B
13. D
14. A
15. B, C, and D

Chapter 2

Q&A

1. B, C, D, E, and G
2. D

3. B, D, and E

4. A, B, and D

5. A

6. B

7. A, C, and D

8. C

9. A

10. C

11. B

12. A, B, and D

13. B

Chapter 3

Q&A

1. A, C, D, and E

2. A, B, and C

3. D

4. B

5. C

6. C

7. A

8. A

9. C

10. B

11. D

12. A and D

13. A, B, and D

Chapter 4

Q&A

1. B

2. A

3. A, C, and D

4. C

5. C

6. D

7. A, C, and E

8. B, C, and E

9. C and E

10. A, B, and D

11. A

12. C

Chapter 5

Q&A

1. C

2. B and C

3. D

4. A

5. B

6. D

7. C

8. A

Chapter 6

Q&A

1. D
2. A
3. B and C
4. B
5. C
6. A
7. B
8. C
9. D
10. A, C, and D
11. A and C
12. D
13. B
14. A
15. C
16. A
17. D

Chapter 7

Q&A

1. A, B, and D
2. C
3. A
4. D
5. A and C
6. C

7. A and C

8. B

9. B and C

10. D

Chapter 8

Q&A

1. B

2. D

3. A, C, and D

4. B, D, and E

5. A

6. C

7. D

8. B

9. C

10. B and C

Chapter 9

Q&A

1. B

2. A, C, and D

3. B

4. B and C

5. C

6. D

7. B

8. B

9. B

10. C

11. A and C

Chapter 10

Q&A

1. A

2. A and B

3. B and D

4. B

5. D

6. B and D

7. B

8. C

9. A and C

10. B

11. A

12. B and D

13. B

14. B and C

15. A, C, and D

Chapter 11

Q&A

1. C and D

2. A

3. B and C

4. D

5. B

6. A, B, C, and E

7. C

8. A, B, and D

9. B

10. A

11. C

Chapter 12

Q&A

1. D

2. C

3. A

4. A, B, and D

5. B

6. A, C, and D

7. D

8. B

9. C

10. A

11. C

12. D

13. C

14. B

15. D

Chapter 13

Q&A

1. A and E

2. D

3. A and C

4. D

5. B, C, and E

6. B

7. B and C

8. B, D, and E

9. D

10. B and C

11. B

Chapter 14

Q&A

1. B

2. C

3. D

4. A and D

5. A, D, and E

6. A, D, and E

7. B

8. B, D, and E

9. D

10. C

Chapter 15

Q&A

1. A

2. B

3. A and C

4. B and D

5. C

6. B

7. D

8. C

9. A

10. B

11. B

12. B and C

13. A, B, and D

14. B

Glossary

access control list (ACL)   ACLs can provide basic traffic-filtering capabilities on Cisco routers. ACLs can be configured for all routed network protocols to filter packets as they pass through a router or security appliance. An ACL may be used for packet filtering (a type of firewall), as well as for selecting types of traffic to be analyzed, forwarded, or influenced in some manner.

accounting   Tracking users' consumption of network resources. This information may be used for management purposes, planning, billing, or other purposes. Typical information that is gathered includes the user's name, the nature of the service delivered, when the service began, and when it concluded.

Advanced Encryption Standard (AES)   The AES initiative was announced in 1997, when the public was invited to propose candidate encryption schemes to be evaluated as the encryption standard to replace DES. The Rijndael cipher was selected as the AES algorithm in October of 2000 by the U.S. National Institute of Standards and Technology (NIST). In 2002 the U.S. Secretary of Commerce approved the adoption of AES as an official U.S. government standard.

application layer firewall   This third-generation firewall technology evaluates network packets for valid data at the application layer before allowing a connection. Data in all network packets is examined at the application layer and maintains complete connection state and sequencing information. Application layer firewalls also can validate other security items that appear only within the application layer data, such as user passwords and service requests.

asymmetric algorithm   Employs a two-key technology: a public key and a private key. Often this is simply called public key encryption. In this key pair, the public key may be distributed freely, whereas the private key must be closely guarded. If it is compromised, the system as a whole will fail. The way that public key encryption works is that the public key is used to encrypt the data. After it is encrypted, only the private key can decrypt the data. The opposite is also true.

asymmetric encryption   Employs a two-key technology: a public key and a private key. Often this is simply called public key encryption. In this key pair, the public key may be distributed freely, whereas the private key must be closely guarded. If it is compromised, the system as a whole will fail. The way that public key encryption works is that the public key is used to encrypt the data. After it is encrypted, only the private key can decrypt the data. The opposite is also true.

auditing   The process of recording the actions of an authenticated user. An example is tracking how long a user is authenticated on the network and the resources he or she works with while on the network, as well as the length of usage. Auditing can produce a history of network usage on the part of a given user or users.

authentication   The confirmation that a user who is requesting a service is a valid user of the network services requested. Authentication is accomplished by presenting an identity and credentials. These might be such things as passwords, one-time tokens, or digital certificates.

authentication, authorization, and accounting (AAA)   These three primary services give a network security as well as a record of user activity. AAA identifies who the user is, what the user can access, and what services and resources the user is using when he or she makes a connection with a server.

authentication server   A RADIUS server (such as Cisco Secure ACS) that validates a client's credentials against its user database.

authenticator   A device (such as a Cisco Catalyst switch) that provides access to a network. The authenticator typically does not authenticate the supplicant. Rather, the authenticator acts as a gateway, relaying authentication messages between the supplicant and an external authentication server.

authorization   The granting of specific types of service to a user, based on his or her authentication, the services he or she is requesting, and the current system state.

AutoSecure   An automated approach to applying security best practices to a router that is invoked from the CLI.

auxiliary VLAN   The VLAN used by a Cisco IP Phone to carry voice traffic is often called an auxiliary VLAN.

availability   The availability of data is a measure of its accessibility. For example, if a server were down only 5 minutes per year, it would have an availability of 99.999 percent (that is, "five nines" of availability).

awareness   Awareness makes the end-user community conscious of security issues, without necessarily any in-depth procedural training. For example, distributing an e-mail or pamphlet describing the issue of viruses and the importance of virus protection creates awareness of the issue.

block cipher   Derives its name from the fact that it transforms a fixed-length "block" of plain text into a "block" of ciphertext. These two blocks are the same length. When the reverse transformation is applied to the ciphertext block, by using the same secret key, it is decrypted. Block ciphers use a fixed length or block size. This generally is 128 bits, but they can range in size. For instance, DES has a block size of 64 bits.

bootset   The collection of a router's image and configuration files that can be protected using the Cisco IOS Resilient Configuration feature, which keeps a secure copy of the bootset.

brute-force attack   Attempts to match password credentials by guessing a sequence of patterns (for example, the letter a through the letter z, followed by the letters aa through zz, followed by aaa through zzz, and so on). In such an attack, all possible combinations are used until the password is discovered. This may require a great deal of time, but it always eventually succeeds in discovering the password.

buffer overflow   A programming error that may result in erratic program behavior, a memory access exception and program termination, or a possible breach of system security.

call agent   Replaces many of the features previously provided by Private Branch Exchanges (PBX). For example, a call agent can be configured with rules that determine how calls are forwarded. Cisco Unified Communications Manager (UCM) is an example of a call agent.

catastrophe   A disruption category in which all resources at a site are destroyed, and normal business operations must be moved to an alternative site.

certificate   A document issued and signed by the certificate authority (CA) that binds the name of the entity and its public key.

certificate authority (CA)   A trusted third party responsible for signing the public keys of entities in a PKI-based system.

Challenge Handshake Authentication Protocol (CHAP)   An authentication scheme used by Point-to-Point Protocol (PPP) to validate the identity of remote clients. CHAP periodically verifies the client's identity by using a three-way handshake. Verification is based on a shared secret. CHAP also is the mandatory protocol for iSCCI, as chosen by the Internet Engineering Task Force (IETF). CHAP is based on shared secrets. It periodically verifies the client's identity by using a three-way handshake. This verification is based on a shared secret. With CHAP, the password never actually crosses the wire, just a hash of the challenge, hostname, and password.

checksum   A mathematical computation used to verify that the contents of a message have not been altered.

ciphertext   The representation of plain text in an unreadable form.

Cisco Discovery Protocol (CDP)   A Layer 2 protocol that permits adjacent Cisco devices to learn information about one another (for example, protocol and platform information).

Cisco Security Agent (CSA)   A host-based IPS (HIPS) solution. The CSA software can be installed on selected host systems and optionally report suspicious activity to a centralized management server.

Cisco Security Device Manager (SDM)   Provides a graphical user interface (GUI) for configuring a wide variety of features on an IOS router.

Cisco Security Manager   An application that can be used to configure security features on a wide variety of Cisco security products.

Cisco Security MARS   The Cisco Security Monitoring, Analysis and Response System. The MARS product offers security monitoring for security devices and applications. In addition to Cisco devices and applications, Cisco Security MARS can monitor many third-party devices and applications.

Cisco Self-Defending Network   The Cisco vision for using a network to recognize threats and then prevent and adapt to them.

class map   A way of identifying a set of packets based on their contents using "match" conditions. Classes generally are defined so that you can apply an action to the identified traffic that reflects a policy. The class itself is designated via the class map. Class maps are created using the **class-map** command. After it is created, the class map is used to match packets to a specified class.

cold site   A cold site offers an alternative site where business operations can be conducted, unlike a hot or warm site. However, a cold site typically does not contain redundant computing equipment such as servers and routers. As a result, the data network would need to be rebuilt from scratch, which might require weeks. Therefore, although a cold site is less expensive initially, as compared to hot or warm sites, a cold site could have more long-term consequences. In fact, the financial consequences could be far greater than the initial cost savings.

collision   When two separate messages have the same message digest. A hash "collision" or hash "clash" happens when two distinct inputs entered into a hash function produce identical outputs. Each hash function has the potential for collisions. However, if you are working with a well-designed hash function, collisions should occur less frequently. In terms of hash functions, collisions inhibit the distinguishing of data, making records more costly to find in hash tables and data processing.

community VLAN   Ports belonging to a community VLAN can communicate with one another, but not with ports in other community VLANs.

confidentiality   Data confidentiality is provided by encrypting data. If a third party intercepts the encrypted data, he or she cannot interpret it.

Context-Based Access Control (CBAC)   Represents a significant advance over ACLs in that it provides stateful packet filtering capability. CBAC provides the capacity to monitor several attributes in TCP connections, UDP sessions, and Internet Control Message Protocol (ICMP). This monitoring is done in an effort to be sure that the only traffic allowed through a firewall ACL is the return traffic for a dialogue that was originated on the private side of the firewall.

cryptographic hash   This function is a transformation that takes an input and returns a string, which is called the hash value. Cryptographic hash functions begin with the assumption that an adversary can deliberately try to find inputs with the same hash value. Creating a well-designed cryptographic hash involves a one-way operation in which there is no practical way to calculate a particular data input that will result in a desired hash value. This one-way nature makes the hash very difficult to forge.

cryptography   The practice and study of encoding information to protect the original contents. In modern terms this is considered the breach between mathematics and computer science, combining to provide a means of securing information both in computer systems and on networks.

data diddling   The process of changing data before it is stored in a computing system.

Data Encryption Standard (DES)   Typically operates in block mode, where it encrypts data in 64-bit blocks. Like other symmetric algorithms, DES uses the same algorithm and key for both encryption and decryption. DES has weathered nearly 35 years of cryptographic scrutiny. To this point, no significant flaws have been found. Adding to its appeal, DES may be easily implemented and accelerated in hardware.

Defense in Depth   A design philosophy that uses a layered security approach to eliminate a single point of failure and to provide overlapping protection.

demilitarized zone (DMZ)   Sometimes called a screened subnet. A segment of the overall network that is cordoned off through the use of two firewalls. One of these firewalls sits between the DMZ and the Internet, and the other sits between the DMZ and the internal network. This configuration may also be referred to as creating a "perimeter" network.

denial of service (DoS)   A class of attack in which the attacker seeks to make a given resource unavailable to legitimate users by overwhelming the resource with requests for service that appear legitimate. The resource, such as a server, seeks to handle all requests but ultimately fails. It either becomes unavailable for legitimate purposes or struggles to such an extent that it cannot respond to legitimate requests in a timely manner.

detective control   Can detect when access to data or a system occurs.

deterrent control   Attempts to prevent a security incident by influencing a potential attacker not to launch an attack.

DHCP snooping   The Dynamic Host Configuration Protocol snooping feature on Cisco Catalyst switches can be used to combat a DHCP server spoofing attack. With this solution, Cisco Catalyst switch ports are configured in either a trusted or untrusted state. If a port is trusted, it is allowed to receive DHCP responses. If a port is untrusted, it is not allowed to receive DHCP responses. If a DHCP response attempts to enter an untrusted port, the port is disabled.

dictionary attack   Attempts to match password credentials by guessing passwords from a "dictionary" of common words.

Diffie-Hellman (DH) algorithm   A key exchange algorithm that was invented by Whitfield Diffie and Martin Hellman in 1976. The Diffie-Hellman algorithm derives its strength from the difficulty of calculating the discrete logarithms of very large numbers. The functional usage of this algorithm is to provide secure key exchange over insecure channels such as the Internet. DH is also often used to provide keying material for other symmetric algorithms, such as DES, 3DES, and AES.

Diffie-Hellman Challenge Handshake Authentication Protocol (DHCHAP)   A variation of CHAP that may be used to authenticate devices connecting to a Fibre Channel switch so that only trusted devices may be added to a fabric. DHCHAP adds a DH exchange that both strengthens CHAP and provides an agreed-upon secret key.

digital signature   Also called a digital signature scheme. A form of asymmetric cryptography that is used to simulate the security characteristics of a written signature in digital form. Digital signature schemes typically use two algorithms that employ a pair of public and private keys. One of these is used for signing, which involves the user's secret or private key. The other is used to verify these signatures. This typically involves the use of the user's public key.

Digital Signature Algorithm (DSA)   The Digital Signature Standard (DSS) outlines the use of the DSA by a signer to generate a digital signature to be applied to data and by a recipient of the data to verify the signature's authenticity. To create the digital signature, you need both a public key and a private key. The private key is used to generate the signature, and the public key is used to verify it. For both signature generation and verification, the data, which is called a message, is reduced through the use of the Secure Hash Algorithm (SHA).

disaster   A disruption category in which normal business operations are interrupted for one or more days. However, not all critical resources at a site are destroyed.

disaster recovery plan   Sometimes called a business continuity plan. Addresses actions taken during and immediately following a disaster.

Dynamic ARP Inspection (DAI)   Uses trusted and untrusted ports. ARP replies are allowed into the switch on trusted ports. However, if an ARP reply enters the switch on an untrusted port, the contents of the ARP reply are compared to the DHCP binding table to verify its accuracy. If the ARP reply is inconsistent with the DHCP binding table, the ARP reply is dropped, and the port is disabled.

dynamic firewall   This fourth-generation firewall technology, sometimes called a stateful firewall, keeps track of the communication process through the use of a state table. This firewall operates at Layers 3, 4, and 5.

EAP   Extensible Authentication Protocol. Dictates the specific authentication messages transported by 802.1x and RADIUS protocols used in an IEEE 802.1x solution.

education   More comprehensive than training because it covers a larger body of knowledge. Obtaining a college degree focusing on IT security is an example of a comprehensive security education.

elevation of privileges   The act of exploiting a bug in a software application to gain access to resources that normally would be protected from an application or user. The result is that the application performs actions with more privileges than intended by the application developer or system administrator.

Encapsulating Security Payload (ESP)   An Internet standard that allows for the authentication and encryption of IP packets. ESP over Fibre Channel provides a means of protecting data in transit throughout the Fibre Channel network. However, it does not address the need to secure data while it is stored on the Fibre Channel network.

endpoint   The final point of connection in a communication channel.

exploit   A malicious program designed to take advantage of a vulnerability.

extended access control list (ACL)   Made up of a series of statements created in global mode. With extended ACLs, IP packets may be filtered based on a number of attributes. Extended ACLs can filter packets according to protocol type, source and IP address, destination IP address, source TCP or UDP ports, destination TCP or UDP ports, and optional protocol type information if finer granularity of control is required.

Extensible Authentication Protocol-Flexible Authentication via Secure Tunneling (EAP-FAST)   Protects authentication messages within a secure Transport Layer Security (TLS) tunnel using shared secret keys. Security is provided by an SSL (Secure Socket Layer)/TLS certificate on the "server side"/ACS and by a username and password on the client side.

Extensible Authentication Protocol-Message Digest 5 (EAP-MD5)   A standards-based EAP type that uses an MD5-Challenge message. This is much like the challenge message used in PPP CHAP (Point-to-Point Protocol Challenge Handshake Authentication Protocol), which also uses MD5 as its hashing algorithm.

Extensible Authentication Protocol-Transport Layer Security (EAP-TLS)   Developed by Microsoft Corporation to address weaknesses found in other EAP types (such as the one-way authentication used by EAP-MD5). EAP-TLS uses certificate-based (X.509 certificate-based) authentication. It requires both a supplicant and an authentication server to possess a digital certification to perform mutual authentication.

Extensible Authentication Protocol-Tunneled Transport Layer Security (EAP-TTLS)   Uses a secured Transport Layer Security (TLS) tunnel to send other EAP authentication messages.

Fibre Channel   In terms of SAN networking, this is the primary SAN transport used for host-to-SAN connectivity.

Fibre Channel Authentication Protocol (FCAP)   Born from Switch Link Authentication Protocol (SLAP), the first authentication protocol proposed for Fibre Channel. This optional authentication mechanism may be employed between any two devices or entities on a Fibre Channel network. It uses certificates or optional keys to provide security.

Fibre Channel over IP (FCIP)   Represents the implementation of Fibre Channel in an IP implementation that relies on TCP/IP as the network protocol.

Fibre Channel Password Authentication Protocol (FCPAP)   An optional password-based authentication key-exchange protocol. It may be used in Fibre Channel networks to provide mutual authentication between Fibre Channel ports. As compared to FCAP, FCPAP does not require a PKI to operate.

Fibre Channel Security Protocol (FC-SP)   Designed to overcome the security challenges for enterprise-wide fabrics by providing switch-to-switch and host-to-switch authentication. The focus of FC-SP is protecting data in transit throughout the Fibre Channel network.

Fibre Channel zoning   The partitioning of a Fibre Channel fabric into smaller subsets for security purposes.

firewall   Allows for the segmentation of networks into different physical subnetworks, thereby helping limit the potential damage that could spread from one subnet to another. This term comes from firewalls in buildings, which limit the spread of a fire. A firewall may be a piece of software or hardware that acts as a barrier between the internal (trusted) network and the external (untrusted) network, such as the Internet.

gatekeeper   Can be thought of as the "traffic cop" of the WAN. For example, because bandwidth on a WAN typically is somewhat limited, a gatekeeper can monitor the available bandwidth. Then, when there is not enough bandwidth to support another voice call, the gatekeeper can deny future call attempts.

gateway   Can forward calls between different types of networks. For example, you could place a call from an IP phone in your office, through a gateway to the PSTN, to call your home.

hashing   Used to provide data integrity. Hashes are based on one-way mathematical functions that can be easy to compute but extremely challenging to reverse. The way that hashing works in practice is that data of an arbitrary length is input into the hash function and is processed through the function, resulting in a fixed-length hash. The resultant fixed-length hash is called either the digest or fingerprint.

heap overflow   A type of buffer overflow that occurs in the heap data area. Memory on the heap is dynamically allocated by the application at runtime and typically contains program data. A heap overflow is not as likely to result in a condition permitting remote code execution as a buffer overflow.

HMAC   Keyed Hash Message Authentication Code. An HMAC in cryptographic terms is a type of message authentication code calculated by using a cryptographic hash function along with a secret key. This may be used to simultaneously verify both the data's integrity and the message's authenticity. An iterative cryptographic hash function such as MD5 or SHA-1 may be used to calculate the HMAC. When these are used, the resulting MAC algorithm is called HMAC-MD5 or HMAC-SHA-1, for instance. The cryptographic strength of the underlying hash function, along with the key's size and quality and the hash output length in bits, define the cryptographic strength of the HMAC.

host-based intrusion prevention system (HIPS)   An IPS in which the intrusion-prevention application resides on that specific host, typically a single computer. The IPS monitors system activities for malicious or unwanted behaviors. It can react in real time to block or prevent those activities. The key benefit is that HIPS is behavior-based as opposed to signature-based.

Host Bus Adapter (HBA)   Connects a host system to other network and storage devices. This term primarily refers to devices for connecting SCSI, Fibre Channel, and eSATA devices, but devices for connecting to IDE, Ethernet, FireWire, USB, and other systems may also be called host adapters.

hot site   A completely redundant site that has equipment very similar to that at the original site. Data is routinely copied from a primary site to a hot site. As a result, a hot site can be up and functioning within a few minutes (or even seconds) after a catastrophe at the primary site.

IEEE 802.1x   A standards-based approach for providing port-based network access. Specifically, 802.1x is a Layer 2 protocol that defines how Extensible Authentication Protocol (EAP) frames are encapsulated, typically between a user's network device (such as a PC) and a switch or wireless access point.

IKE proposal   Internet Key Exchange proposal. A collection of security protocols and algorithms that can be used to establish an IKE Phase 1 (ISAKMP) tunnel.

in-band management   An approach that allows management traffic to be transmitted across a production network.

inline mode   Inline mode operation requires at least two monitoring interfaces on an IPS sensor, because the sensor resides inline with the traffic. (In other words, traffic enters the sensor on one monitoring interface and exits the sensor on another monitoring interface.) Therefore, a sensor running in inline mode supports IPS operation and can drop malicious traffic before it reaches its intended target.

Integrated Services Router (ISR)   As its name suggests, this kind of Cisco router integrates various services (such as voice and security services) into a router's architecture.

integrity   Data integrity ensures that data is not modified in transit. For example, routers at each end of a tunnel could calculate checksum values or hash values for the data. If both routers calculate the same values, the data most likely was not modified in transit.

intrusion detection system (IDS)   Can recognize network attacks by analyzing a copy of network traffic. Can deliver a comprehensive, pervasive security solution for combating unauthorized intrusions, malicious Internet worms, and bandwidth and e-business application attacks.

intrusion prevention system (IPS)   Provides end-to-end protection for the network via a network-based defense that can identify, classify, and stop known and unknown threats, including worms, network viruses, application threats, system intrusion attempts, and application misuse.

IP spoofing   An attack in which an attacker falsifies packets' source IP address (for example, causing the source IP address to be a trusted IP address).

IP telephony   Similar to VoIP, sends voice traffic over an IP network. However, the primary distinction from a VoIP network is that an IP telephony environment contains endpoints that natively communicate using IP.

isolated VLAN   Ports belonging to an isolated VLAN lack Layer 2 connectivity between one another. However, they can communicate with a promiscuous post.

key pair   In terms of a PKI, the key pair is composed of one public key and one private key. These two keys work together to provide a means to both encrypt and decrypt data. The public key may be widely distributed publicly, but the private key should be closely held by its owner. Data encrypted with the public key can be decrypted only by the matching private key.

keyspace   The keyspace of an algorithm represents a defined set of all possible key values. For each key of n bits, a keyspace is produced that has $2n$ possible key values. This means that if 1 bit were added to the key, this would effectively double the size of the keyspace.

Lightweight Extensible Authentication Protocol (LEAP)   Uses a username/password combination to perform authentication. Typically is found in a Cisco wireless LAN (WLAN) implementation.

LUN masking   A Logical Unit Number is an address used by the SCSI protocol to differentiate an individual disk drive that makes up a common SCSI target device. LUN masking represents a defense against attacks. In this authorization process, a LUN is made available to some hosts and unavailable to other hosts.

Management Information Base (MIB)   Information about a managed device's resources and activity is defined by a series of objects. The structure of these management objects is defined by a managed device's MIB.

Media Gateway Control Protocol (MGCP)   Originally developed by Cisco and considered to be a client/server protocol. The client (such as an analog port in a voice-enabled router) can communicate with a server (such as a Cisco Unified Communications Manager server) via a series of events and signals. For example, the server could tell the client that if an attached phone goes off-hook, play the signal of dial tone to that phone.

message   In cryptographic terms, a collection of plain text. Messages may be anything from an e-mail, to a username-and-password combination, to a string of data.

Message Digest 5 (MD5)   An iterative hash function that breaks a message into blocks of a fixed size and then iterates over them with a compression function. Defined in RFC 1321, MD5 with its 128-bit hash value has been employed in a wide variety of security applications. It is also commonly used to check the integrity of files. An MD5 hash typically is expressed as a 32-character hexadecimal number.

method list   A sequential list that defines the authentication methods used to authenticate a user. Method lists enable the designation of one or more security protocols to be used for authentication, ensuring a backup system for authentication in case the initial method fails. Cisco IOS software uses the first method listed to authenticate users. If that method does not respond, Cisco IOS software selects the next authentication method in the method list. This process continues until either successful communication with a listed authentication method occurs or the authentication method list is exhausted, in which case authentication fails.

microengine   Handles a group of similar signatures. A sensor contains multiple microengines and decides which one(s) it will use to analyze traffic. It uses criteria such as the network protocol being used by the traffic, the signature's associated operating system, the port number being used by the session, and the type of attack the sensor is looking for.

Microsoft Challenge Handshake Authentication Protocol (MS-CHAP)   Microsoft's version of CHAP. This protocol exists in two versions: MS-CHAPv1 (RFC 2433) and MS-CHAPv2 (RFC 2759).

Multipoint Control Unit (MCU)   Useful for conference calling. During a conference call, several people might be speaking at the same time, and everyone on that conference call can hear them. It takes processing power to mix together these audio streams. MCUs provide that processing power. MCUs might contain digital signal processors (DSP), which are dedicated pieces of computer circuitry that can mix together these audio streams.

National Institute of Standards and Technology (NIST)   The U.S. government body that is responsible for defining and publishing U.S. Federal Information Processing Standards (FIPS).

network access device (NAD)   The system that provides network access in an enterprise network environment.

network access server (NAS)   Provides enterprise access services and implements security mechanisms for those connecting with a corporate network. A NAS is the intermediate device between an end user and authentication server. It could be a router, VPN endpoint (perhaps ASA), WiFi access point, or Catalyst switch running 802.1x. Any device that handles user credentials via

Telnet, SSH, HTTP, IKE, EAP, PPP, and so on and then passes these credentials to a RADIUS/TACACS server on the back end would qualify as a NAS.

Network Address Translation (NAT)   Employed by networks that use private IP addresses. In terms of security uses, it is used by the application inspection function of firewalls to help identify the location of embedded addressing information. NAT is used to translate embedded addresses and to update any checksum or other fields that are affected by the translation.

Network Admission Control (NAC)   Refers to the Cisco NAC appliance, which provides network access features to enterprise environments to help ensure a secure and clean environment.

Network Time Protocol (NTP)   Allows a router to act as a time source, helping to ensure that the time is consistent across multiple network devices. Synchronizing clocks in this manner makes event correlation much easier.

nondisaster   A disruption category in which normal business operations are briefly interrupted.

nonrepudiation   Blocks the false denial of a particular action.

out-of-band (OOB) management   Keeps management traffic isolated from production data traffic.

parameter map   Specifies parameters to be applied to classified traffic. Using the **parameter-map type** command you may specify parameters that control the behavior of actions and match criteria specified under a policy map and a class map.

phreaker   A hacker of a telephony system.

Point-to-Point Protocol (PPP)   A data link protocol commonly used to establish a direct connection between two nodes over serial cable, phone line, trunk line, cellular telephone, specialized radio links, or fiber-optic links. Most Internet service providers use PPP for customers' dialup access to the Internet.

policy map   Actions are associated with traffic classified by class maps using policy maps. An action is defined as a specific functionality and typically is associated with a traffic class. Some common actions are **inspect**, **drop**, and **pass**.

preventive control   Attempts to prevent access to data or a system. This could be any number of things that attempt to block this access.

private key   One half of a public key/private key key pair. This key must remain privately held and should be guarded by its owner. As soon as data has been encrypted by the associated public key, only the private key may be used to decrypt the data. With regard to digital signatures, its function is to sign a message. The message signature may then be verified through the use of the associated public key.

privilege level   An IOS EXEC mode that allows an administrator logged into that privilege level to access all commands available to that privilege level and all lower privilege levels. Cisco IOS routers support privilege levels in the range 0 to 15. By default, when you attach to a router, you are in unprivileged mode, which has a privilege level of 1. Privilege level 0 may be assigned to a user account. Those who have this level may then be assigned a subset of the commands available at level 1. After entering the **enable** command and providing appropriate credentials, you are moved to privileged mode, which has a privilege level of 15.

promiscuous mode   Uses a single monitoring interface on an IDS/IPS sensor. When running in promiscuous mode, a sensor receives a copy of selected network traffic. If the sensor detects malicious traffic, it can take a variety of actions. For example, it can trigger an alarm or instruct a security appliance to drop traffic coming from a specific source. Because a sensor running in promiscuous mode is not inline with the traffic, IDS operation is supported, but not IPS operation.

Protected Extensible Authentication Protocol (PEAP) Microsoft Challenge Handshake Authentication Protocol version 2 (MS-CHAPv2)   An EAP type that increases protection of authentication messages by creating a protected Transport Layer Security (TLS) tunnel. Then, within the protection of the TLS tunnel, an authentication protocol such as MS-CHAPv2 can be used.

proxy server   Acts as an intermediary between networks, often your internal network and the Internet at large. In such configurations there is no direct connection between an outside user and internal network resources. The proxy provides the only visible IP address on the Internet. Clients connect to the proxy server to submit their application layer request. These requests include the actual destination as well as the data request itself. Based on the proxy server settings, the proxy analyzes the request and may even filter or change the packet contents before proceeding. The proxy server also makes a copy of all the incoming packets and then changes the source address. It does this to hide the internal address from the outside world before it sends the packet to the destination address.

public key   One half of a public key/private key key pair. This key may be made available publicly. It can be used to encrypt data that may then be decrypted only by the matching private key. With regard to digital signatures, its function is to verify a message signature. In this case, the message would be signed with the sender's private key, and then the recipient would verify the signature's authenticity using the sender's public key.

Public Key Infrastructure (PKI)   Taken as a whole, a set of technical, organizational, and legal components that combine to establish a system that enables large-scale use of public key cryptography. Via a PKI, an organization can provide authenticity, confidentiality, integrity, and nonrepudiation services.

public switched telephone network (PSTN)   The North American public telephone network.

rainbow table   A precomputed table of all possible combinations of characters and the hashes they create. If an attacker were to discover the contents of a password file, such as the SAM file in Windows, he could load the hashes stored in the SAM into a rainbow table. The rainbow table then displays the input required to generate that hash. This is often referred to as a time-versus-space trade-off attack. An attacker does not have to spend time trying every possible combination until he finds a match. However, he must sacrifice more than 50 GB of hard drive space to store these tables, or have access to an online rainbow table.

Real-time Transport Protocol (RTP)   Carries the voice payload in VoIP streams. Interestingly, although RTP is a Layer 4 protocol, it is encapsulated inside UDP (also a Layer 4 protocol). The UDP port numbers used can vary by vendor, but in Cisco environments, RTP typically uses even UDP ports in the range 16,384 to 32,767.

registration authority (RA)   To make the operation of the CA more secure, many key management tasks may be effectively offloaded to RAs. These RAs are PKI servers that are responsible for performing management tasks on behalf of the CA. These include authenticating users when they enroll with the PKI, key generation for users who cannot generate their own keys, and distributing certificates after enrollment.

Remote Authentication Dial-In User Service (RADIUS)   An authentication, authorization, and accounting (AAA) protocol for controlling access to network resources. RADIUS is commonly used by ISPs and corporations to manage access to the Internet or internal networks across an array of access technologies, including modems, DSL, wireless, and VPNs.

risk analysis   Beyond basic identification of threats, a key design decision revolves around analyzing the probability that a threat will occur and the severity of the consequences if the threat does occur. This is called risk analysis.

Rivest Cipher (RC) algorithms   A number of widely used RC algorithms or RC ciphers exist, and many were developed by Ronald Rivest. Four of the most widely used RC algorithms are RC2, RC4, RC5, and RC6. Of these, RC4 is the most popular. It is a variable key-size stream cipher that employs byte-oriented operations and is based on the use of a random permutation.

Rivest, Shamir, and Adleman (RSA)   Invented by Ron Rivest, Adi Shamir, and Len Adleman in 1977, RSA is one of the most common asymmetric algorithms in use today. This public-key algorithm was patented until September 2000, when the patent expired, making the algorithm part of the public domain. RSA has been widely embraced over the years, in part because of its ease of implementation and its flexibility.

role-based command-line interface (CLI) views   Can be used to provide different sets of configuration information to different administrators. However, unlike making commands available via privilege levels, using role-based CLI views you can control exactly what commands an administrator has access to.

RTP Control Protocol (RTCP)   Provides information about an RTP flow, such as information about the quality of the call. In a Cisco environment, RTCP typically uses odd-numbered UDP ports in the range 16,384 to 32,767.

salami attack   A collection of small attacks that result in a larger attack when combined.

salt   A series of random bits added to a password. When the password is hashed, and that hash is stored in a database, two identical passwords do not create the same hash. This also protects the passwords from attacks involving rainbow tables.

Secure RTP (SRTP)   Secures the transmission of voice via Real-time Transport Protocol (RTP). Specifically, SRTP adds encryption, authentication, integrity, and antireplay mechanisms to voice traffic.

Secure Shell (SSH)   A protocol that provides encryption and authentication functions for remote terminal sessions. This allows an administrator to securely attach to and exchange information with a router, for example. Cisco recommends that SSH be used instead of Telnet because Telnet sends data in plain text.

security level   Defines the type of security algorithm performed on SNMP packets. Examples of security levels are noAuthNoPriv, authNoPriv, and authPriv.

security model   Defines an approach for user and group authentication. Cisco IOS supports the SNMPv1, SNMPv2c, and SNMPv3 security models.

security policy   A continually changing document that dictates a set of guidelines for network use. These guidelines complement organizational objectives by specifying rules for how the network is used.

security zone   Consists of a group of interfaces to which a policy can be applied. Grouping interfaces into zones involves two steps. First, a zone must be created so that interfaces may be attached to it. Second, an interface must be configured to be a member of a given zone.

Session Initiation Protocol (SIP)   Like H.323, SIP is considered a peer-to-peer protocol. SIP is a very popular protocol to use in mixed-vendor environments, perhaps because of its use of existing protocols, such as HTTP and SMTP.

SHA-1   Secure Hash Algorithm 1. One of five cryptographic hash functions known as SHA hash functions. They were designed by the National Security Agency (NSA) and published by the National Institute of Standards and Technology (NIST) as a U.S. Federal Information Processing Standard. SHA-1 computes a fixed-length digital representation (a message digest) from an input data sequence (the message) of any length.

signature definition file (SDF)   A database of signatures used to identify malicious traffic. Modern routers typically ship with an SDF file installed in flash memory. However, the administrator usually needs to periodically update the router's SDF, because Cisco routinely updates these files to address emerging threats.

Simple Network Management Protocol (SNMP)   A management protocol that allows an SNMP manager to collect information from an SNMP agent.

Skinny Client Control Protocol (SCCP)   A Cisco-proprietary signaling protocol often called Skinny protocol. SCCP is often used for signaling between Cisco IP Phones and Cisco Unified Communications Manager servers. However, some Cisco gateways also support SCCP. SCCP is considered a client/server protocol, such as MGCP and H.248.

Small Computer Systems Interface (SCSI)   In terms of SAN networking, the SCSI communications model serves as the basis for all the major SAN transport technologies. In fact, you could say that a SAN can best be described as the merging of SCSI and networking.

SNMP agent   A piece of software that runs on a managed device (such as a server, router, or switch).

SNMP GET   A message that is used to retrieve information from a managed device.

SNMP manager   Runs a network management application. Sometimes called a Network Management Server (NMS).

SNMP SET   A message that is used to set a variable in a managed device or to trigger an action on the managed device.

SNMP trap   An unsolicited message sent from the managed device to an SNMP manager. It can be used to notify the SNMP manager about a significant event that occurred on a managed device.

snooping   Broadly defines a class of attacks focused on compromising the confidentiality of data. In terms of SAN deployments, these attacks seek to give an attacker access to data that would otherwise be confidential.

Software Encryption Algorithm (SEAL)   This kind of encryption uses a 160-bit encryption key. It offers the benefit of having less of an impact on the CPU compared to other software-based algorithms. It is an alternative to software-based DES, 3DES, and AES.

spam over IP telephony (SPIT)   VoIP spam. A SPIT attack on your Cisco IP Phone could, for example, make unsolicited messages periodically appear on the phone's LCD screen or make the phone ring periodically.

spoofing   Imitating a given resource by alternative means. In network terms this might represent the spoofing of an IP address, where an attacker poses as the valid recipient at a given IP address to intercept traffic.

standard access control list (ACL)   Standard ACLs allow traffic to be permitted or denied from only specific IP addresses. With these ACLs, the packet's destination and the ports involved are not taken into account.

static firewall   This first-generation firewall technology analyzes network traffic at the transport protocol layer. IP packets are examined to see if they match one of a set of rules defining which data flows are allowed. These rules specify whether communication is allowed based on information contained in the network and transport layer headers as well as the direction of the packet flow.

storage-area network (SAN)   In a SAN, storage devices are shared among all networked servers as peer resources. A SAN may be used to connect servers to storage, servers to each other, and storage to storage.

stream cipher   Uses smaller units of plain text than what are used with block ciphers. Typically they work with bits. Transformation of these smaller plain-text units also varies, depending on when during the encryption process they are encountered. One of the great benefits of stream ciphers as compared to block ciphers is that they are much faster. Generally they do not increase the message size because they can encrypt an arbitrary number of bits.

supplicant   A user device (such as a PC) that requests permission to access the network. This device must support the 802.1x standard. For example, a PC running the Microsoft Windows XP operating system supporting 802.1x could act as a supplicant.

Switch Port Analyzer (SPAN) port   Can receive a copy of traffic crossing another port or VLAN.

symmetric algorithm   Because of the simplicity of its mathematics and the speed at which it operates, a symmetric algorithm is the most commonly used form of cryptography. Symmetric encryption algorithms are also stronger. Therefore, they can use shorter key lengths compared to asymmetric algorithms. This further helps increase their speed of execution in software.

syslog   A protocol used to collect log information. The logs are transmitted in clear text. A syslog logging solution consists of two primary components: syslog servers and syslog clients. A syslog server receives and stores log messages sent from syslog clients.

System Development Life Cycle (SDLC)   Describes the life cycle of a component, which is broken into five phases: initiation, acquisition and development, implementation, operations and maintenance, and disposition.

Terminal Access Controller Access-Control System Plus (TACACS+)   A protocol that provides access control for routers, network access servers, and other networked computing devices via one or more centralized servers. TACACS+ provides separate authentication, authorization, and accounting services.

threat identification   The process that network security designers use to identify what potential threats exist, regardless of the probability that the threat will be carried out.

training   Creates competence on the part of the end user to perform a specific task or to serve in a specific role. Conducting a class for network administrators about the features of a Cisco Adaptive Security Appliance (ASA) is an example of training.

transform set   A collection of security protocols and algorithms that can be used to establish an IKE Phase 2 (IPsec) tunnel.

Transmission Control Protocol (TCP)   One of the core protocols of the Internet protocol suite. TCP provides reliable, in-order delivery of a stream of bytes, making it suitable for applications such as file transfer and e-mail. It is so important in the Internet protocol suite that sometimes the entire suite is called "the TCP/IP protocol suite." TCP is the transport protocol that manages individual conversations between web servers and web clients. TCP divides HTTP messages into smaller pieces, called segments, to be sent to the destination client. It is also responsible for controlling the size of messages and rate at which they are exchanged between the server and the client.

transparent firewall   A Layer 2 firewall that behaves like a "stealth firewall." In other words, it is not seen as a router hop to connected devices. In this implementation, the security appliance connects the same network on its inside and outside ports. However, each interface resides on a separate VLAN.

transport mode   Uses a packet's original IP header, as opposed to adding a tunnel header for packets traveling over an IPsec-protected VPN. This approach works well in networks in which increasing a packet's size could cause an issue.

Triple Data Encryption Standard (3DES)   Applies the DES algorithm three times in a row to a plain-text block, but each application uses a different key. Applying DES three times with different keys makes brute-force attacks on 3DES unfeasible. This stems from the fact that the basic algorithm has stood the test of time, weathering 35 years in the field, proving quite trustworthy.

Trojan horse   A piece of software that appears to perform a certain action but in fact performs another action, such as a computer virus. This action, generally encoded in a hidden payload, may or may not be malicious in nature.

tunnel mode   Unlike transport mode, tunnel mode encapsulates an entire packet traveling over an IPsec-protected VPN. As a result, the encapsulated packet has a new IPsec header. This new header has source and destination IP address information that reflects the two VPN termination devices at two different sites. Therefore, tunnel mode is frequently used in an IPsec site-to-site VPN.

turbo access control list (ACL)   Processes ACLs into lookup tables for greater efficiency. Turbo ACLs use the packet header to access these tables in a small, fixed number of lookups, independent of the existing number of ACL entries.

user datagram protocol (UDP)   A communications protocol that has no error recovery features and is mostly used to send streamed material over the Internet.

VACL   VLAN access control list. An ACL applied *within* a VLAN, as opposed to an ACL applied when traffic travels from one VLAN, or subnet, to another (as typically seen on a router).

virtual private network (VPN)   A logical connection (sometimes called a tunnel) that can be established over an "untrusted" network (such as the Internet). An IPsec VPN can use a series of security protocols and algorithms to protect the traffic flowing over a VPN tunnel.

virtual SAN (VSAN)   Created from a collection of ports that are part of a set of connected Fibre Channel switches. Together these ports form a virtual fabric. Ports within a single switch may be partitioned off to form multiple VSANs. Conversely, multiple switches may be used together, and any number of their ports may be joined to form a single VSAN.

virus   A computer program that can copy itself and infect a computer without the user's permission or knowledge. A virus may spread from one computer to another only when its host is taken to the uninfected computer. For instance, a user sends the virus over a network or the Internet, or carries it on a removable medium such as a CD or USB drive. Compared to other malicious code, a virus generally requires end-user interaction. A worm, on the other hand, is based on a system vulnerability. A virus attaches itself to a file, whereas a worm lives in RAM.

vishing   Maliciously collecting private information over the phone.

VLAN hopping   An attack that allows traffic from one VLAN to pass into another VLAN without first being routed.

voice over IP (VoIP)   Sends packetized voice over an IP network. VoIP networks use devices such as gateways to interconnect traditional telephony equipment (such as POTS phones, PBXs, and key systems) to an IP infrastructure.

vulnerability   A weakness in an information system that an attacker might leverage to gain unauthorized access to a system or its data.

warm site   Like a hot site, a facility that has very similar equipment to that on the original site. However, a warm site is unlikely to have current data because of a lack of frequent replication with the original site. Therefore, disaster recovery personnel typically need to go to the warm site and manually bring systems online. As a result, critical business operations might not be restored for days.

World Wide Name (WWN)   Fibre Channel networks use this kind of 64-bit address to uniquely identify each element in a Fibre Channel network. These WWNs may be used in zoning to assign security permissions.

worm   A self-replicating computer program that lives in RAM, rather than attaching itself to a file like a virus does. It uses a network to send copies of itself to other nodes in the network and may do so without user intervention.

X.509v3   An industry standard that has been incorporated to define basic PKI formats. Areas that are based on X.509v3 include the certificate and certificate revocation list (CRL) format.

zone-based firewall   In this kind of firewall, zones establish the network's security borders. The zone itself defines a boundary where traffic is subjected to policy restrictions as it crosses into another region of the network. The default policy between zones is deny all. This means that if no policy is explicitly configured, all traffic moving between zones is blocked.

zone pair   Used to specify a unidirectional firewall policy between two security zones. To define the zone pair, the **zone-pair security** command is used. The direction of the traffic flow is defined by specifying a source and destination zone. These must be security zones. The same zone cannot be defined as both the source and the destination.

CCNA Security Exam Updates: Version 1.0

Over time, reader feedback allows Cisco Press to gauge which topics give our readers the most problems when taking the exams. Additionally, Cisco may make small changes in the breadth of exam topics or in emphasis of certain topics. To assist readers with those topics, the author creates new materials clarifying and expanding upon those troublesome exam topics. As mentioned in the introduction, the additional content about the exam is contained in a PDF document on this book's companion website at http://www.ciscopress.com/title/ 1587202204. The document you are viewing is Version 1.0 of this appendix.

This appendix presents all the latest update information available at the time of this book's printing. To make sure you have the latest version of this document, you should be sure to visit the companion website to see if any more recent versions have been posted since this book went to press.

This appendix attempts to fill the void that occurs with any print book. In particular, this appendix does the following:

- Mentions technical items that might not have been mentioned elsewhere in the book

- Covers new topics if Cisco adds topics to the IINS exam blueprints

- Provides a way to get up-to-the-minute current information about content for the exam

Always Get the Latest at the Companion Website

You are reading the version of this appendix that was available when your book was printed. However, given that the main purpose of this appendix is to be a living, changing document, it is very important that you look for the latest version online at the book's companion website. To do so:

1. Browse to http://www.ciscopress.com/title/1587202204.

2. Select the **Downloads** option under the **More Information** box.

3. Download the latest Appendix C document.

> **NOTE**   Note that the downloaded document has a version number. If the version of the PDF on the website is the same version as this appendix in your book, your book has the latest version, and there is no need to download or use the online version.

Technical Content

The current version of this appendix does not contain any additional technical coverage, but when there are technical content updates they will be placed in this section. This appendix is here simply to provide the instructions to check online for a later version of this appendix.

Index